SAILS AND STEAM
IN THE MOUNTAINS

SAILS AND STEAM
IN THE MOUNTAINS

A Maritime and Military History of
Lake George and Lake Champlain

Russell P. Bellico

PURPLE MOUNTAIN PRESS
Fleischmanns, New York

To Jane and Bill

Sails and Steam in the Mountains:
A Maritime and Military History of Lake George and Lake Champlain

Revised Edition 2001

published by
PURPLE MOUNTAIN PRESS, LTD.
1060 Main Street, P.O. Box 309
Fleischmanns, New York 12430-0309
845-254-4062, 845-254-4476 (fax), purple@catskill.net
http://www.catskill.net/purple

First edition 1992, reprinted with minor changes: 1993, 1995, 1998
Copyright © 1992 by Russell P. Bellico
Revised edition copyright © 2001 by Russell P. Bellico

Library of Congress Cataloging-in-Publication Data

Bellico, Russell P. (Russell Paul), 1943-
    Sails and steam in the mountains : a maritime and military history of Lake George and
Lake Champlain / Russell P. Bellico.--Rev. ed.
        p. cm.
    Includes bibliographical references (p.) and index.
    ISBN 1-930098-33-2 (alk. paper) -- ISBN 1-930098-17-0 (pbk. : alk. paper)
    1. George, Lake, Region (N.Y.)--History, military. 2. George, Lake, Region
(N.Y.)--History, Naval. 3. Champlain, Lake, Region--History, Military. 4. Champlain,
Lake, Region--History, Naval. 5. Underwater archaeology--New York (State)--George,
Lake, Region. 6. Underwater archaeology--Champlain, Lake, Region. I. Title

F127.G3 B48 2001
974.7'5--dc21   2001034963

Cover, frontispiece, and title page:
"British fleet bearing down on Lake Champlain [1777]"
Painting by Greg Harlin. (Wood Ronsaville Harlin, Inc. Used by permission)
Back cover: Anchor, Lake George. Photo by the author.

Manufactured in the United States of America on acid-free paper.

5 4 3 2 1

Contents

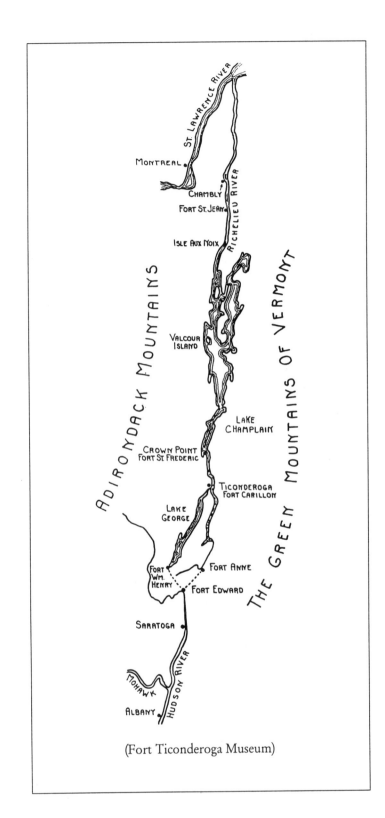

(Fort Ticonderoga Museum)

Acknowledgments

I AM INDEBTED TO MANY INDIVIDUALS for their assistance with my research on Lake George and Lake Champlain that has extended for more than three decades. To begin with, I am especially appreciative of my father's interest in history which resulted in a vacation trip to Lake George and Fort Ticonderoga in 1952. As a nine-year-old, I was thoroughly impressed by my first real contact with tangible American colonial history. Two years later, the observation of the ongoing archaeological excavation at the site of Fort William Henry and another visit to Fort Ticonderoga solidified my life-long interest in the history of the two lakes. When I began my diving excursions to the lakes in the late 1960s, Frank Pabst, a well-known entrepreneur residing in Plattsburgh, helped renew my interest in the maritime history of the two lakes with his wealth of information on the war fleets. Nearly 20 years later, Pabst, then operator of the tour boat *Juniper*, was the first to suggest that I write a book on the maritime history of Lake Champlain.

Special appreciation is due to the staffs of the many libraries that helped me ferret out a variety of historical materials. The following libraries were primarily useful in my investigation: The New York State Library and Archives in Albany; the University of Massachusetts Library in Amherst; the Bailey/Howe Memorial Library at the University of Vermont; the Benjamin F. Feinberg Library at SUNY, Plattsburgh; the Boston Public Library; the National Archives of Canada in Ottawa; the Massey Library of the Royal Military College in Kingston, Ontario; the National Archives in Washington, D.C.; the Connecticut State Library in Hartford; the Crandall Library of Glens Falls; the Starr Library at Middlebury College; the Fort Ticonderoga Thompson-Pell Research Center; the Bixby Library of Vergennes; the Amherst College Library; the Lake George Historical Association; the American Antiquarian Society in Worcester, Massachusetts; the Massachusetts Historical Society in Boston; the Ticonderoga Historical Society; the Bolton Historical Society; the Nimitz Library of the U.S. Naval Academy; the Huntington Library in San Marino, California; and the town libraries of Port Henry, Westport, and Willsboro, New York.

I owe a singular debt of gratitude to Helen Lent, a former administrative assistant at Westfield State College, whose support, endless corrections of my manuscript, and typing were crucial to the completion of the original project in 1992. In addition, special thanks are due to the many work-study students at the college for their diligent transcription of my handwritten draft onto a word processor. I am very grateful to Danielle Bramucci, an administrative assistant at Westfield State College, whose word processing and editing expertise made my task of integrating new material into the text of the new edition much easier. Proofreaders Drs. Wallace Goldstein and Frank Salvidio corrected errors and recommended textual changes. I am very appreciative of their efforts. Historian Donald Wickman's proofreading of the material covering Mount Independence was very helpful. Credit is due Catherine Handy, Jennifer Hanna, and Maryann Nesto, reference librarians at Westfield State College, for their persistent attention to my requests for interlibrary loans. Support for the project from the Committee on Professional Development and a sabbatical leave from Westfield State College enabled me to complete the research and writing of the original manuscript. Advice on photography and the printing of my black and white photographs by the late John Morytko, former director of photographic

1

services at the college, and from David Harris-Fried, the present director of photographic services, is gratefully acknowledged. I also appreciate the help provided by Kenneth Haar and Deborah Samwell, who graciously corrected several computer disk glitches.

Vital historical information from Peter Barranco, Gary Zaboly, Hudson Hagglund, Arthur B. Cohn, Kevin J. Crisman, Craig Williams, Anthony F. Hall, Joseph W. Zarzynski, Christopher D. Fox, Scott Padeni, Donald Wickman, Morris Glenn, Robert Benway, Timothy J. Todish, Richard Strum, Betty Ahearn Buckell, Marilyn Mazzeo, and Grace MacDonald and oral history from Captain Marty Fisher, Captain Gordon Burleigh, Captain Merritt Carpenter, Harmel Burton, and Peter Smith helped piece together the history of the two lakes. The diligent efforts of artists Montserrat Centeno and Gary Zaboly to comply with my requests for illustrations and the use of Kevin J. Crisman's drawings are gratefully recognized.

I received valuable help and encouragement from Joseph W. Zarzynski, executive director of Bateaux Below, Inc., and worthwhile advice and knowledge of the book-publishing market from William Cowan.

I am appreciative of having been included in the side-scan sonar expeditions of three separate teams during the 1980s on Lake Champlain in search of Benedict Arnold's lost gondola. The sound archaeological work on Lake Champlain shipwrecks carried out in recent years by the Lake Champlain Maritime Museum deserves credit for breathing renewed interest into the long history of these freshwater fleets. Similar efforts by Bateaux Below have also created a new emphasis on the preservation of historic vessels. I am also exceedingly grateful to diving associates who were willing to pose for my underwater photographs on numerous expeditions in search of shipwrecks: Richard A. Bellico, Joseph W. Zarzynski, Frank Canosa, Dan B. Couture, Jack Sullivan, and Robert Benway. Captain Dan B. Couture (Marine Explorers) provided excellent diving charters to the shipwrecks of Lake Champlain. My most memorable diving at the two lakes occurred during the late 1960s and 1970s and were shared with my brother Richard A. Bellico, whose enthusiasm for exploring shipwrecks further kindled my interest in the history of the lakes. Fellow members of the *Land Tortoise* project at Lake George are deserving of special recognition for their efforts in documenting a unique vessel in American history.

The encouragement and support of my books by Wray and Loni Rominger of Purple Mountain Press are deeply appreciated. Their 28-year-old firm publishes 20 or more regional titles each year and has 90 books in print at this writing. Generations of readers to come will be grateful for their efforts in nurturing the expansion of regional history titles.

Finally, I owe thanks to my wife, Jane, for her proofreading, encouragement, and patience. I also appreciated my son's occasional suggestions during the original project. In particular, his discovery that young Paul Revere served at Fort William Henry in 1756 provided an assurance that interest in the history of the two lakes transcends generations.

Introduction

N O LAKES HAVE A GREATER CLAIM to a place in American history than Lake George and Lake Champlain. While visitors to the lakes today gaze upon tranquil waters filled with pleasure boats, three wars fought between 1755 and 1814 saw deadly cannon fire, vessels engaged in devastating attacks, and the ascension and decline of the French and English empires in North America. Most military histories of the lakes are limited to these wars, but numerous raids by both the French and English occurred via the lakes during the seventeenth century, and three major English expeditions reached the lake valleys in 1690, 1709, and 1711. These now-distant events have been recorded and passed on by history-minded residents and tourists to new generations in oral and written chronicles and have been kept alive in part by the forts that line its shores and the shipwrecks lying on the bottom of the lakes. The lakes are the common element of the past that provide the foundation for the retelling of historic events. They are special places that generations have embraced for both their beauty and history.

In their first two centuries of European habitation, the Lake George-Lake Champlain valleys witnessed a continual struggle for control of their strategic waterways in a period when the only viable means of transportation was by water. Some of the initial chapters of this book, covering the early expeditions and the French and Indian War, deal extensively with land engagements; however, these events are integral to the total history of the lakes and are interwoven with their maritime activity. In each of these cases, land battles were the consequence of the larger struggle over control of the water route. The long navigable lakes were the logical entryway from Canada into the center of the English colonies. Expeditions were continually raised and forts erected in defense of rival claims to the water highway of the two lakes. In nearly all of these early battles, large armies were transported on the lakes in massive fleets of bateaux accompanied by radeaux, row galleys, schooners, and sloops. The most extensive naval battles, on the other hand, would await the American Revolution and the War of 1812. Although the hastily-constructed Champlain fleet in 1776 under Benedict Arnold was vanquished by a more heavily-armed British armada, the presence of the American fleet delayed the British advance and ultimately changed the course of the American Revolution. The clouds of war were to engulf Lake Champlain once again in a renewed rivalry with Great Britain over control of the strategic Champlain waterway during the War of 1812. The decisive defeat of the British flotilla at Plattsburgh Bay in 1814 by the American fleet under Thomas Macdonough was instrumental in bringing the war to a conclusion with the Treaty of Ghent.

How accurately can we recount these events, some of which occurred over two centuries ago? Surprisingly, we may have more documents written about these military campaigns than about some expeditions during twentieth-century wars. Without modern technology, most military communications were written down and carried by messengers. The soldiers themselves, realizing that they were making history, carried journals and diaries in their packs. Although the journals manifest rudimentary spelling, punctuation, and grammar, they provide a means of untangling fact from myth and have added a firsthand dimension to the narrative of this book. The history of these events can be clarified but will never be final, for other documents will surely be uncovered and events reinterpreted in the future.

Following the wars, a commercial period initiated a new era in the history of Lake George and Lake Champlain. Before railroads and trailer trucks, the water highway of the lakes provided the only economical means of transporting cargoes of pulpwood, iron ore, coal, granite, marble, graphite, and lumber from the resource-rich areas of the north to the marketplaces of the middle-Atlantic and New England states. Lake Champlain was a natural trade route from Canada to the United States which increased in importance with the building of the Champlain Canal in New York with its connection to the Hudson River and the Chambly Canal in Canada. Schooners, canal boats, and majestic steamboats plied the water passageway of Lake Champlain for more than a century. The luxurious steamers of Lake George conveyed passengers to scores of picturesque summer hotels along the lake or to the stagecoaches (later railroad) at the northern landing which transported passengers to the steamer landing on Lake Champlain at Ticonderoga. From the earliest times, tourists found the scenery of the two lakes breathtaking: Traveling aboard the steamboat *Mountaineer* on Lake George in 1827, Margaret Hunter Hall suggested that "I never saw anything more beautiful. It is really quite exquisite"; and during the early 1850s, S. H. Hammond aboard the steamer *America* remarked that Lake Champlain "is one of the most beautiful sheets of water in the world."[1] Although most journeys were pleasant, the history of the steamboat epoch is replete with dramatic tales of steamer disasters.

The book is not only a testament to the past but closely ties the historic events to the exciting archaeological discoveries of the present. True underwater exploration of wreck sites in the lakes began with a survey of the Revolutionary War flagship *Royal Savage* by a commercial diver in 1909 and the subsequent examination and raising of that vessel and the gondola *Philadelphia* by Lorenzo Hagglund during the 1930s. At the same time a crude diving apparatus enabled a diver at Lake George to investigate bateau wreck sites from the French and Indian War.

As a result of the availability of modern scuba diving equipment during the 1950s and 1960s, the exploration of shipwrecks at the lakes became a popular sport for hundreds of people. Unfortunately, many archaeological sites were quickly torn apart for souvenirs. Many wooden and iron artifacts retrieved from these wrecks deteriorated and were eventually discarded. Likewise, some of the vessels raised from the depths of Lake Champlain during the twentieth century, including one of Benedict Arnold's gondolas, Amherst's brig *Duke of Cumberland*, and the 1809 steamboat *Vermont*, were allowed to deteriorate after their exposure to the elements. Fortunately, several vessels did survive their salvage from the lakes, such as a French and Indian War bateau displayed for many years at the Adirondack Museum, the Revolutionary War gondola *Philadelphia* exhibited at the Smithsonian, and the War of 1812 schooner *Ticonderoga* on display at Whitehall.

By the 1980s a new era of conservation and preservation of wrecks had begun in the lake valleys. During the first half of the decade, the Champlain Maritime Society provided leadership in sound archaeological studies on a variety of shipwreck sites. Many groups, including the New York State Divers Association, now recognize that these wrecks are finite resources that need to be preserved for future generations to study and enjoy. The widespread deployment of side-scan sonar has resulted in the discovery of many important intact shipwrecks in Lake Champlain. Following several significant underwater discoveries, the state of Vermont initiated a number of successful underwater historic preserves for visiting divers which have resulted in the reorientation of the diving public toward the concept of preservation. The discoveries have renewed interest in the history of the lake basins and encouraged a re-examination of the maritime heritage of Lake George and Lake Champlain. Widespread support has enabled the Lake Champlain Maritime Museum at Basin Harbor to expand its exhibits of the lake's maritime history, build full-size replicas of a bateau from Lake George and Benedict Arnold's 1776 gondola *Philadelphia*, begin construction of an 88-foot canal schooner, and continue side-scan sonar surveys and archaeological studies of historic shipwrecks. The LCMM survey team has discovered scores of intact vessels at the bottom of the lake, including Benedict Arnold's last unaccounted-for gunboat, *Spitfire*. Likewise, the 1990 discovery of the intact 1758 radeau *Land Tortoise* has focused attention on the archaeological treasures of Lake George. Through the efforts of Bateaux Below, Inc., the *Land Tortoise* has been designated a National Historic Landmark and a New York State Submerged Heritage Preserve. Working with the New York State Department of Environmental Conservation, Bateaux Below was also the driving force behind the creation of Submerged Heritage Preserves for seven sunken bateaux and the wreck of the 1906 launch *Forward*.

In recent years the Lake George-Lake Champlain valleys have witnessed a renewed dedication to the preservation of the history of the region. In addition to the growth of the Lake Champlain Maritime Museum, new and expanded museums include the Mount Independence State Historic Site Visitor Center, Ethan Allen Homestead, Chimney Point State Historic Site, Crown Point State Historic Site Visitor Center, Iron Center of Port Henry, Skenesborough Museum and the restoration of the steamboat *Ticonderoga* at the Shelburne Museum, as well as plans to restore the East Barracks at Fort Ticonderoga, to open a Battle of Plattsburgh Bay Museum at the former air base, and establish a visitor center at Fort George.

The second edition of this book integrates additional original materials from manuscript collections and other sources, spanning the French and Indian War through the steamboat era. In some instances these materials have resulted in an important reinterpretation of historic events. In addition, significant archaeological discoveries, which have occurred during the past decade, have been incorporated into the text.

Drawing by Gary Zaboly

1. Years of Conflict

LAKE GEORGE AND LAKE CHAMPLAIN, intertwined by history and geography, rank as two of the most significant water routes in the settlement of North America. Melting glaciers thousands of years ago left the lake basins with a myriad of deep channels, islands, towering palisades, and rock outcroppings surrounded by lofty mountain peaks. While the receding ice gave Lake George its present shape, the Champlain Valley was inundated by salt water forming the Champlain Sea. Remnants of the oceanic past, including marine fossils, bones of walruses, and a skeleton of a whale, have been discovered along the shoreline of Lake Champlain. Without the weight of the glaciers, the Champlain Valley rose and the waters of Lake Champlain gradually changed from salt to freshwater. Fish such as the ling, sheepshead, and sturgeon trace their origins to this earlier sea. Both Lake George and Lake Champlain drained south to the Hudson River during the last period of glaciation, but later the geological rise of the surrounding land mass caused the water of both lakes to empty to the north.

Today Lake Champlain is the largest body of deep freshwater in the United States exclusive of the Great Lakes. Champlain spans 120 miles from Whitehall, New York, at the southern end to its northern outlet in the Richelieu River. At the widest point, it reaches 12 miles across with a maximum depth of 400 feet. The lake's nearly 500 square miles encompass 71 islands. Over 90 percent of the water in Lake Champlain comes from tributaries that drain into its basin. Lake George, by contrast, receives most of its water from springs. The 32 miles of Lake George, surrounded by steep mountain sides reaching heights of 2,500 feet along the middle of the lake, resemble a pristine fjord. The 172 islands that dot its clear water, coupled with its breathtaking scenery, have endeared the lake to visitors to the region throughout history.

The lakes have not always been tranquil, however. During their turbulent history, these now placid waterways were the sites of three wars and many disastrous shipwrecks, producing a legacy of stories of the American past. They were the scenes of heroic acts of courage, deeds of treachery and torture, and perilous encounters between eighteenth-century soldiers and Native Americans. The interest in the history of these stormy events stems not from a glorification of war but from a fascination with the lakes as special places whose beauty and past are interwoven. The names of islands and landmarks often reflect the historic incidents of the wartime period: Floating Battery Island, Sabbath Day Point, Rogers Rock, Prisoners Island, Arnold's Bay, Carleton's Prize, Schuyler Island, etc. As part of a natural water route from Canada to the Hudson River and the Atlantic Ocean, Lake Champlain and Lake George were of strategic importance to rival colonial powers. Colonel Louis Antoine de Bougainville, pondering strategy during the French and Indian War while at Ticonderoga, noted in his journal in 1758 that "the lakes and rivers are the only outlets, the only open roads in this country."[1] Bougainville, like many military leaders who would follow, concluded that "the only way to assure ourselves the possession of Lake Champlain. . .is by a strong naval force."[2] Radeaux, brigs, sloops, row galleys, and gunboats would become a familiar part of the scenery during periods of war. When peace finally arrived during the nineteenth century, it was time for new fleets of commercial schooners, sloops, steamboats, and canal boats to once again follow the natural water route that the lakes provided.

Although most of the early history of Lake George and Lake Champlain has been written from the ethnocentric view of the European inhabitancy, there is ample evidence that native civilizations had occupied the area for thousands of years. Stone points discovered at Highgate, Vermont (east of Maquam Bay), indicate the presence of a hunting society of Paleoindians about 9300 B.C. The Archaic period in Vermont, rooted in a broad-based hunting and gathering culture, has been dated from 3500 B.C. to perhaps 2000 B.C., based upon relics uncovered at two sites along Otter Creek (Vergennes). Artifacts from the Woodland period found at the Winooski River, Swanton, and East Creek range in date from 60 A.D. to after 1000 A.D. In 1997 scuba divers discovered a 2,000-year-old intact Native American pot in 50 feet of water near Thompson's Point in Charlotte, Vermont. (The clay pot was subsequently preserved at the Lake Champlain Maritime Museum's conservation lab.) East Creek, lying on the Vermont side across from Fort Ticonderoga, was the apparent site of a large village before the Iroquoian tribes or Europeans arrived at Lake Champlain. During the 1930s an excavation of a site on East Creek by the Museum of the American Indian yielded pottery, 15-inch spearpoints, arrowheads, and strings of copper beads. The creek marshes had teemed with muskrat, beaver, and water fowl, while the adjacent north slope of Mount Independence held the best source of flint in the lake valleys. During the British occupation of Boston in 1775, Henry Knox delivered two barrels of flint from East Creek to George Washington, along with the cannons from Ticonderoga.

The Iroquois, who inhabited New York for more than a thousand years, eventually spearheaded one of the most important confederacies of North American Indians, known as the Five Nations (after 1713 Six Nations). While fishing and hunting were pervasive, agriculture, with corn as the staple crop, played a significant role in Iroquois life. Their well-developed political structure included councils composed of democratically-elected members which met in long, bark-covered communal houses. Fine pottery, mats of husk corn, baskets, and orchard fruits were produced and traded, with wampum as a medium of exchange. Wampum was usually made from pieces of shells strung on threads, and were often worn as bracelets or necklaces. More importantly, wampum, in the form of belts, was a symbolic record of intertribal transactions as well as a way of recording historic events.

Evidence of a village site on the Ticonderoga peninsula, alternately occupied by both Algonquin and Iroquois tribes, includes large quantities of tools and arrowheads. Likewise, a village site on Missisquoi Bay where 1,000 artifacts have been unearthed may have been inhabited both by Iroquois and Abenaki Indians (Algonquin Confederacy). By 1575 the Algonquin and Iroquois tribes were mortal enemies vying for control of the region. The Iroquois laid claim to the western shore of Lake Champlain while the Algonquin tribes held the eastern shore.[3] Many of the place names along the lake are Europeanized versions of the original Indian names.[4]

While there is limited evidence that other European travelers may have seen Lake Champlain first, the honor of discovery by a European is credited to 39-year-old Samuel de Champlain who named it after himself in 1609. Prior to that, Champlain had fought in France against Spanish invaders. Five years later, in 1599, he made his first Atlantic voyage to the Caribbean and Central America as a guest aboard his uncle's ship. After several more voyages to North America during the early years of the seventeenth century, Champlain established himself as a map maker and explorer as well as a successful fur trader. His ability to build friendly relations with the Indian tribes along the St. Lawrence River established France in the region and enhanced its lucrative fur trade. Return trips to France found Champlain eagerly seeking backing for new expeditions to North America. One of Champlain's goals on many of his expeditions was to locate a Northwest

Passage to the Orient; to this end he explored the waters of Lake Huron, Lake Ontario, the Ottawa River, and perhaps the Oswego and Genesee Rivers. Champlain spent a brutal fourth winter of 1608-1609 in North America at present-day Quebec City. Twenty of the 28 French explorers died; Champlain himself contracted scurvy. The following summer he met with the Algonquins and Hurons who had been driven north by the Iroquois. They persuaded him to join in a campaign against their enemies at a lake to the south (Lake Champlain). Since Champlain needed the Hurons for the fur trade and geographic information on the region, he felt obligated to participate in the expedition or risk compromising France's harmonious relations with the northern tribes.

In July 1609 Champlain and his crew traveled as far as the Richelieu River in a "shallop" (small sailing galley). Encountering the rapids in the Richelieu, Champlain and two Frenchmen transferred to Indian canoes. The war party of Algonquins, Hurons, and Montagnais proceeded in 24 canoes up "the River of the Iroquois" or Richelieu. Upon entering the lake, Champlain saw "four beautiful islands" but spent more time describing a five-foot fish "as big as my thigh, and had a head as large as my fists, with a snout two feet and a half long, and a double row of very sharp, dangerous teeth. Its body has a good deal the shape of the pike."[5] His description of a garpike has often been misinterpreted to suggest that he had seen the illusive Lake Champlain monster.[6]

The Indians informed Champlain that the place where they anticipated meeting their Iroquois enemies had a "rapid" [falls at Ticonderoga] and beyond that area lay a "lake which is some nine or ten leagues [Lake George]."[7] Traveling at night to avoid detection, Champlain and the Indians met a party of Iroquois paddling in canoes at ten o'clock on July 29, "at the extremity of a cape which projects into the lake on the west side."[8] There has been some debate over the years regarding the location of the cape where Champlain and the Iroquois met. Some writers suggest that the cape was Crown Point, while others insist that it was the Ticonderoga peninsula on which the fort stands today. Since there is ample evidence that the Ticonderoga area had once been a Native American camp and that Champlain later observed the "rapid" at Ticonderoga, it is probable that this was the cape rather than Crown Point.

Both Indian parties began shouting at each other with the Iroquois withdrawing to their camp on the shore. Champlain had encountered a Mohawk party of the Iroquois Nation. The Mohawks onshore began cutting trees to form a barricade or circular stockade as a defense while the Algonquins and Hurons pulled their canoes together offshore. The Indians with Champlain sent a contingent in two canoes to the Mohawks to ask if they wished to fight. The Indians onshore expressed their desire to engage the Algonquins, but persuaded the latter to await daylight in order to distinguish one group from another. During the rest of the night both parties traded verbal insults while the Mohawks danced and sang. The next morning, Champlain prepared his arquebus (a matchlock musket) with four balls, donned his armor, and went ashore with his Native American allies. Until that point Champlain had not been seen by the Mohawks. Two hundred Mohawks with three "chiefs," identified by the big plumes in their headdress, walked out of their stockade as Champlain and the Indians advanced. The chiefs were probably only war captains since chiefs did not participate in battle and would have worn horns, not feathers.[9] Champlain recorded what was probably the first engagement involving Europeans in the lake valley: "When I saw them make a move to draw their bows upon us, I took aim with my arquebus and shot straight at one of the three chiefs, and with this shot two fell to the ground and one of their companions was wounded who died thereof a little later."[10]

Arrows from both sides thickened the air amid loud shouts from the combatants. The Mohawks, according to Champlain, used shields made of wood woven together with cotton thread. These were no match for the arquebus, however, as one of Champlain's two companions who had hidden in the trees fired into the Mohawks. Frightened by the blast of this unknown weapon, the Mohawks finally fled deep into the forest. In addition to the dead, ten to twelve Mohawks were taken prisoner and later tortured. Fifteen or 16 of Champlain's Indians were wounded with arrows, but their wounds healed quickly, according to Champlain. The Algonquins gathered up the abandoned shields and corn, departing northward within three hours. Champlain modestly noted in his journal that "where this attack took place is in 43° and some minutes of latitude, and was named Lake Champlain."[11] After several days of travel, Champlain returned to Quebec with the Montagnais.

Champlain's encounter with the Iroquois has been linked to the collision course with the Six Nations in later years. Although some Iroquois would side with the French during the French and Indian War, for the most part they remained enemies. Champlain would subsequently return to North America several more times and fight two more battles with the Iroquois. Between 1603 and 1632 Champlain had four volumes of his adventures published, which included maps and illustrations. The primary result of his exploration in 1609, however, would be the discovery of a route through Lake Champlain and Lake George to the Hudson River—a route that would be the most contested waterway in North America during wars that would span the seventeenth, the eighteenth, and early nineteenth centuries.

In September 1609, shortly after Champlain's voyage into Lake Champlain, Henry Hudson, supported by the Dutch East India Company, sailed into New York's coastal waters. During the next month, Hudson explored the Hudson River as far as present-day Albany in his 80-ton vessel *Half Moon*. His career in North America, however, was much shorter. The following year Hudson made his final voyage in the English ship *Discovery*, during which his vessel became frozen in the winter ice of Canada's Hudson Bay while searching for the Northwest Passage. After a bitter winter of deprivation, the crew mutinied, sending Hudson, his son and seven others adrift in a small boat, never to be seen again. Four years after Hudson's exploration of the river that bears his name, the Dutch concluded a treaty with the Iroquois and established a trading post at Fort Orange (Albany). The Dutch would dominate the economy of southern New York for the next half century.

During the seventeenth century the French were largely engaged in the fur trade with the Canadian Indians, exporting as many as 150,000 skins a year. Large felt hats, made from beaver pelts, were the basic fashion of the day for European men. During this period, the French tried to convert the Indians to Christianity, beginning with four missionaries who accompanied Champlain to Canada in 1615. Ten years later, Jesuit priests arrived in Quebec to provide instruction in Christian faith and doctrine to the Hurons. Father Isaac Jogues, perhaps the most famous Jesuit missionary, had spent six years with the Hurons before being captured by an Iroquois war party in August 1642. Although he might have escaped, Father Jogues rushed to the aid of two lay brothers who had been wounded. The Mohawks took their captives back to their villages, stopping the first night at Isle La Motte in northern Lake Champlain and later on "Jogues Island" (near present-day Westport, N.Y.). On the latter island the captives were forced to submit to a "salvo, which consists in having the prisoners pass between two rows [of Indians], each discharging upon them blows from sticks."[12]

Whether the war party transported the brutalized Jogues through "Lake Andiatarocté" (an Indian name meaning "where the lake is shut in"—present-day Lake George) or through southern Lake Champlain is subject to some debate. Upon reaching their villages along the Mohawk River, Father Jogues had all but two of his fingernails

pulled out, his knuckles smashed, and his remaining fingers mutilated into stumps. The next year, while accompanying the Iroquois, Jogues was a few miles from the Dutch settlements on the Hudson River. Arendt Van Corlaer, a Dutch merchant friendly with the Mohawks, and a Dutch Reformed minister, Jan Megapolensis, after learning of Father Jogues' tortured captivity, assisted his escape from the Indians. Jogues returned to France after being shipwrecked on the coast of England.

After receiving special permission from the Pope to celebrate mass with his mutilated hands, Jogues returned to Canada and

Left: Samuel de Champlain, from *The Summer Paradise in History* by Warwick Stevens Carpenter. (The Delaware and Hudson Company)

Below: The 1609 battle of Samuel de Champlain and the Mohawk warriors, drawing from the 1613 edition of his *Voyages*.

was sent as an ambassador on a peace mission to the Mohawks with two Algonquins and Sieur Bourdon, a French engineer. Father Jogues stopped at Isle La Motte and Otter Creek before reaching "Lake Andiatrocte." Upon viewing the lake in 1646, Jogues christened it "Lac du Saint-Sacrement," a name that was used until the English changed it to Lake George in 1755.[13] Upon reaching the Iroquois villages along the Mohawk River, Father Jogues set the stage for peaceful relations with the French, leaving gifts and religious articles before departing for Canada on June 16. He returned to Canada with an invitation to establish a mission at the Mohawk villages. Upon approval by the Jesuits, the 39-year-

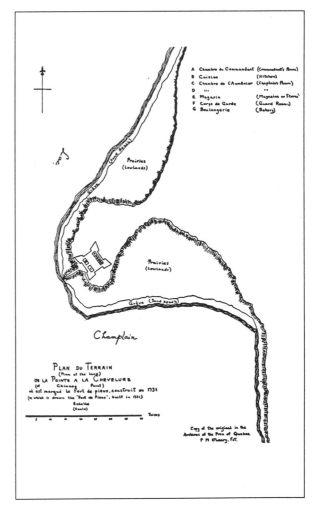

Right: Outpost at "Pointe a la Chevelure" (Chimney Point, Vermont) in 1731. Reconstruction of a map by Guy Omeron Coolidge.

Below: "Fort Orange, 1635." Painting by L. F. Tantillo.

old Jogues returned with René-Jean LaLande in late August. By early October, after caterpillars had consumed the Mohawks' grain and an epidemic had occurred, Jogues was charged with bringing the blight to the village and was murdered. On October 18, 1646, Jogues and LaLande had their decapitated heads mounted on stakes at the Mohawk village. Father Jogues was canonized a saint in 1930; his statue today gazes upon the waters of Lake George from Battlefield Park in Lake George Village.

As the colonial powers vied for trade outlets, the potential for conflict increased. By the middle of the seventeenth century the English were ready to challenge the Dutch presence in North America. From 1652 through 1675 three periods of warfare between the two rival commercial powers took place. In 1664 the Dutch colony on the Hudson River was captured by the English, but subsequently retaken by the Dutch in 1673. It was quickly seized again by the English. By 1675 the Dutch were permanently driven from North America. The Dutch colonists, however, remained at the Hudson River settlement, retaining their cultural and religious heritage.

The elimination of the Dutch and the growth of New France ultimately led to a collision course between the French and English colonial empires in North America. Under King Louis XIV in 1661, France revived its interest in the economic potential of North America. Under several effective governors of New France, ambitious plans for settlement and trade alarmed England and its colonists. Three wars: King William's War (1689-1697), Queen Anne's War (1702-1713), and King George's War (1744-1748) would ensue before the final confrontation of the French and Indian War (1755-1763). Each war escalated the size of the armies and the ferocity of battle as each nation attempted to oust the other from North America.

Initially the conflict began with the Iroquois challenge to the French settlements and forts along the St. Lawrence River. In 1641 the French built Fort Richelieu at the mouth of the Richelieu River, which was burned five years later by the Iroquois. By 1663 the Iroquois had grown bolder, attacking farms and towns in Canada and spreading fear throughout New France. The threat led to the rebuilding of Fort Richelieu and construction of several other fortifications along the St. Lawrence and Richelieu Rivers. A regiment of tough French Carignan-Salières regulars, who had achieved fame in the wars against the Turks, landed in Quebec in 1665 to establish the military power of New France.

Although an Iroquois peace ambassador visited Canada in December, the new governor-general of New France, Daniel de Courcelles, planned a daring mid-winter raid against the Mohawk villages in New York. On January 9, 1666, Courcelles, carrying his own 25-30 pound pack, led nearly 600 snowshoe-clad troops over Lake Champlain, then overland to the Hudson River. However, as early as the third day of the expedition, the ears, fingers, noses, and knees of some of the men had become frost-bitten. The French troops, who had become lost following their Indian guides, found themselves near the Dutch village of Schenectady by February 14, instead of the Iroquois settlements along the Mohawk River. The troops had only a minor skirmish with the Mohawks. Arendt Van Corlaer, who had earlier helped Father Jogues, came to the rescue of the French detachment with provisions of peas and bread. The Dutch also offered shelter, but Courcelles refused, fearing that his troops might desert if they were made comfortable. For his help, Governor Courcelles invited Van Corlaer to Canada.* The French party retreated northward but was forced to march all night in a blinding snowstorm. Sixty soldiers died of starvation and exposure or were taken prisoner by the pursuing Mohawks before the army returned to Canada on March 8.

* The following year Van Corlaer drowned "crossing a great bay" during a storm on Lake Champlain. While there is some debate regarding where he actually drowned, the bay south of Port Kent, New York, adjacent to Schuyler Island is named Corlaer Bay.

Courcelles and Canadian Viceroy Alexandre de Prouville de Tracy did not abandon the plan to crush the Iroquois villages. To this end, they sent Captain de la Motte (Pierre de Saint-Paul, Sieur de la Motte-Lussière) and the regiment of regulars to an island on Lake Champlain to build a fourth fort. The outpost, called Fort St. Anne, was completed by July 26, 1666, on the northwest end of present-day Isle La Motte. The 144-foot fort, constructed with four log bastions, was abandoned as a fortified outpost around 1671, but its remnants were still clearly observable in the late nineteenth century.

By the summer of 1666, a peace offer from ambassadors of the Five Iroquois Nations, meeting with the French in Quebec, seemed to offer hope of a durable accord. But within a few days the news that a captain in the Carignan Regiment and nephew of the Marquis de Tracy had been killed by the Mohawks set the stage for another French expedition to the Iroquois villages. September 28, 1666, was set for a rendezvous of French forces involved in the operation. Both Governor Courcelles and Viceroy Tracy led a 1,300-man expedition in 300 vessels "consisting partly of very light batteaux,* and partly of bark canoes."[14] The army paddled south on Lake Champlain, left some troops with provisions to build a stockaded fort at Ticonderoga, portaged to Lake George, and proceeded to its southern shore where the French hid their vessels for the return trip. The French army marched to the Mohawk River and burned four Iroquois villages, consisting of 100 large sturdy cabins with "a triple palisade, surrounding their stronghold, twenty feet in height and flanked by four bastions."[15] In the spring of 1667, to the surprise of the small garrison at Fort St. Anne, several Iroquois ambassadors appeared, requesting peace with the French and asking for missionaries. On May 22, 1667, ten Iroquois ambassadors met in Quebec with the French to conclude a treaty of peace.

By the 1680s, rising tension over land claims by the French and English was the harbinger of future conflict. Beginning in 1684, land patents north of Fort Orange (Albany) bestowed by the governor of New York, Colonel Thomas Dongan, were the first in a succession of grants that moved the English closer to areas claimed by the French. The French believed the English were arming the Iroquois and secretly encouraging them to break the peace and so they staged additional raids against the Iroquois. Jacques de Brisay Denonville, the Canadian governor, proposed a strategy in 1688 to extend French influence with a garrisoned outpost at Crown Point.

For several years Denonville and other French officials developed elaborate proposals to attack the English through Lake Champlain, Lake George, and the Hudson to New York City. The plan, similar to those devised in later wars, would be aimed at dividing the English colonies. By June of 1689, Louis XIV, the king of France, approved the plan. "He has the more readily consented thereto since he knows that the English inhabiting that country have contemplated of late years, exciting the Iroquois nations, his Majesty's subjects, with a view to oblige them to make war on the French."[16] In addition, the king charged the English with usurping trade in territories belonging to New France. Before the plan was put into action, 1,300 Mohawks in 250 canoes invaded Canada, totally destroying the village of La Chine on the island of Montreal, murdering its residents, and taking 130 captives.

The response to the La Chine raid was combined with a long-range plan of attack on the English colonies. Several French raids on northern New England and New York villages would signify an escalation of the conflict. Although the leadership had once again changed in New France with the recall of Denonville and the reappointment of the vigorous 69-year-old former governor, Count de Frontenac (Louis de Buade de Frontenac), the military and political objectives remained the same. At the beginning of February

---

* Bateaux were flat-bottomed vessels 27-36 feet in length used for carrying men and cargo on inland waters (see chapter 2).

1690, the long-planned attack on New York finally commenced with a scaled-down force. The expedition consisted of 210 men, including 96 Indians. After the Indians balked at the proposed assault on Fort Orange, the raiding party diverted to Schenectady, burning the village and massacring 60 men, women, and children. The significance of this action, along with two other raids on New Hampshire and Maine, was to engulf the colonies in the European wars. King William's War (1689-1697), part of a larger war fought by Europe's Grand Alliance against France, would initiate a conflict that would last on and off for the next 73 years, culminating with the Seven Years' War.

A more ambitious invasion through the Champlain Valley was planned for the spring by Governor Frontenac of New France. In the meantime, officials of New York were not idle, sending Captain Jacobus de Warm from Albany in March 1690 with 12 English troops and 20 Mohawks to establish a base near Crown Point. The contingent constructed "a little stone fort" on Chimney Point across the lake from Crown Point.[17] Another small English party was subsequently sent to Otter Creek and later to Fort Chambly on the Richelieu River. Lieutenant Governor Jacob Leisler of New York busily corresponded with other colonies in an effort to mount a defense against a rumored French invasion.* After meeting with delegates from Massachusetts and Connecticut, Leisler and others initiated a strategy for assembling an 800-man army in Albany, along with the Mohawks, to invade Canada through Lake Champlain. Coinciding with the Champlain offensive, a naval expedition would attack Quebec. Following a lengthy debate, Fitz-John Winthrop of Connecticut, who had had some military experience in England, was chosen to lead the army. Winthrop, the son of former Connecticut Governor John Winthrop and a grandson of the first Massachusetts Bay governor, would later become a governor of Connecticut.

Arriving in Albany in late July 1690, Major General Winthrop "found the design against Canada poorly contrived and little prosecuted, all things confused and in no readiness or posture for marching the forces towards Canada."[18] Despite these problems, the army, which approximated 750 troops and an equal number of Mohawks, advanced toward Lake Champlain in early August. Winthrop, nearing Saratoga on August 2, received dispatches from Boston and Connecticut that the fleet was ready to sail against Canada. By August 6 the army reached Wood Creek at the very southern end of Lake Champlain in present-day Whitehall, New York.

After a few days, the lack of provisions and canoes, along with smallpox which had infected the army, made the problems of the ill-planned expedition all the more obvious. The troops attempted to make canoes on the site, but "the t[i]me being so far spent, the bark would not peel, and so no more canoes could be made."[19] The area around Whitehall in that period had mostly elm rather than birch trees. Since it was too late in the season for elm bark to be peeled, the expedition was doomed. After a two-day council of war with the Indians and officers, Winthrop noted in his journal on August 15 that the lack of provisions and canoes made it "adviseable to return with the army."[20] The expedition, however, did not entirely end with Winthrop's withdrawal. Captain John Schuyler, brother of the mayor of Albany and grandfather of Major General Philip Schuyler of Revolutionary War fame, dissatisfied with the council's hesitation to proceed, requested orders from Winthrop to raid the French outposts in Canada. During the month of August, Schuyler's volunteer party of 29 militiamen and 120 Mohawks raided La Prairie near Montreal, returning to Albany by the end of the month with "19 prisoners and 6 scalps."[21] While the raid was not much of a military victory, it served notice to the French that English colonists could strike deep into French territory.

---

* During the seventeenth and eighteenth centuries, lieutenant governors often handled most of the actual work in administering the colonies.

The second prong of the expedition into Canada had even worse luck. Sir William Phips, a provincial from present-day Maine who achieved knighthood for his salvage of a sunken Spanish treasure ship in the West Indies, captured Port Royal in Acadia for the English in 1690. Phips returned triumphantly to Boston in time to take charge of the fleet that had been assembled to invade Quebec. After a late start, Phips succeeded in maneuvering his fleet through the difficult stretches of the St. Lawrence River. He engaged in a cannon duel with shore batteries at Quebec City and landed 2,000 men; but he failed to take the city and returned to Boston.[22]

Although plans were formulated during subsequent years for major expeditions, including French schemes to invade Boston and Manhattan, the hostilities during the period of the 1690s consisted mainly of raiding parties. Finally, the Peace of Ryswick in 1697 created a temporary cessation of hostilities in the region. Peace was unfortunately short-lived as the War of Spanish Succession in Europe resulted in Queen Anne's War (1702-1713) in North America. The French in Canada planned to destroy all the colonial settlements along the New England frontier. Following a route through Lake Champlain, 250 French and Indians destroyed Deerfield, Massachusetts, in February 1704, killing 47 villagers and taking 112 prisoners. After enduring several years of raids on New England settlements, the English developed a plan for the conquest of French territories in North America. The military plans and outcome were similar to the 1690 English expeditions to Canada. The war in North America would be inconclusive, with armies mustered and dissolved. Years of bloodshed along the frontier and one tragic naval catastrophe would end with another stalemate.

The 1709 British strategy involved a campaign through Lake Champlain with a separate naval force attacking Quebec. In late May the lieutenant governor of New York chose Colonel Francis Nicholson as the commander in chief of the new expedition against Canada. His orders included building canoes and boats at Wood Creek on Lake Champlain and plans to "cut a road from Albany to the Wood Creek for the marching of the men and carrying of the provisions."[23] Colonel Nicholson would later serve at various times as a governor or lieutenant governor of five different colonies. He began his military career as a young ensign in Flanders before going to Tangier as a lieutenant in 1680 and, after service in England, was transferred to North America.[24] Two veteran officers of King William's War, Peter and John Schuyler, would also join the expedition to Canada. The expeditionary force of approximately 1,600 men proceeded as far as Wood Creek by July. A road was cut along the east side of the Hudson River to present-day Fort Edward and to Wood Creek. Along the way, three forts or outposts were also built. At Wood Creek about 100 bateaux and many canoes were constructed to move the troops on Lake Champlain.While awaiting news of the English fleet that was to be dispatched against Quebec, the army at Wood Creek was ravaged by disease.

Meanwhile, the governor of New France, Philippee de Rigaud de Vaudreuil, raised 1,500 troops for a campaign to oppose Nicholson's army. Only a few skirmishes occurred and the main French army never left Chambly to engage the English expedition. By October, Nicholson learned that the promised warships had been sent instead to Lisbon, Portugal. Decimated by smallpox and dysentery, the discouraged troops burned their bateaux, canoes, and forts before marching back to Albany. Governor Vaudreuil soon learned from his Indian scouts that the English had burned their forts and vessels. His report to French officials, however, attributed the retreat of the English troops and the evacuation of the Mohawk villages to the threat of the French army: "so great was the terror among the enemy on account of my encampment at Chambly, that the Mohawk had left their village and retired to Corlar [Schenectady]."[25]

The following winter Francis Nicholson and Peter Schuyler, along with four Mohawk leaders, went to England to seek aid for a renewed expedition against New France. It was not until 1711, however, that the expedition came to fruition. The plan again called for a force to attack through Lake Champlain while a naval fleet with marines would assault Quebec by way of the St. Lawrence River. Sir Hovendon Walker, a relatively obscure naval commander, was chosen to lead a convoy of 70 ships from Boston with 6,400 English soldiers and 1,500 provincial troops commanded by Brigadier General Jack Hill. The admiral sailed with his vessels at the end of July.

Francis Nicholson, now a lieutenant general, was again the commander in chief of the forces in New York. Two thousand troops from the colonies were assembled at Albany where nearly 600 flat-bottomed bateaux were built for the trip to Canada. The plan in 1711 was nearly identical to that of 1709 except for a change of route through Lake George, which was thought to be healthier for the troops than Wood Creek. The militia first reached the ruins of Fort Schuyler, destroyed in the 1709 retreat. Nicholson's troops rebuilt and renamed the outpost Fort Anne. By September, as some of the advance units of the army reached Lake George, Nicholson at Fort Anne heard the news of a disaster that struck the British naval fleet in the St. Lawrence River.[26]

By August 18 the massive fleet had reached Gaspé before entering the St. Lawrence River. Ignoring the warnings of a seasoned French navigator, Admiral Walker sailed into the tricky waters of the St. Lawrence without knowledge of the proper bearings. Sailing past Anticosti Island at the mouth of the river, the fleet ran into a heavy fog on August 20. When land was sighted, Walker misunderstood the sighting and ordered a tack in the wrong direction before going to bed. In a short period of time, Walker, in his night clothes, was called to the deck since the wind was blowing the fleet toward the rocky shores of the river. Most of the ships were able to anchor, but eight transports and two supply ships were smashed on the rocks. Walker, shaken by the catastrophe, abandoned the expedition and sailed back to England.

Upon hearing the news of the end of the naval expedition on the St. Lawrence River, Nicholson, having little choice, abandoned the campaign, burned Fort Anne, and again returned with his troops to Albany. The Treaty of Utrecht in 1713 brought peace to Europe and in turn to North America. The treaty established the boundary between New France and English New York at Split Rock on Lake Champlain (between present-day Westport and Essex, N.Y.). The boundary, however, was never fully accepted by the French. Years of uneasy peace would subsequently lead to an inevitable struggle.

The years following the treaty brought relative quiet to the region. After a long period of successful trade with Canada, John Lydius, a Dutch trader from Albany, was exiled from New France in 1730. The next year he built a stockaded trading post at the "Great Carrying Place" (present-day Fort Edward) on the Hudson River to continue his business. At the same time (1730) Charles de Beauharnois de la Boische, governor of New France, sent a 30-soldier detachment under Michel Dagneaux to drive out English traders who had penetrated Lake Champlain to trade with Native Americans allied with the French. On October 15, 1730, Beauharnois sent a letter to the king of France with a recommendation to build a fort at Crown Point on Lake Champlain. Beauharnois suggested that, "When in possession of Crown Point the road will be blocked on the English should they wish to pass over our territory. . .whilst, seizing on the fort we could harass them by small parties, as we have done from 1689 to 1699 when we were at war with the Iroquois."[27] On May 8, 1731, Louis XV approved the construction of a stockaded fort at Crown Point.

A few French families might have settled at Chimney Point across from Crown Point before French troops arrived in 1731.[28] The Chimney Point settlement may have utilized some of the materials remaining from the small fortification built by the English in 1690. The evidence, including a map, points to 1731 as the construction date of the first fort in the Crown Point area, which was actually located across the lake at Chimney Point.[29] Governor Beauharnois sent Zacharie-François Hertel de la Fresnière and 20 workmen and soldiers from Montreal on August 16, 1731, to build the stockaded fort. By September 22 the outpost at "Pointe a la Chevelure," including interior buildings, was completed.

By November 1731 the English began to protest the fort as an encroachment on their territory. The objections fell on deaf ears and the king approved the building of a "redoubt" in 1734 that eventually became the fort on the opposite shore. By 1737 the stone fortress on the western shore was substantially complete and named after Jean-Frédéric Phélypeau, Comte de Maurepas, a minister of France. By tradition most French forts were given the prefix Saint (Fort St. Frédéric). The fort, mounting only four usable cannons, needed considerable work in 1740, as François Beauharnois, the nephew of the governor, noted: "fortifications without ditches and without ramparts. . .no barracks, guard-rooms on the third floor, no cells, no prison."[30] Fort St. Frédéric underwent additional construction and enlargement. The walls were raised higher and a four-story citadel became a fort within a fort. Stone barracks and a chapel within the walls were also finished with the use of limestone from a nearby quarry. By 1742 Fort St. Frédéric, in size and armament, was second only to the stronghold at Quebec. The fort building on Lake Champlain was only part of the larger picture of English-French rivalry for control of North America.

In 1742 the first major sailing vessel on Lake Champlain was built at Crown Point. A sloop of 45 tons was built by the Corbin brothers ("Kings Carpenters") of Quebec.[31] The captain of the vessel was Joseph Payant St. Onge, who supervised its construction and later became known as the "Admiral of Lake Champlain." The vessel, which might have been named *St. Frédéric*, made regular trips well into the 1750s between Fort St. Jean on the Richelieu River and Crown Point. Major General William Johnson in 1755 noted that the French "have a Vessel which sails and brings all sorts of Supplys from Crown Point."[32]

By 1744 England and France were once again at war in Europe—The War of the Austrian Succession was known as King George's War (1744-1748) in North America. Fort St. Frédéric would serve as a base of operations and staging area for military forays into the surrounding region. Before the new fort became an important post during the war, however, the large French fortification of Louisbourg on Cape Breton Island became the focus of attention. By 1744, after years of construction, Louisbourg, mounting 116 cannons, was a formidable military structure. John Bradstreet, an English officer at Nova Scotia and owner of a small trading schooner, was captured and sent to Louisbourg. Bradstreet, who would later play a role in the Lake George and Lake Champlain campaigns of the French and Indian War, was paroled and sent to Boston. In Boston he was able to provide specific information about Louisbourg to Governor William Shirley of Massachusetts who organized an expedition of New England militia to capture the fortress. With little military training, the 4,300-man army, after a month-and-a-half siege, forced the surrender of the fortress on June 15, 1745. Historian Edward Hamilton would later conclude that the expedition "gave the Yankee colonists confidence in their own abilities, and it was a training ground for the leaders of the two wars yet to come, the last French war and the Revolution."[33]

In the fall of 1745 French raids on New England and New York from their stronghold at Fort St. Frédéric intensified. Captain Paul Marin de La Malgue, who had arrived at St. Frédéric following the French defeat at Louisbourg, headed a party of 509 regulars and Indians in a late November attack on Saratoga. The village was burned and 109 prisoners were taken. On the return trip the French also burned the trading post of John Lydius at the "Great Carrying Place." Lydius subsequently traveled to Boston to plead for military action against the French at Fort St. Frédéric. Although Governor Shirley of Massachusetts formulated plans for an assault on St. Frédéric, nothing came of the proposal in the immediate period. Large-scale raids from Fort St. Frédéric continued in 1746 and 1747, but no English expedition ever materialized.

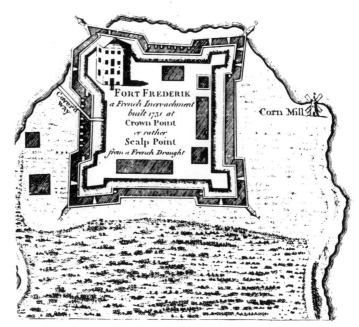

Early drawing of Fort St. Frédéric at Crown Point showing the four-story citadel. (Library of Congress)

In 1748 France and England signed the Treaty of Aix-la-Chapelle which ended the war. Louisbourg was returned to the French while the northern boundary at Lake Champlain was left unclear. Fort St. Frédéric remained a French stronghold with troops periodically camped as far south as Lake George. The Iroquois were quite displeased with the performance of their English allies but valued the trade with them enough to maintain the alliance. In his letter to the governor of Canada on May 9, 1749, Governor Shirley protested French settlers at Fort St. Frédéric as an intrusion on English territory.[34] The French responded by sending the army out with lead plaques to be installed along the frontier that France recognized.

Fort St. Frédéric continued as a bastion of French strength in the lake valleys. In the summer of 1749, Peter Kalm, a Swedish professor traveling in North America, described the French fortress: "The fort is built on a rock, consisting of black-lime or slate. . .It is nearly square, has high, thick walls made of the same limestone. . .On the eastern part of the fort, is a high tower, which is proof against bomb-shells, provided with very thick and substantial walls, and well stored with cannon from the bottom almost to the very top."[35]

In 1750 Governor George Clinton of New York dispatched an observer to size up the fort. Lieutenant Benjamin Stoddert (Stoddard) noted ramparts and bastions, high thick stone walls, a dry ditch with a drawbridge and a subterranean passage to the lake, and a citadel "four story high each turned with arches, mounts twenty pieces of cannon and swivels. . .The walls of the citadel are about ten foot thick the roof high and very taut covered with shingles."[36]

By 1754 the French renewed their raids with an assault on Fort Number 4, the northernmost English settlement located near Charlestown, New Hampshire. Subsequent events in 1755 would lead to another planned expedition to capture Fort St. Frédéric. The most involved and bloodiest war with the French and Indians would follow. The stage was set for the final showdown in North America.

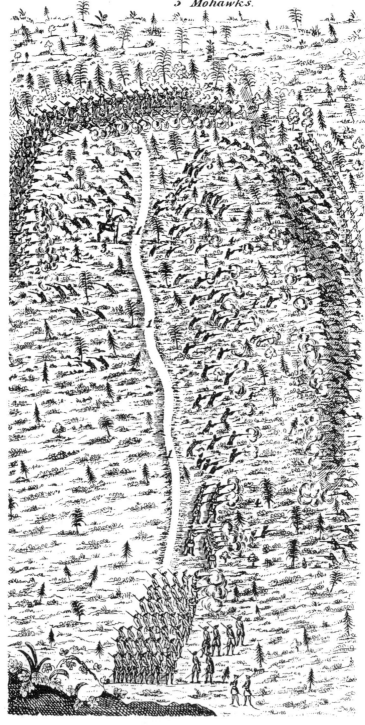

Ambush of troops under Colonel Ephraim Williams on September 8, 1755, from "A Prospective-Plan" by Samuel Blodget. (American Antiquarian Society)

2. Battle of Lake George

AFTER 1750 THE BALANCE OF POWER between Britain and France in North America was undermined by the rapid increase of population in the English colonies. From a quarter million people in 1700, the population of the English colonies soared to 1.2 million by 1750. Population pressure led to the formation of land companies which began to infringe on territories claimed by the French.

One crucial issue was control of the strategic Ohio Valley, which the French considered an essential link between their Canadian and Louisiana territories. The French built a series of forts and trading posts along the Mississippi, Ohio, and St. Lawrence Rivers to protect their frontiers. Subsequently, English land dealers and traders were dislodged from the Ohio Valley by the French, and Fort Duquesne was established at the junction of the Ohio, Allegheny, and Monongahela Rivers (modern-day Pittsburgh). George Washington, then a 22-year-old lieutenant colonel in the Virginia militia, was dispatched in 1754 to reinforce British claims in the area. With only 300 men at a hastily-constructed entrenchment called Fort Necessity, Washington was forced to surrender to a larger French detachment, leaving the valley in the control of the French.

That same year a congress, attended by delegates from seven colonies, was called at Albany to establish a collective plan for the impending war and to win the Iroquois Nation to the British side. Despite the approval at the convention of a well-conceived plan by Benjamin Franklin, colonial assemblies later rejected the proposal.[1] By late 1754, decisions leading to an ultimate confrontation in America would be made in London and Paris with the assignment of several thousand troops to North America by each side. A conference of governors called in April 1755 by Major General Edward Braddock, the British commander in chief, endorsed plans to oust the French from Forts Duquesne, Niagara, St. Frédéric, and Beauséjour (Nova Scotia).[2]

Braddock, a 60-year-old professional officer, would initiate the first part of the plan by leading troops to capture Fort Duquesne, while Governor William Shirley of Massachusetts was to attack Fort Niagara on Lake Ontario (north of present-day Buffalo). The latter campaign, which was to advance through Oswego, New York (southeast shore of Lake Ontario), would cut communications between Canada and the French forts and settlements in the west. William Johnson, a colonel in the Albany County militia and a respected emissary to the Iroquois, was appointed superintendent of Indian affairs and head of the Crown Point expedition with the rank of major general. Last, the leadership of the Acadian (Nova Scotia) expedition would be given to an experienced regular officer, Lieutenant Colonel Robert Monckton.

The opening campaign under Braddock began on June 10 with a long, slow march of regular and provincial soldiers to Fort Duquesne. Although advance troops under Lieutenant Colonel Thomas Gage were employed, Braddock's army was surprised and ambushed by French troops and Indians on July 9, 1755, just before reaching its objective. The panic-stricken British forces, not accustomed to forest warfare, were annihilated by French troops and Indians hidden in the brush and trees. The valiant Braddock had four horses shot from under him before he fell with a mortal wound. Colonel George Washington, a militia aide to Braddock, had two horses shot from under him and four musket balls tear through his clothes. Governor Shirley's oldest son, also an aide to Braddock, was not as lucky and died in the battle. The ensuing war for control of the colonial empires in America, later called the French and Indian War (often dated from 1754-1763), would be the North American phase of the Seven Years' War (1756-1763).

Following the death of Braddock, Governor William Shirley was appointed the commander in chief of all British and provincial forces in North America. Governor Shirley, an architect of the Louisbourg campaign of King George's War (1744-1748), was a lawyer by profession without formal military training. Although Shirley's contribution to colonial politics and military campaigns would later be recognized by historians, his handling of financial matters would be highly criticized. Shirley's personal fortunes increased in wartime, with additional patronage distributed among his supporters in the colonial legislature. War created an abundance of military commissions, supply contracts, credit, and hard currency in colonial America.[3] Ultimately, this would prove the undoing of Shirley, who was recalled to England in 1756 under suspicion of misconduct. Audits of his financial embroilments would not be settled until 1763.

Shirley's Niagara campaign of 1755 never proceeded farther than Oswego. Departing with a smaller force than planned, he became bogged down with short provisions and preparations for an expected attack by French troops from Fort Frontenac, which lay across the lake from Oswego. Shirley, tragically, suffered the loss of a second son in the 1755 campaign with the death of Captain John Shirley at Oswego due to disease. The campaign under Monckton in Acadia, however, achieved its objectives. Unfortunately for the Acadians, thousands were forcibly deported from their homes.

The expedition sent to Lake George and Lake Champlain under William Johnson would have the only military success of 1755. Although Johnson, like many other provincial officers, had no military training, he had successfully worked with the Iroquois during King George's War and had been placed in charge of Indian affairs in April 1755. Since the expedition would take place in the colony of New York, Johnson's appointment as a major general in command of the Crown Point expedition by Governor Shirley would assure cooperation from New Yorkers. His commission stated that the army under his command was "to be employed in an attempt to erect a strong fortress upon an eminence near the French fort at Crown Point, and for removing the encroachments of the French on His Majesty's land there."[4] Appointed second in command and a major general, Phineas Lyman was a prominent Yale-educated lawyer who also had no formal military training. The 39-year-old Lyman was an energetic and competent politician who founded one of Connecticut's first law schools at his home in Suffield. Despite his business and scholarly background, Lyman would prove to be an effective officer under fire. The lack of experience by Johnson and Lyman, however, was compensated for by a number of seasoned officers who served in King George's War and at the siege of Louisbourg in 1745.

Since this was to be an expedition of provincial troops, the colonial governments solicited volunteers to join the foray to liberate Lake Champlain from the French. Connecticut raised 1,000 men, New Hampshire 500, Rhode Island 400, Massachusetts 1,200; and New York provided 500 and paid for 300 troops supplied by Connecticut.[5] By June many of the colonial troops began to assemble near Albany. Three days after the July 14 review of the troops by Governor Shirley and Major General Johnson, Phineas Lyman departed for the north with the first contingent of New Englanders, who began clearing a wagon trail for the rest of the army. While at Saratoga, some of the men were assigned "to S[e]arch for Cannon Ball and Dug up about 1100 Shot" at the site of the former Fort Clinton, abandoned in 1747.[6] The Lyman party, battling mosquitoes and black flies, alternatively moved supplies by river in bateaux and on land, advancing about 50 miles to a sharp bend in the Hudson River called the "Great Carrying Place."

Arriving at the portage on August 3, Lyman began construction of storehouses and a stockade. A more formal fort was subsequently "laid out" by Captain William Eyre of the Royal Engineers.[7] First called Fort Lyman, the stockaded fort would be renamed Fort Edward on September 21, 1755, by William Johnson after a grandson of the British king.[8] On August 14, Johnson, with the rest of the army, had managed to reach the camp at the portage with additional supplies, bateaux, and artillery. Nearly "2/3ds" of the supplies had to be transported by wagon to Lyman's camp because of insufficient "Water in the River to float a Battoe" with heavy provisions.[9] When 30 Mohawks arrived with Johnson's army, James Gilbert with the Massachusetts troops reacted negatively to their appearance: "They had J[ew]els in Their noses. Their fa[c]es painted with all colors. They app[e]ared very odious to us."[10] Shortly thereafter, Johnson ordered a halt to construction of a road to Lake Champlain, despite eight miles having been cleared. After a council of war with the provincial officers, a new road, far more practical than the Wood Creek route, was started to Lake George.* At the end of August the provincial army had grown to 3,100 and 250 Indians.

In all probability, the most essential piece of equipment for the expedition to successfully reach Fort St. Frédéric at Crown Point was the bateau. The bateau was the workhorse of the military during the French and Indian War and the American Revolution, and was even used during the War of 1812. Provisions and light military supplies were often moved by bateaux, but their most important function was to carry troops. The typical bateau on Lake George during this period was 25-35 feet long and carried approximately 22 soldiers with provisions. The vessel was a flat-bottomed, double-ended boat with oak frames (ribs) and bottoms of pine planks. While the vessels were usually rowed or perhaps poled in shallow water, sails were improvised if the wind blew in the right direction. One or two "steersman" would control the direction of the bateau from the stern by use of a long sweep (oar). Later British and provincial expeditions on Lake George (1758) would mark each bateau with a regimental number. The origin of the bateau remains somewhat of a mystery. Apparently, English colonists did not bring the flat-bottomed construction from England. However, as early as Queen Anne's War (1702-1713), colonial carpenters were constructing bateaux in the Mohawk Valley. Six hundred bateaux were built in Albany in 1711 alone. The name implies a French origin, but there is evidence that the influence was actually Dutch. The French, however, used "light batteaux" in the 1666 expedition on Lake Champlain.[14]

The Dutch controlled the Hudson River from its date of discovery in 1609 until 1674. The first permanent settlement in 1624, Fort Orange (later Albany), was Dutch. Dutch boatbuilders had developed vessels strikingly similar to the Lake George bateaux nearly two centuries earlier for the fishing trade in Europe. Albany was still essentially a Dutch community when hundreds of bateaux were constructed during the years of the French and Indian War.[15] In 1755 each colony except New Hampshire brought bateaux with them to Albany, but an inadequate number forced construction of several hundred additional vessels in Albany, requiring the recruitment of carpenters from as far as Boston.

---

* At Fort Lyman one lingering squabble concerned female camp followers (laundresses, nurses, prostitutes), who had trailed the Rhode Island and New York regiments from Albany. While camp followers were a typical occurrence with armies of the period, some officers were particularly worried about the consequences of "immoralities." Major General Lyman wrote to Johnson complaining that "I perceive that there is a number of women coming up with the [New] York forces and Rhode Island which gives a great uneasiness to ye New England troops."[11] On July 27 Johnson wrote from Albany to Lyman regarding the "bad women" in the camp: "I hope we shall not soil the Justice of our Cause with a Conduct rebellious against that Almighty Power upon whose Favour depends the Success of all human Enterprises."[12] The issue reached a turning point at the council of war on August 18. Lyman made a motion that all the "Women in the Camp should be removed from the same and forbid to return."[13] Several days later they were sent off to Albany.

Bateau construction has been well documented in a number of archaeological surveys completed at Lake George since the 1960s (see chapter 4).

By August 28, 1755, Johnson, with 1,500 troops and 40 Indians, had reached the virgin shores of Lake St. Sacrement, the first sizable English force ever to reach the lake. The following day King Hendrick,* the noted Iroquois sachem, and 160 Mohawks arrived at the lake, prompting a ceremony to greet Johnson's allies: "Our army was drawn up to receive them with respect and honour...They began to march through us ye gun[n]er fired five cannon...Their king is a man of Great el[o]quency. He made a long spe[e]ch to his Indians...to be faithful and true."[16] While the army was busy clearing all the trees around the camp, teamsters were hauling supplies needed for the expedition. On September 4 and 5 the army began construction of a storehouse and "Laid out the fort" at the lake.[17] Johnson, an astute politician, promptly changed the name of the lake to Lake George, after King George II, and sent word of his action to Britain.

According to Johnson, the army immediately faced problems at Lake George. The hired wagon drivers threatened to leave the army unless they had more guards to protect them along the crude road from Fort Lyman. Johnson complained that the wagoners discarded cannonballs, plundered provisions, and deserted; "in short they are a set of great Rascals."[18] The New York and Connecticut companies threatened to leave the army unless they were paid. Johnson, presuming that they would have no place to spend it during the expedition, had originally agreed to defer payment until the troops returned. The troops had other ideas which caused Johnson to quickly dispatch a request for the compensation to be sent to Lake George. Thirty men from Colonel Timothy Ruggles' Massachusetts regiment "marched off" after being refused "our back [al]lowance of Rum," but they were quickly brought back by a detachment of troops.[19] Johnson repeatedly expressed his disappointment with his men: "the Troops & the officers with few Exceptions [are] a set of low lifed Ignorant people, the Men lazy, easily discouraged by Difficulties."[20] On top of this he suspected an officer of conspiring with one of his soldiers to sell rum to the Indians. At the council of war on September 5, Johnson informed the officers that his orders had not been obeyed since "Rum was constantly and plentifully sold to the Indians who were in great numbers daily made Drunk."[21]

With the knowledge of the approach of the British expeditionary force, the French at Fort St. Frédéric were not idle. Jean-Armand Dieskau (Baron de Dieskau), born in the German duchy of Saxony and a protégé of the famed Maréchal de Saxe, prepared to intercept the provincial army. The 54-year-old Dieskau was the most experienced professional soldier in the northern theater. In August Major General Dieskau arrived in Montreal and without delay proceeded to Fort St. Frédéric. He examined Braddock's captured papers which outlined the British plan to take Fort St. Frédéric. By late August, Dieskau had an army of 774 regulars, 1,585 Canadian militia and colonial troops, 67 artillerymen, and 659 Indians at Crown Point.[22] In quick order, the general mounted an expedition to cut the supply lines of the intruders. Indian scouts brought an English prisoner to Dieskau while the French were camped at Carillon (Ticonderoga).** The

---

* The 75-year old sachem of the Mohawks was the most influential of Johnson's Indians among the Iroquois. King Hendrick (Theyanoguin), was born to a Mohawk mother and a Mohican father in Westfield, Massachusetts, around 1680, and served as a warrior, statesman, and preacher. Hendrick was one of the four Mohawk leaders who accompanied Peter Schuyler to England in 1710.

** Translated as a chime in French, the name Carillon was derived, according to tradition, from the cascade of water from the falls along the La Chute River in Ticonderoga. Although there is no absolute proof, the name Carillon may actually be related to Philippe de Carrion, a former officer of the French Carignan regiment, who erected a log shed at Ticonderoga for use in smuggling furs between New France and Albany.[23] In early 1756, Major General William Johnson sent a map and list of place names, derived from Native American words, to England. The English word Ticonderoga was derived from an Iroquois term "signifying a Mass or Confluse of Waters."[24]

prisoner skillfully fabricated a story that only 500 men were at Fort Lyman with the remaining provincial force retreating back to Albany.[25]

Based on this information and other considerations, Dieskau left a sizable portion of his troops at Carillon, ignoring the Canadian governor's instructions to keep his troops together. Dieskau would later suggest that the small size of his expeditionary force was needed to move swiftly through the wilderness. In addition, a lack of provisions and the fact that the British had only provincial troops who were "the worst troops on the face of the earth" influenced the decision to leave so many troops at Carillon.[26] Dieskau embarked with 600 Indians, 680 Canadians, and 220 regulars on September 4 to surprise the troops at Fort Lyman, according to Lieutenant Colonel Pierre-André Gohin, Comte de Montreuil, later second in command of the expedition.[27] One hundred twenty troops were left to guard the vessels at South Bay while the main force followed an Indian trail toward Fort Lyman, camping less than four miles from the fort. Meanwhile, approximately 2,200 provincial troops were at the Lake George camp, according to Johnson's aide Peter Wraxall.[28]

Sir William Johnson.
(New York State Library, Albany)

King Hendrick, Mohawk Chief.
(Albany Institute of History and Art)

On September 7, Johnson received information from his Mohawk scouts that "a large army of French and Indians near Wood Cr[ee]k" was marching "in three columns" toward Fort Lyman.[29] One wagoner, Jacob Adams, volunteered to warn the garrison at Fort Lyman, and Johnson also sent two Mohawks and two soldiers on foot with the identical message.[30] At the same time, the soldiers at Lake George hurriedly constructed a makeshift breastwork of logs. After a brief meeting, many of the other hired wagon drivers, apprehensive over the imminent attack, bolted from the camp without notice and headed for Fort Lyman with their wagons.

The messenger sent earlier by Johnson, unfortunately, was tortured and killed. Some of the other wagon drivers who had also been captured apparently provided Dieskau with an accurate account of the provincial forces. Still confident of victory, the French general gave orders to attack Fort Lyman the next morning. The Caughnawaga Indians with Dieskau, however, absolutely refused to move against the fort, which influenced the Algonquin, Abenaki, and Nipissing Indians to take the same stance. The main issue concerning the Indians was the probability of facing cannons at the fort. Many of them had seen a single cannonball cut a tree in half or smash down a wall and were sure that the English had a great many cannons there. While they would not attack the fort, they agreed to assault Johnson's camp at the lake. The Indians suggested to Dieskau that they were unwilling to attack Fort Lyman along the Hudson River since it was "on territory rightfully belonging to them," whereas the Lake George camp was on Indian territory and "surrounded with Woods and still exposed, & without lines."[31]

Nine of the deserting wagoners returned to Johnson's camp with two Indian scouts and two soldiers about midnight. They had heard wagoner Jacob Adams plea for mercy, which meant that the garrison at Fort Lyman had not been warned of an impending attack.[32] The next morning, September 8, a council of war at Lake George voted to detach 1,000 men and 200 Indians to intercept the enemy retreating from the presumed attack on the garrison at Fort Lyman (The council had first intended to send 500 troops to South Bay and 500 to Fort Lyman, but King Hendrick and the other Mohawk leaders convinced them to keep the army together.) The 1,000 troops were sent under the command of Colonel Ephraim Williams of Deerfield, Massachusetts, and 200 Indians under King Hendrick. The provincial soldiers and Indians departed "cheerfully" between eight and nine o'clock in the morning, anticipating the French to be close to Fort Lyman about 13 miles away.[33] But Dieskau, learning of the provincial advance from his scouts, deployed his forces in the shape of a hook along both sides of the rough road that connected Lake George to Fort Lyman. Williams' troops had gone only three to four miles from the base camp when they found themselves in a French trap along a ravine formed by French Mountain. The Mohawks led single file, but Williams had not sent out scouts, even though Braddock's army a month earlier in Pennsylvania had been similarly ambushed in a heavily-wooded area.

King Hendrick paused to inform Williams that he had "scented Indians."[34] Soon musket fire by the French Indians pierced the silence. Dieskau was enraged that his Indians had sprung the ambuscade too quickly, convinced that the Caughnawaga (Iroquois nation) had purposely fired early (reportedly in the air) to warn their relatives among the Mohawks.[35] Dieskau had harbored negative feelings toward the Iroquois from the beginning. Following the battle at Lake George, he wrote to the governor-general of Canada, Pierre de Rigaud de Vaudreuil de Cavagnial, "I prophecied to you, Sir, that the Iroquois would play some scurvy trick; It is unfortunate for me that I am such a good prophet."[36] Daniel Claus, Johnson's interpreter and associate, later recounted a slightly different version of the ambush. Claus reported that a French Caughnawaga Indian addressed King Hendrick in the Iroquois language, suggesting that the French Indians had no "quarrel or trespass against any Ind[ia]n Nation" and urged him to "keep out of the way lest we...involve ourselves in a War among ourselves."[37] But Hendrick made an argument supporting the British, whereupon "one of Hen[drick]'s young warriors fired upon one French Indian that spoke [from] behind the Bushes" and the running battle began.[38] The Massachusetts troops near the head of the column were nearly in the trap when the entire French force opened fire from behind trees and bushes. The musket fire, pouring in from an unseen enemy, devastated the ranks of the provincial soldiers. Williams, at the head of his regiment, tried gallantly to rally his troops but was swiftly cut down with a shot through the head.* The provincial troops soon fell into a panic, wildly retreating back to the lake. The silver-haired Hendrick had his horse shot from under him and was attempting to retreat at the rear of the provincial troops when he was confronted by the "baggage g[u]ard" of the French Indians composed "of young Lads and women who having no fire arms sta[bbe]d him in the back with a Spear or Bayonet...the Manner of his being scalped it is probable a woman did it."[39] Lieutenant Colonel Nathan Whiting now assumed command of the troops and established some defense as they retreated. The sounds of heavy gunfire were heard at the Lake George camp an hour and a half after Williams' detachment had left. The camp immediately "beat to arms"; as the fire drew closer, Johnson sent Lieutenant Colonel Edward Cole of Rhode Island with 300 men to cover the retreat of the detachment. The provincial force reached a small pond about two miles from the Lake George camp where they made a brief stand before continuing their retreat to the lake. At ten o'clock the vanguard of the surviving troops under Whiting began to rejoin Johnson's army at Lake George.

Hearing the musket fire drawing closer and closer, the soldiers at Lake George continued to prepare for the oncoming French assault by desperately adding wagons and bateaux to their rudimentary barricade of logs.[40] Several field pieces and heavy cannons were placed behind the breastwork with one field piece located in a strategic position on the high ground of the left flank. The onslaught was slowed, however, as the Indians stopped to scalp the dead, disobeying Dieskau's order to postpone scalping until the provincials had been defeated. The French commander's plan was to follow the retreating provincials closely, rushing with them into Johnson's camp during the confusion of the returning detachment. However, as the Indians and Canadians approached the breastwork, a few cannonades sent them scurrying for cover. According to Johnson, the French regulars appeared in sight before noon "and marched along the road in very regular order directly upon our center: They made a small halt about 150 yards from our breast-work, when the regular troops (whom we judged to be such by their bright and fixed bayonets) made the grand and center attack."[41] The Indians and Canadians beseeched Dieskau for time to rest and care for their wounded before assaulting the provincial entrenchment. But Dieskau was determined in his strategy. The Indians pleaded, "Father! you have lost your reason—listen to us!"[42] But Dieskau was intent on seizing the moment to crush the provincials.

By noon the renewed battle heated up. Behind the rough barricade, the provincial troops, untested under fire, grew panicky upon hearing the Indian war whoops and musket fire. The rout of the Williams' detachment had likewise unsettled the fresh recruits. Williams' retreating detachment passed through the fresh troops, causing the men at the barricades to turn and run after them. Major General Phineas Lyman of Connecticut ordered the officers to stop them. When the troops did not respond, Lyman himself ran after them, ordering one soldier "to the front and march up and defend it or I would kill him in a minute. . .they all marched back and the fight came on right before me."[43] With brave resolution Dieskau advanced against the provincials who, in the main, held their ground. Captain William Eyre, the director of artillery, used his cannons effectively to keep the camp from being overrun by the French. The Canadians and

---

*Preceding the campaign to Lake George, Ephraim Williams wrote a will bequeathing his land to the town of Williamstown, Massachusetts, with the condition that the money would be used for the establishment of a free school. The school, incorporated in 1773, adopted the name of Williams College in 1793. After the Battle of Lake George, the body of the 41-year-old Williams was hidden by his men to prevent mutilation by the Indians. Later he was buried by the side of the military road four miles from Lake George at a site marked by a large irregular stone (west side of Route 9). In 1854 Williams College alumni erected a marble monument to mark the location where Colonel Williams had been shot (east side of Route 9). In 1920 Williams' remains were reinterred at Williamstown's Thompson Memorial Chapel.

Indians besieged the provincials in a disorganized fashion from the woods. This left the frontal assault to the vastly outnumbered French regulars. Johnson, while directing operations early in the battle, received a musket ball in the "fleshy part of his thigh" and later retired to his tent.[44] Lyman, however, aggressively guided the provincial recruits throughout the entire battle. The French advance of regulars, firing by platoons in a line six across, was brought to a halt far from the breastwork. One of Eyre's gunners later remarked that the artillery "made Lanes, Streets, and Alleys thro' their army."[45]

The blast of cannons and bellow of musket fire became persistent. "My heart trembled," wrote Chaplain Daniel Emerson at Fort Lyman after hearing "great Volleys of small arms" followed by bursts of cannons.[46] Thomas Williams, a Massachusetts surgeon and brother of Colonel Ephraim Williams, described the battle as "the most awful day my eyes ever beheld. . .there seemed to be nothing but thunder & lightning & perpetual pillars of smoke...the bullets flew like hail-stones about our ears."[47] The cannon fire finally forced the grenadiers to seek shelter behind trees and stumps. Mortar bombs lobbed into the Indians' position on the flanks also caused them to pull back further. The casualties, however, were mounting on both sides after several hours of devastating fire that had raked both armies. As the wounded provincial troops were carried back from the breastworks, even some of the heretofore uncommitted wagoners stepped forward with muskets to continue the fight.

In an effort to revitalize his troops, Dieskau apparently risked exposure and was subsequently wounded in the leg a short distance from the provincial lines. Dieskau's adjutant, Pierre-André Gohin, Comte de Montreuil, despite a musketball to his own arm, washed Dieskau's wound with brandy. Dieskau, however, was hit again in the leg. Two Canadians were called to rescue him, but one was killed immediately. At this point, Dieskau refused to be moved and was propped up against a tree where he ordered Montreuil to organize a final assault on the provincial entrenchment.

By five o'clock the French forces had been shattered while the provincials were flush with self-confidence. The provincial troops and Indians leaped over the breastworks and rushed the French, sending them dashing in retreat; "our men sprang over the breastwork and followed them like lions and made terrible havoc and soon brought arms full of guns, laced hats, cartridge boxes."[48] Many of the French were slaughtered and a number of prisoners were taken in the turbulent withdrawal. In the ensuing chaos, Dieskau was left behind. An advancing provincial soldier pointed his musket at Dieskau, while the French general gestured wildly not to shoot. But the soldier, apparently thinking that Dieskau might have a pistol, fired a shot that "traversed both my hips."[49] The provincial soldier who had emigrated from Canada spoke French to Dieskau. Dieskau shouted, "You rascal, why did you fire at me? You see a man lying on the ground bathed in his blood, and you fire, eh?"[50] Eight provincial soldiers finally carried Dieskau to a cot in Johnson's tent for medical attention.

A party of Canadians and Indians, who had earlier left the battle, was busy looting and scalping the dead provincial troops near the scene of the morning ambush of Williams' men when a detachment of 120 New Hampshire and 90 New York troops from Fort Lyman surprised them. A deadly fight caused the remnants of Dieskau's force to retreat to their bateaux at South Bay. Tradition has it that many of the Canadian and Indian bodies were thrown into the pond, thereafter named "Bloody Pond."[51]

According to Johnson, the whole engagement and pursuit by the provincial troops had ended by seven o'clock. The wounds of Johnson and Dieskau were attended to by surgeons in Johnson's tent. While in the tent that evening, a group of Mohawks quarreled with the provincial commander. When they departed, Dieskau inquired about the wishes of the Indians. Johnson retorted that they wanted him to turn over his prisoner "in order to burn you in revenge for the death of their comrades."[52] Dieskau was obviously relieved that their wishes were not accommodated. Johnson assigned a detachment of 50 soldiers and a captain to escort Dieskau to another tent. Despite these steps, an officer barely prevented a Mohawk from stabbing Dieskau the next morning.

The badly wounded Dieskau, shot through the bladder, remained at the Lake George camp until September 16. A mutual respect developed between the rival commanders. Johnson referred to Dieskau as "a man of Quality, a soldier & a Gentleman."[53] Later Johnson had the French general stay at his own house where he was cared for by his sister, whose husband had been killed at Lake George. Dieskau, writing in October from Albany, expressed "gratitude which I owe for all your kind favors."[54]

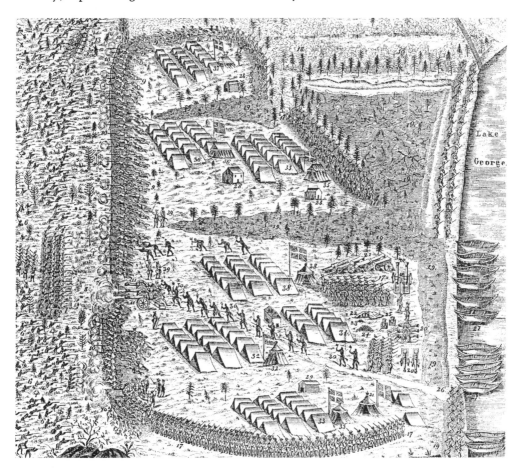

"A Prospective-Plan" of the Battle of Lake George, September 8, 1755, by Samuel Blodget. Blodget was an eyewitness to the battle who first published the "Plan" in Boston in 1755 with the engraving by Thomas Johnston. The "Plan" was republished in London the following year by Thomas Jeffreys. (American Antiquarian Society)

The losses suffered by both sides have been subject to wide variation in different accounts. Johnson's initial report of the battle gave the provincial loss at 130 killed and 60 wounded with the French casualties at 500-600 men.[55] However, the provincial camp surgeons reported 216 provincials dead and 96 wounded, while the French reported a loss of 132 killed and 103 wounded.[56] The wounded often died of convulsions or shock from amputations, resulting from devastating injuries caused by large lead musket balls. In addition, the musket balls found in the bullet pouches of the dead French soldiers were thought to be poisoned with copper and yellow arsenic. Daniel Claus disclosed that Major General Lyman "pestered" the wounded Dieskau, charging that his troops had fired "poisoned balls," but the French general denied any knowledge of it.[57]

According to Lieutenant Colonel Seth Pomeroy, the day after the battle the army began "ye m[e]l[a]nc[h]oly work of bur[y]ing our Dead."[58] The grisly burials continued for three days after the engagement. At the same time, the Mohawks were busy scalping those killed on the French side, "already near 70, and were employed after the battle last night, and all this afternoon, in bringing in scalps; and great numbers of French and Indians yet left unscalped," Johnson reported on September 9.[59] The practice of scalping became widespread during the French and Indian War since the French offered bounties for British scalps while the British raised the ante by offering bounties for both French and Indian scalps. Rather than bring back live prisoners, it was more efficient to bring back scalps tied to a belt. The economic incentive, though, created short cuts for the Indians. A good-sized scalp could be cut and trimmed by the Indians to produce two or even three scalps.

Some of the provincials engaged in looting the enemy bodies before burial. It was a common practice to loot the bodies of the enemy since the only safe place to carry one's possessions or money was on oneself. Ironically, the French arms included British muskets that the French had taken after Braddock's defeat in Pennsylvania. The belongings collected from the French bodies were never equitably distributed among the men. The Mohawk Indians had taken a good deal of it and departed quickly from Johnson's camp. On October 14, Colonel William Cockcroft, on behalf of his troops, petitioned Johnson for an "Equal Dividend" of the plunder, resulting in the formation of a committee by a council of war "to take acc[oun]t of all the Plunder."[60] Notwithstanding, further official action was not taken by the council—apparently, a sale by auction of many of the items ameliorated the controversy.

Rather than being buoyed by the victory over the French, the men at the Lake George camp were disheartened. Seth Pomeroy described the camp as "a Mel[a]nc[h]oly Place [with] So many of our near Fri[e]nds taken away."[61] Shortly thereafter, Pomeroy fell ill and noted that sickness was prevalent in the camp. Nine days after the engagement, Johnson observed that "our sick daily increase."[62] After ten days there were so many sick that wagonloads of men were sent home. The troops at Lake George were not seasoned regulars of the British army, but fresh recruits from small villages across New England who had never experienced the emotional impact of the conflagration of battle. By October 20, the minutes of the council of war indicated that nearly one third of the army was "Sick and unfit for duty their spirits Exhausted ."[63] Part of the malaise of the army was probably caused by the death of relatives and friends in the battle. Colonial troops were often composed of neighbors and family members. The saddest task was to write home of the loss. Surgeon Williams' letter to his wife unhappily reported the death of his brother Ephraim as well as the severe wounding of his brother Josiah. Seth Pomeroy also had the heavyhearted duty to write his sister-in-law of his brother Daniel's death in the engagement.

The main mission of the army was to drive the French from Crown Point. Although there were still two hours of daylight after the main engagement had ended on September 8, Johnson did not allow the army to pursue the retreating French, nor did he attempt to intercept them the following day. Johnson had the army remain at Lake George for a number of reasons: Dieskau indicated that the French had more troops nearby; there was a lack of information about the total size of the French forces at Fort St. Frédéric; and an insufficient number of bateaux to transport troops; and sickness and exhaustion pervaded the provincial troops. After the defeat at Lake George, the French retreated to their camp at Ticonderoga by September 11. After a report from the "king's engineer," Michel Chartier de Lotbinière, Governor Vaudreuil approved the location for a new French fortification, which would "command both the [La Chute] river" and the southern section of Lake Champlain.[64] The work on the four-bastioned fortress under Lotbinière, the governor's cousin, continued for the rest of the season.* French officers were later critical of the fort because it was located too far from the narrows of the lake, and later required the building of a redoubt (small fort) closer to the water.

William Johnson's decision to remain at Lake George and construct a fort renewed a smoldering conflict between Johnson and William Shirley, the Massachusetts governor and commander of all the British forces in North America. In a letter to Lieutenant Governor Thomas Pownall of New Jersey before the Lake George engagement, Johnson complained that Shirley had the "Insolence of a man drunk with power, envenomed by Malice and burning with Revenge—his Arguments are weak and confused they bear the evident marks of Passion overruling reason—he asserts facts notoriously false."[66]

Apparently, the dispute originated over Shirley's negative representation of Johnson to some of the Iroquois and a conflict over Johnson's appointment as the sole Superintendent of Indian Affairs by Major General Braddock. Shirley was upset over Johnson's failure to provide 100 Indians to escort him to Oswego and was unhappy with Johnson's progress in attacking Crown Point. When Johnson refused to send the Indians to guide Shirley to Oswego, Shirley commissioned John Lydius, owner of the former trading post at the "Great Carrying Place" (Fort Lyman). The appointment of Lydius infuriated Johnson, who considered him a duplicitous character. When Johnson wrote his long, detailed report to Shirley on September 9 of the engagement at Lake George, he sent duplicate letters to the governors of the colonies but did not send the letter directly to Shirley. In New York Shirley received a copy of the letter that had been sent to the lieutenant governor of Massachusetts, Spencer Phips, with instructions "to despatch a copy of this letter to General Shirley; my time and circumstances won't permit my writing to him immediately."[67] The letter was an interesting summary of the events of September 8, but omitted any credit in the battle for Major General Lyman of Connecticut.

Although Shirley urged that the French be driven from Ticonderoga, Johnson was not inclined to move northward with the army. Lyman and others, however, wanted to proceed with the expedition while the French were still disorganized. Johnson's immediate plans included building a fort at Lake George. The type of fort, however, became the subject of debate among the men at the lake. At the council of war on September 14, Johnson and Captain William Eyre, the chief engineer, pushed for a strong fortification with earthen bastions, but temporarily yielded to the wishes of other officers who wanted a simple picketed fort of logs. Their decision was based on the views of the officers and troops who had "an Aversion to digging."[68]

In subsequent letters from Lake George, Johnson complained of the "Obstinacy and Ignorance" of the officers regarding the issue of a more elaborate fort and the "averseness of Labour" of the troops building it.[69] Upon hearing of the fort, Shirley immediately wrote to Johnson, disagreeing with the project: "the Fort, you design to build at the End of the Lake will be of little or no utility for carrying on another Expedition"; and in a second letter, "I can by no means adopt your engineer's opinion of the urgent necessity of immediately erecting a strong fort at Lake George."[70] Johnson, however, simply ignored Shirley's opinion.

* Lotbinière made a fortune at Fort Carillon with a franchise on a profitable canteen, the only entertainment for the garrison. Lotbinière also profited by using teams of horses that he owned to haul sand for the mortar.[65]

On September 22, 1755, Johnson called a council of war in his tent to seek his officers' opinions on proceeding toward Crown Point. In a unanimous opinion, the officers advised Johnson to arrange to proceed as soon as reinforcements and provisions arrived. Shortly thereafter (September 25), Shirley again wrote to Johnson, recommending that Major General Lyman be ordered against the French army at Ticonderoga if Johnson could not lead the troops himself. On the 27th, one soldier was placed in confinement for stating that the expedition to Crown Point would not go forward that year since Johnson had stopped Lyman from proceeding. On September 30 Johnson instructed his aide, Captain Peter Wraxall, to deliver to the governors of the colonies the minutes of the council of war and other reports in order to seek advice regarding proceeding with the expedition. On October 14, upon learning of the materials sent to the governors, Shirley criticized the action because by the time all the opinions were gathered by Johnson, it would be "the End of November which will be Extrem[e]ly late for me to send you Directions."[71]

There were many reasons for Johnson's hesitancy. The musket ball that wounded Johnson in what was diplomatically called "the thigh" had never been extracted and continued to bother him. By early October Johnson was stricken "By a violent Inflamation in my head and ear, I have been for some days mostly confined to my bed wholly to my tent." He was "bled, blistered and purged" which did not alleviate the illness, for good reason.[72] Obviously, his personal illness, which confined him to his tent for nearly three weeks, along with the sickness among the troops, affected his willingness to proceed north.

One major problem for the expedition was the failure to bring the bateaux from Fort Edward (called Fort Lyman until September 24). By the end of October there were only 85 fit for service at the lake. More importantly, the artillery boats that Johnson ordered built in September had never been completed. Two days before the September 8 battle, Private James Hill from Newbury, Massachusetts, had been assigned to cut timber for "Flabo[a]ts" that were "about 40 feet Long and to ro[w] With 20 oars, to Car[ry] the artiller[y]."[73] At the end of September, although Johnson had ordered 100 carpenters to work on the flat-bottomed boats, not one had been finished.

Since the report on the failure to finish the vessels was included in the council of war minutes sent to the colonial governors, the issue of the vessels became an additional point of concern for the governors, who wanted to know why they were not finished. By early October Stephen Webster, the captain of the carpenters, formally replied to Johnson concerning the controversy. Webster maintained that the problem was that Johnson's orders to build the fort had left the garrison without enough carpenters to construct the boats. However, one vessel had been completed, two were partly caulked, and another was half-built.[74] On October 22 Johnson wrote to the governor of New York that he had renewed the work orders for the artillery boats. What these vessels actually looked like is not quite certain. However, a detailed set of instructions for a more elaborate "float" had been sent by John Dies, a ship outfitter from New York City, to Johnson in late August. Dies proposed a vessel with a bottom of "squared loggs 8 or nine inches thick. . . trunnel'd together, the sides of this flatt should be Raisd, high Enough for a Breast work to Cover the Men with portholes cut. . . Mount Some of your Field Pieces, Man'd with 40 or 50 men."[75] Variants of this type of vessel would later be called a radeau or floating battery. The radeau was a wide, partially-enclosed floating barge with both sails and oars, mounting heavy guns which could be used in defense of a fleet of bateaux (see chapter 4).

Johnson's own hesitancy to proceed was reflected in his perception of the circumstances at Lake George. By late September he noted that most of the troops wanted to return home. He also worried about the adequacy of provisions, complaining that the reinforcements, especially those from Connecticut, ate the provisions as fast as the wagons delivered them. With his Indian scouts drifting away, troops still weary from the September engagement, the inadequacy of supply wagons, and the near universal insubordination of troops at Lake George, Johnson had a multitude of reasons for not pressing north. Following the advice of Governor Charles Hardy of New York to make an effort to proceed or at least give the appearance of proceeding, Johnson, sensing the loss of resolution of the army because of many delays, called a council of war on October 9. Major General Lyman presided since Johnson was still sick in his tent at the time. Johnson's charge to the council was whether the army should move against the French, and if the advice were in the negative, the reasons should be given for not moving. The council was "Unanimously of Opinion that in the present Circumstances of this Army an immediate attempt upon Ti[c]onderog[a]. . . is not advisable." The reasons were "The Want of sufficient Number of Men and sufficient Quantity of Provisions."[76] They also suggested that the work cease on the flat-bottomed boats in order to finish the fort. At the time there were about 3,600 men at the lake, 500 at Fort Edward, and 2,500 recruits in Albany or in transit.

Nine days later Johnson asked for a council of war to consider sending a detachment to attack the French at the northern end of Lake George. Lyman again presided over the council, which postponed consideration of the detachment until additional scouting reports were forthcoming. On the 20th, the council, with Lyman presiding, again answered Johnson's question about proceeding with the expedition by voting in the negative because of a lack of supplies, the danger of ice, and the sickness of the army. Johnson was pressing the council for an opinion on proceeding against the French army when he already knew the answer because of the lost initiative and lateness of the season. He was, in effect, transferring the criticism to the council for the inaction of the army.

While the army vacillated at the lake, two Mohawk scouts mistakenly reported a large French army on the east side of the Narrows. Captain Robert Rogers and his rangers, on the other hand, placed the French troops at Ticonderoga. Johnson, panicky over an impending French attack, wrote to Shirley on November 11, asking that the reinforcements at Albany be sent to Lake George with all possible dispatch. Rogers was correct; no attack occurred. Robert Rogers, with his New Hampshire volunteers, quickly established a reputation for the bravado of his scouting forays into French territory. The first naval engagement on Lake George occurred between Rogers, using bateaux mounting small swivel cannons, and French troops in vessels at Isle of Mutton (Prisoners Island) in the fall of 1755.[77]

After being ignored during the fall, Shirley called a council of several governors and provincial officers at Albany on November 17, 1755, which recommended "that the Army under the Command of Major General Johnson, do advance against the Enemy."[78] At the same time the Connecticut troops at Lake George insisted on their own dismissal. By the 21st of November, the minutes of the Albany meeting reached Lake George. Johnson reported the Albany decision to his council of officers as "next to an absolute Order for this Army proceeding forthwith against the Enemy, he would recommend that an attempt be made with the utmost Dispatch and Vigour."[79] The provincial officers were not intimidated, voting again not to move forward and adjourned the meeting until the next morning when they would state their reasons. The following morning the officers saved time by referring to the reasons given at the council of war in October. They were, however, able to add cold weather as a new rationale. The next day Johnson wrote a short letter to Shirley, informing him that if he ordered the men to go forward, the majority would flatly refuse; the officers and men simply wanted to go home. This ended the 1755 expedition.

The fort, nevertheless, was substantially complete by late fall. At the council of war on September 29, the provincial officers finally had approved Johnson's and Eyre's plan for a strong earthen fort that could hold a 500-man garrison. By the beginning of November, four bastions and ramparts were completed, and most of the parapet and magazines were finished, as well as one of the barracks, while a second one was nearly ready. Captain Nathaniel Dwight of Belchertown, Massachusetts, noted in his 1755 journal the detailed dimensions of the fort, which included a 30-foot thick main wall, two-story barracks, storehouses, magazines, and a large encampment protected by a breastwork lying to the east of the fort.[80] Johnson named Fort William Henry "after Two of the Royal Family."[81] By the middle of November the artillery was moved into the fort; the two barracks were completed and timber for a third had been cut. Although the mission of challenging Fort St. Frédéric had not occurred in 1755, nonetheless the foothold at Lake George had advanced the British frontier significantly northward.

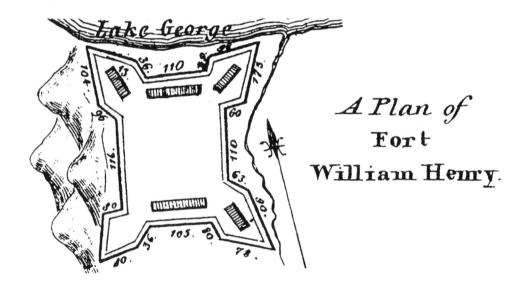

A plan of Fort William Henry, from "A Prospective-Plan" by Samuel Blodget.
(American Antiquarian Society)

What happened to the main protagonists in the Lake George battle? After a month's stay in Albany, Major General Dieskau was sent to New York City where he was further treated for his wounds. Still a prisoner in 1757, he sailed for England where he remained until the end of the war in 1763. Four years after returning to France, he died from the wounds suffered at Lake George. William Johnson, however, received accolades and rewards for his role in the battle. The victory at Lake George, coming after Braddock's fiasco, led Britain to award him the title of baronet, one of only three ever issued to a colonial, and parliament granted him 5,000 pounds for his service. Sir William Johnson was then appointed the Royal Indian Agent and Superintendent of the Six Nations by King George II. He would play a prominent role in the years of the French and Indian War as the most competent British Indian agent. Phineas Lyman, who never received credit for his role during the battle at Lake George, was to serve with dedication each year of the northern campaigns from 1756 to 1760, despite more lucrative business and legal opportunities in Connecticut.[82] Four years after the Battle of Lake George, *The London Magazine* concluded that the expedition in 1755 was "expensive without having gained either glory or advantage to the nation; for a little fort which the enemy could so easily reduce [in 1757], cannot be called an advantage," but because there was no other success in 1755, it was called a "victory."[83]

The idea of death and destruction on a primitive lake in the wilderness is in odd contrast to the resort that Lake George later became. In 1755 only bateaux were on the lake, laboriously hauled to this backcountry. If these provincial soldiers could gaze today upon the lake and observe the flotilla of pleasure boats, tour ships, waterskiers, and parasail riders, what would they make of it?

John Campell, the Earl of Loudoun and British commander in chief
in America from 1756 to early 1758.
(New York State Library)

3. Defeat at Fort William Henry

THE SPRING OF 1756 saw a solidifying of positions in the valleys of Lake George and Lake Champlain. The Crown Point expedition, rekindled in 1756, again failed to move northward, largely due to the problems associated with a change in the commander in chief of the British forces in North America. In June, Major General William Shirley's command was temporarily turned over to Major General Daniel Webb and then to Major General James Abercromby. Sir William Johnson, Lieutenant Governor James De Lancey of New York, and William Pownall, lieutenant governor of New Jersey, had successfully discredited Shirley among their influential friends in England. The new British commander in chief, John Campell, Earl of Loudoun, was an experienced officer from the British upper class. Lord Loudoun's personal belongings alone virtually filled an entire transport ship on the voyage to America. In July he arrived in New York with sixteen servants and his mistress.

Loudoun had developed a distrust for Shirley before arriving in the colonies. Upon reaching New York, Loudoun heard additional criticism of inefficiency, profiteering and irregular commission purchases involving Shirley. The problem of insubordination among the provincial officers was, to Loudoun's mind, Shirley's fault. In 1756 Shirley appointed John Winslow, an experienced provincial officer from Massachusetts, to the rank of major general in command of a new expedition against the French forts on Lake Champlain. To raise the provincial troops for another Crown Point campaign, Shirley promised that the soldiers would serve within a limited geographical region and solely under the provincial officers who enlisted them.

Shirley had placed limited emphasis on the official "Rules and Articles of War" laid down by the British army. Under these regulations, all provincial officers of company grade would be junior to regular officers of the same rank in the British army. Majors and colonels, for example, would only rank as "eldest captains" when marching with British regular officers. Just before Loudoun had actually taken command, Abercromby had queried Winslow, in command of the provincial troops, concerning the integration of the regulars with the provincial army. After a council of war at Fort Edward, Winslow's provincial officers held that any change in the arrangement under which the troops had been recruited would end the Crown Point expedition. The officers replied that "it is our opinion that the effect will be a dissolution of the greater part of the army and have a direct tendency to prevent the raising [of] any provincial troops for his majesty's service for the future."[1]

Loudoun, however, intended to place the colonial troops and officers firmly in a subordinate position. Meeting with Shirley in late July, Loudoun blamed him for the insubordination and mutinous conditions that existed among the provincial troops during the period of his service as commander in chief. Shirley contacted Winslow and wrote to Loudoun in an attempt to explain the views of the provincial officers. After arriving at his new headquarters in Albany on July 31, Loudoun summoned Major General Winslow from Lake George, but, not receiving Shirley's earlier ominous letter, Winslow thought the invitation was merely a social call and declined. Loudoun perceived the refusal as evidence of insubordination. A second order to appear caused Winslow and his officers to ride immediately to Albany, a distance of 60 miles. Apparently Winslow did not alter his initial viewpoint of the arrangements and purpose of the provincial army. In a reply to a letter written by Loudoun the day after their meeting in Albany, Winslow stated that his officers were willing " to act in conjunction with his majesty's troops. . .so that the terms and conditions agreed upon and established by the several governments to whom they belong and upon which they were raised, be not altered."[2]

While agreeing to follow the orders of Loudoun as commander in chief, Winslow had stood his ground by reasserting the conditions under which the provincial troops had been mustered. Not having enough regulars to do without the provincials, Loudoun did not integrate the two forces. Winslow remained in command of the troops at Lake George. However, further squabbles with the civil authorities of Albany over quartering troops and problems with provincial arrangements for supplies compromised any further advance toward the French forts on Lake Champlain. Loudoun finally decided that America was a lawless country without rules, "but the rule every man pleases to lay down to himself."[3] These differences and others would ultimately provide the roots of a rebellion 20 years later. He resolved that the provincial troops were useless and were not to be trusted.

The turning point in the 1756 campaign came during the summer with British capitulation of the Oswego garrisons at a three-fort complex to a 3,500-man French force. As many as 100 British prisoners were butchered by the Indians before the French troops intervened, a portent of the massacre to come at Fort William Henry in 1757. Loudoun had decided to attack Fort Carillon in 1756, but after the news of the Oswego disaster, he ordered Winslow to assume a defensive position. Despite having a force twice the size of the French, Loudoun tabled plans to move northward for the duration of the season. Governor Shirley was recalled to England in the fall of 1756 where he faced questions of his intricate financial dealings and military affairs. Although subsequently passed over for the governorship of Jamaica, in 1761 he was appointed governor of the Bahamas. Shirley returned to Boston in 1769, where he spent the last two years of his life.

For the men at Lake George, scarcely a shot was fired during the 1756 season. Most of the provincial troops, including 21-year-old Paul Revere, swatted mosquitoes during the summer at Fort William Henry. The fort, however, was strengthened and a large number of bateaux as well as several sloops were constructed at the edge of the lake. According to the report of Lieutenant Colonel Ralph Burton, who had been sent by Loudoun to inspect Fort William Henry, Lake George had a considerable fleet in the summer of 1756: "They have two small Sloops of about Twenty Tons each, have four Swivels mounted on each, one Sloop of 30 Tons launched the 23d [August], another of the same size to be launched in a few days, they propose having in each of those Vessels, four small Cannon or Royals—Two large Scows, and one a Building, a good many whaleboats, and more building."[4] The first sloop was "nam'd the Earl of Loudoun" and the second was apparently called the *George* according to a depiction on a powder horn of a provincial recruit at Lake George.[5] French scouts, after observing the activity at the fort, reported that the British had two armed vessels on the lake, two others under construction, and about two hundred bateaux.

Meanwhile, Captain Robert Rogers and his rangers made forays northward to gain intelligence of the French positions, observing the comings and goings of canoes, bateaux, and a schooner on Lake Champlain. Rogers reported that French laborers were "engag'd in heigt[e]ning ye walls of the Fort" at Ticonderoga and building fortified posts at the north end of Lake George.[6] According to Rogers, from 4,000 to 5,000 men were at Ticonderoga with bateaux and "cannons ha[u]l'd up upon the Beach."[7] The action during the 1756 season consisted of skirmishes between scouting parties. In one action in July, Rogers reported pursuing two vessels, "lighters" or "shallops" (probably small sailing galleys), which were sunk with their cargoes near Button Bay on Lake Champlain.[8] In early October, the French found four whaleboats abandoned in a little cove on the eastern shore above Crown Point; one "mounted with three swivels."[9] The whaleboats had been hidden by Rogers following a scouting expedition to St. Jean on the Richelieu River in late August. The vessels had been laboriously carried over the mountains on the east side of Lake George near present-day Huletts Landing to Lake Champlain. However, another trail at Glenburnie to Lake Champlain, known to the British in 1756, would have been an easier route.

The relative calm was broken in January 1757 when Rogers with 74 rangers captured seven French prisoners and three sleighs on Lake Champlain. Pursued by a force of 179 French regulars, Canadians, and Indians, the rangers were overtaken at a ravine near Ticondergoa which resulted in a bloody engagement known as the First Battle on Snowshoes. After a harrowing escape and heavy losses, Rogers and his men returned to Fort William Henry on January 23, 1757. [10]

In March 1757, on the heels of Rogers' battle, Fort William Henry became the object of a major French assault. Pierre de Rigaud de Vaudreuil de Cavagnial, governor-general of French Canada, sent a force of 1,600 men to surprise the small garrison at Fort William Henry. The command of the expedition was given to the governor's younger brother, François-Pierre de Rigaud de Vaudreuil, an appointment that outraged other regular French officers. Rigaud, however, was a veteran officer who had razed Fort Massachusetts in 1746 after a short siege. One of his men described 54-year-old Rigaud as a thin "little man" who appeared younger than his age and who "always marched in the Front, and had no other Accommodations than a Soldiers Tent."[11] The French army remained at Carillon from March 9 to March 15 to organize rations and await more favorable weather. Nearly every fourth man was given a five-foot scaling ladder that could be pieced together to make a ladder three times the original length. Twelve days' rations to be transported on sleds were issued and the men were supplied with snowshoes, iron ice creepers, tomahawks, bearskins, and waistcoats.[12] On March 16 the army of regulars, Canadian troops, and Indians camped below Sugar Loaf Mountain in the vicinity of present-day Huletts Landing. The next night the men camped on the ice near Northwest Bay without making fires. At eleven o'clock on the evening of March 18 the army left for the "Bay of Niacktaron," which would be the depot for the provisions and sleds several miles from Fort William Henry.[13]

Meanwhile, the Fort William Henry garrison of 346 men and 128 invalid troops was not aware of the impending attack. According to John Stark, captain of the rangers at the fort, the troops were planning a celebration for St. Patrick's Day. Stark had instructed the sutler not to issue rum without a written order; but the Irish troops, who composed most of the garrison except for the rangers, nonetheless proceeded with "a drunken carouse" in the desolate outpost.[14] The rangers, however, remained sober, and an alert sentry noticed the French party before they arrived.

According to Major William Eyre, the fort's commander, "about two o'clock [in the morning] a Noise" was heard followed by the "Enemy's approach...upon the ice" and "an Attempt to set on Fire our Largest Sloop [and]...the most remote Bateau[x]."[15] The fort's cannons roared their welcome to the invading men. Troops from the fort were dispatched to extinguish the fires but were driven back with a number of losses. During the day the French continued their attack with musket fire that did little damage to the fort. That evening two hundred additional Canadian militia were sent to help burn vessels, bateaux, and storehouses. Two sloops that were trapped in the ice and a large number of bateaux on shore were burned before daylight on March 20.

About noontime the French force paraded across the ice, prominently displaying their scaling ladders in an attempt to intimidate the small garrison. The army stopped at a safe

Louis Antoine de Bougainville.
(National Archives)

distance from the fort; subsequently, several men walked forward with a red flag.(Since the French flag was white, a red flag was used as a flag of truce.) Eyre sent an officer and four men to receive a letter from the French commander. Rigaud's lengthy surrender proposal included a guarantee that the troops would be allowed the honors of war and could keep their valuables, except for something to appease the Indians from whom the British had nothing to fear! If the British did not surrender, the French warned of dire consequences at the hands of the Indians. Captain François Le Mercier, a Canadian artillery officer, was escorted into the fort blindfolded to receive an answer from Eyre. The British commander provided Mercier with a short answer: "my fixt Resolution was to defend His Majesty's Garrison to the last Extremity." [16] The extra time allowed the fort's garrison to pull the roofs off the storehouses so that the fires set by the French would not spread to the rest of the fort. The French renewed the attack against the fort but retired late in the day.

That night another attack occurred, but the purpose was simply to burn the British outbuildings and boats. Little occurred in the next two days because of heavy snow. By eleven o'clock on the night of the second day (March 22), a volunteer force of 20 French regulars finally succeeded in burning "a vessel pierced for sixteen guns" that was on its stocks.[17] In all, the French reported burning hundreds of bateaux, four larger vessels, two storehouses, the sawmill, the ranger huts, wood planks, and a small fort (probably the hospital).[18] Fort William Henry, surrounded by a sea of fire for several days, was virtually the only structure left standing by the time the French were finished. Although the French force outnumbered the garrison at Fort William Henry by four-to-one, the French troops finally trudged northward on March 23, exhausted after more than a week without shelter. Governor Vaudreuil's report to his superiors in France praised his brother's expedition as a feat of accomplishment at a considerable risk. The casualties on both sides were light; Captain John Stark was grazed by a musket ball, the only time that he was wounded during the French and Indian War or the Revolution. Although Eyre initially listed only "the whaleboats, scows or Gundoles & Bayboats [having] Escaped the Conflagration," two of the sloops that had been damaged by the fires were salvaged.[19] The following summer Major General Daniel Webb noted "two of the Old Sloops and five Whale boats remaining."[20]

The early summer of 1757 brought feverish activity at Fort Carillon as the French army prepared to make a renewed attack on Fort William Henry. Bateaux with white-coated regulars, vessels with cannons and supplies, and Indians in canoes were arriving daily at the fort on Lake Champlain. Although the British knew of the intention of the French to capture Fort William Henry in 1757, the fort had a relatively small garrison because Lord Loudoun had diverted many of the troops for an expedition to capture the French base of Louisbourg on Cape Breton Island. The British preparations for the Louisbourg expedition involved sending a good portion of the troops for a lengthy campaign, first to New York City and then after weeks of delay to Nova Scotia. A tardy British advance allowed the French time to prepare. Reinforcements at Louisbourg, a large French fleet mounting 1,360 cannons, and severe weather forced the British to abort their attack in August. In the meantime, New York had lost some of its

Louis-Joseph de Montcalm.
(National Archives of Canada)

best troops, including Robert Rogers and a good part of his rangers. The French knew of the diversion of the British troops and decided to move against the fortification at Lake George. In June 1757 Louis Antoine de Bougainville, a French officer and aide to the French commander, Louis-Joseph de Montcalm, noted that "In order to take advantage of the absence of Lord Loudoun, who has led away the best troops, . . .the Marquis de Vaudreuil has determined to lay siege to Fort George, called by the English William Henry."[21]

After receiving scouting reports of the heightened activities of the French force at Carillon, Colonel John Parker with approximately 350 troops, composed mainly of the New Jersey regiment, "went out on the 21st [of July] in order to attack the advanced guard at Ticonderoga by water in whale and bay boats. They landed that night on an island and sent, before the break of day, to the main land three battoes, which the enemy way-laid" and later used as "a decoy" to trap the rest of Parker's detachment, according to a member of the garrison at Fort William Henry.[22]

The French presence in the area stemmed from an earlier incident at an island in the upper Narrows of the lake. After a French reconnaissance bateau under the command of Lieutenant de St. Ours had been attacked by an English party near "Isle de la Barque" on July 20, a large detachment of Indians was sent by the French to reconnoiter and ambush any enemy troops.[23] On July 22 Bougainville noted that "Three hundred men, Indians and Canadians are now lying in ambush, part in canoes, part on land, and plan to capture them."[24] After the French viewed six provincial vessels near "Isle de la Barque," Bougainville reported that 450 additional men, mainly Indians under Sieur de Corbière, were sent, "to lay an ambush among the islands with which this part of the lake is covered."[25] At nightfall Corbière observed "twenty barges [whaleboats] and two skiffs" of the provincials. (Colonel James Montresor listed the vessels as whaleboats; both bateaux and whaleboats were usually translated as "barges" in contemporary French military journals.[26])

At daybreak the French and Indians captured three vessels at Sabbath Day Point without firing a shot. Apparently the provincial fleet was widely separated, for the next three vessels, unaware of the ambush, were also captured. The provincial prisoners later reported to the French "that they had separated in the course of the night."[27] The remaining flotilla of 16 vessels similarly fell into the trap. As the Indians darted out of the green foliage, screaming and firing muskets at the unsuspecting soldiers, the provincials tried to retreat southward but were stopped by a flotilla of Indian canoes at their rear. Nearly all of the vessels were sunk or captured. Parker and 60-70 men escaped in a few boats. One hundred sixty-one prisoners were taken, but many provincials drowned in the mayhem. Bougainville recounted the battle: "the Indians jumped into the water and speared them like fish, and also sinking the barges [whaleboats] by seizing them from below and capsizing them. . . The English, terrified by the shooting, the sight, the cries, and the agility of these monsters, surrendered almost without firing a shot."[28]

The captives of the Parker detachment were taken back to the Indian camp at Ticonderoga. The rum from the captured vessels was consumed by the Indians, and at least three of the provincials were "put in the pot and ate."[29] Father Pierre Roubaud, a Jesuit missionary priest who had originally accompanied the Abenaki Indians of St. Francis to Carillon, observed the Ottawa Indians "eating, with a famished avidity, this human flesh. . .drinking skullfuls of human blood."[30] Roubaud carefully approached a young Ottawa to dissuade him from cannibalism, but instead the young warrior offered the priest "a piece of the broiled Englishman."[31] After meeting a provincial officer, Father Roubaud beseeched an old Ottawa to purchase the freedom of the captive but was rebuffed in a threatening tone. The Indians made "touching" visits to the captives, bringing white bread, according to Bougainville, but "Just the same, they ate one of them up at this camp."[32] On July 26 the remaining provincials were sent as prisoners of the Indians to Montreal on a schooner. In early September the prisoners were ransomed by the French from the Indians, sent to Quebec, and then on to Halifax, Nova Scotia.

Upon hearing of the disaster, Major General Webb began calling for reinforcements and also sought to distance himself from the "Ambuscade of French & Indians at a place called Sabbath day point" in a letter to Lord Loudoun on August 1 by suggesting that the detachment had departed "without my knowing any thing of the matter till too late to prevent it."[33] Webb submitted that he was unaware of the intent of the expedition: "to what purpose I real[l]y cannot tell, all the reason they can give for it, was to take some prisoners." [34] The memory of the disaster was renewed the following year when Major General James Abercromby's army landed at Sabbath Day Point: "At 6 o'clock in the evening we had already arrived at Sabbath-day Point, 24 miles, a spot famous by the unfortunate defeat last year of Colonel Parker, who lost there 300, out of a detachment of 350 men, he had under his command. We beheld there its melancholy remains, both in the water and on the shore."[35]

By the end of July 1757, the French were ready to embark on their largest military expedition to date in an effort to destroy Fort William Henry. Forty-five-year-old Major General Louis-Joseph de Montcalm, one of the finest French generals of the French and Indian War, was in command of the French forces at Fort Carillon. Montcalm was a warm, enthusiastic leader who inspired his men and had the strong allegiance of the Indians. He had been appointed to command the French forces in 1756 and had demonstrated his military ability by successfully attacking the British forts at Oswego. In addition to Montcalm's military prowess, his second in command, Brigadier General François de Lévis, was another excellent officer who would later become a marshal of France. Other distinguished officers who would prove themselves in the northern theater included Colonels Louis Antoine de Bougainville and François Charles de Bourlamaque.

Montcalm assembled a massive force of 3,081 French regulars, 2,946 Canadian militia, 188 artillery men, and 1,806 Indians.[36] The unusual part of the expedition was the representation of 40 Indian nations, which included a large number from the regions of the Great Lakes and the Mississippi River. Why would so many come so far to help the French? They believed that the French were less of a threat to their lands. The French had not tried to settle the land as extensively as the English colonists had. In a grand council of the 40 Indian nations held at the portage in Ticonderoga on July 27, Kisensik, the famous Nipissing chief, addressed the nations of the far West: "We domesticated Indians thank you for having come to help us defend our lands against the English who wish to usurp them."[37] Montcalm responded that "The great King has without doubt sent me to protect and defend you."[38] Nearly all of the Indians were convinced of the importance of the mission and cooperated with the French, expecting to gain plunder, prisoners, and scalps.

Since the French did not have enough bateaux to move the entire army by water, one division would follow an old Mohawk trail along the west side of Lake George while the main force would travel by water. On the morning of July 30, a detachment of 2,488 men, which included approximately 500 Indians, began their trek through the virgin forest west of the lake. Meanwhile, the work of the previous six weeks to bring the artillery, bateaux, and provisions from Carillon to the departure point on northern Lake George was nearly complete. Five hundred workmen continued the portaging of supplies all night. Supplies were kept to a minimum, with soldiers taking only one coat and a blanket apiece, weapons, and only three tents per company. Montcalm himself did not bring a mattress along. The cannons and mortars, mounted on their carriages, were held on a platform between two bateaux. Thirty-one of these "pontoons" were utilized.[39] Bateaux

Fort Ticonderoga. Photo by the author.

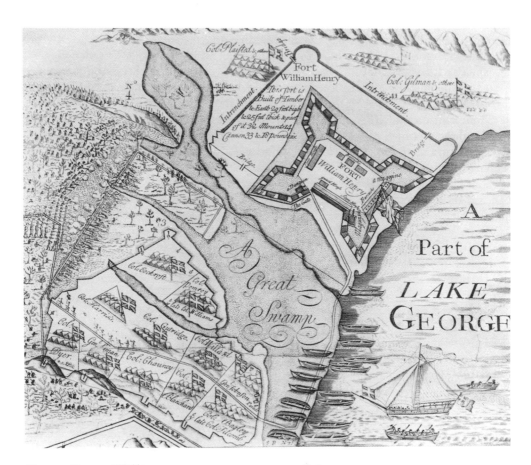

Above: Fort William Henry in 1756, engraved and printed by Thomas Johnston in Boston, April 1756.

Right top: Detail of above showing the sloop. (American Antiquarian Society)

Middle: One of the British sloops built in 1756 at the southern end of Lake George. (Crown Collection, New York State Library)

Bottom: Detail of "A Plan of Fort William Henry" showing sloop *Earl of Loudoun.* (Crown Collection, New York State Library)

were also used for provisions and a few had crude tent-like canopies for the priests.

On August 1 Montcalm with his main force in 250 bateaux set out at two o'clock in the afternoon. The Indians had departed a day earlier in more than 150 canoes. The bateaux fleet, manned by swiftly-paddling soldiers in their varied-colored dress, blanketed the lake. South of Bald Mountain (later called Rogers Rock) a severe storm near Anthony's Nose brought the fleet to a temporary halt. Resuming the voyage, the bateaux and canoes maneuvered through the green islets and majestic slopes of the Narrows as darkness descended. At two in the morning the fleet approached the end of Tongue Mountain, which was later named Montcalm Point on early Lake George maps. At three o'clock in the morning, after observing the prearranged signal of three fires on the dark hillside of present-day Bolton Landing, Montcalm continued across Ganousky Bay (Northwest Bay) to rendezvous with Lévis and his army. The armies reunited somewhere on the Bolton Landing shore at daybreak.

Lake George at the Narrows. Photo by the author.

At ten o'clock on the morning of August 2, Brigadier Lévis renewed his march southward, while Montcalm departed at noon for the southern part of the lake. The bateaux now hugged the bays and indentations of the western shoreline to avoid detection by the British. The fleet halted at "Great Sandy bay" about nine miles from the southern end of the lake. The journey southward was soon renewed with a final disembarkation at Lévis's camp, located near a small peninsula several miles north of Fort William Henry. At ten that night two whaleboats from the fort approached the area where the Indians had pulled their canoes ashore. According to Father Roubaud, 1,200 Indians gave chase to the two vessels, one of which was captured and some of the men massacred; the other crew made their escape back to the fort.[40] The English prisoners were able to give Montcalm important information about the position and number of troops at Fort William Henry. In the middle of the night Montcalm issued orders for the army to move toward the fort at daybreak. Suddenly, a single cannon shot from the fort echoed up the lake, a signal to arms that one of the prisoners had divulged earlier to Montcalm.

At dawn the French army began marching toward the fort, apprehensive that the British might be preparing to intercept their position, but still optimistic that the British could be defeated outside the fort, thus avoiding a long siege. The force under command of Lévis established a position on the west side of the road to Fort Edward, southwest of the entrenched camp of the British and on the south side of the fort. The French army, preparing to besiege the fort from the northwest side, began making fascines (bundles of sticks fastened together like wicker baskets) that would be filled with dirt to build earthworks. At five in the morning the Indians, in 120 canoes, had formed a chain across the lake while yelling war cries to frighten the fort's garrison. Cannons mounted on platforms between two bateaux fired at the fort but were too far away to be effective. During the rest of the day, the Indians fired their muskets from behind tree trunks in the cleared land near the fort.

At three on the afternoon of August 3, Montcalm sent one of his aides, Sieur Fonvive, with a message calling for the British garrison to surrender, warning that the fort was surrounded by the French army, superior artillery, and savages whose cruelty had already been experienced by a detachment from the fort. Montcalm used the Indians to threaten the garrison: "I have it yet in my power to Restrain the Savages, and to oblige them to observe a Capitulation, as hitherto none of them have been killed."[41] The commander of the entrenched camp and Fort William Henry, Lieutenant Colonel George Monro of the 35th Regiment of Foot, replied that he was "determin'd to defend both the fort and the Camp to the last."[42] During the siege Monro remained in the entrenched camp with the majority of the troops, while Captain John Ormsby, also of the 35th Regiment, directed the defenses from within the fort. Ormsby would be severely injured during the subsequent battle but would survive.

In 1757 the fort appeared to be an irregular square with four bastions and ramparts of heavy logs set in cross tiers like cribs with dirt sandwiched between. Barracks for approximately 500 men, storehouses, casemates, and a magazine were inside the fort. The thick log walls, about 17 feet high, were strong enough to resist infantry and light artillery, but vulnerable to heavy siege guns. The fort was protected by standing rows of logs with sharpened ends, a dry moat on the sides facing land, and by a swamp on the east. The fort had 18 cannons, 1 howitzer, 2 mortars, and 17 swivel guns. What were conditions inside Fort William Henry during the French and Indian War? A year earlier, Lieutenant Colonel Ralph Burton had written to Lord Loudoun about the "dirty" conditions at the garrison where sickness and daily burials were prevalent:"The Fort stinks... their Necessary houses, Kitchens, Graves and places for Slaughtering Cattle, all mixed through the encampment."[43] To the southeast of the fort lay the entrenched camp on higher ground bordering the road to Fort Edward. At a meeting of officers at Lake George on July 28, it had been agreed to move the main camp from the "North West side of the Fort, to the Rocky Eminence to the South East" because the former site "was not defensible."[44] "A Breast Work of Logs [was] erected" on the high ground, but at the time when "the Enemy appeared," Monro later wrote, "our Breast Work was not finished."[45] The crude defensive barricade mounted six cannons and a few swivel guns.

By early August the garrison at Lake George was clearly outnumbered by the French army. Major General Daniel Webb, in command of Fort Edward on the Hudson River, had visited Fort William Henry on July 25, returning to the former fort on the 29th. After a scouting party under Israel Putnam observed the movement of Montcalm's flotilla on Lake George, Webb wrote to the governor of New York for reinforcements and suggested that "I am determined to march to Fort William Henry with the whole army under my command as soon as I shall hear of the farther approach of the enemy."[46] A few days later Webb dispatched 800 Massachusetts provincials under Colonel Joseph Frye and 200 regulars under Lieutenant Colonel John Young to Fort William Henry. The French were aware of this reinforcement on August 2 when they questioned the prisoners captured from the bateaux late that night. The total number of troops at Lake George after Webb's reinforcements were approximately 2,300 effectives, with 1,600 remaining at Fort Edward. Most of the troops were stationed at the entrenched camp, while the fort normally contained fewer than 500 soldiers.

During the siege Colonel Monro sent several letters to Webb asking for more reinforcements. The first at nine o'clock on the morning of August 3 and the second at six o'clock that evening concluded: "I make no doubt that you will soon send Us a reinforcement."[47] George Bartman, Webb's aide-de-camp, had forwarded a letter late on the afternoon of August 3 to Monro stating that "every thing will be done for the best on yours and Colonel Youngs part, and [Webb] is determin'd to assist you as soon as possible with the whole army if requir'd."[48] Webb instead sent letters to the governors of the New England colonies asking for immediate reinforcements which, of course, could never arrive in time. The next evening Monro sent another message, requesting that "the whole Army [be] march'd" to Lake George.[49] However, Monro was unaware that Montcalm's Indians had killed Webb's messenger along the Fort Edward road. In the lining of the messenger's jacket was a letter dated noon August 4, which informed Monro that General Webb "does not think it prudent (as you know his strength at this place) to attempt junction, or to assist you till reinforc'd by the Militia of the Colonies" and that a Canadian recently captured had informed him that the French army was 11,000 strong.[50] Webb believed his 1,600 men would prove useless in trying to help the beleaguered garrison and suggested surrender.

By August 4 the French had further solidified their position in preparation for the siege. A decision was made to place the two main batteries on the northwest side of the fort so that cannon fire would cross onto the ramparts. The pontoon arrangement of bateaux with the artillery was finally brought into the small cove on the southwest shore of the lake after nightfall. Twelve cannons and a few mortars were unloaded. (The little inlet later became known as "artillery cove.") While the Indians continued to fire away at the fort during the day, the troops inside were busy tearing off the roofs of wooden shingles from the barracks and storehouses and throwing them into the lake. This was to inhibit the spread of fire in an attack. The Indians, fearing that the English troops might be throwing something of value away, asked Montcalm for troops to stop it.

Eight hundred men assigned to the trench digging continued working all night, nearly completing the left battery by daybreak of August 5. At four o'clock in the morning the night shift of trench diggers were relieved by the day workers. Some of the French troops who had camped too close to Fort William Henry were pulled back since some had been killed in their tents from cannonballs and mortar bombs from the fort. One thousand workers that night completed the trenches for the left battery and brought the cannons from the lakeside. At six o'clock that morning, a battery of eight cannons, including three large 18-pounders and a 9-inch mortar, commenced firing on the west side of the fort and the north side facing the lake, and upon the vessels below. When a shot that cut the pulley for the fort's flag was accompanied by cheers from the French troops, a brave volunteer rehoisted the flag but in "doing this had his head Shot off with a Ball."[51] Again, during the night (August 6), 500 workers labored to complete the right battery. This elaborate digging and maneuvering in trenches seems an eerie forerunner of the debilitating trench warfare to come over 150 years later during World War I. Finally, at six o'clock on the morning of August 7, the right battery, with its two 18-pounders, five 12-pounders, one 8-pounder, two howitzers and a mortar, began firing on the fort; some shells ricocheted on the entrenched camp. Some of the same cannons, captured from Major General Edward Braddock in 1755, had been used by the French to besiege Oswego in 1756.

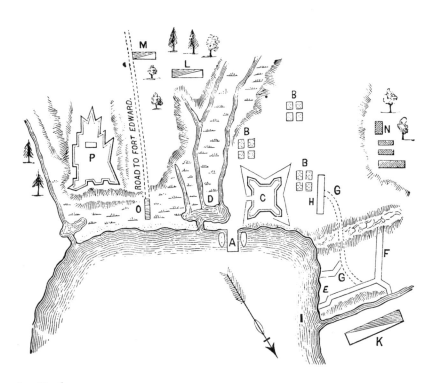

FORT WILLIAM HENRY

A. Dock
B. Garrison gardens
C. Fort William Henry
D. Morass
E. Montcalm's 1st battery
F. Montcalm's 2nd battery
G. Montcalm's approaches
H. Two intended batteries
I. Place where Montcalm landed his artillery
K. Montcalm's camp
L. M. DeLevy's camp
M. M. De La Corne with Canadians and Indians
N. English encampment before retrenchments were made
O. Bridge over morass
P. English retrenchment

A plan of Fort William Henry in 1757 and the English and French camps.
(*History of Lake Champlain* by Peter Palmer)

MONTCALM'S ATTACK

A.   Artillery cove
B.   Road to trench
C.   First battery—length, 70 yd.;
     width, 20 ft.;
   height, 7 ft.; embrasures, 9 ft.
C. to D.—Line of trenches, 578 yd.
D.   Second Battery—length, 74 yd.;
     width, 26 ft.; height, 8 ft.; em-
     brasures, 10 ft.
E. to G.—Line of approach, 890 yd.

F.   Third battery—not opened
H.   Line up the hill and at the crest
     of the Garden
I.   Garden
K.   Fort William Henry
L.   Morass
M.   La Corne and Canadians
N.   Fort George
P.   Docks
Q.   [Fort William Henry Hotel]
R.   [Lake House]

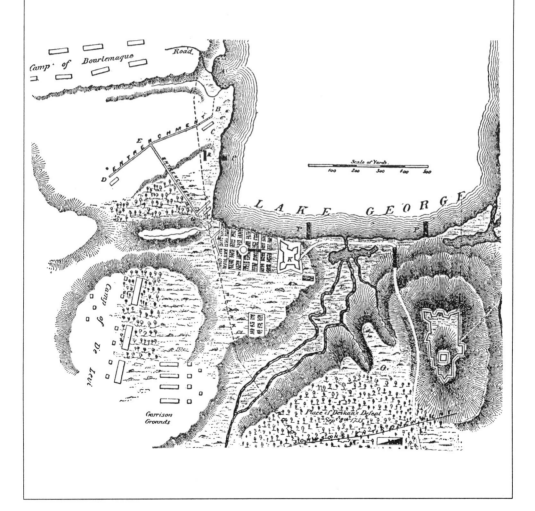

Map of the siege of August 1757.
(*History of Lake Champlain* by Peter Palmer)

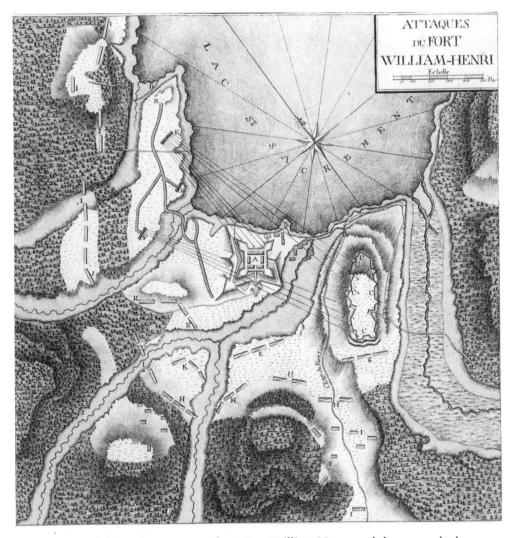

French map of the August 1757 attack on Fort William Henry and the entrenched camp.
(National Archives of Canada)

After a double salvo from both batteries, Montcalm sent Bougainville under a flag of truce, accompanied by a drummer along with 15 grenadiers, with the captured letter written by Webb. Fifteen British soldiers and several officers met Bougainville outside the fort where they "blindfolded me, led me first to the fort, and then to the entrenched camp where I handed to the commandant the letter of the Marquis de Montcalm and that of General Webb."[52] Monro thanked Bougainville for the French politeness and generosity. The letter obviously was a devastating psychological blow to the garrison. They were outnumbered by more than three to one with no hope of reinforcements. After the detachments returned to their respective lines, the cannonades resumed with thundering echoes reverberating from French Mountain. The steadfast Monro issued orders to the garrison "that if any person proved cowardly or offered to advise giving up the Fort that he should be immediately hanged over the walls of the Fort."[53] Although Monro later suggested that the men from the Massachusetts regiment "behav'd and did their duty, better, then either, the Jersey or Hampshire men," he concluded that "the Provincials in the Fort, behav'd scandalously, when they were to fire over the Parapet, they lay down upon their faces and fir'd str[a]ight up in the Air, I sent orders, to the Capt[ai]n [John Ormsby] who Commanded in the Fort to take the first man, that behav'd in that manner, and hang him over the Wall."[54]

The distant cannon fire from Fort William Henry could be heard each day by Major General Webb and others at Fort Edward.[55] "I have not yet received the least reinforcement," Webb complained to Lord Loudoun, "but I fear it cannot long hold out against so warm a Cannonading, if I am not speedily reinforced by a sufficient number of Militia to March to their relief."[56] Two thousand militia did arrive at Fort Edward shortly thereafter, but to Webb it was too little and, in hindsight, too late. Sir William Johnson, after learning of the siege of Fort William Henry, marched to Fort Edward with 800 provincials, Mohawks, and Mohicans (by August 12, there were 4,239 militia encamped at Fort Edward).[57] Webb, however, was unmoved when Johnson pressed him to advance against the French lines. Before reinforcements came to Fort Edward, Webb, sustained by a council of war, had planned to abandon Fort Edward. While Webb seemed more willing to entertain the idea of reinforcing Fort William Henry after the arrival of fresh troops, serious preparations for such an advance were never made. Although a letter on August 6 to Monro suggested that the troops at Fort Edward were ready to "set out in the night with the whole join'd together," two days later another letter postponed the promised assistance "owing to the delay of the Militia."[58] William Johnson later described Webb as a "coward" who "was nearly beside himself with physical fear after the fall of Fort William Henry. His army was in good spirits and anxious to fight. The general alone was panic stricken."[59]

About midnight on August 7, some of the volunteer Canadian militia and their Indian allies made an attack on the entrenched camp from a newly-dug trench, but a contingent of 300 provincial and British regular troops left the barricade to counterattack. Twenty-one Canadians and Indians were killed in the exchange. The French reported 60 English soldiers killed in the battle. That night the French continued their trench-making ever closer to the fort. The following day, August 8, the diggers worked on an elaborate "wet ditch" or causeway over the marshy areas northwest of the fort. Two hundred workers continued their toil during the early morning hours of August 9. By that time the predicament of the encircled garrison had reached a critical stage. In addition to the casualties from the siege, smallpox had spread throughout the fort. Only seven small-bore cannons were left in operation, according to Colonel Joseph Frye of the Massachusetts regiment; all the large cannons and mortars had burst or had been disabled by enemy fire.[60] (It was fairly common for cannons to burst from metal fatigue after repeated firings.)

Following a recommendation of surrender from Monro's council of officers early on the morning of August 9, a white flag was raised. With drums beating repetitiously, Lieutenant Colonel Young rode on horseback to Montcalm's tent. A lengthy set of terms involving nine articles was agreed to by Monro. The British garrison was to march out with the usual honors of war with their guns; all artillery and military provisions were to be turned over to the French; none of the troops could serve against the French or Indians for 18 months, all French prisoners would be exchanged for an equal number of British upon delivery at Fort Carillon within three months; all sick and wounded were to be transported under French protection to Fort Edward; and "the Marquis de Montcalm, being willing to show Colonel Monro and the garrison under his command, marks of esteem, on account of their honorable defence, gives them one piece of cannon, or six pounder."[61]

Aware of the Indians' desire for plunder, Montcalm postponed signing the agreement until he assembled a council of chiefs from all the Indian nations to inform them of the articles of the capitulation and motives behind his actions. Montcalm had gone to great lengths during the expedition to consult with the Indians and treat them respectfully. He "asked their consent and their promise that their young men would not commit any disorder. The chiefs agreed to everything [or acquiesced] and promised to restrain their young men," noted Bougainville, an eyewitness to the meeting.[62] At noon the fort was turned over to the French, whereupon the British forces from the fort were brought to the entrenched camp. The Indians promptly entered the fort to pillage. The sick and wounded men who could not be moved were immediately butchered. Father Roubaud again witnessed several atrocities: "I saw one of these barbarians come out of the casemates. . .[with] a human head, from which trickled streams of blood, and which he displayed as the most splendid prize that he could have secured."[63]

Finding little plunder in the fort, the Indians and some Canadians could not be stopped from entering the entrenched camp and pillaging the British prisoners even though Montcalm had assigned guards. While the women and children were frozen with horror, the Indians roamed the camp and assaulted some of the men for personal belongings. Montcalm and his officers personally went to the entrenched camp to end the misconduct. It took until nine o'clock that evening to bring order to the British camp. Bougainville advised the British officers and troops to throw away all wine, brandy, and any other intoxicating liquor since the French had seen the consequences of the Indians during drunken escapades. A subsequent French account suggested that English soldiers "in spite of all the advice given on the subject, had given the Indians rum to drink," but Colonel Frye noted that "to prevent their being drunk the Liquour was all stove by order."[64] Fearing a renewal of the previous disorder, "Monro [with Montcalm's consent]...determined we should march out that night about 12 o'clock ...the men paraded, and began their march," but a report that Indians were waiting along the road caused the orders to leave to be rescinded.[65] "All the Remainder of this night the Indians were in great numbers round our lines and seemed to sh[o]w more than usual malice," Frye wrote.[66] The Indians, although acceding to the terms of surrender, were unhappy since they had been promised plunder by Montcalm before embarking on the expedition. It was later reported that "an English officer heard the Indian Chief violently accuse the French General with being false and a l[i]ar to them; that he had promised them the plunder of the English, and they would have it."[67]

The next day (August 10) the British were to march to Fort Edward under a French escort. By five o'clock in the morning the Indians, still seeking trophies and pillage, entered the huts and tents of the wounded, dragged 17 men out, and tomahawked and scalped them while Miles Whitworth, a Massachusetts surgeon, watched helplessly.[68] By now panic had seized the British camp. Captain James Furnis, the British Comptroller of Ordinance in America, wrote that the plundering began as "we were preparing to march" when the Indians "got over the Breast Work."[69] According to the French account, the terror-stricken British began their march to Fort Edward before the French escort had fully assembled.[70] The march had barely begun when the Indians began menacing the captives. Although Colonel Monro complained to the French officers, no action was taken. Frye recalled that "the French officers however told us that if we would give up the baggage of its officers and men, to the Indians, they thought it would make them easy."[71] In an attempt to pacify the Indians, the British and provincial soldiers turned over their packs. The packs, however, did not satisfy Montcalm's allies who then "began to take the Officers Hats, Swords, guns & Cloaths, stripping them all to their Shirts...and then took out from our troops all the Indians and negros, and Carried them off."[72] When some of the Indians returned to their camp with plundered articles, others naturally rushed to the English entrenchment to obtain their share of the trophies of war. "By this time the war-hoop was given" by the Indians and with "great difficulty" the troops left the entrenched camp.[73]

Although the British and provincials were verbally promised "to march o[u]t with the honours of War with their Arms & one charge of Powder & ball & one p[iece] of Cannon," a provincial soldier noted that "we were permitted to carry off our arms, yet we were not allowed a single round of ammunition."[74] The soldiers were advised not to offer any resistance "lest it should be Construed as a Breach of our part of the Capitulation and those that were in the rear Should fall a Sacrifice to their [Indians] unbounded fury."[75] Soon the carnage began at the rear of the long column with men, women, and even children killed. Webb's letter to Lord Loudoun, written the following day, reported that troops as well as "the Women and Children [were]...most inhumanly butchered."[76] Captain Samuel Angell described the same episode as "the horrible scene of massacre."[77] Private Seth Metcalf at Fort Edward noted in his diary that the Indians had "Rav[i]sh[ed] the women and then put them to the Slaughter. Young Children of the Regular forces had their Brains Dash[ed] out Against the Stones and trees."[78] An "Express" from Albany printed in the October 1757 editions of *The London Chronicle* and *The London Magazine* referred to the incident as a "massacre [of] all the sick and wounded" and added "the throats of most, if not all the women, were cut, their bellies ript open, their bowels torn out."[79] The troops were nearly stripped naked as the Indians literally tore their belongings from them; hundreds fled terrified into the woods. The British desperately appealed to the officers of the French escort, but they did not intercede in the chaos. Frye recorded that the French officers refused protection and "told them they must take to the woods and shift for themselves."[80] Hundreds more were taken captive by the Indians. The reason for the actions of the Indians was the denial of the spoils of war by the French that had been expected and promised when the campaign began. The European tradition of the honors of war meant nothing to the Indians who regarded the captured troops as enemies.

Upon hearing the cries and commotion, Montcalm and his officers ran to the scene and immersed themselves among the Indians in an attempt to stop the carnage. "Kill me, but spare the English who are under my protection," Montcalm reportedly demanded.[81] A few of the French officers were wounded in the melee. Montcalm arrived, however, after most of the butchery had been completed. Eventually, the French restored order and retrieved 400 captives from the Indians.[82] The French and British officers then divided the few spare clothes remaining among the half-naked troops. Many of the men who had escaped into the woods staggered piecemeal, disoriented, and hungry into Fort Edward on August 10 and for the next several days. Colonel Frye, who had fled into the wilderness, arrived at Fort Edward on August 12.

After the massacre, some of the western Indians dug up the fresh graves of the British and scalped them. Unbeknownst to the Indians, many of the British had died of smallpox. The disease later decimated their villages at home. Most of the Indians, loaded with the prizes of war, left that day; others departed the following morning. One unfortunate ranger, John McKeen from New Hampshire, was tied to a tree by the Indians the night after the massacre and used for target practice with knives and tomahawks, then set afire. Several hundred British prisoners, whom the French could not immediately retrieve, were taken to Montreal by the Indians. After lengthy negotiations at Montreal from August 19 through early September, the French were finally able to ransom most of the prisoners from the Indians. However, the captive Black provincial soldiers were not returned but instead sold into slavery.[83]

The remaining British soldiers were brought back to the entrenched camp at Lake George where they remained until August 15. On that morning 250-300 French and Canadian troops escorted 400 British prisoners from the entrenched camp at Lake George

Above: Artifacts found in 1954 at the possible site of a blacksmith's shop in the area of the East Barracks. (All: Fort William Henry Museum)

Left top: Staff archaeologist Ernest Clute examining mortar shell found in October 1954. The shell was uncovered with a tomahawk blade on top and a human scalp with black hair attached to the opposite side of the shell.

Left: Skeletons of four individuals, believed to be massacre victims, were discovered in 1957 in a casement of the East Barracks.

part way to Fort Edward.[84] Halfway to Fort Edward, a British detachment met the French and escorted Lieutenant Colonel Monro and the survivors the rest of the way. If there were only 400 left, most of the survivors would have had to reach Fort Edward on their own after fleeing the Indians on August 10.[85]

The actual losses of British and provincials during the siege and massacre are somewhat uncertain. Approximately 300 troops that had been at Fort William Henry, over half from the provincial ranks, were dead or missing at the end of 1757.[86] The French listed their losses on August 22 as only 17 killed and 40 wounded.[87]

The French immediately began a demolition of Fort William Henry which lasted for three days. The fort, with its crib-like structure for ramparts with earthern layers, proved difficult to break up and burn. At the time of the siege of Fort William Henry, the British vessels included"2 Galliots [galleys under construction], 2 Scows, 5 whaleboats, 3 Batos, 2 Sloops."[88] On August 14 the victorious French troops burned the "two Row Galleys [on stocks] which were ready to launch."[89] The French used the captured vessels to transport a tremendous amount of provisions, including 1,237 barrels of salt pork and 1,737 quarters of flour, to Ticonderoga. Although the British reported that they were down to only seven small cannons when the fort surrendered, the French transported 23 cannons (8 bronze), 1 howitzer, 2 mortars, 17 swivels, 38,835 pounds of powder, 2,522 shot and other munitions back to Fort Carillon.[90] They also recovered six chests of "fireworks" from the fort. Satisfied with their accomplishment, the French departed on August 16, never to return again in force.

A few weeks after the fall of Fort William Henry, Captain Israel Putnam's ranger patrol noticed "one of our [captured] Sloops lies out in the Lake, at Anchor, in order to give the earliest Intelligence."[91] Shortly thereafter, Major General Daniel Webb wrote to Lord Loudoun with information that the two captured sloops had been "dismasted...and sunk" at the northern end of Lake George; three months later rangers observed the "Boats taken at Fort William Henry...under water."[92] In September 1759 provincial troops raised "two Large flat Bottomed Boats [scows]" taken from Fort William Henry and sunk at the Ticonderoga landing on Lake George, but another large vessel remained underwater.[93]

During the winter of 1757-1758, Robert Rogers and his rangers, after their return from the aborted Louisbourg expedition, walked through the broken ruins of Fort William Henry. One of the bodies that had been dug up and scalped by the Indians was that of Rogers' brother Richard, who had died of smallpox just before the French siege. The undisturbed earthern mounds of Fort William Henry could still be seen more than 100 years later on the edge of the lake. The area remained relatively undisturbed until archaeological work began on the site during the reconstruction of the fort in the early 1950s.[94]

Robert Rogers and his rangers examine the ruins of Fort William Henry, December 1757. Drawing by Gary Zaboly. (Lake George Historical Association)

Major General James Abercromby. Oil painting by Allan Ramsay (ca. 1760).
(Private collection, Fort Ticonderoga Museum)

4. Debacle: Abercromby Expedition

On A TYPICAL JULY EVENING, tourists leisurely stroll down to the tranquil waters of Lake George, but few realize that an epic struggle for a continent occurred in this valley more than 240 years earlier. Yet here, a flotilla exceeding 1,000 vessels conveyed the largest military expedition of the French and Indian War to its doom. As the boats weaved through the islands, the regimental flags fluttered in the breeze and the blare of fifes and trumpets accompanied the shrill cry of bagpipes piercing the silence of the wilderness. Who among the 15,000 men of that expedition could foresee that their exuberance and camaraderie in anticipation of an easy victory would turn into terror and despair a few days later?

As the battle for North America continued between Britain and France, the 1758 British campaign called for the capture of Fort Carillon, constructed on a rocky promontory called Ticonderoga overlooking Lake Champlain, and then a push northward into Canada. By 1758 Carillon had superseded Fort St. Frédéric as the largest French fortress on Lake Champlain. The French had experienced considerable success in their control of the lake valleys: holding their forts at Crown Point and Ticonderoga on Lake Champlain, destroying Fort William Henry on Lake George, and defeating Robert Rogers and his rangers in the Second Battle on Snowshoes in March 1758. In the latter engagement 180 rangers were nearly annihilated by a force of French and Indians in the vicinity of Trout Brook in Ticonderoga.*

William Pitt, the reinstated secretary of state, recalled Lord Loudoun early in 1758 for political reasons as well as for the military setbacks during 1757 at Oswego and Fort William Henry, and the failure of the Louisbourg expedition. Pitt informed provincial legislatures that the position of commander in chief would be reduced to a military head only, thus ending interference with colonial governors and assemblies. Legislatures would have more autonomy and direct financial assistance from England, which guaranteed renewed support for military expeditions.

Although faced with hostilities in Europe, in 1758 Pitt focused a good deal of his attention on the war in North America. The three-pronged strategy not only included a plan for an attack on Carillon, but renewed expeditions against Louisbourg and Fort Duquesne. Pitt recalled Colonel Jeffery Amherst, a cautious but resolute and energetic officer, from the German theater of the Seven Years' War. The seizure of Louisbourg on Cape Breton Island (Nova Scotia), the strongest fortification in North America, would be a first step toward the capture of Quebec. Promoted to major general and assigned leadership of the Louisbourg campaign, Amherst reached the British armada under Admiral Edward Boscawen, as it left Halifax harbor for Louisbourg. Although hampered by severe weather, the troops finally disembarked on the craggy shore on June 8. Among the three brigadier generals with Amherst was 31-year-old James Wolfe, a gallant field officer who would later lead the attack on Quebec. In an effort to block the fort's harbor, the French sank six of their own vessels at its entrance. The French efforts were to no avail; the garrison was forced to capitulate by the end of July. Several hundred cannons and 5,637 prisoners were taken by Amherst upon surrender of the fort. The new

* The subject of a surviving legend, Rogers' daring escape was supposedly made by deceiving his Indian pursuers into thinking that he had slid down the 500-foot cliff of Bald Mountain. Although Rogers did not mention the incident in his journal, land petitions in 1766 referred to the landmark as "Rogers's Leap" and "Rogers's Rock."[1]

commander in chief of British forces in North America, Major General James Abercromby, was given the assignment of the Ticonderoga operation. Abercromby, whose earlier political activity aided his military advancement, had spent most of his career in staff positions in the army. At 52 and in imperfect health, he had a reputation as an inactive and uninspiring commander. A young recruit from Massachusetts noted in his journal that Abercromby was "an aged gentleman, and infirm in body and mind."[2] Rufus Putnam, a youthful, provincial soldier who would later serve as a general in the American Revolution, noted that Abercromby was "an old man and frequently called granny."[3]

William Pitt intended that the officer second in command, 34-year-old George Augustus Howe, who held the rank of brigadier general in North America, be the field commander of the Ticonderoga expedition. The young nobleman breathed life into the body and soul of the army. While many British officers looked down on the provincial troops, Howe was extremely popular and on very close terms with both colonial officers and their troops. He scrapped tradition to suit the needs of warfare in the wilderness. To understand fighting in the wilds of America, he had accompanied Robert Rogers and his rangers on scouting forays, carrying his own blanket and bearskin. As a result of these experiences, he had his men cut their hair and the tails on their redcoats, brown their musket barrels to eliminate glare, discard wigs and other unwieldy baggage, and wear leggings as protection from briars. Howe ordered that no women accompany the troops to wash the soldiers' clothing. He instead set an example by going to a brook and washing his own clothes. The eighteenth-century armies typically provided a separation between

Departure of the Abercromby expedition on July 5, 1758. Painting by F. C. Yohn, The Glens Falls Collection, Continental Insurance Corporation.
(*The Summer Paradise in History* by Warwick Stevens Carpenter, 1914)

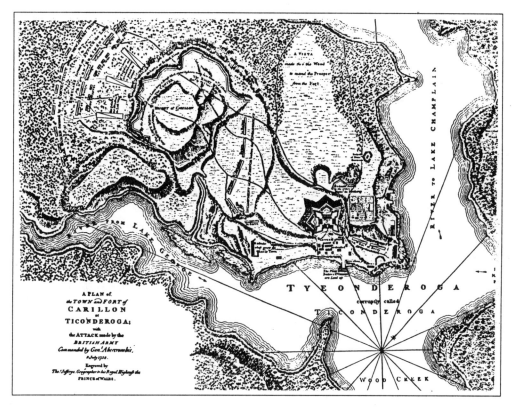

Thomas Jeffreys' map of Abercromby's attack on Fort Carillon on July 8, 1758.
(*History of Lake Champlain* by Peter Palmer)

men and officers, but Howe, scorning the trappings of rank, purposely became familiar with the common troops, which endeared him to the army.[4]

In late June Major General Abercromby declared the 1757 capitulation agreement of Fort William Henry "null and void" since the French had immediately broken it.[5] He called for the reenlistment of officers and soldiers of the 1757 garrison who, by the surrender terms, would have been prohibited for 18 months to "serve in the same manner."[6] Abercromby notified the governor-general of Canada, Pierre de Rigaud de Vaudreuil de Cavagnial, of his decision. However, by early June the French knew that something was impending when prisoners, taken by their Indian allies, divulged that the British army was assembling at Lake George. By June 19 the French discerned that the attack was to be on Carillon; by the end of the month they anticipated that the assault on the fort would involve twenty to twenty-five thousand men. Major General Louis-Joseph de Montcalm, the highly energetic and very successful field commander of the French army in North America, listened to the conflicting advice of his officers. Some felt a retreat north on Lake Champlain was prudent while others recommended making a stand, despite the overwhelming British force. Montcalm, the victor at Fort William Henry a year earlier, decided to oppose the British army. In Montcalm, the French had a career officer with nearly the opposite temperament of Abercromby.

By early July Montcalm still had slightly fewer than 3,000 troops at Carillon, although reinforcements were expected. Governor-general Vaudreuil had decided to assemble 5,000 men at Carillon in mid-June, but political and personal rivalry with Montcalm delayed reinforcements to the fort. Vaudreuil, the Canadian-born son of a former governor of

New France, was an ambitious leader with limited military experience. He never believed that the British would attack at Carillon and continued plans for a diversionary expedition to the Mohawk Valley. It was only at the last moment that troops were ordered to reinforce Montcalm. Even then the largest contingent arrived three days after the battle.

In early July 1758, an army of 6,367 British regulars and 9,024 provincial troops had gathered at the ruins of Fort William Henry on the southern shore of Lake George.[7] Many of the provincial regiments, hurriedly called up, had little training. Two days before embarkation, the Massachusetts non-commissioned officers were yet uncertain how to execute commands, while the troops from Connecticut were attempting to learn how to change from a column to a line. A few men had never fired a musket. The provincial regiment of Private Amos Richardson had just a single day of training the day before leaving for Ticonderoga. Richardson noted a "fine firing" of the muskets during the afternoon but recorded that "some of our men did shoot one of the regulars through the head, which killed him dead."[8] The following day Richardson's regiment was left behind at Lake George.

Provincial troops were typically raised by officers (appointed by a colonial governor), who in turn had the authority to commission lower-ranked officers based on their success in enlisting troops. Militia officers were expected to support the recruitment effort by ordering musters of their units for the solicitation of volunteers or impressment of conscripts. Unlike in the regular army, many of the men and officers were related by blood or neighborhoods. If not enough men were enlisted despite enlistment bounties, conscription of idle men in the town would occur. A conscripted man, nevertheless, could hire a substitute to take his place by paying a small fine to the colonial government and a larger payment to his replacement. As the war dragged on, the payment increased.[9]

On the clear summer morning of July 5, the largest army ever assembled at that time in North America departed on approximately "900 bateaux and 135 Whale Boats, the Artillery. . .being mounted on Rafts," according to Abercromby.[10] Other vessels were also present with the fleet. In late June shipwright William Sweat noted that "they are making a floating Ba[t]tery."[11] Likewise, James Searing, a young New York regimental surgeon, observed that "three redeaus or floating batteries were prepared, two upon batteaux."[12] The floating batteries and rafts were hastily constructed at Lake George while most of the bateaux were built in Albany and Schenectady under Colonel John Bradstreet, commander of the "Battoe Service."[13]

An eyewitness reported that the entire surface of the lake was completely obscured by the fleet, when the vessels were three miles from the departure point.[14] The sun gleamed down on the crystal clear water of the lake as the flotilla, organized in "four columns," stretched for six miles, slowly moving on its way northward through the Narrows.[15] The scene must have been spectacular, with the red coats of the regulars, along with the regal kilts of the Scottish 42nd Black Watch regiment in the middle and the blue uniforms and homespun browns of the provincial soldiers on both flanks, passing by the lush green mountains overlooking the lake. Major Robert Rogers called the scene "a splendid military show and "Beautiful to Se[e]," noted Samuel Fisher.[16] The men were filled with optimism as the vessels made their way along the lake to the intermittent tune of the musical instruments of each corps—bagpipes, drums, fifes, and trumpets. Two weeks later a wounded officer recalled that "I never beheld so delightful a prospect."[17] It would seem that this force would be truly invincible compared to the French army at Fort Carillon with only a quarter as many men. By two o'clock in the afternoon, the French had received a signal that British bateaux were sighted on the lake.

Before sunset, the expedition landed at Sabbath Day Point, about two-thirds of the way to Ticonderoga. The troops had supper there and waited for the artillery and

provisions on the rafts to catch up. Several fires were made to confuse the French about their plans for the night. By eleven o'clock in the evening the army renewed its voyage to the north. At five o'clock in the morning of July 6, the vanguard of the fleet reached the northern end of Lake George, disembarking at a point on the west shore later referred to as Howe's Cove or Landing.

At daylight the French observed their signal flag being raised and lowered on the mountain side, indicating the British bateaux landings. Captain François-Joseph, Chevalier de Germain, with an advance party of French at the lakeside, fired on the British vessels before fleeing to the French camp. The British and provincial troops quickly plundered the belongings left by the French soldiers. A scouting detachment of 350 troops under Captain de Trepézec and En-

Top: "Abercromby's Spearhead," showing Robert Rogers aboard a whaleboat during the Abercromby Expedition. Drawing by Gary S. Zaboly. *Above:* Major Robert Rogers. (National Archives)

sign Jean-Baptiste Levrault de Langis (Langy) Montregron, which had been sent the day earlier to a post between Bald Mountain (later Rogers Rock) and the lake, were now cut off by the British and provincial troops. The detachment was forced to try to reach the French camp via the thickly-wooded area near Trout Brook in present-day Ticonderoga.

According to French officers at Carillon, Captain de Trépezec "told us that he had lost his way through the fault of his guides" in the dense forest. [18] Meanwhile, Abercromby's army began a march in four columns from the landing site "towards the Fort," following a route to the west of the La Chute River.[19] About four o'clock, the advance units led by Brigadier General Howe with Major Israel Putnam accidentally stumbled upon the French party led by Trépezec. "Qui vive [Who goes there]?" "Francais," replied the British, but the French were not deceived.[20] Suddenly, shots rang out and musket balls pierced the green foliage. The young brigadier general, Lord Howe, was killed instantly at the first volley by a ball that penetrated both his heart and lungs. Rogers recalled that Howe with his detachment "had broke the enemy, and hemmed them in on every side; but advancing himself with great eagerness and intrepidity upon them, was unfortunately shot and died immediately."[21] Sixteen-year-old David Perry, who had marched to Lake George with his provincial unit from eastern Massachusetts, experienced his first action with the detachment: "[The] whistling of balls and roar of musquetry terrified me not a little."[22] Captain Joshua Loring, commander of the naval vessels, reported that Major General Phineas Lyman with the Connecticut regiments also "Fell in with a party of French killed many and took one Hundred and Seven Prisoners."[23] The action "ended in Confusion," which was further exacerbated late in the day when "some Provincials & Rangers [accidently] fir'd on each other."[24] That night many of the troops remained in the woods, returning to the Lake George landing the next morning.

The British units decisively overwhelmed the French, who suffered substantial losses, including 148 captured. Trépezec made it back to the French camp but later succumbed to his wounds. The day after the skirmish, Joseph Nichols, a hired replacement in a

View of Baldwin from Rogers Rock. Photo by the author.

Langy and Trepezec at Bald Mountain (Rogers Rock) observing the approach of Abercromby's army on July 6, 1758. The armada consisted of three columns of 900 bateaux, 135 whaleboats, rafts, and three small radeaux, two of which were built from bateaux. Drawing by Gary Zaboly.

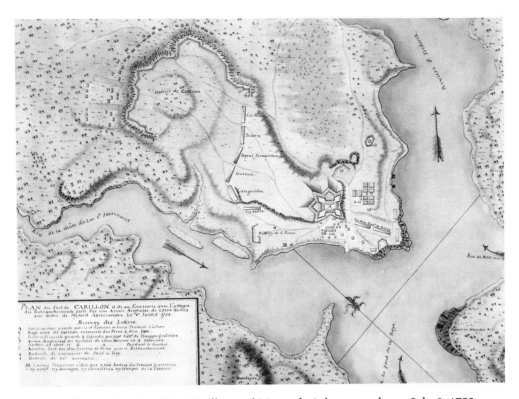

French map showing Fort Carillon and Montcalm's breastworks on July 8, 1758.
(National Archives of Canada)

Massachusetts regiment, "Observ'd in the Woods Many Slain men, An Awful Sight to Behold."[25] The prisoners were held on Mutton Island (later renamed Prisoners Island) and sent to southern Lake George two days after the skirmish (July 8).

The death of Howe, the idol of the army, paralyzed the expedition. The stunned army floundered for the rest of the day. As the body* was brought into the camp, Howe's aide, Captain Alexander Monypenny, remarked that "scarce an eye was free from tears."[29] Robert Rogers observed that his death "seemed to produce an almost general consternation and languor through the whole [army]."[30] Abercromby, realizing that the field strategy would now rest on his shoulders, vacillated on the following day (July 7), ordering the army back to the original landing site on Lake George. The troops being "greatly fatigued" was the explanation that Abercromby provided in his report to William Pitt for the return of the army to the landing site at Lake George.[31] At 11 o'clock on July 7, Colonel John Bradstreet, an American-born regular officer who commanded the "Battoe Service," was sent by Abercromby with a large force of regulars and provincials to the outlet of Lake George to capture the French sawmill and rebuild the bridge.

The hesitation of the British army provided valuable time for the French to fortify their position. At dawn on the 7th, the whole French army—officers and men alike—were busy building an entrenchment about a half-mile in front of the fort. The "Heights of Carillon," the highest part of the ridge before one reaches the fort, had been chosen as

*Contrary to nineteenth-century stories that Lord Howe was buried in Ticonderoga, eyewitnesses corroborate Abercromby's report that the body was "sent to Albany."[26] Amos Richardson, stationed at the camp at the southern end of Lake George, noted on July 8 that "th[e]y Brought Lord How[e's] corps[e] into our Camps and th[e]y car[r]ied him to Alb[a]ny."[27] Samuel Thompson also recorded the same entry in his diary on July 8.[28]

the site of a defensive breastwork of logs on July 1. Montcalm's engineers, Nicolas Sarrebource de Pontleroy and Jean-Nicolas Desandrouins, designed the breastwork about one-third of a mile long, following the sinuosity of the land with sections of the works flanking one another. According to Montcalm's report, the log wall "was formed by falling trunks of trees one upon the other and others felled in front, their branches cut and sharpened produced the effect of a chevaux-de-frize [projecting spikes]."[32] British participants in the campaign later described the breastwork as "Logs well squar'd and Dove tail'd" about "Seven feet above the Ground...cut full of Loop holes which they fir[e]d through."[33]

A number of "Wall pieces" and small swivel cannons capable of firing grapeshot had been mounted at the breastwork.[34] The forest was cleared a short distance in front of the breastwork and the ground covered with sharpened branches. While it may not have appeared substantial viewed from a distance, it would prove to be a fatal trap for the British. By the evening of the 7th the treacherous abatis was completed. Later that night Brigadier General François de Lévis finally arrived with his small reinforcements, which enlarged the total French army to approximately 3,500. Not all the French were occupied making preparations to defend the fort. Michel Chartier de Lotbinière, the fort's engineer and canteen franchisee, was busy putting his cash box in order with a bateau ready to sail if the engagement went badly. Just before the battle the price of a drink of brandy in the canteen fell but increased five times after the engagement.

While the French were busy building their defenses, Abercromby's army had moved only a short distance to the abandoned French sawmill but had left the 40 pieces of artillery (cannons, mortars and howitzers) and other provisions at the landing site. Some of the provincial troops were engaged in building a breastwork adjacent to the outlet from Lake George. Thus far the British operations had obviously been very slow, but at this point Abercromby panicked and suddenly decided to begin action, because the French prisoners had reported that Montcalm had 6,000 men with the expectation of 3,000 reinforcements. However, British spies correctly reported to him that Montcalm had fewer than 4,000 troops.

Twice, Abercromby dispatched scouting parties with his engineer, Lieutenant Matthew Clerk, to reconnoiter the French defenses. Although Clerk was only a "commissioned sub-engineer," and considered by some officers, "a stripling, who had never seen the least service," the young Scottish engineer was held in high regard by others and had had experience scouting Carillon the previous fall.[35] The duties of chief engineer were relegated to Lieutenant Clerk since Colonel James Montresor, the chief engineer in North America, was very ill at the time and Major William Eyre, an experienced engineer, chose to command the 44th Regiment as a result of a dispute with Abercromby. The reconnaissance parties, which included Captains James Abercrombie and John Stark with 400 rangers, viewed the French breastwork from Rattlesnake Hill (later Mount Defiance) late on July 7 and on the morning of July 8 when Abercromby "sent them out again."[36] (The latter scout included "an Ingineer, who was a foreigner," probably Charles Rivez, an engineering assistant.[37]) According to Captain Joshua Loring, the engineers reported "a Slight Bre[a]st work...so weakly bound together that it would be easy to push them down by the Light Infantry"; similarly, Captain William Hervey of the 44th Regiment noted that the engineers had concluded that "we might easily get to and push down [the breastwork] with our shoulders."[38] However, Captain John Stark* disagreed with the

---

*Many of the provincial and British officers who fought side by side at Ticonderoga would find themselves on opposite sides at the Battle of Bunker Hill in 1775. Brigadier General Thomas Gage, appointed second in command by Abercromby after Howe's death, 17 years later ordered the British assault on Bunker Hill during the American Revolution. Captain James Abercrombie, who served on this expedition and Amherst's the next year against Ticonderoga, was killed at the Battle of Bunker Hill. John Stark of the rangers, who disagreed with Clerk's assessment

assessment of the strength of the breastwork.[39] Young Clerk became a victim of his own faulty appraisal and was mortally wounded later the very same day.

When the scouting report of July 8 "Confirmed their former intelligence...a council of war was immediately called, wherein it was unanimously determined to attack the enemy in their lines," Captain William Grant of the 42nd Regiment later wrote from his hospital bed at Fort Edward.[40] Fearing large French reinforcements and "having no Doubt of the Practicability of carrying those works if attacked before they were Completed," Abercromby issued orders to begin the assault on the French position.[41] In reality, Montcalm's army was in a rather precarious situation with its back to Lake Champlain and provisions that might last only a week. Having arrived on the evening of July 7, Sir William Johnson with 440 Indians staked out a position the following morning on Rattlesnake Hill "where he and his Indians fired upon the fort."[42]

About noon the line of march against the main entrenchment began, with the "rangers & c., in the front, regulars next, and provincials in the rear."[43] By half past twelve in the afternoon under a hot July sun, the regulars with their bayonets fixed, in steady formal columns, attacked the French lines. As the drums rolled and the bagpipes screamed their challenge, the tight red ranks of the regulars trudged forward to their deaths. The stern regularity of the march broke down as soon as they attempted to traverse the field of sharpened branches lying in front of the breastwork. The men struggled up the wall only to be shot or impaled on the spiked branches—masses of courageous red-coated and kilt-clad souls were left dangling in front of the entrenchment as the first attack was repulsed by the French. Young Abel Spicer, serving in Nathan Whiting's Connecticut regiment, observed that the regulars marched ten deep to the French breastwork and fired volleys point blank but "fell like pigeons."[44] Private David Perry's provincial regiment had simple instructions to run to the breastwork, but the men were killed so quickly that his regiment sought cover behind trees and logs: "the ground was strewed with the dead and dying. . .I could hear the men screaming and see them dying all around me."[45]

Although most historians in the past believed that Abercromby had remained at the sawmill during the entire battle, his aide-de-camp, Captain James Abercrombie, two days after the battle wrote that the "General. . .came up with the Highlanders" and apparently viewed the battle on the right side of the rear guard of provincial troops above a rock outcropping on the La Chute River.[46] Critics of Abercromby's leadership would later focus on his failure to bring the siege train of artillery to the field of battle. But Captain Hugh Arnot of the 80th Foot recorded in his journal that "it is said the attack would have stop'd there [after the first British assault] until our Cannon came up if it had not been from a very heavy fire the Irregulars and Provincials gave with a huz[z]a[h] at the same time, which made our gen[l] believe & was so told (for He could not see what was doing) that part of the Army had enter'd their Lines."[47] Private Lemuel Lyon in Colonel Eleazer Fitch's Connecticut regiment chronicled that "at noon set out down to the Mil[l]s with the Artillira & we got near the Mil[l]s and we had orders to leave" it there.[48]

However, some light artillery was brought to the front. Abel Spicer recorded that "six small brass cannon and 3 cohorns [howitzers] which was brought up the night before and they had them on a floating battery."[49] Benjamin Glasier, a Massachusetts' ship carpenter, noted that two floating batteries were constructed "to car[r]y the Cann[on] on"; Rufus Putnam added that the vessels were "buil[t] below the Falls" on the La Chute River.[50] "At 12 o'clock," Dr. James Searing observed, "by the directions of Mr. Clerk, engineer, in pursuance of his reconnoitre, r[a]deaus with two six pounders each and one royal

---

of the breastwork, went on to fight on the side of the colonists at Bunker Hill, later becoming a noteworthy general in the Continental Army. Major Israel Putnam, who served with the rangers at the Ticonderoga battle, commanded the Connecticut troops as a militia brigadier general at the Battle of Bunker Hill.

howitzer, was ordered down the lake towards the fort...till he came to an open place...and there to enfilade [fire at] the enemy's works in reverse."[51] Spicer suggested that "the engineer" had gone earlier to Rattlesnake Hill "to see if he could find any place...to plant their artillery."[52] A friend of Matthew Clerk's family later wrote that the young engineer "had intended to have erected a Battery upon that Hill [Rattlesnake Hill]."[53] However, the effort proved fruitless since the two vessels carrying the cannons were quickly driven back by cannon fire from the fort.

As a fresh attack began, the red-coated soldiers charged up the log wall only to be repulsed again and again. The efforts to storm the breastwork were to no purpose, reported one unidentified British officer, "for we were so intangled in the branches of the felled trees."[54] The 42nd Foot, the Scottish Black Watch, was able to fight its way "upon the top of the French Lines every time an attack was made...but not being properly supported they were as often cut off as they entered."[55] The abatis caught fire several times during the engagement, but the French troops quickly put out the flames. Uninjured soldiers under cover from the fire of the rangers would move forward to collect the wounded. Abel Spicer reported a trick by the French that became standard fare in Western movies two centuries later: "the French set their hats just above the top of the breast work for to deceive the soldiers" who would shoot their hats to pieces.[56] In another incident, Captain Jean d'Anglars de Bassignac, a captain in the French Royal-Roussillon, placed a red flag on the end of his musket as a signal. The British, interpreting it as a flag of truce, moved forward to accept their surrender. The French soldiers, on the other hand, thought the British were surrendering and allowed them to approach the breastwork. When another officer, Captain Pierre Pouchot, saw the British advance, he ordered his troops to fire, "which laid two or three hundred upon the ground."[57] In all there were seven frontal assaults that day, but each time the British were thrown back, leaving the clearing before the wall more densely cluttered with the dead and wounded than before.

Montcalm, casting his coat off in the blazing heat of the summer, scampered over his lines, encouraging his troops by word and deed. The French had formed themselves into three lines behind the breastworks—each line taking its turn of fire at the vulnerable, but dauntless crusaders. Of their British adversaries, the French later wrote, "We must do them justice in saying that they attacked us with the most ardent tenacity."[58] Montcalm reported that the "English grenadiers and Scotch highlanders, continued charging for 3 hours without retreating or breaking, and several were killed within fifteen paces of our abbatis."[59]

At five o'clock in the afternoon, the start of another frenzied attack on the impenetrable log barrier occurred. A column of British regulars stormed the center of the wall while provincial troops at the French left flank provided a diversionary effort. This was followed swiftly by a massive attack by the 42nd Black Watch, led by Major Duncan Campbell of Inverawe, Scotland.* As they approached the wall, the Canadian militiamen climbed the nearby trees to rain a deadly fire down upon the British. It was a spark of desperation that drove the Black Watch and regulars forward, only to be repelled by French musket fire. Colonel Bougainville noted that the grenadiers and the Scotch Highlanders "returned unceasingly to the attack, without becoming discouraged or broken."[61] At six o'clock the British troops made their last attempt to charge the log wall.

---

*The legend of Duncan Campbell of Inverawe, Scotland, inspired many published versions, including Robert Louis Stevenson's poem "Ticonderoga," published in 1891. According to the story, Campbell was warned by the ghost of his slain cousin that they would meet again at Ticonderoga. Unknown to Major Campbell was the fact that Fort Carillon was situated at a point that the Indians had named Ticonderoga. Actually, Ticonderoga had been known by that name by provincial and British troops for years. The ghost reappeared in Campbell's tent the night before the attack. Campbell died from his wounds at Ticonderoga and his gravesite today lies in the Union Cemetery between Hudson Falls and Fort Edward.[60]

The utter hopelessness of the strategy was obvious as the slaughter continued, leaving the bodies of the fallen warriors piled at the foot of the wall or hanging from the sharpened stakes. At one point the disorder caused some of the British to fire on their own troops.

By seven o'clock the defeat of the British was apparent to everyone. Major Duncan Campbell lay wounded, as did many of his 1,000 Highlanders who had suffered the most casualties during the battle. Finally, orders were given to stop the senseless massacre, although in the confusion many soldiers actually never heard them. After six hours of bloody slaughter, Abercromby decided that his brave troops "sustained so considerable a Loss, without any Prospect of better Success, that it was no longer prudent to remain before it."[62] At the end of the battle "Abercromb[y] came from left to Ri[gh]t in the rear of the troops [e]ngaged and Ordered a Retreat Beat," Peter Pond later recalled.[63] While the rangers and light infantry provided a covering fire, the vanquished army slowly retreated

Gravesite of Duncan Campbell,
Hudson Falls, New York.
Photo by the author

"The Marquis de Montcalm congratulating his Troops after the Battle of Carillon, 8 July 1758." by Harry A. Ogden, watercolor on board, 1930. (Fort Ticonderoga Museum)

to the hurriedly-constructed breastworks near the sawmill on the La Chute River. Initially, there was "no sort of panic having seized the Army but on the Contrary everybody was Eager for renewing the attack the Next Morning," Captain Joshua Loring wrote.[64] A few hours later orders were issued to some of the regiments to retreat to the Lake George landing with the stores and artillery.[65] The orders were received by individual regiments at different times--some units, however, were never officially informed of the withdrawal. Private David Perry later recalled that "We lay there till near sunset and, not receiving orders from any officer, the men crept off, leaving all the dead, and most of the wounded. . . We started back to our boats without any orders and pushed out on the Lake for the night."[66] The unit of Lieutenant Archelaus Fuller, a provincial officer, retired at sunset to a position in the rear where it was to hold its ground. However, many of the soldiers fell asleep, including Fuller, who awakened to find "that the army was chiefly gon[e]."[67] Fuller's unit did not take to its bateaux until daybreak the next morning (July 9). When Rufus Putnam's unit was ordered to march at midnight he assumed that it was "to take Post on the hill East of Ticonderoga," but instead the men were directed back to the bateaux.[68]

Most of the broken army moved back to the camp at the lake on the night of July 8. The trails leading back to the landing site were so clogged with the dead and wounded that one "could hardly walk without treading on them."[69] The movement of the regulars and provincials was reduced to a panic as the defeated army degenerated into an uncontrollable mob. Colonel Bradstreet took charge of the army, attempting to prevent the men from leaving in wild fright and confusion in the darkness. Although Abercromby did his best to establish firm control over the army on the morning of July 9, an irresistible panic overcame the soldiers as they rushed in terror to the bateaux, convinced that they were being pursued by the French. Joseph Nichols of the Massachusetts militia heard that "the Enemy was coming to fall upon us," which created a frenzy over the bateaux that were lined fifteen deep on the shore; "The Cry of Enemy made our People Cry out & make Sad Lamentations."[70] Similarly, the Connecticut unit of Lemuel Lyon departed in a panic during the early morning hours of July 9 after smashing "200 Barrels of Flour."[71] For most of the soldiers the retreat was confusing.

In contrast to the gallant spirit of confidence on the trip to Ticonderoga, the British army returned "in great confusion and sorrow," arriving at the southern end of the lake at sunset on July 9.[72] The disembarkation surprised and disheartened the army. John Cleaveland, a chaplain with a Massachusetts provincial regiment, declared that "this morning, to the general surprise of the whole army we were ordered to embark in the battoes, to leave the ground we had possessed. . .all dejected, partly on account of our returning, and partly on account of our being without much Food for Three Days."[73] Prior to reaching the Lake George camp, Abercromby "directed to forward all the heavy artillery back to New York," but the order was apparently never carried out.[74]

While some of the eyewitnesses placed the British loss at 5,000 killed or wounded, the actual number from Abercromby's official report was a still devastating 1,944 killed or wounded.[75] By contrast, the French listed their losses as between 375-444 men.[76] Although the British and provincial units tried to evacuate their wounded, in the pandemonium apparently many were left behind. "We got away the wounded of our company; but left a great many crying for help, which we were unable to afford them . . .none of those that we left behind were ever heard of afterwards," wrote young Perry of the provincial forces.[77] In rare instances there were a few survivors. After being badly wounded during the attack on the French breastwork, Jacob Towne, a provincial recruit from Topsfield, Massachusetts, was covered with a severed tree top by a comrade. Four days later he was discovered under the tree by the French and eventually recovered from his wounds.[78]

Seventeen days after the battle, French scouts discovered "a great number of corpses on litters," the remnants of the wounded who were left by the British during the chaotic retreat.[79]

On the evening of July 8, with expectation of a renewed attack, the French worked with feverish resolve to repair their breastwork and finish their batteries on the right and left flanks. Montcalm's forces spent the next day burying the French and British dead on the field of battle. A company of volunteers sent to reconnoiter the British position later in the day found to their surprise that the invasion force had departed. The following morning Montcalm detached Brigadier General François de Lévis with eight grenadier companies along with some Canadians and volunteers to find the British. The French retraced the steps of the British army, finding many soldiers in the woods who were lost, and 700 quarts of partially destroyed flour. "We found in the mud, on the road to the Falls, more than five hundred pairs of shoes with buckles."[80] Wounded men, provisions, 200 barrels of flour, and abandoned equipment were discovered in addition to the "remains of [bateaux] and burned pontoons [rafts]."[81]

On July 11, François Pierre de Rigaud de Vaudreuil, brother of the governor and veteran of the two assaults on Fort William Henry in 1757, finally arrived with the long-awaited reinforcements, consisting mainly of Canadians and Indians. The 3,143 reinforcements brought troop strength to 6,669, still less than half of Abercromby's army. The following day Montcalm reviewed his army, which had been formed into a square on the battlefield. The victorious general made a speech thanking the soldiers in the name of the king and called upon a priest to celebrate a mass. Montcalm later dedicated a roughly hewn cross, painted red, at the French lines. A replica of that cross still stands on the access road to the fort. This was the last significant victory for the French in the war. It was also one of the largest and bloodiest battles in North America until the U.S. Civil War.

After two centuries, the lingering question remains. How could James Abercromby, a career officer, make such a tragic blunder in his conduct of the offensive against the French lines? In the first place, Abercromby had counted on Howe to provide the field command while his role would focus on logistical management. When Howe was killed, he hesitated as the army faltered for 24 hours which gave the French precious time to complete their log wall. Why hadn't the siege artillery been brought from the lake to smash the log wall? Although on July 8 an attempt was made to raft several cannons eastward on the La Chute River to Rattlesnake Hill, the effort was poorly coordinated and failed. While additional artillery was transported as far as the sawmill on the La Chute River, the main siege train remained at the Lake George landing. Bringing the artillery to the French breastwork would have taken "several Days," Abercromby later mused; but concern over the "Enemy...every Minute strengthening their Works, and every Hour Reinforcements...coming" led to the decision to storm the wall without the aid of the siege train.[82] Abercromby's fear of immediate French reinforcements had some justification since François-Pierre de Rigaud's troops did reach Carillon within days of the engagement. However, Abercromby would still have had twice the troops of the French.

Abercromby, however, had little faith in the 9,000 provincial troops that were part of the expedition. Throughout the French and Indian War, British officers looked down on the provincial troops with undisguised contempt. British opinion on provincial military effectiveness stemmed partly from the background of political freedom and flexibility in military service of the provincial troops. The provincials were simply not willing to provide the blind allegiance and discipline required by the professional officers of the British army. A young Massachusetts officer resentfully suggested that British officers treated Americans like "Orderly Serjeants."[83] Abercromby used the regulars for the frontal assaults and treated the provincial troops as scapegoats for his defeat at Ticonderoga. "It is with Concern that I tell you, that, from every Circumstance that I have seen, and which has happened, no real dependence is to be had upon the Bulk of the Provincials. . . Their Officers, with a very few Exceptions, are worse than their Men."[84] Abercromby argued that more than two-thirds of the provincials retreated in haste to the landing site on Lake George on July 8, requiring him to post a guard at the bridge to stop them. A letter, however, by Captain Joshua Loring reported that Major General Lyman's Connecticut line had wanted to hold their ground after the defeat and carry on with the siege.[85]

The provincials, at the same time, reflected negatively on Abercromby's command of the Ticonderoga expedition. Colonel William Williams, who commanded a provincial regiment at Ticonderoga, wrote three days later to his uncle in Deerfield, Massachusetts, that "leaving the place we went to capture, the best part of the army is unhinged. I have told you enough to make you sick, if the relation acts on you as the facts have on me."[86] John Cleaveland remarked that "the conduct is thought to be marvellous strange, to order the entrenchment to be forced with small arms, when they had cannon not far off."[87] Rufus Putnam in his memoirs reflected on Abercromby's leadership: "I considered it the most injudicious and wanton sacrifice of men that ever came within my knowledge or reading."[88]

The experience of the Abercromby expedition and other battles in the French and Indian War would set the stage for the next confrontation in North America. At the beginning of the American Revolution, the British were convinced that they could easily overwhelm an inept American army. Captain Charles Lee scoffed at the British derision of American troops. He noted that the parade maneuvers and formal training of the regulars were of little military value in the American wilderness. His presence at Abercromby's defeat had an obvious impact on the myth of the invincibility of the British military. The experience of provincial troops during the French and Indian War made them less apprehensive in the face of British threats after the war and more confident in their ideals and military ability.

While the Abercromby expedition to Carillon was a major failure in 1758, the British did achieve success in other campaigns during the year. Amherst's capture of Louisbourg was but one of three effective operations. Lieutenant Colonel John Bradstreet, head of the bateau service and a participant in the Abercromby expedition, was finally granted permission at a council of war in mid-July at Lake George for a campaign against Fort Frontenac on Lake Ontario. Bradstreet moved quickly along the Mohawk River with his army to present-day Rome, New York, where construction of Fort Stanwix was to begin. Moving forward on August 12 with 2,600 troops and 300 bateau men, Bradstreet, with considerable secrecy, moved his artillery, supplies, and troops in 123 bateaux and 95 whaleboats toward Lake Ontario. On August 27 the undermanned Fort Frontenac, at present-day Kingston, Ontario, fell to Bradstreet's army. A lightning raid, by eighteenth-century standards, it was a logistical triumph which yielded an immense quantity of French provisions, artillery, furs, and vessels. After destroying a substantial portion of the fort and war material, Bradstreet returned to Oswego with some of the provisions in the two largest warships. The two vessels were burned before Bradstreet's army embarked for Albany.

The Fort Duquesne expedition, renewed in 1758, was commanded by 48-year-old Brigadier General John Forbes, a Scottish veteran who had earlier served on Lord Loudoun's senior staff. Forbes decided to forge a new direct route through the Allegheny Mountains in Pennsylvania rather than make use of the existing road where Braddock had been annihilated three years earlier. Although Colonel George Washington and other

Virginians opposed the plan, Forbes proceeded on his arduous expedition by mid-summer. Most Virginians favored the old road through Virginia, mainly for economic reasons. The ailing Forbes, often carried on a litter, established a number of staging areas, or supply depots, as the army cut its way through the primeval forest. On November 24, as the British army approached Fort Duquesne, the French blew up the fort and retreated. As a result of the cutting of supply lines with the fall of Fort Frontenac at the hands of Bradstreet, the French garrison had little choice but to evacuate since provisions were insufficient to withstand a siege. With his health failing, Forbes was carried back through snowstorms to Philadelphia where he died in March 1759.

During the rest of the 1758 summer at Lake George, Abercromby and his army remained relatively idle at the southern end of the lake. The rangers were actively engaged in warding off French raiding parties while the rest of the troops built breastworks and vessels while trying to avoid camp diseases which spread through the army. The French likewise had a relatively uneventful season after the July battle. On July 24 a detachment of 600 Indians and Canadians departed from Fort Carillon. They were to have left sooner, but games of lacrosse between the Iroquois and Abenaki Indians, in which 1,000 crowns of belts and strings of wampum were at stake, delayed their departure.

Canadian Governor Vaudreuil, during the remaining season, pressed Montcalm to attack the British at Lake George. Because the provisions at Carillon were inadequate to sustain a major military expedition and the lack of any real military target at Lake George, Montcalm, for the most part, simply ignored Vaudreuil. British wagon convoys mainly carried wine, spirits, and other provisions of the sutlers (private merchants) to the garrison at Lake George and were not worthy of attack by the whole French army.

The relative tranquility at the British posts was broken on July 20 when ten soldiers were ambushed near the Halfway Brook fort, a stockade manned by Massachusetts troops. Officers and men from the post marched to their assistance, only to be attacked themselves by the same Canadian and Indian raiding party. Joseph Holt subsequently listed the names of 26 men who had been killed, wounded, or missing in the attack—"a terrible day as ever I saw."[89] Eight days later a second detachment of 400-500 Canadians and Indians, led by St. Luc de la Corne, attacked a convoy of more than 40 wagons on the military road between Fort Edward and Lake George. Although French sources mentioned that "80 scalps and 60 prisoners, including men, women and children," were taken in the ambush and Major Robert Rogers later recorded 116 killed, provincial diaries place the numbers much lower.[90] With a force of 700 troops, Major Rogers was dispatched after the raiders; the French and Indians, however, eluded the detachment. A few days later Rogers and Major Israel Putnam and Captain James Dalyell, with a detachment of regulars, returned to the southern end of Lake Champlain in search of the enemy. On August 8, after camping near Wood Creek, the 530-man detachment encountered a slightly smaller French party under Joseph Marin de La Malgue, a Canadian captain. Marching at the head of the provincials, Putnam, along with a lieutenant and two others, was captured.* After two hours of intense musketry, the French retreated with their prisoners. The English losses amounted to 33, while the French reported their losses at 13; but provincial soldiers recorded more than 50 French and Indian scalps taken.[92]

---

*Major Putnam's ordeal after his capture is one of the extraordinary tales of the war. The Indians hauled the major to the rear, lashing him tightly to a tree. One young Indian entertained himself by throwing his tomahawk as close to the head of Putnam as possible without hitting him. Then a French or Canadian officer pressed his musket to his chest and squeezed the trigger. The flint struck, but the musket did not fire. The officer turned the weapon around and smashed Putnam in the face with its butt. At this point, Putnam may have been caught in a crossfire between the French and British. He was untied, stripped of his coat, shoes, and stockings and forced to carry many of the French knapsacks. Upon arriving at the encampment for the night, the Indians again lashed him to a tree, stripped him and heaped brush around him. As the flames leaped upward, a sudden shower doused the fire. When it ended, the Indians repeated the preparations and soon relit fresh brush. At this point Captain Joseph Marin de La Malgue, realizing what

"A Map of the retrenched Camp at Lake George in 1758." (Fort Ticonderoga Museum)

The sloop *Halifax*, built at Lake George in August 1758, was sunk in the lake for winter storage and raised the following year. Drawing by Montserrat Centeno.

was occurring, broke through the crowd of Indians, kicked the brush aside, and cut Putnam down.[91] The 40-year-old Putnam was later exchanged for French prisoners and continued in military service to the end of the war. In 1762 he again cheated death as one of the few survivors of a shipwreck off Cuba during the ill-fated Havana expedition. At 57 Putnam commanded the Connecticut troops at the Battle of Bunker Hill in 1775, and two days later was appointed a major general in the Continental Army. The energetic, persevering Putnam became the subject of many legends that continue to be debated by historians today.

A major shipbuilding effort at Lake George began in the summer of 1758 under the direction of Captain Joshua Loring of Hingham, Massachusetts. Loring, a privateer during King George's War (1744-1748) and Royal Navy post captain in 1758, was the first experienced seaman in charge of the naval activity on the lakes. Some of the most closely-recorded notes on the vessels constructed at Lake George during 1758 were written by Captain Samuel Cobb, who had commanded a company from a Massachusetts regiment during the attack on Carillon. The 39-year-old captain was a well-known shipwright from Maine (then a part of Massachusetts) who built more than 150 vessels during his lifetime. On July 19, barely a week after the disaster at Ticonderoga, Cobb noted in his journal that he "Began to Work on a Sloop to Draft and Mould her."[93] The sloop and other vessels were built at the southeast end of Lake George. On July 25 Colonel Henry Champion, with a provincial regiment from Connecticut, recorded that troops were "building a shipyard at ye southeast corner of ye Lake, building a breast work round it, building saw-pit in it, sawing ship plank and getting ship timber."[94] The Lake George camp in July consisted of a "Piqueted Fort where W. H.[William Henry] stood another opposite on East side of ye Swamp," a hospital, a rudimentary brickyard, cabins for the wounded, and another breastwork located on Diamond Island.[95] Abercromby referred to two of the "picketed forts" as "a Stockaded Post, where the late Fort stood & another Work of the same kind on the Rising Ground where the entrenched camp was last year."[96] Another fortification was begun in late July, according to Abel Spicer, who recorded that men from Colonel Nathan Whiting's Connecticut regiment were "clearing a place to build a breast work on a small hill which lieth about 100 rods south from the southwest corner" of the picketed camp at the remains of Fort William Henry.[97] The new outpost would later be named Fort Gage.[98]

Pressured by Loring, Cobb and his carpenters worked on the sloop every day despite filthy living conditions and the illnesses that plagued the camp. The sloop became stuck in her ways during an attempted launch on August 9 but was successfully launched on the following morning. According to Abercromby, building the sloop was "not only for Protection and Security...but also... Cruising to and fro, up the Lake to watch and discover the Motions of the Enemy."[99] A contemporary newspaper described "the Earl of Halifax, 51 Feet Keel, about 100 Tons Burthen...to carry 18 6 & 4 pounders, 20 Swivels, 50 Sailors, and a Company of Marines," but Joshua Loring indicated that the vessel was designed for "Sixteen Guns four pounders" and Abercromby mentioned "14 Six & four Pounders"; another eyewitness suggested that the armament consisted of "ten four pounders carried aboard, and there was two more...to be carried and twelve swivels."[100] During the course of the remaining season, the *Halifax* would complete six cruises on Lake George. After receiving reports from scouts, the French called the *Halifax* "a bark carrying twelve four-pounders" and worried that the activity at Lake George was in preparation for a siege of Carillon in October.[101] The vessel was used by the British in 1758 and 1759, and depicted in a "View of Lake George, 1759" by Thomas Davies while he was serving with Amherst's army (the original painting is now in the Fort Ticonderoga Museum).

By the end of August, Cobb and ten carpenters began work on "a Row Gally of 40 feet long 15 feet wide 5 feet deep to carry 12 pounders in the stern and 5 Swivels on a Side to go with 24 Oars."[102] The journal of Dr. Caleb Rea on September 14 disclosed the readiness of the two row galleys: "the Row Gallys mounted with Guns & tryed by fireing their Can[n]on."[103] These stubby vessels were the forerunners of the gunboats that the Americans would construct on Lake Champlain in 1776.

In late September Reverend John Cleaveland, with the Massachusetts provincial soldiers, provided a rare delineation of the construction of Indian canoes in his journal. After dinner one evening, he walked down to the shore of Lake George to view two captured birch bark canoes, the largest of which was 35 feet in length, five feet wide, and designed to carry 20 men. The inside was made "with Cedar Clap-Boards thin as brown paper and laid lengthways of ye Canoe upon which crossways of ye Canoe is another laying of Cedar."[104]

On September 18 Cobb and his carpenters were reassigned to Captain Thomas Ord, a British officer in charge of the artillery who had been supervising the building of a large radeau. The radeau, designed as a floating fort, was an idea that had surfaced earlier, as evidenced by the detailed instructions sent to William Johnson at Lake George in 1755 by John Dies (chapter 2). In 1756 William Shirley had recommended to James Abercromby that the capture of Ticonderoga or Crown Point could be facilitated "by attacking it with a floating Battery from the Lake at the same time, that it is attacked by Land."[105] "Radeau," meaning "raft" in French, denoted the flat-bottomed nature of the ship. The lower sides of a radeau inclined slightly outward while the upper sides or bulwarks curved inward at a steep angle over the interior of the vessel. The upper sides, were "planked up higher than a man's Head Shelving in or arching inwards to defend ye men's Bodys & Heads with Port-Holes for ye Cannon" and "contriv'd so that tis impossible for the Enemy to board her."[106] The radeau was equipped with a large number of sweeps (oars) with a design for one or two masts and square sails.

Cobb's journal entries for each succeeding day mentioned working on the "Raddow." Only on Sundays and days on which he was incapacitated by the "Bloody flux" or dysentery did Cobb fail to labor on the radeau. Colonel Henry Champion, a provincial officer from Colchester, Connecticut, became an interested observer of the radeau construction. On October 7 Champion drew a sketch of the radeau in his journal with notation that "it is 51 feet in length, about 16 or 18 wide, straight flat bottom, flaring waist about 5 feet high, then turns with an elbow. . . The name of this creature is Tail and End, or Land Tortoise."[107] Dr. Rea also walked to the lakeside shipyard on October 7 to examine the new vessels under construction and drew a sketch in his journal of a type of vessel that he had never seen before. "One," according to Rea, "is very odd, being seven squared sided like this figure, besides she Tumbles in & makes seven squares more, so that she is truly fourteen square besides her bottom & top."[108] Christopher Comstock, from a Connecticut regiment, likewise made a drawing of the radeau which he labeled "Tail and End" and tried to explain the strange configuration as "Something Like a gambrel Roof house."[109]

With winter approaching the desolate region, the men strained to finish the vessels at Lake George. By mid-October, artillery and some of the bateaux had been hauled southward. The two row galleys were sunk in the lake on October 16 for safekeeping over the winter.[110] Finally, on October 20 Cobb reported that "we launched 2 Raddows," one measured 50 feet with a 19-foot width and 6-foot depth while the second was only 30 feet by 7 feet.[111] "We tryed the Raddows and Rowed well they went with 26 Oars," Cobb noted on October 21.[112] Snow in the air provided a new incentive for the troops to begin their long march homeward. On Sunday, October 22, only two days after their launching, Cobb wrote "Working on the Raddows Sinking them in the lake."[113] By then, some of the provincials had begun to refer to the strange-looking *Land Tortoise* as the "ark" or "Ord's Ark" while one New Hampshire soldier called it "the most odd vessel" at the lake.[114]

The sloop *Halifax, Land Tortoise*, row galleys, and other vessels at the lake, including 260 bateaux, were sunk in the depths of Lake George for protection. Because Fort William Henry had been destroyed by the French during the summer of 1757, the ships could not be safeguarded at a garrisoned fort over the winter. Leaving the vessels exposed would certainly result in their destruction, as had occurred during a French raid across the ice in March 1757. Placing them in cold storage at the bottom of the lake with retrieval planned for the spring of 1759 was the only option available.

Given the state of eighteenth-century technology, how were these large vessels sunk? One clue is provided by Henry Champion, who noted that stone-filled cribs had been attached to the *Halifax* and *Land Tortoise* to sink them.[115] A majority of the bateaux were carried by wagon to Fort Edward.[116] Joshua Loring's "Accounts of Stores Left at Lake George" enumerated "about 200 Batteaus, 7 Whale Boats, 3 Row Gallys, 1 Large Luggarde Boat [radeau *Land Tortoise*], the Sloop [*Halifax*] Sunk in Different Parts of the Lake."[117] Before sinking the *Halifax*, the rigging and cannons were removed and buried onshore. The buildings, including "the barracks within the new Picket Fort," were dismantled and boards buried or burned.[118] On October 23 Cobb's regiment began its long, cold march home; three days later Champion and his regiment departed.

Later, scouting Lake George, the French were taken by surprise when they found the camp completely abandoned with defensive works, storehouses, and huts burned. Colonel Bougainville reported that the English had "buried bombs and shot and sunk their bark and part of their barges [bateaux]."[119] Montcalm immediately sent out a detachment with some "specialists" to try to dig up the shot and haul out the "bark" (*Halifax*) and "barges" (bateaux). "This detachment found twenty quarters of salt pork, two hundred barrels of lime, the location of the bark, fifty sunken barges [bateaux], and several other caches in a neighboring swamp."[120] The French apparently did not raise any of the vessels; the *Halifax* was hoisted out the following spring with some difficulty by the British. Colonel Bougainville concluded that the decision by Montcalm not to attack the English at Lake George, as Vaudreuil had urged, was the correct one since they had burned their own entrenchments and departed.

Although some preparations were made in anticipation of a second attempt on Fort Carillon, another expedition in 1758 failed to materialize. Colonel William Williams, who had led a Massachusetts regiment during the July campaign, appealed to Governor Thomas Pownall of Massachusetts to assist in the formation of a second expedition in which provincials would play a larger role. On July 18, 1758, Abercromby requested reinforcements from Major General Jeffery Amherst, who was then besieging Louisbourg.[121] On August 20, Brigadier General James Prevost (local rank in America) sent Abercromby a specific proposal for an attack on Carillon which would "afford you Still an opportunity to end this Campaign with honour."[122] Under pressure, Abercromby ended his vacillation the next day.

Receiving word from Amherst that he was proceeding to Lake George with "five Battalions," Abercromby apparently made preparations for a possible renewal of the campaign, but when Amherst reached Stillwater on October 4, he was ordered by Abercromby to hold his troops at Albany.[123] Amherst reached Lake George late on October 5 and after meeting with Abercromby and his officers on the following day, plans for a renewed attack on Carillon were shelved due to "the Strength of the Enemy at Ticonderoga, both in Troops & Works, and the Season advancing past wherein the Troops cannot hold the field."[124] Abercromby soon received a letter of recall from Pitt and returned to Britain. In spite of his dubious record, the beleaguered Abercromby was promoted to lieutenant general, but he never saw active duty again, and Amherst replaced him as the commander in North America. A year after the fateful expedition of 1758, a British force nearly the size and composition of Abercromby's army advanced again on Fort Carillon. This time, with a more cautious commander, the results would be dramatically different.

Archaeological Discoveries

The vessels from the French and Indian War lay unnoticed at the bottom of the lake for many years. The first vessel to attract attention was a sunken hull in 15 feet of water near the steamboat dock at Lake George Village, often described in guidebooks during the late nineteenth century. Seneca Ray Stoddard's 1887 guidebook noted "the charred remains of an old hulk, her blackened ribs and keel half hidden in the sand. It appears to be about forty feet in length...Shell and cannon balls have been taken away at different times, and in 1820 two small cannon were removed from the wreck."[125] The vessel, built of black oak, was 44 feet long, 14 feet wide, and 7 feet deep.[126] The sloop-like vessel, raised by William S. Tuttle on July 2, 1903, yielded old military buttons and buckles, pewter spoons, pipes, grapeshot, and a 1743 Spanish coin. The following week the *Lake George Mirror* described the wreckage as "the keel, outer planking and the ribs, the ends of which are charred from the fire that burned them to the water's edge," and speculated that the vessel had been a sloop destroyed by the French during their March 1757 raid on Fort William Henry.[127] Unfortunately, the vessel was dismantled for souvenirs. Several frames, apparently from this vessel, were donated to the Lake George Historical Association in 1990.

Another vessel that has fascinated Lake George history buffs lay in the waters off Floating Battery Island, north of Black Mountain Point in the Narrows. Although there are several versions of how the island received its name, the dominant story relates to the abandonment of one of the floating batteries used by Abercromby in the ill-fated 1758 expedition. In 1888 Charles Possons' guide to Lake George suggested that on the south side of the "Southernmost Island are the remains of two floating batteries built to accompany Abercrombie."[128] The daughter of the first forest ranger on the lake recalled seeing the vessel with all its frames in place during the 1920s. In the 1950s Colonel Lorenzo Hagglund, the New York salvage engineer who had raised the Revolutionary War schooner *Royal Savage* and the gondola *Philadelphia* from Lake Champlain in the 1930s, searched for a gunboat or floating battery around the island. After searching the south side of the island in the 1970s, I discovered remnants of the vessel. By then it was totally broken up with a few pieces scattered around a wide area. The surviving parts definitely appeared to be of the hand-hewn construction characteristic of the period. A keel, strakes (side boards), and a large bateau-type rib are identical to vessels of the eighteenth century. A larger frame (rib) from the vessel is presently in the Fort Ticonderoga Museum collection.

In July 1960 two divers discovered a 28-foot bateau-like vessel from the French and Indian War with approximately 40 large, 13-inch mortar bombs off the southern shore of Lake George.[129] The 150-pound mortar bombs were subsequently raised and are presently displayed at Fort William Henry, Fort Ticonderoga, the Skenesborough Museum, and the Smithsonian Institution. In 1960 two teenage divers recovered two ornately-engraved French bronze swivel cannons from a pair of bateaux sunk in Warner Bay. The young salvagers sold the rare guns for $25 each!

The most extensive archaeological discoveries in Lake George have been bateaux. Published reports on locations of sunken bateaux appeared as early as 1893.[130] Using a homemade apparatus, an amateur diver observed a group of bateaux along the southeast shore of the lake in the 1930s. It was not until July 1960, however, that two teenage scuba divers rediscovered the bateaux.[131] In total, about 14 bateaux were located that summer. The archaeological work that ensued drew widespread attention, involving the staff of the Adirondack Museum, a team of divers from the Smithsonian, and U.S. Navy divers

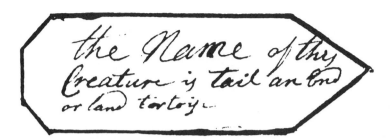

Above: Original drawing of radeau *Land Tortoise* by Henry Champion. (Connecticut State Archives) *Right:* Klein side-scan sonar record shows the 18th century radeau shipwreck *Land Tortoise* found in Lake George, N.Y. on June 26, 1990 by the LGBRRT. (Copyright 1990 by Joseph W. Zarzynski, Klein Assoc., Inc.) *Facing page, top:* French and Indian War sloop raised from Lake George in 1903. (Ed Bethel Collection, Cooper's Cave Ale Company) *Bottom:* Bateau from Lake George had been on display at the Adirondack Museum for many years. Raised in the early 1960s, the vessel has a bottom length of 32 feet with an overall length of 34 feet. Photo by the author.

from Washington, D.C. Three bateaux were eventually raised and preserved under the supervision of Robert Inverarity, then director of the Adirondack Museum. The sunken vessels were part of the "wet storage" ordered by Major General Abercromby in October 1758. Colonel John Bradstreet's report on the "State of the Battoes" on December 31, 1758, to the new commander in chief, Major General Jeffery Amherst, noted: "Sunk in Lake George—260" and "hid in the woods near Lake George—30."[132]

The bateaux found on the bottom of the lake in 1960 lay in orderly rows, indicating that they were probably sunk purposely. The recovered bateaux had bottom lengths of 32 feet and 34-foot overall lengths, making them larger than those commonly used in rivers or streams where portaging would be a problem.[133] An examination of the curved frames of the bateaux also indicated that the whaleboat had influenced the design of the Lake George bateaux. During the summers of 1963 and 1964 the Adirondack Museum sponsored "Operation Bateaux" directed by Dr. Robert Inverarity. Terry Crandall was charged with the search and underwater processing of the archaeological sites in Lake George for the museum. His extensive examination of over two dozen sites in the lake was a significant early archaeological study of French and Indian War vessels.

In July of 1965 the state police, with 15 qualified scuba divers and 17 trooper candidates, held a training exercise on several bateau sites. While the acting state historian identified the remains of the vessels, hundreds of relics including ribs, planking, and musket balls were taken from the bateaux piece by piece.[134] In retrospect, this, unfortunately, was not a desirable archaeological project since the vessels were not measured, relics were mixed up, and the sites were disturbed for future research.

Twenty-seven years after the discovery of bateaux in 1960, an archaeological workshop at Lake George held under the auspices of the Atlantic Alliance for Maritime Heritage Conservation would focus once again on one of the main bateau sites. The workshop at Lake George was organized by Joseph Zarzynski, author and lecturer, and taught by R. Duncan Mathewson, then chairman of the Atlantic Alliance and chief marine archaeologist for the seventeenth-century shipwreck *Atocha*. After classroom and pool

The Radeau *Land Tortoise*

1

1. Bow showing mooring rings. 2. Mooring ring and sweep port on the stern port section. 3. Open gunport. 4. Port side bow. 5. Inside of starboard section showing frames and sweep port holes. 6. Gunport lid on starboard side. The vessel is presently protected in a New York State Submerged Heritage Preserve. Photos by the author.

4

2

5

3

6

instruction in the fundamentals of proper underwater archaeology, 21 sport divers began a thorough study of some of the remaining bateau wrecks. Philip Lord, Jr., senior scientist, Office of Archaeology, New York, was able to observe the survey through a monitor connected to a Remotely-Operated-Vehicle (ROV), a tethered underwater robot with a video camera. At the same time, the Lake Champlain Maritime Museum at Basin Harbor built an exact reproduction of one of the Lake George bateaux that had been recovered in 1960.

Other bateau clusters were discovered during the 1990s on the southeastern shore of the lake. Further study of these sites may determine how these vessels were sunk and retrieved, the use of sails, whether they were rowed by standing or sitting, and whether the vessels were tied together when they were sunk. Unfortunately, with the expansion of scuba diving, many wreck sites have been dismantled piece by piece for souvenirs. Although a 1958 New York law prohibited disturbing any archaeological or historic site, many of the sunken bateaux were systematically stripped of everything but their bottom boards. A new era which recognizes that our historic underwater wreck sites are finite resources is slowly dawning. In 1993 seven sunken bateaux, lying offshore from the Wiawaka Holiday House, were designated New York State's first "Submerged Heritage Preserve." The bateau preserve site, listed on the National Register of Historic Places, has been maintained through a partnership between the New York State Department of Environmental Conservation and Bateaux Below, Inc., a not-for-profit educational corporation. In 1995 Bateaux Below made an interesting discovery connected to the 1960 search for bateaux at Lake George. A 15-foot, 3,700-pound research submarine, built to photograph bateau wrecks, mysteriously disappeared from her dock at the lake in 1960.[135] Using side-scan sonar, a Bateaux Below research team found the vessel in deep water.[136]

In June 1990, 232 years after her sinking, the ghostly outline of the radeau *Land Tortoise* appeared on the printer of a side-scan sonar unit. Led by Joseph Zarzynski, the Lake George Bateaux Research Team (later Bateaux Below, Inc.), which had been awarded an Explorers Club flag to search for French and Indian War vessels, discovered the vessel. The *Land Tortoise*, last observed by provincial soldiers in 1758, had been sitting perfectly upright for more than two centuries. The group had discovered the oldest completely intact warship ever found in the Western Hemisphere and the only radeau known to exist.[137] Over the next three years, an archaeological survey was completed that included the use of an underwater robot (ROV), photography, and physical measurements by divers, wood sample identification, videography, and photomosaic documentation. I served as the historian on the project and an underwater still-photographer.

The archaeological survey of the *Land Tortoise* revealed a number of features that had not been disclosed in the wartime journals. The seven gunports, three on the starboard side and four on the port side, were designed asymmetrically to avoid interference between gun crews during the recoil and loading of the cannons. One gunport in the bow and another in the stern section allowed firepower from all sides of the radeau.[138] Sweep ports on six sections of the *Land Tortoise* permitted complete maneuverability of the vessel, while two mast steps found in the hull floor indicated that the ship was intended for sail on the open lake. The upper-bow sections have a view hole on each side that would have allowed an observer to scrutinize a military engagement or the forward progress of the radeau without being exposed to enemy musket fire. The measurements taken in 1990, approximately 52 feet in length and 18 feet wide, are virtually identical to those given in the Cobb and Champion journals. The 26 sweep ports found on the vessel coincide with Cobb's description, while the configurations drawn by Champion, Comstock, and Rea parallel the outline of the radeau.

During 1991 the team continued its documentation of the radeau site under a permit from the state of New York. Prior to the 1991 archaeological survey, the state provided plastic permit signs to the team that warned other divers of the on-going archaeological study of the vessel. The free-standing signs encircled the radeau on the floor of the lake. Divers, working under the direction of archaeologists Robert Cembrola and D. K. Abbass, measured all frames, planks, and stanchions on the vessel, including their exact location and spacing. Each stanchion was assigned a small numbered flag to aid the divers in the recording process. Each side of the vessel has 16 hardwood frames with an adjacent knee that serves as a stanchion for the upper sides. The vessel was constructed of a combination of oak and pine, which is consistent with historical records.[139]

Our group struggled with the mystery of the 107-foot depth of the radeau given its planned retrieval. The mystery was largely solved by the diary of a provincial shipwright from Massachusetts, William Sweat, who related the difficulty in sinking the flat-bottomed vessel which ended in the loss of the radeau during a haphazard operation after dark: "Sunday 22 Day, I was forced to go to work, a sinking our Radow, which we got Ready at the Sun sect [set], & we Sunk her once; But one side Rise again, so that we were forced to work the chief of the night, Before we could keep her Down."[140]

In 1994 volunteer divers from Bateaux Below, Inc., with authorization from state agencies, installed an underwater fence, consisting of PVC posts and plastic chain, around the radeau *Land Tortoise* to serve as a passive protective reminder to visiting divers of the fragility of the vessel.[141] On August 7, 1994, the radeau was officially opened as a controlled public access (permit only) "Submerged Heritage Preserve." Four years later, under the dedicated stewardship of Joseph Zarzynski, executive director of Bateaux Below, Inc., with the assistance of many history-minded citizens, the nomination of the radeau *Land Tortoise* as a National Historic Landmark was approved by the Department of Interior, making the vessel one of only six shipwrecks to receive this honor.

The northern end of Lake George was the focus of an archaeological study (1993-2000) under the direction of Scott A. Padeni with the assistance of Bateaux Below, Inc., and the Lake Champlain Maritime Museum. Remnants of vessels from the colonial period to the steamboat era were discovered during the survey. Although known as a "shipwreck graveyard," the outlet at Lake George may have been impacted by the salvage efforts of William S. Tuttle, who was authorized by the state legislature (1894-1903) to remove sunken vessels from the lake.[142] Working with a state permit, the survey team documented numerous vessels, including wrecks of barges, steamboats, a wooden sledge, a sailboat, and the remains of a vessel that may have dated to the French and Indian War.[143]

Partially funded by a grant from the Lake Champlain Basin Program, Bateaux Below, Inc., completed the first seamless photomosaic of a shipwreck, the 1758 radeau *Land Tortoise*. The photomosaic, made from 200 color photographic images, shows an overhead view of the upper bulwarks of the vessel. The vessel is presently preserved in a New York State Submerged Heritage Preserve. Photographer, Robert Benway; computer assembler, Kendrick McMahan; project director, Joseph Zarzynski.

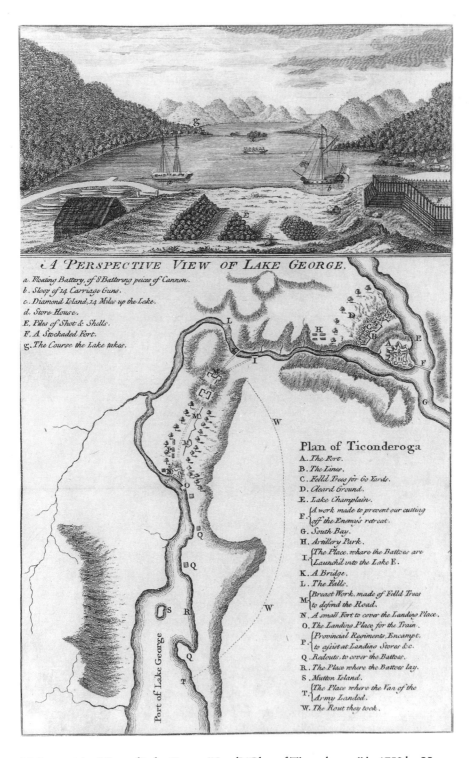

A PERSPECTIVE VIEW OF LAKE GEORGE.

a. Floating Battery, of 8 Battering peices of Cannon.
b. Sloop of 14 Carriage Guns.
c. Diamond Island, 14 Miles up the Lake.
d. Store House.
E. Piles of Shot & Shells.
F. A Stockaded Fort.
g. The Course the Lake takes.

Plan of Ticonderoga

A. The Fort.
B. The Lines.
C. Felld Trees for 60 Yards.
D. Cleard Ground.
E. Lake Champlain.
F. A work made to prevent our cutting off the Enemu's retreat.
G. South Bay.
H. Artillery Park.
I. The Place where the Battoes are Launch'd into the Lake E.
K. A Bridge.
L. The Falls.
M. Breast Work, made of Felld Trees to defend the Road.
N. A small Fort to cover the Landing Place.
O. The Landing Place for the Train.
P. Provincial Regiments, Encampt to assist at Landing Stores &c.
Q. Redouts to cover the Battoes.
R. The Place where the Battoes lay.
S. Mutton Island.
T. The Place where the Van of the Army Landed.
W. The Rout they took.

Port of Lake George

"A Perspective View of Lake George" [and] "Plan of Ticonderoga" in 1759 by Henry Skinner with the radeau *Invincible* and sloop *Halifax*. First published in *The Universal Magazine*, London, 1759. (Fort Ticonderoga Museum)

5. Amherst Sweeps the Lakes

WILLIAM PITT'S OVERALL PLAN FOR 1759 not only included Jeffery Amherst's primary campaign to take the French forts on Lake Champlain and proceed to Canada, but also involved expeditions against Fort Niagara on Lake Ontario and Quebec City. In the early summer, Brigadier General John Prideaux and Sir William Johnson were sent to re-establish the British base at Oswego and then move to capture Fort Niagara, the vital French fortress linked to other western posts. Leaving about 1,300 troops at Oswego under Lieutenant Colonel Frederick Haldimand, Prideaux and Johnson advanced to Niagara with approximately 2,200 troops and 900 Indians. A week after the siege had begun, Prideaux was accidently killed by a mortar discharged from his own lines. On July 25, following the defeat of a French relief force, Pierre Pouchot, a captain in the French regulars, surrendered his outnumbered force to Johnson.

In June, 22 British warships and a larger number of transport vessels, carrying an army of 9,000 men under Major General James Wolfe, arrived at Quebec City. The British army, however, soon became stalemated in its attempt to establish a foothold near the city. The French, meanwhile, sent fireships (vessels set ablaze, loaded with munitions) against the British armada in the St. Lawrence River. Wolfe, wracked by illness during the summer, launched a successful assault in September on the Heights of Abraham above Quebec. The dramatic British victory came after more than 4,000 troops scaled the rocky ledges in the early morning hours of September 13. Without waiting for Louis Antoine de Bougainville's 3,000 reinforcements, Major General Louis-Joseph de Montcalm, the successful commander at Carillon in 1758, decided upon an immediate attack on Wolfe's army. Marching straight into the muskets of the British line, the French ranks were decimated by two doubled-shotted volleys at close range. Both Montcalm and Wolfe were mortally wounded during the battle. The governor of New France, Marquis de Vaudreuil, fled to Montreal, as did Bougainville and his army.

The late spring of 1759 saw the gathering of a British and provincial army at Lake George for the fifth consecutive year. Once again the objective would be to drive the French from their fortifications on Lake Champlain. The leadership of Britain's main campaign for 1759 rested with the army's 42-year-old commander in chief, Major General Jeffery Amherst. Although Amherst had little command experience before coming to North America, his successful direction of the Louisbourg expedition in 1758 instilled confidence in his leadership. Amherst was essentially a careful military manager and firm disciplinarian who took few risks and planned for all eventualities. While the cannon and musket were the essential tools of his trade, he was also partial to the shovel and the hammer. He would leave his mark on Lake George and Lake Champlain with the construction of several forts and the building of the first British fleet on Lake Champlain.

The campaign of 1759 ushered in a new military era in the history of Lake Champlain that would not end until the close of 1814. The use of large naval fleets would forever change military strategy in the struggle for the continent. As Colonel Bougainville, the erudite French journal keeper, observed in 1758, "the only way to assure ourselves the possession of Lake Champlain. . .is by a strong naval force."[1] A race to build armed schooners, sloops, and radeaux would now determine the control of the two lakes.

By early June the British army began its trek to Lake George. Amherst himself reached Fort Edward by June 6. Preparations for the renewed campaign included moving

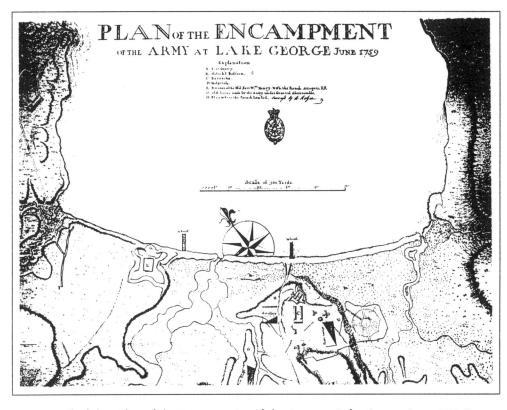

Detail of the "Plan of the Encampment of the Army at Lake George June 1759."
(National Archives of Canada)

provisions, artillery, ammunition, and bateaux to the lake. Many officers who were with
the ill-fated Abercromby expedition returned for another attempt on the French fortifications. Veteran officers of the Lake George and Ticonderoga campaigns included Major
General Phineas Lyman, Lieutenant Colonel William Eyre, Colonel John Bradstreet,
Major Robert Rogers, and Captain John Stark, among others. At Fort Edward on the
evening of June 17, a Canadian major and four men under a flag of truce arrived with
letters from the French generals, Montcalm and François-Charles de Bourlamaque,
concerning the exchange of prisoners. Amherst had expected the French flag of truce as
a way of observing the preparations of the British army. The French at the time had a
force of only 3,000 regulars and Canadian militia under Bourlamaque at Fort Carillon.
The French by June were nervously awaiting Amherst's army, which was erroneously
estimated at 25,000. Meanwhile, Amherst's troops were rebuilding the Fort Edward-Lake
George road and constructing a series of stockaded outposts along the way, including the
Four-Mile Post, Fort Amherst, and Fort Williams, and rebuilding the Halfway Brook
Post and Fort Gage. The Fort Edward camp was a major assembly point for the troops
who arrived almost daily from distant colonies. On June 21 the drums beat a half hour
before daybreak, signaling the start of the army's move to Lake George. The total army
that Amherst commanded at Fort Edward included 6,537 regulars and 4,839 provincial
troops.[2] Amherst ordered intricate precautions against an ambush, but the march to Lake
George was uneventful. By nine at night the rear guard had finally arrived at the southern
end of the lake.

"A View of the Lines at Lake George, 1759" by Thomas Davies shows Amherst's Lake George camp with the radeau *Invincible* and sloop *Halifax*. (Fort Ticonderoga Museum)

The very next day Amherst met with his chief engineer, Colonel James Montresor, to plan the location for a new fort at Lake George. The site of the fort was the high ground used as the entrenched camp during the siege of Fort William Henry in 1757. Within three weeks "about 2 or 3 acres of foundation" were laid; a month later a provincial officer noted "the Walls [are] about 14 Feet thick Built of Stone & Lime."[3] Named Fort George, the fortification would encompass a wooden fort, barracks, and a hospital, but the stone fortress was never completely finished; the remnants of one bastion still stand in Lake George Battlefield Park.*

Two of the biggest tasks for the army were retrieving the vessels sunk in 1758 and building new ones. By June 25 Captain Joshua Loring, the commander of the naval forces, was busy trying to bring the sloop *Halifax* to the surface. Amherst noted the next day that "Capt. Loring can't get his sloop up which was to have come up very easily."[5] On July 4, after ten days of labor, the *Halifax* was brought slightly above water and dragged to one of the docks on the southern shore of Lake George.[6] It took several more days to remove the water before repairs could be made and a new mast cut. The cannons from the vessel that had been buried the previous fall were also successfully retrieved. Similarly, "a Row galley that had been sunk last fall was found and got up to shore," according to

* A visitor to the lake in 1767 described Fort George as a "redoubt amounting to 12 guns, about 200 yards from shore, and some barracks."[4] Additional work on the fortification occurred during the Revolutionary War. An ambitious reconstruction of the fort began in 1921 but was never completed.

Lemuel Wood, a 17-year-old provincial from Massachusetts.[7] Henry Skinner, a Captain-Lieutenant in the Royal Artillery, recorded the depth of the vessel at "40 feet water."[8] The 40-foot row galleys were later described in a Boston newspaper as mounting one cannon which "fires out of the Head, they row with 14 Oars on each side, carry 30 Men each."[9] While only two row galleys accompanied Amherst's flotilla to Ticonderoga later in July, a few original sources suggest the presence of three row galleys on Lake George.[10] A row galley with an 18-pound cannon was employed in an action on July 12 against French and Indians on an island in the Narrows, but the latter escaped in 20 canoes.[11]

Apparently the army at Lake George mistakenly believed that the French had raised the radeau *Land Tortoise*, for Skinner noted that "the only thing of any consequence that they have found is a floating battery."[12] Without the recovery of the *Land Tortoise*, another large radeau was constructed under the supervision of Major Thomas Ord, the commander of the artillery train. Although slightly behind schedule, the radeau *Invincible* was built in less than two weeks. On July 16 Ord's radeau splashed into Lake George at five o'clock in the evening. As a result of the record construction time, Amherst found

Radeau *Invincible* leading a column of artillery rafts on Lake George as part of Jeffery Amherst's expedition to Fort Carillon in 1759. Drawing by Gary S. Zaboly.

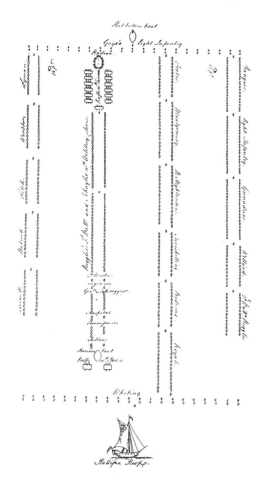

General Jeffery Amherst.
(National Gallery of Canada)

"Line of Vessels on Lake George under General Amherst, 1759" showing the English flat-bottomed boat, radeau *Invincible*, row galleys, rafts with cannons, and columns of bateaux, and the sloop *Halifax*. (Public Record Office, London)

one problem, "a little mistake in the height of the Port Holes of the Radeau, but she will do."[13] A 1759 painting by Captain Thomas Davies, presently in the Fort Ticonderoga Museum, depicts a single-masted *Invincible* similar in design to the *Land Tortoise*; but a second contemporary drawing by Skinner shows the *Invincible* with two masts.[14] When completed the radeau *Invincible* was armed with "four 24 pounders, and four 12 pounders."[15]

Other vessels that were built as part of the 1759 navy on Lake George included "Thirteen rafts...for Cannon" and two additional rafts for horses.[16] The rafts "were made by building a stage on three battoes."[17] A large elliptically-shaped vessel named the *Snow Shoe* was launched on July 5 and subsequently employed as a provision vessel that could transport 70 horses at a time.[18] Another vessel, which had been hauled from the Hudson River to the lake, was described as "the English flat-bottomed boat with a three-Pounder in her [bow] mounted as swivel"; and it carried 50 men.[19]

Finally, when all the vessels were completed and loaded, the British and provincial army would again make an attempt on Carillon after four years of preparation and disappointment at Lake George. At two o'clock in the morning of July 21, the drums beat for the army to assemble. By six o'clock the vessels began to depart. By nine o'clock the rear of the armada set forth. Once again the lake witnessed the majestic pageant of an optimistic army with its banners fluttering and the various colors of the regular regiments and provincials against the steep green mountains. The expedition consisted of 5,854 regulars and 5,279 provincials, a somewhat smaller number than Abercromby's 1758 army.

The vessels were organized into four double columns headed by the English flat-bottomed boat with the advance guard of Brigadier General Thomas Gage's light infantry in 43 whaleboats.* The first column on the right of rangers, light infantry, and grenadiers rowed whaleboats, accompanied by a row galley with one 12-pound cannon; the second column of regulars and Highlanders rowed bateaux; the third column with the radeau *Invincible* in the lead was followed by 13 rafts with the artillery on their carriages and bateaux carrying the hospital, sutlers, engineers, and carpenters preceding the provision vessel *Snow Shoe* and two rafts with horses; and the fourth column of provincial troops in bateaux was escorted by a row galley mounting one 18-pound cannon. Bateaux with provincial troops at the rear extended across the four columns, followed by the sloop *Halifax*.[21] Signals, consisting of colored flags, were to be made from the *Invincible* and *Halifax*. The men were ordered to row slowly and in turns to avoid fatigue; those not rowing were to sleep. Amherst was a careful leader who considered all the circumstances and details.

Whenever the wind favored the fleet, the soldiers deployed blanket sails on their bateaux. Each bateau, carrying nine barrels of pork or twelve of flour and approximately 20 men, was marked and numbered to aid in organizing the fleet. Rain during the day, however, hampered the efforts to keep the columns of vessels straight. Before sunset the fleet came to anchor in present-day Hague in sight of "ye great smooth rock [Rogers Rock]" where the troops "Lay in our boats all night."[22] The radeau *Invincible* anchored with the supply rafts moored alongside. At the break of light on July 22, the fleet renewed its voyage northward. Between nine and eleven o'clock in the morning the army landed on the east side of the lake, just below present-day Black Point in Ticonderoga at Weeds Bay. The advance guard of light infantry and rangers proceeded toward the sawmill, where they met the French posted in three positions.

Brigadier General François-Charles de Bourlamaque, who was wounded during the battle with Abercromby's army in 1758, was now in command of Carillon. While the French had troops at Carillon nearly equal to the numbers that Montcalm had mustered a year earlier, rations were short and disease raged inside the fort. (Reinforcements, food, and supplies for North America from France were minimal in 1759 because the French council of ministers decided to concentrate its efforts on the European theater of the Seven Years' War.) Bourlamaque himself led 300 Indians and some grenadiers in a skirmish with the invading troops. The French commander did little to stop the British from reaching the high ground at Ticonderoga: "twas impossible for me to induce the Indians to march against the enemy. . .and I was obliged, after having got the other light troops to fire for some time, to make them fall back within the entrenchments of Carillon."[23]

Amherst's method of command involved a calm, precise, and methodical movement of troops toward an objective. Eli Forbush, a Massachusetts soldier, wrote that the march to Ticonderoga "was performed with ye greatest regularity, ye least noise, a noble calmness and intrepid resolution, ye whole army seemed to pertake of ye very soul of ye commander."[24] That night Amherst set up posts at several locations: the high ground, sawmill, and Rattlesnake Hill. He had done his homework on Carillon and was sure of every move. The previous winter, the British command had sent Rogers and his rangers with Lieutenant Diedrick Brehm, an engineering officer from the 60th Regiment, to reconnoiter the fort and entrenchments. The engineer stalked the snow-covered landscape at midnight, producing a detailed report on the fortifications.[25]

---

* Amherst described the whaleboats in 1759 as "28 feet in the Keel, 5 feet 2 inches broad, 25 Inches Deep, 34 feet from stem to Stern. . .with Seven Oars besides the Ste[e]ring Oar."[20]

The next morning, July 23, Amherst received reports from the provincial units posted on Rattlesnake Hill that the French had taken their tents down and had departed in three sloops and bateaux. The British and provincial troops proceeded to the high ground of the French entrenchment that had been used so effectively against Abercromby in 1758. A cannonade from the fort caused the soldiers to entrench themselves behind the French breastworks. In the past year the French had greatly strengthened the earthen and log entrenchment. Ironically, the French breastworks, where so many British had died a year earlier, now protected them. Only about 400 soldiers were left inside Carillon under Captain Louis-Philippe Le Dossu d' Hébécourt. Bourlamaque, according to a prearranged plan and orders from Governor Vaudreuil, had abandoned the fort and moved to Fort St. Frédéric, taking with him about 2,600 regulars and Canadian militia and 400 Indians. In the meantime, the British and provincial army erected a redoubt to defend the landing site and a breastwork along the road from the landing area to the sawmill. By afternoon more cannons were brought forward. Major Ord's total artillery train consisted of 38 cannons, 11 howitzers, and 5 mortars.

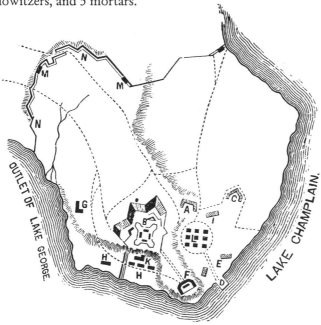

Plan of Fort Carillon, 1759.

A. Stone battery
B. The fort
C. Earth battery
D. Wharf
E. Stone houses for
   naval stores

F. Redoubt
G. Battery
H. Stone houses
   for prisoners
I. Lime kilns
K. Nine ovens

L. Gardens
M. Batteries in the lines
N. French lines

(*History of Lake Champlain*
by Peter Palmer)

The cannonading from the fort lasted all day as the British and provincial troops dug in behind the wall. The garrison at Carillon fired a large number of huge 13-inch mortar bombs into the British lines. Although the cast iron shells made a frightening noise, they landed in the dirt before exploding. On July 24 the British troops continued their digging closer to the fort while Amherst ordered the "artillery to be got up as fast as possible."[26] Amherst's orders for the troops were to hold their fire until all the batteries were in place.

The road to Lake Champlain had been improved to facilitate moving some of the whaleboats and bateaux to the new launching area on the lower lake.

Late that night an accident occurred in the British entrenchment. Amherst had ordered the troops never to fire at night, but instead to wait for the enemy with fixed bayonets. After some of the troops became alarmed that the French were making a raid on their lines, the British troops began firing on one another, leaving two killed and 12 wounded. As a result of the incident, different passwords were used each night in the trenches. On July 25 Robert Webster, a soldier with the Connecticut provincials, reported that "This day we got the General's boat [English flat-bottomed boat mounting a three-pound swivel] over in to Lake Champlain and three or four whale boats."[27] Some of the 24-pound cannons and the 13-inch mortar were brought to the entrenchment. The troops by then had dug within 600 yards of the fort, although the French had kept a continuous 24-hour fire on their position. Colonel Roger Townshend, a personal friend of Amherst, was killed by a cannonball as the British troops became more vulnerable in their advance toward the fort.[28]

On July 26 the *Snow Shoe* arrived at the northern Lake George landing at noon "with 60 horses on Bo[a]rd her [along with] Wagons on Bo[a]rd Battoes" which were immediately employed in carrying ammunition and stores to the trenches.[29] By the evening of the 26th, much of the artillery was in place, with Amherst preparing to open fire at daybreak with a battery of six 24-pounders and another of mortars. However, before any of the batteries were ever used, three deserters appeared in the British trenches with news that the French had abandoned the fort, setting the wooden sections on fire and lighting a delayed fuse to blow up the magazine and the guns loaded up to their muzzles with powder. Amherst offered 100 guineas to the deserters if they would go into the fort and cut the fuses. Not knowing if they would survive to collect the money, the deserters insisted that they didn't know where the fuses were.[30] Shortly thereafter, a tremendous explosion in the fort sent flames leaping into the summer sky. Fifty horses stabled above the fort's magazine were killed instantly in the explosion. The heat, flames, and secondary explosions made it impossible to approach the fort for most of the night. Amherst sent Colonel William Haviland with the light infantry and Major Robert Rogers with his rangers in the English flat-bottomed boat and whaleboats to attack the rear of the fleeing French troops. (Rogers had earlier received orders from Amherst to cut the French log boom "which the enemy have laid across from the point below, the Fort to the opposite shore."[31]) Several French bateaux were found adrift, loaded with powder; other bateaux had sunk. In all, 16 prisoners were taken, some of whom were from a French scouting party that had returned to Carillon expecting to find their own army but instead became captives of the British.

Although the fort was still in flames, at six o'clock in the morning a sergeant from a regular regiment volunteered to go into the fort to pull down the French flag and hoist the Union Jack of Great Britain. By eight o'clock in the morning the British and provincial troops entered the fort to attempt to extinguish the fires and defuse the artillery that had not been reached by the fire. Later that day Amherst totaled up 30 pieces of various caliber cannons and mortars and a howitzer from the fort, and ordered the retrieval of sunken French vessels and the construction of new boats at Ticonderoga "for carrying 24-Pounders."[32] However, it was not until September 13 that provincial troops succeeded in raising "two Large Flat bottomed Boats...taken when Fort William Henry was and Sunk at ye [northern Lake George] Landing."[33] A sloop, also captured by Montcalm's forces in 1757, was visible underwater but was never raised by Amherst's troops.[34]

Eli Forbush was quite impressed by the size and construction of Carillon. "The strength of ye Fort exceeds ye most sanguine imagination, nature and art are joind to render it impregnable, and had not ye enemy behaved like cowards and traitors they might have held out a long siege."[35] Young Lemuel Wood wrote a long, detailed description of the fort in his 1759 journal. Fort Carillon impressed Wood as the strongest fortress in North America; he noted stone walls 24 feet high on the west and northwest sides with rooms beneath for soldiers and "Dark Prisons," a neatly arched room housing two large ovens in the northeast section of the fort, a two-story stone barracks spanning the fort's length, redoubts, and a breastwork to the west of the fort that crossed the entire Ticonderoga peninsula.[36]

The total casualties reported by Amherst in taking Carillon included 16 men killed, 51 wounded, and one missing.[37] While other accounts have slightly higher casualty figures, the operation was a far cry from the devastating losses of a year earlier. Amherst issued a public thanks at the head of each unit for the conquest of the fort.

The fire inside the fort reignited from time to time until July 30. Only one bastion and two walls had been demolished; the walls of the barracks, artillery casemates, the covered way, and 11 ovens were essentially untouched. Amherst ordered the rebuilding of the fort by Lieutenant Colonel William Erye along the same lines that the French had originally constructed it. By using the same plan, he could minimize the labor involved and save the engineering effort for a new fortification at Crown Point. Construction of a new barracks for the garrison, however, was part of the rebuilding effort at the fort, as was completing the French redoubt closer to the lake.

However, an immediate push to Crown Point was hampered by a small French naval fleet on Lake Champlain. While Carillon was still burning, Amherst received scouting reports from Crown Point that "the two sloops and a Schooner are there to cover their boats."[38] The 10-gun schooner, rigged with topsails, was *La Vigilante*, constructed by Nicolas-René Levasseur at St. Jean, Quebec, in the fall of 1757. Joseph Payant St. Onge, who had earlier piloted a 45-ton sloop built by the French at Crown Point in 1742, now commanded the "King's bark" *La Vigilante*. Payant's long naval career on Lake Champlain earned him the unofficial title of "Admiral of Lake Champlain."[39] The French also had three "xebecs" on the lake that were sloop rigged with overhanging sterns. The three sloops or "xebecs"—*La Musquelongy* (The Muskellunge), *La Brochette* (The Pike), and *L'Esturgeon* (The Sturgeon), constructed by Levasseur and assistant shipbuilders Pierre Levasseur (son of Nicolas-René) and Louis-Pierre Poulin de Courval Cressé at St. Jean in the fall of 1758 and spring of 1759, carried eight guns each, with a crew of 40 to 50. Joannis-Galand d'Olabaratz (Laubaras), a former privateer and port captain, was appointed by the Marquis de Montcalm as the fleet commander on Lake Champlain in the spring of 1759.

On July 27, the morning after the fort had been abandoned, Amherst instructed Captain Joshua Loring to repair the sawmill in order to begin construction of a brig for Lake Champlain to be completed as soon as possible.[40] The previous morning "3 Ro[w] gal[l]eys [were] Drawn out of Lake George" and relaunched in Lake Champlain.[41] The sunken French bateaux were also to be raised and the British bateaux and whaleboats transported from Lake George to Lake Champlain. Two small radeaux were also hurriedly constructed, according to Eli Forbush. Forbush described the British vessels on Lake Champlain just before the departure for Crown Point: "We have two rydaus [radeaux] that carry Six 12 pounders in [their] sides and one 24 in ye bow. four ro[w] galleys...carry one 18 in each of [their] bows one flat boat and one six pounder and four bayboats with swiv[e]lls and a brig in great forwardness."[42] At noon on August 1, a scouting party returned with the news that the French had abandoned Fort St. Frédéric. At two o'clock in the morning on August 4, the drums beat assembly once again for a renewed voyage northward. The army, in bateaux and whaleboats, again formed in columns for

Views by Captain Thomas Davies of the Royal Regiment of Artillery, 1759.

Above: "A South View of the New Fortress at Crown Point." showing the radeau *Ligonier*, sloop *Boscawen*, and brig *Duke of Cumberland*. (Winterthur Museum)

Below: "South East View of Crown Point." (National Archives of Canada)

Above Right: "A South West View of the Lines and Fort of Tyconderoga." (National Archives of Canada)

Right: Detail of "A North View of Crown Point," which shows the 84-foot radeau *Ligonier* built on Lake Champlain under the supervision of Major Thomas Ord, who had also supervised construction of the *Land Tortoise*. (Library of Congress)

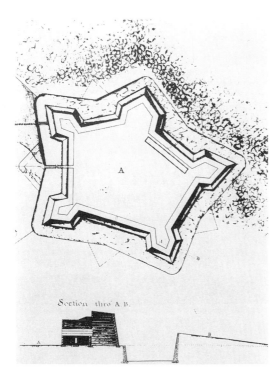

Section thro' A. B.

the journey, but a strong north wind delayed the landing at Crown Point until the evening.

Upon reaching the French fortress, Amherst was ready with his building ideas: "I ordered the Engineers to reconnoitre the best place for erecting a Fort that I may set about it as soon as possible."[43] Fort St. Frédéric, named for a French minister, had taken its basic shape by 1737 but would be improved in the early 1740s. Nearly square in shape with four bastions with sentry huts at each angle, St. Frédéric had a medieval castle or citadel standing four stories high with ten-foot thick limestone walls. The self-contained citadel was a fort within a fort, entered by a drawbridge over a ditch. The four-story structure contained all the essential facilities to withstand a siege, including 20 cannons. The outer walls enclosed bar-

Top: Plans for the fort constructed under Jeffery Amherst in 1759 at Crown Point. (National Archives of Canada) *Above:* Crown Point showing remains of British fort (left) and Fort St. Frédéric (right). Photo by the author.

racks, an additional magazine, storage buildings, and the chapel. Outside the walls were numerous structures, including a hospital, windmill, redoubts, and a small village. Fort St. Frédéric had been blown up when the French evacuated the fortress on July 31. When the provincial troops finally viewed St. Frédéric, there was little left to impress them: "They have destroyed all their Buildings of value. They Blew up their Ci[t]adel or Magaz[i]ne it is a very Large heap of Stones."[44] Although Colonel Nathan Whiting found Crown Point "a very pleasant place presenting a fine view of the Lake," he remarked that "the old Fort is very trifling for one that has made so much noise in the World."[45] After the destruction of St. Frédéric, Brigadier General Bourlamaque moved his army to the southern end of the Isle-aux-Noix in the Richelieu River (north of Lake Champlain) where the French army entrenched itself with 3,040 men and 100 cannons.

At Crown Point, Amherst ordered 100 rangers to open a road to Ticonderoga, 200 rangers to cut a road across present-day Vermont to the Connecticut River, and troops to build several redoubts or small forts; he sent scouting parties to explore the source of the Hudson River and creeks in Vermont. Two days after landing at Crown Point, Amherst marked the ground out for the new fort. Within a few days 400 men were at work on it, and by August 13 Amherst had assigned 1,500 men to the project. Although he had assured Pitt that he would move to Canada with the "utmost vigor and despatch," the varied construction projects slowed progress.[46] Captain Loring had been left at Ticonderoga to build a brig, but the sawmill there was constantly breaking down due to the increased demand for sawed lumber for the new fort at Crown Point. In addition, many rainy days delayed the work.

On August 16 a deserter from the French squadron that had been anchored below Four Brothers Islands accurately reported the numbers, names, armaments, and officers of the French fleet to the British. Amherst immediately summoned Loring from Ticonderoga to reassess the need for a larger British fleet. Loring, upon learning of the size of the French fleet, suggested that the brig under construction would not be sufficient for control of the lake. After a meeting on the problem, Loring and Ord agreed that the fastest solution would involve building a radeau to carry six 24-pound cannons. The vessel, to be built in ten days, was very similiar to the radeaux *Land Tortoise* and *Invincible* that Ord had completed at Lake George. On the first of September, a scouting party under Sergeant Joseph Hopkins returned with news that a new sloop "pierced for 16 guns" had been launched by the French.[47] Actually, the new French sloop, the 65-ton *Waggon*, mounted six to eight 4-pound cannons.[48] Amherst immediately embarked on two courses of action. He ordered Ord to prepare "fire darts" (a type of incendiary device) and hand grenades to burn the new French sloop. More significantly, he ordered Loring to build a sloop when the brig was finished. Amherst and Loring decided on a sloop of 16 guns, which further delayed the movement to Canada.

Two weeks later the scouting party that had been sent against the French sloop was back after failing to burn the vessel. The men had boarded the sloop with the combustible materials but were discovered by guards. The guards and troops in the French camp fired on the saboteurs, who luckily escaped unharmed. Amherst was unhappy with the raid since his orders were to try to burn the vessel at two o'clock in the morning, but the men instead attempted the operation at ten o'clock in the evening.[49]

While awaiting the completion of the vessels during September, Amherst dispatched Rogers and 190 men on a long expedition into Canada to destroy the Indian village of St. Francis (Odanak) on a tributary of the St. Lawrence River. The daring raid was in retaliation for the holding of Captain Quinton Kennedy and his party, whom Amherst had earlier sent to the village with a peace offer under a flag of truce. (The onerous journey became the subject of Kenneth Robert's book *Northwest Passage*.)

In the meantime, breakdowns at the sawmill at Ticonderoga extended the planned time for the three vessels under construction. However, the radeau *Ligonier*, built at Crown Point, was finished in the time promised and launched on September 29. "She is 84 feet long & 20 feet broad on the Platform, where the Guns run out she is 23 feet & to carry six 24-Pounders."[50] The *Ligonier* had two masts, with the lower hull angling outward and the upper sides angling inward with gunports, according to a contemporary sketch (1759), "A North View of Crown Point" by Thomas Davies. When Major Ord tried the *Ligonier* against the wind in early October, the vessel apparently did not sail well.

After many disagreements over supplies, logs, and the sawmill operation among the principal officers, the brig and sloop finally arrived at Crown Point on October 10 and 11. Although the 155-ton brig, christened the *Duke of Cumberland*, had been launched more than a month earlier, Loring needed more time to construct the quarterdeck and rig the two-masted vessel.[51] On August 29, Amherst had written that the "Brigantine...will Mount Twenty guns," but other reports noted "six 6 pounders, twelve 4 pounders, and 20 swivels."[52] Crews with experience were hard to come by. Eventually 70 crew members and 60 troops to be used as marines were assigned to the vessel. The morning after the brig arrived at Crown Point, the new 16-gun sloop, commanded by Lieutenant Alexander Grant, joined the fleet. The sloop *Boscawen* carried "four 6 pounders, twelve 4 pounders, and 22 swivels, 60 seamen, and 50 marines."[53] The 115-ton *Boscawen*, built of oak, had a length of 80 feet and a 24-foot width. At one point in September, Amherst had been so anxious to get underway that he considered advancing against the French "with the Brig [and] Radeaux boats without waiting for the Sloop," but in the end he decided to wait for the *Boscawen*.[54]

At the same time, Brigadier General Bourlamaque kept his four vessels cruising the lake with scouts observing the British position. Bourlamaque noted that Amherst "employed his army in erecting at St. Frédéric a fort much larger and stronger than that I had destroyed, until he should have a navy built superior to that we had on the lake."[55] In late August and early September, in two letters to Governor Vaudreuil, Bourlamaque calculated that Amherst would not attack in 1759. "Wise people believe they will defer to next spring. . .the odds are that Mr. Amherst has no intention to come here this year, and that he is satisfied with the building of a large fort at St. Frédéric."[56] However, as soon as the sloop arrived, Amherst wasted no time in his advance against the French. Loring did not think that the *Duke of Cumberland* and *Boscawen* were strong enough to engage the four vessels of the French fleet, but Amherst, undeterred, gave orders to sail past the French, unobserved if possible, and cut them off from their base at Isle-aux-Noix. "You will at all Events do Your utmost to Come up and Attack them."[57]

During the afternoon of October 11, Amherst and his troops departed from Crown Point. According to one provincial officer at Crown Point, Amherst's fleet not only consisted of the 20-gun *Duke of Cumberland*, 16-gun *Boscawen*, and 6-gun *Ligonier* (with one large mortar), but included "two arke" or small radeaux with a 24-pounder each and mortars, and three row galleys mounting one 18-pounder each, as well as an assortment of other artillery.[58] The fleet of bateaux was divided into four columns with the radeau *Ligonier* placed in advance of the center columns with Amherst aboard. Ranger Captain James Tute's method of rigging blanket sails (which had been used earlier) was adopted, with each bateau rigged with two blankets.[59] At four o'clock the *Duke of Cumberland* and *Boscawen* set sail with a fair wind and easily outdistanced the main fleet later that day.

The fleet rowed all night, following a lantern hung on Amherst's radeau. During the night an error occurred when troops in bateaux under Major John Reid from the Highlander Regiment followed "the light in the Brig for the one in the Radeau [*Ligo-*

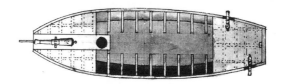

Plan, Elevation and Section of a Galliot to Row with 22 Oars besides Main Sail and Fore-Sail on Occasion, to be Mounted with one 18 or 12 Pounder for a Chase two 6 or 4 Pounders 16 Wall Peices or Swivels and 250 Men. This Vessel in its Construction will partake of the Advantages of a Galley or Zebeque in its Agility, and of a Sloop in its Sailing and defence with the Addition of a Prow for Boarding or Landing.
S Davies fecit 1759

Plan for a typical English row galley in 1759. (National Archives of Canada)

nier]."[60] At daybreak the errant detachment found itself among the French sloops south of Four Brothers Islands. Lieutenant (Hugh?) MacKay and 20 men were taken prisoner.[61] "I made all the sail with the Radeau I could," recorded Amherst after hearing the firing from the north.[62] Shortly thereafter, returning Highlanders reported the skirmish with the French sloops. With the wind blowing hard against them, the radeaux, the row galleys, and the fleet of bateaux continued their advance until it was nearly dark, when Colonel Peter Schuyler of New Jersey recommended stopping in a nearby bay on the western shore. According to Commissary Wilson's orderly book, Amherst's fleet landed at "Ligonier Bay" (just south of present-day Ligonier Point on Willsboro Point); Amherst "ordered the rangers on an island."[63]

On the first night, Loring with the brig and sloop had sailed past the three French sloops at Four Brothers Islands, commanded by Joannis-Galand d'Olabaratz. The schooner *La Vigilante*, commanded by Joseph Payant St. Onge, was stationed further north on the lake near Grand Isle. At daybreak on October 12, Loring observed the French schooner apparently moving toward the two British ships. The *Vigilante* fired and the *Cumberland* and *Boscawen* gave chase, whereupon the French schooner maneuvered into shallow water between the Sister Islands (Bixby and Young Island) on the west side of South Hero Island. The experienced French pilot had drawn the British vessels into a trap, with both British ships running aground. The *Boscawen* got off the shoal easily, but the *Cumberland* was forced to take eight cannons and all the troops off to lighten the vessel. By the time the British were free of the shoal, the *Vigilante* was long gone. After a time the British noticed the sails of the three sloops beating against the strong wind as they tried to reach Isle-aux-Noix. Instinctively, Loring dropped his sails and began to pursue the French fleet. D' Olabaratz turned his vessels in a desperate attempt to elude the larger British ships. The French vessels, sailing into a setting sun, entered Cumberland Bay. They moved into a position off the western shore near present-day Cliff Haven, west of Crab Island. Loring, with the *Duke of Cumberland* and the *Boscawen*, followed the three sloops and anchored in a position that would block their escape.

D' Olabaratz called a conference aboard *La Musquelongy* at which the French officers decided to scuttle their ships and walk back to Isle-aux-Noix.[64] Onshore in the darkness, two scouting parties that had been sent by Amherst heard banging and hammering from the French sloops. Two long boats, however, escaped to Isle-aux-Noix to inform the garrison of Amherst's advance. The remaining crews of the sloops cut the masts and dumped some of the cannons, swivel guns, and muskets overboard. The next morning the crews of the British vessels were surprised to find the *Musquelongy* abandoned, with guns spiked and the mast cut, and the two other sloops sunk "in five fathom[s] [of] water."[65] The beleaguered French crews took nine days to reach Isle-aux-Noix overland. One last crew member eluded the British until October 24. *La Vigilante*, at the same time, had hidden in the lee of Isle La Motte. The old lake pilot brought his vessel into Bourlamaque's headquarters on October 16 to the wonder of the garrison, whose men had thought the ship had been captured. Bourlamaque was infuriated, nevertheless, over the scuttling of the rest of the French squadron without a fight. Amherst's report to Lieutenant Governor James DeLancey of New York suggested a reason for the French sinkings. After an "officer" of the captured Highlanders had "greatly magnif[ied] our naval strength," the French had scuttled their vessels "in Such a Manner that they might easily get them off or up again."[66]

On October 13 Loring took the *Cumberland* to search for the French schooner, leaving Lieutenant Grant and the crew of the *Boscawen* to retrieve the *Musquelongy* and some of the sunken war materials from the other two sloops. Amherst and his army were grounded at Ligonier Bay for five days due to severe wind and stormy conditions. The temperature continued to drop each night with hard frosts on the last two nights. Men in two whaleboats dispatched to Captain Loring on October 13 returned on the evening of the 17th after an unsuccessful attempt to reach his position because of rough water.

At last on the 18th of October the weather calmed down and Amherst received letters with the news that Quebec had been taken by the British. Surmising that the whole French army would now move to Montreal, Amherst decided to suspend the expedition and move back to Crown Point to finish the fort. Several days and nights of cold, blustery October weather also influenced Amherst's decision to end the campaign. Amherst did sail to the site of the scuttling of the French sloops, landing his troops on Crab Island. By then the *Musquelongy* had been repaired and was ready to join the British fleet. Amherst ordered a contingent of Gage's light infantry and rangers in whaleboats to help Loring, aboard the *Duke of Cumberland*, search for the missing French schooner. The next day the wind picked up from the north again; Amherst realized that it would take ten days to get to Isle-aux-Noix and decided to return to Crown Point with his men.

By October 21 Amherst had returned to Crown Point and ordered the troops to work on the fort. Five days later the brig and sloop, along with the French prize *La Musquelongy*, arrived at Crown Point. After Loring reported that it was possible to raise the sloops *La Brochette* and *L'Esturgeon*, Lieutenant Grant was sent on October 27 with the *Boscawen*, the *La Musquelongy* (renamed the *Amherst*), and the two small radeaux with 200 men and equipment to raise the sloops.[67] Shortly thereafter, Grant reported to Amherst that he had "raised the Stern of one of the vessels above water after great Labour being assisted by the other Sloop and have now three Cables under the Said Wreck which I believe will answer."[68] By November 1 some of the provincials had mutinied and threatened to go home, but Amherst marched out the regular troops to stop them. Four days later 100 deserters were captured, but they were pardoned by Amherst. On November 10, to observe the king's birthday, the garrison at Crown Point held a celebration. But the next day more provincials began deserting, finally leading to a march home by several regiments over the following days. On the morning of November 16, Grant arrived at Crown Point with the two French sloops raised from the waters at present-day Cliff Haven. Lieutenant MacKay informed Amherst that "the Enemy had thrown over board two Brass Guns from Each Sloop," leaving the carriages on the vessels.[69] The next day all the sloops sailed for Ticonderoga to be laid up for the winter at the King's Dock just north of the Grenadiers Redoubt. Later, Thomas Ord's "Return of Guns, Ammunition & Stores, Found on board the Three French Sloops" listed twenty 4-pound cannons and 11 swivel guns.[70]

By mid-November "His Majesty's Fort of Crown Point" had taken substantial shape as the last chimney was completed and the shingles set on the barracks roof. The fort, three or four times bigger than Fort St. Frédéric, would eventually be the largest British fortress in colonial America. Fort Crown Point would be formed into a pentagon with five bastions and three Georgian-style barracks which enclosed a parade ground of six acres. Redoubts, blockhouses, storehouses, and a village outside the walls would be completed over the years. Amherst also concluded construction for the season at Ticonderoga with completion of the barracks in November. Despite the priority construction at Crown Point, the Ticonderoga fort underwent substantial reconstruction, as evidenced by Ensign Ebenezer Dibble's journal, which listed a 90-foot stone barracks, a framed 173-foot barracks, a 209-foot magazine with casements, and another 190-foot stone structure.[71]

After considering the construction of a blockhouse to defend the vessels in their winter berths at Ticonderoga, Amherst and his officers agreed on a wooden palisade or pickets adjacent to the wharfs with guards to be stationed on the vessels, which were to have "two

Guns out of their Sterns and also two in their Bows."[72] Another method to protect vessels over the winter was apparently tried unsuccessfully with the *Ligonier*. In December Major John Campbell, in command at Ticonderoga, reported to Amherst that he "could not by any means get the Rad[e]au Sunk."[73]

With winter fast approaching, Amherst departed in late November for New York City. Because of bad weather and ice on the Hudson, he did not use the sloops on the river but was forced to walk a good part of the way to the city. While walking, he envisioned new construction projects, including bridges.

The campaign of 1760 would bring the final collapse of the French empire in North America. The strategy involved a three-pronged attack on the French forces in Canada which would ultimately converge on Montreal for the final blow. Brigadier General James Murray, in command of Quebec after Wolfe's successful battle for the city in September 1759, would move west on the St. Lawrence River toward Montreal. Amherst, leading the main army on the most difficult route, would move east on the St. Lawrence from Lake Ontario, while Brigadier General William Haviland (local rank in America), in command of Crown Point in 1760, would move north on the lake, capturing Isle-aux-Noix before pushing to Montreal.[74] The easiest passage to Montreal for the entire army would have been through Lake Champlain, but a pincer attack from the east and west via the St. Lawrence River would prevent the French from escaping and thus ensure the end of the war.

Forty-two-year-old Brigadier General Haviland had extensive experience in the Lake George and Lake Champlain theater during the French and Indian War. In 1757 Haviland had led his regiment to America, where he commanded Fort Edward in the winter of 1757-1758 and fought under Abercromby in the aborted attack on Carillon in 1758. In 1759 he served with Amherst and commanded Crown Point during the following winter. During the spring of 1760 Haviland would be delegated a major role in the last campaign of the war in North America.

On May 25, before all provincial troops had arrived at Crown Point, Amherst ordered Major Robert Rogers to raid the port of St. Jean on the upper Richelieu River and destroy the French vessels, provisions, and other war material that could be utilized at Isle-aux-Noix. He was then to attack Fort Chambly. Rogers and his 213-man raiding party successfully defeated a larger French detachment in a battle on the Point au Fer peninsula. Although unsuccessful in destroying any of the French vessels, the daring operation was a well-coordinated amphibious operation utilizing the *Duke of Cumberland*, commanded by Lieutenant Grant, and the four sloops in the British fleet. The larger ships acted as floating bases for the whaleboats and bateaux which had been carried to the northern waters on the decks of the brig and sloops.

During June and early July the army slowly mobilized as the provincial troops reached Crown Point. While Amherst's instructions to Haviland stressed his sole objective of "the Reduction of the Remains of all Canada," he ordered "finishing the Works at Crown Point, Rebuilding the Barracks at Ticonderoga; & Completing the Works at Fort George" during the time before the army departed.[75]

Upon arriving after a march of six weeks, Lieutenant Thomas Moody from present-day York, Maine, was impressed by the fortress on Lake Champlain. "Crown Point, Far surpasses the Idea that I conceived of it."[76] Reverend Samuel MacClintock, a chaplain with a New Hampshire regiment, was similarly impressed: "It is a pentagon with 5 bastions & 5 redoubts—the wall 40 foot thick, made of timbers and earth—a Casemt is round ye inside 18 foot deep, bomb pro[o]f."[77] While some troops were engaged in various construction projects, others target practiced, unloaded bateaux, and sweltered in extremely hot July weather. During the idle days before the expedition was to proceed northward, the troops entertained themselves with whaleboat races on the lake.

Following several days of feverish activity, the army at Crown Point embarked at ten o'clock on the morning of August 11. The diverse fleet included the *Duke of Cumberland*, the sloop *Boscawen*, the three captured French sloops (*Brochette, Esturgeon, Musquelongy*), the radeau *Ligonier* and two other small radeaux, three row galleys or "prows" with one cannon each, two long boats, 263 bateaux, 12 canoes, and 41 whaleboats.[78] Although the weather was clear the first day, the wind blew strongly against the vessels. The 3,300-man army moved only approximately five or six miles in the wind, landing on a rocky area on the western shore for the night. The next day the adverse wind again handicapped their progress, requiring a tow of the radeau *Ligonier* "with 6 Battoes."[79]

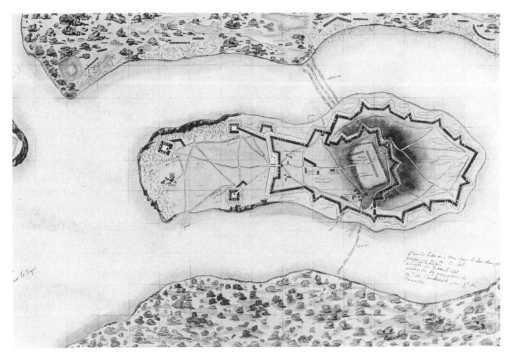

Plan of Isle-aux-Noix by Louis Antoine de Bougainville 1760.
(National Archives of Canada)

After camping at Button Bay, the fleet renewed its voyage. The wind out of the north, however, continued and the army once more covered but a short distance. On August 14 the army was propelled to Schuyler Island by south winds accompanied by heavy seas and rain. One "birch canoe" split open and eight rangers drowned.[80] Seven bateaux were "Missing Supposed to be gon[e] to the Bottom."[81] On the following day the favorable winds pushed the armada to Isle la Motte. On August 16 the army finally reached Isle-aux-Noix, disembarking south of the French fort on the eastern shore of the Richelieu River. To protect the troops during the landing, the radeau *Ligonier* and row galleys maintained a fire on the French fort and vessels. The army began construction of a breastwork nearly a mile long on the eastern shoreline of the mainland, eventually erecting three batteries of cannons and one of mortars.

The following morning a bloody encounter occurred "on board...a Small Artillery R[a]deau, Bore away Towards the fort whose orders was to go on till fir'd upon," when a French cannonball struck six men sitting on the deck of the vessel.[82] One or both legs of all six men were blown off. The captain died and the survivors were moved to a small island just to the south, since named Hospital Island.

For several more days the British and provincial army worked on their breastwork and batteries while the French bombarded the British entrenchment with their artillery. On the afternoon of August 23, the British batteries of cannons and mortars were finally ready: "at 3[o'clock], all ye music in camp play[ed] 10 minutes and then open[e]d ye Batteries...on ye fort...which soon made the houses fly to p[i]e[c]es."[83] The ensuing cannon duel resulted in severe casualties on both sides. In a bold move on August 25, Colonel John Darby, with two light infantry companies, and Major Robert Rogers, with four of his ranger companies, sought to break the siege by dragging two howitzers and a six-pound cannon through the forest along the river bank adjacent to Isle-aux-Noix just to the north of the fort and a defensive boom of logs that the French had laid across the channel. At this point the British battery separated the French fort from their vessels. The French vessels included the schooner *La Vigilante*, the 65-ton sloop *Waggon*, two row galleys or "tartans," the *Petit Diable* and *Grand Diable*, and several small gunboats or jacaubites.[84] The first shot cut the cable holding the row galley *Grand Diable* (also called a radeau), while another shot severed the head of its captain.[85] The vessel drifted onto the shore where it was easily captured. The other vessels weighed anchor, with their crews pulling furiously on the long oars to evade the dreaded rangers. Rogers and his men crossed the river and scurried along its shore through the dense foliage to prevent the French vessels from escaping into open water. Rogers beat the vessels to the end of the channel and fired on the lead vessel, which soon ran aground on a muddy shoal. Brandishing tomahawks, the rangers swam to the vessel and captured the crew. The schooner *La Vigilante* piloted by 60-year-old Joseph Payant St. Onge, who had outmaneuvered Captain Joshua Loring the year before, was now finally captured. The other French vessels met with the same fate in the shallow channel. The three vessels taken in the action were listed as "one Rideau one Topsail Schooner & a Sloop" by Sergeant David Holden from Groton, Massachusetts.[86] British records listed the "Schooner Vigilant[e], Sloop Waggon, Row Gall[e]y Grand Diable, [and] Row Gall[e]y Petit Diable" as captured at Isle-aux-Noix in 1760.[87]

The British and provincial troops opened new batteries closer to the French fort on August 26 but not without a cost. On the following day one French shot caused the explosion of a British magazine, resulting in numerous casualties, including one provincial soldier who was thrown 40 feet into the air. The troops on Isle-aux-Noix were now in a precarious position without ships to evacuate them. The French had only about 1,650 troops at the island under Colonel Louis Antoine de Bougainville, the bright young officer who had served as an aide to Montcalm during the siege of Fort William Henry and at Abercromby's defeat the following year. While Bougainville had much to report in his journal in the years of French victories, by 1760 his chronicle became notably brief. By midnight on August 28, Bougainville and his men deserted their fortress following an order of Canadian Governor Vandreuil, leaving a token crew to maintain a cannonade on the British position. The French army crossed to the western shore, probably in bateaux, and marched 12 miles through the dense forest to St. Jean. When the British and provincials entered the fort at Isle-aux-Noix the following morning, they "found one Capt. and 30 Privates together with a great many that were sick & Wounded."[88] Rogers and his men were sent by Haviland to follow the fleeing French army. By the time Rogers reached St. Jean, Bougainville had left the port village on fire and was halfway to Montreal. Rogers pursued the French army, which he estimated at 1,500, until he encountered the rear guard, who fled under the rangers' attack. Rogers' small force, however, did not engage Bouganville's main army but awaited Haviland's arrival at St. Jean.

By September 6 the French armies, pursued from the east and west, had converged on Montreal. Bougainville, deserted by the militia, entered Montreal from the south with his regulars. The three armies of Amherst, Haviland, and Murray now surrounded Montreal with 17,000 troops. Inside Montreal were the remnants of the entire French force in Canada, only 2,200 troops and several hundred soldiers from French colonies. That night Governor Vaudreuil called a council of war with his officers who unanimously accepted his proposal for surrender. Ironically, Colonel Bougainville, who had formulated the terms of capitulation for the surrender of the British at Fort William Henry in 1757, now carried the surrender terms of the French. Amherst, recalling the atrocities of the war, demanded complete surrender of the French army without the "honors of war."[89] Bougainville and some other officers instead presented a letter to Governor Vaudreuil "containing sharp protests against these humiliating conditions and the offer to attack the enemy at once."[90] But on the next morning of September 8, 1760, Vaudreuil, with little real choice, signed the 55 articles of surrender. Although Amherst had little sympathy for the French army, his treatment of the civilian population of Canada was remarkably compassionate. Colonel Nathan Whiting noted that Amherst's march to Montreal was "very peaceable"—his army "did not the least damage to them [settlements], the General having forbid all plundering."[91] French military officers and high civil officials were sent back to France in British ships. Many accusations of corruption and incompetence would be made as the result of the fall of France in America. Bougainville joined the French navy in 1763, making a two-year scientific voyage around the world, and later served with the French fleet fighting for the Americans during the Revolution.

After the victory, Amherst returned to New York City by way of Lake Champlain, inspecting Isle-aux-Noix and ordered "the fortifications...entirely Destroyed."[92] He arrived at Crown Point on October 15, noting his displeasure at the progress on the fortress. Amherst immediately set the men to work again. His interest in building even extended to a beaver dam which he dismantled on October 21 to see how it was constructed. On his trip to New York, Amherst inspected the fortification at Lake George. "The bastion enclosed at Fort George is very neat, mounts 15 Guns, is very small and a bad defence, but 'twas the shortest, cheapest & best method of finishing what was begun of the Fort."[93] Amherst was treated as a hero upon his arrival in New York City. The British government appointed him governor of Virginia, a largely perfunctory position with a substantial income, and governor-general of British North America. He returned to England in late 1763 but was urged to return by the king as the commander in chief in America at the beginning of the Revolutionary War. Amherst, however, declined the request despite many efforts to convince him otherwise.

In the fall of 1760, while the colonies were rejoicing with parades at the defeat of the French, most of the provincial soldiers were still stationed at Crown Point and Ticonderoga, where they were ravaged by many serious illnesses. As late as November 9, Thomas Moody noted "extreme Cold lying in open tents" at Crown Point.[94] Finally, on November 19, Moody's provincial regiment began its long march home, battling the cold and snow squalls along the rough road (Number 4) built in 1759 through the wilderness of Vermont and New Hampshire.

Most of the vessels were brought to Ticonderoga at the end of the 1760 operations and remained under the direction of Lieutenant Alexander Grant through 1763.[95] In May 1761 Grant suggested sinking "the vessels that are not put in use this season," but Amherst did not concur and nearly all the vessels in the Lake Champlain fleet were rigged in 1761.[96] Amherst concluded that the soldiers at Ticonderoga were not entitled to "any Extraordinary pay" for their labor but instead should be rewarded with "Some Rum: They are not Entitled to any thing More."[97] The most dramatic incident in Lieutenant Grant's tenure occurred during a storm at Crown Point on October 22-23, 1761, when the *Grand Diable* "during the night...was drove from her anchor" with 150 barrels of provisions aboard and "the water Dashing in at the row Ports fill'd in [a] few minutes & Sunk."[98] Several attempts were made to "weigh her but to little or no Purpose"; but the provisions and some planks were recovered from the vessel.[99] With the loss of the *Grand Diable*, the *Petit Diable* was employed for the remainder of 1761 carrying provisions between Ticonderoga and Crown Point.[100]

The forts on Lake Champlain were not shuttered after the last campaign of 1760. As late as 1762 several thousand troops were stationed at Crown Point with work continuing on the fort and redoubts.[101] After the peace treaty of 1763, however, the British maintained only small garrisons at Crown Point and Ticonderoga. Francis Grant, a visitor at Crown Point during the summer of 1767, noted that the "barracks on the inside. . .not finished" and the fort was "now going fast to decay, and it is said will be abandoned."[102] At Ticonderoga Grant was most impressed by the size and condition of Montcalm's breastwork, which had stopped Abercromby.* Grant described the war fleet "laid up here, consisting of a large Brigantine which mounted 20 guns, two Schooners, two sloops, and some small craft; also a sloop [*Musquelongy*] constantly employed in the summer season between this place and St John's."[104] In all likelihood, the last official accounting by the British of the rival fleets from the French and Indian War was made on July 30, 1778. The brig *Duke of Cumberland* and sloop *Boscawen* were noted as "Lay'd up And Decay'd"; the sloops *Brochette*, *Esturgeon*, and *Musquelongy*, listed as "taken in 1759" were "In Service till Decay'd," and the schooner *Vigilante*, sloop *Waggon* and row galley *Petit Diable* were recorded as "Taken in 1760...Lay'd up till Decay'd."[105]

Fort George remained an active post during the early 1760s and several vessels were employed to carry provisions and troops on Lake George. In May 1760 Amherst ordered provincial troops "to Bale out the Sloop [*Halifax*] there"; but the following summer John Cowley wrote to Amherst that he collected "all the Stores...in the storehouse at Fort George belonging to His Majesty's Sloop the Earl of Halifax and Sent them on bo[a]rd the Snow Shoe."[106] A "List of Vessels built, taken & c on the Lakes" recorded the *Halifax* as "broken Up 1760"; but the 1778 British return of the "Provincial Navy," which listed vessels from the French and Indian War, included a sloop built at Lake George in 1758, with the notation "Lay'd up And Decay'd."[107] In June 1761 the radeau *Invincible*, which had been at the northern Lake George landing, mired "in Mud & Water was by a strong squal[l] of wind forced out of her bed and carr[i]ed almost to the Little Falls."[108] The vessel was repaired and used the following month to move artillery stores to Fort George.[109] The vessel employed most often on Lake George during this period to transport troops and provisions was the *Snow Shoe*. Little is known about the exact construction of this vessel, and a letter written in 1760 referred to "the new Snow shoe," which raises the possibility of more than one vessel with the same name; other original sources indicate that the *Snow Shoe* could be sailed or rowed and hauled "16 Barrels of Flo[u]r, 20 Barrels Beef, 229 Barrels of Pork" and was considered "more convenient for carrying the troops" than the radeau *Invincible*.[110] Five years later William Gilliland, the original settler of Willsboro, New York, shipped "all [his] Cattle in the Vessel Called the Snow Shoe."[111]

---

* Nine years later Ammi Robbins, a chaplain with the American army of 1776, observed the mass graves at the site of the Abercromby defeat where "numbers of bones,—thigh, arms, etc.—above ground."[103]

Archaeological Discoveries

A decade after the last battle, many of the vessels used by the British and French on Lake Champlain during 1759 and 1760 were still tied up to the military dock or "King's Shipyard" at Fort Ticonderoga north of the old grenadier battery. The vessels, with cannons and rigging removed, eventually sank in the shallow water of the wharf area. During the Tercentenary Celebration of Lake Champlain, plans were made to salvage the hull of a vessel reported to be Arnold's 1776 schooner "*Revenge*," which had sunk near the old military dock at Fort Ticonderoga. A vessel "about ninety feet long and twenty-two feet wide" was raised during the winter of 1909 and subsequently displayed as the "*Revenge*" near the shoreline for many years.[112] The remains of the "*Revenge*" were shown in various publications including Max W. Reid's *Lake George and Lake Champlain* published in 1910. In the spring of 1948, a roof collapsed on the vessel, causing major damage to the hull. However, as late as 1954 the Fort Ticondergoa Museum reported that it was planning to move the vessel and display it adjacent to the fort.

During the early 1950s the museum began exploratory diving on two wrecks that officials had surmised dated to the Revolution: "We commenced exploratory diving last summer [1953] to determine the best possible means to raise the *Enterprise* and *Trumbull* lying in the mud off the shore at the fort."[113] These names were surprising because historical evidence did not indicate that these two vessels had sunk at the fort. One of these vessels, claimed to be the *Trumbull*, was raised in 1954, but the 75-foot vessel was probably not a war vessel and was burned in 1959.[114] Although one researcher in 1964 speculated that the "*Revenge*" hull was actually the *Duke of Cumberland*, the identification of these vessels at the Fort Ticonderoga dock remained a mystery until 1982.[115] During a survey of the area by the Champlain Maritime Society in cooperation with Fort Ticonderoga, the badly deteriorated hull of the "*Revenge*" was examined. Based on the remaining dimensions, construction, and historical data, the ship was identified as the 1759 brig *Duke of Cumberland*. Three additional wrecks were discovered sunk in the mud at the old fort dock, including the sloop *Boscawen*, one of the French sloops, and a bateau.

A major underwater archaeological project was undertaken in 1984 by the Champlain Maritime Society and the Fort Ticonderoga Museum to study the wreck of the *Boscawen* and recover artifacts. The project, directed by Arthur B. Cohn with Kevin Crisman as the project archaeologist, was successful in anaylzing the construction of the vessel, obtaining accurate dimensions, and recovering 600 artifacts for conservation. Using a water dredge, archaeologist William Bayreuther and other divers were able to clear the mud from the vessel to obtain precise calculations of the remaining hull. A grid system of plastic pipe was placed over the wreck, creating five-foot-square excavation units to properly identify areas of study and artifact removal. The artifacts that were removed were immediately subjected to a preservation process using techniques developed for Texas A&M's study of the Revolutionary War brig *Defense* in Castine, Maine. The archaeological finds, preserved under the direction of conservator Heidi Miksh, included tools, grapeshot, cannonballs, gunlocks, a flask, buttons, buckles, clay pipes, eating utensils, coins, keys, blocks, and deadeyes. The excavation of the *Boscawen* over two summers represented the first state-of-the-art archaeological study and conservation of an eighteenth-century shipwreck in Lake Champlain.[116]

Other French and Indian War vessels have not fared as well. Most of the *Duke of Cumberland's* rotting frames remained exposed to the elements at Fort Ticonderoga until 1999. By then the vessel had virtually disappeared. In 1909 Fred Nadeau of Crown Point raised the wreckage of a vessel near the Crown Point ferry slip and at a later date pulled

Above: Salvage of the 90-foot brig *Duke of Cumberland* at Ticonderoga in 1909. (New York Lake Champlain Tercentenary Commission).

Below: Duke of Cumberland, built in 1759, raised in 1909, mistakenly identified as *Revenge*. (Postcard, collection of the author)

Facing page, top: Wreck, possibly the row galley *Grand Diable*, raised in 1909 at Crown Point. (Fort Ticonderoga Museum)

Bottom: Remains of the *Duke of Cumberland* in 1984. Photo by the author.

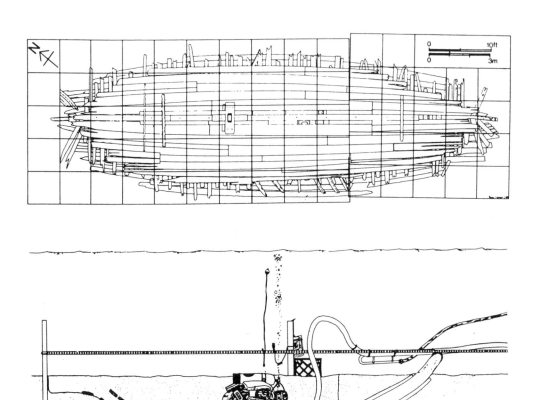

Hull of sloop *Boscawen* excavated during the Champlain Maritime Society's 1984-1985 archaeological survey at Fort Ticonderoga, and a diver using a water dredge to remove mud from the sloop's hull. Drawings by Kevin J. Crisman. (Lake Champlain Maritime Museum)

the remains of the ship onto the parade ground inside the fort. The vessel, measuring 70-72 feet in length and 12 feet in width, was vandalized in 1921 and destroyed in a grass fire years later.[117] The existing photographs of the vessel indicate that it may have been the row galley *Grand Diable*, which had sunk in the area in 1761. A five-day, in-water archaeological survey by the Lake Champlain Maritime Museum for the New York State Bureau of Historic Sites in 1990 found a "total absence of cultural materials [including shipwrecks] from the 18th century" at Crown Point.[118]

Much of the armament that the French tossed overboard when they abandoned the *La Musquelongy* and scuttled the *La Brochette* and *L'Esturgeon* in October 1759 has been discovered near Cliff Haven in Plattsburgh. When the British brought the French sloops to Crown Point in November, they had their rigging and guns "except two brass 12 pounders, that Monsr. de L'oberatz [Joannis-Galand d'Olabaratz] threw over board, while Lt. McKoy [MacKay] was there."[119] Mackay had earlier been captured by the French near Four Brothers Islands. The two cannons were among the British armament that the French took back to Carillon after their victory at Fort William Henry. Upon the evacuation of Carillon in 1759, they were placed on the French sloop *La Musquelongy*, then dumped into Lake Champlain.

The two sunken cannons remained undiscovered for 209 years until three young scuba divers in September 1968 found the cannons and a large anchor.[120] In subsequent dives, they discovered a swivel deck gun, muskets, a saber, and more anchors. The swivel gun was placed in the Clinton County Historical Museum in Plattsburgh. Unfortunately, without proper archaeological preservation, the muskets and the saber blade fell apart. The remaining portion of the officer's bronze sword and musket were given to the museum by a diver in 1987.[121]

The two elegantly-engraved brass cannons, however, had a longer story. Although New York State authorities indicated that the cannons belonged to the state, little effort was made to acquire the artifacts. In May 1982 the two cannons, offered at public auction by Sotheby Parke Bernet of New York City, were purchased on a conditional sale for $68,000 by the Fort Ticonderoga Museum. Spurred into action by the sale, the state was subsequently awarded the cannons in a court decision. One cannon is now displayed at the Crown Point State Historic Site Visitor Center and the other at the Clinton County Historical Museum. A ruling by the Court of Claims in 1987 awarded $45,500 for expenses and storage to the two original salvagers of the cannons.[122]

The search for vessels from the French and Indian War period has also continued in the Richelieu River. During 1978 and 1979, the Committee of Underwater Archaeology and History of Quebec conducted an extensive underwater survey of the Richelieu River in the vicinity of Isle-aux-Noix.[123] Thirteen archaeological sites, including the remains of a French bateau, were found during the search. The early 1980s ushered in serious archaeological work which has attempted to study wrecks without disturbing or compromising historic sites for future researchers.

Remains of Fort George. Photo by the author.

Mezzotint by R. Purcell showing Benedict Arnold at Quebec City, published by Thos. Hart in London, March 1776. (Library of Congress)

6. From Champlain to Canada

ASIDE FROM THE LIGHTLY GARRISONED military outposts that were beginning to crumble in the lake valleys, the solitude of the wilderness returned when hostilities ended following the French and Indian War. For a short time, the tranquil blue waters and lush green mountainsides witnessed only the occasional traveler. The years of peace, at the same time, saw the beginnings of a few settlements along the two lakes. Among the new migrants were the Stoughton brothers from Connecticut, John, Joseph, and Nathaniel, who had all served with the provincials and British during the war. In a partnership with Samuel Deall from New York City, the Stoughtons established a lumber business with a grant of 2,000 acres at the northern end of Lake George (Ticonderoga). In 1764, after several years of land petitions and after organizing a settlement at the southern end of Lake Champlain, Philip Skene, who had served as a British officer during the French and Indian War at Lake Champlain, received a land grant of 25,000 acres from Lieutenant Governor Cadwallader Colden of New York and 20,000 acres from King George III.[1] Skenesborough (Whitehall, N.Y.) soon flourished with tenants, mills, and a fine manor house. Similarly, William Gilliland, who served with the British army in America until 1758, bought soldiers' land claims near Willsboro and began a settlement along the Boquet River in 1765.[2] About the same time, Charles de Fredenburgh, a former captain in the British army, settled in present-day Plattsburgh near the mouth of the Saranac River and petitioned for a land grant. In 1769 he was awarded 30,000 acres, but by late 1772 his house and sawmill were apparently unoccupied.[3]

As former soldiers, many settlers received land grants from the king of England in amounts based on their military rank, and others purchased land from the original grantees at low prices. Before the Revolutionary War, settlers inhabited areas along both shores of Lake Champlain and several sections of Lake George. Some of the biggest land speculators included Ethan Allen and his brother Ira, who initially obtained New Hampshire land titles to 12,000 acres in present-day Vermont and expanded their holdings under the Onion River Land Company to 60,000 acres, including land along Lake Champlain.

By 1775 events in distant parts of the colonies would once more engulf Lake George and Lake Champlain in turmoil, eventually transforming the idyllic setting into one of violence and bloodshed. The burgeoning national debt of Britain, largely caused by the Seven Years' War, combined with the prospect of supporting thousands of British troops in North America, resulted in proposals to raise revenue through taxation in America. Although the tax burden on the colonists was actually only a fraction of that placed on British citizens and per capita income was substantially higher in America, the colonists were in no mood for new demands on their economy. The need for revenue came at a time when the colonists no longer needed Britain and its army for protection from the French. As the colonists began nurturing their own identity, the prospects of greater control by Britain in the political and economic arena would prove divisive. Step by step, opposition to arbitrary British policies escalated into an inevitable clash and revolution.

Even before the first shots of the Revolution were fired on April 19, 1775, in Lexington, Massachusetts, military plans were proposed by the Americans for the Champlain Valley. John Brown, an attorney from Pittsfield, Massachusetts, was sent by the Massachusetts Committee of Correspondence on a covert mission to Montreal in

February 1775 to deliver letters to sympathizers and to evaluate the Canadian position in the event of altercations with the British in the 13 colonies. After a rigorous journey to Canada through the broken ice of Lake Champlain, which had frozen his boat to an island for two days, Brown drafted a letter from Montreal to the Massachusetts Committee in Boston which detailed his findings and urged "the Fort at Tyconderoga must be sei[z]ed as soon as possible should hostilities be committed by the Kings Troops."[4]

When hostilities erupted in Massachusetts, colonial forces quickly acted to take the fort. After news of the Lexington battle reached Connecticut, Benedict Arnold, a 34-year-old captain in the militia at New Haven, immediately pressed for action. Arnold, a muscular and energetic man of medium height, was an experienced sailor and merchant. His vigor, physical strength, and daring would make Arnold one of the most notable figures of the American Revolution. Despite the stand of neutrality of the New Haven town fathers, Arnold secured access to the powder magazine and marched with his militia Footguards to Cambridge, Massachusetts, with a proposal to capture Ticonderoga. Within a few days, Arnold received an appointment from the Massachusetts Committee of Safety as "Colonel and Commander-in-Chief over a body of men. . .to march to the Fort at Ticonderoga, and use your best endeavours to reduce the same."[5] At the same time, a group from Hartford, Connecticut, accompanied by several more militia officers from Pittsfield, Massachusetts, with attorney John Brown, marched to Vermont to join Colonel Ethan Allen and his Green Mountain Boys to take the fortress at Ticonderoga.

Traditional view of the capture of Fort Ticonderoga on May 10, 1775, by Ethan Allen without Benedict Arnold, engraving from a painting by Alonzo Chappel.
(National Archives)

Migrating from Salisbury, Connecticut, in 1769, Ethan Allen subsequently led an unofficial militia called the Green Mountain Boys composed of settlers living in present-day Vermont, who successfully harassed any New York land claimants. In 1772 Allen acknowledged that the governor of New York "has advertised me and some Others and Offered Considerable Reward to have us Delivered to New York."[6] However, he refused to take Philip Skene's advice and flee to Connecticut. Allen was a natural-born leader, noted for his physical strength and energy, oratory, and assertive personality. He was said to be able to throw bushel bags of salt over his head with his teeth as fast as two men could bring them to him.

Predictably, a disagreement between the two strong-willed leaders, Arnold and Allen, over command of the Ticonderoga expedition occurred. When Arnold arrived ahead of his troops, the forces preparing to capture the fort were happy with the commitment of Massachusetts to the expedition, "but were shockingly surprised when Colonel Arnold presumed to contend for the command of these forces that we had raised."[7] Allen's men, however, insisted that they would serve only under their own officers. The expedition went forward and, according to Allen, "[Arnold] entered the fortress with me side by side."[8] Before the raid, Captain Noah Phelps of Connecticut reconnoitered the fort on a spy mission and learned that the gunpowder in the fort had been damaged.[9] Although approximately 150 men assembled on the eastern shore of Lake Champlain on the evening of May 9, only about 83 actually captured the fort because of a shortage of boats to ferry them across the lake. At the same time, another detachment of 30 men led by Captain Samuel Herrick was sent to take Skenesborough, where the son of Loyalist Philip Skene was captured along with Skene's trading schooner *Katherine*. Near daybreak on May 10, the American raiders at the fort entered through a wicket gate in the south curtain wall and rushed onto the parade ground and then on to the barracks. Allen, along with Arnold, climbed the stairs to the second floor of the west barracks where they encountered a partially-dressed young lieutenant, Jocelyn Feltham. Assuming that the officer was the fort's commander, Allen demanded the surrender of the post.[10] In a short period of time, however, Captain William Delaplace, the fort's actual commandant, made his appearance fully clothed and surrendered the fortress. The lightly garrisoned fortress (fewer than 50 men) surrendered without a fight. The capitulation of the fort yielded 86 cannons to the Americans.

Colonel Seth Warner of the Green Mountain Boys was later dispatched to capture Crown Point. Crown Point, which had fallen into substantial disrepair after a fire in 1773, held an assortment of 111 cannons including mortars and howitzers, but many were not workable.* The garrison of less than a dozen men quickly surrendered to the Americans. At the same time, Captain Bernard Romans, whose own orders from Connecticut to capture Ticonderoga had been ignored by the invaders, proceeded to the southern end of Lake George to assume control of Fort George. However, before Romans arrived, the fort had already been "given up to 3 or 4 of our men who we sent forward," Captain Epaphras Bull disclosed in his journal.[13]

The capture of Ticonderoga renewed the dispute between Allen and Arnold over the command of the colonial forces. When Arnold tried to take command of the garrison, the committee of war at Ticonderoga gave new orders in writing to Allen as commander.

---

* Most sources indicate that Crown Point was in a dilapidated condition in 1775. However, Aaron Barlow found "the Barracks within it are very beautiful, three in number, three stories high. The wooden work is consumed by fire. The stone work is all good and strong."[11] In 1773 an accidental fire, caused by two soldiers' wives making soap, severely damaged the barracks at Crown Point. Charges of misconduct were brought against the commander at Crown Point, Captain William Anstruther, but a contentious court of inquiry ended inconclusively.[12] The forts at Crown Point passed through a series of private owners during the nineteenth and early twentieth centuries, but in 1910 the property was deeded to the state of New York by the Witherbee, Sherman and Co. of Port Henry.

Arnold had forbidden looting of the fort, but the troops continued "in the greatest confusion and anarchy, destroying and plundering private property, committing every enormity, and paying no attention to the public service."[14] Gallons of rum in the fort also contributed to the lack of discipline.

Arnold's lack of command finally ended on May 14 when Captains Jonathan Brown and Eleazer Oswald, with 50 volunteers raised under Arnold's instructions, arrived at Ticonderoga aboard Philip Skene's captured schooner, renamed the *Liberty*. After arming the schooner with "4 Carriage & 6 Swiv[e]l guns," Arnold departed on May 16 for St. Jean, Canada (called St. Johns in American journals), with 50 men in the *Liberty* and two bateaux.[15] When the schooner became becalmed 30 miles south of St. Jean at eight o'clock in the evening on May 17, Arnold ordered 35 men in the bateaux to oar the larger vessel northward. At six o'clock the next morning the expedition arrived at St. Jean and "surprized & took a S[e]rgeant & his party of 12 Men, the King's Sloop of about 70 tons, with two brass 6-pounders & 7 men, without any Loss on either Side."[16] Arnold and his men remained for two hours loading provisions into the sloop and into four captured bateaux, and burned five other British bateaux before departing for Crown Point. Arnold had been lucky, for a large British detachment from Montreal with additional cannons for the sloop had been expected at any moment. The British named the sloop, which had been built in 1771, the *Betsey*, but other original sources simply called it the "King's Sloop" or "the armed Sloop of George the Third."[17] The sloop was renamed the *Enterprise* by the Americans and later fitted out with "Six Carriage and Twelve Swivel Guns" while the *Liberty* held "Four Carriages & Eight Swivels."[18]

Following the capture of the sloop, Arnold, with the only large vessels on the lake, sailed triumphantly southward, and soon met Ethan Allen about six miles south of St. Jean. Allen, with four bateaux and approximately 90 men, was determined to occupy St. Jean. However, he left Crown Point in such a hurry that he had failed to bring adequate food and supplies to sustain the expedition. Arnold, who tried to dissuade Allen from proceeding, "supplied him with Provisions, his Men being in a starving Condition.— He informed me of his Intention of proceeding on to St. Jean with 80 or 100 Men, & keeping Possession there."[19] Allen camped on the shore across from St. Jean, but was attacked by 200 British regulars the next morning, and was forced to retreat to Crown Point.

Upon returning to Crown Point, Ethan Allen's Green Mountain Boys departed for home, leaving Benedict Arnold, with his 150 enlistees, as the de facto commodore of the lake and commander of the American forces at Ticonderoga and Crown Point. Arnold, however, had another run-in with Allen's officers in June. After an insult by Colonel James Easton, Arnold "took the Liberty of Breaking his head."[20] The incident would have lasting consequences for Arnold.

In the meanwhile, orders arrived from the Continental Congress to inventory the cannons at Crown Point and Ticonderoga and move them to the south end of Lake George. The thought of abandoning the forts on Lake Champlain, however, drew a loud outcry from Massachusetts, the Committee of the City of Albany, Allen, Arnold, and others in the northern colonies who saw the lake outposts as vital to the defense of the colonies. On May 29 Governor Jonathan Trumbull of Connecticut informed Massachusetts that the colony had ordered 1,000 men under Benjamin Hinman to march to Ticonderoga and Crown Point to defend the fortresses. On May 31 the Continental Congress officially reversed its earlier decision by requesting the governor of Connecticut to reinforce the forts on Lake Champlain and retain the cannons necessary for their defense.

Ethan Allen, meanwhile, had written a long letter on May 29 to Congress advocating an advance into Canada. Arnold made the same suggestion two weeks later. Allen and

Seth Warner successfully lobbied the Continental Congress in June for authorization to raise an official, paid regiment of the Green Mountain Boys to serve in the northern theater. Allen's accomplishment in Philadelphia, however, later turned into disappointment when the Green Mountain Boys elected Seth Warner as their commander instead of the impetuous Allen. Arnold, at the same time, did not fare any better with his own command. On May 31 Colonel Joseph Henshaw received instructions from Massachusetts for Arnold to give up his command at Ticonderoga to the Connecticut troops and return to Watertown, Massachusetts, to settle his accounts. The instructions, however, were never given to Arnold and new instructions on June 1 from the Provincial Congress of Massachusetts requested that he stay at his post to command the Massachusetts troops, at least until the Connecticut troops or New York militia assumed control of the garrison. When the Connecticut troops arrived, Arnold disputed the command of the fort. In response, Massachusetts appointed a committee to examine Arnold's conduct, prompting a bitter reply from him. The chairman of the committee, Walter Spooner, in a letter to Governor Trumbull, related Arnold's refusal to serve under the new appointee, whereupon he "disbanded his Forces and resigned his Commission."[21]

Arnold soon left the lake and returned to his Connecticut home in July where his wife had died in his absence. Later that summer he traveled to Massachusetts to settle his accounts and collect his expenses for the Ticonderoga expedition. After receiving only half of what he had spent from his own funds, he resubmitted the bill to the Continental Congress and was eventually granted the remainder of the money.

By now the Revolution had taken a more ominous shape. Following the Battle of Bunker Hill in June 1775, the Second Continental Congress appointed George Washington as commander in chief of the American forces. Washington hastened to Boston, where he commanded the troops until the British occupation of the city was broken the following year with the help of the cannons captured at Fort Ticonderoga.

During its June 1775 organization of the American army, the Continental Congress appointed Philip Schuyler as a major general and commander of the Northern Department. The 41-year-old Schuyler, a fourth-generation member of a well-known New York Dutch family, had served as an officer during the Battle of Lake George and with the unsuccessful Abercromby Expedition in 1758. Following quartermaster duty with John Bradstreet, Schuyler spent the last years of the war in private business that involved supplying provisions to Amherst's army. Soon after his appointment in 1775, Schuyler received orders to "exert his utmost power to destroy or take all vessels, boats, or floating batteries, preparing by sd Govr [Governor Guy Carleton of Canada] or by his order, on or near the waters of the lakes."[22] By the end of the month Congress had decided on an aggressive policy, which included "making an Impression into Canada," and provided directions for the invasion to Schuyler.[23]

By July 17 Schuyler had arrived at Fort George at the southern end of Lake George, where he found the 334-man garrison in a filthy, undisciplined state. He immediately established work schedules, limits on drinking, and orders on cleanliness and the appropriate use of military supplies before departing for the northern landing on Lake George. When he reached the 102-man contingent at the blockhouse on northern Lake George at ten o'clock at night, Schuyler was annoyed to find the guards asleep at their posts. Proceeding to Ticonderoga the next morning, the new general found an inactive army of 335 men under Colonel Benjamin Hinman and the fort in poor shape. Soon a stream of orders to the men and requests for supplies and equipment for the invasion of Canada invigorated the garrisons at Fort George and the two Lake Champlain fortresses.

One of the most formidable tasks facing Schuyler was the construction of vessels that would carry the invaders into Canada. Lake George soon became a center for boat building with 30 bateaux completed by the end of July. In addition, two flat-bottomed boats measuring 40 feet by 12 feet were also built at Lake George. With intelligence that the British at St. Jean were rebuilding their fleet, Schuyler pressed to obtain carpenters and naval supplies to build and outfit an American fleet. The mills of William Gilliland at Willsboro had provided 5,000 board feet of lumber for Schuyler's navy by early August and pledged to double or triple that amount. In a letter written on August 23 to Benjamin Franklin, Schuyler reported that he had enough vessels on Lake Champlain to move 1,300 men with 20 days of provisions and two large, sloop-rigged gondolas that had been built at the lake: "I have two flatt-bottomed Vessels amongst those we have Built they are Sixty Feet long and capable of carrying five twelve Pounders each, but I can unfortunately mount only one, as I have no Carriages."[24] The two gondolas, named *Hancock* and *Schuyler*, eventually sailed into Canada in late August.[25]

By mid-August the American navy on Lake Champlain consisted of the schooner *Liberty*, sloop *Enterprise*, gondolas *Hancock* and *Schuyler*, and two large bateaux armed with small swivel cannons. Other bateaux and large flat-bottomed vessels or scows were also being used on Lake Champlain at this time. Included among these was one formerly owned by Philip Skene that had been taken by Allen's men to ferry his troops across the lake during the May 1775 capture of Fort Ticonderoga.

After mustering troops and aiding his commander's efforts to organize supplies for the Canadian invasion, Brigadier General Richard Montgomery, Schuyler's second in command, reached Lake Champlain in August. Montgomery, with an impressive stature and likable personality, was later described by a soldier on the expedition: "His air and manner designated the real soldier."[26] Thirty-seven-year-old Richard Montgomery had spent nearly half of his life as an officer in the British army. After graduating from Trinity College in Dublin, he began his military career as an ensign in 1756, subsequently serving during the French and Indian War with Amherst at Louisbourg, Crown Point, Ticonderoga, and Montreal. As a captain in the 17th Regiment of Foot, he sold his commission in 1772 in an apparent dispute over a promotion and sailed for America. While farming in New York, Montgomery reluctantly accepted a commission from the Continental Congress as a brigadier general.

By August some of Brigadier General David Wooster's troops, led by Colonel David Waterbury of Connecticut, had arrived at Ticonderoga. While the men and provisions filtered into Ticonderoga and Crown Point, Schuyler sent scouting parties to Canada to observe British preparations. Early in August Schuyler had word from several sources that two vessels were under construction by the British at St. Jean.[27] Major John Brown, who had earlier in 1775 reconnoitered Canada, again returned in the summer to procure new intelligence of British activities. Brown journeyed into Canada with a number of men, including Bayze Wells, a young sergeant from Connecticut, who would later record the naval battles on the lake in 1776.

On August 28, fearing new British reinforcements and the completion of the two vessels at St. Jean, Montgomery embarked from Ticonderoga for the invasion of Canada with 1,200 men, leaving approximately 1,000 troops at the forts. Although Montgomery set out without waiting for Schuyler, there is ample evidence that both generals agreed on the military plans for Canada. Thus Montgomery was not usurping Schuyler's authority when he departed with the army, but simply putting into motion a plan that had already been formulated by Schuyler. By August 30 the fleet of bateaux and larger vessels departed from Crown Point just as Schuyler arrived at Ticonderoga from Albany. Montgomery reached Isle La Motte on September 2; Schuyler, despite being sick, met the army on the island at noon on September 4. Schuyler immediately issued orders to re-embark, which brought the army, by now reduced by illness to 900-1,000 men, to

Isle-aux-Noix at seven o'clock in the evening. Only 15 years earlier, provincial troops with the British army had landed on the eastern shore of the Richelieu River to prepare an assault on the French at Isle-aux-Noix and St. Jean (chapter 5).

On September 6 the expedition advanced 12 miles to the fort/redoubts at St. Jean, where they were met by a fiery cannonade. While marching forward on the western shore, the Americans were ambushed by Indians and Canadians, but the former rallied and "charged them with great Spirit & Firmness."[28] The troops built a small breastwork, but soon withdrew after the fort's cannon fire reached the barricade. Another breastwork was hastily constructed about three-quarters of a mile farther south. The next morning, Schuyler decided to retreat with the army back to Isle-aux-Noix because of inadequate munitions and artillery. At Isle-aux-Noix, a boom, or "Chevaux-de-frise," was constructed across the main channel of the Richelieu River on the west side of the island to prevent the passage of British ships. On September 10 another attempt on the fort at St. Jean was made by the Americans, without success. An American detachment sent to sever the route between Chambly and St. Jean was dispersed by enemy fire. Fearful of fire from a British schooner at St. Jean, the men refused to return to Chambly. Court-martials at Isle-aux-Noix followed the mutiny. On September 14, orders called for volunteers to try to capture the British schooner. According to Dr. Benjamin Trumbull, who served as a chaplain and volunteer orderly with the 1775 army, the men publicly declined the call. Trumbull thought the volunteer call odd and mused that "He [Montgomery] feared that much Blame would fall on him, and to shift this from himself and lay it on the troops."[29]

Brigadier General Richard Montgomery.
Engraving by E. Mackenzie from a
painting by Charles Willson Peale.
(New York State Library)

Schuyler and Montgomery, however, were handicapped by their minimal artillery, sickness among the army, and troops who thus far had been reluctant in the face of the enemy fort and a well-armed schooner. Schuyler later reported to John Hancock that more than 600 troops of the American army were sick at the time at Isle-aux-Noix. Although bedridden on the island himself, Schuyler continued to play a crucial role in the strategy to take St. Jean. Suffering "from a Bilious Fever & violent rheumatic Pains," Schuyler was carried to a covered bateau on September 16 and returned to Ticonderoga.[30] At Ticonderoga Schuyler carried on the management of supplies and reinforcements to Montgomery with a corresponding stream of letters to the Continental Congress, George Washington, and others. Although Schuyler anticipated returning to his troops in Canada, recurrent bouts of violent fluxes, sweats, and rheumatic gout prevented him from rejoining the army.

Even though many troops were ill at Isle-aux-Noix, new reinforcements, including the Green Mountain Boys, had swelled the ranks of the army. When Colonel David Waterbury and Major William Douglas, the "Commodore" of the American fleet, renewed the call for volunteers to capture the British schooner, 320 men were eventually raised for the operation. With approximately 1,400 effective troops, Montgomery launched a third assault on St. Jean on Sunday morning, September 17. Although some artillery had now been set in place south of the fort by the Americans, it proved inadequate to besiege the fort. Montgomery sent Colonel Timothy Bedel with a large detachment of troops to establish a position north of St. Jean, cutting the road to the fort at Chambly. For the next week the Americans constructed breastworks and batteries in preparation for a siege of the fort from the south side. By three o'clock on the afternoon of September 25, a battery of cannons and another of small mortars finally began to fire on the fort at St. Jean. The next day, however, began a week of stormy, cold, and wet weather that bogged down the discouraged troops in their muddy camp.

Unfortunately, the discouragement was caused by more than the rain. Some of the Canadians who were fighting with the Americans grew fearful of the outcome and left the army. Colonel Ethan Allen, who no longer commanded the Green Mountain Boys, had set out on September 18 with a small group of followers in an effort to raise a regiment of Canadians. Collecting about 30 Americans and only 40 or 50 Canadians, he rashly decided to march on Montreal. A separate party commanded by Major John Brown was to meet with Allen's men near Montreal. On September 25 Allen's detachment, which never saw any of Brown's group, became encircled by British regulars, Canadians, and Indians about two miles from Montreal. Some of Allen's men fled the scene leaving "but forty-five men with me. . . The enemy kept closing round me. . .with vast unequal numbers" until Allen surrendered, despite a futile attempt to retreat.[31] Immediately, two Indians tried to kill Allen, but the resourceful insurgent grabbed hold of an officer and spun him around as a shield until rescued by a regular with a fixed bayonet.[32] Allen, clapped in irons, was sent to England, where he spent several years in prison. "Colonel Allen's misfortune will, I hope," wrote Washington to Schuyler, "teach a lesson of prudence and subordination to others who may be too ambitious to outshine their general officers, and regardless of order and duty rush into enterprises which have unfavorable effects to the public and are destructive to themselves."[33]

On September 25 at St. Jean "the Row Galley was launc'd," according to a journal attributed to Lieutenant John André, a British officer at the fort who would later play a major role in the treason of Benedict Arnold.[34] The vessel, armed with "a 24 pounder of Brass in her Bow & on each side 1, 4 pounder, besides swivels" and carrying 12-16 oars, crossed the lake on October 4 and fired on the Canadians, who had constructed breastworks on the east side.[35] By this time the Americans had most of their vessels in the vicinity of Isle-aux-Noix: "The Force on the Lake consisted of the Schooner Liberty mounting 2, 4 Pounders and two 2 D° with 8 or 10 Swivels. The Sloop Enterprise mounting 2 Brass 6 Pounders and four 3 D° with 11 Swivels. The Gundalo Schuyler mounting one 12 Pounder in her Bow and twelve Swivels on her Sides. The Gundalo Hancock mounting the Same metal. Two Bat[e]aux with Swivels."[36]

By the fifth of October, a 13-inch mortar called the "old Sow" arrived from Ticonderoga and was placed on duty the following day, lobbing mortar shells toward the fort. After nearly a week of ineffective fire on the fort, a council of war was held to discuss strategy. During a council of war, officers would voice their opinions in a hierarchy of rank with the highest-ranking officers speaking last. Nearly all officers including David Waterbury, second in command, favored strengthening the battery on the east side of the river to destroy the British ships rather than Montgomery's plan to erect a new battery northwest of the fort. Although contrary to his own view, Montgomery acceded to the demands in order to maintain harmony. The battery, opened on October 14, paid dividends in only two days with the sinking of the British schooner. The vessel, which had been used only sparingly by the British, had been employed a few times to send a raking fire of grapeshot against the Americans on the shoreline. The 70-ton schooner *Royal Savage* was described by Captain Henry Brockholst Livingston as "very long and something flat bottom'd—elegantly built & finish'd...mounts 14 brass 6 pounders besides a number of swivels. . .a very handsome elegant vessel."[37] The schooner had sunk in shallow water by her dock and could easily be raised. However, the British defenders continued a steady bombardment of "our Camp & at our two Batteries by throwing dead

Shot [solid cannonballs], Shells & Grape [shot] incessantly amongst us—Sometimes a hundred Shells a Day & three Times the number of Shot, which happily did us little or no hurt," according to Lieutenant Colonel Rudolphus Ritzema.[38]

On October 18 Major John Brown and James Livingston, with help from nearly 300 Canadians and 50 Americans, forced the surrender of Fort Chambly on the banks of the Richelieu River. The capitulation of Chambly brought more artillery and provisions and six tons of gunpowder to the invading Americans. Cut off from Chambly and Montreal, the besieged garrison at St. Jean was reaching the end of the line. On October 21, British troops at St. Jean watched solemnly as bateaux filled with prisoners

The schooner *Royal Savage*, described by an American officer as "a very handsome elegant vessel," was captured from the British at St. Jean in 1775. Drawing by Montserrat Centeno.

from Chambly "pass'd the Forts."[39] Washington, upon hearing the news of the surrender at Chambly, praised Schuyler "on the Success of your enterprize So far I Congratulate You, as the acquisition of Canada is of unmeasurable importance to the Cause we are engaged in."[40]

Proceeding to St. Jean with reinforcements, Brigadier General David Wooster was delayed for three days at Ticonderoga by heavy rains and gale winds. The sixty-four-year-old Wooster, a crusty veteran of King George's War and the French and Indian War, including a presence at Abercromby's defeat in 1758, became second in command upon his arrival at Montgomery's camp on October 26. With Wooster at the head of the Connecticut troops, Montgomery accelerated the placement of batteries on the west side of the Richelieu River. Although Major General Guy Carleton in Montreal tried to break the siege at St. Jean with 800-1,000 regulars, Canadians, and Indians, his army was repulsed on October 30 by Colonel Seth Warner with 300-350 of the Green Mountain Boys after five hours of fighting at Longueil on the banks of the St. Lawrence River.[41]

On November 1 Montgomery's new battery, located northwest of the British position, opened fire. After six hours of bombardment, Montgomery sent a letter proposing terms of surrender to the garrison at St. Jean. The next day, two officers from the fort requested a cessation of hostilities for four days and stated that if relief did not arrive by then, the garrison would surrender. The British officers from the fort expressed their doubt that Carleton's forces had been defeated. Montgomery provided a prisoner to verify the British defeat of the relief force on October 30 and allowed officers from the fort to examine other prisoners held on the sloop *Enterprise*. Following the examination of the British prisoners, the commanding officer, Major Charles Preston, signed six "Articles of Capitulation" at nine o'clock at night. The following morning the garrison of 600 (28 officers, 425 regulars, 75 carpenters, sailors, and Canadians, 72 women and children) marched out of the fort with the "Honors of War." The surrender of Fort St. Jean was the biggest triumph to date for the American forces. During the siege, the British had fired 2,500 cannon shot with an equal number of musket balls at the Americans, but succeeded in killing only 20 men.[42]

The victory at St. Jean provided two more vessels for the American fleet on Lake Champlain. According to Dr. Trumbull's notes, the captured naval stores included: "The Schooner, called by the regulars the Brave or Royal Savage, of about 70 T[o]ns full rig[g]ed pierced for 14 Guns 6 and four Pounders. One Row gall[e]y carrying in her Bow one Brass 24 Pounder, and pierced for 2 Six Pounders—Besides she would have carried 20 Swivels. . . . The victorious Americans named the Schooner The Yankee, and gave the Name of Douglas to the Row Gall[e]y in honor to Comm[o]dore Douglas."[43] The new names for the vessels, however, did not endure. The schooner, which was raised by Captain William Douglas, soon reverted to its original British designation, *Royal Savage*. The row galley has a more elusive record. It had been referred to as a "Gundoloe" by Robert Barwick, who served with a New York company during the campaign, and as one of "two Schooners" captured at St. Jean, according to Lieutenant Colonel Ritzema.[44] Nevertheless, the vessel was called a row galley by most of the other eyewitnesses, and its original name might have been the *Revenge*.[45] By the end of November both vessels had made the voyage through a bitter storm from St. Jean to Ticonderoga.

While the attack on Canada by the Lake Champlain route was taking place, a more dramatic episode in American history was occurring along the rugged back rivers of present-day Maine. After meeting with George Washington in Cambridge, Massachusetts, Benedict Arnold was selected to lead a perilous expedition through the wilderness of Maine to attack Quebec City. Recognizing the energy and optimism of the Connecticut native, Washington gave Arnold his first independent command, which he eagerly embraced. The stalwart volunteers marched on September 13, 1775, for Newburyport, Massachusetts, where they embarked on 11 coastal sailing vessels for the trip to Maine six days later, to the cheers of hundreds of spectators. At Pittston, Maine, on the Kennebec River, over 1,100 men loaded 225 bateaux for a journey to Quebec that was expected to take three weeks. The army included militia, farmboys, several wives, and a black soldier. Among the troops was 19-year-old Aaron Burr, who later served as vice-president under Jefferson after missing the presidency himself by one vote. Burr, however, is perhaps best remembered as the man who killed Alexander Hamilton in a duel in 1804.

Arnold and his men were unfamiliar with the rough terrain of Maine, which required lugging the poorly-built, 400-pound bateaux and 65 tons of supplies over numerous rapids along the Kennebec River and beyond. By October 13 Arnold wrote to Washington at the second portage, from the Kennebec to the Dead River, describing his difficulties: "we have had a very fatigueing time, the Men in general not understanding Batteaus have been obliged to wade & haul them more than half way up the River."[46] By then he was down to 25 days of provisions and 950 effective men. The men slogged through knee-deep mud in heavy rains (undoubtedly, the same rains that mired Montgomery's forces down at St. Jean) and were pressed forward by the determined optimism of Arnold.

In the rear, Lieutenant Colonel Roger Enos, after holding a council of war without Arnold, decided to turn back with his three companies consisting of 300 men. The remaining troops, now running low on provisions, much of which had spoiled, were bitter when they received news of Enos's departure on October 27. Henry Dearborn, a 24-year-old militia captain and New Hampshire physician, noted that the news "disheart[e]ned and discouraged our men," since Enos's troops had departed with more than their share of the provisions and ammunition: "Our Men made a General Prayer, that Colo: Enos and all his men, might die by the way."[47] Enos was later court-martialed, but was acquitted largely because his main would-be accusers were in Canada.

By the beginning of November the men were starving and reluctantly killed and ate Captain Dearborn's faithful Newfoundland dog, even consuming the animal's "guts and skin."[48] Although the men had "a very great feast" on the dog, the next "morning when we arose, many of us were so weak that we could hardly stand; we staggered about like drunken men."[49] The dauntless invaders were finally reduced to eating their "shaving soap, pomatum, and even the lip salve, leather of their shoes, cartridge boxes, etc."[50] More than 70 miles from Quebec, some of the men were forced to march barefoot in the snowy weather after their moccasins had been worn to shreds. At the same time, Arnold had pushed ahead to buy food for the army at friendly Canadian homesteads. Soon French farmers were driving cattle to the famished troops. Slightly more than 600 survivors made it to the St. Lawrence River opposite Quebec on November 9, 1775, after a journey of 45 days. Pleased with his unfaltering colonel, George Washington wrote to Arnold: "It is not in the power of any man to command success, but you have done more—you have deserved it."[51]

"A general view of Quebec from Point Levy, September 1, 1761."
(New York State Library)

The ragtag army of gaunt survivors, without artillery or boats and only about 400 usable muskets, gazed across the river at fortress Quebec. A letter from Arnold seeking help from one of John Brown's contacts in Quebec had instead been delivered to the acting commandant of the city, who destroyed the boats on the south shore of the river before Arnold arrived. Undaunted, Arnold ordered the building of scaling ladders, procured 25-35 canoes, and slipped past two British warships (the *Hunter* and *Lizard*) to land with 500 men at four o'clock in the morning of November 13 on the Quebec side of the river. On the Plains of Abraham, where Wolfe and Montcalm had fought and died in 1759, Arnold assembled his men. The following day, a messenger with a flag was sent forward by Arnold demanding the surrender of the garrison. The flag was immediately fired upon that day and the next. Without equipment, there was little Arnold could do but await the arrival of Montgomery's army.

Meanwhile, Montgomery's Champlain army, after the surrender of the British fort at St. Jean, pushed immediately toward Montreal, with the first troops departing on November 5 and 6. Over the next several days some of the cannons were loaded on bateaux and moved to Chambly to be used in the siege of Montreal. Heavy rains, however, caused wagons, loaded with baggage, to sink in mud up to their hubs. As the Americans approached Montreal, Governor Guy Carleton evacuated his army and ships toward Quebec. The retreat apparently left the families of the British soldiers to fend for themselves. On a cold and wet November 10, Dr. Trumbull lamented the "miserable" condition of the British refugees from Montreal, consisting mostly of the wives and children of regulars: "women badly clothed, children bare foot. . .covered with Mud and Water" who had to travel by foot to New England.[52] On November 13 the American army marched into the undefended city of Montreal. The remaining inhabitants proposed terms of surrender to the Americans, but they were not negotiated since the city had no army or military equipment to surrender at that point.

Before Carleton left on the evening of November 11, his men destroyed the remaining cannons at Montreal and most of the bateaux , then fled downriver in an assortment of 11 vessels. The Americans attempted to intercept Carleton and his fleet by racing to Sorel about 40 miles distant. Near the mouth of the Richelieu River, three batteries of artillery and "the Gondola mounting one double fortified 12 Pounder and carrying a large Number of Swivel Guns was also got down."[53] Apparently the Americans were able to transport the two gondolas, the *Hancock* and *Schuyler*, over the rapids at Chambly and eventually into the St. Lawrence River. In his November 17 report to Schuyler, Montgomery disclosed that "Colo: Easton has 6 Guns mounted on shore [three] 12 Pounders 1 Nine... & two sixes at the Sorel & the two Row Gallies [gondolas]."[54]

Carleton's forces tried to by-pass the American batteries but were repulsed and bluffed into believing the Americans had heavy batteries in place on the shore. After the British threw powder and provisions into the river, eleven vessels, including three schooners, two sloops, and a brig were surrendered by Brigadier General Richard Prescott to the Americans. Earlier, Carleton, disguised as a peasant, had escaped during the night by rowing through the American lines in a whaleboat. Carleton, as a major general of British forces in Canada and governor of Quebec, took control of the defenses of the city of Quebec on November 20. In Carleton, the British had a shrewd politician as well as a competent military leader. Carleton had wisely pressed for passage of the Quebec Act of 1774, which he had had a hand in drafting. The religious tolerance that the act provided brought support from the French Catholic clergy while other provisions favored the French propertied classes. Although Carleton misjudged the amount of support that the lower classes would give to defend British interests in Canada, the Americans also miscalculated when they counted on widespread help for the American attack on Canada. Once secure in Quebec, Carleton immediately issued a proclamation ordering all "useless, disloyal and treacherous persons. . .to quit the Town in four Days."[55]

On December 1, "to the Great Joy of our Men," Captain Henry Dearborn noted, "Gen[l]. Montgomery arriv'd...with Three Arm'd Schooners, with men, Artillery, Ammunition, Provision[s] & Clothing."[56] At Quebec, the British still had the sloop *Hunter* with

32- and 24-pound cannons and the schooners *Lizard* and *Magdalen* and at least four other vessels. The *Hunter* continued to harass the Americans while the other vessels, whose cannons had been used to fortify the city, were laid up for the winter. Montgomery dispatched a letter to Carleton requesting the surrender of Quebec. Carleton, who regarded Montgomery with his 16 years of service in the British army as a traitor, had the letter tossed unopened into his burning fireplace. For the next two weeks the Americans organized their provisions and erected more batteries. Cannons and howitzers lobbed shells into the city with little effect, and Carleton's gunners returned the fire on the American batteries.

In the meantime, another saga in American history was unfolding at Fort Ticonderoga and Lake George, where Henry Knox, dispatched by Washington, was to bring back artillery to relieve the occupation of Boston. On December 4 Colonel Knox reached Fort George, where he met one of the prisoners from St. Jean, Lieutenant John André, whose conspiratorial activity with Benedict Arnold was yet to occur. Two days later at Ticonderoga, Knox noted that the troops were "Employ'd in getting the Cannon from the fort on board a Gundaloe in order to get them to the bridge [La Chute River]."[57] This vessel may have been the row galley *Revenge* captured from the British at St. Jean, which Robert Barwick had earlier described as a "Gundeloe." [58] Other cannons were apparently hauled by cattle to the Lake George landing where they were loaded onto the "Scow, Pettiaugre [a double-ended vessel with two masts] & a Battoe."[59] Fifty-nine cannons and mortars weighing 119,000 pounds were taken from Fort Ticonderoga and Crown Point. On December 9 Knox sailed ahead on Lake George aboard the "Pettiaugre," but the scow carrying his 19-year-old brother William Knox hit a rock on the morning of December 10. The scow was dislodged from the rock and in the evening reached Sabbath Day Point, where the vessel sank. The scow was bailed out, repaired, and all the artillery reached the southern end of Lake George by December 15. With the help of Philip Schuyler, Knox employed enough men, oxen, and sleds (including 124 teams of horses) to begin the Herculean trek from Albany to Boston by early January.

In addition to the bitter weather, two problems hindered the American army at Quebec: a lack of hard money and expiring enlistments of the troops. The local population in Canada would not accept Continental money. When American soldiers used it in Canada, they were forced to accept less than face value, as it had quickly depreciated. A second pressing issue involved the enlistments of many of the soldiers, which were to end on January 1. If Montgomery did not act by then, he might not have enough troops to take the Quebec garrison that winter. Montgomery also had to deal with the "Resentment against Arnold" from some of the officers who would have been willing to stay on but not under Arnold's command.[60]

The capture of Quebec, however, was critical to the American cause since it would deny the British an essential base for their invasion of the 13 colonies via Lake Champlain. On December 25 Montgomery addressed Arnold's troops "in a very sensible Spirit'd manner" and "asked us if we w[e]re wil[l]ing to storm the city."[61] With the support of the majority, plans proceeded for an attack on December 27 during a storm, but a clearing of the night sky canceled the operation. The only hope for a successful attack on the city with so few troops was a surprise assault under the cover of a stormy night. During the early hours of December 31, in the midst of a fierce snowstorm, Montgomery and Arnold launched a dual offensive on the Lower Town, hoping to break through the gates leading to the Upper Town. At two o'clock in the morning, the army mustered for the attack.[62] Arnold approached the Lower Town from the northeast and Montgomery moved close to the Lower Town from the southwest, while Colonel James Livingston and the Canadian volunteers made a diversionary attack from the Plains of Abraham (above the

"Montgomery's Assault on the Lower Town, Quebec."
(National Archives of Canada)

Upper Town) near the St. John's Gate to the city. (Another diversion would occur at the Cape Diamond bastion.)

As the two columns approached the Lower Town, sky rockets suddenly lit the sky green above the Plains of Abraham, an American signal that the diversion had begun. Unfortunately, the rockets that were also to signal the general attack were fired before the real invasion forces had reached their positions in the Lower Town and alerted the British defenders.[63] Montgomery's men hurriedly sawed the posts of a wooden stockade as the general drew his sword to enter the city. The men passed the barricade and began cutting through a second barricade below a blockhouse. Abruptly, a deadly burst of cannon fire punctured the darkness from the second floor of the blockhouse. The brave Montgomery was smashed by grapeshot "thro' the Head & both his thighs."[64] Other officers and men were similarly cut down by the lethal fire from above. Colonel Donald Campbell, who now assumed command over Montgomery's men, ordered an immediate retreat, although the firing had stopped, leaving the bodies of Montgomery and the other officers.

On the other side of the town, Arnold and his troops approached the first barricade to be crossed for entry into the Lower Town. As they attempted to force their way through the barricade, a langrage shot (nails, hunks of iron, etc.) and muskets spread flying metal into the troops, wounding Arnold in his lower left leg. Lieutenant John Starke of the British navy described the defenses of the city: "Some Guns judiciously placed in a house, formed a kind of masked Battery, which raked the Street which the Rebels occupied, and being loaded with grape Shot, they did effectual execution."[65] Arnold, although wounded, spurred his men on, now led by Captain Daniel Morgan. Morgan broke through the first wooden barrier and chased the British guards into a house where 50 British soldiers surrendered, followed by scores of local inhabitants who also gave themselves up to the Americans. By now the bells in the city were ringing their alarm. The Americans seized the dry muskets from their captors and rushed to the second barrier. Finding the second barrier deserted by the defenders, Morgan was ready to rush through to the Upper Town, but other officers persuaded him to wait until Montgomery's force reached the planned rendezvous point (not realizing that Montgomery's forces had retreated). The moment was lost, however, since in a short period of time new British defenders arrived at the barricade. Morgan's men threw up their scaling ladders, but many of the attackers were cut down by a hail of flying musket balls from the other side. "We got some of our ladders up," Captain Simeon Thayer of Providence, Rhode Island, noted, "but were obliged to retreat, our arms being wet, and scarcely one in ten would fire."[66] Carleton had now sent out several hundred soldiers to cut off the retreat of the Americans.

Captain Henry Dearborn, whose contingent had become lost in the narrow streets in the blizzard, was now faced with British regulars who could not be distinguished from his own army: "I was at a Stand to know whether They were our men, or the enemy, as they were dress'd like us."[67] The reason for the confusion stemmed from the use of the British uniforms, brought by Montgomery from Montreal, that the Americans were forced to wear due to a lack of clothing. The Americans put small hemlock branches in their hats to distinguish themselves, but in the snowy darkness the branches were of little use. (Some of the Americans had slips of paper pinned to their caps with "Liberty or Death" written on them.[68]) The British had the same problem and hailed Dearborn, asking who he was, "I answer'd a friend; he asked me who I was a friend to, I answer'd to liberty, he then reply'd God-damn you."[69] Outnumbered by six to one, Dearborn's detachment surrendered after their muskets failed to fire. Morgan, Thayer, and Lieutenant Colonel

Death of Brigadier General Richard Montgomery at Quebec City, January 1, 1776.
Engraving by W. Kelterlinus from a painting by John Trumbull.
(National Archives)

Christopher Greene with 130 prisoners did not retreat immediately, "having been for upwards of 4 hours victorious in the Lower town," but were soon to become prisoners.[70] With 70 to 90 Americans lying dead or wounded on Quebec's streets (with total American casualties estimated as high as 221), Morgan and his men fought from house to house in their retreat. The realization that they were totally surrounded forced them to surrender between nine and ten in the morning.

In all, the British captured 426 men. Captain Thayer noted wryly that "were altogether imprisoned on the first of January, being a bad method to begin the new year."[71] It was, however, preferable to the fate of their fallen comrades, whose distorted bodies the prisoners observed in horse-drawn carts "heaped in monstrous piles. . .Many of our friends and acquaintances were apparent."[72]

Brigadier General Montgomery was given a burial with honors in the city of Quebec by the British. The circumstances of his death left a bitterness toward Colonel Campbell in many of the soldiers. John Joseph Henry, a 16-year-old rifleman from Lancaster, Pennsylvania, later wrote a narrative on the "Death of General Montgomery," in which he called Campbell a "poltroon [coward]. . .The disgust caused among us, as to Campbell, was so great as to create the unchristian wish that he might be hanged."[73]

For the most part, the prisoners at Quebec were treated humanely by Carleton, although nearly a quarter of them who were of British birth were forced to join the Royal Highland Emigrant Regiment or be sent to England for trial as traitors. The others were eventually exchanged. Many American soldiers and officers who fought at Quebec, including Aaron Burr, Henry Dearborn, Daniel Morgan, and Simeon Thayer, would fight many more battles during the Revolutionary War. Morgan was to play a decisive role on the Saratoga battlefield and as a brigadier general at the "Battle of Cowpens" in January 1781 that reversed American losses in the South, setting the stage for the final victory at Yorktown.

Arnold was promoted to brigadier general by the Continental Congress on January 10 for his role in the Canadian campaign . At the same time, however, he again planted seeds of distrust for his detractors, who would later make accusations against his character. On February 1 Arnold wrote to John Hancock disputing a promotion to colonel for John Brown, a promotion which, according to Brown, had been promised by Montgomery. Arnold insisted that Montgomery felt that Easton and Brown were under a cloud, accused of "plundering the Officers, Baggage taken at Sorell, Contrary to Articles of Capitulation, and to the great scandal of the American Army."[74] Arnold would not support his promotion.

On February 15, following a recommendation from Philip Schuyler, the Continental Congress approved a committee to be sent to Canada to present American ideas about Canada's future, including an assurance of freedom for Canada, the need to establish an independent Canadian government, the possibility of Canada's becoming a sister colony, and a proposal for cooperation in the struggle against Great Britain. The three-man committee, granted far-ranging powers by Congress, included Benjamin Franklin, Samuel Chase, and Charles Carroll. The committee did not reach Lake George until April 18, where they found Fort George in "ruinous" condition. The trip to Canada was unsuccessful, but Carroll's journey provided an interesting description of the two lakes in 1776. Franklin, Chase, Carroll, and Schuyler traversed Lake George in a bateau, described as "36 feet long and 8 feet wide. . .and carry 30 or 40 men . . . They are rowed. . .[and] have a mast fixed in them to which square sail or a blanket is fastened."[75] Carroll described Lake George as " fine deer country and likely to remain so, for I think it never will be inhabited."[76] He was very interested in a "machine," devised by Schuyler for raising the boats at the northern end of Lake George and easing them onto four-wheel carriages to be drawn overland to Ticonderoga by six oxen. An eighteenth-century description of the waters in parts of Lake George and Lake Champlain provides an insight into the condition of the lakes then and now. As Carroll reached the very northern end of "Lake George the water suddenly shallows from a great depth to 9 or ten feet or less. This change is immediately discoverable by the different colors of the water. The water is of deep bluish cast and the water of this river of whitish color" which he attributed to "white clay" along the banks.[77] The water in the southern basin of Lake Champlain along Crown Point and Ticonderoga has a distinctive milky cast today. John Trumbull, who served as the deputy adjutant general of the Northern Army at Ticonderoga in 1776, described the waters around Crown Point as "the filthy water of that peculiarly stagnant muddy lake."[78] Some eighteenth-century maps actually separated Lake Champlain into two sections, calling the southern part of the lake the St. Frédéric River.

At Ticonderoga, Carroll observed "3 schooners and one sloop. . .of these 3 schooners, two were taken from the enemy on the surrender of St. Jean."[79] The vessels were the sloop *Enterprise*, schooners *Liberty*, *Royal Savage*, and *Revenge*. Apparently, the *Revenge* was the captured row galley that was later re-rigged as a schooner. After Crown Point, Franklin, Chase, and Carroll next stopped at the home of Peter Ferris on Ferris Bay (now Arnold's Bay). The committee reached Montreal on April 29, where it proceeded no farther, realizing that it was too late to influence the outcome of the American siege.

On May 11 Franklin left Montreal for the long trip back to Fort George and eventually to the Continental Congress. Samuel Chase and Charles Carroll stayed in Canada several more weeks, penning a discouraging report to Congress on the state of military affairs. Although by then the tenuous military foothold in Canada was rapidly collapsing, they recommended that 6,000 men be sent immediately.

The siege of Quebec had continued in the spring of 1776, as supplies and reinforcements slowly arrived in Canada. In early April Brigadier General David Wooster took charge of the troops at Quebec, while Arnold, still suffering from his leg wound and a subsequent fall from a horse, assumed command at Montreal. Wooster praised Arnold's siege in a letter to Washington: "General Arnold has, to his great honour, kept up the blockade with such a handful of men that the story, when told hereafter, will be scarcely credited."[80] By April Arnold had nearly 2,800 men, but 800 were incapable of service due to illness (mainly smallpox). The problem of buying supplies with Continental currency had never been resolved, leaving Schuyler's supply lines from Albany overextended. A dozen bateaux loaded with provisions were required from Albany each day to supply the threadbare army in the north. Schuyler was successful in building large numbers of bateaux at the southern end of Lake George in the winter and spring of 1776. By March 22, 100 new bateaux were completed there, and Schuyler expected another 110 to be completed by May 10 with 50 more planned.

On May 2, 1776, after three weeks in Albany, Major General John Thomas of Massachusetts reached Quebec to become the senior commander, replacing the ineffectual Wooster. Thomas was left with approximately 1,900 men as a result of enlistments running out and desertions. Of that number, 800-900 were estimated to be sick with smallpox. With news that large British reinforcements would be arriving soon, Thomas held a council of war with his officers on May 5, deciding on a plan to retreat to a point 25 miles west of Quebec at Deschambault. That evening reports came into the American camp that 15 British ships had been sighted 120 miles from Quebec. Early the next morning (May 6), however, the British fleet arrived sooner than expected, landing 1,800 troops immediately. Thomas initially attempted to make a stand but could rally only 250 men. As "all the bells in the town rang for joy," the Americans began a desperate retreat and "were obliged to leave all their baggage and bring nothing away but the cloaths upon their backs."[81] The American retreat was so sudden that the British troops found "the Commanding officer's Dinner which he had left at the fire and discovered abandoned "cannon, mus[k]ets, ammunition...the road strew[n] with ...clothes, bread, pork."[82] The Americans initially planned to hold Deschambault, then Three Rivers, but eventually made their camp at Sorel about 100 miles southwest of Quebec on the St. Lawrence River.

The Americans set fire to most of their ships before retreating from Quebec, but at least three schooners were recaptured by the British. The American army, nevertheless, still had vessels in Canada and were building more gondalos at Chambly on the Richelieu River. Benedict Arnold drafted a letter on May 8 in Montreal describing the American fleet on the St. Lawrence River as two armed gondolas, a ten-gun schooner, and "four other Gondaloes are building at Chambly."[83]

The camp at Sorel was in miserable condition as smallpox swept the army. Many of the desperate soldiers, despite prohibitions, inoculated themselves against smallpox. Arnold devised a plan to inoculate all the soldiers on a rotating basis in Montreal. Major General Thomas, adamantly opposed to inoculation, reversed Arnold's orders, insisting "that it should be death for any person to inoculate."[84] According to Dr. Lewis Beebe, a physician from Sheffield, Massachusetts, the very next day Thomas showed symptoms of smallpox himself. When it was evident on May 21 that Thomas had the disease, his command was relinquished to newly-arrived Brigadier General William Thompson, a 40-year-old Pennsylvania native who had had a questionable record during the 1775 Boston siege. In less than two weeks Thomas died of smallpox at Chambly. When the commissioners from Congress, Charles Carroll and Samuel Chase, reached Sorel, they discovered "little or no discipline among [the] troops. . .in want of the most necessary articles . . .an army broken and disheartened."[85]

Although dismayed by the reports of the retreat from Quebec, Congress was still determined to make a stand in Canada. Brigadier General John Sullivan, a lawyer and militia veteran from New Hampshire, led several thousand fresh reinforcements by way of the lakes to hold Canada. By June 4 the confident Sullivan arrived at Sorel to take command of the disorganized, broken army. The news of 500 Americans captured two weeks earlier west of Montreal at "The Cedars" and an expected offensive by the British army did not permit optimism, however.

Without proper information of the enemy forces, Sullivan quickly approved an earlier plan by Brigadier General Thompson to stop the British advance at Three Rivers, seventy miles southwest of Quebec. Sullivan, with knowledge of the presence of 18 British ships but no more than 300 troops on land, dispatched Thompson "with about two Thousand of our best Troops to attack them."[86] Before the engagement, Thompson's estimate of British strength was uncertain, ranging from 500-1,500 men. The Americans crossed the St. Lawrence River on the night of June 7 guided by a Canadian peasant who purposely led the invaders through 13 miles of deep swamp. Tired and disoriented, the men emerged from the swamp to find a much larger British force entrenched at Three Rivers, along with shiploads of British troops offshore.[87] The Americans attacked the British advance guard at six in the morning; then, with their drums beating, unsuccessfully assaulted the infantry at seven o'clock. The British, however, were not surprised since American drums had been heard as early as three o'clock in the morning. After repeated attacks, British armed schooners continued a raking fire into the dense foliage. Eventually, the Americans retreated as the British troops tried to race them to their bateaux. Although some American versions of the story have Thompson and his officers surrounded by the British troops after wandering through the woods the following night, Ensign John Enys, an eyewitness serving with the British 29th Regiment of Foot, noted "About 7 or 8 in the Morning [June 9] great Numbers began to come in to us and give themselves up as

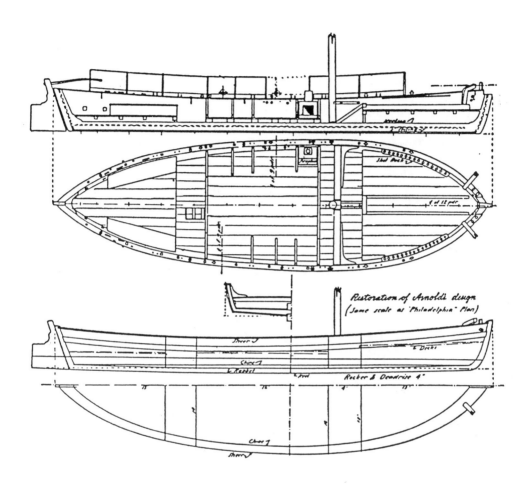

Benedict Arnold's gondola design at Chambly, Canada in 1776. The design was nearly identical to that of the gondolas later built at Skenesborough. (Smithsonian Institution)

prisoners, among whom was General Thom[p]son who commanded."[88] Most of the Americans escaped, but 22-30 were killed while 300-500 were made prisoners.

Although Benedict Arnold had suggested aggressive strategies in May 1776 for the holding of Canada, including making a stand at Deschambault on the St. Lawrence River, by June he became more pragmatic in view of the collapse of the American army. By June 6, even before Thompson's defeat, he proposed retreating to St. Jean and Isle-aux-Noix to make a stand. Four days later with no hope of American reinforcements, he pressed Brigadier General Sullivan by letter not to lose one minute in securing a retreat from the superior British force. Arnold's letter, both rational and eloquent, obviously had an impact on the final decision to retreat: "Shall we sacrifice the few men we have by endeavoring to keep possession of a small part of the country which can be of little or no service to us?...These arguments are not urged by fear for my personal safety: I am content to be the last man who quits this country, and fall, so that my country [may] rise. But let us not fall all together."[89]

Arnold's resolute stewardship of his forces in Canada, however, still had detractors. Dr. Lewis Beebe, a brother-in-law of Ethan Allen and a former Yale classmate of John Brown, described Arnold in his journal as an "infamous, villainous traitor"; and later at Crown Point following Arnold's arrest of several officers, Beebe wished that "some person would try an experiment upon him, (viz) to make the sun shine thro' his head with an ounce ball; and then see whether the rays come in a Direct or oblique direction."[90]

Faced with overwhelming odds (about 13,000 British troops) and the devastating sickness that affected half the troops, Sullivan retreated from Sorel on June 14, 1776, hours before the British landed there. Arnold, after expropriating a variety of supplies from merchants in Montreal, evacuated his troops to St. Jean. When Arnold's 30 wagons of merchandise reached Chambly on their way to St. Jean, Colonel Moses Hazen (a former ranger of Robert Rogers) interfered with the shipment, suspecting that it was plunder. The event would have some lasting consequences, including a charge of insubordination against Hazen by Arnold. Sullivan's army dragged the bateaux loaded with supplies and the sick through the rapids to Chambly. Once there, "Genl Sullivan set fire to all the armed vessels, 3 Gundalows & fort at Chambly" and retreated to St. Jean.[91] With 3,000 men already sick at Isle-aux-Noix, Sullivan on June 18 moved the rest of his army to the island to await orders from Schuyler as the British approached St. Jean.

Again, the American army just missed the British. Ensign Enys later reported that "some of their Rear boats [American] were Still within Sight of St. Johns [Jean] when our people arrived at that Place."[92] At St. Jean the Americans had burned a schooner still on the stocks and were forced to leave 22 pieces of artillery behind. Arnold, however, was able to send the frames from a vessel being built at St. Jean to Lake Champlain. The Americans also stripped two and a half tons of lead roofing from one of the houses in the fort, which later would be used to make ammunition. Arnold was the last man to leave St. Jean, pushing a canoe into the water himself. Without vessels at St. Jean, the British could not immediately follow the Americans on the Richelieu or Lake Champlain.

A horrible scene awaited the fleeing Americans at Isle-aux-Noix as smallpox and dysentery quickly spread to the rest of the army. Dr. Beebe vividly noted his impressions in his journal of the spectacle of a large barn filled with the sick, "many of which could not See, Speak, or walk. . .two had large maggots. . .Crawl out of their ears."[93]

In the last week of May, Schuyler had shipped 1,515 barrels of provisions to the army in Canada. A few weeks later he rushed empty bateaux from Lake George and Lake Champlain to rescue the 6,000-7,000-man army at Isle-aux-Noix. On June 20 Sullivan gave orders to transport the sick to Crown Point. From June 21 to the 27th, the sick men and their baggage were transported south to a temporary camp at Isle La Motte. With a shortage of bateaux, many troops marched along the lake for 20 miles before being ferried to Isle La Motte. On June 28 the army reembarked for Crown Point from Isle La Motte aboard bateaux. The sloop *Enterprise* and the schooners were also used in the evacuation. After days of rain and intermittent thunderstorms, the troops reached Crown Point at midnight on July 2, 1776. The sick were sent across the lake to Chimney Point. (The name Hospital Creek, north of Chimney Point, appeared on land surveys following the French and Indian War.) Later the invalid soldiers were sent to the hospital at Fort George, where 2,000 sick were cared for.

Although the Americans felt that the Canadians did not give them enough support in their fight against the Crown, the view of British soldiers was quite different. "Many of the Canadians had taken a decided part in their favor, rendered them essential services," wrote one soldier, while another maintained that "the peasantry of Canada are more friends to the Americans than to the British troops."[94] Two regiments of Canadians had been organized (1775-1776), but any real Canadian support for the colonies subsided after the American retreat from Canada in 1776. Although approved by Congress, a renewed invasion plan in 1778 was cancelled as impractical.

While the incursion into Canada was seemingly a total failure, in reality it forestalled a British invasion through Lake Champlain, the gateway into the colonies, during 1776. In particular, Arnold's raid on St. Jean in May 1775 and Montgomery's capture of the fort and vessels in November deprived the British of a navy on Lake Champlain. Because the Americans occupied St. Jean until June 18, 1776, the British were not able to complete construction of a new fleet to challenge the American superiority on Lake Champlain until the fall of 1776. In the meantime, the Americans made major additions to the existing fleet of vessels that had been captured earlier. The assignment of additional British troops to Canada, caused by the American foothold in Quebec, diverted British resources from other strategic areas. This diversion ultimately delayed General William Howe's attack on New York and gave George Washington time to prepare for operations there.

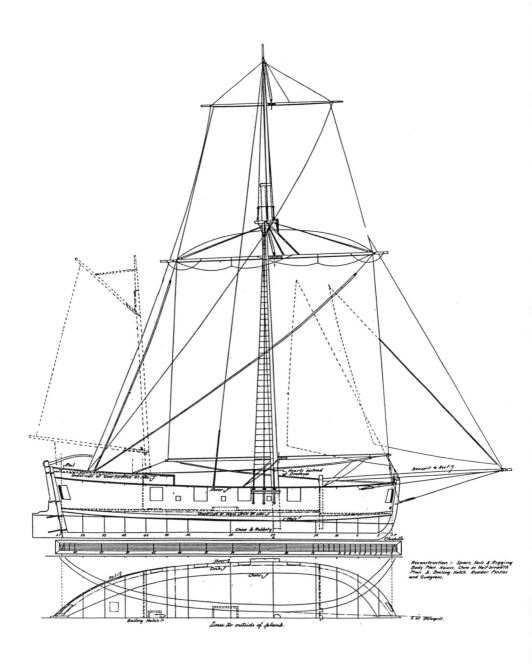

The 62-foot gondola *Loyal Convert* was captured on the St. Lawrence River by the British during the American evacuation and dragged through the rapids at Chambly to St. Jean. Reconstruction of an Admiralty drawing by H. I. Chapelle. (Smithsonian Institution)

7. Battle of Valcour Island

As ONE APPROACHES THE CRAGGY SHORE of the southern tip of Valcour Island on Lake Champlain, it is hard to imagine that over two and a quarter centuries ago this was the scene of a desperate struggle between 15 American warships and an overwhelmingly superior British fleet. The primitive island, with its tall, white spruce trees, evinces solitude as gentle waves break against the gray cliffs on its southern shore. Yet here cannon fire echoed from each shore; men were raked by devastating grapeshot, and vessels were smashed and sunk. Today's picturesque scene of blue water meeting the grays and greens of this detached bluff of land disguises the onslaught that sealed the fate of America's first naval fleet. Only a stone monument on the distant shore "Commemorating the Valor of American Forces Led by Benedict Arnold at the Battle of Valcour, October 11, 1776" signifies its stormy past.

To facilitate their invasion of the colonies, the British began a furious race to construct a naval fleet at St. Jean during the summer of 1776. The British strategy involved an invasion through Lake Champlain to the Hudson River with Lieutenant General John Burgoyne's army, while General William Howe's forces, after capturing New York City, would join with the northern army near Albany. (Both Burgoyne's and Howe's ranks were local in America.) If successful, these operations by the British army would effectively split the colonies in two, severing vital military, political, and economic links necessary to carry on the war. George Washington, following the British withdrawal from Boston in March, was engaged in defending southern New York from Howe's offensive during the summer and fall of 1776. Recognizing Lake Champlain and Lake George as the gateway to the north, Americans made a major military commitment to stop the British advance on the lakes. This would involve building a fleet of ships on Lake Champlain to augment the existing four vessels in the American fleet (sloop *Enterprise* and schooners *Liberty*, *Revenge*, and *Royal Savage*).

As the British army advanced southward on the Richelieu River in June 1776, Brigadier General John Sullivan, with the American army at Isle-aux-Noix, wrote to George Washington on the 24th suggesting the building of "Row-gallies to Command the Lakes."[1] The following day Benedict Arnold, with the knowledge that the British had brought the frames of vessels from England to be used on Lake Champlain, dispatched a similar request to Washington, urging that the lakes be immediately "secured by a large Number of (at least Twenty or thirty) Gundaloes, Row Gallies & floating Batteries."[2] Arnold was involved in the construction of gondolas in Canada in 1776 and formulated a design for these vessels on the St. Lawrence River that is quite similar to the design of the vessels that were later constructed at Skenesborough, New York (Whitehall).

Although Arnold is often credited with much of the management and construction of the American fleet on Lake Champlain, several other officers had as much to do with its creation as did Arnold. As early as May, Major General Philip Schuyler, the commander of the Northern Department, who had a large number of bateaux built in the spring of 1776, made preparations for the construction of gondolas in Skenesborough. Schuyler was in contact with George Washington about materials for the gondolas a month before letters by Arnold and Sullivan proposed such a fleet. Skenesborough was chosen as the construction site for the fleet because of its iron forge and two sawmills. At a considerable distance from Ticonderoga, the Skenesborough location would separate

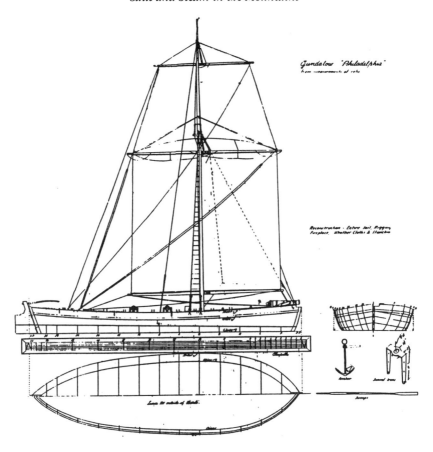

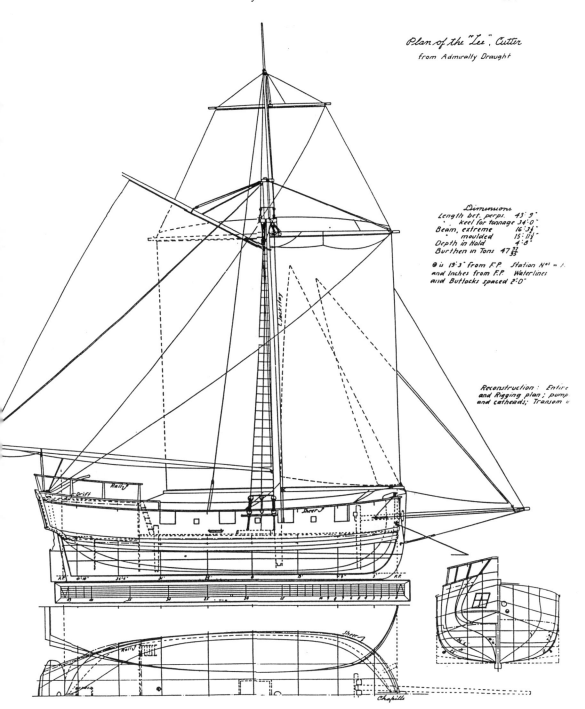

Plan of the "Lee", Cutter
from Admiralty Draught

Above: The cutter *Lee* was built from frames taken by Benedict Arnold during the American evacuation of St. Jean in June 1776. Drawing by H. I. Chapelle from an Admiralty draught. (Smithsonian Institution)

Facing page, top: The gondola *Philadelphia* was built in 1776 at Skenesborough (Whitehall, N.Y.). Line drawing by H. I. Chapelle. (Smithsonian Institution)

Bottom: American gunboats 1776. Painting by Ernest Haas.

the army from the highly-paid shipwrights and carpenters who were employed building the fleet.

By June 24 Schuyler reported to Washington that "one gundalo is finished at Skenesborough and a second is already planking."[3] By then, Schuyler had plans for five more gondolas with a timetable of one constructed every six days. The Lake Champlain gondolas were flat-bottomed with an approximate length of 54 feet and a 15-1/2 foot beam. The vessel had a square sail and topsail on its one mast but could be propelled by sweeps (oars). The gondolas were later fitted with either a 12- or 9-pound cannon in the bow, and nearly all carried two 9-pound cannons on the midship gun deck (one on each side) and a number of swivel guns mounted on brackets on the gunwales. Although gondolas and row galleys have received the most attention from the action on Lake Champlain, they were not unique to the lake. Indeed, John Adams and George Washington recommended such vessels during the same time period for use on the Delaware River and at New York City. Fifty carpenters from Philadelphia, one contemporary newspaper reported, were at Skenesborough "building Row Gallies, on the construction of those in the river Delaware."[4]

After the evacuation of Canada, the American army retreated as far as Crown Point in early July. Upon arriving at Crown Point, Colonel John Trumbull, deputy adjutant general and the son of the Connecticut governor, described the garrison: "at that place I found not an army, but a mob, the shattered remains of twelve or fifteen very fine battalions, ruined by sickness, fatigue and desertions."[5] With the death of Major General John Thomas in May, Congress procrastinated until June 17 before naming Major General Horatio Gates as the commander of the American army in Canada. The 48-year-old Gates, noted for his offensive personality, was a veteran of the French and Indian War and a personal friend of George Washington. By the time Gates reached Albany on June 26, the American army under Brigadier General John Sullivan had retreated from Canada. Since the Northern Army was no longer in Canada, a dispute over who was in charge of the army, Schuyler or Gates, arose in early July. In addition, Sullivan, irritated at being replaced by Gates, later traveled to Philadelphia to tender his resignation to the Continental Congress but withdrew it before Congress acted. On July 8 Congress solved the Schuyler-Gates dilemma by placing Gates subordinate to Schuyler. Although Schuyler remained the commander of the Northern Army, Gates was its field commander.

Despite the dispute, on July 7 a council of war held at Crown Point with Generals Schuyler, Gates, Sullivan, Arnold and De Woedtke agreed on a plan to abandon Crown Point and move the army to Ticonderoga and the eastern shore opposite the fort, with the sick to be sent to Fort George. The council resolved to build gondolas, row galleys, and armed bateaux to attain superiority on Lake Champlain. Gates, in a letter to Governor Jonathan Trumbull of Connecticut, described the broken-down condition of Crown Point at the time: "The ramparts are tumbled down, the casemates are fallen in, the barracks burnt, and the whole a perfect ruin, that it would take five times the men of our army, for several summers, to put it in defensible repair."[6] Twenty-one field officers at Crown Point, nevertheless, petitioned Schuyler to reconsider the withdrawal to Ticonderoga. When the news of the abandonment of the famous fortress reached George Washington and his staff, it created a "general chagrin and consternation."[7] The criticism of the move was so widespread that Schuyler felt compelled to write a very long letter to John Hancock, president of the Continental Congress, spelling out in minute detail all of the rationale for the decision. Crown Point, in reality, was never completely abandoned because a Pennsylvania regiment under Lieutenant Colonel Thomas Hartley garrisoned the fort until the British ships arrived after the Valcour battle in October 1776.

By early June construction of a fleet at Skenesborough was well underway while Schuyler continued to press for much-needed marine supplies and carpenters. The Marine Committee of the Continental Congress authorized a pay of 34-2/3 dollars per month with a month's pay in advance for shipwrights, a premium to attract skilled craftsman to the backwoods of New York. Although most of the workers were actually house carpenters, shipwrights from Connecticut, Massachusetts, Pennsylvania, and Rhode Island eventually formed a core of experienced marine craftsmen. In addition, blacksmiths, armorers, oarmakers, sailmakers, and other skilled workers arrived at Lake Champlain.

Becoming increasingly concerned with the progress of construction, Gates noted that the gondolas ordered by Schuyler "as he had no model to direct him, are in nothing but in name like those at Philadelphia."[8] Two of the gondolas had been finished by July 16 with two more expected to be completed within a week. While some of the vessels were at least partially rigged at Skenesborough, many of the later vessels were also rigged and armed at Fort Ticonderoga.

After several surveys by the engineers and officers in early July, the land at Mount Independence was soon cleared for a fortified post. Under the supervision of engineer Jeduthan Baldwin, the new military camp on the eastern shore grew in scope in 1776 with the construction of batteries, redoubts, storehouses, and barracks, and substantial progress on a star-shaped fort enclosed by pickets (logs), encompassing four and a half acres.[9] Although the post had several names, after a reading of the Declaration of Independence by Colonel Arthur St. Clair to the cheers of his assembled troops on July 28, 1776, the name Mount Independence began appearing in soldiers' journals.[10]

In the spring and early summer of 1776, the command of the four existing vessels of the American Champlain fleet, upon Schuyler's recommendation, was assigned to Captain Jacobus Wynkoop of the Fourth New York Regiment, who had previous experience with the American fleet on Lake Champlain. By July Gates became increasingly unhappy with Wynkoop, whom he regarded as inefficient in command of the emerging fleet. With only a few gondolas completed by July 22, Arnold traveled to Skenesborough to expedite the building of the vessels. As Gates' confidence in Arnold increased, he wrote John Hancock on July 29, 1776, that "General Arnold (who is perfectly skilled in maritime affairs) has most nobly undertaken to command our fleet upon the Lake."[11] Although Gates had not sought consultation on the appointment of Arnold, both Washington and Schuyler wholeheartedly approved of the selection. Jacobus Wynkoop, however, was not immediately informed of the change in command.

Arnold's boundless energy and enthusiasm were contagious among the workers at Skenesborough. This was in contrast to earlier reports received by Gates that the carpenters at Skenesborough had complained that the soldiers assigned to help them in the woods "would sit down by the trees instead of working."[12] Gates remarked that Arnold had gone to Skenesborough "to give life and spirit to our dock-yard."[13] At the end of July, Arnold informed Schuyler that he had left 200 carpenters at the Skenesborough shipyards with orders to "begin four Row Gallies, Nearly of the Constructions of those Built in Philadelphia."[14] The row galleys were to be 72 to 80 feet in length with a beam of 18 feet, carrying two masts with lateen (triangular) sails and 36 sweeps (oars). Galleys, like the gondolas, could be propelled by hand-pulled sweeps as well as by sail and were designed for operation in shallow water.

Controversy again dogged Arnold at Ticonderoga in the summer of 1776. His charges against Colonel Moses Hazen for refusing to accept responsibility for goods seized by Arnold in Montreal during the Canadian evacuation resulted in a court-martial of Hazen in July. The goods, whose seizure was authorized by the Congressional Commissioners in Canada, were broken open, plundered, and stolen after Hazen failed to take charge of the goods delivered by Major Scott for Arnold. When the court of 13 field officers refused to hear testimony from Scott during the stormy court-martial and found Hazen not guilty, Arnold vigorously protested. The court took strong offense to Arnold's protest and demanded an apology, which Arnold refused to make, suggesting that when the war ended, "I will by no means withhold from any gentleman of the Court the satisfaction his nice honour may require."[15] With that challenge, the court turned to Gates, demanding Arnold's arrest. After studying the situation, Gates dissolved the court and sent the records to Congress with the warning that "the United States must not be deprived of that excellent officer's service at this important moment."[16] The incident would not be forgotten by Arnold's enemies. Although Arnold would be cleared of these accusations, the controversy would follow him throughout his American career.

Arnold's contribution to the naval fleet on Lake Champlain included his vigor in finding supplies, crews, and materials to complete the new vessels. He dispatched work crews to the Onion River (Winooski River) and beyond for timber, pressed for seamen to man the vessels, and requested an experienced captain who had been convalescing at the Fort George hospital. Gates was similarly aggressive, as was Schuyler, who was away at Albany and German Flats meeting with Indian representatives of the Six Nations to obtain their neutrality. Schuyler demonstrated his ability to administer through correspondence.

The results of the renewed vigor in the construction process were evident by early August. By August 5, three gondolas had sailed: the *New Haven*, *Providence*, and *Boston*; the *Spitfire* was completed and nearly rigged; and another gondola, the *Philadelphia*, was finished but not rigged. The names of the gondolas, for the most part, reflected the communities that the carpenters represented.

Another vessel, initially called a row galley, was sent to Ticonderoga on August 8 to be armed and rigged. This vessel, named the *Lee*, was built from frames belonging to a vessel that had been under construction at St. Jean when the Americans were forced to evacuate in June 1776. The frames, taken by Arnold, were numbered for easy reassembly later. The stubby *Lee*, with a length of only 43 feet, 9 inches, was called a row galley, cutter, sloop, and gondola by various contemporary sources because she apparently had characteristics common to all of these vessels.

As Arnold worked to put the fleet together, Captain Jacobus Wynkoop, aboard the schooner *Royal Savage*, continued to act as the commander of the naval forces despite the change of command. The pompous Wynkoop was deflated on August 10 when he mistook seagulls for the sails of the British fleet. After a "Large flock of White Gulls" appeared in his looking glass, Wynkoop ordered the boatswain to hail the American fleet with his trumpet.[17] Wynkoop called all the officers aboard his flagship for a council of war. After some time, however, Captain Isaac Seaman of the *Revenge* climbed the mast and identified the seagulls through his looking glass.

After scouts observed a signal fire on August 17, which could indicate the approach of the British, Arnold gave orders to Captains Seaman and Premier of the schooners *Revenge* and *Liberty* to proceed seven or eight miles north to scout for the enemy and cover 100 American troops returning to Crown Point. When the vessels at Crown Point attempted to make sail, Wynkoop fired a swivel cannon from the *Royal Savage*, halting their progress. This contradiction of Arnold's orders was based on Wynkoop's insistence that he was commander of the navy on Lake Champlain through his appointment by Philip Schuyler. Arnold boarded the *Royal Savage* and confronted Wynkoop and presented his appointment letter from Gates. While Wynkoop insisted that Arnold had not made clear his command earlier, Arnold, in an exchange of letters later that day, wrote that he was surprised by Wynkoop's attitude "as I acquainted you some time since that the Commander in chief had Appointed me to take command of the Navy on the Lakes."[18] Arnold warned Wynkoop that unless he followed his orders, he would have the disagreeable task of immediately arresting him. Wynkoop persisted in his belief that Schuyler's appointment gave him command of the fleet.

After Gates had ordered Wynkoop's arrest, Arnold noted that the discharged commander was sorry for his insubordination and suggested to Gates that Wynkoop "may be permitted to return home without being cashiered."[19] Following Arnold's request, Gates sent Wynkoop with a pass without arrest to Schuyler in Albany but insisted that he not be returned to Ticonderoga. Wynkoop made an appeal to Congress, which was largely ignored, but he was never cashiered (forcibly discharged) from the service.

With reports that the British were building a fleet at St. Jean, the Americans pressed forward to deploy their fleet under Arnold during August. By August 18 Gates reported that he had nine vessels "fit for action" which included the *Enterprise, Royal Savage, Revenge, Liberty,* and the new gondolas *New Haven, Providence, Boston, Spitfire,* and *Philadelphia.* The first four vessels had been captured by the Americans in 1775. The *Revenge,* taken at St. Jean, had been referred to as a row galley by contemporary accounts of 1775 but was apparently re-rigged as a schooner at Ticonderoga.[20] The gondola *Jersey* and cutter *Lee* were not yet rigged. The other row galleys that Arnold had ordered were not finished as planned. The delay, Gates later reported to Congress, was caused by the "excessive sickness of that place [Skenesborough] [which] has greatly retarded the finishing of the galleys."[21]

Meanwhile, the British, cognizant that the Americans were enlarging their fleet, were rushing to complete their own flotilla for Lake Champlain. Their strategy involved building some very large ships which would result in "our acquiring an absolute dominion over Lake Champlain."[22] To that end the British planned to bring vessels from the St. Lawrence River into Lake Champlain via the Richelieu River and build additional ships at St. Jean. The 14-gun schooner *Maria,* named for Governor Guy Carleton's wife, had been captured by the Americans in November 1775 on the St. Lawrence. Recaptured by the British on May 6, 1776, during the American evacuation of Quebec, the 66-foot *Maria* was to be transported overland on a newly-built road from Chambly to St. Jean. However, the road in July was found to be too loose to support the *Maria* or two other hulls that were also to be moved overland. The *Maria* was subsequently taken apart and shipped by water to Chambly and then to St. Jean, where it was to be reassembled. The largest vessel, an 80-foot ship under construction at Quebec, later to be named the *Inflexible,* was likewise disassembled and transported in long boats and bateaux to Chambly. At Chambly some of the frames were transferred to wagons, while other sections were shipped by water to St. Jean for completion. The *Inflexible* would be finished at St. Jean in a remarkable 28 days. The 59-foot schooner *Carleton,* recaptured from the Americans at Quebec in May, was similarly dismantled and reconstructed at St. Jean.[23]

A 62-foot gondola, named the *Loyal Convert* by the British, was dragged through the rapids at Chambly to St. Jean. This vessel had also been taken from the Americans during the May 6 retreat from Quebec. The vessel was possibly one of the American gondolas, *Hancock* or *Schuyler,* built by Philip Schuyler on Lake Champlain in 1775, that had been dragged northward over the same rapids the previous November. The length is approximately that given by Schuyler in 1775 for the gondolas.[24] The British also moved 30 long boats, many from their fleet on the St. Lawrence River, over the Chambly rapids to St. Jean. The long boats, typically ranging from 20 to 40 feet in length, carried the frames and materials for the fleet to be constructed at St. Jean. In addition, some flat-bottomed boats and 400 bateaux were dragged over the rapids.

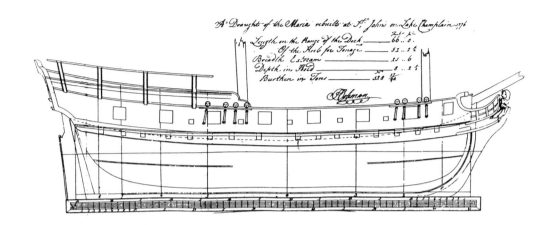

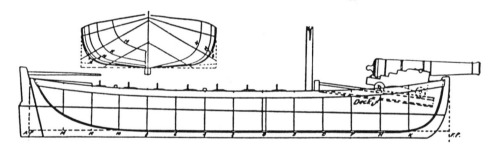

Above: British gunboat of 1776 used at the Valcour engagement. Admiralty draught, Chapelle Collection. (Smithsonian Institution)

Below: Admiralty drawing of radeau *Thunderer*. (Public Record Office, London)

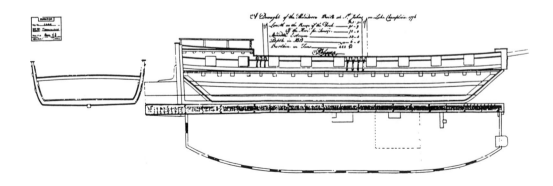

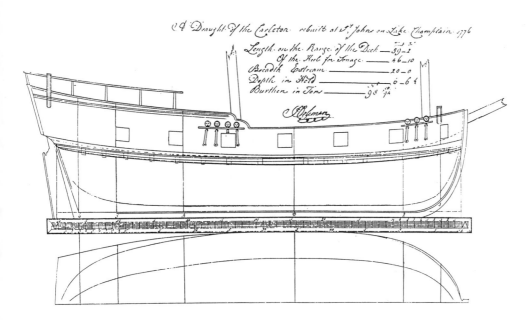

Above: Admiralty drawing of 59-foot schooner *Carleton*. (National Maritime Museum, Greenwich, England)

Facing page (top): Admiralty drawing of 66-foot schooner *Maria* which had been dismantled and rebuilt at St. Jean in 1776. (National Maritime Museum, Greenwich, England)

At St. Jean the British built "Twelve Gun Boats" from the frames brought from England and either built or dragged across the rapids "16 Canadian Built Boats."[25] Eventually, 22 or more of these gunboats would face the Americans in October 1776. The names of these vessels, listed on a "Return of Gun Boats...Commanded by Captain [John] Carter 7th October 1776," included the *Carcase, Invincible, Firebrand, Renown, Desperate, Revenge, Dreadful, Blast, Infernal, Tartar, Destruction, Vesuvius, Thunderbolt, Etna, Resolution, Terrible, Repulse, Furious,* and *Pluto* (three armed bateaux on the list were not named.).[26] The standard gunboat employed by the British was 37 feet long with a 12-foot beam, and carried one mast and one cannon in the bow.

The most powerful vessel to be built by the British at St. Jean in 1776 was the large square-rigged, two-masted radeau *Thunderer,* which would mount 2 howitzers, 6 twenty-four-pound cannons, and 6 twelve-pounders. The 91-foot *Thunderer* carried "6-24 pound cannon on the lower deck" and the rest of the artillery on the upper deck and was "built in a square of strong rafters, fitted however with masts."[27] Although the vessel was unwieldy to sail, if the wind blew in the right direction the vessel was remarkably fast.

By the time the Americans were ready to sail, the British at St. Jean were still feverishly working on their vessels. On August 24 the American fleet, under the command of Benedict Arnold, departed from Crown Point with the *Royal Savage* and *Enterprise* in the lead, followed by the gondolas *New Haven, Boston, Providence, Spitfire, Philadelphia,* and *Connecticut* with the schooners *Revenge* and *Liberty* in the rear, as well as a large number of bateaux. Gates' sailing orders, given over two weeks earlier, suggested that the "ultimate end" of Arnold's command would be to prevent the enemy invasion but warned that it was a defensive war and urged that "no wanton risk or unnecessary display of the power of the fleet is at any time to influence your conduct."[28] The fleet was to be stationed in a narrow pass of the lake to thwart the British advance. If the British fleet was stronger, Arnold was advised to retire to Ticonderoga after making every effort to retard its progress.

On the second night of the cruise, the American fleet was anchored off Willsboro when a violent gale from the northeast forced Arnold to sail to Buttonmould Bay (Button Bay, near present-day Panton, Vermont) for a safe harbor from huge waves set in motion by the storm. The gondola *Spitfire*, however, was stranded by the storm near Willsboro and presumed "foundered or drove on shore," but later rejoined the fleet undamaged at Button Bay.[29] The American fleet renewed its voyage northward on September 1. Three days later, Arnold moored the fleet across the narrow span of the lake at Windmill Point. At that time the cutter *Lee* and gondola *New Jersey* joined the American flotilla. On September 5 and 6 Arnold sent some of the crews to cut "Facines [branches] to fix on the Bows and Sides of the Gondolas to prevent the Enemies boarding and to keep off the small Shot."[30] On the second day, crew members of the gondola *Boston* were ambushed by Indians led by a British regular officer. The crews rushed back to the boat, but the melee resulted in the deaths of three men, with six more being wounded. Believing the British were erecting batteries on the shoreline at Windmill Point, Arnold moved the fleet to a wider part of the lake at Isle La Motte on September 8.

At the northern anchorages, Arnold complained to Gates that his crews were "very indifferent Men, in general, [a] great part of those who shipped for Seaman know very little of the Matter."[31] He pleaded with Gates for swivel cannons for the vessels, warm clothing for the crews, more seamen, and provisions while proposing arming bateaux with swivel guns. At Isle La Motte, Arnold waited for the galleys that were far behind schedule. According to Colonel Jeduthan Baldwin, the first two row galleys did not reach Ticonderoga for rigging and arming until September 11 and 12. The galleys *Congress* and *Trumbull* would require more than two weeks to be fitted out. Although Arnold and others worried about the construction delays during the summer of 1776, in retrospect the building process was a remarkable achievement in itself given the circumstances. Building this fleet in a few months, including some of the gondolas in a matter of weeks, largely with hand tools, was a feat of ingenuity and hard work.

The eighth and last gondola, *New York* (called the *Success* earlier), joined the fleet on September 11. After eliciting information from British prisoners regarding the size of the British fleet under construction at St. Jean, on September 18 Arnold wrote to Gates of his intention to move to the bay west of Valcour Island (Plattsburgh, N.Y. today) "where is a good harbour, and where we shall have the advantage of attacking the enemy in the open Lake."[32] The next day the American fleet anchored at Bay St. Armand, north of Cumberland Head. The *Liberty*, cruising near the western shore opposite Isle La Motte, was lured by a man dressed in French clothing. The man waded into the lake and requested the *Liberty* to come closer. Suspecting a trap, the captain sent a smaller boat near the shore. When the crew refused to be decoyed closer, 300-400 Indians, Canadians, and regulars rose up on the shore and fired on the vessel, wounding several crew members. The boat "returned the fire with its swivels and small-arms" and the *Liberty* "fired several broadsides of grape" before returning to the fleet.[33]

The fleet sailed for Valcour Bay on September 24. At Valcour, Arnold wrote Gates, reiterating his strategy "that few vessels can attack us at the same time, and those will be exposed to the fire of the whole fleet."[34] Although a few historians have criticized Arnold for not following Gates' original sailing instructions of not risking the fleet, Gates had plenty of time to order the fleet out of Valcour Bay. On September 21 Arnold again informed Gates of his intention to anchor at Valcour Bay but suggested moving if Gates did not approve: "I make no doubt you will approve of this measure; if not, I will return to any of my former stations."[35] Gates, however, never questioned Arnold's choice of anchorages and had full confidence in Arnold's leadership. Gates dispatched a letter to Arnold on October 12 (not having news of the previous day): "I. . .am pleased to find You, and your Armada, ride in Valcour Bay, in defiance of the power of our Foes in Canada."[36] Gates, for most of the period before the engagement, had been optimistic about the power of the American fleet. In mid-August, he wrote confidently that the naval force, after completion, would command Lake Champlain. Even in early October, after examining intelligence reports of British preparations, Gates was not entirely convinced that the British would engage the American fleet: "I am inclined to suspect they are rather Acting upon the Defensive."[37]

Scouts had continually observed the growth of the British fleet at St. Jean, but most reports underestimated the strength and size of the vessels. A September 20 report indicated the "sloop and schooners" were not finished, only two out of seven gondolas were completed, and "no other vessels building" at St. Jean, although timber was being cut.[38] Arnold felt that the British would have a considerable naval force on the lake, but the intelligence that he received in mid-September of one ship of 20 guns on the stocks (*Inflexible*), several schooners, and some smaller craft at St. Jean still underestimated the fleet by omitting the large number of gunboats and the radeau *Thunderer*. Information from a Frenchman concerning the vessels at St. Jean, however, did mention a floating battery under construction, but Arnold thought the man a British spy and didn't believe the report.[39] An undated intelligence report that more accurately portrayed the British squadron at St. Jean was not reflected in the letters of Gates or Arnold before the engagement at Valcour.[40] On the day before the engagement, Arnold had no recent intelligence because of the loss of the fleet's only two canoes.

During the last two days of September and early October, the American fleet rode at anchor in Valcour Bay awaiting the British fleet. The weather was cold and windy as the crews practiced firing at marks and maneuvering their vessels. On September 30 the galley *Trumbull*, carrying 8 cannons and 16 swivels and under the command of Captain Seth Warner, arrived at two o'clock in the afternoon. While the galley was a much-needed addition to the fleet, Arnold complained that the vessel was only half-rigged, mounting cannons considerably smaller than he had ordered. Cannon salutes pierced the wilderness six days later on October 6 when the galleys *Congress* and *Washington*, under the command of Captains James Arnold and John Thatcher respectively, finally joined the fleet. Brigadier General David Waterbury, who had been directing the work on the vessels at Skenesborough and Ticonderoga, arrived in the galley *Washington* to take his post as second in command of the fleet. The crews were glad to see the *Washington* since a barrel of rum for each gondola was part of its cargo. Anxious to hear news of the American army on Long Island, Arnold wrote to Gates on the following day. In his letter, he suggested moving the fleet back to Button Bay if the British did not appear by the middle of October, but the fleet was ready for action: "I make no doubt of giving a good account of them."[41] In early October, Arnold was still confident, believing the British "naval force, by the best accounts, near equal to ours."[42] As the American flotilla pitched and rolled in the stiff autumn gales of October 1776, the brave crews were unaware of the juggernaut coming their way.

On October 4 General Guy Carleton, governor of Canada, and Royal Navy Captain Thomas Pringle, commander of the fleet, set sail from St. Jean southward on the Richelieu River aboard the schooner *Maria*. A few days later the largest British ship, the *Inflexible*, joined the fleet, barely a week after her launching. The fleet anchored at Point au Fer on the western shore of Lake Champlain, where a blockhouse was erected on the peninsula and four companies of soldiers assigned to defend it. The majority of British and German

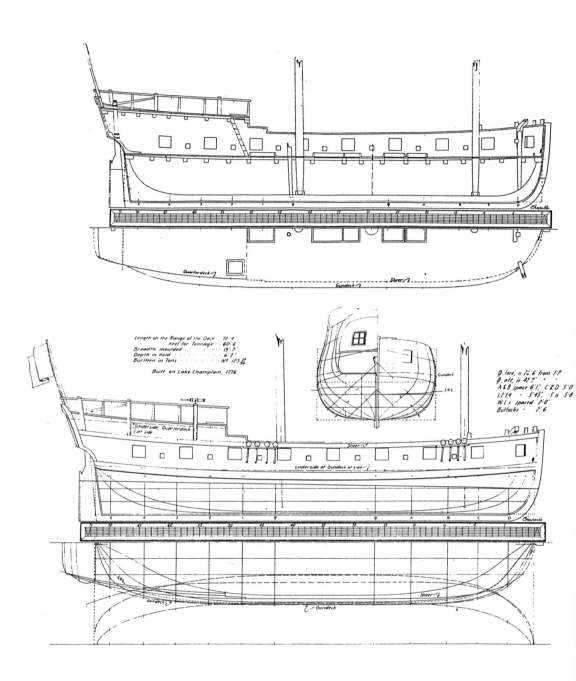

The galley Washington was built by the Americans in 1776 at Skenesborough.
From Admiralty draughts by H. I. Chapelle, Chapelle Collection.
(Smithsonian Institution)

troops bivouacked at camps on the Lacolle River and at Isle-aux-Noix. The British fleet remained at Point au Fer until October 10 while scouting parties searched for the American fleet. On the tenth of October, Carleton received an erroneous report that the Americans had been seen in Cumberland Bay (or near Grand Isle). Based on that report, the second inaccurate sighting of the Americans, the British fleet sailed and came to anchor near "the Southern end of Isle au Mot[t]e."[43] The night before the battle, Captain Pringle was said to have received accurate information on the location of the American fleet, but other eyewitnesses noted that the American fleet was expected at Cumberland Bay.[44] The next morning, the British fleet, consisting of the ship *Inflexible*, schooners *Maria* and *Carleton*, radeau *Thunderer*, gondola *Loyal Convert*, and 20 or more gunboats, as well as long boats, bateaux, and canoes made uneven progress as the cold, blue water lapped their hulls.* As the British fleet neared Cumberland Bay, "to our great mortification we cou'd discover no ships," Dr. Robert Knox, the chief medical officer to the British army in Canada, disclosed in his journal.[46]

Schooner "*Royal Savage* sallies forth" to engage the British fleet. Painting by Ernest Haas.

The sky was clear and a crisp northerly wind blew through the American fleet anchored in Valcour Bay on the morning of October 11. The Americans could see snow on the Adirondack Mountains to their west as the crews began their seventeenth day at the bay. The American fleet consisted of 15 vessels and some bateaux. The schooner *Liberty* had departed for another trip to Ticonderoga for provisions and the row galley *Gates* was still being outfitted at Ticonderoga. At eight o'clock in the morning, the guard boat of the American fleet fired an alarm as it brought the news of the approaching fleet. At half-past nine, Arnold ordered Colonel Edward Wigglesworth, a former shipmaster

---

* Although most contemporary British sources do not name a sixth vessel in the British fleet, the contemporary painting of the Valcour battle by Henry Gilder in the Royal Collection, on display in Windsor Castle, depicts another sailing vessel with a bowsprit at the stern of the *Thunderer*. Likewise, the original drawing by Charles Randle in the National Archives of Canada shows what may be the same vessel labeled a long boat. Major General Friedrich Riedesel, a German commander with the British force on the lake, mentions six vessels in his memoirs.[45]

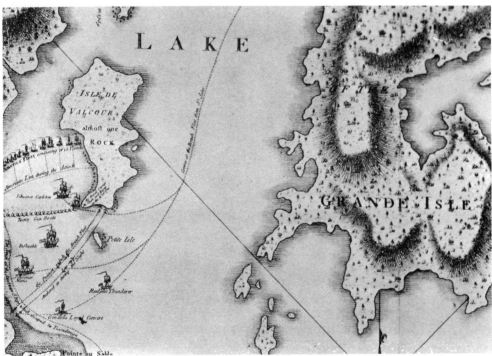

Above: "The Attack and Defeat of the American Fleet under Benedict Arnold by King's Fleet Commanded by Captain Thomas Pringle, Upon Lake Champlain, the 11th of October, 1776" by William Faden, London, 1776. (Special Collections, Bailey/Howe Memorial Library, University of Vermont)

Top: The Battle of Valcour Island 1776 by Henry Gilder. (Windsor Castle, Royal Library, Her Majesty Queen Elizabeth II)

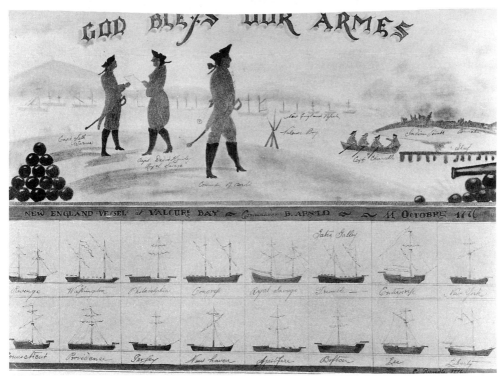

Above: "God bless our Armes" depicts the American fleet at Valcour Bay on October 11, 1776. Watercolor by Charles Randle, 1777. (Fort Ticonderoga Museum)

Top: "A View of New England Armed Vessels, on Valcure Bay on Lake Champlain, 11 October 1776" by Charles Randle. (National Archives of Canada)

Middle: "A View of His Majesty's Armed Vessels on Lake Champlain, 11 October 1776" by Charles Randle. (National Archives of Canada)

from Newburyport, Massachusetts, serving as third in command of the fleet, out into a yawl to observe the motions of the British fleet. Arnold moved his flag from the *Royal Savage* to the galley *Congress*, probably because he believed that the row galleys would be better equipped for maneuvering during battle.

As the British fleet with its larger ships came into view, it must have stirred apprehension among the 500 green hands on their makeshift shoal vessels. Brigadier General Waterbury immediately boarded Arnold's vessel to give his "opinion that the fleet ought immediately to come to sail, and fight them on a retreat in main Lake, as they were so much superior to us in number and strength."[47] But Arnold, undeterred by the size of the British fleet, ordered the American vessels in a line across the bay to receive the invading force. Arnold was probably correct since a haphazard retreat on the open lake against the faster British ships would have been a disaster, as the events of October 13 would later prove. To some extent the fleet had been built to be sacrificed to slow the British invasion; to save it and allow the British invasion to go forth unchecked was not a strategy Arnold would have supported.

The British fleet had almost twice the weight in cannons, more vessels, and more men who were trained sailors, and drew its Royal Navy officers from the British fleet in the St. Lawrence River. The fleet was accompanied by some bateaux, long boats, and canoes, but the main army consisting of 7,000 men in 300-400 bateaux did not depart from Point au Fer until October 14. Fewer than 1,000 men in bateaux accompanied the fleet as boarding parties. The British ships sailed past Valcour on the stiff northerly wind and then, sighting the American vessels, had to sail upwind, as Arnold had anticipated, to attack them. The British gunboats, however, were successful in reaching a position, in a line from the southwestern tip of Valcour Island to the New York shore, which faced the American line to the north. Although many of the participants noted 20 gunboats in the British line, estimates ranged as high as 28 armed gunboats and longboats.[48]

After the Americans heard the news of the oncoming British fleet, Arnold "ordered the 2 schooners and 3 galleys under way immediately" to entice the ships into the bay.[49] Between ten-thirty and eleven o'clock the battle began. The *Royal Savage*, the only American craft in a class with the British warships, ran aground on the southwestern corner of Valcour Island after its masts and bowsprit were damaged and its rigging shot away by three shots from the *Inflexible*. The gunboats then brought an incessant fire on the stranded *Royal Savage* as the *Loyal Convert* entered the bay. The crew of the *Royal Savage* abandoned the schooner, but not before Lieutenant Edward Longcroft, commander of the *Convert*, boarded the vessel and captured as many as 20 crew members before they could escape. Longcroft then turned the guns of the *Royal Savage* back on the Americans. When half of the boarding party were killed by return fire, Longcroft left the *Royal Savage* for his gondola.

For the next several hours the crews of the British gunboats and American vessels engaged in a savage duel as cannons fired solid shot, barshot, and grapeshot. Smoke from the American guns floated with the wind over the British boats as carriages recoiled from each blast. Arnold, aboard the *Congress*, anchored in the hottest part of the crossfire and aimed the cannons himself on the open deck amid flying shot and splintering wood. Many of the American shots, however, missed their mark since "the [British] G[un] Boats being low in the Water made the Shot go over their heads."[50] The British gunboats, on the other hand, were quite effective in lobbing shot upon the American vessels with devastating results. According to Lieutenant James Hadden, "each Gun Boat carried 1 Gun in the Bow (or Howitzer), 7 Artillery Men, and 11 Seamen, the whole under an Artillery officer."[51] In the heat of battle, Captain Georg Pausch, chief of the Hesse-Hann artillery in the engagement, observed the gunboat of Lieutenant Dufais explode: "a chest went up into the air, and after the smoke had cleared away, I recognized the men by the cords around their hats."[52] Pausch rescued most of the crew (the gunboat *Infernal*, under Lieutenant Smith, took Dufais, the Bombadier, and an artillery man) which increased the number of men on his gunboat to 48, nearly sinking the vessel. The gunboat that had exploded burned and sank in Valcour Bay.[53]

While the Americans were fighting the crews on the British gunboats, Indians led by Captain Christopher Carleton, nephew of Governor Guy Carleton, and Captain Alexander Fraser with another group of Indians and Canadians fired ineffectively from both the shore and Valcour Island. Pascal Charles Joseph De Angelis, a recruit from Connecticut not quite 13 years old, who served with his stepfather Captain Seth A. Warner aboard the galley *Trumbull*, wrote that during the "time of action the Regulars and Indians Fired with Small arms From the Shore at the Galley Washington who soon put them in Sil[e]nce by a few Cann[i]ster Shot."[54] The schooner *Carleton*, under the command of Lieutenant James Dacres, by mid-afternoon had sailed into Valcour Bay to a position north of the British gunboats. The schooner was now exposed to the full force of the American line. The vessel became totally disabled as the American vessels concentrated their fire on the *Carleton*. Massachusetts militiaman Jahiel Stewart recorded that "we Cut her Rig[ging] most all away & bored her threw and threw."[55] Lieutenant Dacres was wounded and knocked senseless, and the officer second in command, Robert Brown, lost his right arm. Nineteen-year-old Midshipman Edward Pellew took command of the *Carleton*, while Captain Pringle, lying far back in the schooner *Maria*, signaled recall to the *Carleton*. Pellew, who in later years would become one of Britain's most famous admirals, crawled out on the bowsprit amid flying shot to deploy a jib sail. When one of the tow ropes was cut by a shot, Pellew once more risked his life when no one else volunteered by again exposing himself on the bowsprit to secure the tow rope to the long boats of the *Inflexible*.[56] Eight men were killed and six wounded on the *Carleton* during the attack.

"Battle of Valcour Island." Painting by Ernest Haas. (Lake Champlain Maritime Museum)

"The *Philadelphia* sinking, assisted by the galley *Washington*, Battle of Valcour Island,
Lake Champlain, October 11, 1776." Painting by Ernest Haas.
(Lake Champlain Maritime Museum)

While the battle was raging, the 14-gun schooner *Maria*, reportedly the best sailing
vessel in the fleet, remained far south of the action with her sails furled. Captain Thomas
Pringle only vaguely directed the naval operations during the battle, while Governor-
General Guy Carleton and his younger brother, Colonel Thomas Carleton, observed the
engagement from the open decks. The next year, after learning of Pringle's account, which
failed to mention the efforts of all the officers involved, Lieutenants John Schank
(*Inflexible*), John Starke (*Maria*), and Edward Longcroft *(Loyal Convert)* wrote a scathing
letter to Pringle, accusing him of mismanagement of the battle and of making no attempt
to use the *Maria* "while yourself in the Maria lay too with the topsails, and was the only
person in the fleet who showed no inclination to fight."[57] Probably the only shots fired
by the *Maria* were at the beginning of the engagement when the *Maria* "opened a lively
cannonade" and "was replaced by the frigate 'Carleton'; and as she in turn retreated, the
'Inflexible' took her place only to retreat as others had done."[58] The *Inflexible* may have
entered into the action at the end of the clash since the vessel was said to have "sunk one
of the rebel Gundalos."[59]

"The most Desp[e]rate can[no]nading without intermis[si]on continued till about half
after 5 oclock...about 6 oclock the firing Ceas[ed]," young De Angelis wrote in his diary.[60]
The British gunboats withdrew about 600 to 700 yards away but continued their fire until
dark. By then the American fleet, with three-fourths of its ammunition gone, had been
badly damaged; the galley *Congress* receiving "Seven Shot between Wind & Water, was
hulled a doz[en] times, had her Main Mast Wounded in Two places & her Yard in One."[61]
The galley *Trumbull*'s mainmast was broken "about half way up the mast and s[l]iv-
ered...almost to pcascs [pieces] and one Twelve pound Shot under our Counter [overhang-
ing stern section] between Wind and water and about 20 or 30 more in Different Places."[62]

The galley *Washington*, likewise, had her hull pierced by shot, her main mast shot away, and was leaking. The *Washington* also lost her first lieutenant and had her captain wounded. The gondola *New York* had lost all her officers except the captain. At the end of the battle "a boat came a Long side [of the galley *Trumbull*] and took our Wounded...on board of the Hosp[i]tal Sloop Enterprize."[63] Jahiel Stewart, aboard the hospital sloop, observed "the Doct[o]rs Cut of[f] great many legs and arm[s]" and saw the dead tossed overboard.[64] In total, approximately 60 men were killed or wounded on the American side during the engagement. At the end of the engagement the gondola *Philadelphia* sank from damage suffered during the cannonading. When the vessel was recovered in 1935, a 24-pound ball was found lodged in the outside planking of the bow. The shot that sank the *Philadelphia* may have come from one of the gunboats, two of which carried 24-pound cannons. Before dusk a British boarding party set the *Royal Savage* afire, resulting in an explosion of the remaining powder on the vessel. The fire burned all night before the hull settled into the water off the island. Benedict Arnold's personal papers, which had not been transferred to the *Congress* from the *Royal Savage*, were saved by the British.[65]

At dusk Arnold called a council of war in his cabin aboard the *Congress*. With little choice, Generals Arnold and Waterbury and the captains of the vessels agreed to retreat immediately to Crown Point with the crippled fleet. Some of the officers proposed sailing around the northern end of Valcour Island, but Arnold elected to take the fleet through the British line.* In the darkness, shrouded in a dense fog, the fleet inched its way along the western shoreline. With the galley *Trumbull* in the lead and a hooded "Lantern at our St[e]rn" to show only directly behind, the fleet carefully passed single file "with so much secrecy that we went through them entirely undiscovered."[67] Captain Pringle's letter to the secretary of the admiralty on October 15 stated that he "brought the whole fleet to anchor in a line as near as possible to the Rebels, that their retreat might be cut off."[68] Schank, Starke, and Longcroft, however, later disputed the report, suggesting that "the fleet was not brought to anchor as near as possible to the rebels. . .the rear of the British line was at least one mile from the western shore, and the van beyond the small island at the Southern end of Valcour."[69] The American fleet with the *Congress* and *Washington* in the rear made its way to Schuyler Island seven and a half miles to the south of Valcour.

At the break of dawn, the British peered at Valcour Bay, ready to finish the destruction of the American fleet. To their surprise the Americans were gone. According to Major General Friedrich Adolphus Riedesel, "General Carleton was in a rage" and sailed away to find the rebel fleet, but "forgot to leave instructions for the army on the land. . .the wind, however, being adverse, and nothing having been seen of the enemy, he returned" to Valcour Island.[70] Riedesel's story has been the most commonly accepted and repeated version of the events of October 12, but Reidesel was not actually there. General Carleton wrote that the American fleet was "still in our sight, this morning, but the wind blowing very strong from the southward we have been obliged to give over the cha[s]e for the present."[71] Ensign John Enys, aboard the radeau *Thunderer*, also noted "at day light some of their fleet were Seen at a distance. Our fleet attempted to pursue them but the wind was so hard against us we were obliged [to] put back again."[72] Enys reported that the *Thunderer* was in some danger when her lee boards caved in, causing the radeau to heel over and water to flood in through the gunports.

---

* An interesting controversy arose in the late nineteenth century when some historians argued that Arnold had actually escaped with his fleet by sailing around the northern end of Valcour Island. As more journals were published, it became clear that this had not occurred. The story is also linked to the tale of "Carleton's Prize," a solitary rock island three and a half miles east of Valcour Island, which was mistakenly assumed to have been bombarded by the British fleet the next morning. The tale seemingly has no basis in fact although some have claimed to have found cannonballs there.[66]

Early on the morning of October 12 the American fleet became widely separated. The galley *Trumbull* and some of the other vessels had only paused briefly at Schuyler Island while Arnold in the *Congress*, Waterbury in the *Washington*, and most of the gondolas eventually anchored at Schuyler to stop their leaks and mend the sails. During the early hours of October 12, two of the gunboats were abandoned in the course of the retreat southward. In a letter to Major General Schuyler, Arnold reported "two gondolas sunk at Schuyler's Island," and De Angelis was told that "one of our G[o]nd[o]l[a]s was taking [water] and the other sunk."[73] Abandoned or partially scuttled by the Americans, the gunboat *New Jersey* was recorded as "taken" by the British on October 12.[74] Ensign John Enys wrote that "a party of Canadians found a Gondola Named the Jersey on the opposite Side [from the eastern shore] of the lake."[75] The second gunboat, Captain Philip Ulmer's *Spitfire*, was "quitted...& sunk" in deep water.[76] Arnold wrote to Major General Gates from Schuyler Island requesting a dozen bateaux to tow the vessels back to Crown Point in the event of southerly winds. The vessels came to anchor at Schuyler Island at markedly different times. The journal entry of Bayze Wells, aboard the *Providence*, "Arivd to Sch[uy]lers Isleland and Came too the wind being hard against us," was made during the night of October 11-12.[77] Arnold's letter to Philip Schuyler on October 15 stated that the fleet only remained at Schuyler Island long enough to stop leaks and mend sails on the *Washington* when "at two o'clock, P.M., the 12th, weighed anchor with a fresh breeze to the southward."[78] Waterbury's account written on October 24 (and a later version on Feb. 26, 1777) suggested that the *Washington* was still under sail north of Schuyler Island on the morning of October 12: "The wind being against us, and my vessel so torn to pieces that it was almost impossible to keep her above water. . . I was obliged to come to anchor at twelve o'clock, to mend my sails. When we had completed that, we made sail, just at evening."[79]

By contrast, the galley *Trumbull* on the morning of October 12 had proceeded as far as Four Brothers Islands. On October 12 Colonel Edward Wiggesworth, third in command, noted "up with Schu[yl]ers Island. At 10 came to anchor under Ligonier Point to wait for the fleet & stop our leak & sew our M[ai]n Mast, which was shot in two."[80] The *Trumbull* remained anchored at Ligonier Point for repairs until "half after one at Night...whereupon we got under way and Beat down the Rest of the Night."[81]

The weary, half-starved American crews battled strong southerly headwinds on the evening of October 12. Whitecaps slapped against the bows of the leaking vessels and the crews shivered in the cold wind while futilely pulling on their long sweeps all through the night. The British, meanwhile, had renewed their pursuit of the Americans during the evening of the 12th. As the wind moderated, Arnold's fleet made some progress: "at six o'clock next morning we were about off Willsborough. . . The enemy's fleet were very little way above Schuyler's Island."[82] At the same time, Captain Thomas Pringle aboard the *Maria* "saw eleven sail of their fleet" on the morning of October 13.[83] The chase began in earnest after the early sightings. With the wind from the north on October 13, the ship *Inflexible* and schooners *Carleton* and *Maria* made better headway on the lake than the shattered, leaky American gondolas and galleys. The British gunboats and other vessels trailed the three lead vessels southward in a piecemeal fashion. The *Trumbull*, *Revenge*, *Enterprise*, and *New York* were well ahead of the two galleys, *Congress* and *Washington*, and the four American gondolas as the three British ships closed in. The crew of the hospital sloop *Enterprise* "manned all our oars with three men to an oar and the generals boat Came up and ordered us to make all the Speed we could to ty [Ticonderoga]."[84] Although British sources reported that the cutter *Lee* had been "Run into a Bay," and abandoned by her crew, an American "Return of the fleet" dated October 22, 1776, noted that the cutter had been left at the "Onion [Winooski] River."[85] The vessels still with

Engagement on Lake Champlain on October 13, 1776. Engraving printed
in London for Robert Sayer and Jno. Bennett on December 22, 1776.
(Special Collections, Bailey/Howe Memorial Library, University of Vermont)

Arnold desperately tried to escape the British, but "by the time we had reached Split-Rock,
were alongside of us."[86] Just before Split Rock, Waterbury asked permission from Arnold
to run his vessel onshore and blow it up, but Arnold refused, instructing Waterbury "to
push forward to Split Rock, where he would draw the fleet in a line, and engage them
again"; but when Waterbury reached Split Rock, he found the other vessels still fleeing
"and left me in the rear, to fall into enemy's hands."[87] Arnold had sent orders via his yawl
at nine o'clock for Wigglesworth "to lie by for the fleet, which I did, by stretching across
the Lake."[88] De Angelis recalled that "we received orders from General Arnold to heave
to and engage the British," but the vessels with Wigglesworth were apparently too far
away from Arnold to regroup effectively.[89]

The *Inflexible*, *Carleton*, and *Maria* immediately poured deadly broadsides into the
two American galleys.* Although Captain Pringle aboard the *Maria* noted "the action
began at twelve o'clock, and lasted two hours," Colonel Wigglesworth recorded "at 10
A.M., the enemy began to fire upon the two galleys in the Rear" and both Pascal De
Angelis and Jahiel Stewart suggested that about nine o'clock the action began.[91] Thirty
miles away at Ticonderoga, Persifer Frazer reported that "the greater part of the forenoon
we heard distinctly at this place an almost continual cannonading which ceased about 3
O'Clock."[92]

As the three British vessels surrounded the *Washington*, about "five Mil[e]s Belo[w]
Split Rock," the men left their oars "and after four or five shot the Washington galley
str[uc]k without firing one gun."[93] At this point Colonel Wigglesworth, as third in
command, with three other vessels nearby, "thought it my Duty to make sail & endeavour
to save the Trumbull galley if possible," subsequently double-manning the oars, and
throwing the ballast overboard to escape the British fleet.[94] Arnold on the *Congress*,
following the eastern shore, faced the full brunt of the large enemy warships as their fiery

---

* While there is no apparent historical evidence that any part of the engagement began north of Split Rock, cannonballs
discovered on the beach in Whallons Bay and Essex indicate that some action occurred in this area.[90] The cannonballs,
however, may be related to a raid by a British flotilla under Daniel Pring in May 1814.

Above: Galley *Congress* under attack by British vessels at Ferris Bay (later Arnold's Bay), *Inflexible* in foreground. *Top:* Galley *Congress* approaching Ferris Bay. *Facing page:* American vessels burning at Ferris Bay, British schooners *Carleton* and *Maria* in foreground. Paintings by Ernest Haas.

blasts pounded the already devastated galley. The rigging and sails were torn to pieces, and the first lieutenant and three others were killed in the cannon duel. Two vessels at the stern of the *Congress* and one alongside poured round after round of grapeshot and solid cannonballs into the striken vessel. On an open deck, Arnold directed his return cannon fire on the British vessels. The battle was a running engagement under a northerly wind during which the vessels sailed approximately nine miles from Split Rock to present-day Panton, Vermont.

With no hope for escape, Arnold ran the *Congress* and four gondolas (the *Boston, Connecticut, New Haven,* and *Providence*) into a shallow bay, named for homesteader Peter Ferris, and beached the vessels on the northeastern shore: "I set her [*Congress*] on fire with four gondolas."[95] As the vessels were ignited, Arnold "ordered the colours not to be struck; and as they grounded, the marines were directed to jump overboard, with their arms and accoutrements, to ascend a bank about twenty-five feet elevation, and form a line for the defense of their vessels and flags against the enemy, Arnold being the last man who debarked."[96] The British fleet, which included seven vessels at that point, continued a cannonade from a distance. The house of Peter Ferris on the southeastern bank of the bay (which from that day has been known as Arnold's Bay) was struck by several cannonballs and grapeshot.

After observing the burning and explosion of the galley *Congress* from the deck of the *Maria*, Dr. Robert Knox noted that Arnold "remained on the beach till he set fire to them [vessels], burning the wounded and sick in them."[97] The story quickly circulated among other British officers and men as Major General Riedesel soon noted "a dreadful report was current, viz: that General Arnold. . . had also burned about thirty sick and wounded men who were on board."[98] Using Riedesel's journal, Max Von Eelking later embellished the story of the wounded, "their cries being heard above the crackling on the flames and the noise of the guns."[99] Among the American eyewitnesses to the events in the bay was fourteen-year-old Squire Ferris, son of Peter Ferris. Interviewed years later, Ferris told of only one wounded man accidentally left on the *Congress*.[100] Lieutenant Goldsmith, severely wounded by grapeshot, was lying helpless on the deck, according to Ferris. Arnold ordered Goldsmith removed, but the gunner set fire to the galley, ignoring the wounded officer's pleas: "He remained on deck at the explosion, and his body was seen

when blown into the air. . . . To the credit of Arnold, he showed the greatest feeling upon the subject and threatened to run the gunner through on the spot."[101] From a distance, viewing a body blown into the air, Dr. Knox concluded that Arnold had consciously burned the wounded with the vessels.

Peter Ferris and his family accompanied Arnold and his men through the woods along the eastern shore of Lake Champlain, only two hours ahead of the Indians dispatched by the British. The British destroyed the Ferris farm and shot all the cattle, horses, and hogs. "We trav[e]l[e]d by Land as far as against Putn[a]m Point," wrote Bayze Wells "and th[e]re met boats which took us on board we Ar[r]iv[e]d to Ticonderoga about Sun Set" on October 14.[102] After briefly stopping at Crown Point, Arnold had reached Ticonderoga at four o'clock in the morning on October 14 "exceedingly fatigued and unwell, having been without sleep or refreshment for near three days."[103]

Colonel Jeduthan Baldwin, the chief engineer at Ticonderoga, on October 13 recorded that"about 3 o'Clock our Schooner [*Liberty*] came in Sight, Soon after a Sloop [*Enterprise*] & then another Schooner [*Revenge*], & then the Row Galley [*Trumbull*] & after a gundalow [*New York*], & they were followed by the Inhabitants from Crown point & from Panton."[104] The *Liberty*, on its way back to the fleet, had promptly turned about and joined the urgent flight southward with the other four vessels. As early as eleven-thirty in the morning on October 13, Colonel Thomas Hartley's message to Major General Gates stated "I am told two sails are just in sight."[105] When the defeat of the Americans was known and the advance of the British imminent, Hartley's regiment at Crown Point burned the buildings and evacuated to Ticonderoga.

The British anchored in sight of Crown Point on October 13. Pringle's handling of the fleet on October 13 was later criticized by the commanders of the *Inflexible*, *Maria*, and *Loyal Convert*, who contended that by ordering the fleet to try to prevent the burning of the American vessels at Panton, which had already been set ablaze, "the Galley, the Schooner, and the Gondola that escaped, must inevitably have been taken, or shared the same fate."[106] The following morning the British rangers and Indians landed and took possession of Crown Point. In the meantime, Carleton, while having doubts about pursuing the campaign further that year, dispatched orders to the British army at their camps at Point au Fer on Lake Champlain and at the Richelieu River to embark immediately for Crown Point. Not all of the troops embarked for Crown Point, however. German regiments at Isle-aux-Noix journeyed only as far as Point au Fer, and other British units never left Canada due to a shortage of bateaux.[107] Lieutenant General John Burgoyne was the first to depart with his troops from Point au Fer, but not before his adjutant rallied the troops by "waving the enemies colors, thirteen stripes, [and] declared the day was all our own."[108] The flag, probably taken from the galley *Washington*, had 13 stripes with a union jack in the left hand corner (the 13 stars came in 1777).

Before Carleton set foot on Crown Point, he released Brigadier General David Waterbury and 106 prisoners at ten o'clock in the morning on October 14. Carleton, who appeared reserved to some of his own officers, was magnanimous and friendly to the American prisoners, treating the wounded with as much concern as the British, entertaining the prisoners with "grog" aboard the *Maria*, and praising their bravery. Whether Carleton was attempting to win over the Americans with his magnanimity or his actions were genuine remains uncertain. In a letter to Burgoyne, Carleton suggested that because the victory "was obtained over the kings subjects...we should suppress all signs of triumph on the occa[s]ion."[109] The prisoners, under a flag of truce, were brought to Ticonderoga and paroled with the promise that they would not take up arms again in the war. Colonel John Trumbull, deputy adjutant general to Gates, received the prisoners but quickly recognized Carleton's shrewd psychology. When the parolees related the "kindness" of their treatment, Trumbull ordered the men confined to the boats and advised Gates of the "danger" in permitting the men to speak to the troops at Ticonderoga: "accordingly they were ordered to proceed immediately to Skenesborough, on their way home, and they went forward that night, without being permitted to land."[110] The following day "Capt. Rew [Benjamin Rue from the *Philadelphia*] came in through the woods with 16 men, they left Genl. Waterbury Just before he Struck. went into a battoe & went on Shore."[111] Ironically, the prisoners had an easier time than the crew that escaped through the rugged mountainside.

On board the *Maria* on the 14th, Carleton wrote the British secretary of state for the American colonies, Lord George Germain, summarizing the lake battles, listing the American vessels, and concluding that "the season is so far advanced that I cannot yet pretend to inform your Lordship whether any thing further can be done this year."[112] Carleton's list included the names of the gunboat *Jersey* and the cutter *Lee*.[113] Undoubtedly, the British learned the names, with some errors, from the prisoners from the *Washington* (and the *Royal Savage*) before their release. The loss of most of the fleet, while a disappointment, did not unnerve Gates, who had the highest praise for Arnold's handling of the fleet. "It has pleased Providence to preserve General Arnold. Few men ever met with so many hairbreadth escapes in so short a space of time."[114]

The Americans at Fort Ticonderoga and Mount Independence began strengthening their fortifications in anticipation of a British attack. Most of the American artillery was mounted in redoubts (small forts) on the Ticonderoga peninsula and in batteries on Mount Independence. Second Lieutenant Ebenezer Elmer of the Third New Jersey Regiment listed five redoubts (Jersey, Sandy, Oblong, Circular, and Stone), totaling 38 cannons, 14 pieces of artillery at the French lines (originally built in 1758), 33 cannons at the two Mount Independence batteries, but only three "in the old Fort [Ticonderoga]."[115] Philip Schuyler called up more militia to bolster the 9,000-10,000 men already at Ticonderoga, but George Washington advised against the reinforcement: "Instead of calling up a number of useless hands and mouths, (for such I deem Militia in general), I would advise a collection of as much provision as could possibly be got together," which would be sufficient to keep the British at bay until the weather forced their retreat.[116]

Between eleven and twelve o'clock on the evening of October 15, the edgy garrison was called to alarm "by 5 or 6 guns fired by the century [sentry]," recorded Dr. Lewis Beebe; "thro mistake the fire was at an ox, which was taken for one of the enemy, for not giving the Countersign when demanded."[117] Colonel Baldwin began supervision of a log boom across the lake on the 17th as rumors circulated that "Carleton said he would be in possession of Ticonderoga before Sunday & on his way to Albany where he was to have his Winter Quarters."[118] The men worked at a feverish pitch to complete the log boom across the lake by the 25th and began a floating foot bridge connecting Fort Ticonderoga to Mount Independence. Behind the boom was the remaining American fleet. The bridge was completed on October 29 and four barracks raised at Mount Independence in November.

On October 17 some of the British army that had departed from the upper reaches of Lake Champlain three days earlier arrived at Crown Point. Battling "great swells," the bateaux carrying other troops did not reach Crown Point until October 20. Only a small portion of the British army ever landed at Crown Point since there were not enough bateaux to bring them from St. Jean and Isle-aux-Noix. The British troops at Crown Point had erroneously estimated the American force at Ticonderoga to be as high as 20,000 men.[119]

By October 20 Carleton had made up his mind to return to Canada. Carleton's letter to Major General William Howe, who was fighting Washington's army in lower New

York, disclosed "I fear the want of time (the severe season approaching very fast) to put. . . Crown Point in a state to quarter troops . . .will force us back to Canada."[120] However, the decision was made several days earlier—the German regiments "received orders on Oct. 20 to move into winter quarters" when Lieutenant General Burgoyne returned to Point au Fer aboard the captured galley *Washington*.[121] Within days, Carleton began making proposals to use the navy on Lake Champlain for a renewed campaign in 1777, which would include building another ship the size of the *Inflexible*.

British troops remained at Crown Point and made one advance toward Ticonderoga. Carleton had hoped that the Americans would evacuate Ticonderoga, but that was never considered by the garrison. Strong southerly winds prevailed in October, hampering the British fleet from reaching Ticonderoga."Monday the 28th. . .in the morning our advanced boat made the signals that the enemy were approaching; alarm guns were fired from our different batteries & in a few minutes every person able to carry a musket was at his post," Persifer Frazer, of the Fourth Pennsylvania Regiment, wrote in a letter to his wife.[122] Three to five of the British gunboats, followed by 13-15 other vessels, appeared at Three Mile Point where a landing was made by the British troops. When one gunboat appeared within gunshot, the Jersey Redoubt, another battery to the east, and the galley *Trumbull* opened fire. The *Trumbull*'s fire hit the gunboat, killing one man and wounding another. Before long a rumor spread that 3,000 British troops had landed and were advancing on the American lines. The colors of the various regiments were mounted defiantly on top of the breastworks as a challenge to the British, wrote Frazier "to win them and wear them.—I never had greater satisfaction than to see the order with which our men were possessed."[123] By sunset, the British had retreated to Crown Point. The Americans believed their resolute appearance helped to dissuade the British from attacking. "The number of our troops under arms on that day (principally however militia) exceeded thirteen thousand," observed Colonel Trumbull: "Our appearance was indeed formidable, and the season so far advanced . . .that the enemy withdrew without making any attack."[124]

The British troops disembarked from Crown Point on November 1st and 2nd for their winter quarters in Canada. The British regiments that departed on November 2 were forced to anchor in a "creek" due to severe weather. Lieutenant William Digby recorded that "our soldiers called this place Destruction Bay, and not unaptly, as there we saw the great execution the enemy suffered from the fire of our fleet in the engagement on the 11th and 13th of October. Some of their dead were then floating on the brink of the water, just as the surf threw them; these were ordered to be directly buried."[125] Although the bay was an estimated 17 miles from Crown Point according to Digby, the inlet was probably Arnold's Bay.

By the evening of November 3, the first scouting reports reached Ticonderoga that the British had departed from Crown Point. The militia units at Ticonderoga were soon dismissed and most of the regular troops later sailed south on Lake George and the Hudson River with Major General Gates to join Washington's dwindling army, which had retreated to New Jersey in the face of reverses at the hands of General Howe.

Colonel Anthony Wayne, who marched with Brigadier General Thompson at the Three Rivers battle in Canada during June 1776, became commandant of Ticonderoga and Mount Independence for the winter. Wayne also supervised the remaining fleet from the Valcour engagement, which included the schooners *Liberty* and *Revenge*, sloop *Enterprise*, galley *Trumbull*, and the galley *Gates*, which was completed following the battle. One surviving gondola, unnamed in almost all contemporary accounts, was the *New York*. The vessels were still manned in early winter when Wayne recorded in his orderly book that 26 men were to "go on board the New York Gundalow" on January 1, 1777.[126]

The praise for Arnold's courage and dedication during the Valcour engagement came from many quarters, including recognition by the British for his skill and boldness under fire. Surgeon Julius Friedrich Wasmus of a German regiment remarked that "the American General Benedict Arnold has shown that he was equally able as admiral in command of a fleet."[127] Gates noted the "gallant behavior and steady good conduct of that excellent officer" in a letter to Governor Trumbull of Connecticut, ten days after the engagement.[128] But Arnold also had his detractors. Colonel William Maxwell, who had served at Ticonderoga with Abercromby in 1758 and in Canada at Three Rivers in 1776, referred to Arnold as "our evil genius to the north, [who] has, with a good deal of industry, got us clear of all our fine fleet" in a letter from Ticonderoga on October 20.[129] Richard Henry Lee, a member of the Continental Congress, wrote Thomas Jefferson criticizing Arnold as "fiery, hot, and impetuous, but without discretion" who failed to obtain proper intelligence and retire when faced with a superior force.[130]

Some historians argue that if Arnold had retreated to Crown Point with the fleet intact, the British would still have retired to Canada in 1776.[131] Any retreat on the open lake, once the British arrived, would have ended in a fiasco. Without the naval battle, Carleton could not have returned to Canada empty handed, not having engaged the Americans. The naval success was enough to allow Carleton to call off the northern invasion in 1776. Had the British taken and held Ticonderoga and Lake George in 1776, the fate of the United States, with a British base secured on Lake Champlain, might have been quite different in 1777. The delay at Valcour cost the British more than a week in a season of rapidly deteriorating weather. By the time Carleton had cleared the lake, sent for his troops at Point au Fer, and had them row to Crown Point, it was October 20. The fleet was expendable in Arnold's view, but he manipulated it with great proficiency before it was lost.

The real value of the Valcour navy lay in its mere existence, which delayed the British advance until it was too late. Major General Riedesel, in reflecting on the termination of the British campaign, mused that "If we could have begun our last expedition four weeks earlier, I am satisfied that everything would have ended this year."[132] The completion of the *Inflexible* alone took four weeks, and it was not finished until October. The year of delay that the Valcour fleet provided gave the Americans valuable time to organize a viable defense at Saratoga in 1777. That victory and French help turned the tide of the Revolution. As the famous naval historian Admiral Alfred T. Mahan so aptly concluded, "The little American navy on Champlain was wiped out; but never had any force, big or small, lived to better purpose or died more gloriously, for it had saved the Lake for that year."[133]

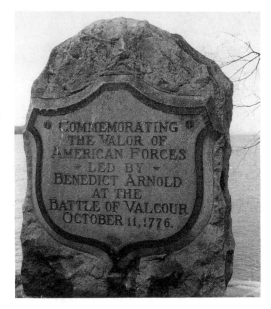

Monument overlooking Valcour Bay.
Photo by the author.

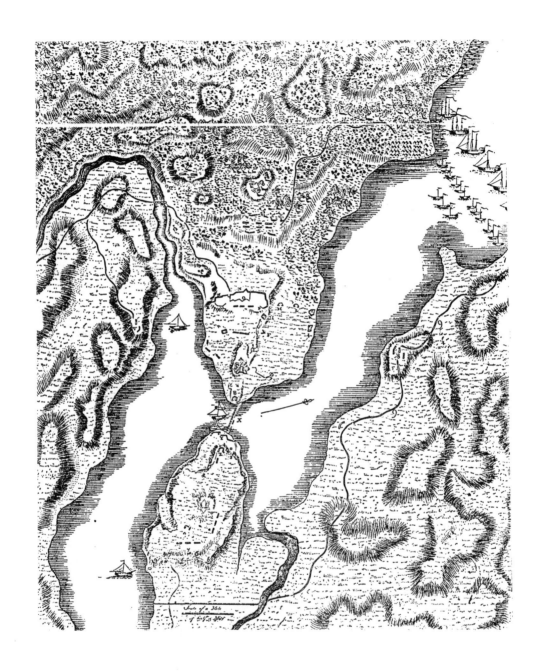

Map of American and British positions at Fort Ticonderoga
and Mount Independence in early July 1777.
(Collection of New-York Historical Society)

8. Invasion of the Lakes

In LATE 1776, as the two opposing northern armies settled into their winter quarters, plans were already being formulated for a new round of naval construction on the lakes. On December 28, 1776, Congress authorized "two large floating batteries" for Lake Champlain based upon Major General Philip Schuyler's recommendation to protect a proposed bridge and boom connecting Mount Independence and Fort Ticonderoga.[1] Carleton had already recommended that a new vessel, the size of the ship *Inflexible*, be added to the existing British fleet on Lake Champlain. The British felt compelled to enlarge their navy, especially after receiving a December 9 report which suggested "the rebels at Ticonderoga having put a 20 gun ship on the stocks . . .are making great preparations for another engagement on Lake Champlain next year."[2] The next month a British officer, who had been held prisoner and recently exchanged, erroneously suggested that the Americans at Ticonderoga "had laid the keels of 26 boats, large and small."[3] The Americans, however, did not build another major vessel at the lake in 1777; but the British would complete a new 96-foot, 26-gun ship named the *Royal George*.

The garrison at Fort Ticonderoga was in no condition during the unusually bitter winter months of 1777 to build a 20-gun ship. The undermanned garrison was ill-clothed and ill-fed. Colonel Joseph Wood, with his Pennsylvania battalion, related that one-third of the men were barefoot at Ticonderoga. Following a visit to the makeshift hospital, Wood found "one man laying dead at the door, the inside two more laying dead, two living lying between."[4]

By the end of 1776, George Washington's army had been pushed into New Jersey after military reversals in lower New York. Faced with expiring enlistments, Washington called on Congress for more reinforcements. When the prospects looked darkest for the patriot cause, Washington and his men boldly crossed the Delaware River from Pennsylvania and successfully attacked the Hessian troops at Trenton the day after Christmas. Marshaling over 7,000 troops before daybreak of January 2, Lieutenant General Charles Cornwallis (local rank in America) marched from Princeton to Trenton, hoping to trap the rebel army. The British army, delayed by mud and skirmishes along the way, took ten hours to reach Trenton. The Americans repulsed a limited British and Hessian attack late that day, causing the British to retire for the evening in anticipation of wiping out the ragtag army the following day. Washington, however, outwitted Cornwallis by slipping out of the American encampment in the middle of the night to attack the rest of the British force at Princeton. Following two badly-needed triumphs, the Continental Army marched to Morristown, New Jersey, for winter quarters.

In early 1777 orders to supplement the defenses at Mount Independence were issued by Major General Schuyler in anticipation of a renewed invasion of Lake Champlain during the summer. Schuyler's instructions on February 13 to Colonel Jeduthan Baldwin, the chief engineer, included "Cassoons to be sunk in the Water at small Distances from one another and joined together by Stringpieces, so as at the same time to serve for a Bridge between the Fortifications."[5] The caissons at Ticonderoga were constructed of heavy logs formed into cribs and filled with rocks. The log cribs, probably built one tier at a time, were carefully lowered into holes cut in the ice and guided to the lake bottom with long poles. After several courses of logs, a platform was placed across the square opening and rocks added, followed by more log tiers and a second platform of rocks close to the top of the structure.[6] By the end of March 1777, most of the caissons or cribs had been placed on the bottom. In all, 22 of these piers were constructed to support a 1,700-foot-long floating bridge and boom across the lake. The bridge, as described by James Thacher, a hospital surgeon's mate with the American army, consisted of floats between the piers "each about fifty feet long and twelve wide, strongly fastened together with iron chains and rivets."[7]

Anticipating the British route of invasion through Lake George as well as Champlain, the Americans made a commitment to build vessels on the smaller lake. As early as February 21, the New York Committee of Safety authorized shipwrights to be sent to Lake George to build vessels. On March 24 Schuyler sent Captain Jacobus Wynkoop, the controversial commodore of the 1776 American fleet before Arnold assumed command, to Fort George to "employ the Carpenters in constructing two strong Schooners of Sixty feet Keel & twenty feet Beam. . .besides three other vessels are to be built without Decks, These shou'd be so contrived as to Row fast and to carry a Cannon of twelve pounds...in the Bow, and as many on each side as possible."[8] A week earlier, Schuyler had ordered his deputy quarter master general to overhaul the existing schooner on Lake George.

Progress in building the new vessels, however, was very slow. To some extent, Schuyler's absence during the spring of 1777 caused a slowdown in organizing resources for the Northern Department. In late March, following a long smoldering controversy over the command of the Northern Army, Congress directed Major General Horatio Gates to proceed immediately "to Ticonderoga, and take command of the army there."[9] Engaged in dealings with Congress and on special assignment with the Pennsylvania forces, Schuyler was absent from New York from late March until the first of June. Following Schuyler's reinstatement as commander of the Northern Department, Gates departed from Albany (where he had remained since his appointment) rather than serve as Schuyler's deputy at Ticonderoga.

The British strategy of 1777 was quite similar to their aborted plans of the previous year. The British army with its German mercenaries was to invade through Lake Champlain under Lieutenant General John Burgoyne, nicknamed "Gentleman Johnny" for his flair and popularity. Governor Guy Carleton, the commander of the invasion force in 1776, was replaced in 1777 by the over-confident Burgoyne, who boasted that he would be back in England, victorious within a year. Lieutenant Colonel Barry St. Leger, with a local rank of brigadier general in America, was to advance with a force of 2,000 Indians, Tories, British regulars, and German troops from Oswego on Lake Ontario to the Mohawk Valley. Eventually St. Leger's forces, which were intended to provide a diversion from the main invasion through Lake Champlain, would join with Burgoyne's army in Albany. Ultimately, General William Howe's army, in possession of New York City, would move northward to unite with Burgoyne's forces.

The plan to advance northward to meet Burgoyne, however, was not made clear to Howe by Lord George Germain, the British secretary of state for the American colonies. The American plans for 1777 included blocking any British invasion at Fort Ticonderoga and Mount Independence. As early as January 30, 1777, Schuyler had written to George Washington recommending at least 10,000 men for Ticonderoga to blunt the expected British incursion through Lake Champlain. However, both Congress and Washington incorrectly believed that many of the troops in Canada were destined for Howe's campaign in the south. Consequently, Ticonderoga remained drastically undermanned during the spring and early summer of 1777.

The British army and naval fleet made their final assembly at St. Jean on the Richelieu River in June. At St. Jean new fortifications had been erected, the ship *Royal George* constructed, and the frames of gunboats from England assembled. The latter gunboats, however, were not completed in time to depart with the invasion force. On June 5 advance units and some of the Indians, under the command of Brigadier General Simon Fraser, departed from their Richelieu River bases and arrived at the Boquet River (north of today's Essex) on June 11. Four gunboats from the 1776 campaign accompanied the advanced corps to the Boquet camp. On June 15 Burgoyne, characteristic of his theatrical style, set forth from St. Jean amid a grand spectacle of booming cannons and bands playing. Governor Guy Carleton and other dignitaries watched as Burgoyne boarded the schooner *Maria* while the flotilla maneuvered to begin its long journey of anticipated triumph.

The British had amassed 7,390 men for the campaign.[10] Over 3,000 of the soldiers were German mercenaries

John Burgoyne. Painting by Sir Joshua Reynolds (1767). (Library of Congress)

under the command of Major General Friedrich Adolphus Riedesel, who had also headed the Hessian and Brunswick troops in 1776. It was common practice during the American Revolution for Britain to hire German troops. German princes profited from the arrangement while most of the troops, given the generous bounties and an eagerness for adventure in the New World, signed up voluntarily.

The British fleet on Lake Champlain in 1777, under the command of Captain Skeffington Lutwidge, consisted of the ships *Royal George* and *Inflexible*, the schooners *Carleton* and *Maria*, the radeau *Thunderer*, the gondola *Loyal Convert* (also called *Royal Convert*), and the captured American vessels from 1776: galley *Washington* (re-rigged as a brig), gondola *Jersey*, and cutter *Lee*. The *Thunderer* was rebuilt in 1777, for Surgeon Julius Friedrich Wasmus suggested that the radeau "has even grown taller by one story"; while another German eyewitness, Lieutenant August Wilhelm Du Roi, observed that the vessel was "fitted...with masts, sails, wheel and a cabin, like a ship."[11] The guns of the *Loyal Convert*, *Washington*, and *Lee* were removed just before embarkation to make room for other artillery, stores, and provisions. Twenty-four to 28 gunboats, 25 bateaux for each regiment, and a dozen sloop-rigged long boats were part of the flotilla. Other British vessels listed on "A General Return" at the end of 1778 may also have been on the lake in 1777.[12]

Thomas Anburey, a young lieutenant in the 29th Regiment of Foot, described the fleet as "one of the most pleasing spectacles I ever beheld. . [a] splendid regatta."[13] Burgoyne sailed with the fleet ahead of the main army which followed in the slower bateaux, rendezvousing with the troops at Cumberland Head. By June 20 the fleet had landed at the Boquet River, where Brigadier General Fraser with some of the advanced corps and Indians had made camp earlier. In an elaborate banquet at the camp, Burgoyne rallied his 400 Native American allies but implored them to spare women, children, and prisoners from their hatchets.[14] Burgoyne also issued a detailed proclamation which outlined the reasons for the invasion and encouraged loyal citizens to support his forces. The British army expected vital support from local inhabitants along the way, but the use of Indians actually galvanized resistance against the invaders.

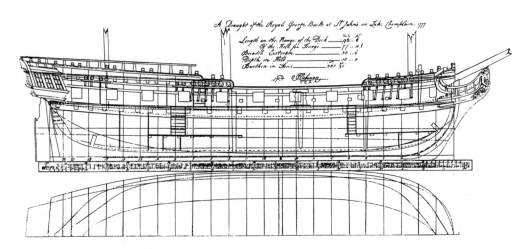

Admiralty drawing by P. Coleman of the 96-foot *Royal George*. The ship was constructed at St. Jean in 1777 for the invasion through Lake Champlain. (National Maritime Museum, Greenwich, England)

While Burgoyne celebrated with the Indians, Riedesel with the main army was forced to remain at Willsboro Bay due to violent weather. When his bateaux fleet made a second attempt to move south, an intense thunder and hail storm was followed "by a fog so dense that the drummers in the advance were obliged to beat their drums continually to keep the fleet together and indicate the course to be pursued."[15] After the fog, high winds and waves forced five of the boats onto Four Brothers Islands. Riedesel's troops stopped at the Boquet River and Button Bay before reaching Crown Point.

The small garrison at Ticonderoga was only vaguely aware of the massive force moving its way in June 1777. The command at Ticonderoga and Mount Independence on June 12 had been turned over to 40-year-old Major General Arthur St. Clair, a veteran of Amherst's campaign against Louisbourg and Wolfe's assault on Quebec during the French and Indian War. St. Clair had also served at the Three Rivers disaster in 1776 and the more recent actions at Trenton and Princeton. Less than a week into his command, he reported to Major General Schuyler that scouts observed enemy vessels above Split Rock. By the 24th, St. Clair related a sighting of "three vessels under sail beating up, one at anchor about one mile above Split Rock, and the Thunderer behind it" to Schuyler.[16] On June 20, 1777, there were "under 2,500 effectives" at the American fortifications, according to the "Council of General Officers."[17] (Nine hundred reinforcements would arrive in early July.)

During the spring of 1777, the fortifications were strengthened around Fort Ticonderoga and at Mount Independence, but the American naval fleet on Lake Champlain was not enlarged. The bridge and boom across the lake were substantially complete in

Major General Friedrich Riedesel and his troops were forced to remain in Willsboro Bay due to violent weather in 1777. Photo by the author.

Below: Watercolor of a British cutter and gunboat for Lake Champlain from journal of Simon Metcalfe, 1782.
(Fort Ticonderoga Museum)

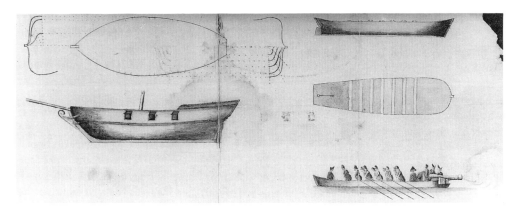

April, although subsequent ice and wind damage would later require major repairs. On May 5 chief engineer Jeduthan Baldwin "laid out the ground" for a 250-foot-long hospital on Mount Independence.[18] A week later Colonel Thaddeus Kosciuszko, a Polish military engineer, joined the ranks of Baldwin's engineering assistants. Nearly 20 acres of timber had been cut around Mount Independence to accommodate the picketed fort, gun batteries, huts, artificer's shops, lookout posts, and other structures at the camp. British and German troops were subsequently impressed by the entrenchments and the "octagonal, star-shaped palisaded fort, where there are cannon and about 8 barracks" and thought that a full siege would be required because of the abundance of heavy artillery.[19]

The Americans had also strengthened the entrenchments at the old French lines, held an outpost at Mount Hope overlooking the connection between the lakes, and maintained a blockhouse at the lower falls in Ticonderoga on the north side of the La Chute River. Since Fort Ticonderoga itself was in poor condition in 1777, many of the Americans were spread out along breastworks and redoubts outside the fort. The extent of the American fortifications was revealed to the British in June when a local settler, James MacIntosh, was taken by Brigadier General Fraser's men, and "from his intelligence, and some other sketches in my possession...a very distinct drawing of Ticonderoga, Mount Independence and the country round it" was provided to Burgoyne by Fraser.[20] (The British, however, had obtained intelligence regarding the American forts as early as March from Samuel Adams, taken prisoner by Captain Samuel Mackay, and from 20 American soldiers captured during an ambush at Sabbath Day Point by Mackay and his Indian party.[21])

The biggest addition to the American naval strength occurred at Lake George since the waterway was perceived as the obvious invasion route to Albany. Five large new vessels were to be built in the spring of 1777. The shipbuilding, however, which was to begin in March was considerably behind schedule. Major General Schuyler reported to Congress on June 25 that "one of the schooners at Lake George is launched: She is to carry fourteen guns. Another will be in the lake by the first of next month."[22] Although lumber had been cut for three row galleys, apparently none was completed. By early July Schuyler complained to George Washington that he did not have enough cannons, "not a sufficient number even for the two small schooners on Lake George."[23]

In late June and early July, the British forces began their advance toward Ticonderoga and Mount Independence. The British strategy was to flank the American forts on land while moving their artillery into key positions. A full frontal assault with their fleet would draw deadly fire from the American batteries. On June 18, even before the British appeared in force, St. Clair warned Schuyler that it would be dangerous to give up Ticonderoga or Mount Independence; "yet it is certain we cannot with our present numbers hold both."[24] His plan envisioned holding Ticonderoga as long as possible before retreating to Mount Independence. A week later, he again warned that there was no prospect of defending the forts unless the militia was called in.

On June 30 Brigadier General Fraser's corps of advance troops camped at Three Mile Point and the British fleet, including the larger vessels and gunboats, sailed into a line spanning the lake. At five o'clock the next morning, troops in two divisions, under Major Generals William Phillips and Friedrich Adolphus Riedesel, embarked from Crown Point in bateaux accompanied by the music of the different regiments. The corps under Phillips moved along the west side of the lake, while Riedesel's men pressed forward on the east shore. Despite the presence of the British fleet, St. Clair's letter to Schuyler on July 1 seemed to lack the urgency of the situation: "We have now two ships, eighteen gun boats, and three sloops, lying off the Three Mile Point, and they are forming a camp upon the point, and retrenching it. This does not look like their being strong."[25] From the British position, some of the armed vessels of the American fleet were observed behind the floating bridge. The vessels at the American outposts, all remnants of the 1776 fleet, included the galleys *Gates* and *Trumbull*, schooners *Liberty* and *Revenge*, sloop *Enterprise*, and gondola *New York*.

At noon on July 2 the American batteries opened fire on Fraser's advance troops, but without proper sighting, the artillery barrage had little effect. Riedesel, with Colonel Heinrich Breymann and the German advance corps, moved forward to occupy a position to the north of Mount Independence. The fire resulted in a number of casualties on both sides during that day and the next. Phillips' troops, which had advanced along the western shore, took Mount Hope (evacuated by the Americans), cutting off American communication with Lake George. By then the blockhouse and sawmill on the La Chute River had been abandoned. The cannonading along the lake continued as the radeau *Thunderer* was brought down to bombard the Americans. After the radeau proved too unwieldly to maneuver, her heavy guns were dismounted on July 4 to be used as siege artillery on land.

Fort Ticonderoga. Photo by the author.

Nine hundred militia reinforcements arrived at the American forts from the east before the British could intercept them. As the siege preparations continued on July 3, a 750-foot hill south of Fort Ticonderoga and across the Lake George outlet, called Sugar Hill (also Sugar Loaf Hill) or Mount Defiance, became the object of attention by the British. Captain James Henry Craig, accompanied by 40 soldiers of the light infantry, was dispatched to "reconnoiter this hill" and reported that it was a "very commanding ground."[26] The engineer, Lieutenant William Twiss, along with Brigadier General Fraser, surveyed the position the following day, reaffirming that the hill had "the entire command of the works and buildings both of Ticonderoga and Mount Independence."[27] Shortly thereafter, Major General Phillips directed 400 men to build a road to the summit and a battery of six cannons was expeditiously hauled to the top.[28] In his journal on July 5, James Thacher expressed "astonishment that we find the enemy have taken possession of an eminence called Sugar-loaf Hill" which he noted "is said ought long since to have been fortified by our army."[29] A year earlier, Colonel John Trumbull, deputy adjutant general to Gates, had recommended a battery for Mount Defiance and climbed the hill with Benedict Arnold and Anthony Wayne to prove that the summit was accessible. Likewise, in May 1777 Thaddeus Kosciuszko suggested that a cannon could be raised to the summit, but the idea again fell on deaf ears.

Until then, Major General St. Clair still harbored hopes of defending the American position, but when the British were observed building a battery on the summit of Mount Defiance, St. Clair quickly changed his mind. Turning to Colonel James Wilkinson, St. Clair remarked, "We must away from this, for our situation has become a desperate one."[30] At issue was the possibility that the battery could sever the line of retreat on the lake for the Americans in the face of the overwhelming British force.

"A View of the old French fort, Redoubts and Batteries at Ticonderoga on Lake Champlain and his Majesty's ship Inflexible" in 1777 from Mount Independence by Henry Rudyerd.
(Fort Ticonderoga Museum)

In the early evening of July 5, St. Clair called a council of war with his other generals. The council of war, consisting of St. Clair and Brigadier Generals Matthias Alexis Roche de Fermoy, Enoch Poor, John Patterson, and Colonel Pierce Long, unanimously decided to retreat "as soon as possible."[31] The orders to abandon, however, came piecemeal to the officers and troops. Major Ebenezer Stevens first heard the orders from St. Clair at seven o'clock, while Colonel Baldwin was told at nine o'clock that departure would be at two A.M.[32] But the orders to strike their tents and load baggage was not given to some of the regiments until midnight. Most of the men were asleep when the orders were issued. Confusion soon overtook the surprised troops as they grappled in the darkness with heavy equipment and supplies. To avoid detection by the British, St. Clair gave orders not to burn the buildings. At the same time, cannons from the Jersey battery were fired every seven minutes upon the British position to disguise the activity of several thousand men in retreat. The evacuation was aided by the fact that most of the large cannons and barrels of provisions had already been moved to Mount Independence in anticipation of making a stand there or retreating from that point. Many of the cannons that could not be loaded during the night of the retreat were spiked by the Americans. At one o'clock on the morning of July 6, one participant later testified that "I saw the General [St. Clair] again on Mount Independence, who begged that we would make all the dispatch possible, and carry off all that we could in boats by day light."[33] While St. Clair's initial reaction to the advance of the British seemed restrained, his aide, Major Isaac Budd Dunn, later indicated

"A View of Ticonderoga from a point on the Shore of Lake Champlain, 1777," by James Hunter which shows a British gunboat in the foreground and American vessels in the background. (National Archives of Canada)

Below: "Plan of Carillon or Ticonderoga. . .1777," showing Mount Independence, the floating bridge, and the fortified works at Fort Ticonderoga. (National Archives of Canada)

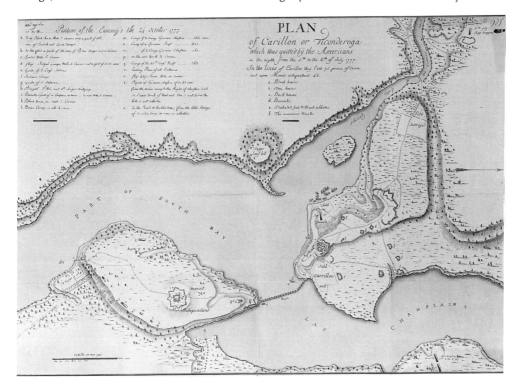

that "after they landed at Three Mile Point, . . . I do not believe he slept one hour in four and twenty, on an average, till the evacuation took place."[34]

James Thacher, who had been awakened at midnight, tried to load the sick and wounded (about 100 men) and hospital supplies into bateaux as quickly as possible. Only four wounded men who could not be moved safely were left behind. Against St. Clair's orders, Brigadier General Fermoy, a French volunteer at Mount Independence, burned his house there. The fire lit up the movement of the troops on the Mount and further lowered the spirits of the men. (Although Fermoy's house was "set on fire" during the night, several German officers also observed "in the afternoon...unusually heavy smoke on Mount Independence."[35])

At three o'clock in the morning most of those retreating by water departed. "Our fleet consisted of five armed gallies and two hundred batteaux and boats deeply laden with cannon, tents, provisions, invalids, and women," wrote James Thacher.[36] Six hundred troops, under Colonel Pierce Long of New Hampshire, accompanied the vessels on their voyage to Skenesborough. In contrast to the bewilderment of the departure, the trip was almost tranquil, according to Thacher: "The night was moon-light and pleasant, the sun burst forth in the morning with uncommon lustre, the day was fine, the water's surface serene and unruffled. . . . The drum and fife afforded us a favorite music; among the hospital stores we found many dozen bottles of choice wine, and, breaking off their necks, we cheered our hearts with the nectareous contents."[37]

The troops who remained at Mount Independence, preparing for their retreat on foot, however, did not have time to sample any wine. Led by St. Clair, the main body of troops, amounting to 2,500 men, retreated about an hour after the boats had departed, marching along the unfinished road through the wilderness to Castleton, Vermont, with the intention of rejoining the other American evacuees at Skenesborough. At sunrise, the last of the soldiers left Mount Independence. Open powder kegs in the picketed fort on Mount Independence and a trail of gunpowder were left outside to be touched off by four men after the retreat. Cannons, likewise, were to be touched off upon the advance of the British. The next day the British discovered the four men "dead drunk by a cask of Madeira" with the lighted matches close to the cannons.[38] Although the Americans tried to take as much as possible on their retreat, Major General Riedesel claimed that "Eighty large cannon, five thousand tons of flour, a great quantity of meat and provisions, fifteen thousand stand of arms, a large amount of ammunition, two hundred oxen, besides baggage and tents, were found in the camps of the enemy."[39]

Despite months of strenuous work, the floating bridge and boom were breached in a short time.[40] The British gunboats, commanded by Captain John Carter, passed promptly through the opening in the bridge followed by the ships *Royal George* and *Inflexible* a half-hour later. About an hour after the Americans arrived, the British gunboats entered the narrow channel of Skenesborough and "fired on us very Smartly...which occasioned great Confusion."[41] Some of the Americans were "posted in a stockaded fort and their armed gallies in the falls below."[42] "The well directed fire of [the British gunboats] obliged the crew[s] of two of their ships to quit them, 3 other vessels were burnt, and blown up."[43] A British list of the vessels taken and destroyed at Skenesborough included: "1.— Tru[m]bull Galley — Taken, 2—Liberty—schooner—loaden with Powder—Taken; 3—Revenge—[schooner]—loaden with Powder—Blown up;—4.—Gates Galley— Blown up; 5.—Enterprize Cutter—laden with provisions—Burnt."[44]

While most American and British journals report only five American vessels burned, blown up, or captured at Skenesborough, the gondola *New York* was also destroyed there. Lieutenant James Hadden noted that the Americans, upon the appearance of the British gunboats at Skenesborough, abandoned their vessels, "Five in Number, and one Skow with an Iron Howitzer, thus ended irresistible Naval Armament Built last year."[45] The latter vessel may have been the *New York*. Two days later surgeon Julius Friedrich Wasmus observed the remnants of the American evacuation at Skenesborough: "the enemy had burned a 2-masted ship [galley *Gates* or schooner *Revenge*] here; it had sunk but the masts could still be seen...Most of the more than 200 bateaux had been burned, a great deal of ammunition, provisions and other items had been thrown into the water."[46] At Skenesborough, the Americans fled under the attack of the British. Most ran through the woods to Fort Anne, "so closely pressed by the pursuing enemy, that we frequently heard calls from the rear to 'march on, the Indians are at our heels.'"[47] The desperate refugees ran most of the night, reaching Fort Anne at five o'clock in the morning. Some of the bateaux with the sick and wounded escaped by way of Wood Creek, but a good deal of the provisions, baggage, and cannons fell into the hands of the British.

Although bordering on panic and suffering from sweltering heat, the troops that departed from Mount Independence under St. Clair made good headway on their retreat toward Castleon. On the morning of July 6, Brigadier General Fraser with 850 light infantry and grenadiers, followed by Major General Riedesel's troops, began a pursuit of the retreating Americans. On the hot, sultry July day, the British marched swiftly before stopping late in the afternoon. By then Fraser had learned from stragglers of the slower rear guard of the Americans. While Fraser's troops were resting, Riedesel with his force of grenadiers had caught up to the advance corps. Fraser and Riedesel decided to march a few more miles toward the Americans and camp until early the next morning.

The rear guard, under Colonel Ebenezer Francis of the Massachusetts regiment, Colonel Seth Warner of a Continental regiment of Green Mountain Boys, along with Colonel Nathan Hale of the 2nd New Hampshire Regiment, was ordered by St. Clair to wait for the rearmost men and proceed to Castleton. The 1,000-man detachment camped six miles from Castleton in present-day East Hubbardton, Vermont. "At three in the morning our march was renewed," wrote Lieutenant Thomas Anbury with the British; "about five we came up with the enemy [2nd New Hampshire Regiment], who were busily employed in cooking their provisions."[48] The Americans rallied as Fraser's men pressed the attack on Francis' and Warner's regiments—"as hot a fire as ever was kept up," remarked Captain Enos Stone.[49] Fighting "bravely to the Last," Colonel Francis "drop'd on his face" dead, following a second wound.[50] Singing their national hymns, Riedesel's troops arrived after Fraser's initial attack and marched headlong into the brisk fire of 400 American musketmen. After nearly an hour and a half of fighting, the Americans realized that they were nearly surrounded and fled into the wilderness."After the action was over, a Colonel [Nathan Hale], with the remains of his regiment...came and surrendered himself prisoner," wrote Anburey.[51] The battle resulted in a substantial loss of life and more than 100 officers and soldiers wounded on each side and approximately 230 Americans taken prisoner.[52]

St. Clair's main force, rejoined by the remnants of the rear guard, proceeded on a circuitous route to Fort Edward, arriving there on July 12. Initially, St. Clair was to rendezvous with Colonel Long at Skenesborough, but Burgoyne's immediate attack there and the presence of British and German troops in eastern Vermont forced a long march, impeded by dwindling provisions, around the British positions. The British chased the American evacuees from Skenesborough to Fort Anne (about 11 miles below Skenesborough), where the Americans later counterattacked. Cognizant of a renewed British advance with fresh reinforcements, the Americans "left Fort Ann in flames...traveled without Stop[p]ing to Fort Edward 14 miles in a heavy rain."[53] Although the British could have remained at Fort Anne, they chose to return to Skenesborough.

The British failure to occupy Fort Anne allowed Philip Schuyler at Fort Edward to slow Burgoyne's advance by destroying the road connecting Skenesborough to Fort Edward. Schuyler first sent Brigadier General John Fellows with the Massachusetts militia followed by a larger force of Continental troops under Brigadier General John Nixon to break up bridges, divert streams, cut trees into the roads and creeks, and place obstructions to block the passage of Burgoyne's army. Captain Rufus Lincoln's diary suggested that Burgoyne "had 40 Bridges to Construct one of two mil[e]s in length, besides others to repair and Some Skirmi[sh]ing & firing on every Days march."[54] The failure to stop the Americans was the first error of many that led to Burgoyne's disaster at Saratoga. The retreat from Fort Anne by the British, with the concomitant failure to prevent the destruction of the corridor south, may have been the crucial blunder of the Burgoyne campaign. The route through Wood Creek cost the British valuable time—24 days to move less than 25 miles.

Why Burgoyne chose Wood Creek instead of Lake George for his passage to the Hudson River has been a question that has intrigued historians for years. Upon arrival at Skenesborough, Burgoyne settled into Philip Skene's grand house to ponder his strategy. Philip Skene, who had been exchanged as a prisoner of war from the Americans, returned for a short period to England before sailing to Quebec with his son. From there, Skene and his son joined Burgoyne at Crown Point. Skene, as a friend and advisor to Burgoyne, promised support and provisions from loyal families during the invasion. He was said to have convinced Burgoyne to make his way from Skenesborough to the Hudson River because Skene wanted a good road built that would enhance the value of his property (assuming the British would win the war).[55] Skene's interest in property values, ironically, might have changed the course of history. Burgoyne later defended his decision not to move back to Ticonderoga and the northern end of Lake George by suggesting that the action would have created the impression of "a retrograde motion" on the minds of enemies and friends.[56] Burgoyne also maintained that the Lake George route would delay his advance by requiring a siege of Fort George, and that employing vessels for "the transport of troops over Lake George" would slow the conveyance of "provisions, artillery, and ammunition."[57] Had Burgoyne gone back to Ticonderoga, it might have appeared that his army had given up the pursuit of a retreating army.

Burgoyne, however, decided to use Lake George to carry provisions, ammunition, and other military supplies to his advancing army. Once in control of Lake George, the British planned to rebuild the road from Fort George to Fort Edward to carry the provisions. On July 11 Burgoyne wrote to Carleton of his plans: "My present purpose, Sir, is to get a sufficient number of gun-boats upon the Lake George to scour that lake as expeditiously as possible, to support them with a proper force to attack Fort George."[58] On July 15, Major General Riedesel was ordered to Ticonderoga to supervise the transfer of vessels onto Lake George.

By late July Burgoyne had given directions to disarm all the larger vessels on Lake Champlain except the schooners *Maria* and *Carleton*, so that the fleet could be used to transport provisions for the army. Only four armed "Tenders" would patrol Lake Champlain and four gunboats assigned to protect Fort Ticonderoga. "For Lake George and Hudson's River. Fourteen Armed Gun Boats at 7 Men each [and] Four Armed Gun Boats with 6 Pounders to cruize in Lake George" were hauled from Lake Champlain to Lake George.[59] The time that it had taken to bring the gunboats to Lake George further delayed Burgoyne's advance southward.

Schuyler had ordered the commander at Fort George, Major Christopher Yates, to move the ammunition to Fort Edward and abandon Lake George if the British arrived in strength. Yates set fire to the fort on July 16 and marched with 700 men to Fort Edward.

In the days prior to the evacuation, the provisions, stores, and bateaux were removed to Fort Edward. The Americans at Fort George, noted Lieutenant Hadden on July 27, had "destroyed their Vessels (5 in number) including two on the Stocks."[60] Fort George, in Hadden's 1777 description, was "a small square Fort faced with Masonry and contains Barracks for about a hundred Men secured from Cannon Shot. . . The Rebels. . .blew up the Magazine on the side next [to] the Water, which demolish'd that Face."[61] Philip Schuyler described the fort as "an unfinished bastion of an intended fortification" with barracks that would hold only 30 to 50 men.[62]

Under the direction of Major General William Phillips, the British soon began building the road from Fort George to Fort Edward. Two companies of soldiers were assigned to Fort George and two more to Diamond Island with requisite gunboats for their defense. At Skenesborough Burgoyne had issued a proclamation to the inhabitants of the region to ally themselves with the British to save their property. Convinced of the dissension among the residents on the New Hampshire Grants, Burgoyne directed citizens, under threat of military action, to meet with Philip Skene, who would "communicate conditions upon which the person and property of the disobedient may yet be spared."[63] Only several hundred took the offer, contrary to Skene's more optimistic prediction, leaving the British without the support that they had anticipated. The death and scalping near Fort Edward on July 26 of young Jane McCrea, a local inhabitant betrothed to a Tory officer, at the hands of Burgoyne's Indians has long been thought to have coalesced opinion against the British. The impact of the event, however, has been minimized by modern researchers, although it is still subject to debate over two centuries later.[64]

Burgoyne finally advanced to Fort Edward by the end of July. Schuyler, meanwhile, continued retreating from posts but employed a scorched-earth policy to deny the British any provisions. Schuyler's forces, however, numbering 4,400 men on July 20, began to increase as time passed. New officers also arrived, including Major General Benedict Arnold on July 22. Nevertheless, Schuyler continued retreating, moving his headquarters between Moses Creek, to which St. Clair's army had retreated, and Saratoga at the end of July. In early August Schuyler moved his army further south to Stillwater.

On August 3 Burgoyne received the confounding news from General William Howe that his army would be in Pennsylvania rather than poised in New York to march north. After learning the news of the fall of Ticonderoga, Howe felt comfortable in departing with his armada southward. On August 16 Howe finally received instructions to cooperate with Burgoyne from Britain's American secretary, Lord George Germain, who was in charge of coordinating the military operations in America. According to one report, Germain was about to send a letter to Howe outlining the coordination of the two armies soon after approving Burgoyne's invasion plans but departed for a weekend in Sussex and forgot about the letter.[65] Subsequent letters to Howe also failed to spell out the strategy of support for Burgoyne until it was too late. The failure to communicate and coordinate the armies would prove deadly for Burgoyne's invasion force. Burgoyne, however, was less than forthright with his officers, informing Brigadier General Johann Friedrich Specht (local rank) that Howe's message, received on August 3, indicated that "we could be absolutely certain that not only was his army progressing in accordance with our wishes but that we would see a respectable corps of theirs join our army in a short time."[66]

Following the evacuation of Fort Ticonderoga and Mount Independence, there had been accusations of cowardice and treachery against St. Clair and Schuyler. James Wilkinson, an officer during the Ticonderoga retreat, found the daily rumors that the two generals were traitors to be without precedent. One outrageous rumor suggested that the two generals received "an immense treasure" from the British for their treachery when "silver balls, fired by Burgoyne into St. Clair's camp, and by his order [were] picked up and transmitted to Schuyler at Fort George."[67] The loss of Ticonderoga was a severe setback for the patriots, who considered the fortress akin to the Rock of Gibraltar. In retrospect, the retreat set the stage for the ultimate trap of Burgoyne's army. Congress acted within a month to change the commander of the Northern Department. After Washington declined to name a replacement for Schuyler, Congress voted on August 4 to replace the beleaguered general as head of the Northern Army with their earlier choice, Major General Horatio Gates.

Schuyler and St. Clair were court-martialed the following year for the loss of Ticonderoga. St. Clair, who had not received orders from Schuyler to evacuate Ticonderoga, was charged with neglect of duty, cowardice, and treachery. Officer after officer, however, testified that St. Clair was not a coward and had acted in a proper manner under the circumstances. The court unanimously found St. Clair not guilty with the highest honor. Similarly, Schuyler, charged with neglect of duty and incompetence, was unanimously found not guilty with the highest honor.[68]

Before Schuyler turned over his command, another battle in Vermont would add one more nail in the coffin of the British advance. In an attempt to obtain draught animals, cattle, horses, and carriages for the Brunswick dragoons, Lieutenant Colonel Friedrich Baum of the dragoons was to lead a combined force of 800 Germans, Canadians, Indians, Tories, and British regulars into Vermont. John Stark, a former ranger with Robert Rogers during the French and Indian War, had been commissioned a brigadier general of the New Hampshire militia and had raised 1,492 men and officers. Stark met Seth Warner and his Green Mountain Regiment of the Continental Army at Manchester, Vermont. In Manchester, Stark turned back a request by Major General Benjamin Lincoln of the Continental Army to take command of the New Hampshire and Vermont troops.

Instead, Stark marched his troops to Bennington, where he received intelligence from scouts that 200 Indians followed by 1,500 Germans and Tories had arrived at Cambridge, New York, about 14 miles northwest of Bennington. Stark immediately dispatched a message to Warner and his men to reinforce his New Hampshire militia at Bennington. The German dragoons, with their heavy boots, leather breeches, and unwieldy 12-pound swords, trudged toward Bennington, where they halted late on August 14. After receiving reports of the size of the American force, the dragoons entrenched themselves. Originally expecting easy pickings at Bennington, Baum now called for reinforcements from Burgoyne. Rain on August 15 delayed the battle and slowed reinforcements of approximately 600 men led by Lieutenant Colonel Heinrich Breymann. On the morning of the 16th, the Americans began their assault on the Germans entrenched on a sodded bluff. Baum first saw men in shirt sleeves moving forward, who the "provincial" (probably Philip Skene) advised "were all loyalists and would make common cause with him."[69] The engagement began shortly thereafter in earnest as Stark's men attacked Baum's position from two sides. Just before the battle, Stark addressed his yeoman farmers turned soldiers: "There are your enemies the red coats, and Tories—We must have them in half an hour, or my wife sleeps a widow this night."[70] The Americans dislodged the Germans and British after heavy fighting, including hand-to-hand combat on the hill occupied by the Germans.

Baum was fatally wounded, and the first engagement was over when at three o'clock in the afternoon, Colonel Breymann met Philip Skene two miles from the battle site. As the fatigued troops began to advance, they noted a force on a nearby hill. Skene assured Breymann that they were not rebels, but an immediate volley of muskets proved him wrong again. Fortunately for the Americans, Seth Warner's men arrived at about the

Battle of Bennington, August 16, 1777, engraving from a painting by Alonzo Chappel. (National Archives)

same time. After a renewed battle, Breymann was wounded and discovered five bullet holes through his clothing. The German drummers beat a call for a surrender meeting, but, unaware of its meaning, the American militia continued its fire. Finally, the remnants of the British and German army escaped into the woods in the darkness.

Stark reported 207 enemy killed in the battle and 750 taken prisoner with only 30 Americans killed and 40 wounded.[71] The Americans also seized muskets, ammunition wagons, swords, and four brass cannons. The cannons, originally captured from the French by Wolfe in 1759 at Quebec, were later used in the War of 1812. The Battle of Bennington was a memorable American victory. The best-trained European troops were defeated by rural militia who earlier had been scoffed at by British officers. The event was a milestone in the northern campaign and brought new confidence and recruits to the American cause. Tied together, the Tory prisoners were paraded through Bennington. Ironically, the funds to pay the militia were drawn from the proceeds of confiscated Tory property.

Another event would further strengthen the American position against Burgoyne's army. Barry St. Leger with his force of regulars, Tories, Hessians, and Indians (half of the total) had besieged Fort Stanwix (also called Fort Schuyler) at the head of navigation of the Mohawk River (present-day Rome, N.Y.) for three weeks in August. A relief force of militia under Brigadier General Nicholas Herkimer was turned back in the bloody Battle of Oriskany on August 6. In response, Schuyler called for a new relief force for the besieged garrison and Benedict Arnold volunteered for the command. Just before the Americans arrived at Fort Stanwix, a plan by one of Arnold's officers for releasing a prisoner (in one account, his brother remained as a hostage) to exaggerate the size of

Arnold's force among St. Leger's Indians was put into effect. At the time, St. Leger's army was within 150 yards of Fort Stanwix. Arnold force marched his troops the last 10 miles but before arriving received a message from the fort that St. Leger had begun retreating. Several days later, St. Leger's letter to Burgoyne attributed the departure of the Indians to reports of American reinforcements: "Arnold was advancing by rapid and forced marches, with 3000 men."[72] Whether the ruse had worked or the Indians were ready to abandon St. Leger, the result was the same. The second arm of the invasion from the north had been turned back. Now Burgoyne was alone in New York, deep in American territory with supply lines stretched to their limit.

On September 13 Burgoyne's army crossed the Hudson River and marched south along the western shore in present-day Schuylerville. On September 19 the two armies finally met in the first engagement of the Saratoga battles. Entrenched at Bemis Heights in Saratoga, the American army, commanded by Major General Horatio Gates, had now grown to 7,000 men. Bemis Heights, a rise of land named for a local tavern owner, had been selected earlier for fortification by Thaddeus Kosciuszko and Benedict Arnold. Burgoyne's forces advanced to the clearing of Freeman's Farm, about a mile north of Bemis Heights, on the morning of September 19. Gates initially planned to meet the British on the Heights, but Arnold vehemently argued for an immediate attack on the advancing British columns. The indecisive Gates finally acquiesced, dispatching riflemen and light infantry under Colonel Daniel Morgan and Major Henry Dearborn, both veterans of the Quebec assault in 1775. Arnold played a major role in the field direction of the ensuing battle. Although the Americans withdrew from the field at the end of the day, the victory was clearly theirs, with about half the casualties compared to the British. Arnold and Gates, who once had seen eye to eye at Ticonderoga in 1776, were now at odds over many issues. Arnold's arrogant demeanor, his alignment with former aides and friends of Philip Schuyler, and differences over strategy had worn an earlier friendly relationship thin.

As the first Battle of Saratoga was taking place, new engagements occurred at Lake Champlain and Lake George. Major General Benjamin Lincoln, who had over 2,000 militiamen at Pawlet, Vermont (south of Castleton), sent three detachments of 500 men each to Ticonderoga, Mount Independence, and Skenesborough. Lincoln's strategy was not designed to capture the posts, but to provide a diversion by moving on the rearward position of Burgoyne:"this menace would oblige him to make heavy detachments and secure the several points necessary to cover his rear."[73] Lincoln's letter to Gates on September 14 also makes clear that the primary goal was not to capture Ticonderoga, but "to divide and distract the enemy...to release the prisoners & destroy the stores there [at the northern Lake George landing]."[74] Thiry-three-year-old Lieutenant Colonel John Brown, who had accompanied Ethan Allen and Benedict Arnold on the 1775 capture of Ticonderoga, was assigned the Ticonderoga operation by Lincoln. (Brown remained one of Benedict Arnold's strongest antagonists. At one point in late 1776, Brown passed out handbills against Arnold on the streets of Albany with the prophetic words "Money is this man's God and to get enough of it he would sacrifice his country."[75])

The three-pronged raid began without a snag as Brown advanced through the forest near Lake Champlain. Colonel Samuel Johnson, who was to attack Mount Independence, used the wilderness road from the Castleton-Hubbardton area, and Colonel Benjamin Ruggles Woodbridge and the third detachment marched to Skenesborough. Woodbridge, who met no resistance at Skenesborough, was joined by Lincoln's main force before both parties returned to Pawlet, Vermont. After marching all night, Brown, along with Colonel Samuel Herrick of the Vermont Rangers, reached the Ticonderoga area at dawn on September 18. At Ticonderoga Brown faced the 26-year veteran, Brigadier General

Henry Watson Powell, with 1,000 British and German troops, many of whom were scattered at several outposts around the fort. In short order, Captain Ebenezer Allen with 40 Vermont Rangers climbed the summit of Mount Defiance and overwhelmed the garrison of an unfinished blockhouse. At the same time, Brown and Herrick surrounded a British encampment east of Lake George (south of the La Chute River), taking many prisoners. The seizure of the sawmills brought additional prisoners.

Captain Lemuel Roberts with some of the Vermont Rangers then captured the vessels and men at the outlet of Lake George before attacking a house on the eastern shore of the lake. A nearby barn was opened and 70 to 100 American prisoners, mostly from the Hubbardton battle who had been used by the British for work details, were released. The Americans also took possession of the old French lines and Mount Hope. Finally, the American raiders, equipped with one cannon, demanded from Lieutenant Simeon Lord of the 53rd Regiment the surrender of a blockhouse near the sawmills on the north side of the La Chute River. After Lord was allowed to observe the American forces from a hillside, he tearfully surrendered his garrison.

Brown demanded the surrender of Ticonderoga and Mount Independence, suggesting to Brigadier General Powell that "it will very soon be out of your power to stop the Mighty Army of the Continent surrounding you on every side."[76] Powell, however, regarded the demand as a bluff. In a letter to Carleton the next day, Powell related Brown's letter: "Mr. John Brown, who stiles himself Colonel Commandant summoned the Garrison to surrender...I...answer[ed], I should defend the Garrison to the last."[77] Powell, nevertheless, sought reinforcements.

When the day was over, Brown wrote to Lincoln that he had 293 prisoners and "150 batteaus below the falls in Lake Champlain 50 above the falls including 17 gun boats and an armed sloop."[78] The gunboats on Lake George, most of which had been used in the Battle of Valcour Island in 1776, had been carried from Lake Champlain in late July. The captured sloop had been "armed with three 6 Prs., because she was found unfit for the transport service for which she was ordered," John Starke of the schooner *Maria* noted.[79] Ironically, the "armed sloop [had been] stationed to defend the carrying-place," according to Burgoyne.[80]

Brown and his men began a cannon fire from the old French lines onto Fort Ticonderoga, which was returned promptly by the fort's garrison. The British vessels at the forts, the *Carleton, Maria,* and two gunboats were moved to a position north of the floating bridge to be out of range of the captured battery on Mount Defiance. After testing the defense at Mount Independence, Colonel Johnson's detachment of 500 men, supported by Brigadier General Jonathan Warner of the Massachusetts militia, never made a serious attack on the fort, although a surrender demand was sent to the garrison. Starke, aboard the *Maria,* noted that the "Mount was never attacked by the Rebels"; the only approach after September 18 was that of a stray cow during the night of September 21 which caused "a most thundering cannonade" from the fort and vessels which lasted until daybreak "when the lawless plunderer who had been so daring, was taken prisoner and carried into the garrison in triumph."[81]

The British fired from their vessels and batteries into the woods each night as a precaution against the Americans. Brown discharged some cannon shells into Fort Ticonderoga for four days; but with no chance that Mount Independence could be taken, and fearing reinforcements under Sir John Johnson, he decided to withdraw. About 100 German troops arrived from Canada on the 21st, followed by provision vessels and the *Loyal Convert* from Crown Point the next day, hastening the decision of the Americans to leave. The 300 or more British prisoners and their American guards were sent to Skenesborough. Prior to departure, Brown also "destroyed four Gunboats at this end [north] of Lake George, and two Gun Boats and some batteaux which lay about the bridge on this side of the Sawmill," according to Powell.[82] Brown's plans now called for an attack on the British post on Diamond Island in Lake George, a vital link to Burgoyne's army in Saratoga. Two companies of the 47th Regiment under Captain Thomas Aubrey were stationed on the island "for the security of the stores at the south end of Lake George," Burgoyne wrote later in his dispatches to Lord George Germain.[83] Late in the afternoon of September 22, Brown departed with 420 troops aboard "20 Sail of Boats three of which were Armed Viz one Small Sloop mounting 8 Guns & 2 British Gun Boats."[84]

The fleet, battling heavy winds, came to anchor with great difficulty at Sabbath Day Point that night. A sutler (merchant) on the voyage, who had been dealing with the British and had been captured with his small boat at the northern landing by the Americans, escaped before reaching Sabbath Day Point. Brown had ordered the sutler "Terry & his Associates on board the Gun boats," but another officer ordered them off the boat to follow at the stern of Colonel Herrick's gunboat.[85] Upset over the disappearance of the sutler, who might alert the island's garrison, the officers suspended their attack the next morning and made camp on an island six miles to the north of Diamond Island.[86] The sutler did warn the British garrison; Powell's contingent account recorded that 30 pounds, 10 shillings were later paid "To Terry. . .for informing Captain Aubrey of the rebels' intention to attack Diamond Island."[87]

Forewarned, the two companies under Captain Aubrey readied their cannons behind breastworks on the small island. The size of "Captain Aubrey's Detachment," Powell recorded, "on the Island and Fort George consisted of about two hundred men, half of them Germans."[88] At nine o'clock in the morning the sloop and gunboats advanced to cover an attempt to land troops in the 17 bateaux on the other side of the island. The booming cannons from the island batteries soon altered Brown's plans. For more than an hour, the armed ships and shore batteries kept up a heavy cannonade. The sloop, hit between "wind & Water," had to be towed off, and "one of the Gun Boats [was] so damaged I was obliged to quit her."[89] Two Americans were killed, two others mortally wounded, and several more wounded in the engagement.

Brown ran the flotilla into a bay on the eastern shore (probably Dunhams Bay) a "considerable distance and burnt them."[90] Thomas Wood with the Massachusetts militia later suggested that "our vessels moved down the outlet of Lake George into a bay, on the south side, where they were burnt."[91] . After burning the vessels, the Americans donned packs weighing as much as 97 pounds and marched off toward Skenesborough before the British had reached the eastern shore. Burgoyne later wrote that British gunboats from Diamond Island pursued the Americans to the east shore where "two of their principal vessels were retaken."[92] However, Lieutenant George Irwine, commander at Fort George, noted that only one gunboat was retaken.[93] Likewise, General Powell's letter to Carleton a few days after the engagement stated that the Americans "went into a Creek, not far from the Island*. . .brought from thence a Gun Boat, with a twelve pounder on board."[100]

---

* One lingering question regarding the battle concerns the location of the island and the bay where the vessels were burned. The small size of Diamond Island (erosion, however, accounts for some of its present size) makes it difficult to believe that it could hold two companies and supplies. Since the contemporary maps often did not label Diamond Island, and erroneous mileage estimates were typical of the eighteenth century, some modern writers have proposed that the British supply depot was on Dome Island and Brown's vessels were burned in Warner Bay rather than Dunhams Bay.[94] Major General Riedesel's 1777 journal noted, however, that Diamond Island was "seven miles from Fort George," while at the same time Lieutenant General Burgoyne stated that the island was "three miles distant from the land" and, in a subsequent letter, "at the lower end of Lake George"; this coincides with Brown's estimate that Diamond Island "lies within 5 Miles Fort George."[95] The name of Diamond Island had been known at least as far back as the French and Indian War. The island received its name from the quartz crystals that were once easily found

On October 7, two weeks after the action on Lake George, the British and American armies met for their final, decisive confrontation. As Burgoyne readied his attack on Bemis Heights, he still held out hope for reinforcements from Howe's second in command, Major General Henry Clinton, in New York City. Although Clinton moved northward on the Hudson River, capturing two forts, the diversion never helped Burgoyne's army, nor did Clinton try to reinforce Burgoyne. Clinton's message to Burgoyne, which disclosed that no reinforcements were to be expected, was intercepted on the lower Hudson River by the Americans. Upon capture, the messenger swallowed a small silver ball containing the message. The Americans gave the messenger a large dose of "tartar emetic," which brought forth the silver ball. Refusing to talk, the messenger was hanged.

By early October Burgoyne had fewer than 6,000 troops, but the Americans had massed more than double that force at Saratoga. Burgoyne's wait for Clinton's advance allowed American strength to grow steadily, nearly 1,000 a day toward the end. Given the size of the American force, Burgoyne was persuaded by his officers not to risk the entire army in an advance on its position. On the 7th Burgoyne led a large reconnaissance force composed of 1,500 regulars and 600 or more auxiliaries in three divisions toward Bemis Heights "to discover whether there were any possible means of forcing a passage."[101] Much as in the first battle on September 19, Colonel Daniel Morgan's riflemen and Major Henry Dearborn's light infantry were in the forefront of the action. While the bloody battle raged, Arnold remained idle, stripped of his command by Gates as a result of heated altercations with the commander of the Northern Army. When Arnold announced earlier that he would leave to join Washington's army, a petition was circulated among the general officers, including some previous antagonists, requesting Arnold to stay on. Arnold finally burst out of his quarters on the afternoon of October 7, mounted his chestnut horse and galloped into history. Gates ordered an aide, Major John Armstrong, to bring Arnold back to headquarters. Taking charge of three regiments, Arnold turned the engagement into a major battle by breaking through the British lines and assaulting one of the British redoubts. After being drawn to a standstill, Arnold daringly galloped to the American left, riding within feet of blazing muskets, to lead American troops against a redoubt manned by German soldiers. After Arnold charged into the redoubt on his horse, a musket ball smashed the same leg that had been hit during the Quebec assault.

The British were finally decisively beaten on the 7th, losing five times as many men as the Americans and all the cannons that had been taken into the battle. Brigadier General Simon Fraser and Sir Francis Clerke, Burgoyne's aide, were mortally wounded in the clash, while Colonel Heinrich Breymann was shot and killed by one of his own men after using his sword on four of his soldiers to keep them in the battle. Burgoyne survived the battle unscathed, despite shots passing through his hat and waistcoat. While credit for the American success deservingly goes to other American officers and men, Arnold's role was important to the outcome. Burgoyne, three weeks after the battle, credited his defeat to Arnold.[102]

---

there (especially on the east side). In 1758 Amos Richardson, a soldier from Massachusetts, "went to Looking [for] Dimons in the Lake" while stationed on Diamond Island, which he indicated was located in the vicinity of Long Island.[96] Captain Alexander Monypenny's Orderly Book in the same year specifically mentions troops stationed on "the first island down the Lake."[97] The crystals found off Diamond Island were described in 1819 as "six-sided prism[s]" which "are hardly surpassed by any in the world for transparency and perfection of form."[98] While nineteenth- and early twentieth-century writers agreed on Diamond Island as the location, there was a diversity of opinion regarding the bay where Brown abandoned his boats. One late nineteenth-century account suggested that "the remains of old boats may be seen in the water here [Dunhams Bay], which, it has been conjectured, were those of the plucky Brown"; but another described Warner Bay "where the remains of these boats [Brown's] have been dug up from the shallow water near the shore."[99]

On October 8 Burgoyne's army began its futile retreat; the next day the sick and wounded of the British army fell into American hands. The British, in an attempt to retreat through Forts Edward and George, sent parties out to repair bridges on the northern route, but they were stopped by Americans who were in full control of the region. The American troops lined the east shore of the Hudson River and poured fire on the British troops in bateaux near the west shore. On the 13th, a council of war held by Burgoyne was unanimous in seeking "a capitulation upon honourable terms" with the American army.[103] With the uncertainty of Clinton's advance, Gates consented to the easier terms of a convention rather than capitulation by Burgoyne. Burgoyne delayed the final surrender after hearing an optimistic story from a Tory of a possible British advance by Major General John Vaughan under Clinton's command. However, Vaughan and his 1,700 troops never intended to join Burgoyne's forces and were satisfied raiding communities 50 miles south of Albany.

British surrender at Saratoga, October 17, 1777. Painting by John Trumbull.
(National Archives)

On October 17, as the American army assembled in "two lines, flags flying and fifes and drums shrilling 'Yankee Doodle,' while the enemy entered the meadow north of the Fishkill...to lay down their arms," the 13 articles of surrender were signed.[104] The British and German soldiers stacked their arms and passed by the American encampment. A German officer remarked that "not a man of them was regularly equipped. Each one had on clothes which he was accustomed to wear in the field, the tavern, the church, and in everyday life."[105] To the vanquished Germans, the Americans appeared erect, soldierly, and larger than life, or at least taller than Europeans.[106] The signed convention allowed free passage of the army back to Great Britain on condition of not serving again in North America. (Although Burgoyne returned to England in 1778, the troops of the "Convention Army" remained prisoners in America until the end of the war.) The surrender, by any standard, was a great victory, with the capture of seven generals, nearly 6,000 officers, men, and auxiliaries and a considerable amount of arms. After the occupation of Philadelphia by the British, the success in the north was met with jubilation by Washington's army. In France Benjamin Franklin was able to use the victory to obtain open support from the French for the American cause. The American army finally seemed to have turned the corner to eventual victory.

Several weeks after Burgoyne surrendered, Brigadier General Powell at Ticonderoga ordered the heavy supplies and most cannons loaded onto the British ships under Commodore Skeffington Lutwidge for shipment to St. Jean. Fort George and the breastworks on Diamond Island were burned and the facilities at the northern Lake George landing, La Chute River, and the "old French line...demolished and the cannon, which we could not take along, were broken and blasted during the last days."[107] Before daybreak on November 8 at Mount Independence and Ticonderoga, "all the newly built blockhouses, huts, barracks, magazines, etc. were set afire...because of some 50 powder barrels lit underneath, Fort Ticond. blew up high into the air."[108] The floating bridge connecting Fort Ticonderoga and Mount Independence was "cut down and burned."[109] Most troops departed for Canada aboard bateaux late in the afternoon on the 8th but were hampered by heavy snow on the first leg of the journey, reaching a small inlet south of Button Bay. Other troops, during their retreat to Canada, marched north on the west side of Lake Champlain with cattle and some supplies. Captain Ebenezer Allen and 50 Vermont Rangers followed Powell's withdrawal as far as the Boquet River, where the Americans captured cattle, supplies, and 59 men.

The lake valleys in the next several years did not return to peaceful solitude as a series of large-scale raids by the British penetrated the interior of New York and Vermont. During this period, the British fleet sailed Lake Champlain freely under the command of Captains William Chambers and John Schank. Although the radeau *Thunderer* had sunk in late 1777, most of the fleet survived to the end of the war. In 1778 a formidable British fleet included the *Royal George, Inflexible, Maria, Carleton, Washington, Lee, Loyal Convert, Jersey, Trumbull*, and *Liberty*. "A General Return of His Majesty's Arm'd Vessels on Lake Champlain" at the end of 1778 by Captain Schank also listed six 30-foot, sloop-rigged tenders: the *Spitfire, Spy, Lookout, Dispatch, Dilligence*, and *Nautilus*, each armed with a few small cannons and swivel guns; five hoy-rigged (fore- and aft-rigged sloops) "Victuallers" or unarmed supply vessels included the 65-foot *Camel*, 56-foot *Commissary*, 42-foot *Ration*, 53-foot *Receipt*, and the 53-foot *Delivery*.[110] In addition, Schank recorded 12 gunboats, 16 long boats "From 20 to 30 feet long," 16 cutters "From 24 foot 5 Inch to 20 long," and two rowing barges with 10 oars and 12 oars.[111]

Following British raids into Vermont in March and July 1778, the British heeded reports from a spy in Saratoga that large amounts of supplies moving between Fort Edward and Saratoga were an indication of an impending invasion of Canada. Although the Americans had formulated plans to invade Canada with Lafayette as commander, the idea had been dropped. After hearing reports of invasion plans, the new governor and commander of the army in Canada, General Frederick Haldimand, was ready with a pre-emptive strike into the Champlain Valley. On October 24, 1778, Major Christopher Carleton, nephew of Sir Guy Carleton, departed from Isle-aux-Noix with 354 British and German troops and 100 Indians aboard a small fleet of vessels (schooners *Carleton* and *Maria*, cutter *Lee*, at least two gunboats, and bateaux) with orders "to destroy all the supplies, provisions, and animals which the rebels may have assembled on the shores of Lake Champlain, to take prisoner all the inhabitants. . .to destroy all the boats. . .sawmills and grist mills."[112]

Carleton, who had led Indians during the Valcour engagement in 1776, sent his raiders deep into Vermont, penetrating as far east as Middlebury. In three weeks Carleton's troops assaulted and burned settlements along the bays, creeks, and shores of Lake Champlain. The total destruction included 47 houses, 48 barns, 103 stacks of wheat and hay, a blockhouse, sawmill, and gristmill. A large number of horses and hogs were killed and 100 head of cattle either killed or driven to Canada. Forty prisoners from both sides of the lake were taken aboard the ships to St. Jean and later imprisoned in Quebec.

Peter Ferris and his son Squire had their house on Arnold's Bay burned, the third time that the family had property destroyed by the British. Several times the two Vermonters had helped the patriots, including Arnold's crews in 1776, and had also entertained the commissioners to Canada (Benjamin Franklin, among others) at their homestead. Captured while deer hunting below Crown Point, Ferris and his son spent several harrowing years in prison. In 1779 Ferris, then 54 years old, and his 15-year-old son escaped but were recaptured by Indians. After another escape attempt, the two were held in separate dungeons for 72 days. When allowed above ground again, they and others escaped by digging under a wall. Lost in the wilderness for much of their 19 days of freedom, both were retaken and were not exchanged until 1782.[113]

Following raids in 1779 and early 1780, the British launched their biggest expedition (since Burgoyne's 1777 invasion) in the fall of 1780 against military targets in the lake valleys. On the 28th of September 1780, Major Christopher Carleton with an army of nearly 1,000 regulars, Loyalists, and some Indians (most of whom joined Carleton several days later) embarked from St. Jean, Canada. At two o'clock on the morning of October 7, Carleton's fleet of eight vessels and 26 bateaux landed at Bulwagga Bay (between present-day Port Henry and Crown Point). There, Carleton dispatched 100 men (rangers, Loyalists, and Indians) under Captain John Munro to march overland to join a second advance from Niagara by Sir John Johnson, son of Sir William Johnson of the Battle of Lake George in 1755. Because of additional Indians, a separate party under Lieutenant Richard Houghton, a participant in the 1778 Vermont raids, was sent to the Onion River (present-day Winooski River). Houghton with his 300 Indians and Loyalists succeeded in burning Tunbridge, Randolph, and Royalton.[114]

Carleton pressed on with the main force aboard bateaux and at least one gunboat, landing at South Bay in the darkness early on October 8. One hundred men and two officers rowed the vessels back to Ticonderoga. From there 30 men were to portage two bateaux loaded with two artillery pieces into Lake George for use in a siege of Fort George. On the afternoon of the 8th, Carleton's army of 800 marched southward. The garrison at Fort Anne quickly surrendered; three officers and 72 privates were made prisoner. The Loyalists with Carleton were sent southward where they destroyed houses, barns, and mills in Kingsbury, Queensbury, Fort Edward, Fort Miller, and in the area east of Saratoga. Captain Munro's party, which had traveled by way of the Schroon River, similarly plundered and burned houses in Ballston.

By October 11 Carleton's army approached Fort George. After a report of "a small party of savages near Blo[o]dy Pond," Captain John Chipman, in command of Fort George, sent Captain Thomas Sill with 48 men to "make discoveries of them."[115] The detachment of Americans under Captain Sill was quickly surrounded and defeated in a brief but bloody engagement, in which 27 were killed and 8 captured; 13 escaped into the forest. Carleton offered Chipman, with only a handful of troops left and little ammunition, agreeable terms of capitulation, similar to those accepted by Fort Anne's garrison. With little choice, Chipman surrendered the fort. John Enys, a British officer who had witnessed the Valcour battle, described the walls of Fort George as "Stone with a thick earth parapet and good Bomb proofs for the Garrison," but the walls had been burned and were in bad shape and the well unusable for the "filth" dumped into it.[116] Carleton ordered his men "to raise all the Boats belonging to the place which were Sunk in several different places."[117]

The next morning, as the fort burned, the recovered bateaux were loaded with two captured cannons, supplies, and prisoners. Since there wasn't room in the boats for everyone, some of the party were forced to march along a crude trail on the west side of the lake called "Rogers's Road." On the morning of the 15th the party marched over "Roger's Rock, from the top of which we had a most beautyfull prospect of Lake George."[118] Shortly after the British departed from the southern end of Lake George, Austin Wells, a 39-year-old American militiaman, arrived at Fort George and discovered "twenty-two slaughtered and mangled men. All had their skulls knocked in, their throats cut and their scalps taken."[119] Recognizing the bodies of two friends, one militia officer "cried like a child."[120]

On October 24 Captain Munro returned from his Ballston raid and rejoined Carleton's fleet on the west shore north of Crown Point. Carleton's raid had taken two forts, burned six sawmills, a gristmill, 38 houses, 33 barns, and 1,500 tons of hay. As the fleet got under way on its voyage back to Canada on October 26, an express boat arrived with a message from General Frederick Haldimand with orders for Carleton to stay on the lake. The purpose was to cover Captain Justus Sherwood, a Loyalist spy sent with a flag of truce to Vermont. Sherwood's mission was related to negotiations between Ethan Allen and the British, supposedly over prisoner exchanges, but actually concerning secret dealings to have Vermont become a neutral state tied to British Canada.* With Congress's ear deaf to Vermont's plea for admission as a state, Allen, Governor Thomas Chittenden, and others were adamantly against Vermont land being split between New Hampshire and New York. Allen and his family, whose earlier controversial involvement over land with the Onion River Company was well known, still held large tracts of land in northern Vermont.

Major Carleton had written Brigadier General Henry W. Powell on October 17 that "I am this moment informed that the despatches forwarded by the Commander in Chief [Haldimand] to Brigadier Allen of the State of Vermont was obligded to be destroyed, the person who carried them being pursued."[121] Allen required a cessation of hostilities in Vermont and New York while negotiations were taking place. As a brigadier general of the Vermont militia, Allen dismissed his army in late October. New Yorkers' suspicions, however, were raised by the dealings. Governor George Clinton of New York wrote to George Washington that the Vermonters passed on no information when the British fleet sailed south on their way to raid New York; Philip Schuyler in a letter to Washington questioned whether Allen had turned traitor or was about to do so.[122]

Ethan Allen's brother, Ira, and Jonas Fay continued as the Vermont commissioners in 1781 during negotiations with the British which would make Vermont a Royal Province, neutral in the war and free to trade with Canada. General Haldimand, with the support of Lord Germain, was eager for the deal. The Vermont commissioners, however, stalled the agreement. In mid-October 1781, Haldimand sent Colonel Barry St. Leger with the British fleet and a force of 1,000 regulars and Loyalists to Ticonderoga as a show of presence to support the treaty. Philip Schuyler later wrote to George Washington that scouting reports on October 26 indicated that "The Enemy are refortifying Ticonderoga...they had already covered the largest barracks, and had about two hundred people employed in drawing materials for the repair of the Fort."[123] In an attempt to obtain a Vermonter as a messenger, St. Leger's men unwittingly shot a militia sergeant. A letter

---

* After his release from British captivity, Allen was appointed a brigadier general in the Vermont militia in 1779.

of apology, sent to Governor Chittenden by St. Leger, was opened by the courier, Simon Hathaway, who exposed its contents to everyone along the way. By the time Hathaway reached the Vermont Assembly, the citizens of the area were up in arms over the meaning of the letter.[124] At the same time news of the British surrender at Yorktown reached St. Leger at Ticonderoga; the army soon retreated to Canada without orders from Haldimand.

Ira Allen later contended that the truce with the British held off their armies, preventing bloodshed in Vermont. Supporters of the conspirators also argued that the ploy was successful in eventually bringing Vermont to statehood. But the duplicity during a period of the nation's greatest need raised questions that are still being debated. Nearly a year after Yorktown, Ethan Allen, intransigent in his views, wrote to General Haldimand that "I shall do anything in my power to render the State a British Province."[125]

The two years after Yorktown brought a semblance of tranquility to the lake valleys while military readiness continued as the peace treaty was finalized. During this period, George Washington established his headquarters at Newburgh on the Hudson River. With little to do, Washington embarked on inspection tours during 1782 and 1783. During late July 1783 Washington and his party moved north on Lake George in three bateaux, inspected Fort Ticonderoga and Crown Point, and returned south to the Mohawk River, where his inspection party traveled to Fort Stanwix (Schuyler). The

Ruins of Fort Ticonderoga by W. H. Bartlett.
(Author's collection)

peace treaty was finally signed in Paris on September 3, 1783. Although the British evacuated New York City several months later, they remained at their post at Point au Fer on Lake Champlain (south of Rouses Point, N.Y.) until June of 1796. Before the British departed from Lake Champlain, however, a fresh round of defensive structures was constructed in New York. In response to the continued British presence at Point au Fer and increased military tension between Great Britain and the United States during 1793-1794, the state of New York completed a chain of four small blockhouses located at Plattsburgh, Peru, Willsboro, and Whitehall. As a result of a political resolution of the issues, the blockhouses were never manned or equipped with weapons.[126]

After the peace treaty of 1783, the settlers returned to the lake valleys to reestablish their communities and lives. Fort Ticonderoga and Crown Point became accessible quarries for new settlers to the region seeking foundation stones. Furniture, floors, doors, and windows, were removed from Fort Ticonderoga and reinstalled in farm houses. Even abandoned cannons, most spiked and unusable, were melted down to be reused for their iron. The only objects from the turbulent years of the Revolution that remained untouched were those that had fallen to the bottom of the lakes.

Archaeological Discoveries

The search for the vessels from the American Revolution has been a history in itself, luring historians, divers, and the Lake Champlain citizenry into more than a century of tales about the sunken wrecks of Benedict Arnold's navy. All of the original 15 vessels that were present at the Valcour engagement (including two schooners, the *Revenge* and *Royal Savage*; one sloop, *Enterprise*; one cutter, *Lee*; three row galleys, the *Congress*, *Trumbull*, and *Washington*; and eight gondolas or gunboats, the *Boston*, *Connecticut*, *New Haven*, *New Jersey*, *New York*, *Philadelphia*, *Providence*, and *Spitfire*) eventually sank in Lake Champlain or the Richelieu River. Two other American vessels, the schooner *Liberty* and row galley *Gates*, were not present at the Valcour engagement, since the latter vessel was unfinished and the *Liberty* had sailed to Ticonderoga for provisions at the time of the battle. Both suffered the same fate as the rest of the fleet. The cold freshwater of the lake provides an ideal time capsule, because the teredo worms that would ordinarily destroy submerged wood in salt water are absent in freshwater. Additionally, the only damage to iron objects has been simple corrosion, rather than the more severe destruction of iron in salt water through electrolysis. However, some of the vessels were carelessly handled by salvagers and dismembered by souvenir hunters, which has resulted in nearly total destruction. Others were destroyed during canal construction and one lies intact at the bottom of the lake. Presently, both New York and Vermont have laws to prevent the removal of historically-significant artifacts from the lake. Unfortunately, the laws came too late to save some vessels that were recovered but subsequently burned or allowed to deteriorate. Only one of the 15 vessels of the fleet remains on display for the American public at the Smithsonian Institution.

About half of the fleet sank along the north-south path of the running battle of October 11-13, 1776. Valcour Island in the north to Schuyler Island and on to Arnold's Bay in Vermont have been the major search areas for the vessels. In 1777 several of the remaining vessels were scuttled at the very southern end of the lake at Whitehall. Corroborating information about specific events of the Valcour battle has been difficult because of a lack of detail in the few original American journals available and the insufficiency of direct observation of events recorded in many of the journals of British officers.

The flagship *Royal Savage*, the first vessel to sink in the battle after running aground on Valcour Island, had most of her guns salvaged by the British in November 1779. Until 1860 the schooner's hull remained undisturbed. At that time, the bow was pulled out of the water in an attempt to raise her, but she slipped back into deeper water.[127] In 1866 Peter Palmer in his *History of Lake Champlain* observed that "the hull of the schooner lies on the spot where she sunk, and her upper timbers can yet be seen during low water in the lake."[128] Local relic hunters soon stripped the exposed structure for souvenirs. In 1868 the *Plattsburgh Republican* reported that Captain George Conn anchored his vessel over the wreck and pulled up oak planking with a grappling iron. The oak pieces were later made into a cane, gavel, and rulers.[129] On June 20, 1901, a Chicago diver, J. G. Falcon, raised "three gun carriages and about thirty cannon balls and shot" from 30 feet of water at the site of the wreck.[130] In 1908 the *Glens Falls Daily Times* reported that the *Royal Savage* was to be raised for the Champlain Tercentenary (1909) for display in Plattsburgh. After retrieving a frame, silver spoons, cannonballs, and musket balls, a diver from Boston, hired by the Tercentenary Committee, related "that about forty-five feet of the hull is in a fair state of preservation and can be raised practically as it is."[131] Artifacts from the *Royal Savage* were displayed in the Hotel Champlain in Plattsburgh before their subsequent destruction by fire in 1910. During the early 1930s the *Royal Savage* could still be seen off the island. John Ferguson, as a teenager, searched for the wreck in 15-20 feet of water when he observed the vessel: "I realized that this was my chance to make history come alive, to grab a piece and hold it. I dove to the wreck several times grabbing anything within reach—wood, square nails, even grape shot that lay all around the hulk."[132] Working for the staff of the Fort Ticonderoga Museum, young hard-hat divers "recovered the remains of a rotted old gun carriage" near the site of the *Royal Savage* during the summer of 1933.[133]

In the early 1930s Lorenzo F. Hagglund, manager of the Under-Water Metal Cutting Company affiliated with the Merritt-Chapman and Scott Corporation, initiated an effort to locate and raise the *Royal Savage*. He had originally heard of the vessel's history when he was in Plattsburgh for officer training in preparation for overseas duty during World War I. Hagglund's interest was further kindled during the construction of the Crown Point bridge in 1929 when several of his divers recovered military relics, including a small cannon.[134] On September 9, 1929, Hagglund notified the director of the New York State Museum, Charles C. Adams, of his plans to organize "a small expedition to recover some Revolutionary relics" from Lake Champlain and requested cooperation from the museum.[135] In subsequent correspondence, Hagglund proposed raising the *Royal Savage* for the state museum, providing an estimate of his expenses ($495 to $1,000).[136] Without a commitment from the state, Hagglund finally began his search for the vessel during a vacation in the summer of 1932. Hagglund trudged along the bottom of the lake off Valcour Island with hard-hat diving gear without luck, although he discovered cannonballs, bar shot, grapeshot, and other artifacts from the wreck. On the last day of his vacation, he rowed further out on the lake and caught the dim outline of the wreck from the surface in less than 20 feet of water. The position of the wreck was 150 feet offshore, just outside of the area that he had covered with his diving gear. Shortly thereafter, he wrote to Adams, offering "to secure this for the museum."[137]

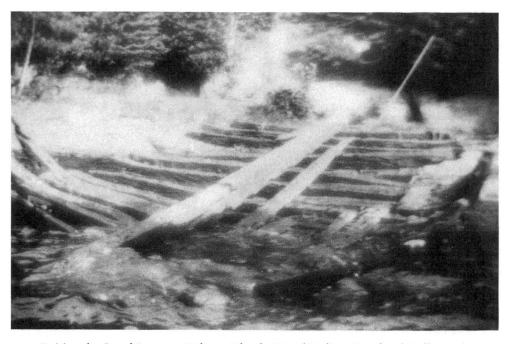

Raising the *Royal Savage* at Valcour Island, 1934. (Hudson Hagglund Collection)

In April 1934 Hagglund met with Adams at the museum and a week later wrote that "during this coming summer I plan to raise and condition the remains of this hull and collect as much Revolutionary [War] material as possible from the surrounding lake bottom. The proper place for this collection would be the New York State Museum and it is my idea to offer the material recovered to your museum as a loan exhibit and also give the museum the option to acquire the exhibit at any time upon payment of the cost of obtaining and preserving this material...less than $1,000."[138] After failing to gain any government backing, Hagglund returned in 1934 to salvage the vessel with his own resources. However, several weeks before Hagglund returned, another hard-hat diver, Lieutenant Horace Mazet of the United States Navy, explored the wreck of the *Royal Savage*: "Walking slowly toward her, we were able to see her full length, picking out some 14 ribs still standing. . .Whitened musket balls of lead gleamed dully against dark oak timbers, and we were soon finding groups of rust-welded grape-shot oxidized to planks. . .cannon balls, coated with thick encrustations of rust, a bar-shot."[139] Because of the continuing dismemberment of the wreck, Hagglund decided to salvage the *Royal Savage* in August 1934.[140] Using 20 drums, Hagglund raised the surviving wreckage, measuring approximately 35 feet with a beam of 15 feet, consisting of the keel, keelson, bottom planking, 13 frames, and over 100 individual artifacts. According to a 1935 article in the *U. S. Naval Institute Proceedings*, the wreck was dismantled and the timbers carefully marked and placed "aboard a box car and on their way to storage in the vicinity of New York City."[141] Unfortunately, the New York State Museum did not acquire the *Royal Savage* at this time because it "did not have sufficient space to exhibit such a piece" and had a "storage problem."[142] Hagglund apparently housed the wreck in several locations in New York State and subsequently stored it in a building north of Essex, New York. The relics were stored on Long Island, in Vermont, and in upstate New York. Hudson Hagglund, Lorenzo's son, consigned the wreck of the *Royal Savage* to a Gettysburg (Pa.) military antiques dealer, who sold the vessel for $42,500 in 1995 to the city of Harrisburg (Pa.) for display in a new city-owned museum (National Civil War Museum). At the time of this writing, some local interest had been generated for the return of the relic to the Champlain Valley for display.

Two decades after Hagglund had raised the vessel, Montreal divers found part of the vessel's 1,500- pound keel, a large anchor, and numerous cannonballs.[143] The anchor and a six-foot section of the stern, holding a pin and ring (gudgeon), were displayed at the David M. Stewart Museum on St. Helene's Island in Montreal before being permanently loaned to the National Canadian War Museum in Ottawa. In the 1960s more relics were recovered by area divers off Valcour Island. A summer 2000 archaeological survey of Valcour Bay, under the direction of the Lake Champlain Maritime Museum, was slated to continue in 2001 and involve the raising of three large cannon fragments.

In the summer of 1935 Lorenzo F. Hagglund returned to Valcour Island with a crew of volunteers, including J. Ruppert Schalk and his yacht *Linwood*, to search for the gondola *Philadelphia*. Schalk, an assistant secretary of the Jacob Ruppert Brewing Company and nephew of the owner, had earlier formed a "joint enterprise" with Hagglund to raise the *Philadelphia*.[144] Although Hagglund mentioned the *Philadelphia* in a letter to Director Adams of the New York State Museum in 1930, he was not candid about his plans in 1935, writing Adams on July 22 that he "hoped to find a few more items connected with the Royal Savage" during his vacation at Lake Champlain.[145] On August 1, using a sweep chain suspended from the *Linwood*, Hagglund and his crew discovered the *Philadelphia* intact, sitting upright mid-channel in Valcour Bay in 57 feet of water. Hagglund later described her position on the bottom of the lake: "We advance towards it, and it takes shape. It is the hull of a vessel. . . Now we are abreast of her mast. It is still

Gunboat *Philadelphia* recovered at Valcour Island in 1935.

Top row, left: Cannons on the recovery barge. (Special Collections, Benjamin F. Feinberg Library, State University of New York at Plattsburgh)

Right: Raising the gunboat. (Smithsonian Institution)

Middle row, left: At the Shelburne Shipyard. (Vermont Historical Society)

Right: Lorenzo F. Hagglund (with helmet) and crew on recovery barge at Valcour Island. (Vermont Historical Society)

Bottom row, left: On display at the Smithsonian Institution. (Smithsonian Institution)

Right: Being lifted into the new Museum of History and Technology at the Smithsonian Institution, 1962. (Vermont Historical Society)

standing upright."[146] Using a high-pressure jet, William Lilja, a 23-year veteran of commercial diving, "cut three holes through the sands beneath the 'Philadelphia'...[and ran] rope slings through each of the holes...and fastened to logs, extending crossways of the ship, across the gunwales, to act as spreaders."[147] On August 9 the wreck was brought to the surface with the aid of a derrick "as cheers resounded from the throats of passengers, in the 36 assorted pleasure craft" assembled in Valcour Bay.[148] The recovered wreck included one of the most significant collections of early colonial artifacts ever discovered. Cannons, shot, tools, anchors, pots, china cups, pewter spoons, buttons, shoes, a time glass, and even torn sails were retrieved—virtually everything aboard remained intact.

The *Philadelphia* was housed for the winter of 1936 at Shelburne Harbor, Vermont, with the intention of permanent exhibition on the campus of the University of Vermont. When Charles Adams learned of Vermont's request from Congress for an appropriation for a permanent building for the *Philadelphia*, he wrote to a UVM faculty member, stating that the vessel was the property of the New York State Museum: "It is hardly worthwhile to ask Congress to make an appropriation for something that does not belong to Vermont!"[149] Funds for a building to house the ship were not forthcoming. Hagglund offered the vessel to the U.S. Navy and the Smithsonian Institution, but both rejected the offer.[150] Hagglund then began a tour with the *Philadelphia* on a barge around Lake Champlain. In early December 1936 the *Philadelphia* arrived in Albany on an enclosed barge. After state officials viewed the exhibit, a committee concluded that the gunboat was "a most valuable historic relic...[which] should inspire tremendous interest in the Revolutionary War in young and old. It would be a most desirable exhibit for the New York State Museum."[151] Despite offers from many institutions to purchase the *Philadelphia*, in 1937 Hagglund was "not at all anxious to turn over these boats [*Philadelphia* and *Royal Savage*] to others unless he is compelled to do so by [a] lack of funds to continue their exhibition."[152] Although New York authorities resolved legal issues regarding ownership of submerged artifacts, they were never able to devise a plan to acquire Hagglund's vessels. In 1937 Hagglund towed the *Philadelphia* aboard her barge from Albany to West Point and during the summer displayed the vessel at the Crown Point State Park wharf. The gunboat was also exhibited each summer from 1938 to 1940 at Crown Point, then at Fort Ticonderoga in 1941, 1945-1947, and from 1948 until 1960 in a barn located on Route 22 between Essex and Willsboro. The *Philadelphia* was not shown from 1942 to 1944 because Hagglund, a captain in the army reserves, had returned to active duty, rising to the rank of lieutenant colonel. In 1961, following the death of Colonel Hagglund, the vessel was acquired by the Smithsonian Institution and four years later, after preservation, was placed on permanent display with constant humidity and temperature control in the Museum of History and Technology. The *Philadelphia* is the oldest intact warship presently on exhibit in North America.[153]

Only one sister gondola remains at the bottom of Lake Champlain. Although Benedict Arnold's report of October 15, 1776, mentioned "two Gondolas sunk at Schuyler's Island," only one actually sank.[154] One of the two abandoned gondolas was the *New Jersey*, which was taken by the British on October 12. While some records suggest that the *New Jersey* was captured, the vessel was found by the British abandoned. The British description which most closely matches American records comes from a letter written by Captain Charles Douglass of the Royal Navy. It conveys the dispatches of Lieutenant James Dacres, commander of the schooner *Carleton*, and accurately accounts for the eight gondolas: "One taken the 12th; one sunk the 11th; four burnt the 13th; one escaped, and one missing."[155] The *Jersey* was taken by the British after being scuttled by Arnold's forces. There is no mention in the American documents of the crew of the *Jersey*'s surrendering to the British. Brigadier General David Waterbury's account of the surrender of the galley

Washington makes no reference to another vessel being captured by the British. Likewise, Captain Thomas Pringle, aboard the British schooner *Maria*, writing about the events of the 13th, stated that "The Washington galley struck during the action, and the rest made their escape to Ticonderoga."[156] Brigadier General William Maxwell, writing to the governor of New Jersey from Ticonderoga on October 20, related that the fleet, under orders from Arnold, had separated to escape and subsequently was run ashore or destroyed: "but one row-galley fell into their hands."[157] Obviously, the Americans did not count the *Jersey* as captured. The *Jersey* was recorded as being "taken" by the British on October 12, a day when the American and British fleets were miles apart.[158] The most convincing evidence that the *Jersey* was found abandoned and had not surrendered comes from the journal of John Enys, a nineteen-year-old ensign in the British army, who witnessed the Valcour engagement from the *Thunderer*. Enys recorded that " a party of Canadians found a Gondola Named the *Jersey*."[159]

The search for the last gondola began with Colonel Lorenzo Hagglund's exploratory diving at Schuyler Island and Ligonier Point from 1951 to 1953.[160] Several gondola anchors were raised from the east side of Schuyler Island during the early 1960s and another from a reef near Basin Harbor, Vermont. One of the anchors is presently in the Colchester Lighthouse at the Shelburne Museum, and a second is in the Navy Memorial Museum in Washington, D.C.

In November 1967 New York State issued a permit to the Smithsonian Institution to explore the waters off Schuyler Island. After several days of diving operations in the frigid water, the search was temporarily halted. The following June the Smithsonian returned, aided by a grant from the National Geographic Society and side-scan sonar equipment from the Massachusetts Institute of Technology. A nine-day search, however, was repeatedly hampered by rough weather. The search parties and divers returned in late November of 1968 to continue their sonar probe. Although several targets were indicated on sonar and some wooden fragments found by divers, they did not locate any shipwrecks. In a 1976 report, Dr. Philip Lundeberg, then Curator of Naval History at the Smithsonian, stated that he still hoped to return to Schuyler, concluding that "this Division looks

forward to future opportunities to decipher the mystery of the Schuyler Island gondolas."[161]

The search for the missing gondola was renewed during the 1980s. A six-day side-scan/Loran/ ROV (Remotely-Operated Vehicle) survey of the Schuyler Island area in search of Arnold's lost gondola began in the summer of 1987. The group was led by Joseph Zarzynski, with Garry Kozak of Klein Associates, manufacturers of sophisticated side-scan sonar equipment, and Vince Capone of Kaselaan & D'Angelo Associates of New Jersey, who provided the ROV. Unfortunately, the systematic search did not find the vessel, but it did relocate the wreck of the tugboat *William H. McAllister*, which had sunk in 150 feet of water south of Schuyler Island in 1963. In February 1988 an expedition of the National Geographic Society directed by Emory Kristoff, which utilized sector-scanning sonar, Loran, and a ROV, searched through the ice off the southern end of Schuyler

Right: Cannonballs and other artifacts on the gunboat *Spitfire*. (Photograph courtesy of the Lake Champlain Maritime Museum with special thanks to Benthos, Inc.)

Below: Bow cannon protruding over the lead-lined stem of gunboat *Spitfire*. (Photograph courtesy of the Lake Champlain Maritime Museum with special thanks to Benthos, Inc.)

Facing page: Schuyler Island, site of Benedict Arnold's anchorage in 1776. Photo by the author.

Island without success.[162] Kristoff worked with James Kennard, who had used side-scan sonar around Schuyler Island with Scott Hill earlier in the 1980s. Kennard continued the search for the missing gondola with side-scan sonar in 1989.

The third group within a year to search near Schuyler Island was led by Arthur Cohn, director of the Lake Champlain Maritime Museum at Basin Harbor, with technicians and side-scan sonar equipment from the Woods Hole Oceanographic Institution and the research vessel from the University of Vermont Lake Studies Program. A three-day search off Schuyler Island in April 1988, unfortunately, did not turn up the gondola. The Woods Hole Oceanographic Institution, in conjunction with the Lake Champlain Maritime Museum and the University of Vermont, renewed the search for the missing gondola in 1989 with the most sophisticated equipment deployed to date in the Schuyler Island area. The project, under the direction of noted marine explorer Robert Ballard, included plans to survey the gondola, if found, as part of the Jason Foundation's yearly scientific adventure to motivate schoolchildren via live broadcast satellite transmission to museums around the country and Canada. The search team, supervised by David Gallo of Woods Hole and Arthur Cohn of the LCMM, did not find the gunboat, but discovered two nineteenth-century railroad cars, a ferry boat, and the completely-intact wreck of the 73-foot schooner *Sara H. Ellen*, built at Isle La Motte in 1849. The 50-ton vessel had departed from Ligonier Point for Burlington with a load of stone in December 1860, but it foundered and sank in 300 feet of water during a winter storm.[163]

The Lake Champlain Maritime Museum's team, under Arthur Cohn with lake historian Peter Barranco, continued the search effort during the 1990s with a multi-year, side-scan mapping of the lake bottom. As a teenager in the 1950s, Barranco had worked at the *Philadelphia* exhibit in Willsboro and participated in Lorenzo Hagglund's search for the missing gunboat. In early June 1997 the outline of a double-ended vessel with a protruding object at one end appeared on the side-scan recorder. Cohn and LCMM diver Pierre LaRocque plunged into the depths of the lake to examine the mysterious target. After having disappeared 221 years earlier during a frantic nighttime retreat from Valcour Island, the last undiscovered gunboat of Benedict Arnold's fleet had finally been found. Later, with the assistance of the Benthos Corporation, a Falmouth, Massachusetts firm specializing in Remotely-Operated Vehicles, a survey revealed details of the perfectly-intact vessel. Although the two nine-pound cannons on the midship gun deck were missing, the bow cannon was still on its slide track carriage, pointing eerily into the darkness, as if waiting for a British warship to come into view. The mast stood upright (only a six-foot piece at the top was broken); the rudder remained in place, a section of the awning support frame survived intact, and the hull appeared to be in an excellent state of preservation. Cannonballs and other artifacts lay on the deck and in the recesses of the hull.[164] On June 30, 1997, U. S. Senator Patrick Leahy, an advocate for Lake Champlain, made the official announcement of the gunboat discovery at a press conference held at the LCMM. Philip Lundeberg, curator emeritus of naval history at the Smithsonian Institution, later remarked that the gunboat "could prove to be the most significant maritime discovery in American history in the last half century."[165] The name of the gunboat, however, remained a mystery. After two years of research, the staff of the Lake Champlain Maritime Museum narrowed the list of possible names to two vessels, the *Spitfire* and *Connecticut*.[166] Finally, in the spring of 2000, a breakthrough occurred when the LCMM received an original document, heretofore unknown, entitled, "A Return of the Fleet belonging to the United States of America on Lake Champlain...October 22, 1776," which identified the *Spitfire* as the other gunboat sunk.[167] At this writing, the LCMM, under a "Memorandum of Agreement" with the Naval Historical Center in Washington, D. C., is studying option plans for the long-term management of the gunboat.

The five vessels (galley *Congress* and four gondolas, the *Boston, Connecticut, New Haven,* and *Providence*) that Arnold burned and scuttled in what is known as Arnold's Bay in Panton, Vermont, have met with nearly total destruction. Some of the salvage occurred immediately after the battle. Major General Freidrich Riedesel's journal of October 25, 1776, observed that "Part of the garrison were at this time engaged at Buttonmole Bay [Arnold's Bay] in raising some of the sunken war material especially cannon."[168] When he had passed the bay in late October, approximately 20 cannons had been raised. Lieutenant John Enys stayed overnight at the bay in 1787 and recorded that "the wrecks of this fleet are still to be seen."[169] One brass cannon was retrieved years later from the bay by the Peter Ferris family and was reportedly used in the Battle of Plattsburgh during the War of 1812. An iron 4-pound cannon raised from the bay by Paul Bilhuber in 1934 is presently on display at the Lake Champlain Maritime Museum.[170] Another small cannon, a bronze swivel gun pulled from Arnold's Bay in 1932, was offered for sale on the eBay Internet auction site in January 2000. After several government agencies concluded that the artifact was still the property of the United States, the owner turned over the cannon to the U.S. Navy.[171] Subsequently, the LCMM received the cannon on loan for its Revolutionary War exhibit.

In 1842 Zadock Thompson mentioned that Arnold's fleet was still to be seen in the bay at low water.[172] Writing about Arnold's Bay in 1859, however, A. M. Hemenway suggested that "Of the 5 vessels sunk, 3 are known to have been raised, and 2 of them may still be seen in low water."[173] Philip Tucker, in his short essay "General Arnold and the Congress Galley" written in 1860, noted that "Edrick Adams, Esq., of Addison, who lived many years near Arnold's Bay, informs me that he has seen the remains of three of them in the bay and knows their respective localities. . .near a point of this rock rest the remains of the Congress."[174] Horace Mazet, after diving in the "opaque chalkiness" of Arnold's Bay in 1934, reported that "The wrecks of three of Arnold's vessels lie, stark and broken, held fast in the clay of the bottom, their few remaining ribs and timbers hardly recognizable as once having been boats."[175] Tradition has it that three of the gondolas were dragged out of the water with teams of horses during the nineteenth century and cut up for souvenirs. Eventually, the sparse remains of the vessels rotted away on neighboring farms with at least one of the vessels being burned on the shore of Arnold's Bay.

In October 1891 William Adams raised a large section of the stern of Arnold's galley *Congress,* from Arnold's Bay, and the local newspaper reported that "her bones are now bleaching on the shores"; subsequently, the remains were hauled to Adams' farm, where relic hunters eventually carted away many pieces of the wreck.[176] Some of its ten frames that have been handed down through several generations of families are still in existence. Canes and other souvenirs were fashioned from its timbers and frames.[177] In 1901 a section of a knee (rib) from the *Congress* was displayed at the New York State Fair. In 1910 W. Max Reid's book *Lake George and Lake Champlain* reported that "All that is left of the *Congress* rests on the lawn back of Hotel St. Frederic at Chimney Point."[178] Frames from the stern of the *Congress* were still to be seen in the late 1920s at Chimney Point. The last few frames of the vessel were acquired by Lorenzo Hagglund and are still in existence today. In 1990 two of the original frames were loaned to the Lake Champlain Maritime Museum by Hudson and Mary Hagglund.

In 1960 and 1961, divers William Leege, Robert Leahy, and Oscar Bredenberg discovered the bow section of the *Congress,* undertaking one-week excavations in each year. The trio retrieved over 1,500 artifacts, including buttons, buckles, cannonballs, iron fasteners, musket balls, parts of small arms, woodworking tools, and various fragments. The Leege Collection, the preponderance of the artifacts, was sent to the Lake Champlain

American crews abandoning their battered vessels at Arnold's Bay, October 13, 1776.
Painting by Charles Waterhouse. (Marine Corps Museum Art Collection)

Aerial view of Arnold's Bay where Benedict Arnold scuttled
the galley *Congress* and four gunboats. Photo by the author.

An 1899 photograph of the remains of the row galley *Congress* retrieved
from Arnold's Bay in 1891. Two surviving frames are on display at the
Lake Champlain Maritime Museum. (Vermont Historical Society)

Maritime Museum for conservation and curation in 1996. In 1984 the Champlain
Maritime Society began a side-scan sonar and diving survey of Arnold's Bay to determine
if any portions of the historic vessels still remained in the bay. Using information provided
by William Leege, the Society subsequently discovered the ends of the frames of a vessel
buried in the mud. A section of a gun carriage, a grapeshot, and frames were examined
and determined to be from part of the bow area of the *Congress*.

What is considered the last gondola in Arnold's Bay was raised in 1952 by Lorenzo
Hagglund and several partners, towed across the lake and sunk along the New York shore
to prevent deterioration.[179] The vessel which had been deeply buried in the mud was in
remarkable condition—much of the hull nearly as intact as that of the *Philadelphia*. The
runners for the bow cannon were still present when the vessel was pulled out of the mud.
The gondola was raised again in October 1954 and set alongside the remains of the early
nineteenth-century steamer *Vermont* near Ausable Chasm, New York, in what was to be
a private naval museum owned by the Lake Champlain Associates. The group planned
to build a huge masonry exhibition hall for the "Museum of American Naval History"
with an issue of $300,000 in shares of common stock. The museum backers intended to
display the *Royal Savage*, the *Philadelphia*, the gondola from Arnold's Bay, the 1809
steamer *Vermont* and other artifacts.[180] Attempts to raise funds to preserve and display
these relics never materialized. One last opportunity to save the Arnold's Bay gunboat
occurred in 1958 when the Whitehall Bicentennial Committee received a letter from
"Payson Hatch, head of a proposed naval museum at Ausable Chasm, stat[ing] that the
remains of the gundelo *Boston* would be made available to Whitehall" for its new
Skenesborough Museum.[181] But the gunboat remained in the woods.

Gunboat raised nearly intact from Arnold's Bay in 1952 and at Ausable Chasm in 1961.
(Lake Champlain Maritime Museum) The vessel remained outside after funding
for a maritime museum failed to materialize. (Smithsonian Institution)

In the 1960s Howard Chapelle, the noted naval historian, and Philip Lundeberg of
the Smithsonian determined that the abandoned wreck in the wooded area near Ausable
Chasm was indeed one of Arnold's gondolas. According to Dr. Lundeberg, the gunboat
"revealed structural details virtually identical with those of the *Philadelphia*, including
comparable over-all dimensions, flat-bottomed construction, similar frame and floor
spacing, iron and treenail fastenings, and the characteristic keelson."[182] A stem piece of
this gondola was given to the Navy Memorial Museum at the Navy Yard in Washington,
D. C. After nearly 20 years of disintegration and dismemberment by souvenir hunters

The gunboat *Philadelphia II* under sail on Lake Champlain.
(Lake Champlain Maritime Museum)

while it lay exposed in the woods, a few pieces of the gondola were removed in 1973 to make way for a campsite. Some of the frames from the gondola are presently held by the LCMM. Raising of historic shipwrecks without prearranged preservation facilities has often resulted in total destruction of the vessels. Many archaeologists now believe that building full-size replicas of historic ships may be preferable to raising fragile shipwrecks. In 1989 the Lake Champlain Maritime Museum began construction of a full-scale working reproduction of the gondola *Philadelphia* at an estimated cost of $430,000. Built from plans made available by the Smithsonian Institution, the replica *Philadelphia* is an exact copy of the original. The finished gondola was launched in 1991 as part of the Vermont Bicentennial and toured the lake in 1992, welcoming over 12,000 visitors. The following year the *Philadelphia II* cruised the lake once more, journeying as far north as St. Jean, Quebec.[183] The vessel is a featured permanent exhibit at the Lake Champlain Maritime Museum today.

What happened to the rest of the vessels? The *Enterprise, Liberty, Revenge, Trumbull,* and *New York* escaped the 1776 disaster and spent part of the following year at Fort Ticonderoga. Most of them, however, sank to the bottom of the lake during the British invasion of 1777. When Lieutenant General John Burgoyne's forces placed a battery on Mount Defiance on July 5, 1777, the Americans evacuated Fort Ticonderoga and Mount Independence during the early morning hours of July 6 and fled to present-day Whitehall. The *Revenge* and *Gates* (a galley completed after the Valcour engagement) were set afire and blown up by their crews near Wood Creek Falls. The *Enterprise* burned and sank. The *Trumbull* and *Liberty* were taken by the British. During the construction of the Champlain Barge Canal from 1910-1911, several cannons were salvaged, and years later two were placed on the lawn of the State Armory in Whitehall and another in the Skenesborough Museum. Two four-pound cannons, probably from the galley *Gates,* were raised on August 10, 1910.[184] According to one local newspaper account in late 1911, "two more large cannons, making a total of four, were taken from the bed of the harbor at Whitehall by the dipper dredge [steam shovel mounted on a barge]."[185] Parts salvaged from the other vessels found near Lock 12 are still in Whitehall, having been fashioned into checker boards, billiard cues, and canes.

What happened to the gunboat *New York* remained a mystery for many years. Most British and American lists of the vessels captured or destroyed at Whitehall do not include the gunboat *New York.*[186] However, in 1990 the Lake Champlain Maritime Museum acquired a stem piece, originally recovered during the construction of the barge canal at Whitehall in 1910, which is identical to the gunboat *Philadelphia's* stem piece.[187] Apparently, the *New York* had reached Whitehall during the evacuation of 1777.

In May 1782 Captain William Chambers of the Royal Navy reported that the *Washington, Jersey,* and *Lee* (all taken from the Americans in 1776) were still carrying provisions from St. Jean.[188] The "Return of His Majesty's Vessels on the Undermentioned Lakes" in January 1784 listed only eight vessels in service on Lake Champlain which included the captured American vessels *Washington, Trumbull,* and *Liberty.*[189] However, a March 1784 list based on a "Return of Vessels...at St. Johns...3d Sept 1783" indicated that the *Washington* "can not come down [to Lake Champlain]"; the *Trumbull* and *Lee* had the same remark with the added note "without some trouble and Expense"; the *Liberty* was listed as "Ha[u]led up on the stocks not worth the trouble," but the *Jersey* was suitable for service.[190]

Nearly all the British ships and captured American vessels that sailed Lake Champlain during the Revolutionary War eventually settled to the bottom of the Richelieu River or were broken up in the vicinity of St. Jean. The radeau *Thunderer,* loaded with the sick and wounded from the Saratoga battles, sank in Lake Champlain after hitting a rock near

Windmill Point in late 1777. A few of the British vessels continued in military or commercial service for quite a few years after the American Revolution. The armed schooner *Maria*, for example, was used for cargo inspection of trading vessels until 1794 at Point au Fer on Lake Champlain (replaced by the 16-gun schooner *Royal Edward*).[191] Two war vessels were acquired from the British in 1790 by Gideon King of Burlington for commercial use on Lake Champlain. Remnants of the British fleet which had sunk at St. Jean were found when the Chambly Canal was constructed during the nineteenth century. An extensive side-scan sonar and underwater survey between 1978 and 1980 by Canadian archaeologists discovered numerous wreck sites in the Richelieu River. Although many wrecks were canal boats, artifacts recovered from the site of an old wharf near St. Jean dated from the Revolutionary War.[192]

A schooner, identified as the *Revenge*, was raised off Fort Ticonderoga in 1909 and placed on display at the museum. The vessel deteriorated substantially after a shed collapsed on it in 1948. The wreck was not the *Revenge*, which had been blown up in Skenesborough (Whitehall) in 1777. The Champlain Maritime Society examined the scant remains of the vessel in 1983 and identified the wreck as the brig *Duke of Cumberland*, built under the command of Major General Jeffery Amherst in 1759 for use in the naval campaign of the French and Indian War (see chapter 5). In September 1954, a 75-foot vessel, at the time called the *Trumbull*, was raised at Fort Ticonderoga, but the wreck "was not a war vessel (or even a sailing vessel)" and was burned in 1959.[193]

A section of a wreck was pulled out of East Bay in Whitehall in 1949 and rested for many years at Fort Mount Hope in Ticonderoga. While an old sign over this vessel stated that it might be one of the gunboats from Arnold's fleet, an inspection of its construction suggested something else. On the portion of the vessel that was dragged out of the bay in 1949 were found an 1812 Canadian coin in the step of the mizzen mast and a split 13-inch mortar that had been used at Fort Ticonderoga during the American Revolution. After Colonel Henry Knox hauled cannons from Ticonderoga to Boston in the winter of 1775-1776, two mortars, among other munitions, were returned to the fort in the spring of 1776. On August 1, 1776, one of the mortars was fired from a gondola and burst in half; the second mortar, fired the next day, also burst. The split mortars were subsequently used for ballast in the American row galleys. The galley *Trumbull* escaped the Valcour Island disaster in 1776 but was captured by the British at Skenesborough in 1777 following a brief battle. After serving with the British navy, the vessel was broken up or sunk at her moorings at the British shipyard at St. Jean. When the British built their fleet during the War of 1812 they apparently used the broken mortar as ballast.[194] The victorious American navy under Thomas Macdonough escorted its captured prizes to Whitehall in late 1814. Through research and actual measurements, the Champlain Maritime Society identified the vessel in East Bay/Mount Hope as the 82 1/2-foot brig *Linnet*, built by the Royal Navy. This would explain the broken mortar and the 1812 Canadian coin on the same vessel. Many of the cannonballs, bar shot, and other relics found on the half of the vessel pulled out of East Bay were subsequently sold piece-by-piece to tourists.

In recent years several other significant archaeological surveys have enhanced the understanding of historic sites from the period of the American Revolution. An archaeological study by Dr. David Starbuck and a crew of 40 volunteers working with the Vermont Division of Historic Preservation from 1989 to 1990 unearthed a large number of relics at the site of Mount Independence, including musket balls, bayonets, buckles, buttons, coins, tobacco pipes, pottery, bottles, spades, nails, etc.[195] An underwater survey conducted by the Lake Champlain Maritime Museum in 1992 under the direction of Arthur Cohn and Dr. Kevin Crisman revealed structural details of 21 crib caissons from the 1777 Great Bridge which connected Fort Ticonderoga to Mount Independence. The archaeological team discovered 900 artifacts, including a 12-pound cannon, musket balls, bar shot, mortar bombs, grapeshot, cannonballs, tools, and wine bottles.[196] In 1996 the state of Vermont opened a new visitor center at Mount Independence to interpret the site and display the artifacts found during the archaeological survey of the area.

In the summer of 2000, Dr. David Starbuck and a team of volunteer archaeologists began a multi-year excavation of Fort George, garrisoned during both the French and Indian War and the American Revolution. During the first year of the project at Fort George, the team uncovered foundations and eighteenth-century artifacts, including buttons, buckles, cuff links, musket parts, musket balls, a cannonball, spade, key, and fragments of cups and dishes. A new interpretive center at Fort George has been recommended by many in the regional community.[197]

A cannon being raised from the waters near Mount Independence in 1993.
(Lake Champlain Maritime Museum)

While much progress has been made in educating the public regarding the preservation of invaluable archaeological sites, both on land and underwater, additional enlightenment and vigilance are essential. Groups such as the Lake Champlain Maritime Museum, Bateaux Below, Inc., and land-based archaeological field schools have raised public awareness of the important artifacts that deserve preservation for future generations. Additional measures are needed to discourage piece-by-piece dismemberment of historic shipwrecks and the destruction of important land sites.

The discovery of these priceless relics preserved in the cold waters of Lake Champlain has kept the story of the Revolutionary War fleet alive. The observation of a bit of history, untouched since it fell to its watery grave, creates a tangible link between the past and present. There is a certain degree of immortality attached to the surviving relics as they have been passed from generation to generation in the Champlain Valley. It is to be hoped that these artifacts will not be lost but at some point brought forth to be displayed in museums.

Master Commandant Thomas Macdonough by John Wesley Jarvis.
(City of New York Art Commission)

9. War of 1812: Plattsburgh Bay

T HE LAKE VALLEYS on the eve of the War of 1812 were no longer the wilderness that once dominated the region during the eighteenth century. While Lake George experienced a much slower rate of growth, by 1810 over 100,000 people lived in counties adjacent to Lake Champlain. Stimulated by trade with Canada to the north and commercial traffic to the south and east, communities grew rapidly along the lake. Burlington, Plattsburgh, Whitehall (formerly Skenesborough), and Vergennes, experiencing remarkable economic growth during the early nineteenth century, became dominant centers for commercial activity on Lake Champlain. The clouds of war, however, were soon to engulf Lake Champlain once again.

As a neutral party to the war between Great Britain and France, America experienced enormous growth in trade on the high seas by the turn of the century. The belligerents, Britain and France, soon began a series of actions that interfered with American ocean shipping. Although trouble with France on the Atlantic Ocean resulted in a virtual undeclared naval war (Quasi-War 1798-1800), harassment of American merchant vessels by the British navy would have more lasting consequences. With the desertion of English sailors eager for the higher wages of the American merchant fleets, Britain stopped American ships and impressed seamen into the Royal Navy. The British arrogantly forced many legitimate United States citizens (estimated at 6,000–9,000 men) into their navy. Provoked by the harassment, President Thomas Jefferson called for an embargo that essentially forbade all foreign trade. The disastrous effect of the embargo led to the passage of the Nonintercourse Act of 1809, which permitted trade with all nations except Britain and France. This legislation, upon expiration, was replaced by the Macon Bill of 1810, which reopened trade with the offending countries, but promised reimposition of the nonintercourse on Britain or France if one should withdraw its restrictions on American shipping. Napoleon lifted his maritime restrictions on American shipping, prompting President James Madison's threatened renewal of the trade ban with Britain.

With no compromise on the maritime interference by Britain, a 90-day embargo was signed into law in April 1812. Responding to increasing pressure as the altercations with Britain continued, Madison asked for a declaration of war in early June. Ironically, Britain had announced its intention to suspend the offending Orders in Council several days before the U.S. declaration, but without modern communication, America prepared for war. The reasons for war, however, were broader than simply Britain's maritime harassment. Support for the war was strongest in the West and South as frontiersmen were determined to defend and expand U.S. borders against Indians allied with Britain. Support of Indian claims by the British, who supplied weapons to Indians, created a charged atmosphere on the frontier. The desire for annexation of Canada, an idea relatively dormant since the American Revolution, became more prominent as expansionist motives flourished. The war, however, was not popular, especially in the New England states.

While British merchant ships were on their way to America with the good news of the end of the Orders in Council, Americans had begun planning their first advances into Canada. An immediate offer of peace by the British was rejected since it failed to make assurances that impressment of American seamen would end. Appointed brigadier general in April 1812, William Hull, a former Revolutionary War officer and governor of the

Michigan territory, advanced into Canada in July with more than 2,000 troops. Americans had thought that Canada could be taken easily, but unfolding events would soon dispel their optimism. After a series of defeats at the hands of a smaller force of British and Indians, Hull was forced back over the border, resulting in the capture of Detroit by the British. Two subsequent invasion attempts by Major General Stephen Van Rensselaer and Brigadier General Alexander Smyth at the Niagara River (near present-day Buffalo) were turned back, in part due to the refusal of the New York militia to cross the border and the incompetence of Smyth in the second attempt.

Sixty-two-year-old Major General Henry Dearborn, a veteran of Arnold's 1775 assault on Quebec and the Battle of Saratoga in 1777, was selected to lead the northeastern sector of the army. In the fall of 1812 a large force of regular troops and militia was massed at Plattsburgh and Burlington, poised for an attack across the border. Dearborn had earlier accepted a proposed armistice from the governor-general of Canada, Sir George Prevost, based on the repeal of the Orders in Council, but the arrangement was denounced by President Madison.[1]

In late September 1812, Secretary of Navy Paul Hamilton ordered Lieutenant Thomas Macdonough to Lake Champlain to command the small fleet at the lake. Macdonough, son of a Revolutionary War officer, entered the U.S. Navy as a midshipman at the age of 16. After distinguished service in the war with Tripoli and subsequent experience on navy frigates, Macdonough commanded a small flotilla of gunboats headquartered in Portland, Maine. The 28-year-old lieutenant departed from Portland on October 5, arriving in Burlington four days later after an arduous journey through the mountains of New Hampshire and Vermont. The American plans for the war included control of the Great Lakes and Lake Champlain. Thus far in the war, the only success had been the remarkable naval victories on the high seas of the *Constitution, Wasp,* and *United States* over four British ships. The Americans hoped to duplicate these triumphs on the lakes with competent, vigorous officers.

The Champlain fleet was begun in 1809 with the construction of two small gunboats (numbers 169 and 170) at Whitehall by shipbuilder John Winans under the direction of navy Lieutenant Melancthon T. Woolsey, son of the New York Customs Collector. The 40-ton vessels, authorized by Jefferson in April 1808, were to check the smuggling with Canada, which remained rampant throughout the period along the Champlain route despite the embargo.[2] When the war began, the two gunboats were at Basin Harbor in Vermont, one partially sunk. They were placed under the command of Lieutenant Sidney Smith, who repaired the vessels and returned them to service on the lake. As the army mobilized on the northern frontier of the lake, six sloops were acquired by the War Department.[3] These vessels included the 65-foot *President,* 60-foot *Hunter,* 64-foot *Bull Dog* and three small sloops (*Champlain, Juno,* and *Jupiter*), which remained as War Department transports after being found too old to carry guns.[4] The 75-ton *President,* built in Essex, New York, as the sloop *Fox* in 1812, was purchased from John Boynton, while the smaller *Hunter,* built in 1809, was procured from Gideon King.[5]

The largest sloop, the *President,* was initially retained by Dearborn. The energetic Macdonough, however, soon sailed for Whitehall where he refitted the *Hunter* and *Bull Dog* and the gunboats. The *Hunter* was armed with two 12-pound cannons, four 6-pounders, and one 18-pounder on a pivot, while the *Bull Dog* had six 6-pounders and an 18-pounder on a pivot. Each gunboat carried one 12-pound cannon. Later, after her hull was reinforced to support the heavier load, the *President* was given six 18-pound cannons and two 12-pounders. Sometime in late 1812, Macdonough renamed the *Hunter* the *Growler* and the *Bull Dog* the *Eagle.*[6]

Macdonough's fleet returned to the northern end of the lake in early November to escort the transports and bateaux, which were ferrying troops from Burlington to Plattsburgh, and to patrol the lake. Arriving in Plattsburgh on November 10, Major General Dearborn began preparations for another invasion of Canada. An estimated 5,000–6,000 regulars and militia began their move toward the Canadian border on November 16. At the border, Dearborn assumed command of the army on November 19. At dawn, a detachment under Colonel Zebulon Pike (who had earlier discovered Pike's Peak) forded the Lacolle River about five miles from the border and besieged a blockhouse. Most of the Canadians and Indians in the blockhouse escaped, but a second American detachment mistakenly fired on Pike's men in a skirmish that lasted half an hour. Dispirited over the error and threatened by a British counterattack, the Americans, with their much larger army, hastily retreated to Plattsburgh.[7]

Macdonough sailed his fleet into Shelburne Bay for winter quarters and additional refitting, and departed for a short time to marry Lucy Ann Shaler on December 12 in Middletown, Connecticut. Returning with his bride to Burlington, the young lieutenant skillfully began the task of refitting and enlarging the Champlain fleet. Fifteen carpenters arrived from New York in mid-February; supplies, carronades (short cannons firing heavy shot at close range), ammunition, and gun carriages arrived the following month. The *President* was fitted out with four more guns while the *Growler*, commanded by Lieutenant Sidney Smith, and the *Eagle*, under Sailing Master Jairus Loomis, had their quarter decks removed to increase their armament from seven to eleven guns.

Much of the military activity in 1813 focused on the Great Lakes region. The withdrawal of regular troops from Plattsburgh earlier in the year had left the defense of the border areas in the hands of militia. In one of the earliest actions of 1813, Brigadier General Zebulon Pike attacked and burned York (modern-day Toronto) but was killed in the raid when a magazine exploded. During the early part of 1813, a naval construction race occurred between the British and Americans at Lakes Erie and Ontario. Captain Isaac Chauncey had been sent to Sackets Harbor, New York, in late 1812 to command the existing vessels and direct the building of a larger squadron. The Americans initially had relied on converted merchant schooners, as was the case on Lake Champlain, but the top-heavy vessels were no match for men-of-war. The Ontario schooners *Hamilton* and *Scourge* in Chauncey's fleet, for example, were blown over and quickly sank in a squall in 1813. At Kingston, Ontario, Captain James Lucas Yeo, who would later be the overall commander of the British fleet on Lake Champlain, engaged in a massive shipbuilding effort to gain absolute superiority over the American fleet. On Lake Erie, the navy sent Lieutenant Oliver Perry to present-day Erie, Pennsylvania, to command a fleet built by the New York shipwrights, Adam and Noah Brown.

In April 1813 the three largest vessels on Lake Champlain, the *President*, *Growler*, and *Eagle*, sailed for Plattsburgh. The American fleet at the time was far superior to the gunboats that the British had stationed at Isle-aux-Noix on the Richelieu River, but in a surprisingly short time the fleet would be lost. The flagship *President* was severely damaged when she ran aground at Plattsburgh, and the gunboats were temporarily taken out of service when one capsized in a squall.

At the beginning of June, Macdonough ordered Lieutenant Smith with the *Growler* and Sailing Master Loomis of the *Eagle* to proceed north as far as the border to confine the British gunboats to the Canadian side of the boundary line. After a report that the British were planning to attack, Smith and Loomis were reinforced at one A.M. on June 3 by troops under Captain Oliver Herrick and Ensign Washington Dennison.[8] At five A.M. Smith decided that their present position was unsafe and ordered the two vessels further north across the border, where he anchored below Hospital Island (about six miles from the border). Despite the assurances from Pilot Abraham Walters that the channel was wide enough to navigate, Smith immediately realized that his two sloops could no longer maneuver in the strong current and light south winds. Smith quickly ordered the vessels to return to Lake Champlain. To their horror, "At 15 minutes past six [we] discovered four [actually three] of the enemy's gunboats in chase of us," Loomis later recorded in his report to Macdonough.[9]

The three British gunboats, which could readily maneuver upstream with oars, were sent by Major George Taylor from Isle-aux-Noix. At the same time, British troops were landed on both banks of the Richelieu River to close the trap on the American vessels. By six-thirty A.M. the naval engagement had begun. The 24-pound cannons on the British gunboats soon began to inflict substantial damage to the American sloops. The pilot of the *Eagle* was severely wounded early in the battle; a short time later, the guns of the *Eagle* were temporarily disabled due to damage to their breeching and ring bolts. While the vessels were engaged in their cannon duel, Taylor's troops onshore directed musket fire onto the open decks of the American sloops. A council of officers, hastily called by Smith, decided to retreat while still engaging the enemy gunboats, but the strategy was soon changed to a plan to board and capture the British gunboats. At eleven A.M., just before the attempt to board was to be made, a 24-pound ball smashed completely through the *Eagle*'s hull, exiting through three broken planks on the starboard side, causing her to sink in shallow water. The British thereupon boarded and captured her. The *Growler* continued for 15 minutes longer, but with her ammunition nearly expended and her gaff boom (top spar) shot away, Smith had little choice but to surrender.

The *Growler* and *Eagle*, each with 11 guns, were brought to Isle-aux-Noix for repairs, where they were subsequently renamed by the British the *Shannon* and *Broke*. Despite the length of the battle, the casualties were light. Nearly 100 American officers and men were marched to Montreal and then sent to Quebec as prisoners. Some of the prisoners were later exchanged and returned to Lake Champlain. A court of inquiry, held nearly two years later at Sackets Harbor, found that the two vessels had been taken too far north of the border in a narrow channel where they could not maneuver. The court, however, ruled that Smith's general conduct on Lake Champlain was "correct and meritorious," and that the two sloops "were gallantly defended and that they were not surrendered until all further resistance had become vain."[10]

After the loss of the *Growler* and *Eagle*, Macdonough brought the *President* to Burlington on June 17. William Jones, Madison's new secretary of the navy, wrote to Macdonough with instructions to procure the necessary vessels, men, material, and munitions to regain control of the lake. Jones, a veteran of the Continental Navy during the Revolution with subsequent merchant shipping experience, was a successful and knowledgeable manager of navy resources, unlike his predecessor. The navy secretary authorized Macdonough "to purchase, arm, and equip in an effective manner two of the best sloops or other vessels to be procured on the lake."[11] He also gave Macdonough permission to build, if necessary, four or five barges or gunboats, 50 or 60 feet in length.

During the summer of 1813, Macdonough and his men were busy outfitting additional vessels at Burlington. The most significant purchase at the time was that of the 50-ton merchant sloop *Rising Sun* from Elijah Boynton, a vessel built in 1810 at Essex, New York, by Richard Eggleston.[12] The *Rising Sun* probably received its name from the widespread use of the rising sun symbol in early architectural designs on Essex buildings. The sloop was renamed *Preble* before she was ready for the open lake in late summer. Another sloop, the *Montgomery*, is presumed to have been purchased in the same period of time. Some historians, however, suggest that the *Montgomery* was one of the three transports retained by the army the previous fall and turned over to Macdonough in

1813.[13] Two smaller vessels, the *Francis* and *Wasp*, were rented and armed by Macdonough later in the summer of 1813. On July 24 the enterprising Macdonough was promoted to master commandant. Although he was referred to as "Commodore" Macdonough, the title was actually a courtesy and not a commissioned rank.

With the sudden increase in the size of the British navy at Isle-aux-Noix, requests for officers and seamen to man the new sloops were dispatched to the Royal Navy in Quebec. Following a letter from Sir George Prevost, governor-general of Canada, proposing a raid on public stores on Lake Champlain, Captain Thomas Everard of the sloop *Wasp* volunteered for 14 days to lead the raid with 50 of his crew and 30 crewman from transport vessels. Everard and his men soon proceeded to the Richelieu River aboard a steamboat. At the same time, Captain Daniel Pring was sent by Prevost from Kingston, Ontario, to command the fleet after Everard's departure. In late July Lieutenant Colonel John Murray, the commandant at St. Jean, was given instructions for the raid by the commander in lower Canada, Major General Roger Sheaffe: "The chief objective. . .will be to create a diversion" with the destruction of public buildings, military stores, and vessels, "but all private property. . .are to be respected."[14]

The expedition, led by Colonel Murray with 1,000 men aboard the sloops *Broke*, *Shannon*, three gunboats, and 47 bateaux, departed on the morning of July 29 from Isle-aux-Noix. The naval command was temporarily under Captain Everard, the senior officer, while Captain Pring served as second in command. The British landed unopposed at Plattsburgh on the afternoon of July 31, since Major General Benjamin Mooers, head of the New York militia at Plattsburgh, had withdrawn with 300-350 men to a point three miles west of the town. Alerted on the 29th of the approach of the British fleet, Mooers called up the militia and futilely requested help from Major General Wade Hampton, stationed at Burlington with army troops. After a contingent of prominent Plattsburgh residents pleaded "not to put up resistance, which could destroy the town," Mooers retreated because of his inadequate forces.[15] Before the British arrived, however, the Americans had removed supplies from the state arsenal.

With a map from a Canadian immigrant living in Plattsburgh, Murray's troops raided and burned the arsenal, a blockhouse, warehouses, and barracks. Despite Murray's orders not to plunder private property, houses were looted of their contents. On the morning of August 1, the British departed from Plattsburgh after taking a 32-foot commercial sloop, the *Burlington Packet*, and burning a storehouse on Cumberland Head. The expedition then split in two. Murray, with two gunboats and the bateaux, sailed north stopping at Point au Roche, where more private property was compromised before reaching Maquam Bay, whereupon his troops marched to Swanton, Vermont. At Swanton, the British burned the barracks and hospital in addition to destroying bateaux and private property.

On August 2 "at half past two o'clock P.M. the two sloops [*Broke* and *Shannon*] and row galley. . .came within one and a half miles of the shore [Burlington] and commenced a cannonading which was returned by the vessels and battery and continued about twenty minutes," according to an eyewitness at Burlington.[16] The British vessels under Everard and Pring withdrew southward, and later Macdonough with several vessels moved out of the harbor firing one gun in defiance. The British sailed for Shelburne Bay, where they captured several small commercial vessels and at least one other vessel off Charlotte, Vermont. The biggest prize was the 50-ton sloop *Essex*, owned by Gideon King and Ezra Thurber, which was becalmed 15 miles south of Burlington following a delivery of 19 sailors to Macdonough. After being unable to tow the *Essex* back to the *Broke* and *Shannon*, the British boat crews burned the vessel.

Everard's report, written aboard the *Broke* on August 3, disclosed the observation of three sloops, two schooners, two one-gun scows (gunboats), and a floating battery at Burlington: "Having captured and destroyed four Vessels, without any attempt on the part of the Enemy's armed Vessels to prevent it, and seeing no prospect of inducing him to quit his position, where it was impossible for us to attack him, I am now returning."[17]

On the morning of August 3, the British fleet was observed passing Cumberland Head with two captured sloops. At Chazy the fleet halted to plunder and expropriate stores and a schooner prior to withdrawing to Isle-aux-Noix. At about the same time, a detachment from Murray's force marched to Champlain, New York, and burned two blockhouses, a storehouse, and barracks before returning to Isle-aux-Noix on August 4. The successful raid exposed the vulnerability of the towns along the upper lake, which in turn created incentives to build a more substantial American fleet the following year, and revealed a need for more military cooperation between Vermont and New York.

With men borrowed from Major General Hampton's troops, Macdonough re-emerged on Lake Champlain in early September 1813 with the armed sloops *President*, *Preble*, *Montgomery*, *Francis*, *Wasp* and two gunboats. Two new 50-foot gunboats (presumably the *Alwyn* and *Ballard*) were launched a month later at Plattsburgh.[18] The four gunboats, mounting one long 18-pounder each, were later named the *Ludlow*, *Wilmer*, *Alwyn*, and *Ballard* (honoring the names of four navy lieutenants killed in action).[19] Macdonough now had the edge over the British fleet. When the American fleet approached the British squadron north of Plattsburgh in September, the latter retreated to the Richelieu River.

Further west on September 10, Commodore Oliver Perry, with a fleet superior to that of Captain Robert Barclay, decisively defeated the British in a bloody naval battle on Lake Erie. Perry's victory paved the way for Major General William Henry Harrison's defeat of the British at the Thames River battle in which the famous Indian leader Tecumseh was killed. The twin victories forced the British to evacuate Detroit. The military success, however, was not duplicated in the east. Major General James Wilkinson, veteran of the Champlain theater during the American Revolution and implicated in the Aaron Burr conspiracy (1807), arrived at Sackets Harbor in August to assume Major General Dearborn's command. Wilkinson's plans included a two-pronged attack from the east and west on Montreal. After a letter from Wilkinson, Secretary of War John Armstrong ordered Major General Hampton, then stationed at Burlington, to capture Isle-aux-Noix and St. Jean in the Montreal operation. Subsequently, the Isle-aux-Noix plans were dropped when Macdonough, unwilling to risk his fleet again in the narrow channel of the Richelieu River, declined Hampton's joint operation proposal. Macdonough, however, did agree to prevent the British fleet from entering Lake Champlain while Hampton's troops advanced northward.

After assembling at Cumberland Head, Hampton's army proceeded in bateaux west on the Great Chazy River, arriving at the village of Champlain on September 20. Four thousand American troops, including cavalry and artillery, had reached Champlain by a land route. The army had barely crossed the border when it turned back for lack of water. Hampton instead decided to attempt to reach Montreal by way of the Chateaugay River. Marching to present-day Chateaugay, New York, Hampton's army waited nearly a month for Wilkinson's advance from Sacket's Harbor. On October 21 Hampton's army finally moved toward Montreal. But Hampton's regiments were soon stopped by a much smaller force of French Canadian regulars, militia, and Indians on October 26 at a fortified position on the banks of the Chateaugay River. The Canadians successfully repelled the American army with heavy firing and repeated bugle calls in all directions, which duped

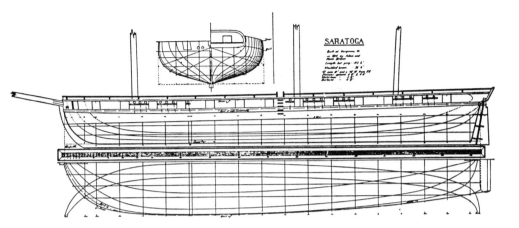

Above: The 143-foot *Saratoga*, launched at Vergennes in a remarkable 40 days, served as the flagship of the American fleet at the Plattsburgh Bay engagement.
Chapelle Collection. (Smithsonian Institution)

Below: Gunboat and galley designs by William Doughty, naval contractor, intended for use on Lake Champlain.
Chapelle Collection. (Smithsonian Institution)

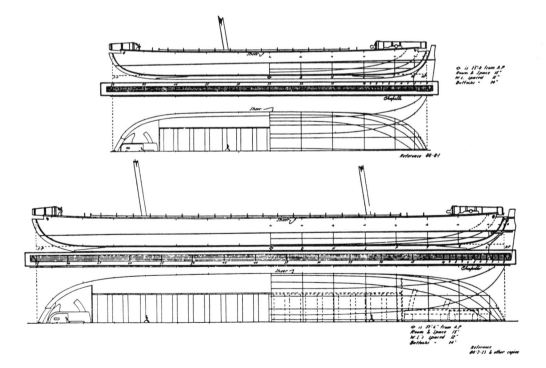

Hampton into thinking the Canadians had a much larger force. The Americans retreated to Chateaugay and soon returned to Plattsburgh.

On November 12 Wilkinson's force of 8,000 men also retreated after a 2,000-man American detachment was defeated along the St. Lawrence River by 800 British troops in a muddy field about 90 miles from Montreal (Battle of Chrysler Farm). Two American armies of more than 12,000 men had been turned back by fewer than 2,500 British and Canadian troops. The incompetent Wilkinson charged Hampton with the expedition's collapse, ordering his arrest in Plattsburgh for "disobedience of orders."[20] Hampton escaped on the steamer *Vermont* to Whitehall and then to Washington, D.C. After an unauthorized advance into Canada that ended in another fiasco (Lacolle Mill) in early 1814, Wilkinson was himself called before a court of inquiry but exonerated in 1815.

On December 4, British gunboats commanded by Captain Daniel Pring ventured as far as Cumberland Head, where troops burned an empty storehouse. Four American gunboats under Lieutenant Stephen Cassin, second in command to Macdonough, pursued Pring for three hours, but the British vessels escaped into the Richelieu River. Two and a half weeks later, on December 21, Macdonough brought his fleet seven miles up Otter Creek to Vergennes for winter quarters.

Macdonough had chosen Vergennes for winter quarters in anticipation of a major shipbuilding program early in 1814. In addition to stands of oak and pine around Vergennes, the village's falls powered a host of industries, including eight forges, two furnaces, a wire factory, a rolling mill, and sawmills. Supplied by bog iron beds nearby, Vergennes had one of the most developed iron industries in the region. Vergennes not only had a secure lake access but was also connected by roads to Burlington and Boston. Before moving to Vergennes, Macdonough had received instructions during December from Navy Secretary William Jones to make preparations for building 15 galleys on plans drawn of vessels under construction for Chesapeake Bay service: "The first class, 75 feet long and 15 wide, to carry a long 24 and a 42 pound carronade, row [with] 40 oars...Second class, 50 feet long and 12 wide to carry long 18 and 32 carronade and row [with] 26 oars."[21] On January 28 the navy secretary authorized Macdonough to build either 15 gunboats or a ship and three or four gunboats. Early in February Macdonough's suspicions were confirmed when an intelligence report suggested that the British were building a large vessel of approximately 20 guns.

Macdonough decided upon building a large ship, whereupon the navy engaged Adam and Noah Brown of New York City, who had built Perry's successful fleet on Lake Erie the year before. Secretary Jones informed Macdonough on February 22 that a contract "to launch a Ship of 24 Guns, on Lake Champlain, in 60 days" had been signed with the firm on February 14.[22] In addition, Jones wrote in the same letter that "Lt. Cassin says there is a New Boat 120 feet long, near Vergennes, intended for a Steam Boat; if she will answer, you are authorized to purchase her for use of the Navy."[23] By late February Noah Brown and his shipwrights had arrived in Vergennes and they soon began cutting timber and constructing a makeshift shipyard. Early in March the keel of a 26-gun ship was laid and the construction of five row galleys (also referred to as gunboats) had begun. In the end, six 70-ton row galleys with lengths of 75 feet and widths of 15 feet were built. The galleys, carrying two masts with triangular sails (lateen-rigged) and 40 oars each, mounted one 24-pound cannon and one 18-pounder. The galleys, completed by late April, were named the *Allen, Borer, Burrows, Centipede, Nettle,* and *Viper*.[24]

In an amazing 40 days, the 26-gun ship (sloop of war) with a length of 143 feet and width of 36 feet was launched at Vergennes on April 11. Guns for the new vessel were taken from the frigate *John Adams* at Boston and transported by oxcarts over muddy roads to Vergennes. Originally, Macdonough intended to name the vessel *Jones,* but later called it the *Saratoga*, upon learning that a new American brig on Lake Ontario already had the same name.[25] After the launching of the *Jones/Saratoga*, Macdonough and Brown examined the hull of the unfinished steamboat owned by the Lake Champlain Steam-boat Company which Secretary Jones had suggested buying in his February 22 letter. Work on the vessel by the steamboat company had continued during the interim, but the company was apparently eager to sell the vessel. The governor of New York, after being informed of the company's desire to sell the vessel to the government, wrote a detailed letter to Secretary Jones recommending the purchase of the vessel for $15,000-$17,000 and its use as a steam-powered war vessel.[26] Noah Brown, however, appraised the empty hull at $5,000. Macdonough, who felt steamboat machinery was unreliable after observing the *Vermont* on Lake Champlain, decided with Brown to convert the vessel to a schooner. The company wanted $22,000 for the vessel and sent Jahaziel Sherman, who, as the steamer's future captain had supervised the building of the hull, to Washington, D.C., where he negotiated a price of $12,000 with Secretary Jones.[27]

The new schooner, named *Ticonderoga* by Macdonough, was launched on May 12. Brown had added a substantial false keel to the relatively flat-bottomed *Ticonderoga* to provide stability under sail. The 120-foot vessel with a beam of approximately 26 feet was soon fitted, rigged, and mounted with 17 guns. The guns were taken from the two small sloops, *Francis* and *Wasp*, which were relegated to transport duty before being returned to their owners. Macdonough temporarily removed guns for use on the *Ticonderoga* from "the four old Gallies; two of which are very rotten, as they were built in 1808 [1809]."[28] Macdonough's entry, "four old Gallies," is somewhat puzzling since two of the vessels were supposedly constructed in 1813.

On May 8, 1814, Captain Daniel Pring, aboard the new 16-gun, 82-1/2-foot brig *Linnet*, "with the Chub and Finch [previously the sloops *Shannon* and *Broke*, renamed for the fourth time], Canada [formerly the 44-foot sloop *Mars* captured from the Americans], the Flotilla of Gun Boats, a Tender. . .[and] two merchant vessels," was dispatched to attack the American fleet at Otter Creek or block the channel.[29] The flotilla of gunboats consisted of seven or eight vessels; one of the merchant sloops included the *Icicle*, formerly the sloop *Burlington Packet*. While the purpose of the raid was to attack the American fleet before it could be completed, the chief benefit was to gain detailed information about the American vessels from two prisoners captured in a small boat on the lake.

Hampered by southerly winds, Pring's flotilla did not appear at the mouth of Otter Creek until daybreak of May 14. In early April Macdonough received warnings from Peter Sailly, the collector of customs, and Major General James Wilkinson that the British might block Otter Creek, and both suggested erecting a battery at the mouth of the waterway. On April 20 Macdonough and Wilkinson settled on a site for the defensive artillery. Fifty light artillery troops were subsequently sent under Captain Arthur Thornton from Burlington to man the battery, consisting of seven long 12-pound cannons on ship carriages, mounted behind horseshoe-shaped earthworks at the mouth of Otter Creek. Lieutenant Stephen Cassin was also dispatched with a detachment of sailors to assist Thornton's troops. (The battery site later became known as Fort Cassin.)

The engagement on May 14 lasted less than two hours, causing little damage to either side. Without a sufficient landing force, Pring withdrew his fleet from the mouth of Otter Creek. Macdonough brought almost all of the vessels to the mouth of the creek, including the *Saratoga*, but the ships reached the site of the engagement after the British had departed. Macdonough reported the action immediately to the secretary of war, describing an attack of "One hour & a half" between the American battery and "Eight of the Enemy's Gallies [gunboats], with [a] Bomb Vessel" accompanied by the "new Brig, with

Fort Cassin at the mouth of Otter Creek was the site of the May 14, 1814, battle with the British fleet under Captain Daniel Pring. Photo by the author.

Three of the British gunboats ascended the Boquet River after the Otter Creek engagement to raid government flour stored in a gristmill at the falls. (One galley had also chased a small boat up the Boquet before the Otter Creek battle.) Brigadier General Daniel Wright described the militia's fire from the banks of the Boquet upon one of the gunboats which was "so disabled as to oblige them to hoist a flag of distress when a sloop came to their assistance and towed her off."[31] The result of Pring's raid was another escalation of the naval race on Lake Champlain. With the detailed information on the entire American fleet, including the specifics on the 26-gun *Saratoga* from the two prisoners, Britain would later make plans for the largest warship ever to sail Lake Champlain.

The American fleet finally left Otter Creek on May 26. Macdonough's vessels now included the *Saratoga*, *Ticonderoga*, *Preble*, *President*, and *Montgomery*, and the six new galleys: *Allen*, *Borer*, *Burrows*, *Centipede*, *Nettle*, and *Viper*. The four smaller gunboats, temporarily disarmed, would wait until additional crews and cannons were available. The problem of recruiting had delayed the embarkation of the fleet and would continue to hamper the American navy on Lake Champlain throughout the summer of 1814. Lake service was disdained by most trained seamen, forcing Macdonough to request army troops. After his repeated requests, several hundred soldiers were finally sent to Vergennes, which allowed the fleet to achieve enough manpower by the end of May to patrol the lake.

Macdonough reached Plattsburgh on May 29, whereupon he reported to the navy secretary that the *Saratoga* was a "fine ship," as was the *Ticonderoga*, and the galleys were "also remarkably fine vessels."[32] The American fleet spent the next few days escorting transports and bateaux loaded with troops from Burlington.* Macdonough's fleet later moved northward to Point au Fer, forcing the British squadron to relocate near Ash

---

* Richard Eggleston, a shipbuilder at Essex, New York, built over 250 bateaux for the American army during the war.[33]

Island, about a mile into the Richelieu River. On June 11 Macdonough reported to Navy Secretary Jones that the British had laid "the Keel of a Ship...to equal, at least, the Saratoga."[34] A string of letters ensued from the Champlain commandant pleading for orders from Jones to build a new 18-gun brig. The navy secretary, having trouble meeting the debts incurred for the *Saratoga*, *Ticonderoga*, and galleys, failed to respond to Macdonough's requests for the new ship. For the only time during the war, President James Madison, not willing to chance the loss of Lake Champlain, overruled Jones' decision in late June. In early July, Jones authorized Adam and Noah Brown to build a brig of 18 guns immediately at Lake Champlain. Macdonough, however, first learned of the decision to build the brig on July 18 when Adam Brown reached the *Saratoga* at Point au Fer to discuss the plans for the vessel.

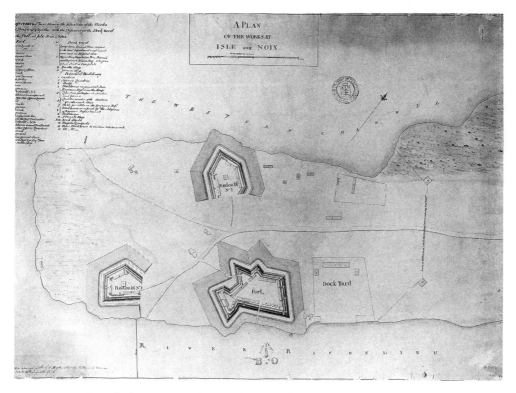

Plan of Isle-aux-Noix during the War of 1812 showing the shipyard
on the east side of the island. (National Archives of Canada)

While the shipbuilding race proceeded at Isle-aux-Noix and Vergennes, the problem of smuggling along the Lake Champlain corridor to Canada continued. From the Jefferson administration through Madison's war years, commercial relations with Canada along Lake Champlain flourished despite prohibitions. Even Gideon King, who sold vessels to the American forces, had been characterized by some as a "notorious smuggler" from Burlington.[35] Since the British paid more for cattle, Americans simply drove cattle (in one case 120 yoke of oxen) across the border.[36] On July 31 Major General George Izard reported to Secretary of War Armstrong that revenue officers were unable to stop the outrageous smuggling: "on the eastern side of Lake Champlain ...supplies of cattle...are pouring into Canada. Like herds of buffaloes they press through the forest, making paths for themselves."[37]

Governor-General Prevost had plans in August 1814 for an invasion of northern Lake Champlain but resolved not to take offensive action on the Vermont side of the lake. Prevost was well aware of the mixed political role that Vermont had played in the last war. As late as 1813, Governor Martin Chittenden prohibited Vermont militia from serving on the New York side of Lake Champlain. In an August 5 letter to the British colonial secretary of state, Lord Bathurst, Prevost suggested that Vermont displayed "a decided opposition to the war. . .I mean for the present to confine myself in any offensive Operations which may take place to the west side of Lake Champlain."[38] Three weeks later on August 27, Prevost's letter to Bathurst disclosed that "Two thirds of the army are supplied with beef by American contractors, principally of Vermont and New York."[39]

Americans were even smuggling naval supplies to the British shipyards at Isle-aux-Noix. Sailing Master Elie La Vallette of the galley *Burrows* destroyed two spars, 80 and 85 feet long, being towed to the border. A little more than a week later Midshipman Joel Abbot, in a covert operation four miles over the border, destroyed four more spars, resembling a mainmast and three topmasts. The smugglers never gave up; on July 23 two American galleys intercepted a large raft loaded with planks, spars, and 27 barrels of tar a mile from the border.[40]

Although bottled up in the Richelieu River, the British worked furiously to finish a fleet they hoped would command the lake. In anticipation of the larger fleet, Captain Peter Fisher had been appointed to command the British naval fleet on Lake Champlain in June. Pring, however, remained commander of the brig *Linnet*. The fleet consisted of the 60-foot sloop *Chub* with 11 guns, the 64-foot sloop *Finch*, also with 11 guns, and 12 gunboats, mounting either one or two cannons ranging from 18 to 32 pounds, named *Sir James Yeo*, *Sir George Prevost*, *Sir Sidney Beckwith*, *Brock*, *Murray*, *Wellington*, *Tecumseh*, *Drummond*, *Simcoe*, *Marshal Beresford*, *Popham*, and *Blucher*.[41]

The British pinned their hopes for naval supremacy on one huge ship. The vessel, hastily built under the direction of William Simons at Isle-aux-Noix, would mount 37 guns. The 831-ton, square-rigged, three-masted ship with a length of 147 feet and a 37-foot beam with two gun decks in the bow and stern was the largest fighting vessel ever used on the lake.[42] Launched on August 25, the frigate would be named *Confiance*, after a French ship which Commodore Sir James Lucas Yeo had captured and commanded early in his naval career.[43] Yeo had overall naval command on the Great Lakes and Lake Champlain. Short of men and fittings because Yeo had channeled much of the naval stores to Kingston on Lake Ontario for his own shipbuilding needs, the *Confiance* would require another 17 days to complete.

At the American shipyard at Vergennes, Adam Brown and his carpenters launched the new brig on August 11 in a record 19 days following the laying of her keel. It would take another two weeks, however, to finish the 117-foot brig. Just before the vessel's completion, recently-promoted Master Commandant Robert Henley, an ambitious officer with experience on the *Constellation* during the undeclared naval war with France, arrived with an appointment from Secretary Jones to command the new brig. Henley had commanded a gunboat division only briefly during an engagement in 1813 and was anxious to distinguish himself in the war. The independent and self-important 31-year-old officer immediately wrote directly to the secretary of navy with his name for the brig, the *Surprise*.[44] Macdonough, however, had written to Secretary Jones in early August asking his suggestion for a name "for the Brig or may I call her the Eagle."[45] On the morning of August 27, fresh southerly breezes snapped the new white sails of the *Surprise* as the brig reached Macdonough's anchorage near the Canadian border. The American fleet was now complete, mounting 92 cannons, which included six on the sloop *Montgomery* and one gun each on the four older gunboats.

The American fleet began training with the expectation of a strong British naval force leading an invasion of British troops into the Champlain Valley. In late July and early August, Governor-General Prevost noted the arrival of brigades from the Duke of Wellington's army, which had just defeated Napoleon's best troops in the Peninsular War (1809-1814). Two huge naval convoys of 60 transports, loaded with Europe's most experienced soldiers, sailed directly from France to Canada. At the end of August, more than 13,000 troops had been transferred from Europe. This was in addition to the thousands of regulars and militia already in Canada.

The traditional interpretation of the British strategy, still reflected in some modern histories of the war, suggested that the British planned to move through Lake Champlain and advance south along the Hudson River, thus severing the New England states from the rest of the country.[46] Soon after the battle at Plattsburgh, Governor Daniel Tompkins presented this interpretation to the New York legislature: "One great object...was to penetrate. . .Lake Champlain and the Hudson, and, by a simultaneous attack with his maritime force on New York, to form a junction which should sever the communication of the states."[47] Prevost's instructions from Lord Bathurst on June 3, however, were only to establish a foothold at Lake Champlain: "any advanced position on that part of your frontier which extends towards Lake Champlain, the occupation of which would materially tend to the security of the Province," but not to risk "being cut off by too extended a line of advance."[48] A dispatch by Prevost on August 5 lamented the lack of progress of the fleets which were to cooperate with "the occupation of Plattsburg."[49] After the battle Prevost described his intention "to establish the Army at Plattsburg and to detach from thence a Brigade for the destruction of Vergennes & its Naval establishment."[50]

In early August of 1814, commissioners from Great Britain and the United States met at Ghent, Belgium, to negotiate an end to the war. The initial claims were unrealistic in light of the final settlement, but at the time at least some were plausible given the military build-up. The British demanded land cessions in the upper part of Maine, west of the Great Lakes, the Champlain Valley, and land between the Ohio River and the Great Lakes. The Americans, not to be outdone, wanted the cession of Canada along with solutions to issues surrounding violations of American rights on the high seas. For the British to support their land claims, there would be a need to occupy some of the regions they demanded.

The American operations in 1814 were generally more successful, but the news was not all good. In early July tough American troops under Major General Jacob Brown and Brigadier General Winfield Scott were successful in several fierce battles on the Niagara frontier but withdrew to Fort Erie. As the main army was disembarking in Canada, a British diversionary force under Vice Admiral Alexander Cochrane and Rear Admiral George Cockburn roamed the American seaboard with troops of Major General Robert Ross to destroy any vulnerable cities along the coast. After a brief skirmish, the militia protecting Washington, D.C., fled in the face of Ross's experienced regulars. The British burned the city and withdrew with plans to raid Baltimore.

In the northern theater, delays due to the continuing naval construction race on Lake Ontario between Commodores Yeo at Kingston and Chauncey at Sackets Harbor left the main British thrust into America at Lake Champlain. Major General George Izard, a competent officer who had served a year earlier under Hampton, was assigned the main command of the American army at Plattsburgh. Brigadier General Alexander Macomb, a 32-year-old professional soldier who had graduated from West Point, was assigned by Izard to Burlington to head several regiments. In August Izard commanded a force of

5,100 men, including Macomb's regiments brought from Burlington. Six hundred troops were assigned to the construction of forts at Plattsburgh and Cumberland Head, while 4,500 were camped at Chazy and Champlain. On July 19, assuming that hostilities would occur on the Niagara frontier, Izard had asked for a transfer to the west. Once aware of Prevost's troop increases, Izard wrote back to Secretary of War Armstrong to rescind his request. By then, however, Armstrong had already made the decision that it would be good policy to "carry the war as far westward as possible while we have ascendency on the Lakes."[51] Izard warned Armstrong that he would go, "but I shall do it. . .with the certainty that everything in this vicinity...will in less than three days after my departure be in the possession of the enemy."[52] Izard departed with several thousand troops at the end of August, remaining at Lake George for two days hoping for a change of orders. His march to the Lake Ontario frontier was largely a wasted effort. (Following the burning of Washington, Armstrong was forced to resign on September 3.)

After the last of Izard's troops left on August 29, Macomb had approximately 1,500 effective regular troops left with another 900 sick from dysentery and typhus. Two days after Izard's main army had departed, the first elements of the British invasion crossed the border into New York. As a result of the presence of British troops on the New York shore, Macdonough decided to move his fleet from Point au Fer to Plattsburgh. The redeployment of the fleet began on August 31, but on the following afternoon light winds required the use of the row galleys to tow the *Saratoga*, *Ticonderoga*, and *Eagle* the remaining distance to Plattsburgh. When the British invasion began, Macomb immediately called on Major General Benjamin Mooers of the New York militia and Governor Chittenden of Vermont for militia. Mooers, on his own authority, called out the militia from the counties of Clinton, Essex, and Franklin, while Chittenden, following the earlier precept that Vermont militia would not serve outside her borders, appealed for volunteers. About 700 New York militia from the three counties marched immediately to Plattsburgh as the residents fled in panic with word of the British approach. Just before Prevost's army reached Plattsburgh, Macomb had assembled only 3,400 troops, but 1,400 were sick and 250 were serving on Macdonough's fleet; his instructions to the troops declared "The eyes of America are on us. . .Fortune always follows the brave."[53] By the time the battle began on September 11, 2,500 Vermont volunteers under Major General Samuel Strong had arrived in New York from towns across Vermont. Luckily for the Americans, the delay in bringing the British fleet to Plattsburgh caused Prevost to postpone his attack on the American position. Three redoubts or forts in Plattsburgh— Fort Scott, Fort Brown, and Fort Moreau—were strengthened in the meantime.

Prevost's army, consisting of thousands of veterans of the Napoleonic Wars, did not reach the Plattsburgh area until September 6. While contemporary reports and subsequent writers estimated the size of Prevost's army at Plattsburgh as high as 14,000 men, only 8,200 reached Plattsburgh with 2,100 troops assigned to outposts between the town and the Canadian border.[54] When the British troops reached Dead Creek in Plattsburgh on the morning of the 6th, the American galleys, which had been stationed there the day before, opened fire on the invaders. The British soon brought up some of their artillery to bear on the American vessels. Macdonough dispatched Acting Lieutenant Silas Duncan in the *Saratoga*'s gig (launch) to order the galleys back. Unfortunately, Duncan was severely wounded (later losing his right arm) but still delivered his orders. Most of the town fell to the British in one day, but the Americans sabotaged roads and removed planks from the bridges across the Saranac River. Macomb, whose men occupied the three forts south of the Saranac River, conspicuously paraded his troops to exaggerate his numbers and planted false information of additional troops nearby for British consumption.[55] With fewer than one-third the troops (over 700 American sick had been sent to Crab Island), Macomb faced Europe's best army.

Oftentimes, the chronicle of the battle of Plattsburgh neglects the vital role played by Brigadier General Alexander Macomb. Had he accepted the counsel of some of his officers to abandon the forts and retreat southward in the face of an overwhelming British army, the outcome of the naval engagement may have been different. With British control of the cannons at the forts, Macdonough's strategy based on an anchorage in Plattsburgh Bay could have been compromised. But Macomb was unequivocal in making a stand at the forts.

Macdonough's strategy for engaging the British had striking similarities to that of Benedict Arnold at Valcour Bay in 1776. A northern wind that would carry the British to Plattsburgh would also make it difficult for the enemy fleet to position itself in the bay. A close-range battle in the bay would permit the American fleet to use its carronades, more effective at shorter distances, than would a more distant battle on the open lake where the British had superiority in long-range guns. By September both sides had fairly accurate intelligence of the composition of each other's fleet. Macdonough moved his fleet to a position, presumably out of range of the shore batteries, about 100 yards off Cumberland Head, where the vessels, in a north-south line, were set in an intricate anchoring system with spring lines. With two anchors dropped on each side of the bow and the stern anchored, the vessels could be turned end to end to bring fresh guns from the opposite side of the ship to bear on the enemy should the guns on the original side become disabled.

Macdonough's fleet included the *Saratoga*, *Ticonderoga*, *Surprise*, *Preble* and ten galleys/gunboats. The sloops *President* and *Montgomery*, former merchant vessels, had been assigned to transport duty with the latter vessel transferring 16 of its crew to the undermanned brig on September 2. (The sloop *President* probably would have been included in Macdonough's final war fleet at Plattsburgh Bay, but a squall had damaged the vessel, requiring removal of her guns for repairs.[56]) Four days later, the brig *Surprise* (a name that Macdonough personally had never used) was redesignated the *Eagle*.[57] In all probability, Macdonough made the decision himself to change the name from Master Commandant Henley's designation to his original selection. Joseph Smith, the first lieutenant of the short-handed *Eagle*, approached Brigadier General Macomb on September 7 with a note from Macdonough requesting more troops. When Macomb refused, the enterprising lieutenant asked for Macomb's prisoners. Forty prisoners (all American soldiers) in ball and chain were freed and taken aboard the *Eagle* for a regimen of gun training. A few days later, six musicians in the army band (one brought along his wife) were recruited as crew members aboard the *Eagle*. From September 7 through 11, the two armies and Macdonough's navy awaited the arrival of the British fleet at Plattsburgh Bay.

The flagship of the British fleet, the 37-gun *Confiance*, was still being completed in early September when Commodore Yeo sent Captain George Downie from Lake Ontario to command the ship and the British fleet, replacing Captain Peter Fisher, who subsequently protested the change in command. Downie, unfamiliar with Lake Champlain and his new crews, arrived at the Isle-aux-Noix shipyard on September 1, but he did not assume command until the 3rd.[58] On the same day, Captain Daniel Pring, leaving the brig *Linnet* in the hands of her first lieutenant, sailed with the sloops *Chub* and *Finch* and the gunboats to protect the advancing British army on the New York shore. Pring established a three-gun battery at Isle La Motte to guard the mouth of the Little Chazy River, the intended landing site for British supply vessels.[59] With pressure from Prevost to sail, Downie departed from Isle-aux-Noix with the unfinished *Confiance* on September 7. After temporarily grounding the vessel in the river, Downie moved as far as Ash Island with the *Confiance* and the brig *Linnet*.

On the 8th at Point au Fer, Downie indignantly answered Prevost's letter, written earlier in the day, which had again pressed for the arrival of the *Confiance*: "I stated to you that this Ship was not ready. She is not ready now, and, until she is ready, it is my duty not to hazard the Squadron before an Enemy who will be superior in Force."[60] Downie anchored off the Little Chazy River opposite Isle La Motte, where finishing work continued and crews had their first opportunity for gun practice. While the crews were "Exercising the Great Guns," workers "were employed in making Shot lockers, altering Beds and Coins [supports and quoin wedges for the elevation of cannons] and driving in belaying pins & c."[61] Downie informed Prevost of his intention to depart at midnight on September 10, but unfavorable winds delayed the departure, affording the naval commander time to host a grand banquet at Chazy Landing, where many toasts of wine and rum were offered to a British victory.[62] The following morning Dowie sailed with his fleet for Plattsburgh. The artificers and riggers left the vessel only a short time before the battle, but shipbuilder William Simons made the fatal decision to remain aboard the British flagship. Prevost and Downie agreed upon a scaling of guns (shooting cannons without balls) as a signal to prepare for a joint land and naval assault on the American positions. At quarter past five in the morning, the British fleet fired their blank shots just north of Cumberland Head.[63] All the commanding officers were shortly called aboard the *Confiance* by Downie for directions as to which American vessels they would each engage. "Having approached within a League of Cumberland Head the Enemys Mast Heads were seen over the Land," recounted First Lieutenant James Robertson of the *Confiance*, "Captain Downie accompanied by the Master went in his Gig [small boat] to reconnoiter their position."[64] After inspecting the deployment of the American vessels, Downie returned in his boat to the fleet with final instructions for the officers and crews. The *Linnet*, supported by the *Chub*, was to attack the *Eagle*; the *Confiance* would fire her starboard guns into the *Eagle* and her port battery into the *Saratoga*; the gunboats were to attack the *Ticonderoga*; and the *Finch* would support the gunboats and later engage the *Preble*. The supply/hospital sloop *Icicle* would remain at a distance.

The British fleet moved into Plattsburgh Bay by eight o'clock on the morning of the 11th (there are slight differences in the recorded time of the battle by original participants).[65] The two fleets were nearly evenly matched, although the British vessels, primarily the *Confiance*, had greater weight in long-range cannons. Both fleets (particularly the American) had a hodgepodge of crews consisting of trained seamen and inexperienced land troops. None of the crews was prepared for the devastating savagery of the ensuing battle. The British commander decided to engage Macdonough on the latter's pre-arranged position in the bay rather than try to fight at a distance on the open lake. Although pressure from Prevost played a role in Downie's decision to engage immediately, the British naval commander was overconfident of his frigate's ability to destroy the American fleet. Two days before the engagement, Prevost had reported to Downie that the American fleet was "insufficiently manned" and had staffed the new brig *Eagle* with prisoners. Downie was said to have felt that the *Confiance* alone was a match for the whole American fleet.[66]

As the British sailed closer, the American fleet lay in a line from north to south with the *Eagle* the farthest north, adjacent to the *Saratoga*, *Ticonderoga*, and *Preble*. The six larger American galleys and four smaller gunboats were stationed in four divisions west of the larger ships. (One division of three galleys was northwest of the *Eagle*.) On the shores of Cumberland Head, anxious residents viewed the scene as history was about to unfold. Similarly, British and Canadian civilians, including women, watched the battle from a small vessel at a safe distance, confident of a British victory.[67] Meanwhile, the prearranged, coordinated attack on land had a delayed start. The British troops were ordered by Prevost to make breakfast as the British fleet approached Plattsburgh Bay.[68] Although the British batteries opened on the American forts as the naval engagement commenced around nine o'clock, the orders to the British army to ford the Saranac River did not come until an hour later.

The British fleet, tacking against the light northerly breeze, had difficulty reaching its planned position in the bay. Macdonough and his men, amid the anxiety and grim expectations, knelt on the deck of the *Saratoga* for a brief prayer before the onslaught began. As the *Confiance* maneuvered into position, Master Commandant Robert Henley directed a hasty broadside from his long 18-pound cannons, but the shots fell short of the British flagship. When the *Linnet* sailed past the *Saratoga* on her way to a position to engage the *Eagle*, a broadside aimed at Macdonough's ship fell short, except for a shot that struck a hen coop aboard the American flagship. The bird, a gamecock kept by the seamen, jumped on a gun-slide, flapped his wings and crowed lustily and defiantly, according to James Sloan, Macdonough's clerk.[69] The *Saratoga*'s crew sent up a cheer, regarding the incident as a good omen. Soon afterward, Macdonough fired a single gun from the *Saratoga* as a signal to his fleet to open fire on the enemy. The *Confiance* was immediately hit with a piercing fire that shot away two anchors on her port bow. Without firing a shot, Downie continued maneuvering the *Confiance* but prematurely anchored the vessel at a distance from Macdonough's flagship. Once in place, a double-shotted broadside from the *Confiance*'s 24-pound guns ripped through the decks of the *Saratoga*, instantly killing or wounding 40 of her crew. The blast shook the *Saratoga* so violently that half the crew were flattened.

"Macdonough Pointing the Gun." Painting by John R. Chapin,
engraving by D. Virtue & Co. (Line of Battle, Inc.)

Above: "The Plight of the English Flagship" *Confiance* from *Naval Action of the War of 1812* by James Barnes, 1896.

Below: "MacDonough's Victory on Lake Champlain." Painting by H. Reinagle, engraved by Benjamin Tanner. E. Newbold Smith Collection. (Independence Seaport Museum)

Right: Maps of "Battle of Plattsburgh Bay." (*Dedication of the Thomas Macdonough Memorial*, 1926)

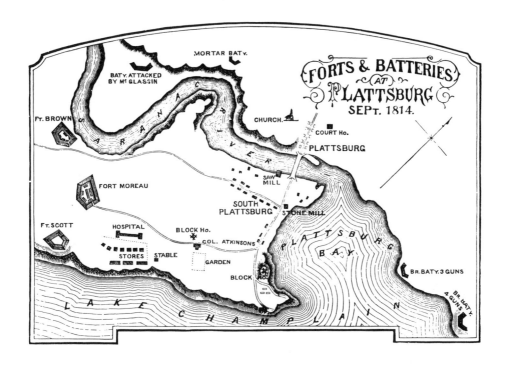

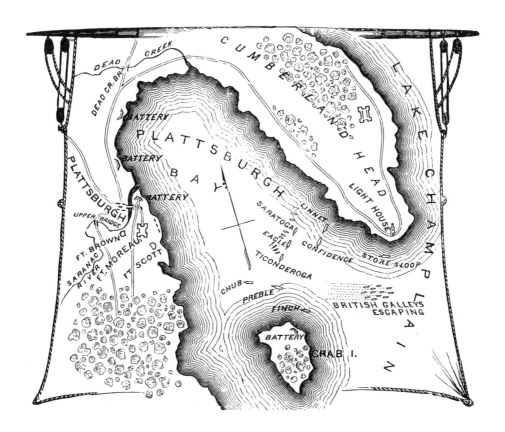

By now nearly all the vessels were engaged in the battle. The *Linnet*, just to the northeast of the *Eagle*, unleashed a raking fire upon the bow of the American brig, while the sloop *Chub* maneuvered to fire on the *Eagle's* stern. Four British gunboats and the *Finch* engaged the *Preble* and *Ticonderoga*. The American galleys and gunboats supported the *Eagle* and *Saratoga* on the northern end of the American line and the *Ticonderoga* and *Preble* at the southern end. Fifteen minutes after the action had commenced, Captain Downie was killed almost instantly when a shot from the *Saratoga* struck a 24-pound cannon on the *Confiance*, throwing it completely off its carriage into the British commander's groin. The fallen commander had no part of his skin broken; the only visible injury was a black streak across his chest. His watch had been flattened upon impact, with its hands pointed to the hour and minute when he received the fatal injury.[70] (The cannon that killed Downie remains at the U.S. Naval Academy at Annapolis on the lawn next to Macdonough Hall.)

Only 15-20 minutes into the action, the sloop *Chub*, commanded by Lieutenant James McGhie, had her cables, bowsprit, sails, yards, and main boom shot away. The *Chub* drifted helplessly through the American lines while most of her crew remained below deck. Lieutenant McGhie, after two of his finger tips were shot off and he had received a wound to his thigh from a splinter, went below deck, where he was later joined by ten soldiers and marines who left their stations. With five dead and three times that number wounded, only six men were left on the deck of the vessel when McGhie ordered Midshipman John Bodell to strike the colors and surrender.[71]

From a vantage point on Cumberland Head, Julius Hubbell observed the thunder and destruction on the water: "The firing was terrific, fairly shaking the ground, and so rapid that it seemed to be one continuous roar, intermingled with spiteful flashing from the mouths of the guns, and dense clouds of smoke soon hung over the two fleets."[72] Macdonough, while sighting a cannon on the *Saratoga*, was knocked senseless onto the deck when a cannonball cut the spanker boom in two, causing the heavy spar to fall upon him. As he regained his composure, he was again knocked to the deck by the flying head of his own gun captain which had been severed by a cannonball.[73] Elie La Vallette, acting lieutenant on the *Saratoga*, was similarly thrown to the deck after being hit by a decapitated head.[74]

At the southern end of the line, the sloop *Preble*, commanded by Lieutenant Charles Budd, and the schooner *Ticonderoga*, under Lieutenant Stephen Cassin, were engaged with the British sloop *Finch* and four gunboats. Only four British gunboats, the *Marshall Beresford*, *Murray*, *Popham*, and the *Blucher* were vigorously engaged in the attack at the southern end of the line.[75] Most of the gunboats, largely manned by French Canadian militia who spoke no English, remained out of range to the leeward off Crab Island during much of the engagement.[76]

The *Finch* initially fired on the *Ticonderoga*, but soon Acting Lieutenant William Hicks turned the sloop's guns on the *Preble*, as did some of the British gunboats. An hour into the battle, to the cheers of the British crew, "the Enemy's Sloop [*Preble*] slip her cable and haul down her Colours to me."[77] Lieutenant Budd moved the sloop to the safety of the Plattsburgh shoreline. (Although Macdonough later stated that Budd's "best Quality is in his Seamanship," he recorded that Budd "did not behave well on the 11th Septr. [1814]."[78]) Lieutenant James Robertson, who assumed command of the *Confiance* when Captain Downie was killed, also observed the *Preble* "retire in shore with her colours struck, where however she afterwards rehoisted them."[79] After the *Preble* left, the fire of the gunboats and *Finch* was directed at the *Ticonderoga*. Although the British gunboat crews had hoped to board the *Ticonderoga*, the schooner successfully fought off its attackers but suffered six men killed and six wounded during the engagement. The

American galleys and gunboats played a less aggressive role during the battle than did the larger vessels. However, the 75-foot American galley *Borer*, commanded by Midshipman Thomas Conover, advanced to the bow of the *Ticonderoga* but was hit directly by the British cannon fire, killing three crew members and wounding one. Seven of the ten American galleys and gunboats had no casualties at all, while the *Centipede* and the smaller *Wilmer* suffered one injured crew member each. The low casualties were probably the result of the vessels' small size and height, which made them less important targets at the northern end of the line where the fire of the *Linnet* and *Confiance* focused on the *Eagle* and *Saratoga*.

Following a crippling broadside from the *Ticonderoga*, the *Finch*, with three and a half feet of water in her hold and the main boom, mast, and rigging severely damaged, drifted out of control toward Crab Island. The *Finch* ran aground on a reef on the northeast side of the island, whereupon convalescing soldiers fired two field pieces at the striken sloop. The *Finch* returned the fire, forcing the gunners to seek cover. Lieutenant William Hicks "then order'd four Eighteen Pound Carronades to be hove overboard but without any Effect to her."[80] The vessel could not be refloated, but Hicks did not strike her colors until the *Confiance* surrendered and the gunboats had fled.[81]

In the heat of the battle between the *Saratoga* and *Confiance*, confusion reigned as the men struggled to cripple one another's flagships. The Americans overloaded carronades, often cramming them with shot as far as the muzzle. The confusion may have been worse on board the *Confiance*. After the battle, one cannon was found to have been loaded with two balls but no powder; another had been loaded without shot, and a third had the wad and cartridge loaded in reverse order. The inexperienced crew on the British frigate often failed to readjust the quoin, or gun-wedge, under the rear of the cannons which loosened after each shot. The muzzle of the guns would thus be raised higher and higher, causing the shots to fly over the heads of the crew on the *Saratoga* and into the lower rigging and hammocks.

At 10:30 the brig *Eagle* had her starboard anchor spring shot away, causing the vessel to turn, so that her remaining guns were no longer effective. By then the dead on her deck included two of the musicians recruited at the last minute for the engagement. When the wife of James M. Hale, one of the army musicians, replaced the powder boy who had been killed, she had to step over the dead on the bloody deck, one of whom she recognized as her husband.[82] A participant in the war later recalled that "Mrs. Hale...with a cool serenity...supplied the gunners with ammunition & other martial materials & to those who lay wounded on the deck she administered every Comfort in her power."[83]

With the guns of the *Eagle* serving no purpose, Henley promptly made the decision to leave his station: "I ordered the cable cut and cast the brig, taking an advantageous position a little south of the *Saratoga*."[84] The *Eagle* anchored between the *Saratoga* and *Ticonderoga*, leaving the flagship endangered by the *Linnet*'s guns. Although Macdonough was restrained in his criticism of Henley, he noted in his report to Navy Secretary Jones two days later that the move left him "exposed to a galling fire from the Enemy's brig [*Linnet*]."[85] In a fitness report to the Board of the Navy Commissioners in 1815, Macdonough noted that Henley was "very deficient in Seamanship and in the equipment of a Vessel of War...[however] he behaved like a brave man on the 11th Sept. last, though his vessel was badly managed."[86]

Late in the battle, Macdonough's starboard guns were nearly all unusable or dismounted. By the prearranged plan, the stern anchor was disengaged and the bow cable cut, allowing the *Saratoga* to be turned end to end. The American flagship could now bring fresh guns to bear on the *Confiance*. By then the British flagship was torn to pieces with mangled bodies strewn across her decks. Many of the dead had been thrown overboard while " numerous wounded below were frequently moved from place to place to prevent their being drowned" as water poured into the shattered hull.[87] Lieutenant James Robertson sought to duplicate the *Saratoga*'s maneuver, but in the middle of the turn, the *Confiance* became stranded with her bow facing the *Saratoga*. By then the British crew had had enough: "the Ship's Company declared they would stand no longer to their Quarters, nor could the Officers with their utmost exertions rally them," Robertson later testified.[88] Desperate to save his ship, Robertson tried to signal the gunboats in the far distance for assistance, but "the Signal book, in consequence of the Captain's Death, had been mislaid."[89] Reluctantly, Robertson called the surviving officers together for a council, which decided upon surrender since "keeping up the Colours any longer would be a Wanton and useless waste of human blood."[90]

The *Saratoga*'s fire was now directed on the brig *Linnet*, whose masts, sails, and rigging had been shot away, making escape impossible. With a foot of water above the lower deck and no chance of being towed away by the elusive gunboats, Pring surrendered his brig about 15 minutes after the *Confiance* had given up. Macdonough initially ordered the American galleys to pursue the 12 fleeing British gunboats but quickly rescinded the command in order to use the vessels and their crews to save the sinking ships. While Macdonough's official report to the secretary of navy mentioned that "Three of their Gallies [gunboats] are said to be sunk," no British gunboats actually sank in the engagement.[91] Macdonough also recorded that 13 galleys (gunboats) accompanied the British fleet, but evidence suggests that 12 or perhaps only 11 were present.[92] Macdonough probably mistook the supply/hospital sloop *Icicle* for a gunboat, as it was among the British gunboats that had retreated from the main action. The gunboats regrouped and hastily retreated north, passing a "public" house near the ferry landing on Cumberland Head. The escaping British vessels were serenaded by the residents with tin pans, bells, and horns, but the chorus was silenced by a cannon shot fired into the house.[93]

The battle, which ended at about 11:20 A.M., had raged for two hours and 20 minutes, with deafening cannon booms accompanied by musket fire, hissing rockets, and artillery fire on shore. At the end of the engagement Midshipman William Lee aboard the *Confiance* found his clothes "literally torn all to rags with shot and splinters; the upper part of my hat was also shot away. There is one of the marines who was in Trafalgar action with Lord [Horatio] Nelson, who says it was a mere fleabite in comparison with this."[94] The rigging, masts, spars, and sails on the *Confiance* and *Linnet* were virtually all shot away. There were 250 to 300 cannonballs lodged in the hull of the *Confiance* (Macdonough's original report had 105), 55 in the *Saratoga*'s hull, 39 in the *Eagle*, and 30 to 50 shot holes in the *Linnet*.[95] Macdonough also recorded that "the *Saratoga* was twice set on fire by hot Shot from the Enemy's Ship," but British officers denied the use of hot shot by the fleet in subsequent court-martial testimony.[96] The casualties were high on both sides: 52 American dead and 58 wounded with estimates of 54 to 57 British killed and 116 wounded. (Lieutenant James Robertson reported that the *Confiance* alone had 40 killed and 83 wounded.)[97] Many of the dead on the *Confiance* had been thrown overboard during the engagement; some of their bodies continued to float to the surface days after the battle.

When the battle on the lake began, Prevost's batteries began a barrage of shells, balls, and congreve rockets which " fell thick as hailstones" on the American forts and land positions, according to William Miller, an army officer at the battle.[98] Prevost, however, did not dispatch troops to ford the Saranac River and attack the American positions until ten o'clock, halfway through the naval battle. At three different points the British army attempted to cross the river. After initially getting lost, the British managed to reach the upper ford of the Saranac River, where they were eventually successful in dispersing a spirited detachment of American militia and volunteers. The British who attempted crossings at the two lower fords located at the bridges were repulsed by American regulars. By the time British troops had crossed at the upper ford, Prevost "had the extreme Mortification" to hear shouts of victory from the Americans over the *Confiance*'s surrender: "This unlooked for event Depriving me of the cooperation of the Fleet without which the further prosecution of the service was...impracticable, I did not hesitate to arrest the course of the Troops advancing to the attack."[99]

The land battle at the Saranac River crossing; opposing fleets in the background.
From an 1816 engraving. (Schaffer Library, Union College)

Late in the day the British ceased their bombardment and then withdrew their artillery at dusk. At sundown the American forts fired one last salute with their guns accompanied by the tune "Yankee Doodle." "At two the next morning," Brigadier General Macomb later reported to the secretary of war that "the whole army precipitately retreated, leaving the sick and wounded to our generosity."[100] During the hasty flight, large amounts of provisions, cannonballs, shells, and tents were abandoned, some dumped in ponds, creeks and Lake Champlain. John Suth Sinclair, commander of the British artillery, later disclosed " that a Sloop laden with Stores (partly Ordnance Stores) unfortunately sank off Isle la Mothe [Motte] and fell into the hands of the Enemy."[101] On November 6 Macdonough reported that "A Transport Sloop has recently been raised at Isle la Motte, which was Sunk by the Enemy loaded with their Naval Stores, and various Instruments of War."[102] In addition, about six tons of shells hidden in the waters off Chazy were also recovered.

Within half an hour of the conclusion of the naval engagement on September 11, Macdonough wrote a simple message to Navy Secretary Jones: "The Almighty has been pleased to grant us a signal victory on Lake Champlain in the capture of one frigate, one brig, and two sloops of war of the enemy."[103] After a short period of time, Captain Pring and Lieutenants Robertson, McGhie, and Hicks boarded the *Saratoga* and presented their swords to Macdonough. The American commander, in a magnanimous gesture, bowed and declared, "Gentlemen, return your swords into your scabbards and wear them. You are worthy of them."[104] The wounded men from both sides were treated at the hospital on Crab Island; 47 of the most seriously wounded were paroled to Isle-aux-Noix by Macdonough. The British and American dead were buried side by side in unmarked graves on the north end of Crab Island. The bodies of 15 dead officers, including Captain George Downie, however, were covered with flags and buried on the shore in a formal funeral ceremony on September 14 (present-day Riverside Cemetery). The next day many of the 367 prisoners, well enough to travel, departed on the steamer *Vermont* for their journey to prisons further south. The officers of the *Linnet* wrote a letter on the steamer just before departure, expressing gratitude for their "honorable treatment" by Macdonough. Similarly, Lieutenant James Robertson, at the request of the surviving officers of the *Confiance*, conveyed a feeling of debt to Macdonough for the "unbounded liberality and humane attention not only extended to themselves but to the unfortunate wounded seamen and marines."[105]

Macdonough, of course, was honored for his part in the victory, receiving public dinners in Plattsburgh and Burlington, gifts of land by Vermont and New York, a gold medal from Congress, and promotion by the navy. Most of the troops who served in Plattsburgh went unpaid during 1814, as did Henry Delord and William Bailey, who had granted $20,000 in credit to officers and soldiers at their store in Plattsburgh. The partners eventually went bankrupt; appeals to Washington for repayment as late as 1841 by Bailey and Henry Delord's widow were unsuccessful.

In 1815 the Royal Navy held a court-martial of Captain Daniel Pring and the other officers who participated in the Plattsburgh naval engagement. The hearings, held aboard the *H.M.S. Gladiator* in Portsmouth Harbor, England, from August 18 to 21, 1815, honorably acquitted the naval officers except Lieutenant James McGhie of the sloop *Chub*, who did not appear at the trial, and Lieutenant Mark Raynham, the commander of the gunboats, who had been cashiered from the service earlier. (Raynham had fled with the gunboat *Yeo* to the safety of the hospital sloop *Icicle* during the battle.) The blame for the naval failure was placed on Governor-General Prevost who had urged the *Confiance* "into Battle previous to its being in a proper state to meet its Enemy by a promised Cooperation of the Land Forces, which was not carried into Effect."[106] The court also "agreed that the Attack would have been more effectual if part of the Gun Boats had not failed in their Duty."[107] Although obviously conjecture, some officers contended that Prevost's shore batteries could have driven Macdonough from the bay before the battle. According to this viewpoint, Prevost could have prevented the defeated British squadron from falling into American hands by providing a covering fire had the British army stormed Macomb's positions. Broken by the negative publicity of the naval court-martial which impugned his reputation, Sir George Prevost died early in January 1816, a month before he had a chance to present his side of the story in a court-martial hearing.

Although the British army and navy had made inroads in Maine, and Commodore James Lucas Yeo in late 1814 had blockaded the American fleet at Sacket's Harbor, the British had been turned back at Baltimore and decisively defeated in Plattsburgh Bay. When London newspapers published the outrageous demands of the British peace delegation at Ghent, the body politic and populace exhibited increased disfavor with the war. Similarly, the Hartford Convention, which met December 15, manifested the disagreement over the war by some of the New England states. With the failure to strike a foothold at Plattsburgh and heightened public pressure at home, the British dropped their territorial claims. The American delegation correspondingly jettisoned the maritime demands that the war had originally been undertaken to end. The result was the Treaty of Ghent, signed on Christmas Eve of 1814, which preserved the status quo on all boundaries. While this was certainly not a victory for America, the young nation proved its resilience against Europe's greatest power and emerged with an enhanced sense of national identity. Ironically, one of the most notable battles of the war, Andrew Jackson's successful defense of New Orleans, occurred several weeks after the signing of the peace treaty without the participants knowing of the settlement because of the slow communications of the day. But Jackson's victory insured ratification of the treaty and put an end to British plans for taking Louisiana.

The engagement at Plattsburgh Bay was the turning point of the war. "The battle of Lake Champlain, more nearly than any other incident of the War of 1812 merits the epithet 'decisive' " wrote the noted American naval historian, Captain (later Admiral) A. T. Mahan in 1905.[108] Theodore Roosevelt's earlier volume, *The Naval War of 1812*, credits Macdonough's foresight and resourcefulness with the victory by forcing "the British to engage at a disadvantage. . . . His skill, seamanship, quick eye, readiness of resource, and indomitable pluck, are beyond all praise."[109]

The American naval squadron remained at Plattsburgh Bay in the fall of 1814, making repairs to the devastated vessels. In early October Macdonough transferred to the *Eagle*, while sending the *Saratoga*, *Confiance*, *Linnet*, and *Ticonderoga* to winter quarters in Whitehall. He retained the six galleys, four gunboats, and the sloops *Preble*, *Montgomery*, *Finch*, and *Chub*. At the end of the fall, the vessels were consigned to winter quarters at Whitehall under Lieutenant Charles Budd. In the meanwhile, Macdonough journeyed to New York City to command the first steamship of war, the 156-foot *Fulton First*, built by Adam and Noah Brown. Orders issued on December 27, 1814, by the new navy secretary, Benjamin Homans, recalled Macdonough to Whitehall to take measures "to repell an expected attempt of the enemy to destroy the fleet."[110] Although there was no raid, Macdonough did obtain intelligence that the British were building more vessels at Isle-aux-Noix. With the news that the Treaty of Ghent had been signed and the possibility of renewed hostilities remote, the American fleet and captured British vessels were laid up in "ordinary" in March 1815 with a dismantling and storing of the guns, sails, and naval stores.

Macdonough soon left Lake Champlain, spending most of the next ten years commanding American navy frigates. On October 24, 1825, after news of his wife's death reached Macdonough, then in command of the Mediterranean fleet aboard the *Constitution*, the ailing commodore decided to return home with his four-year-old son. Six hundred miles from America, on November 10, the hero of Lake Champlain succumbed to tuberculosis aboard the merchant brig *Edwin*.

From left to right: the *Eagle*, *Linnet*, *Saratoga*, *Ticonderoga*, and *Confiance* "laid up at Whitehall. . .Sept. 9, 1816." Watercolor, 1816. (Lake Champlain Maritime Museum)

In May 1815 the fleet at Whitehall was placed under the command of Captain James Leonard, an officer court-martialed during the war and relegated to secondary duty. Following an authorization for a public sale by the navy, the sloops *Preble, Montgomery, President, Chub,* and *Finch* were sold in July 1815 for prices ranging from $805 to $2,430. The four oldest gunboats, *Ludlow, Wilmer, Alwyn,* and *Ballard,* were sold for less than $100, but the sale of the six 75-foot galleys was canceled because bids were too low. The larger vessels remained moored end to end at the "Elbow" north of the center of Whitehall, while the six galleys were sunk for preservation in 1815. The following year, the galley *Allen* was raised and used for survey work on the lake.[111] In later years, the vessel was used for patrol duty.

Traveling through Whitehall in November 1818, Scottish tourist John M. Duncan observed that the remaining vessels were "dismantled and roofed over."[112] In the fall of 1819, Professor Benjamin Silliman, aboard the steamboat *Congress,* also viewed the mothballed fleet at Whitehall: "As we passed rapidly by, a few seamen showed their heads through the grim port-holes. . . . Spareless, black and frowning, these now dismantled ships, look like the coffins of the brave."[113] In January 1820 the rotting *Confiance* settled on the bottom in six feet of water. During the following summer, Captain Leonard brought the *Eagle, Linnet,* and *Ticonderoga* to new moorings along the banks of the Poultney River (East Bay). Late that year, the *Saratoga* and the *Confiance,* after being temporarily pumped out, were likewise brought into the East Bay.[114] When Professor Silliman again passed Whitehall "in June 1821, these vessels were lying a little way down the lake, mere wrecks, sunken, neglected and in ruins."[115]

The *Saratoga* settled in shallow water in 1821 with her upper works, which had been modified as barracks, above water. At least for some of the time, the abandoned vessels were used by local squatters as dwellings. Large sections of the *Confiance* were broken up in 1824 after the vessel washed into the lake channel. Following an unsuccessful auction in June 1825, which required the removal of the vessels, the remaining fleet was sold to salvagers who were not required to remove the hulks. Over the years, salvagers removed all of the exposed wood and iron on the vessels. The *Eagle,* however, sank on her port side before wrecking crews could rip her apart.[116] During the summer of 1873, dredging caused the remaining hull of the *Confiance* to float into the main channel. The vessel was blown up with nitroglycerine, and 300 pounds of copper were salvaged from the hull.[117] The famous vessels that had changed the course of history thus ended their careers ingloriously as junk. (Some walking canes were also made from the wrecks, including the *Confiance.*)

Following the War of 1812, peace finally became a permanent state of affairs along the Lake Champlain corridor but not without new fortifications. In 1817 construction of an American fort began on a site north of Rouses Point. Despite problems related to an inadequate foundation, work continued on the octagon-shaped fort through 1818. A new land survey under the Treaty of Ghent disclosed that the fort's location was partially on Canadian soil. The fort resembled a "great stone castle" when observed by Professor Silliman in 1819.[118] Thereafter, the abandoned fortification became known as Fort Blunder to residents, who subsequently carted away materials for local buildings. Years later in 1842, the Webster-Ashburton Treaty re-established the fort area on American territory. In 1844, construction of a new fort, named Fort Montgomery for the hero of Quebec in 1775, finally began. The immense stone fort with five bastions was surrounded by water and connected by a drawbridge over a moat to the mainland. Although nearly completed, Fort Montgomery's construction was suspended in 1870 and the fort abandoned in 1908 with the cannons given to cities and towns. Although designed for an 800-man garrison, apparently only one sergeant and an engineer ever occupied the outpost. Some of the fort's walls were used as foundation material during the construction of the Rouses Point Bridge during the 1930s. Today the crumbling fort, owned by a Canadian developer, stands in silent vigil over the calm waters of the Richelieu River and Lake Champlain. The ruins of Fort Montgomery are in stark contrast to the excellently-preserved fortification on Isle-aux-Noix. Fort Lennox, built by the British between 1819 and 1829 to guard the Canadian frontier against the Americans, was constructed on the original ruins of the 1759 French fort. Today, the massive stone fort is a Canadian National Historic Park and military museum.

The southern section and the interior of Fort Montgomery.
(Delaware and Hudson Railroad Collection, New York State Library)

Archaeological Discoveries

The wrecks of the *Ticonderoga, Linnet, Eagle*, and galley *Allen* remained relatively undisturbed near the first major bend in the Poultney River until the mid-twentieth century. The *Linnet*, then an unnamed wreck, was broken into two pieces in a clumsy salvage attempt in 1949.[119] Seventy-five feet of the vessel survived until local farmers employed three tractors and horses to haul a section of the wreck from the river.[120] A split 13-inch mortar, 350 cannonballs, and two disabled cannons were also retrieved from the wreck. One of the cannons and the split mortar were purchased by Fort Ticonderoga and the second cannon with "smashed Trunnions" and "105 cannonballs, 38 bar shot and six exploding bombs" were acquired by Carroll V. Lonergan for the Fort Mount Hope museum in Ticonderoga.[121] Although an 1812 Canadian coin had been found in the step of a mast, the artifacts were referred to as "1777 relics."[122] The split mortar and disabled cannons aboard the *Linnet* originally had been used as ballast on the American galley *Trumbull*, captured by the British in 1777.[123]

The retrieved section of the vessel was later displayed at Fort Mount Hope with an erroneous sign identifying the vessel as possibly one of Arnold's gondolas of 1776. Cannonballs and pieces of the wreck were sold in subsequent years at an antique shop in Ticonderoga. A 1995 joint field school of Texas A & M University and the University of Vermont, directed by Dr. Kevin Crisman and Arthur Cohn, examined the wreck of the *Linnet*, which had been first identified during a 1981-1983 Champlain Maritime Society field school. Researchers excavated 23 floor timbers on the starboard side of the 58-foot-long hull section and discovered a 14-foot portion of the keel about eight feet upriver. Careful measurements were taken of the frames of the vessel and the remaining pieces located at Fort Mount Hope, which were then owned by Fort Ticonderoga.[124]

A second vessel, the American schooner *Ticonderoga*, was raised in the fall of 1958 by volunteers working for the Whitehall Bicentennial Committee. A few of the members of the team who had raised the *Linnet* in 1949 directed the salvage operation of the

Remains of *U.S.S. Ticonderoga* raised in 1958 at Whitehall. Photo by the author.

Top: Section of British brig *Linnet* raised in 1949 from East Bay, Whitehall. (New York State Archives)

Above: Remains of *Linnet* (ca. 1980s). Photo by the author.

Right: Archaeological study of the brig *Linnet* at East Bay, Whitehall, in 1995. Photo by the author.

Ticonderoga.[125] The techniques employed by the crew were similar to those employed in 1949: cables were attached to the hull and connected to two bulldozers and a town dumptruck, but the salvors were forced to cut the vessel into sections and to use dynamite to free the wreck from the river bed. A number of artifacts were recovered with the hull, including grape/cannister shot, cannonballs, and a 25-foot-long piece of a shot garland.[126] The six sections of the vessel were reassembled and placed on display under an open shed at the new Skenesborough Museum in Whitehall, which opened in 1959. A full-scale study of the *Ticonderoga* was conducted in 1981 by Kevin Crisman as part of his academic program at Texas A & M University. Measuring the keel, keelson, strakes, and frames, Crisman found the hull in "generally good condition."[127] Fifty-five of the original 59 frames were partially present on the remains of the *Ticonderoga*.

Since the locations of the wrecks in East Bay had been well known for years, scuba divers in the 1950s and 1960s had removed hundreds of artifacts before archaeologists could document the site.[128] In 1957 Carroll V. Lonergan and his sons located the wreckage of three vessels "about one hundred twenty-five feet in length" and planned to return the following summer to recover cannonballs, bar shot, and any cannons that might be present.[129] The next year several hundred cannonballs were removed from the wrecks at East Bay.[130]

The number and names of the vessels remaining in East Bay continued to be a mystery as late as the 1970s. Using scuba equipment and information supplied by a local resident, I explored two wrecks in the bay in October 1970. After crawling through the comparatively intact wreckage of one vessel, I abandoned my survey due to the five-inch visibility.[131] This relatively intact vessel was identified as the brig *Eagle* over a decade later by the Champlain Maritime Society in its comprehensive study of the wreck directed by Kevin Crisman. The 1981-1983 study was sponsored by the Vermont Division for Historic Preservation with federal grant funds and a grant from the Vermont Historical Society. One hundred fifteen feet of the *Eagle* was still intact in the bay with ten of the original 24 gunports still in existence. The results of the study also indicated that the *Eagle* had a very shallow draft (seven feet three inches in the hold), which would contradict early depictions of the battle that showed vessels similar in hull design to ocean warships. In addition to taking thorough measurements of the structure and determining the original dimensions of the vessel, divers discovered shot garlands, iron fittings, two bottles, a few tools and shot on the wreck.[132] Archaeologists also identified a section of a partially-sunk vessel as the remains of the *Linnet* and discovered the 75-foot galley *Allen*. The project resulted in a book by Kevin Crisman, *The Eagle: An American Brig on Lake Champlain*, published in 1987.

The remains of the 75-foot galley *Allen*, located during the Champlain Maritime Society's 1981-1983 Whitehall fieldwork, became the subject of a thorough examination during the 1995 field school directed by Crisman and Cohn (see *Linnet* field school above). Archaeologists discovered that approximately 50 percent of the original hull remained intact, including the 70-foot keel and 67-foot keelson. The team excavated and documented all sections of the wreckage, concluding that the row galleys were hurriedly constructed, and that builder Noah Brown made significant alterations to the plans approved in October 1813 by William Doughty, chief naval constructor at Washington, D.C. Brown's galleys were designed to handle better under sail on the open waters of Lake Champlain than the "barge-like" galley designed by Doughty.[133] Much credit is due to archaeologists and volunteer divers who endured near zero visibility to record these important relics of America's past.

During the late 1990s the focus of public attention returned to Plattsburgh, drawn by the recovery of the largest anchor ever found in Lake Champlain. In August 1996 divers

William Vanstockum and his son Ken discovered a 14-foot, 3,200-pound anchor half-buried in the sediment of Plattsburgh Bay. The huge anchor was temporarily removed from the lake with the assistance of a crane operated by Captain Frank Pabst of the tour boat *Juniper*. The anchor was identified by its British broad-arrow emblem, the word Quebec painted on one of the flukes, and H.M.S. and 1813 carved into the metal. It is believed to be one of the anchors that Macdonough shot away from the bow of the *Confiance*, an event which played a pivotal role in the American victory. The anchor was returned to the lake and raised again in September 1998 for a two-year preservation treatment at the conservation lab at the Lake Champlain Maritime Museum. On August 24, 2000, the LCMM delivered the preserved anchor to Plattsburgh City Hall.[134] Shortly thereafter, the museum began the preservation of a 300-pound British anchor that had been discovered near Cumberland Head in 1981.[135]

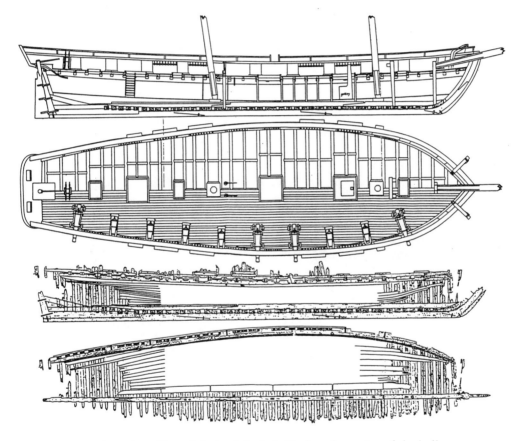

Inboard profile and deck of the brig *Eagle* and remains of the hull.
Drawing by Kevin Crisman. (Lake Champlain Maritime Museum)

As a result of low water and high winds at Lake Champlain during the summer of 1999, two War of 1812 bateaux were uncovered on the shoreline of Plattsburgh Bay. The first vessel, consisting of 33 feet of intact bottom planking and a stem piece, was placed in a freshwater storage tank by the Battle of Plattsburgh Association. A more intact bateau was carefully excavated by New York State Police divers and relocated and buried in deeper water. A brass U.S. Navy button linked to a unit serving during the Battle of Plattsburgh was found on the wreck.[136]

Canal schooner near Vergennes in the1880s.
(Special Collections, Bailey/Howe Memorial Library, University of Vermont)

10. Champlain Canal Boats

WITH THE END OF THE WAR OF 1812, trading schooners and sloops once again sailed the water highway of Lake Champlain in peace. Soon a new type of vessel, the canal boat, would appear on the lake and eventually supersede traditional commercial sailing vessels. "I've seen the water down there solid with canal boats," an old-timer nostalgically remarked earlier in the twentieth century.[1] In the heyday of business traffic on the lake, a "forest of masts" from canal schooners and other commercial vessels could be observed at harbors along the lake. Once men and women toiled on the large canalers, carrying cargoes of lumber, pulpwood, iron ore, marble, granite, and coal to supply the needs of a growing nation. Before trains and trucks, these vessels were the chief means of inland transportation of bulk cargo in the eastern United States. Today, on the bottom of the lake the ghostly images of many of these vessels remind us of the once-thriving commercial traffic on the lake.

In 1761 Philip Schuyler of Albany, veteran of the French and Indian War and later a general in George Washington's army, visited England, where he viewed the operation of the Bridgewater Canal. After returning to the colonies, he recommended the construction of canals in America. Charles Carroll, one of the Congressional Commissioners sent to Canada in 1776, noted in his journal that Philip Schuyler suggested a water route between New York and Quebec via "locks and a small canal cut from a branch that runs into Wood Creek, and the head of a branch which falls into the Hudson River."[2]

By 1785 Elkanah Watson, who had earlier been sent with dispatches to Benjamin Franklin in Paris, had returned to America with information about canals based upon European observations. After a two-day visit to Mount Vernon in which George Washington, as president of the Potomac Company, described plans for a canal between the Ohio and Potomac Rivers, Watson became a strong advocate of canals in New York State. Watson's ideas found fertile ground in Philip Schuyler, who had strong political influence and a predisposition to canals. In 1792, legislation incorporating two private canal companies, the Western Inland Lock Navigation Company and the Northern Inland Lock Navigation Company, was passed by the New York legislature. Schuyler was elected president of both companies and Watson served as a director. Although not a financial success, the Western Company did complete a canal that would be a forerunner of the Erie Canal. The Northern Company, which was to connect the Hudson River to Lake Champlain, spent $100,000 in an unsuccessful attempt to build a waterway through Wood Creek.[3] While the Northern Company was a failure, the project provided a background of experience for the builders of the Champlain Canal.

In 1807 the U.S. Senate instructed the secretary of treasury, Albert Gallatin, to prepare "a plan for the application of such means as are within the power of Congress, to the purposes of opening roads and making canals."[4] The far-sighted plan of federal outlays to improve transportation was aimed at stimulating economic growth. His ideas for northern water linkages included a canal from the Hudson River to Lake Champlain. Although federal help was not forthcoming, the state senate in 1812 appointed commissioners to study New York canal routes. Their report found that "a canal, between Lake Champlain and Hudson's river, is one of those things which are deemed of national importance."[5] Following subsequent reports delineating the economic benefits and cost estimates, the state legislature on April 15, 1817, authorized work to begin on both the Erie and

Champlain Canals.[6] Support for building the canal came from the lumber business along the lake, the iron mining industry on the New York shore, and the Vermont marble cutters.

Although the original plans called for smaller dimensions for the Champlain Canal, early in the construction, the prism of the canal was increased to match the size of the Erie Canal: 40 feet wide at the top, 28 feet wide at the bottom, and four feet deep with locks 90 feet in length and 15 feet wide.[7] In late November 1819 a multitude of spectators at Whitehall, amid "the discharge of cannon and other demonstrations of joy," witnessed the arrival of a canal boat from Fort Edward during the "first trial of the Northern Canal."[8] State Senator Martin Van Buren, later to become the eighth president of the United States, was among the dignitaries present at Whitehall. Three boats made the return trip to Fort Edward. Charles Budd, a naval officer who had participated in the 1814 Battle of Plattsburgh Bay, "kindly permitted the use of one of the boats from the fleet [probably the row galley *Allen*]."[9]

In 1821 a feeder canal from Glens Falls was approved in order to provide a sufficient source of water at the summit of the Champlain Canal; a year later authorization was given to finish the feeder as a navigable waterway (completed 1829). In 1823, after six years of work, the Champlain Canal (also called the Northern Canal) opened for commercial traffic over its entire length from Whitehall to Waterford, New York. The first celebration of the opening occurred on September 10, 1823, when several vessels "ascended the lock, passed up to Waterford, and returned, deeply laden with passengers, greeted by every demonstration of joy and rejoicing from the shores, loud huzzas, the ringing of bells and the firing of cannon, music, processions, and [a] military parade."[10] Welcomed by large crowds at Troy and other cities, the 60-foot sailing canal boat *Gleaner*, built at St. Albans, Vermont, was the first vessel to complete a voyage through the new canal from Lake Champlain. One newspaper recorded that the unique vessel was "built as an experiment. . .[which] sails as fast and bears the changes of weather in the lake and river as well as ordinary sloops and is constructed properly for passing through the canal."[11]

Two basic types of canal boats plied Lake Champlain. One was strictly a canal boat that had to be towed on the open lake; the other was a new class of boats, like the *Gleaner*, which adapted to both lake and canal navigation. These latter vessels, developed by shipbuilders at the lake, had features of both a traditional sloop/schooner and canal boat. The maximum size of these vessels was dictated by the smallest lock in the canal network. The masts would be taken down when the vessel entered the canal in order to pass under low bridges. Along the canal, the boat would be towed by mules or horses, but once out of the canal it would sail on the open lake. This convertible vessel would save three or four days for shippers at Whitehall, the entry point for the canal when going south. Steamers and traditional schooners would have their cargoes reloaded on canal boats, whereas the canal schooners and sloops simply dropped their masts and continued on, sometimes cutting the total time for a voyage in half. This was especially crucial in the sale of Vermont's dairy products. By 1831 even guidebook writers took notice of "numerous canal boats, some fitted with masts for schooners for sailing."[12]

The first class of canal sloops and schooners (1823-1839) was characterized by a randomness of design.[13] One early canal boat design by naval architect William Annesley eliminated the heavy framing typical of most ship construction, substituting "three courses, two fore and aft. . .and [a] middle course" of planking laid at right angles.[14] Visiting the Lake Champlain region in 1823, Annesley sold a half dozen or more of his designs for sailing canal boats. The 75-foot, schooner-rigged canal boat *William Annesley* was built for merchant Matthew Sax of Chazy, New York, who had read of Annesley's ideas in the *New York Evening Post*. A second sailing canal boat of Annesley's design, the *Governor Clinton*, was also completed for Sax. Later that same year, a third Annesley boat was launched at Vergennes by Captain Jahaziel Sherman: "the Ethan Allen, sloop rigged, having a centre drop keel. . .sailed in a very superior manner."[15] (The retractable centerboard in the keel of sailing boats was an invention of John Schank, captain of the British ship *Inflexible* during the Battle of Valcour Island and supervisor of the shipyard at St. Jean in 1776.[16]) Two more Annesley boats were subsequently built in Plattsburgh. Other schooner- and sloop-rigged canal boats of this early class of vessels were constructed at Alburgh, Burlington, Highgate, Milton, South Hero, St. Albans, and Vergennes, Vermont; and at Fort Ann, Essex, Whitehall, and Willsboro, New York.* These vessels, ranging in length from 48 feet to 79 feet, included the *Hope, Hudson, Julia* of Milton, *Lady Byron, Laurel, Mazeppa, Onion, President Washington, Temperance, William Tell,* and *Troy*.[18]

The Champlain Canal fulfilled expectations for economic development as a wave of new enterprises emerged in the port towns along Lake Champlain. During the first year of operation of the Erie and Champlain Canals, more than 19,000 canal boats and rafts passed through Troy.[19] By 1836 revenue from the tolls on the Erie and Champlain Canals completely paid off the remaining original debt incurred during their construction.[20] The chief advantage of canals was a matter of physics as well as economics. A horse or mule could drag a load fifty times heavier through water than on land. While cargoes of iron ore and other natural resources generated much of the canal traffic from Lake Champlain, shipments of butter and cheese increased fivefold and wool fifty times during the period.[21] By 1833, 232 canal boats were registered at the ports of Lake Champlain or along the Champlain Canal; ten years later the number of canal boats had almost doubled to an estimated 450.[22]

Following the opening of the 12-mile-long Chambly Canal in 1843, which connected Lake Champlain to the St. Lawrence River, trade in the region further accelerated. (The proposal for a St. Lawrence River-Lake Champlain canal first came in 1775 from Silas Deane and later from Ira Allen. William Twiss, the same British engineer who helped fortify Mount Defiance in 1777, positively evaluated the possibility of a Canadian canal to Lake Champlain in 1785.) The nine locks of the Chambly Canal, measuring 120 feet in length and 24 feet in width, allowed larger vessels than those using the Champlain Canal to pass through the canal. During 1850, 1,999 sailing vessels and 449 steamboats navigated the Chambly Canal; and the canal became one of the primary avenues for the export of Canadian forest products to the United States.[23]

A second class of sailing canal boats built at Lake Champlain shipyards was generally more standardized in its dimensions—about 79 feet long and 13-1/2 feet wide. The 78-1/2-foot canal sloop *Richard M. Johnson*, built at Burlington by Orson S. Spear in 1841 for the commercial wholesale firm of Timothy Follett and John Bradley, was typical of this new sloop-rigged line of canal boats.[24] (Examples of this second class of sailing canal boats began to appear as early as 1839, and included the 78-foot sloop-rigged *John Tyler*, built in Burlington, the 78-1/2-foot *Hiram*, also built in Burlington, and the 78-foot *Eliza* and 78-foot *Elizabeth*, both completed at Milton, Vermont.[25]) Burlington emerged as the most prominent commercial port on the lake and demand for a fleet of sailing canal boats by Follett and Bradley influenced shipbuilders toward a more standardized design.[26] According to one document, during the period from 1842 to 1857, eleven sailing canal

---

*Traditional schooners and sloops continued to be built during the 1820s and 1830s, including the *Daniel Webster, D. A. Smith, Delaware, Emperor, Franklin, General Scott, Hawk, Henry Clay, Hercules, Hornet, Julia* (Grand Isle), *Lafayette, Linnet, Maria, Mary Jane, Napoleon, Royal George, Vermont,* and the *Water Witch* (converted from a steamboat in 1836).[17]

Above: Burlington docks (ca. 1870s). (Vermont Historical Society)
Below: The 96-foot traditional schooner *John P. Howard* of Burlington.
Built at Champlain, New York, in 1882. (Canal Society of New York State)

Above: Canal schooner *Hiram Walker* at Burlington in 1892.
(Vermont Historical Society)
Below: Burlington, VT. Photo by the author.

boats were built at Essex; seven at Burlington; five at Milton; three each at Swanton and Willsboro; two each at Isle La Motte, Port Jackson, and Ticonderoga; and one each at Champlain, St. Albans, Vergennes, and Whitehall.* In addition, twenty traditional schooners and sloops were constructed at Lake Champlain shipyards between 1842 and 1868.**

The packet canal boat, as another distinct class of canal vessels, dominated passenger traffic in the first three decades of the Champlain Canal. Until the arrival of railroads, packet boats nearly monopolized passenger traffic to New York City and immigrant transportation to Buffalo from the Champlain Valley. A packet canal boat differed from a standard or freight canal boat in the design of its cabin, which extended nearly the entire length of the packet vessel with only narrow walkways along the gunwales. Behind the cabin was a small landing for standing and the steering mechanism. One could also stand or sit on the roof of the cabin but had to duck for low bridges. If a passenger on the roof fell asleep and failed to hear the call "low bridge" from the crew, his nap would end with a rather rude awakening. Long benches or seats lined each side of the cabin, along with a table for dining, and a little stove for cold weather trips. At night the cabin was oftentimes divided with one-third of the forward section for the women separated for privacy by curtains. Some of the bedding was spread across the seats; the rest hung by cords from the ceiling in a berth/hammock arrangement. After a night on a Champlain canal packet, nineteenth-century historian Benson Lossing compared the cabin to a "Turkish bath." [29] Other passengers on packets complained that sleeping was out of the question with the nightlong serenade of children crying in the women's section of the cabin. Charles Dickens likened the rows of bunks in the canal packet to bookshelves and the passengers to large folio volumes that, once placed, could not be moved. In the morning, Dickens found the odors of breakfast mixed with bar smells of gin, whiskey, brandy, rum and "a decided seasoning of stale tobacco." [30] No wonder Dickens later referred to the luxurious Lake Champlain steamers as "floating palaces." [31]

Canal packets utilized the fastest horses along the towpath; when a horse slowed down with age it was relegated to towing freight boats. The packets had the right-of-way over the freight canalers because of passengers, the larger crew, and the vessel's physical dimensions. Packets usually employed one man on the crew with a reputation as a fighter to serve as the "bouncer." His job was to quell any disorderly or rowdy conduct on the vessel, which typically meant throwing the culprit into the canal.

The 1830s and 1840s witnessed the expansion of lake and canal traffic because of the increase in immigrants from Canada on their way west. Nearly every lake port had a line of boats that traveled between the lake and Buffalo. The Vergennes-Troy Line, the Albany-Vergennes Line, and the Westport and Buffalo Line carried many immigrants heading westward with departures once or twice a week. Small steamers such as the *Washington* were used to tow the packet vessels on the waters of Lake Champlain. Once the steamer reached Whitehall, the packet would be towed through the canal, day and night, by relays of horses. At the junction of the Erie Canal, passengers could transfer to

---

*Canal sloops built by Lake Champlain shipbuilders from 1842 to 1857 included the *Amazon, B. Kingsland, C. B. Jones, Columbia, Commodore, D. R. Ferris, P. T. Davis, E. K. Bussing, Elmira, Empire, Giles Harrington, Growler, G. Thurman, Harrison, Stephens, H. H. Ross, H. W. Catlin, Industry, Isaac Nye, J. Bowman, J. D. Kingsland, J. H. Barker, John Bradley, John Jackson, Joseph Blake, J. S. Bussing, L. A. Johnson, M. Bradley, Mike, Nailer, New England, Oregon, Planet, P. T. Barker, P. T. Hewitt, Republic, Rising Sun, S. Barker, S. Boardman, Sea Bird, Valcour, Victorine, W. W. Wright,* and *Young America.* [27]

**Traditional schooners and sloops were still an important segment of the shipbuilding industry at Lake Champlain. A partial list of vessels constructed at the lake between 1842 and 1868 includes the *A. M. Clark, American, Billow, Canada, Col. Jones, Essex, Excelsior, Fortress, Glassmaker, Joseph Clark, Jenny Lind, J. W. Holcomb, Nancy, Swallow, Swiftsure, W. B. Freleigh, Vermont* (rebuilt from the sloop *Delaware*), *Wave, W. H. Blake,* and *Y. D. Chapman.* At least eight more traditional schooners and sloops were built after 1868. [28]

a line of western boats. At the southern end of Lake Champlain, the Emigrants' Line and the Western Line at Whitehall competed for European immigrants who had arrived in Canada and passed through Lake Champlain. Many Irish immigrants, after landing in Montreal, made their way to St. Jean on the Richelieu River where they boarded a Lake Champlain steamer to Whitehall. In 1846 the Emigrants' Line advertised that their boats "are all new, and fitted up in the best style for comfort, convenience and accommodation of the traveling public."[32] Apparently, Dickens missed these boats on his trip to Lake Champlain. To reassure passengers, ads also boasted that "the boats of this line will be commanded by experienced and sober men."[33] The advertisements for the Western Line stressed that "Capts. of Line boats are worthy and trusty."[34] Both lines were also towed by relays of fresh horses which were stationed at points along the canal towpath rather than the old method of carrying fresh horses on the boat, which some passengers found offensive. Usually six or seven days were required to reach Buffalo from Whitehall. In 1848 over 4,000 immigrants, mostly Irish, passed through Lake Champlain and the canals of New York.

Some of the immigrants, upon arrival at Whitehall, would be solicited for passage on freight canal boats by unscrupulous agents. They would be shown the main cabin of the vessel with adequate berths, a cookstove, and other reasonable amenities. After they paid their fare and the boat had departed from the wharf, the captain, in no uncertain terms, would inform them that if they set foot in that cabin they would be thrown into the "drink." Thus many of the immigrants ended up huddled in the recesses between the piles of lumber carried by the canal boats. Day or night, rain or shine, men, women, and children sat out in the elements as the canal boats moved at two or three miles per hour.

A hodge podge of legislation over the years eventually led to an enlargement of the Champlain Canal's locks and prism (surface width, bottom width, and depth of the canal). During the 1830s, locks on the Champlain Canal began to be replaced with larger ones, measuring 100 feet in length and 15 feet in width; by 1850 nearly all the locks had been replaced.[35] An amendment to New York's constitution was passed in 1854, authorizing enlargement of the Champlain Canal locks to match the size of the enlarged Erie Canal (110 feet by 18 feet), "whenever from dilapidation or decay it should be necessary to rebuild them."[36] Work on the Champlain Canal proceeded at an uneven pace in different sections of the canal. By 1859 only 11 of the 25 locks had been enlarged to 110 feet. Due to renewed pressure from the business community, in 1860 the New York legislature authorized an enlargement of the prism of the Champlain Canal to 50 feet x 35 feet x 5 feet and the continued replacement of locks.[37] Although the enlargement of the prism and locks of the Erie Canal (begun in 1836) was completed in 1862, work progressed slowly on the improvements to the Champlain Canal.[38] In a speech to the New York Assembly on April 5, 1864, Andrew Meiklejohn pleaded for further improvements in the canal. While many of the locks matched those of Erie, Meiklejohn suggested that the Champlain Canal was not large enough, resulting in "one-third of our time. . .lost in the effort to navigate the canal."[39] Ten days later, on April 15, 1864, the legislature appropriated $295,000 to continue the enlargement of the Champlain Canal and Glens Falls feeder to a bottom width of 35 feet and a depth of five feet.[40] By the end of 1868, 45 miles of the Champlain Canal's prism had been widened at the bottom to 35 feet and deepened to 5 feet, and 17 locks had been enlarged.[41] But it wasn't until 1877 that all locks on the Champlain Canal matched the 110-foot by 18-foot dimensions of the Erie Canal.[42]

Despite the slow pace of the enlargement of the Champlain Canal, by 1860 shipbuilders began producing slightly larger vessels with lengths of 86 to 88 feet and widths of 14-1/2 feet. This added length allowed sailing canal boats to be schooner-rigged. In 1860 two schooner-rigged canal boats, the 86-foot *John L. Merriam* and 86-foot *Trader*, were

Above: Canal boat *W. N. Sweet* launched in 1902. (Special Collections, Bailey/Howe Memorial Library, UVM) *Facing page, top:* Essex, NY—site of extensive canal boat construction. Photo by the author. *Bottom:* Canal schooner *P. E. Havens* built in Essex, NY, in 1865. Abandoned in 1903. (Special Collections, Bailey/Howe Memorial Library, UVM)

completed at Essex, New York.[43] During the late 1850s, several larger sloop-rigged sailing canal boats had been built at Essex—the 83-foot *Planet* and 86-foot *Richmond.* Although some additional sloop-rigged canal boats, including the *Agnes, Helen Mary, H. H. Adams, James Averill,* and *Henry Stanton,* were built after 1860, a schooner-rigged class of sailing canal boats dominated shipbuilding during this era.*

In sheer numbers, the standard or towed canal boat was the most prevalent type of canal vessel employed in transporting cargo through the canals and the lake. Upon reaching Lake Champlain, towed canal boats were often formed into tremendous caravans of 30 or 40 boats. Since the tolls were lower on the Chambly–Champlain route, cargo from Canada was often routed along the Champlain corridor rather than the more expensive Erie Canal route. Guidebooks, covering Lake Champlain in the nineteenth century, noted "large fleets of canal boats discharging their coal from Pennsylvania, and receiving return cargoes of iron ore" in communities such as Port Henry, New York.[45] The construction of the standard canal boat was often dictated by the type of cargo to be carried. Many of the boats that carried ore and coal were slab-sided with much of their deck open to the cargo hold of the vessel. The average life of a wooden canal boat used on freshwater was approximately 20 years, unless it was rebuilt. The boats often leaked, requiring hours of pumping. If the leak was located, a "Medicine Spoon" was used to plug

---

*A partial list of schooner-rigged Lake Champlain sailing canal boats built from 1861 to 1869 includes the *B. Noble, General Butler, Helen, Henry C. Foot, Hiram Walker, Itasca, J. C. Dean, J. E. Brett, J. G. Witherbee, L. A. Hall, Mary D. Craig, Moneka, O. J. Walker, P. E. Havens, W. G. Lyon,* and *W. H. Roberts.*[44]

the hole without taking the vessel out of the water. A long-handled wooden box with dry horse manure or sawdust would be pushed under the bottom of the boat, and the incoming water would draw the manure into the leaky seams. Similarly, an open potato sack filled with the same ingredients would be hauled back and forth over the bottom of the boat to seal a leak.[46] The design of early canal boats created some problems—when a square-bow canal boat collided with another vessel, it could sheer off the whole side of the boat, spilling its contents into the canal. As early as 1830, the Canal Board promulgated regulations that "squared-headed or sharp-cornered scows or boats shall have a semicircular platform firmly fastened upon the bow," and the state of New York later legislated rounded bows for all canal boats.[47]

Both the sailing canal boat and the towed canal boat were houses as well as cargo carriers. Lake ports before 1875 resembled small floating villages where one would have to cross 40 or 50 boats to reach a wharf. The acre of vessels would also provide a handy marketplace for local merchants serving the needs of the crews living on the boats. The stern section of canal boats contained a cabin for living space, some with only the minimum essentials, while others were slightly more elaborate. Lighting was provided by kerosene lamps and meals were prepared on a wood or coal stove. Typically, the stern had four windows; the top of the cabin, which extended a few feet above the deck, usually had two or three windows on each side. Cabin windows were often not screened, allowing flies and mosquitoes to infest living quarters. Shelves, chests of drawers, tables, chairs, and cupboards were added to cabins. The best cabins had side berths used as bedrooms with sliding doors; others had curtains for privacy. Canal boats had no toilet facilities and used wash water from the canal or Lake Champlain. In a 1921 survey of canal families, it was found that drinking water (described as very clear) came directly from Lake Champlain.[48] The better cabins had fixed basins with gravity-fed water from a tank on the deck; others simply had a barrel of water on the deck or in the cabin. The 1921 survey also found that approximately half of the families did not have sleeping space for every member of the family. During the warmer months, some of the family members would have to sleep under an awning on the deck. On the open lake, independent owners could sail or have their canal boats towed 24 hours a day, but work hours were eventually restricted to 10-12 hours on the Champlain Canal.

Despite these hardships, it was fairly common for children to live on canal boats. At the age of seven, Martha Robbins lived on a Whitehall-built canal boat with her mother and uncle. During the years 1897–1907, her trips included many to Canada through Lake Champlain and to New York City. "The cargo from the north might be lumber, hay, or spruce pulpwood from Three Rivers [Canada] cut in two foot lengths and you had real spruce gum to chew! If the cargo was pulpwood, you might drop off from the tow at Ticonderoga but usually Fort Edward."[49] When the lake turned rough, the tows would pull into harbors such as Ore Bed, Snake Den, or Burlington. Upon reaching Whitehall, the families would usually stock up on groceries to last through Albany or further. Martha recalled: "At that age my one big ambition was to ride one of the mules while towing." After a few years, her uncle finally let her ride on the mule one day, but the towline snapped, sending Martha flying onto the towpath. "That ended my mule riding career."[50] Similarly, Cora Archambault later recalled her childhood aboard her family's two canal boats, which hauled logs, ice, potatoes, and other cargo. Nearly every aspect of life changed for families living aboard the boats: "Word would go up and down the length of the tow to not empty slop buckets or throw anything into the lake as water barrels were to be filled."[51] She recollected that "some canal boats had two cabins, one. . .for living quarters and one for mules. It seemed odd to see the animals with their heads sticking out of the cabin windows."[52] Sometimes Cora would be allowed to ride the mules on the towpath.

Wash flapping in the breeze usually indicated the presence of a family on the canal boat. Family members either loved or hated the gypsy life. Life for the children was not easy with many accidents, irregular school attendance, lack of recreation, and illness. Young children were often tied to the towing post or deck to prevent them from falling into the canal or lake.[53] Boys worked with their fathers until they were old enough to operate their own boat. The job of a canal boat captain became an occupation handed down from father to son. One mother explained the family tradition in canal boating this way: "The children are brought up on the boat and don't know nothin' else, and that is the only reason they take up 'boating'."[54] One youngster with boating experience, who used his inheritance from his deceased mother to purchase his own boat and a team of mules, became a captain at 14. He had virtually no formal education and never learned to read or write. Several of his sons also became boatmen, and a 16-year-old grandson was working with the captain when the latter was still boating at 68.[55]

In the cold months, if an unforseen cold snap closed the navigation for the season, the canalers would be forced to stay in ports such as Ottawa, New York City, or other points away from their winter residences. In that case the whole family spent the winter on the boat. In larger cities the children of canal boat families, trapped by the winter ice, would sometimes attend local schools. One winter, Martha Robbins' family from Whitehall failed to return to the lake and spent the winter aboard the boat in Brooklyn.

Canal towns such as Whitehall have been compared to those of the Wild West, especially on payday. It was standard practice to withhold the canal laborers' pay for the last two months of the season until the last day of navigation on the canal. A drinking, gambling, and fighting spree usually occurred with some workers losing their wages. The hapless crew members who lost their money often spent the winter at the "poor farm" near Whitehall, awaiting the opening of the next canal season.

There were many freight canal boat companies in the Champlain Valley over the years. The firm of Mayo & Follett located in Burlington entered the freight forwarding business with their first canal boat *Vermont* in 1823. The Merchants' Line, established in 1841 by Follett and Bradley of Burlington, used a standardized fleet of 20 or more sloop-rigged sailing canal boats. The New York and Canada Line, begun by W. H. Wilkins of Burlington, conducted business between Quebec, Montreal, and New York City in 1854. By 1859 the New York and Canada Line merged with the Copeland Line founded by C. Copeland in 1856. Together the new company had 31 boats operating on the canals, Lake Champlain, and Canadian rivers. H. G. Burleigh was the force behind the founding of Burleigh and Marshall in Whitehall in 1859, which was succeeded by the firm of Burleigh Brothers. In the 1880s this firm was consolidated with Robert Cook and the Whitehall Transportation Company to form the New York and Lake Champlain Transportation Company. Shortly thereafter, Burleigh and Cook began separate lines which were consolidated into the Lake Champlain Transportation Company after Burleigh's death in 1900. The new company operated six tugs and a fleet of canal boats and barges before being absorbed by the Murray Transportation Company of New York.

The Northern Transportation Line of Whitehall also played an important role in the canal and freight business on Lake Champlain. Asa Eddy began one of the earliest lines of canal boats on the lake at Whitehall when the canal opened in 1823. In 1831 he sold his operation to Peter Comstock, who had a competing line of canal boats at the time. With two partners, Comstock operated his company under the name of the Northern Transportation Line, a name that he had used previously. Comstock was one of the famous characters of Champlain history who was noted for driving a team of horses with

Sailing canal boats engaged in the pulpwood trade at Ticonderoga.
(Ticonderoga Historical Society)

Below: Canadian canal sloops at the Burlington wharf in 1905.
(Special Collections, Bailey/Howe Memorial Library, UVM)

provisions to Plattsburgh during the 1814 battle, racing canal boats, and making deals, as well as for his steamboat rivalry with the Champlain Transportation Company of Burlington. Comstock's company changed hands several times; by 1856 a consolidation of several canal lines created the new Northern Transportation Line. The NTL owned canal boats as well as freight and tow steamboats on Lake Champlain, including the steamers *Oliver Bascom, Ethan Allen, William Birkbeck, Boston,* and *J. H. Hooker.*[56]

Canadian sailing canal boats on the Richelieu River at the turn of the century.
(Postcard, author's collection)

When the Copeland Line and the New York and Canada Line merged in 1859 to compete more effectively with the Northern Transportation Line, the latter firm offered higher salaries and commissions to shipping agents. Shortly thereafter, the NTL began a rate war. After a few years the Copeland--New York and Canada Line was forced into a consolidation with the Northern Transportation Line. Although the NTL was successful in eliminating much of the competition on the lake, there was one source of competition that would eventually win out—the railroad.[57] The support for railroads included the mining and lumber interests on Lake Champlain which wanted year-round transportation. In an effort to protect its investment in canals, the state legislated that railroads could carry only passengers and baggage. Later the state allowed railroad freight traffic, but required the collection of tolls equal to the cost of using the Champlain Canal. Eventually this requirement ended, and by 1875 the Delaware and Hudson Railroad had completed a line from Whitehall to the Canadian border.

The lumber industry along Lake George and Lake Champlain was stimulated by the opening of the Champlain Canal. Essex County, New York, saw new docks and an improvement in existing facilities at Ticonderoga, Crown Point, Port Henry, Essex, and Port Kent. These ports were jammed with canal boats, schooners, and sloops as lumber fever spread throughout the region. Unfortunately, the expansion of lumbering initially meant the denuding of the lake and river shores in the valley. During the first half of the nineteenth century, the village of Ticonderoga overflowed with lumber activity as the outlet for the huge Lake George lumber region. Two-thirds of the lumber business in Ticonderoga was attributed to Joseph Weed, who shipped 340 boatloads of lumber in one year alone. Weed's canal boats included the *Black Mountain, Bolton, Lyon*, and *Swallow*. Boats at the time were able to navigate all the way into the basin at the "Lower Falls" in Ticonderoga before waste from paper mills filled in the waterway. By 1852 Ticonderoga was exporting 600,000 pieces of lumber and Port Douglas 200,000 pieces a year, and 1,625,000 board feet were being shipped from Port Kent.[58]

The opening of the Champlain Canal and later the Chambly Canal touched off a huge import market for Canadian lumber. In 1849 alone, over 15 million board feet of lumber came through the Champlain Canal from Canada destined for Troy and New York City. Part of the trade was in lumber that was bound for New York City from Lake Ontario. Although hundreds of miles shorter, the natural route through the Erie Canal involved 136 miles of tolls. Lumber diverted to the longer Lake Champlain route saved substantially on tolls with the shorter canal mileage of the Champlain Canal. By 1850 roughly twice the amount of lumber reached New York City by the Champlain Canal compared to the Erie Canal.

By the 1880s and 1890s, 400 canal boats and steamers, as well as hundreds of Canadian vessels, were involved in the lumber trade. Since international regulations did not allow Canadian vessels to pass out of the lake, larger canal boats were built that carried 250,000 board feet of lumber. These vessels would still fit the larger Canadian canals. The Canadian vessels were most often unloaded at Burlington where the lumber would be transferred to American canal boats for the trip south or to railroad cars destined for Boston. Burlington, as one of the first markets to import Canadian lumber, became the location of numerous lumber-forwarding companies and manufacturing enterprises. Stockpiles of lumber adjacent to the wharves often covered 30 or 40 acres. The direct connection of Burlington to some eastern cities by railroad made it a natural center for the lumber business. By 1871 Canadian imports into Burlington amounted to 175 million board feet of lumber each year. The volume increased so rapidly that the construction of a breakwater was needed to offer protection for boats that had to wait to be unloaded or cleared by Customs. First constructed in the 1830s, the Burlington breakwater would be rebuilt during the 1860s with additional work during the following decade. As time passed, the railroads took a larger share of the lumber market away from canal boats. However, canal boats continued in some areas for many decades. The Diamond Match Line utilized boats to import thousands of feet of match blocks. The International Paper Line at Fort Edward and the Fort Miller Pulp and Paper Line brought in most of their pulpwood by canal boat right into the twentieth century.

The canal era stimulated the shipbuilding industry in many communities along the lake. In 1846, 14 boats were launched at Ticonderoga, with an average of a dozen a year being built for another decade.[59] Essex, New York, famous for its early shipbuilding even before the opening of the Champlain Canal, built 53 documented vessels between 1814 and 1870.[60] Many were the sloop- and schooner-rigged canal boats that sailed the lake until the turn of the century. One Essex yard—Hoskins, Ross and Company—accounted for a major share of the canal boats built in this era. Although records for Willsboro are incomplete, shipbuilding extended from approximately 1835 to 1865 with the construction of seven sloop-rigged canal boats and scows.[61] Many canal boats were also built at Alburgh, Burlington, Champlain, Chazy, Colchester, Fort Edward, Isle La Motte, Milton, Peru, Philipsburgh, Plattsburgh, Port Jackson, St. Albans, Swanton, Ticonderoga, Vergennes, and Whitehall.

The mining industry in the Adirondacks and the marble quarries of Vermont were some of the biggest users of canal boats on the lake. The iron companies of Crown Point, Moriah, Port Henry, and the Westport area were importers and exporters of raw materials and finished goods. Several mines along the lake at Split Rock Mountain included a granite quarry at Barn Rock Harbor, a graphite mine near the Split Rock Lighthouse, and iron mines at Ore Bed Point and Grog Harbor. These, as well as others, were directly serviced from the lake by canal boats and schooners. By the 1890s the iron ore veins were exhausted at Split Rock Mountain and the mines were closed. The larger mines, however, near Mineville, Moriah, and Port Henry constituted a major industry in the Champlain Valley for more than a century. Andrew Meiklejohn, in his plea for a larger canal in 1864, cited the increased output from Port Henry as evidence: "The iron ore shipped over this canal from Port Henry alone was 7,000 tons in 1850, while last year [1863] it had mounted up to 145,000 tons."[62] Anthracite coal from Pennsylvania was also shipped to the western shore of Lake Champlain for the iron industry. Granite for buildings, breakwaters, and road edging from the Lake Champlain region was carried for years on canal boats. Marble, used in many public buildings throughout the United States, especially the black and grey marble from Isle La Motte, was shipped by Champlain canal boats. Additional marble firms in the region included the Burlington Manufacturing Company Marble Works located adjacent to the harbor.

According to Captain Frank Godfrey, a veteran of the New York canals, during the later years of the ore trade on Lake Champlain three types of canal boats were used. The biggest were strong, heavy canal boats with nine-foot sides and a full deck. These vessels were loaded with 250–255 tons of ore, 110 tons on the deck and 145 tons inside. At Troy the deck ore would be transferred to vessels going to Wilmington, Delaware. On the return trip, the vessel was so high that it would not fit under low bridges unless it was reloaded (usually with coal). The second type were first-class, dry-cargo boats with a full deck and eight-foot sides that would take ore from Port Henry to the Rome Iron Works in Rome, New York, and return with salt or shipments from canning factories for the Spaulding Kimball Line or the O. J. Walker & Brothers Company in Burlington. The third type were old worn-out, open-deck boats that were kept afloat by "Medicine Spoons" and pumps. Godfrey knew one owner with three of these old boats who suggested that "The only thing I don't like about the ore is to get up in the morning with two, or three feet of water in the hold."[63]

Between 1870 and 1915 approximately 1,500-1,800 canal boats worked the Champlain route.[64] Gradually, however, the days of the canalers began to decline in the Champlain Valley despite the fact that tolls were eliminated in 1882. In 1890 the volume of commerce on the Champlain Canal reached a peak of a million and a half tons. By 1907, however, it had dropped to less than half that amount "due to the disappearance of the fleet of sloops and schooner-rigged canal boats" which were unable to compete with the Delaware & Hudson rail lines along the west side of Lake Champlain.[65] Part of the change resulted from the gradual reduction of trade through New York City. Differential rail freight rates often favored other Atlantic ports, including Boston, Baltimore, Philadelphia, Norfolk, and Newport News instead of New York City. By 1902 iron ore traffic had ceased between Port Henry and Wilmington, Delaware, via the Champlain Canal. In spite of the railroads, some canalers continued to work the lake and canal. Canal boats carried pulpwood for the region's paper mills as late as the 1920s.

Efforts were made to make the canal more competitive by enlarging it again. The legislative process leading to an enlarged canal system became divisive, however. Charges of incompetence and fraud were raised after a nine-million-dollar appropriation in 1895 proved to be insufficient to complete a deepening of New York's canals.[66] When the entire

Above: Detail of "Potter Panorama" of Whitehall showing canal boats. (New York State Library)

Left: The Champlain Barge Canal's entrance into Lake Champlain at Lock 12. Photo by Richard K. Dean.

Below: Tugboat and oil barge passing Crown Point. (Postcard, author's collection)

funding was exhausted, less than six miles of improvements to the Champlain Canal had been finished. In addition to the inadequate appropriation, the failure was also due to deterioration of the canal itself, including multiple breaks in the towing path and banks which had collapsed into the canal. By 1898 railroads carried ten times the tonnage of the canals, which had dropped to a 41-year-low. The following year newly-elected Governor Theodore Roosevelt appointed a seven-member committee to study New York's canals and recommend improvements. In 1900 the Committee on Canals urged the enlargement of the Erie, Oswego, and Champlain Canals. Roosevelt endorsed the idea, suggesting that "we cannot afford to rest idle while our commerce is taken away. . .we must act. . .to retain the state's commercial supremacy" and signed into law a request for the state engineer to prepare surveys and cost estimates for a new barge canal.[67] Despite strong opposition from railroad interests, a 101-million-dollar bond issue for the barge canal passed the state legislature and was endorsed overwhelmingly by voters in a November 3, 1903, referendum.[68]

Although the Panama Canal would be the recipient of far greater publicity, the New York Barge Canal was actually ten times longer and rivaled the engineering achievement of the canal through Central America.[69] Ground was broken for the Champlain Barge Canal in April 1905 at Fort Miller. Largely due to the priorities of World War I, only a modest celebration on May 15, 1918, marked the official opening of the entire New York Barge Canal system. (A more gala ceremony in 1915 commemorated the opening of the Waterford to Rexford section of the canal.) The new barge canal was built without towpaths; canal boats were to be towed by tugboats through the canal and the canalled section of the Hudson River. The Champlain Barge Canal from Troy to Whitehall covered a total of 63 miles, encompassing 12 locks, each 328 feet long and 45 feet wide. Vessels as long as 300 feet could be accommodated in the locks. As a result of the new barge canal, the Witherbee-Sherman Company purchased four steam-powered canal boats and a large number of barges, some measuring 150 feet by 33 feet.[70]

The New York Barge Canal did not reach the level of tonnage transported in the peak year of the old canal (1903), until the 1930s. The tonnage on the barge canal attained its zenith in 1951 and thereafter began a slow descent as a result of competition from oil pipelines, railroads, trucks, and the St. Lawrence Seaway. Oil tankers were the last large vessels to navigate the Champlain Barge Canal, carrying fuel to Plattsburgh Air Force Base before its closing in 1995. Because of the Plattsburgh base, Champlain Barge Canal tankers had carried more than half of the entire tonnage transported on New York canals during the early 1970s.[71] Today, the canal has a new life as a recreational waterway. The Canal Corridor Initiative, a Department of Housing and Urban Development program, is expected to generate 700 million dollars in growth for the economies bordering the canal system.[72]

Archaeological Discoveries

For a variety of reasons, many canal boats lie today at the bottom of Lake Champlain. Storms on Lake Champlain could be treacherous, especially for a vessel overloaded with iron ore or marble and using too much sail. When the lake became turbulent during storms, vessels would try to navigate into protected harbors, but some vessels never reached the safety of sheltered inlets. During a storm, steamboat tow captains would often cut loose the tow of canal boats to save the tow vessel. As the boats were blown cross wind, crews would desperately struggle to cut loose the other vessels. Without engines and enough anchor line to reach bottom in deeper waters, the boats were at the mercy of the waves and often sank. Others sank because of human error or were abandoned when they outlived their usefulness.

Boats that sank in canals were either raised or destroyed to clear the waterway. The canal boats that sank in Lake Champlain, however, are still there. In the last 20 years a number of perfectly intact sailing canal boats have been located by side-scan sonar and divers. In 1975 the state of Vermont approved the Historic Preservation Act, which established state ownership of shipwrecks (ten years or older) with the provision of support for research and the protection of submerged cultural resources. Spearheaded by the Champlain Maritime Society, a non-profit organization dedicated to the preservation of the maritime heritage of Lake Champlain, a whir of publicity occurred during the 1980s surrounding the discovery, identification, and conservation of shipwrecks. Art Cohn, then Vice-Chairman of the CMS, headed the Underwater Parks Committee which was successful in 1985 in starting the first preserve with the support and aid of Giovanna Peebles, Vermont's state archaeologist. In 2000, four sunken canal boats were among the vessels protected in Vermont's Underwater Historic Preserve system. The vessels in the

ISLE LA MOTTE CANAL SLOOP.
Left: Mast tabernacle. *Right:* Tiller bar.
Photos by the author.

preserves are identified by yellow buoys, which are connected to cement pads and identification signs on the bottom. Dive boats are secured to the mooring buoys, which protect the sunken vessels from accidental anchor damage while the signs outline safety procedures and remind divers that it is illegal to remove artifacts from the wrecks. Wooden deadeyes, cleats, and other historic objects have been purposely left on the vessels for divers to see and photograph.

A 79-foot canal sloop, one of the first intact sailing canal boats to be discovered, was found near Isle La Motte in October 1978 by a Canadian group led by Marc Theoret, using side-scan sonar operated by Dr. Harold Edgerton of the Massachusetts Institute of Technology. At the time the Canadian team was searching for War of 1812 wrecks and identified the wreck only as a "merchant sloop of the early 19th century."[73] The vessel is a sloop-rigged canal boat which represents a class of canal sloops built during the 1840s. The vessel sank with a full load of marble which is still onboard, including a nine-foot block wedged near the windlass on the deck.[74] (The windlass was employed to raise and lower the mast and centerboard as well as for use loading cargo and deploying anchors.) The Isle La Motte canal sloop has three deck hatches and a large stern cabin (roof missing), a single mast tabernacle (support), folding-stock iron anchor, rudder, wooden tiller bar, centerboard, deadeyes for the rigging, and four windows in the transom.

An Essex-built canal schooner became Vermont's initial Underwater Historic Preserve in 1985. The 86-foot *General Butler*, built at the shipyard of Hoskins and Ross in 1862, was named after the Civil War general, Benjamin F. Butler.[75] On December 9, 1876, the *Butler* was carrying a 30-ton load of Isle La Motte marble and battling ten-foot waves during a winter storm, when its steering gear cracked and the vessel began drifting helplessly. William Montgomery, an experienced lake captain, cast a storm anchor and desperately attempted to save the vessel by chaining a spare tiller bar to the steering mechanism. The anchor line was then cut and Montgomery tried to sail around the southern end of the Burlington breakwater. The effort proved futile and the canal schooner smashed into the breakwater. Incredibly, everyone aboard successfully leaped onto the icy rocks, including Montgomery's teenage daughter and her girlfriend (who were on a Christmas shopping trip to Burlington), a deckhand, and a quarry operator from Isle La Motte. Captain Montgomery was the last to jump to safety; the *General Butler* sank a moment later. The survivors were rescued by ship chandler James Wakefield and his son in a 14-foot rowboat.

In 1980 the vessel was found by divers Dean Russell and Scott McDonald, using information provided by Lake Champlain historians Peter Barranco and Merritt Carpenter. The vessel was discovered in 35-40 feet of water complete with its entire hull, decking, hatches, cleats, deadeyes, anchor, windlass, mast tabernacles, rudder, iron cookstove, and jury-rigged tiller bar.[76] Under project director Arthur Cohn and archaeologist Kevin J. Crisman, the Champlain Maritime Society carried on a three-year (1981-1983) study of the *General Butler*. Because the city of Burlington planned to expand its wastewater system during the 1990s, further study of the *General Butler* occurred in 1993 and 1995. Cohn, executive director of the LCMM, served as the project director, and Crisman and Joseph Cozzi, both from Texas A & M University, were the project archaeologists. The examination revealed more details of the lightly-framed, chine-built hull with edge-fastened construction.[77] All the artifacts from the 1980s and 1990s survey have been catalogued and conserved, including bottles, bowls, cups, crocks, plates, saucers, utensils, cast iron pots, flasks, stoneware jugs, deadeyes, a leather boot, a woman's skirt, a wooden boat model, and a ceramic doll.[78] While the *General Butler* survives in remarkably good condition, the effect of zebra mussels remains to be seen.

The Canal Schooner *General Butler*

The wreck became the first Underwater Historic Preserve in Lake Champlain.

Clockwise from below:
The rudder. Forward tabernacle with broken mast. Tiller bar, jury-rigged during an 1876 storm. Windlass on the bow. Photos by the author.

The Canal Schooner *O. J. Walker*

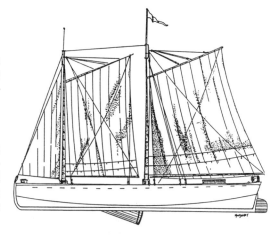

The canal schooner *O. J. Walker* was built in Burlington in 1862. Sunk in 1895, it remains intact today in an Underwater Historic Preserve in Burlington Bay.

Clockwise from right:
Drawing by Montserrat Centeno. Side-scan sonar image (Joseph Zarzynski and Klein Associates, Inc.). Steering wheel. Windlass and anchor. Cabin on deck. Bow with twin deadeyes and anchor. Mast. Photos by the author.

In 1998 a second sailing canal schooner, the 86-foot *O. J. Walker*, was added to Vermont's Underwater Historic Preserve system. The 78-ton, schooner-rigged *O. J. Walker*, named for Burlington merchant Obadiah Johnson Walker, was built in 1862 by shipbuilder Orson Saxton Spear at the northern end of Shelburne Bay for Captain Joseph H. Kirby.[79] After 31 years of service, the *O. J. Walker* was sold to her fifth owners, John W. and Henry W. Brown, a father and son partnership, manufacturing brick and tile at Malletts Bay, Milton, and Burlington. On May 11, 1895, Captain W. J. Worthen departed under a clear sky from Malletts Bay with the 33-year-old canal schooner, carrying a heavy deck load of brick and clay drain tile destined for use at Dr. William Steward Webb's estate at Shelburne. A severe gale arose shortly thereafter—one newspaper account noted a "scene magnificent in its wildness" and suggested that the "boatman no doubt. . .sought a place of safety."[80] Worthen nearly succeeded in reaching the protected waters of Burlington harbor when the old schooner "sprung a leak."[81] Worthen dropped an anchor and deployed a life boat. The *O. J. Walker* rolled on its side, dumping a great deal of the deck cargo, righted itself for an instant, then sank to a depth of 65 feet. Worthen, his wife, and a crew member were blown to shore by the high winds--the yawl had been launched before oars could be found.[82] (Worthen was lucky; one of the schooner's last captains, 75-year-old Shell Parkhurst, died aboard the vessel.[83])

The wreck of the *O. J. Walker* was initially discovered with the use of side-scan sonar in 1983 by James Kennard and Scott Hill, and located and recorded in 1984 by a team sponsored by the Champlain Maritime Society, using side-scan sonar operated by Alan Bieber and John Fish with information provided by lake historian Peter Barranco. The vessel remained virtually intact with masts, booms, deadeyes, blocks, the windlass, anchor, a large wooden steering wheel, an intact stern cabin, a wheel barrow, hand trucks, and clay drain tile and brick still on the deck. Under the direction of Arthur Cohn and Kevin Crisman, the Lake Champlain Maritime Museum sponsored an archaeological survey of the vessel with a permit from the Vermont Division for Historic Preservation (1988-1989). A number of artifacts, including a brass cornet, were raised from the wreck and catalogued.[84] Another LCMM-sponsored survey (1995), under the direction of Cohn with Texas A & M University archaeologists Kevin Crisman and Joseph R. Cozzi, documented the hull construction of the vessel. The survey revealed that the forward mast had been permanently stepped, limiting the *O. J. Walker* to lake transportation during her final years of service. While the fragile nature of some sections of the wreck and the abundance of artifacts on the *O. J. Walker* initially made the vessel an unlikely candidate for an underwater preserve, increasing anchor damage caused by visiting divers led to a decision to include the wreck in the preserve system. By then the roof of the stern cabin had been accidently displaced by an anchor. A special registration system, similar to that used for the radeau *Land Tortoise* at Lake George, was implemented in 1998 to provide a record of divers visiting the site.

During the late 1980s an unidentified sailing canal vessel was found in the shallow water near North Beach in Burlington. Since the chine-built canal boat was considerably broken up, details of the hull's bottom were easily accessible for examination during a 1992 field school sponsored by Texas A & M University and the University of Vermont.[85] Other sailing vessels also ended their careers on the bottom of the lake near Vermont, including the 77-foot sloop *Cornelia*, which "sprung a leak" and foundered with 108 tons of coal on November 17, 1897.[86]

Beginning in the 1990s, the Lake Champlain Maritime Museum, under director Arthur Cohn, conducted annual, systematic side-scan sonar surveys of the lake in an effort to document as many historic shipwrecks as possible before these vessels became encrusted with zebra mussels.[87] Two sailing canal sloops were located and examined by LCMM divers in 1996. Although one near Plattsburgh had substantially deteriorated, the other canal sloop found near Burlington (first located in 1984) was in pristine condition with an intact stern cabin, steering wheel, anchor, mast and boom, cargo of coal, and deadeyes, and with the original paint visible on the hull.[88] Another canal vessel, first discovered during the 1960s north of Schuyler Island and examined by LCMM divers in 1998, may also have been a sloop-rigged vessel since rigging elements (deadeyes, pulleys) were present on the wreck during the 1960s.

Wreck of canal schooner
Troy, sunk in 1825.
Drawing by Kevin Crisman.
(Lake Champlain Maritime Museum)

The LCMM's most interesting discovery during the 1999 survey occurred when the canal schooner *Troy* of Westport, New York, was found in deep water. The intact shipwreck represents the only known example of the earliest class of sailing canal boats. In November 1825 Jacob Halstead, the 25-year-old captain of the vessel, with his 13-year-old brother George, his stepbrother Jacob Pardee, and two crewmen were returning to Westport with a load of ore when a gale arose and the schooner "foundered."[89] The boys' mother and sisters waited anxiously at the Halstead homestead in Westport "listening through the storm for the sound of home-coming footsteps as the night wore on. Suddenly they heard the boys on the doorsteps, stamping off the snow," but when they dashed to the door no one was there.[90] Over the following days the "captain's hat, trunk and pocketbook" were found on shore, but "none of the bodies" were ever discovered.[91] The iron ore cargo apparently shifted forward as the *Troy* descended; the bow section lies buried in the bottom of the lake while the intact stern rises 30 feet above the floor of the lake. The archaeologists at the LCMM speculated that the canal schooner *Troy* may be the "oldest vessel in the world ever located equipped with a centerboard."[92]

A large number of standard (towed) canal boats have been discovered at the bottom of the lake over the past three decades. Sunken canal boats have been found near Plattsburgh, Port Kent, Willsboro Bay, Ligonier Point, Westport, Port Henry, Burlington, Shelburne, Diamond Island, north of Potash Bay, Orwell, and the southern section of the lake, including Whitehall. At this writing (2000), two of these vessels are included in Vermont's Underwater Historic Preserve system. One, the 90-foot *A. R. Noyes*, had broken loose while being towed by the steam tug *Tisdale* on October 17, 1884. The relatively intact vessel, located with side-scan sonar in 1984 by veteran New York divers James Kennard and Scott Hill, lies in 65–75 foot depths. The *A. R. Noyes* is buoyed for the public at Proctor Shoal at the southern end of Burlington Bay. The cargo of coal is still in the *Noyes*, as are two coal shovels with a mule harness nearby. The cabin is well preserved, but the bow section was damaged when the cargo of coal shifted forward as it went down. Artifacts have been intentionally left on the vessel to allow visitors to understand the history of the wreck and to demonstrate that these vulnerable artifacts are in the public trust. It is hoped that divers now realize that souvenir hunting will destroy these historic vessels which would otherwise be preserved for future generations to see. A second standard canal boat, lying in 12- to 20-foot depths on the southeast side

Above: Rudder post on the canal boat *A. R. Noyes,* sunk in 1884. The vessel is part of Vermont's Underwater Preserve system. *Top, left:* Cabin on the canal boat *A. R. Noyes. Right:* Stern section of an intact canal boat wreck near Port Kent. Photos by the author.

of Diamond Island, is now an underwater preserve. The sides of this 93-foot canal boat have fallen off, exposing her cargo of quarried stone blocks.

The annual LCMM side-scan sonar survey, covering approximately 40 square miles each year, has recorded an extraordinary collection of standard canal boats, many completely intact. Archaeological surveys were conducted on ten of these wrecks either by a LCMM diving team, or by researchers using a large ROV supplied by Benthos, Inc., of Falmouth, Massachusetts, for deeper sites. Most of these sunken canal boats had windlasses, tiller bars or steering wheels, anchors, rudders, cabins, and contain a host of artifacts. Many still had a full load of cargo aboard, as did the canal boat *L. A. Hall,* filled with Port Henry pig iron when it sank in 1878; others were loaded with stone or coal;

and one carried a cargo of cast iron stoves, cooking pots, and teakettles. One pristine Erie-type canal boat, lying in deep water, rises eight feet above the floor of the lake with two intact deck cabins, including a bow stable for mules. Several large canal boats have lengths of 96-98 feet and widths of 18-1/2 feet, including one originally discovered during the 1980s near Port Kent. The vessel apparently sank during a storm since the ropes holding the vessel pulled the windlass from its mounting.[93]

Some of these canal boats will be recommended as underwater historic preserve sites in both New York and Vermont.[94] Preserves allow divers safe access to historic vessels, enhancing the public's under-standing of the history of the lake, and protect the vessels from sou-venir hunting and accidental an-chor damage. The wreck of a standard canal boat, the *Vergennes* sunk in 1853 at Barn Rock Har-bor, illustrates the problem. The bow of this wreck once held a large windlass attached to two beams, running from the top of the inside bow to the bottom of the vessel. In 1985 someone ripped the entire windlass out of the boat. This kind of mindless souvenir hunting eventually de-stroys the integrity of these ves-sels by weakening the structures holding them together. Untreated artifacts in private hands are often thrown away. Preserves generate public recognition that historic shipwrecks are finite resources to be left intact for others to see. The LCMM archaeological team ex-amined the *Vergennes* in 1998, and determined that the vessel was a viable candidate for a preserve.[95] Because the bay has become popu-lar with recreational boaters, pre-serve status would also protect the

Canal boat wreckage in Willsboro Bay.
Photo by the author.

vessel from accidental anchor damage. However, some other canal boat wrecks are too deep or archaeologically sensitive to be considered preserve sites at this time. Preserves require complex management strategies, which balance preservation, safety, and public access.

The story of the canal boat era will be kept alive with the building of a full-size replica of a sailing canal schooner, modeled after the *General Butler* and *O. J. Walker*. The replica schooner, named for philanthropist Lois McClure, will be constructed on the Burlington waterfront by the Lake Champlain Maritime Museum, in partnership with the Lake Champlain Transportation Company, and will serve as "a harbor-side educational exhibit illustrating how the lake served as a dynamic highway of commercial transportation during the 19th century."[96]

Captain Ell B. Rockwell ended a career of more than 80 years on
Lake Champlain at the age of 98 as captain of the steamboat *Vermont III*.
(Special Collections, Bailey/Howe Memorial Library, UVM)

11. Steamboats of Lake Champlain

Although the commercial steamboat era on Lake Champlain began as early as 1809, a viable network of trading schooners and sloops had existed for two decades on the lake. Following the migration to Vermont of Gideon King from New Lebanon, New York, and Benjamin Boardman, along with master shipbuilder Daniel Wilcox from Connecticut, shipbuilding and commercial traffic burgeoned at the lake. Gideon King and Job Boynton initiated the shipbuilding boom in the late 1780s with two small cutters for service to Burlington, Essex, and Plattsburgh. In 1790 the two entrepreneurs purchased two old warships in Canada to haul cargo between St. Jean and Burlington. That same year Boardman and Wilcox launched a 30-ton sloop, followed by two more vessels by King and Boynton in 1793. By the early part of the nineteenth century, Gideon King's son (of the same name) emerged as the owner of the largest fleet of vessels and became known as the "Admiral of the Lake."[1] As trade grew, the demand for new vessels mushroomed, encouraging new shipbuilders along the lake. Although a few vessels were built in other locations, Burlington, Essex, and Whitehall dominated the shipbuilding business. When the first steamboat plied the lake, there were more than two dozen sailing vessels exceeding 30 tons in service (see table, page 263).

While much of the technology of steam propulsion had existed for some time during the eighteenth century, it was not until the 1780s that definitive work on a steam-powered vessel occurred in America. In Bath, Virginia, George Washington was present in 1784 when James Rumsey's model boat, powered by a waterwheel with vertical poles, moved upstream. A year later, in a letter to Washington, Rumsey suggested that steam could power his planned vessel. Rumsey obtained monopoly rights for his proposed vessel in both Virginia and Maryland. After two failures, Rumsey eventually succeeded with a steam-powered boat using an early form of jet propulsion. On December 3, 1787, former Major General Horatio Gates of Revolutionary War fame was among the spectators who watched in astonishment as the vessel moved three miles an hour on the Potomac River. Following financial setbacks, Rumsey died of apoplexy (stroke) in 1792 after addressing the Society of Arts in London on his ideas.

Rumsey's more successful rival, John Fitch, an ingenious jack-of-all-trades entrepreneur, built a model of a steamboat and petitioned Congress in 1785 for support. Although failing to gain Congressional backing, Fitch received monopoly rights for 14 years to operate steam-powered boats in New Jersey and three other states. Following mechanical setbacks and rocky financial dealings, Fitch achieved eight miles an hour with his 60-foot steamboat on the Delaware River in April 1790. The small boat ran several thousand miles during the summer of 1790 but was a financial loss due to low passenger use. Had Fitch lowered his prices, a resulting increase in passenger traffic might have changed the historical recording of the first successful steamboat in America.

Others experimented with steamboats during the early 1790s, including Captain Samuel Morey of Vermont, who built a small steam-powered sidewheeler on the Connecticut River. In 1793 Morey's new steamboat, equipped with a stern wheel, traveled from Hartford to New York. His success drew the interest of Robert R. Livingston. Livingston was granted a monopoly in 1798 for boats moved by "fire or steam" on the waters of New York State, but his steamboat, built with his brother-in-law John Stevens, fell apart from engine vibrations. While serving as minister to France (where he negotiated the Louisiana Purchase), Livingston sought out inventor Robert Fulton, then living in Paris, for a partnership in building a steamboat in New York. After the development of an operational submarine, Fulton produced a 74-foot steamboat in 1803, creating a sensation as it crossed the River Seine four times at a speed of three to four miles an hour. However, Fulton's success was not entirely based on his own ideas since he had access to the work of earlier steamboat pioneers, including the drawings of John Fitch. Fulton then traveled to England for a special order steam engine but lingered for two and a half years under contract to the British for the development of his submarine designs.

When his funding ended in Britain, Fulton returned to the United States in 1806 after a 20-year absence and began construction of a 130-foot passenger steamboat for service on the Hudson River. With financial backing from his partner Robert Livingston, Fulton completed a sturdy, well-appointed steamboat in only eight weeks. Powered by side paddle wheels, the steamboat offered an interior cabin, measuring six and a half feet high, and displayed an ornately decorated bow and stern. After a trial run around Manhattan, Fulton made a perfect 32-hour, 150-mile trip from New York City to Albany on August 17, 1807. At the time he simply called the vessel *The Steamboat*. Fulton's steamboat apparently was never called the *Clermont* during his lifetime. Clermont was the name of Livingston's estate on the Hudson River, home port for the boat. The vessel was lengthened during the winter of 1807-1808 and registered as the *North River Steamboat of Clermont*. Fulton had built the first large, mechanically-flawless steamboat to achieve commercial success. He had hoped to build a steamboat empire with monopoly rights, but new competitors, lured by potential profits, dashed those dreams with legal challenges to his New York State monopoly. Attempts to gain a U.S. patent were similarly foiled by partial patent rights obtained by James Rumsey and John Fitch.[2]

John and James Winans, who had worked on the hull of Fulton's steamboat, moved to Burlington in 1808. With their previous boat building experience (James had also been the pilot on Fulton's boat), the two brothers with the support of local businessmen proceeded to build a steamboat that same year. Completed in 1809, the 167-ton *Vermont* measured 125 feet with a 20-foot beam. The vessel had a flush deck, an 18- by 25-foot

The steamboat *Vermont* at Basin Harbor. Painting by Ernest Haas.

EARLY LAKE CHAMPLAIN COMMERCIAL SAILING VESSELS[3]
(1793-1814)

Name	Tons	Year	Owner	Master Carpenter	Where Built
Dolphin	25-30	1793	Gideon King	Wilcox	Burlington
Burlington Packet	30	1793	J. Boynton	Wilcox	Burlington
Lady Washington	25	1795	Gideon King	Jones	Burlington
Maria	30	1796	Gideon King	Fittock	Burlington
Name unknown	30	1800	Gideon King	Fittock	Burlington
Union	30	1800	J. Boynton	Fittock	Burlington
Eliza	40	1800	Daniel Ross	Eggleston	Essex, N.Y.
Jupiter	40	1802	Gideon King	Eggleston	Essex, N.Y.
Juno	46	1802	Gideon King	Wilcox	Essex, N.Y.
Euretta	31	1803	E. Boynton	Eggleston	Essex, N.Y.
Independence	35	1805	S. Boardman	Eggleston	Essex, N.Y.
Privateer	40	1807	Gideon King	Wilcox	Burlington
Hunter	50	1809	Gideon King	Wilcox	Burlington
Emperor	50	1810	H. & A. Ferris	Young	Westport
Rising Sun	50	1810	E. Boynton	Eggleston	Essex, N.Y.
Eagle	60	1810	S. Boardman	Eggleston	Whitehall
Essex	50	1810	Gideon King	Eggleston	Essex, N.Y.
Boston	30	1810	Gideon King	Wilcox	Burlington
Saucy Fox	50	1810	Gideon King	Eggleston	Essex, N.Y.
Gold Hunter	50	1811	E. Boynton	Young	Whitehall
President	75	1812	J. Boynton	Eggleston	Essex, N.Y.
Fair Trader	71	1812	J. Boynton	Eggleston	Essex, N.Y.
Morning Star	50	1812	S. Boardman	Eggleston	Whitehall
Jacob Bunker	65	1812	H. E. Chittenden	n.a.	Burlington
Richard	60	1811	Gideon King	Eggleston	Essex, N.Y.
Leopard	50	1813	J. Boynton	Eggleston	Essex, N.Y.
Boxer	63	1814	Gideon King	Eggleston	Essex, N.Y.
Paragon	75	1814	Gideon King	Eggleston	Burlington

Other sailing vessels during this period included the cutters *Greyhound, Mighty, Topsey,* and *Youth;* schooners *Beaver* and *Liberty;* and sloops *Constellation, Constitution, Champion, Federal Enterprise, Federal Packet, Franklin, Governor Craig, Hope, Laura, Mars, Polly,* and *Resolution.*

cabin below deck with side-by-side berths, rigging for sails, and a 20-horsepower steam engine which powered open side paddlewheels.[4] The rules for passengers of the *Vermont* were similar to those of Fulton's steamboat. The back cabin of eight berths was reserved for women and children and the "great cabin of sixteen berths" was for use by men: "cleanliness, neatness and order are necessary . . . It is not permitted for any person to lie down in a berth with their boots or shoes on."[5]

Although the steamer *Phoenix*, built by John Stevens in 1808 for subsequent use on the Delaware River, preceded the *Vermont*, the latter steamboat is often credited with being the first regularly-scheduled steamboat after Fulton's original vessel. The *Vermont* began regular service in June 1809 with trips from Whitehall to St. Jean, Canada, scheduled for 24 hours, but because of frequent breakdowns the actual schedule was one round-trip per week. The steamer was used during the War of 1812 to ferry troops and supplies along the lake and was nearly captured by the British in May 1814. Warned by an informant, Captain John Winans changed direction before being ambushed. Following the war, the *Vermont* re-established service to St. Jean from the United States. The steamboat sank on October 15, 1815, when its connecting rod broke a hole through the hull, sinking the vessel near Bloody Island in the Richelieu River.

Before the sinking of the *Vermont*, a lawsuit which claimed a violation of the Fulton/Livingston monopoly rights against Elihu Bunker and a group of Albany investors, owners of two Hudson River steamers, the *Hope* and *Perseverance*, set the stage for future steamboat development on Lake Champlain. As part of a September 15, 1812, settlement, the Albany owners could no longer "navigate any of the waters of the state of New York" where Fulton and Livingston held monopoly rights, but the former were granted "the exclusive right of the navigation of the said Lake Champlain by Steam Boats" and subsequently used the engine of the *Perseverance* for a new vessel on the lake.[6] With a license to operate on Lake Champlain, the Albany investors, along with new Vermont business interests, were given a charter from the New York legislature under the name of the Lake Champlain Steam-boat Company. The former captain of the *Perseverance*, Jahaziel Sherman, was sent to Vergennes to supervise the building of the new steamboat. While under construction in 1814, the vessel was sold to the navy for a profit and was converted into the war schooner *Ticonderoga*.

Within four months of the end of the War of 1812, a new steamer was launched at Vergennes by the Lake Champlain Steam-boat Company. The 336-ton *Phoenix*, propelled by a 45-horsepower engine, had a length of 146 feet and a beam of 27 feet with handsomely appointed cabins, a smoking room, barbershop, sitting room, small stateroom, baggage room, kitchen, and captain's office. The hull was more rounded and deeper than the *Vermont*'s with enclosed side paddlewheels amidship, one forward mast with a large square sail, and a bowsprit. The flush main deck, circumscribed by a railing, was partially covered with a canvas awning. The *Phoenix* carried cargo and passengers between Whitehall and St. Jean on a regular schedule for four years. After a new engine was installed in 1817, the *Phoenix* achieved eight miles an hour on her regular runs. That same year the *Phoenix* transported President James Monroe to Plattsburgh and the following year carried the remains of Brigadier General Richard Montgomery, who had been killed during the attack on Quebec in 1775, for reburial in the United States.

On the evening of September 4, 1819, the *Phoenix* departed from Burlington for Canada with 46 passengers and crew: "We left Burlington at 11:00 P.M. with everything in apparent good order about the vessel," Richard Sherman later recollected.[7] Richard Sherman, the 21-year-old son of Captain Jahaziel Sherman, commanded the *Phoenix* that fateful night because his father was confined to his bed in Vergennes, suffering from a fever. About one in the morning near Providence Island, a fire was discovered on the

The steamboat *Phoenix* (1815-1819) and ablaze during the early morning hours of September 5, 1819. Paintings by Ernest Haas. (Lake Champlain Maritime Museum)

vessel by a special messenger from the Bank of Burlington who had gone to check on the $8,500 in Montreal bills of exchange that he was carrying to Canada for collection. The passengers were awakened and two life boats launched, but the second boat departed for Providence Island with extra space available. When one passenger proposed turning back for the remaining people aboard the flaming vessel, the steamer's engineer on the lifeboat threatened "to knock the first man overboard with an oar" who should rise to make the first attempt to turn back.[8] Eleven people were left on board—tables, benches, and boards were subsequently thrown overboard to save the remaining passengers, but six, including a woman and a 12-year-old boy, were lost. "The cries for assistance of those who could not swim were pitiable," a newspaper reported ten days after the incident.[9] Rescuers in the second lifeboat returned to the steamboat to retrieve survivors from the blazing wreck or from the water, but by then it was too late for some of the passengers. Richard Sherman was later remembered as the hero of the disaster. After the last lifeboat departed, Sherman discovered the chambermaid unconscious under a settee. "Lashing her to the plank he had prepared for his own escape," Captain Sherman "sprung from the burning wreck as it was about to sink."[10] Sherman and four others remained afloat in the darkness for nearly two hours before being rescued. One survivor, who had "hung by the rudder" until it burned away, was saved after climbing on top of the detached structure.[11]

The flames leaped into the black sky all night as the *Phoenix* burned to its waterline. The burning hull drifted in the wind until it ran aground on Colchester Shoal, north of Burlington. The cause of the fire was later attributed to a candle left burning in the pantry rather than any mechanical failure. In the confusion after the catastrophe, one passenger absconded with the $8,500, but he was pursued to Grand Isle where he surrendered the money. Rumors that an agent of the commercial sailing interests on the lake might have sabotaged the steamboat were never substantiated. After the engines were removed from the wreck of the *Phoenix*, it apparently began a slow descent down the steep northerly slope of the shoal.

In 1816, before the *Phoenix* burned, the Lake Champlain Steam-boat Company completed the 128-ton, 90-foot steamer *Champlain*, similar in design and appearance to the *Phoenix*. To deter the Winans brothers from building a new steamboat with the engine salvaged from the *Vermont*, the Lake Champlain Steam-boat Company contracted with John Winans for installation of the recovered engine and boilers in the *Champlain*. Although the Vermont legislature in 1815 granted the Lake Champlain Steam-boat Company monopoly privileges for 23 years, the company was inclined to check any potential competition before it began. The steamboat monopolies, however, would be declared unconstitutional in 1824. Following Daniel Webster's fervent arguments against steamboat monopolies in Gibbons V. Ogden, Chief Justice John Marshall ruled that steamboats "can no more be restrained from navigating waters and entering ports" than can sailing vessels.[12] After this decision, steamboat companies would use the route of mergers and acquisition of rival vessels to dominate steamboat traffic on the lake.

The steamboat *General Greene*. Painting by Ernest Haas.

The *Champlain*, commanded by Captain George Brush, was placed on the Whitehall-St. Jean run during 1816. Her four-miles-an-hour speed was increased to six during the following year when the engine was replaced with the original engine from the *Phoenix*. The original engine of the *Champlain*, which had been salvaged from the *Vermont*, was then used for Lake George's first steamboat. With only two seasons of service, the *Champlain* burned at her dock in September 1817 as a result of the faulty location of the boilers. The second engine and boilers on the *Champlain*, which had originally come from the Hudson River steamer *Perseverance*, were now placed in a new steamboat whose construction had begun at Vergennes in late 1817. Completed in 1818, the *Congress* resembled the *Phoenix* in appearance and accommodations. The 108-foot *Congress*, described by Professor Benjamin Silliman in the fall of 1819 as "a neat and rapid boat," made three trips a week between Whitehall and St. Jean at a speed of eight miles an hour.[13] Unlike the first three steamboats on Lake Champlain, the *Congress* did not burn or sink, but was retired without mishap in 1835.

With the destruction of the *Phoenix* in 1819, the steamboat company had only the *Congress* for regular service on the long Whitehall-St. Jean route. Before the end of 1819, the company began construction of the 150-foot *Phoenix II*, the last of the large steamers to be built at the Vergennes shipyard. Somewhat larger than the original *Phoenix*, the new vessel, completed in 1820, used the engine salvaged from the wreck at Colchester Shoal. The *Phoenix II*, decorated elaborately in a patriotic fashion, carried the Marquis de Lafayette on his American tour in 1825; three years later the steamer was temporarily relegated to freight duty, but returned to passenger service under new ownership during the 1830s, carrying the famous Irish actor Tyrone Power (great-grandfather of the American movie star) from Whitehall to St. Jean, Canada.[14]

The *Congress* and *Phoenix II* were the first vessels to initiate "popular excursions" with an advertisement: "to view the remains of those ancient fortresses, Ticonderoga and Crown Point, and. . .the Battle Ground of Macdonough's Naval Engagement—Plattsburgh."[15] While stories of the early nineteenth-century steamboats conjure up romantic images of a period long past, many contemporary eyewitnesses were not impressed. Captain Basil Hall of the British navy had only complaints about his 1827 trip aboard a crowded steamboat on Lake Champlain: "The machinery was unusually noisy, the boat weak and tremulous, and we stopped, backed, and went again, at no fewer than eleven different places, at each of which there was such a racket that it was impossible to get any rest."[16] Hall's wife was no less critical, suggesting that "the boat was without exception the noisiest steamer I have yet been in, all night long I could have fancied that a couple of kettle drums. . .were close to my ear."[17]

Beginning in the mid 1820s, Lake Champlain witnessed an expansion of steamboat services at several locations on the lake. Although sail ferries had existed at several points along the lake before the end of the eighteenth century, it was not until 1825 that a steam ferry was placed in service. In 1824 the Vermont legislature chartered the Champlain Ferry Company to operate between Burlington and Port Kent. Completed at Shelburne Harbor, the 115-ton, 75-foot *General Greene* ran until 1833, when the vessel was converted into a sloop. The 136-foot *Winooski*, completed in 1832 by the Champlain Ferry Company, replaced the *Greene* on the Burlington-Port Kent-Plattsburgh route.

Several ferry crossings on Lake Champlain relied upon horse-powered vessels during this period. The earliest American horse-powered boat was built on the Delaware River in 1794 by John Fitch, the steamboat innovator. As many as 16 horse boat designs were filed with the U.S. Patent Office, including one granted to Barnabas Langdon of Whitehall on June 5, 1819. Langdon's horizontal treadwheel design was a "technological break-through" that would influence the future construction of horse boats.[18] Langdon's horse boats were single-hulled vessels with the horses facing "opposite directions, one to the bow, and the other to the stern. . .their feet cause the horizontal wheel to revolve. . .by a connexion of cogs, moves two vertical [paddle]wheels, one on each wing of the boat."[19] John C. Langdon joined his father in producing five or six horse boats per year during the 1820s at their Troy, New York, factory.

By 1826 the horse-powered ferry *Experiment* plied the waters between Port Henry and Chimney Point. Although the Vermont legislature in 1821 approved a charter for a horse ferry between Essex and Charlotte, the recipients of the permit, Charles McNeil and Henry H. Ross, apparently continued to use their sail ferry at the crossing through 1827. From 1828 to 1847 the partners operated the 68-foot *Eclipse*, employing six horses, on the Essex-Charlotte passage. The horse boat *Eagle* began operating in 1832 between Westport and Basin Harbor, ending her career in 1844 on a shorter route between Westport and Adams' Landing (Arnold's Bay). The horse ferry *P. T. Davis* plied the route between Chimney Point and Port Henry from the mid 1840s to 1857, while the *Gipsey* made the same crossing from 1858 into the 1860s.[20]

On October 26, 1826, the Champlain Transportation Company, which would dominate steamboat commerce on the lake through the twentieth century, was chartered by the Vermont legislature with rights for "transporting by the aid of tow-boats or otherwise, passengers, goods, wares and merchandise. . .upon the said Lake Champlain."[21] With broad powers delineated in the company's charter, the founders decided to build the largest and most powerful steamboat on the lake to date. The 162-foot *Franklin*, built at St. Albans Bay, Vermont, was powered by a 75-horsepower engine which propelled the vessel at 10 miles per hour. Launched in July 1827, the *Franklin* was the first steamer with a covered main deck (promenade deck) and offered 84 berths, which were larger in size and number than those of any vessel to date on the lake. The *Franklin*, under Captain Jahaziel Sherman, immediately offered strong competition to the aging *Congress* and *Phoenix II* on the Whitehall-St. Jean run.[22]

Two years later, the St. Albans Steam Boat Company, also chartered by the state of Vermont in 1826, completed the 89-foot, 30-horsepower *MacDonough*, named after the victorious commander of 1814, for use between St. Albans and Plattsburgh. As a tow boat in the last years of her career, the 137-ton vessel "ran onto a reef opposite Barber's Point on the Vermont side and was wrecked there in a gale of wind," according to Captain Ell B. Rockwell, who spent over 80 years on the lake and had served as a cook on the schooner *Cynthia* in the early 1840s.[23] Other sources indicate that the *MacDonough* was trying to retrieve the canal boat *Citizen* which had broken loose from a tow during a gale on November 16, 1841, when it wrecked upon rocks near Button Bay.[24] The engine was later taken out and the remaining "hull abandoned where it lay."[25] (The Champlain Maritime Society sponsored an unsuccessful field search for the vessel in 1984.)

With more competition developing on the lake, consolidation of steamboat interests began during the late 1820s. On March 13, 1829, the Lake Champlain Steam-boat Company leased the *Congress* and *Phoenix II* to Timothy Follett and Cornelius P. Van Ness, canal freight operators, who formed a pool or cartel arrangement with the Champlain Transportation Company two weeks later whereby only one steamer would make the Whitehall-St. Jean run and the new lessees would "be entitled to one equal half of the whole net earnings."[26] The five-page agreement disclosed that the steamer *Franklin* "shall be considered as a passage boat. . .not exceeding six passages per week through the lake," while the *Congress* "shall continue to run through the lake" and the *Phoenix II* "shall be laid up" and held in reserve.[27] The agreement also assigned the steamboat *Washington* to freight and part-time passenger service. The 92-foot *Washington* had been completed in 1828 at Essex for the McNeil-Ross line as a ferry, but the horse boat *Eclipse* was substituted and the *Washington* was pressed into full lake service. On March 9, 1829, the CTC purchased the *Washington* with "an issue of more capital stock."[28] Facing continuing losses, the Lake Champlain Steam-boat Company was sold at auction in 1830 to Isaiah Townsend of Albany, who signed a pooling agreement on January 29, 1831, whereby "the gross earnings of both said boats [*Franklin* and *Phoenix II*] are to be annually equally divided between the parties."[29] Two years later, on February 22, 1833, Townsend sold the *Phoenix II*, the *Congress*, and all property at Shelburne Point to the CTC.[30] The purchase was financed with an issuance of stock. The Champlain Ferry Company, the St. Albans Steam Boat Company, and a new steamer built for Jahaziel Sherman offered the only remaining competition for the Champlain Transportation Company.

The 83-foot *Water Witch* was built by Samuel Wood at Fort Cassin on Otter Creek for Captain Jahaziel Sherman in 1832.[31] The steamer's narrow beam of 17 feet and relatively powerful 40-horsepower engine moved the vessel at eight miles per hour. Although the passenger accommodations were inferior to those on other steamers, the ability to carry freight made the independent steamer practical on the Vergennes-Whitehall run. Consistent with its monopoly strategy, the Champlain Transportation Company formed a collusive agreement with Sherman on November 21, 1833, whereby he was "at no time to permit his Steam Boat Water Witch to go North of Fort Cassin so as to interfere with the regular business. . .by the Champlain Transportation Company."[32]

On January 27, 1835, the Champlain Transportation Company completed its consolidation on the lake with the purchase (through stock sales) of the Champlain Ferry Company, owners of the *Winooski*, the St. Albans Steam Boat Company with the *MacDonough*, and the *Water Witch* from Sherman.[33] The *Water Witch* was placed in towing service by the company in 1835, but the next year was converted into a two-masted schooner and sold. Captain Ell Rockwell remembered the vessel as a schooner: "her cabin was finely decorated as a steamer and never changed."[34] On April 26, 1866, the *Water Witch* was headed for Burlington loaded with iron ore from the Cheever Ore Bed in Port Henry when it foundered south of Diamond Island during a spring squall. According to the newspaper report on the following day, the vessel sank so quickly that the lifeboat was not deployed "and all would have been lost but for the [canal schooner] Trader, Capt. Edward Eaton, who was near by. Capt. [Thomas] Mock kept his wife and two children above water for nearly twenty minutes, until picked up by Capt. Eaton. An infant child of Capt. Mock's went down on board the schooner."[35]

By 1835 the Champlain Transportation Company owned every steamboat on the lake. The *Congress* was retired in 1835; the *Phoenix II* ended her service in 1837 and the *Franklin* the following year. The steamboat company began a modernization program in 1837 with the completion of the 190-foot steamer *Burlington*. According to an eyewitness, the launching of the *Burlington* turned into "a disappointment to the hundreds of people assembled, as it took three days. . .Yet the people came day after day, many camping on the ground."[36] The *Burlington* was to carry many famous passengers, including President Martin Van Buren and Henry Clay in 1840 and Charles Dickens in 1842. Dickens found the *Burlington* "a perfectly exquisite achievement of neatness, elegance, and order."[37] Although the walking-beam engine design had been used on lake steamers earlier, the *Burlington*'s 200-horsepower engine was the largest and most powerful steam engine to date on Lake Champlain. The walking beam, resembling an oil field pump, was connected to the steam cylinder by a connecting link on one side and to the paddlewheels by a connecting rod on the opposite side. When the engine operated, the iron "walking beam," mounted high amidship, would tilt back and forth as it transmitted power to the paddlewheels. The construction of the early nineteenth-century steam engines was quite remarkable considering the lack of gas and electric arc welding, high-speed electric and pneumatic drills, etc.

While the Champlain Transportation Company was building the *Burlington*, its brief monopoly was challenged by Peter Comstock, an industrious canal boat operator who had started construction of a large steamboat in Whitehall. As a director of the acquired Champlain Ferry Company, Comstock had been "well taken care of" in 1835 by the Champlain Transportation Company.[38] To protect its monopoly, the latter company purchased the unfinished steamer from Comstock in 1836, made him a director, and paid him a salary for eight years as an agent of the company; in return he was "not to build or cause to be built during said term of eight years, any other Boat in opposition to this Company."[39] The Champlain Transportation Company lengthened Comstock's steamboat to 215 feet and added a 200-horsepower steam engine before her completion in 1838. Although considered a sister ship, the *Whitehall* was not as elaborately finished or ever as famous as the *Burlington*.

The elegant steamer *Burlington*, built in 1837 at Shelburne Harbor, carried passengers such as the English novelist Charles Dickens and President Martin Van Buren. (Special Collections, Bailey/Howe Memorial Library, UVM)

In 1842 the Champlain Transportation Company replaced the steamer *Winooski* with the 166-foot *Saranac*, built at Shelburne Harbor for the Burlington-Port Kent ferry service. The company's position seemed secure and profitable with a $5.00 through-passage rate on the steamers *Burlington* and *Whitehall*, but opposition to the high price led to an incipient steamboat company from New York. The new company was incorporated with a broad charter by the New York legislature on January 22, 1841, under "the name of the New-York and Champlain Steam Transportation Company, for the purpose of navigating Lake Champlain."[40] The New Yorkers decried the "complete monopoly" of the Champlain Transportation Company where "boat after boat has been purchased in and laid up."[41] Once again, however, the Champlain Transportation Company bought out the potential stockholders but before any vessel was ever built. The CTC owners

Clockwise from top: Francis Saltus at Whitehall, 1844. (Special Collections, Bailey/Howe Memorial Library, UVM) The 240-foot *United States*, completed at Shelburne Harbor in 1847. (Special Collections, Bailey/Howe Memorial Library, UVM) The 250-foot *R. W. Sherman*, built in 1851 at Whitehall, later renamed the *America*. (Ticonderoga Historical Society) The 260-foot *Canada*, built at Whitehall in 1853. (Special Collections, Bailey/Howe Memorial Library, UVM)

could not relax, however. Peter Comstock, with his agreement expiring, resigned as a director and began building another steamboat at Whitehall. After a policy of acquisition of all competitors, the Champlain Transportation Company abruptly changed its strategy and decided to compete with the new steamboat. Completed in 1844, Comstock's 185-foot steamer *Francis Saltus*, commanded by Captain H. G. Tisdale, offered strong competition for the *Burlington*.

The steamer *Saranac* was recalled from ferry service by the Champlain Transportation Company, refitted and lengthened to compete with the *Saltus*. The resulting rivalry led to an all-out contest of speed between the two vessels as passengers cheered on the captains and crews while placing side bets on the results. Stops were often skipped to make up time as the crews tossed pine pitch into the boilers to raise steam pressure and tied down safety valves. With Comstock's cabin fare cut to 50 cents and deck passage only 25 cents, the CTC cut fares to $3 on the *Burlington* and the *Whitehall* and to 25 cents on the *Saranac*. Because of mounting financial problems caused by low fares, Comstock's control of the *Saltus* was passed to the firm of Grant, Coffin and Church of Troy, New York.

The 224-foot *Montreal*, completed in 1856 at Shelburne Harbor. (Special Collections, Bailey/Howe Memorial Library, UVM)

When an agreement during the summer of 1846 to "divide the gross receipts" of the Champlain Transportation Company's steamers and the *Saltus* was not adhered to by the Troy owners, the CTC commenced building a larger steamboat to compete with the *Saltus*.[42] The steamer *United States*, with a length of 240 feet, beam of 28 feet, and displacement of 648 tons, was easily the biggest vessel to date on Lake Champlain. With elegant staterooms on the second deck and a 250-horsepower engine that propelled the vessel at 19 miles per hour, the *United States* in 1847 far surpassed the performance and amenities of the *Saltus*. As passenger traffic on the latter vessel declined in favor of the more contemporary steamer, the end for the Troy owners neared. On February 10, 1848, the Champlain Transportation Company acquired the *Saltus* and the *Montreal*, a 224-foot steamer hull under construction at Whitehall.

While the passenger steamer traffic was consolidated by one company, the Champlain Transportation Company, the freight and towing service saw several competitors over the years. The Northern Transportation Line, controlled by Peter Comstock in the mid-nineteenth century, built the 136-foot, 50-horsepower steamer *James H. Hooker* in 1846 (converted to a barge in 1879). In 1847 the newly formed Steam Tow-Boat Company completed the 136-foot, 75-horsepower *Ethan Allen* for towing operations. A year later, McNeil and Ross finished the 82-foot, 30-horsepower steamboat *Boquette*.[43] The 127-foot steamer *Boston*, built by the Champlain Transportation Company in 1851, was sold the following year to the Rutland and Burlington Railroad to be used for transfer of freight and passengers. In 1856 the Northern Transportation Line also built the 136-foot, 150-horsepower *Oliver Bascom* for towing service.[44] Some of the towing vessels changed ownership several times in their careers on the lake. The *Ethan Allen*, for example, was owned at different times by the Steam Tow-Boat Company, the Vermont Central Railroad, the Champlain Transportation Company, and the Northern Transportation Line.

After a period of time the Northern Transportation Line consolidated much of the towing and freight operations on the lake. One of their 1870 handbills advertised "the New and Powerful Steamer, *L.J.N. Stark*, exclusively for freight. . .And will run the Steamers *Oliver Bascom, J. H. Hooker, Boston*, and *Ethan Allen* for Towing."[45] The steam towboat *L. J. N. Stark*, completed at Whitehall in 1869, had one of the shortest careers on Lake Champlain. The 185-foot vessel with a 26-foot beam was commanded by Captain Richard Arbuckle during her one-year stint on the lake. While towing six barges on August 5, 1870, the sidewheeler caught fire and sank just south of the Point Au Roche light (north of Plattsburgh). One crewman drowned in the accident. (One hundred fifteen feet of the wreck lies south of the light in 10 feet of water.)

The passenger business on the lake was stabilized in 1848 with control of all the large steamboats by the Champlain Transportation Company. In the following year, several local directors of the company sold their interest in the company to owners of the North River Steamers (a Hudson River line), who inaugurated the "North and South Through Line," which allowed passengers to buy a single ticket for passage from New York City to Montreal via railroads and steamers.

New competition for the Champlain Transportation Company, however, appeared in 1852 with the opposition line of T. D. Chapman and Associates, which placed in service the 250-foot steamer *R. W. Sherman*, built at Whitehall by Thomas Collyer in 1851. Eyeing the competition, the builders of the *R. W. Sherman* designed it for the highest possible speed. The vessel, at 19 miles per hour, set a record of 27 minutes from Port Kent to the northern end of the Burlington breakwater in 1852.

In a move to turn an apparent quick profit, the Champlain Transportation Company sold all its assets (except the charter) to the Rutland and Burlington Railroad on August 31, 1852. Early in 1854, however, the Champlain Transportation Company purchased the *R. W. Sherman* and another steamer, the *Canada*, completed at Whitehall in 1853. In 1854 the *Sherman*, renamed the *America* by the company, and the 260-foot *Canada* were the most modern and efficient steamboats in Lake Champlain service.[46] Late in 1854, following two years of disappointing operations, the Rutland and Burlington Railroad sold back the steamers *United States, Burlington, Whitehall, Saranac*, the unfinished *Montreal*, and the Shelburne facilities to the Champlain Transportation Company for one-third its original purchase price.

The steamer *United States* continued in service on the lake with the *America* and *Canada*, but the *Burlington, Saranac*, and *Whitehall* were sent to Shelburne Harbor to be broken up. The *Francis Saltus*, not included in the buy-back from the Rutland and Burlington Railroad, once again became the subject of controversy on the lake. After its sale to a director of the Plattsburgh and Montreal Railroad and a payment to lay-up the steamer in 1856, the vessel was seized by Captain Lot Chamberlain of the CTC on the basis of an unpaid lien for repairs. Following two court orders and another seizure, the steamer was brought to the CTC facilities at Shelburne where a standoff occurred at

Old steamboat wrecks at Shelburne—steamer *Burlington* in foreground.
(Special Collections, Benjamin F. Feinberg Library, SUNY Plattsburgh)

gunpoint when 100 men from Plattsburgh attempted to reclaim the steamer. The saga of the *Saltus* did not end until 1858 when the Champlain Transportation Company once again purchased the vessel. The following year the company finally ended the wild career of the *Saltus* by ordering her dismantled. The remnants of the old challenger lie today in the shallow water of Shelburne Harbor.

After the aging *Saranac* was dismantled in 1855, her engine was placed in the 224-foot steamer *Montreal*, which had been reacquired by the Champlain Transportation Company. The hull of the *Montreal* had been built at Whitehall in 1847, but the steamer wasn't completed until 1856 at Shelburne.[47] The *Montreal* remained in passenger service through 1868 when the steamer was reassigned to towing duties "in retaliation against the action of the Northern Transportation Co. putting the [*Oliver*] *Bascom* as a passenger boat."[48] The *Montreal* was sold to the latter company in 1872 and accidentally burned eight years later at Maquam Bay.

During the Civil War, the Champlain Transportation Company moved a large number of volunteers and some of their horses from northern New York to Whitehall on their way to join the Union Army. Aside from the 1864 raid by 22 Confederate soldiers on St. Albans, Vermont, the Champlain Valley's role in the Civil War consisted largely of supplying men and materials. Before the end of the war, the CTC made plans for a new steamer to replace the *America*.

The Champlain Transportation Company, under the presidency of Colonel LeGrand B. Cannon (1864-1895), made substantive changes in the financial structure of the firm and services offered to passengers. Cannon's association with the Rensselaer and Saratoga Railroad (controlled by his brother-in-law) led to the railroad's purchase of the Champlain Transportation Company. Following a purchase of the majority of stock in the Lake George Steam Boat Company on January 8, 1868, the Champlain Transportation Company assumed control of the Lake George operation. On May 1, 1871, the Rensselaer and Saratoga Railroad permanently leased all holdings to the Delaware and Hudson Canal Company; thus control of both steamboat companies fell under the Delaware and Hudson. The Delaware and Hudson soon coordinated its train schedules and lake steamer runs with the Hudson River Day and Night Lines to provide continuous service between New York City and Montreal.

In the spring of 1867, the 251-foot *Adirondack*, displacing 1,087 tons, was finally completed at Shelburne Harbor. By the 1860s the Lake Champlain steamers had been converted from wood to coal burning. In 1858 the steamer *United States* had been the first on the lake to make the conversion to coal; the *Adirondack* was the first of the Champlain Transportation Company steamers originally designed for coal. The *Adirondack* was taken out of service in 1875 because of a vibration that could not be overcome by the builders and the reduction in business due to railroad competition. The engines were sold for installation on a steamboat on the Hudson River and her elegant upper works,

The 251-foot *Adirondack*, built at Shelburne Harbor in 1867 and retired eight years later. (Special Collections, Bailey/Howe Memorial Library, UVM)

The 132-foot *A. Williams*, completed in 1870 at Marks Bay, Burlington.
(Special Collections, Bailey/ Howe Memorial Library, UVM)

including cabin fixtures and furnishings, were sold for use on the steamer *City of Cleveland* on the Great Lakes. To replace the 18-year-old *Canada*, in 1871 the Champlain Transportation Company completed the most opulent and powerful steamboat built on Lake Champlain during the nineteenth century. The 1,500-horsepower, 262-foot *Vermont II* could achieve 19 miles per hour. The vessel offered 61 staterooms, a bridal room, barbershop, president's room, a walnut and chestnut stateroom hall 171 feet in length, and a dining room designed to seat 150 people. Many distinguished travelers crossed the lake on the handsome steamer, including President Ulysses S. Grant and General Philip H. Sheridan in 1872.

Several smaller steamers were also built during this period. In 1868 the St. Albans, Grand Isle, and Plattsburgh Ferry Company operated the steamer *River Queen* between St. Albans Bay, Maquam Bay, and Plattsburgh. The small steamer crashed onto a rock ledge at Hathaway's Point on the St. Albans shoreline on October 30, 1868, and sank. The *Grand Isle*, built as a passenger steamer in 1869 at Essex, was later sold to the Northern Transportation Line after failing to generate the expected profits. Other small passenger steamers, including the *Water Lily*, *Curlew*, *Little Nellie*, *Victor*, and *Alexander*, operated between Vergennes and Westport. The 132-foot *A. Williams*, built at Marks Bay in Burlington in 1870 by Andrew Williams of Plattsburgh and Warren Corbin of South Hero, Vermont, was sold to the Champlain Transportation Company in 1874. The vessel had a successful career of 23 years on the lake before retirement and dismantling at Shelburne Bay.

In 1873 the Champlain Transportation Company purchased a 258-foot steamer that had been used as a railroad ferry. Two years later, the steamer would become the most famous shipwreck in the long history of steamboat traffic on Lake Champlain. Originally named the *Oakes Ames* after a Massachusetts congressman and railroad financier, the steamboat was built in 1868 by the Rutland Railroad Company's subsidiary, the Burlington Steamboat Company, to haul loaded rail cars across the lake. Two vertical walking-beam steam engines of 270 horsepower each allowed independent power for both paddlewheels while leaving an unobstructed main deck for two sets of railroad tracks. With an overall length of 258 feet, a beam of 35 feet, and an overall width of 61 feet, the *Oakes Ames* was among the largest vessels ever used on the lake.[49] The steamer was designed to carry 14 loaded railroad cars in addition to freight and passengers.

The 262-foot *Vermont II*, completed in 1871 at Shelburne Harbor.
(Special Collections, Bailey/Howe Memorial Library, UVM)

For five years the *Oakes Ames* made four round trips daily carrying railroad cars between Burlington and Plattsburgh. Nearing the expected completion of a railroad line from Ticonderoga to Plattsburgh, there would be less need for the *Oakes Ames* as a portable railroad bridge. Thus in 1873 the *Oakes Ames* was sold to the Delaware and Hudson Railroad, which controlled the Champlain Transportation Company at the time. The Delaware and Hudson subsequently sold the vessel to their subsidiary, the Champlain Transportation Company, for $85,000 for refitting the next year as a passenger steamer. The Champlain Transportation Company changed the name of the vessel to the *Champlain (II)*, as "indicative of the geographical features of Lake Champlain and its neighborhood."[50] The actual reason for the name change probably had more to do with the notorious reputation Congressman Oakes Ames had acquired from involvement in the Crédit Mobilier financial scandals.

The remodeled vessel displayed thick imported carpeting from Brussels, fine butternut and black walnut wood panels, expensive black walnut furniture, 41 cabins, a post office, barbershop, 115-seat dining room, and a huge 162-foot main stateroom. The *Champlain II* operated as a passenger liner during 1874 and 1875. To change a ship's name, however,

The steamer *Oakes Ames*. Watercolor by James Bard, Museum of the City of New York.
(Special Collections, Bailey/Howe Memorial Library, University of Vermont)

was said to be an omen of bad luck. This magnificent steamer, unfortunately, would fulfill the ominous prophecy.

After mechanical trouble sidelined the steamer *Vermont II* in the summer of 1875, the *Champlain II*, which had been used for charter excursions, was placed in regular line service along the lake. On July 15, 1875, the *Champlain II* left Ticonderoga at 9:30 in the evening for its northern run. At Westport, 23 passengers disembarked, leaving 53 adults and a number of children plus a crew of approximately 47. As the *Champlain II* departed from Westport a few minutes after midnight with "a bright moonlight and with no wind," the Senior Pilot John Eldredge, a veteran of 18 years with the CTC, lit his pipe and took the wheel from Second Pilot Ell Rockwell.[51]

Fifteen minutes later at 12:20 A.M., the vessel, traveling at 16 miles per hour, crashed on the rock ledge at Steam Mill Point, only three miles from Westport. Crewmen Walter Hedding and Edwin Rockwell, nephew of the second pilot, were seated at a table in the hold having a midnight snack when a big rock burst through the bottom of the boat with a thundering crack and a surge of water. Amid splintered walls, buckled floors, and escaping steam, the crew and passengers scurried above, fearful that the steamboat was about to explode. Without vulnerable connecting pipes, the separate engines mounted on each side of the vessel were quickly shut down by the engineers, thus avoiding scalding injuries to the crew and passengers. Second Pilot Rockwell, who had just retired to his cabin before the crash, was the first to reach the pilot house from his adjoining cabin. According to Rockwell, who delighted in retelling the story, Pilot Eldredge was still holding onto the steering wheel after the crash, staring blankly at the mountainside. Eldredge "turned cooly" to the second pilot and asked, "Ell, can you account for my being on the mountain?" Rockwell replied, "Yes, Mr. Eldredge, you were asleep." Eldredge swore that he was steering the vessel on "her true course."[52] In a statement given in Burlington three days later, Eldredge maintained that he "was not con[s]cious of being sleepy" and had "no recollection of [the] vessel being out of her course & was not aware until she struck."[53]

Captain George Rushlow, who "had been asleep but a few minutes" in his room on the main deck when the accident occurred, immediately sprang into action to stabilize the vessel and make accommodations for the passengers to evacuate the *Champlain II*.[54] The frightened passengers, many of whom were still in the "grand saloon," were calmed by the "coolness and presence of mind" of Captain Rushlow.[55] Although there was some initial screaming after the crash with one person fainting, the most serious injury was the broken tooth of a female passenger. Not all the passengers were unsettled by the disaster, however. When the *Champlain II* collided with the shoreline, Mrs. Smith Weed awoke with a shriek which sent her husband to the stateroom window. Observing the stillness outside, Weed concluded that "They must have struck [the] Westport dock pretty hard," and the couple returned to bed.[56] Within eight minutes of the disaster, gangplanks and lights were set up and passengers stood safely on the rocks examining the wreckage. According to a contemporary newspaper account, the bow had been driven "sixty feet upon the rock."[57] The boat began filling with water, breaking in "two where she was lying across the rock" soon after the passengers were on shore.[58] When the vessel broke, both ends settled with the stern sinking into the water up to the promenade deck. By then most of the baggage in the stern had been retrieved.

Rushlow promptly dispatched Second Pilot Rockwell in a life boat to hail the steamer *Adirondack*, which was in sight traveling from the north. The *Adirondack* came alongside

Facing page:
The wreck of the *Champlain II*. (Special Collections, Bailey/Howe Memorial Library, UVM)

the stricken vessel at two A.M. to collect the passengers and their baggage and return them to Ticonderoga. Rockwell was then towed to Young Bay, where he woke Captain Connor of the canal schooner *Mary D. Craig* to take valuables off the *Champlain II*. Later the schooner *J. G. Witherbee* was employed to retrieve freight from the wrecked steamer.[59]

Pilot John Eldredge, meanwhile, sat in disbelief in the pilot house as the rest of the crew scrambled to clear out the vessel. When Alex Markee, the third pilot, entered the pilot house after the crash, he found Eldredge "sitting on the settee swinging his hands up and down and mourning in a pitiful manner."[60] Engineer Joseph Trombly saw Eldredge at the break of dawn "with his valise and coat on his arm" disappear over the mountain.[61] Following wild rumors by the public on the cause of the wreck, the U.S. Local Inspectors of Steam Vessels held formal hearings on the disaster at the end of July. Evidence, corroborated by several witnesses, found that Eldredge had been in the habit of buying morphine, which was widely available from druggists during the nineteenth century. One druggist from Burlington testified that Eldredge had bought two or three bottles of morphine several weeks before the disaster.[62] Sixty-one-year-old Eldredge had a reputation as an excellent navigator of Lake Champlain who knew every inlet and reef on the lake, but he was stripped of his license. When the inspectors told him that his pilot's license had been revoked forever, he was said to reply; "Gentlemen, wait until I ask you for one."[63] The discredited pilot disappeared in the West without taking his last pay. Years later, he wrote the company for money from a home for the aged. The Champlain Transportation Company sent him a small check, and that was the last that anyone in the valley heard of him.

The other two officers, on the other hand, continued their careers on Lake Champlain. Captain George Rushlow, who began his career in 1844 aboard the schooners *Hornet* and *Melvina*, saw 60 years of service on Lake Champlain. The all-time record, however, belongs to the second pilot of the *Champlain II*, Ell Rockwell. Rockwell, who started out in 1844 as a cabin boy on the schooner *Cynthia* on Lake Champlain, eventually became a captain for the Champlain Transportation Company, serving until the age of 98 when he retired as captain of the steamer *Vermont III* in 1928.

The crash of the vessel was a night to remember for most of the crew and passengers but not for everyone. In the wee hours of the morning, the captain sent a waiter through a small hole cut in the bulkhead in order to work his way to the dining room for food. The waiter came flying back with the report that a dead man was lying in a cabin. The hole was made larger to allow Second Pilot Rockwell to enter the cabin. Sure enough, a man lay still on a bed with part of his mattress in the water. "About four feet of water was in the room and his shoes were floating in it," recounted Rockwell.[64] "About four feet from his head was the side which struck the mountain, and timbers and planking were broken right up to his head. I thought he was dead."[65] Rockwell shook him until he woke up. Evidently, the passenger was a law student who had passed the bar exam the day before and had had too much to drink. However, in an interview with the *Burlington Free Press and Times*, the young lawyer attributed his "profound slumbers" to "hard work and previous interruption of sleep."[66]

To prevent the *Champlain II* from slipping into the deep water at Steam Mill Point, the vessel was cabled to the trees onshore. During the following six weeks, the hull was stripped of her superstructure, boilers, and engines. One engine was used on the steamer *Horicon,* built at Lake George in 1877. Souvenir hunters also descended on the vessel, stripping off the black walnut ornamental woodwork. A Plattsburgh newspaper account described the interior dismantling, which "necessitated a voyage through part of the steamer in a small boat . . .the most persistent and daring of this army were women."[67] The Champlain Transportation Company did not collect on its insurance policy which only covered destruction by fire. The company, however, did salvage all of the machinery and even ran tourist excursions for 50 cents to the site of the wreck aboard their smaller steamer *A. Williams*. After the cables were cut, the remaining hull slid into the lake.

After 1875, following the completion of a railroad between Ticonderoga and Plattsburgh (November 1875), steamboat demand on the lake reached a plateau. The expansion of rail lines meant the abandonment of Whitehall as the southern terminus and Rouses Point in 1876 as the northern stop for the lake steamers. Ticonderoga's 1,550-foot semicircular railroad bridge at the base of Mount Defiance became the new southern depot, while Plattsburgh's rail terminal at the lake served as the northern end of the line for the lake steamers. For the first time, steamboats were no longer the vital link between New York City and Montreal. The first casualty of the new economic reality was the eight-year-old *Adirondack*, retired and dismantled at Shelburne Harbor in 1875. This reduced the Champlain Transportation Company's fleet to the *Vermont II* and the smaller *A. Williams*.[68] To turn a profit, the company advertised the steamers to tourists for their access to the geography and history of the lake. The trip through Lake George and Lake Champlain was made more convenient for tourists after 1874 by the construction of a rail line by the Delaware and Hudson between the Baldwin Landing on northern Lake George and the Montcalm Landing at Ticonderoga on Lake Champlain. By 1882 the Delaware and Hudson expanded rail lines from Glens Falls to the southern end of Lake George.

During the early 1880s two medium-sized passenger steamers were built on Lake Champlain, successfully taking advantage of the growing rail connections. The 142-foot *Maquam*, built under master carpenter A. J. Cookson at Grand Isle, Vermont, was completed in 1881 for the St. Johnsbury and Lake Champlain Railroad Company. In 1897 the steamer was purchased by the Champlain Transportation Company to run between Burlington and St. Albans and for special excursion trips. The *Maquam* was used to transport President William McKinley during the summer of 1897 while he vacationed at the Hotel Champlain (now Clinton Community College), just south of Plattsburgh. The vessel had an unusual tendency to roll in the waves, which often caused jokesters to run back and forth across the forward deck to exacerbate the rolling until the captain ordered the crew to interrupt the mischief makers. After 24 years of operation, the *Maquam* was retired from regular service in 1905 and her hull cut up at Shelburne Harbor the following year.[69] A second steamer completed in 1881, the 168-foot *Reindeer*, was built at Alburgh, Vermont, under master carpenter Jermiah Faulks for the Grand Isle Steamboat Company.[70] The *Reindeer*, which began passenger service in 1882 between Burlington and St. Albans, was one of the few steamers in the history of the lake never to operate under the ownership of the Champlain Transportation Company. After many years of excursion service, the steamer sank at the Central Vermont wharf in Burlington in 1902. The *Reindeer* was subsequently raised and taken to Whitehall for dismantling, and her 800-horsepower engine was cut up for scrap iron. (The remains of the *Reindeer* lie in the shallow water on the shore of South Bay in Whitehall.)

With the Champlain Transportation Company's two steamers, *Vermont II* and *A. Williams*, turning a profit during the 1880s, the company decided to build a larger vessel to replace the smaller of the two steamboats. In a departure from previous wood construction, the Champlain Transportation Company built the 1,000-horsepower, 205-foot *Chateaugay* with a steel hull. The *Chateaugay*, a marvel of inland steamboat construction, began passenger and excursion service in 1888. The 1,200-passenger vessel operated until 1917, when it was temporarily laid-up due to a drop in tourism during World War I and did not resume service until September 1919. In 1920 and 1921 the *Chateaugay* was employed as an automobile ferry, but did not operate from 1922 to 1924.

Above: The 142-foot *Maquam*, 1881-1906. *Top:* The 168-foot *Reindeer*, built at Alburgh, Vermont, in 1881. One of the few steamers from this era on Lake Champlain never to have been owned by the Champlain Transportation Company. *Facing page, top:* The 205-foot, steel-hulled *Chateaugay* began service on Lake Champlain in 1888. The hull was hauled to Lake Winnepesaukee, New Hampshire, in 1940, where it continues in service today as the M/S *Mount Washington II. Middle: Chateaugay* was remodeled as an automobile ferry in 1925 for the Burlington-Port Kent route. *Bottom:* The 262-foot, steel-hulled *Vermont III* was built in 1903 and ended service on Lake Champlain after the 1932 season. (Special Collections, Bailey/Howe Memorial Library, UVM)

When the Champlain Transportation Company decided to refit the *Chateaugay* as a car ferry, David Collins of the Steamboat Inspection Service was sent to Shelburne to assess the safety of changing the old steamer. Collins, who had served on Warren Harding's presidential yacht as an engineer, warned the company that "making changes in a boat that was built in 1888 is a waste of money and I can never O.K. it."[71] But after inspection he remarked that "if anybody had told me a vessel thirty-seven years old could be in the shape she is I wouldn't have believed them."[72] The superstructure on the forward and aft decks was removed to allow automobile ferry service. The remodeled *Chateaugay* reentered car ferry service on July 12, 1925.[73] By the end of the decade, the *Chateaugay* had carried over 48,000 cars between Port Kent and Burlington.

The *Chateaugay* plied the lake through 1932 under the CTC banner. Revenue fell drastically during the Great Depression and the *Chateaugay* was leased to Daniel A. Loomis, the CTC general manager, who kept the auto ferry in business on the Burlington-Port Kent route from 1933 to 1935. The auto ferry briefly returned to CTC operation in 1936, but the vessel was sold with other CTC assets the following year.[74] At the end of the Depression, an engineless *Chateaugay* was relegated to service as a clubhouse for the Burlington Yacht Club. Loomis lamented the fate of the *Chateaugay*: "a pretty sad end to a remarkable record of a fine steamboat, into [a] kind of dance hall and boo[z]e joint."[75] Following a fire on December 22, 1939, that totally destroyed the old steamer *Mount Washington* on Lake Winnipesaukee, New Hampshire, the newly formed Mount Washington Steamship Corporation purchased the *Chateaugay* for $20,000. In the spring of 1940 the vessel's hull was cut into 20 sections at Shelburne and loaded onto barges to be taken back to Burlington, where eight railroad cars carried the old vessel to Lake Winnipesaukee. Launched on August 12, 1940, the *Mt. Washington II* survives on the lake to this day. During the winter of 1982-1983, the renamed *M/S Mount Washington* was lengthened by 24 feet. If Inspector Collins could now examine the hull after more than 100 years of service, he would surely be impressed.

Following the success of the *Chateaugay* on Lake Champlain at the turn of the century, the Champlain Transportation Company launched the largest steamer ever built on Lake Champlain. The steel-hulled 262-foot *Vermont III*, completed in 1903, had a beam of 62 feet and displaced 1,195 tons. The 1,800-horsepower engine propelled the vessel at speeds of 23 miles per hour. The *Vermont III* was a floating palace with mahogany furniture, red carpeting, a white-and-gold stateroom hall with an ornate staircase, and 50 staterooms with running water. The retirement of the *Vermont II* in 1902 and the *Maquam* three years later ended the era of wooden steamboats owned by the Champlain Transportation Company. The *Vermont II*, like the *Maquam* later, was hauled out of the lake at Shelburne Harbor and cut up during the summer of 1903.

Because of the need to replace the aging, wooden-hulled *Maquam*, the Champlain Transportation Company decided to build a larger vessel as its third steamer on the lake to complement the *Vermont III* and *Chateaugay*. The 220-foot, 1,500-horsepower *Ticonderoga* was completed at Shelburne Harbor in 1906. The steel hull plates were built by the T. S. Marvel Company in Newburgh, New York, and shipped to Shelburne for assembly and the building of the wooden superstructure. The huge engine, built by the W. and A. Fletcher Company of Hoboken, New Jersey, powered 25-foot diameter iron sidewheels. The superstructure contained a finely decorated main stateroom hall with fluted stanchions, newel posts and banisters of cherry, butternut-paneled stateroom doors, rich patterned carpeting, and gracefully curved timbers supporting a stenciled ceiling.

The *Ticonderoga* was given the St. Albans-Plattsburgh-Burlington-Essex-Westport-Port Henry run while the *Chateaugay* was assigned the excursion trade, formerly the task of the *Maquam*. In 1909 during the Tercentenary Anniversary of the discovery of the lake by Samuel de Champlain, the *Ticonderoga* played an important role in transporting dignitaries, including President William Howard Taft. During 1918 the Federal Railroad Administration controlled the CTC steamers, but local management remained in place. While tourist excursions were curtailed during World War I, the *Ticonderoga* and *Vermont III* transported troops and equipment between the army base at Plattsburgh and Fort Ethan Allen in Vermont and made special trips for officer trainees to the sites of the Valcour and Plattsburgh battles.

The 220-foot *Ticonderoga*, completed at the Shelburne shipyard in 1906.
(Special Collections, Bailey/Howe Memorial Library, UVM)

Returning to service in 1920 after a serious grounding in 1919, the *Ticonderoga* carried passengers throughout the decade, including such notables as General John J. Pershing, who made a tour of inspection of the Plattsburgh army post and Fort Ethan Allen in 1924. The *Ticonderoga* was profitable in 1929, but business fell precipitously thereafter. The CTC also faced competition from Elisha Goodsell's Burlington-Port Douglas ferries: the *Admiral* (1922-1931), the *Legonia* (1929-1933), and the former yacht of William Randolph Hearst, the *Oneida*, purchased at auction in 1932 and operated through 1933.[76] Large financial losses caused by the Great Depression led to the idling of the *Ticonderoga* and *Vermont III* in 1933. However, the *Chateaugay*, which operated from 1933 to 1935 as the "Burlington-Port Kent Ferry" under a lease arrangement, returned to service in 1936 under CTC control, as did the *Ticonderoga*. Continued losses resulted in the Delaware and Hudson's sale of the Champlain Transportation Company to Horace W. Corbin of Burlington on April 1, 1937. Corbin, a World War I pilot and grandnephew of George Armstrong Custer, was the nephew of the co-owner of the steamer *A. Williams*. Corbin had owned ferries at several crossings on Lake Champlain since 1920, including the Grand Isle-Cumberland Head ferry (*Plattsburgh* and *Roosevelt II*), and, under the name of the Green Mountain-Adirondack Ferry Company, had built two 152-foot steel ferries, the *City of Burlington* (1936) and the *City of Plattsburgh* (1937). But Corbin's debts soon mounted and his company collapsed into bankruptcy; the *Chateaugay* was sidelined in 1937, while the *Ticonderoga* operated for excursion parties and was subsequently advertised as a "Showboat."[77] The engines of the *Vermont III* and *Chateaugay* were sold for scrap with the latter hull going to Lake Winnipesaukee in 1940 while the *Vermont III*'s hull was stripped for conversion to a diesel freight boat for duty on the South Atlantic coast after World War II. The once proud steamboat *Vermont III* sank with a cargo of newsprint off the coast of North Carolina during the 1950s. The Delaware and Hudson

Above: The 108-foot ferry *Roosevelt II* was built in 1923 and scuttled in the lake in 1959. The intact wreck was located during a side-scan sonar survey by the Lake Champlain Maritime Museum in 1989 and relocated again by the LCMM in 1997. (Special Collections, Bailey/Howe Memorial Library, UVM) *Below:* Shelburne Shipyard, Vermont. Photo by the author.

also ended its control of the Lake George steamboats during the Depression by first leasing the vessels and facilities and finally selling them in 1939.

During World War II, the *Ticonderoga* was brought to life again as a freight, passenger, and excursion steamer because gasoline rationing did not impinge on the coal-burning steamer. The Shelburne Shipyard, leased to the Donovan Contracting Company of St. Paul, Minnesota, by Horace Corbin in 1941, began construction of war vessels, the first on the lake since the War of 1812. Five sub-chasers, four yard tugboats, and three torpedo lighters (barges) were constructed by shipyard workers and taken through the Champlain Canal to ultimate ocean service for the U.S. Navy.[78] The shipyard was sold by Horace Corbin in 1946 to the wartime yard superintendent Jerry Aske and his brother Wendell. The shipyard subsequently built the 190-foot ferry *Valcour*, 73 motorboats, and 467 landing craft for the U.S. Navy (1952-1958), and 50 private cruisers for the Pembroke Boat Company of New Hampshire.[79] In 1948 Horace Corbin sold the Champlain Transportation Company to Lewis P. Evans, Jr., Richard H. Wadhams, and James G. Wolcott, who renamed the corporation the Lake Champlain Transportation Company, and moved the firm into the modern but less exciting era of steel-hulled ferries. A number of ferries were constructed or rebuilt during the Evans-Wadhams-Wolcott era (1948-1976): *Grand Isle, Adirondack, Champlain, Essex, Abnaki, Algonquin, Juniper, MT. Mansfield, MT. Marcy,* and *Governor George D. Aiken.* The LCTC was sold in 1976 to Ray Pecor, Jr., who initiated year-round service between Grand Isle and Cumberland Head and placed the ferries *Charlotte, Essex, Plattsburgh, Evans-Wadhams-Wolcott, Vermont IV,* and *Cumberland* in operation.[80] Further south, the cable-guided Fort Ti Ferry (tug *Addie B* and barge *Fort Ticonderoga II*) continues to operate as an independent company on its route between Shoreham and Ticonderoga. The history of ferry crossings on Lake Champlain is a chronicle in itself.[81]

The 190-foot ferry *Valcour* during the 1950s.
(Special Collections, Bailey/Howe Memorial Library, UVM)

By 1950 the *Ticonderoga*, which had been purchased by Captain Martin Fisher a year earlier, was in deep financial trouble. Following a fund-raising campaign under the leadership of Ralph Nading Hill and the Burlington Junior Chamber of Commerce, the *Ticonderoga* was able to steam through the 1950 season. An interest-free loan to the Fisher Steamboat Company from the Junior Chamber, however, was not able to keep the company solvent. On January 25, 1951, Electra H. and J. Watson Webb, then assembling a village museum at Shelburne, purchased the *Ticonderoga* for passenger service during the summer months. The Shelburne Steamboat Company operated the last sidewheeler as a marine museum and excursion boat for three more seasons. Although the revenue from the *Ticonderoga* covered her operating expenses every year (30,000 passengers in 1953), the lack of steam engineers, rising fuel prices, and the increasing age of the vessel induced the Webbs to transport the steamer two miles overland to the Shelburne Museum grounds. After the steamer was floated onto 16 railroad freight cars in a berthing basin dug for the maneuver, the *Ticonderoga* inched its way on a set of double tracks for 65 days and 20 hours before reaching its permanent retirement home at the museum on April 6, 1955. A National Historic Landmark since 1963, the *Ticonderoga* remains a star attraction at the Shelburne Museum. A renovation in 1980 and 1981 on this last North American passenger sidewheeler failed to halt the deterioration of the steamboat, but a 1.7 million dollar gift and endowment from J. Warren and Lois McClure in 1991 allowed an extensive restoration of the vessel (completed 1998), insuring its continued display at the museum.

After a 23-year absence of tourist excursions on Lake Champlain, the 65-foot, twin-diesel *Juniper*, sailing from Plattsburgh, renewed the tradition of the cruise boat on the lake. The *Juniper* began her career in 1945 as the *Big Bottle*, a transport vessel for the Pepsi-Cola Company in the waters around New York City. Purchased by the Lake Champlain Transportation Company in 1952, the vessel was renamed the *Juniper* and spent the next 15 years on the ferry run between Essex and Charlotte. After retirement as a ferry and work vessel, the *Juniper* was acquired by Frank Pabst of Plattsburgh and a group of local investors. Pabst, a colorful entrepreneur and marine history enthusiast, rebuilt the *Juniper* and began his nostalgic excursions into the history and adventure of Lake Champlain on June 26, 1976. For a quarter-century Captain Pabst provided his unique personal description of the Battle of Valcour Island, rumrunner hideouts during prohibition, the Garden Island treasure of the French and Indian War, and the tumultuous naval battle fought on Plattsburgh Bay.[82]

The 1980s witnessed the introduction of two additional excursion boats on Lake Champlain. In 1983 the 65-foot, stern-wheeler *Spirit of Ethan Allen*, owned by the Green Mountain Boat Lines, Ltd., began operations at Burlington with scenic narrated cruises, dinner cruises, and sunset excursions. In 1995 the 101-foot, 500-passenger *Spirit of Ethan Allen II*, owned by the Lake Champlain Shoreline Cruises (GMBL renamed), replaced the former vessel, offering the same services as well as live entertainment. The new vessel, originally built in Ohio in 1986, accommodated passengers on three spacious decks. In 1993 the Lake Champlain Transportation Company inaugurated narrated cruises of Burlington Harbor aboard a converted ferryboat, the 100-foot *Essex*, built in 1981. Today, the LCTC offers weekend cruises during the spring and fall months and daily excursions during the summer. The southern section of the lake also witnessed a renewal of tour boat service. In 1986 the 112-foot *Mount Independence* began cruises from its homeport of Whitehall. The ex-submarine chaser (1943) was rebuilt as a 133-passenger tour boat, offering a range of ten separate trips on Lake Champlain and the Champlain Canal, but operations were suspended after only two years. In 1990 the 60-foot M/V *Carillon*, owned by Mahlon and Gena Teachout, began a variety of tours in the area of Fort Ticonderoga and Mount Independence. Built by Scarano Boat Builders of Albany, the 49-passenger *Carillon* was designed to resemble a classic 1920s Thousand Island tour boat with a long mahogany-trimmed cabin and swing-up windows. In 1997 the Westport Marina, Inc.,

Facing page: The *Ticonderoga* (1906-1953), presently on display at the Shelburne Museum. Interior of the *Ticonderoga*. Photos by the author.

began weekend excursions aboard its 50-foot, 46-passenger *Philomena D*, a classic Chesapeake Bay vessel built in 1948.

The future of Lake Champlain for excursion tours, recreational boating, sightseeing, and scuba diving has been the subject of debate for more than 40 years. Lynn Watt's 1969 article "Is Champlain Doomed?" (*Vermont Life*) outlined the continuing deterioration of water quality due to municipal sewage, agricultural contamination, and industrial waste.[83] Although Vermont passed its first pollution control act in 1949, major pollution problems continued to plague Lake Champlain years later. On the New York side of the lake in 1969, 19 municipalities and industries were still discharging raw sewage and industrial waste into the lake. After the Federal Clean Water Act of 1972, both New York and Vermont made significant strides in preventing pollution. In August 1988 a cooperative agreement to chart a new course for Lake Champlain was signed on the tour boat *Juniper* by Governors Madeleine Kunin of Vermont and Mario Cuomo of New York and Quebec Premier Robert Bourassa. The "Memorandum of Understanding" encompassed plans to protect water quality and to regulate shore and lake development.

The 60-foot M/V *Carillon* on the Champlain Barge Canal at Whitehall. Photo by the author.

Under the leadership of the Lake Champlain Committee, founded in 1963, public awareness of the need to preserve the finite resources of the lake basin has been raised. Progress has been made on many fronts during the 1990s: the Lake Champlain Special Designation Act (1990), which committed federal funds over a five-year period to a major pollution control effort; a phosphorous reduction agreement among New York, Vermont, and Quebec as part of the Lake Champlain Restoration Act (1996); fifteen million dollars in funding for 23 projects (as of 2000) through the New York Clean Water/Clean Air Bond Act; improvements in Burlington's sewage system; and land purchases by the Adirondack Nature Conservancy & Adirondack Land Trust, as well as the Lake Champlain Land Trust. Despite intense efforts, problems facing the lake persist and new ones such as an infestation of zebra mussels have emerged. It is hoped that problems of industrial pollution, PCB sludge in Cumberland Bay, agricultural runoff, and stormwater runoff/sewage in Burlington Bay will be resolved. Ironically, the Burlington harbor area contains four of Vermont's Underwater Historic Preserves. Despite the ongoing water-quality problems, the heightened public awareness and government commitment to solve these problems have provided some optimism for the preservation of Lake Champlain.

Archaeological Discoveries

A number of historic Lake Champlain steamboats have been discovered at the bottom of the lake. The steamer *Vermont*, sunk in the Richelieu River near Bloody Island in 1815, was one of the first steamboat wrecks to receive public attention. The steamer lay on the bottom of the river in 15 feet of water until October 1953 when the Lake Champlain Associates, Inc., which included Lorenzo Hagglund, salvager of the *Royal Savage* and *Philadelphia*, raised the remaining hull with oil drums. The *Vermont* was hauled to a site on the Port Kent road near Ausable Chasm, New York, to be displayed in a maritime museum that failed to materialize.[84] The frames and timbers of the *Vermont* were still fairly solid in the early 1970s as it lay abandoned in dense foliage 100 feet from the road. The *Vermont* survived until 1973 when nearly all of the vessel was destroyed to clear the land for a campsite. Ironically, in an effort to save the vessel, the Lake Champlain Associates created the circumstances that led to its destruction. Some of the surviving timbers were stored in a barn and donated to the Lake Champlain Maritime Museum during the 1990s by Edward Hatch, the son of one of the original salvagers of the *Vermont*. The current philosophy among many preservationists is to leave the vessels underwater and protect the sites by the creation of historic preserves.

The hull of the steamboat *Vermont* (1809) was raised from the Richelieu River in 1953 and brought to a site near Ausable Chasm. (*Adirondack Album* by Barney Fowler)

The second steamboat to ply Lake Champlain, the *Phoenix*, burned and sank at Colchester reef in 1819. Although divers had searched for the remains of the *Phoenix*, its location remained undiscovered until 1978 when dive instructor Donald Mayland found the wreck accidentally while practicing a deep dive with two students. The vessel was lying in depths of 60 to 110 feet, untouched for 159 years. Mayland revisited the site in 1978 and the next year joined Arthur Cohn, who earlier had been granted a permit to search for the *Phoenix* from the Vermont Division for Historic Preservation, in an effort to identify positively the wreck as the steamboat *Phoenix*.[85] In 1980 the Champlain

The wreck of the *Phoenix*.

Above: Stern section lying in 110 feet of water near Colchester Shoal. The wreck is a Vermont Underwater Historic Preserve. *Left:* Bow section. *Below:* Iron rods, which once held the engine and boilers on the *Phoenix*. Photos by the author.

Maritime Society was officially organized and initiated the first of two archaeological projects to examine the *Phoenix*. The first CMS team recorded the physical measurements of the wreckage and began photographic documentation; the second in 1983 completed the photo documentation and recovered hundreds of glass and pottery fragments, kitchenware, buttons, spikes, forged iron fittings, and keys.[86] Archaeologists concluded that the *Phoenix* "had a strong, well-fastened hull with a smooth, rounded design, quite unlike the boxy shape of her predecessor *Vermont*."[87]

In 1985 the *Phoenix* became the first wreck site designated an Underwater Historic Preserve by the state of Vermont. Today, the vessel is accessible to all divers with the use of a large mooring buoy which floats over the wreck to which boats can be tied. The buoy is attached to an anchor pad with an underwater sign, which briefly describes the wreck and reminds divers that any removal of artifacts, wood, etc. is forbidden by law. The bow section, which stands about 15 feet from the bottom, lies at a depth of 60 feet; the stern lies in 110 feet of water. The frames, the rudder hardware at the stern, the iron rods that held the engine, the keel, etc., remain on the *Phoenix*.

Another early form of lake transportation, the horse ferry, would become the subject of an intensive archaeological study following the discovery of the only known intact horse boat in existence. Using side-scan sonar in Burlington Bay in 1983, James Kennard and Scott Hill discovered a nearly intact 63-foot horse boat with two eight-foot diameter paddle wheels, lying in 45 feet of water. With the assistance of the Champlain Maritime Society and the Vermont Division for Historic Preservation, Hill and Kennard completed a photomosaic of the wreck in 1984.[88] The Burlington horse ferry, a turntable-type vessel powered by two horses, received national attention in the October 1989 issue of *National Geographic*.[89] To safeguard the vessel from accidental anchor damage by visiting divers, the VDHP opened the horse ferry as the state's fourth Underwater Historic Preserve on September 20, 1989, with a dedication by Governor Madeleine M. Kunin.

Beginning in 1989, the VDHP initiated a four-year archaeological study of the Burlington Bay horse ferry. The first two-week study under the direction of archaeologist Kevin Crisman (Texas A & M University) documented the exposed hull structure and turntable mechanism. During the next three years, the archaeological team, under field school project directors Crisman and Arthur Cohn (LCMM), utilized a water dredge to excavate "slightly less than half of the sediment filling the interior of the ferry" and recorded the structure of the vessel in great detail.[90] The four-year study required 700 dives by team members. Although the name of the Burlington horse boat is still uncertain, evidence suggests that the machinery, and possibly the entire boat, was built by Barnabas and John Langdon.[91]

The 1832 steamboat *Water Witch*, converted to a schooner in 1836, sank south of Diamond Island in 1866, only a short distance from the site where the vessel had been built at the mouth of Otter Creek. The *Water Witch*, first discovered by Canadian diver Derek Grout in 1977 and later relocated by James Kennard with side-scan sonar, lies completely intact in 75-80 feet of water. The vessel's primitive windlass, bowsprit, two anchors, wooden cleats, pulleys, deadeyes, tiller bar, and broken forward mast remain undisturbed in eerie silence after 135 years underwater. The cabin, whose wooden white-trimmed panels have largely fallen into the silt, extends the width of the vessel and is 17 feet long. About 30 feet astern of the vessel lies the small lifeboat that Captain Mock had tied to the stern. The Lake Champlain Maritime Museum archaeologically documented the wreck during 1990 and 1993.[92] The *Water Witch*, which operated as a steamer and schooner during the nineteenth century, may be the nation's oldest completely intact commercial vessel. Because the wreck lies in deep water and visibility is often limited

Horse ferry sunk in Burlington Harbor.

The vessel is one of Vermont's Underwater
Historic Preserves.

Above: Paddle wheels. Photo by the author.

Left: Photomosaic by Scott Hill.
(Funded by National Park Service)

Below: Gears for paddle wheels. Photo by the author.

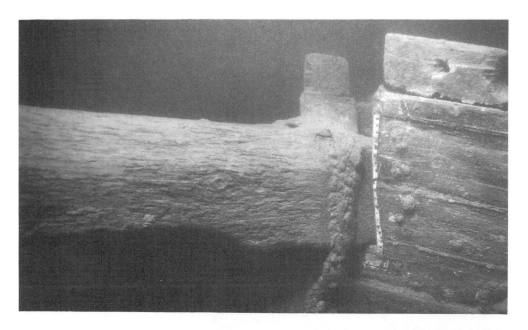

Wreck of the *Water Witch*.

Above: Bowsprit.

Right: Anchor on bow.

Shelburne Bay.

Below: Steamboat wreck.

Photos by the author.

because of silting from Otter Creek, the *Water Witch* is not considered a good candidate for preserve status at this time.

Most of the earlier wooden steamers, outliving their usefulness, were stripped of their engines and the usable portions of their superstructures and left to settle to the bottom of Shelburne Bay. Shelburne Harbor is the graveyard of at least a dozen scuttled lake steamers of a bygone era. Just below the surface in five to ten feet of water, the massive timbers of these vessels unfold like gigantic brontosaurus skeletons. Although some are quite broken up, probably due to shipyard and marina construction as well as ice damage, at least a half dozen of the hulls are substantially together. In 1983 the Champlain Maritime Society examined and measured six of the hulls.[93] Most of the steamers have massive frames, engine mounts, keels, and keelsons that are quite solid, considering that almost all have been on the bottom for more than 100 years.

In addition to the 222 feet of the *Adirondack* lying southwest of Colamers Island in 10 to 15 feet of water, the most visible wrecks are located on the north side of Pine Point (just south of the present Shelburne Marina). The most intact wreckage in this area is the steamer *Burlington*, lying in a north-south direction in shallow water with the bow area facing the shore. Dismantled in 1859 at Shelburne, 161 feet of her length and 25 feet of width exists, along with 83 frames, the stern post, and the rudder. Touching the port side of the *Burlington*'s bow area is another steamer, lying in an east-west direction with an existing length of 210 feet and width of 27 feet. Although an old Shelburne Shipyard drawing placed the *Whitehall* (original length of 215 feet by 23) in this locality, the wreckage may be the *Canada*. As many as 149 frames remain on the port side of the vessel, as well as massive engine mounts about 59 feet from the stern. To the starboard side of the *Burlington* lies 125 feet of the wreckage of either the *Francis Saltus*, abandoned in this area in 1859, or possibly the *A. Williams*, dismantled in 1893. This vessel lies close to the shoreline in an east-west direction in five feet of water. Another steamer wreck, measuring 135 feet by 23 feet, lies on the starboard side of the *Burlington* in an east-west direction and is believed to be the *Franklin*, abandoned in the vicinity during 1838. On the south side of Pine Point are the scattered remains of a steamer thought to be the *United States*. The steamers *Saranac* and *Winooski* and sloop *Hann*, listed on the Shelburne drawing, were hauled further out into deeper water during construction of the present marina. The area north of the old shipyard on Shelburne Point contains the scattered wreckage of the 81-foot steamer *Herald*, the 250-foot *America/Sherman*, tug *Pocahontas*, yacht *General Allen*, the 55-foot shipyard tender *Osceola*, and a scow.[94]

The wreckage of the steamboat *Champlain II*, sunk in 1875, lies in 15 to 35 feet of water about three miles north of Westport and 100 feet south of Steam Mill Point.[95] Listed in guidebooks for scuba divers during the 1960s and 1970s, the wreck of the *Champlain II* became a popular dive site very early. Because Ogden Ross' *The Steamboats of Lake Champlain* (published 1930) noted that "the hull was sunk in the deep water near where she had crashed," many divers concluded that the wreck was in two sections with one undiscovered portion in 150 or more feet of water.[96] In 1980, however, the New York search team of Joseph Zarzynski of Wilton and James Kennard and Scott Hill of Rochester, New York, after deploying side-scan sonar at the wreck site, found no other sections of the vessel. The forward section, representing about one third the length of the *Champlain II*, had been cut off and dismantled on shore before the remaining hull was dragged by ice to its present location. During the summers of 1993 and 1994, the Lake Champlain Maritime Museum conducted an archaeological survey of the *Champlain II* to determine if the wreck would make a good site for a New York State preserve. Arthur Cohn and Kevin Crisman directed the field school and Elizabeth R. Baldwin supervised the survey of the wreck. Although half of the port side of the *Champlain II* has collapsed,

Left: Engine support buttress on the steamboat *Champlain II*. The wreck is now a New York Underwater Preserve. *Right:* Massive timber assembly on the *Champlain II*. Photos by the author.

a sizeable section of the starboard side remains upright, connected to massive engine support buttresses with two cross timbers. The archaeological team observed that "when compared to Lake Champlain's collection of steamers, the *Champlain II* is an oddity. . .the timbers. . .are larger than any other vessel it has been compared to."[97] The sternpost, standing just over 11 feet from the bottom, is only five feet below the surface. (The rudder was salvaged years earlier and is presently displayed in a dining room of the Portside Restaurant at the Essex marina.) The wreck of the *Champlain II*, measuring 163 feet 11 inches in length, was designated New York State's first preserve in Lake Champlain in 1998 and is listed on the National Registry of Historic Places.[98]

Side-scan sonar surveys by the Lake Champlain Maritime Museum have uncovered other relics from the era when steamboats and railroads coexisted at Lake Champlain, including three nineteenth-century drawboats. Completed in 1871, an 1,830-foot-long railroad bridge, utilizing a 300-foot drawboat section to allow for the passage of vessels on the lake, connected Willow Point, Ticonderoga, to the south side of Beadles Cove at Larrabees Point (Vermont). A side-scan sonar survey of the area in 1992 by the LCMM revealed the remains of two drawboats used for the portable section of the bridge. The first of the 300-foot drawboats, in service from 1871 to 1888, lies in one piece near the Vermont shore in approximately 13 feet of water. The second drawboat, in operation from 1888 to 1902, is sunk closer to the middle of the lake at a 20-foot depth.[99] A third drawboat, discovered during a 1999 side-scan sonar survey, was once a section of a long railroad trestle across Bulwagga Bay, linking Port Henry to Crown Point for use in the transportation of iron ore. The 250-foot barge-like vessel is completely intact in relatively shallow water.[100]

Two decades of side-scan operations at Lake Champlain have revealed the most diverse collection of intact shipwrecks in America.

1844.

STEAM PACKET
Wm. Caldwell,

LAKE GEORGE,
L. C. Larabee, Master,

WILL commence her regular Trips on *TUESDAY*, the fourth day of June next—Leaving J. F. SHERRIL'S *Spacious Lake House* at Caldwell, every Morning, (except Sundays) at 8 o'clock. The Boat will remain at the foot of the Lake 3 1-2 hours, giving Passengers time to visit

THE RUINS OF FORT TICONDEROGA,

and Dine and return to Caldwell the same Day, leaving Ticonderoga at 3 o'clock, P. M. Should any alteration be made in the Steam Boat Arrangement on Lake Champlain, the above arrangement will be altered so as to conform thereto. And thus

Form a regular Communication between

SARATOGA SPRINGS AND LAKE CHAMPLAIN THROUGH LAKE GEORGE.

☞Passengers taking or leaving the Champlain Steamers at the Hotel near the Fort. now kept by Mrs. ATHERTON, formerly of the Hotel on the Outlet of Lake George. will find Carriages to convey them from one Lake to the other.

May 1st, 1844.

Broadside (poster) for the steamboat *William Caldwell*, 1844. The same steamboat illustration had been used earlier on other posters to represent different steamboats. (Special Collections, Bailey/Howe Memorial Library, UVM)

12. Steamboats of Lake George

THE BEAUTY OF THE CLEAR, blue waters of Lake George, surrounded by steep mountains reaching heights of 2,500 feet, quickly became apparent to visitors and potential settlers during the late eighteenth century. Writing to his daughter in 1791, Thomas Jefferson observed: "Lake George is, without comparison, the most beautiful water I ever saw; formed by a contour of mountains. . .finely interspersed with islands, its water limpid as crystal."[1]

Early land patents included 500 acres granted to Samuel Adams in 1766 at Sabbath Day Point and 1,595 acres at present-day Lake George Village conveyed to Albany merchant James Caldwell* in 1787.[4] Large land tracts, owned by John Thurman of New York City, were incorporated into the township of Thurman in 1792, covering much of present-day Warren County. From these land tracts and earlier grants, the towns of Bolton in 1799, Rochester in 1807 (changed to Hague in 1808), and Caldwell in 1810 (Lake George Village today) were established as the first permanent communities at Lake George. Although settled earlier, the town of Ticonderoga was not officially defined until 1804. Lumbering initially became one of the area's most important commercial endeavors, but the tourist trade eventually played a major role in life along the lake during the nineteenth century.

The Adams' Tavern, established by 1765 at Sabbath Day Point, was the earliest tavern on the lake.[5] The first tavern at the southern end of the lake had been called the "Long House" and by some reports was a building remaining at the close of the American Revolution. Although a British raiding party burned Fort George in 1780, Professor Benjamin Silliman from Connecticut, traveling in 1819, remarked "on the very shore, we observe one of the old barracks, formerly belonging to the fort, now exibiting a tavern sign, and, till within a few years, constituting the only place of accommodation to those who visited Lake George."[6] By 1821 the town of Caldwell, named for the original promoters of the settlement, James Caldwell and his son William, was inhabited by 500 to 600 people.

Professor Silliman was one of the early writers proclaiming the beautiful scenery and clarity of Lake George to potential visitors: "Everyone has heard of the transparency of the waters of Lake George. . .in fishing, even in twenty or twenty-five feet of water, the angler may select his fish, by bringing the hook near the mouth of the one which he prefers."[7] In 1853 Henry Marvin suggested that "the water is so transparent that a white object may be seen at the depth of near forty feet."[8] James Fenimore Cooper's most famous novel, *The Last of the Mohicans* published in 1826, exposed readers of fiction to vivid descriptions of the beauty of Lake George (called Horicon in the book) and the stirring adventures of his characters during the French and Indian War.** As the reputation of Lake George grew, more and more hotels were built there during the nineteenth century.

---

* James Caldwell manufactured tobacco, snuff, mustard, starch, and chocolate in his mills in Albany during the late eighteenth century.[2] Caldwell and other manufacturers had many political ties and when his tobacco mill burned to the ground in 1794, the New York legislature provided a large loan to rebuild the factory.[3] James Caldwell died on February 1, 1829, at the age of 82 and is buried in a family plot at the cemetery on Mohican Street in Lake George Village.

** Cooper led an unsuccessful campaign to rename Lake George "Horicon."

On the heels of the experience of steam-powered vessels on Lake Champlain, the first steamboat was completed at Lake George in 1817. The Lake George steam boat company, with James Caldwell and John Winans among the directors, was chartered by the state legislature from April 15, 1817, until 1838.* The company's first steamboat was begun in 1816 by John Winans, who had also completed construction of Lake Champlain's first steamer, the *Vermont*, in 1809 at Burlington. The 80-foot, 20-horsepower *James Caldwell* used the engine and boilers that had been salvaged from the wreck of the *Vermont* and used for one season in the steamer *Champlain*. The *James Caldwell* was reportedly built "at Ticonderoga, above the rapids," probably because it was easy to transport the engine and boilers from Lake Champlain.[9] The vessel resembled early Lake Champlain steamers but featured an odd brick smokestack. Traveling at only four miles per hour, the *James Caldwell* took a full day to traverse the length of the lake, making a return trip the following day. Although once struck by lightning, the steamer survived two seasons before burning under mysterious circumstances at her Caldwell dock at the Lake House in 1819. Professor Benjamin Silliman's record of his tour of the lake in 1819 included reference to the "wreck of a steam-boat, recently burnt to the waters edge, lay near the tavern" and suggested that renewed steamboat service would make the lake a "great. . .resort."[10]

Since the steamer *James Caldwell* "did not pay," according to a nineteenth-century newspaper account, it took until 1824 before the next steamboat was constructed at the lake.[11] The 125-ton *Mountaineer* was built at Caldwell by John Baird and Captain Jahaziel Sherman. At the time, Baird owned the Lake House Hotel on the present-day site of Shepard Park in Lake George Village, while Sherman was the builder and master of many early Lake Champlain steamboats. Nineteenth-century sources indicate that the vessel had a keelson but no frames, a hull "made of three tiers of inch oak plank, two of which ran fore and aft," and another course which ran in the opposite direction, fastened by cedar pins.[12] This unusual construction was said to cause the vessel to "weave and twist like rubber," according to Captain Elias S. Harris, whose "first ride on a steamboat was on her."[13] The unique construction was the work of naval architect William Annesley, who had collaborated with Jahaziel Sherman a year earlier at Vergennes during the design stage of the canal sloop *Ethan Allen*. At Lake George, Annesley "set up the moulds of the Mountaineer Steam Boat, 100 feet extreme length, 17 feet wide, and 8 feet deep."[14]

The steamer, painted red, white, and blue, operated for 13 seasons and had a faster schedule than the *James Caldwell* due largely to Captain Lucius C. Larabee's practice of transferring passengers while already underway from rowboats to the steamer's yawl, which was towed astern. The yawl would then be pulled alongside the steamer for boarding. The practice was necessary because the only wharves were located at each end of the lake and at Bolton and Hague. Larabee, however, would always slow down to pick up female passengers. The *Mountaineer* ended service in 1836 and subsequently "rotted down" and sank above the "rapids at Ticonderoga" in an area of Ticonderoga Creek called the "Boat Grave Yard" near the old lime and charcoal kilns.[15] The vessel's remains could still be observed as late as the 1890s.

After the sale of Jahaziel Sherman's steamer *Water Witch* to the Champlain Transportation Company, the steamboat pioneer returned to Lake George to build a more up-to-date steamer. On February 10, 1837, the Lake George Steam Boat Association filed a letter of intent for incorporation in New York to build and operate a steamboat on the lake.[16] However, the company apparently never obtained a state charter. While there are

---

* During the nineteenth century, the company had at least four names, each written differently: the Lake George steam boat company (1817), the Lake George Steam - Boat Company (1819), the Lake George Steam Boat Company (1854), and the Lake George Steamboat Company (1872).

discrepancies in the reported dimensions of the new steamer, an early newspaper account listed the *William Caldwell* as 110 feet in length with a 17-foot beam.[17] Begun in March 1837, the 150-ton steamer was completed in August at a cost of $18,000 at the Homelands Dock (one-half mile north of the present Baldwin Landing) on the Ticonderoga outlet. In a drawing on an 1844 poster, the vessel appears to have had two decks and twin smokestacks. The drawing of the *William Caldwell* on the poster, however, is virtually identical to an 1834 poster advertising the steamer *Phoenix II* and the 1836 poster of the *Franklin*, both on Lake Cham-

plain. The posters, printed by the same firm, used the same drawing for all three vessels. A more accurate drawing by W. H. Bartlett, done in 1838, shows the twin smokestacked *William Caldwell* with one deck and a bowsprit.

The *William Caldwell* era initiated the first through service via land connections by carriage to Lake Champlain. The steamer departed the Lake House at eight o'clock in the morning and remained for three and a half hours at the northern landing to allow tourists time to visit the ruins of Fort Ticonderoga. Taverns at the northern outlet of Lake George also provided rooms and meals for travelers. The area known as Alexandria, named for English land-owner Alexander Ellice at the turn

The steamer *William Caldwell* at Black Mountain, detail of a print by W. H. Bartlett, 1838. (Collection of Betty Ahearn Buckell)

of the nineteenth century, accommodated travelers at the Alexandria Hotel, built before 1825. After a time, the stagecoach line of Captain William G. Baldwin carried passengers to Lake Champlain from the Homelands Dock (also called Cooks Landing). The *William Caldwell* was retired in 1850 and abandoned in the shallow water of a cove north of the Lake House in Caldwell. In 1853 Henry Marvin noted that travelers often made inquiries of the "old hulk" which had been "stripped of all her valuable necessaries and was left lying upon the strand, where she has been subjected to the action of the elements for the past three years."[18]

The story of the next steamboat, the 142-foot *John Jay*, begins in 1846 with convoluted financial arrangements and ends with the tragic sinking of the vessel a decade later. In 1846 an "association" was established to raise capital through the sale of stock at $100 a share to build a new steamboat under the direction of John Jay Harris, an enterprising businessman from Queensbury.[19] On June 7, 1848, the Lake George Steamboat Association, owners of the steamboat *William Caldwell*, entered into an agreement with Harris to purchase half of the steamboat (still under construction) for $4,000 and also had "the privilege of purchasing the remaining half" until June 1 of the following year.[20] However, the purchase was apparently never consummated and the vessel was completed at Ticonderoga by shipbuilder Ferris Collyer for John Jay Harris. Similar to the collusive activity that occurred earlier between steamboat companies at Lake Champlain, on May 7, 1850, the Lake George Steamboat Association called for an "arrangement" with Harris, suggesting two options: "what amount will you take to lay up your Boat this season" or "how much will you give us to lay up the Wm. Caldwell this season."[21] Although details of the agreement are uncertain, the steamboat *William Caldwell* was retired in 1850. The steamer *John Jay* operated for a few years under Lucius C. Larabee, the former captain of both the *Mountaineer* and *William Caldwell*. A steamer captain later described the *John Jay* as "about 145 feet in length, painted white, with a lower and upper deck, the latter being approximately fifteen feet above the guards. In 1855, the company added a wooden roof or canopy over the upper deck."[22] The 250-ton steamer, made entirely of oak, plied the lake at 13 miles per hour with a reliable, wood-burning 75-horsepower engine.

Above: John Jay at the Lake House (present site of Shepard Park, Lake George Village) from *Gleason's Pictorial Drawing-Room Companion*, 1854. (Author's collection)

Left: The steamer *John Jay* at Cooks Landing. (Collection of Betty Ahearn Buckell)

In August 1850 a traveler from Connecticut, Mrs. John Van Winkle, toured Lake George aboard the steamboat *John Jay*. During the trip she observed "a grand sight" of a bald eagle as it "sailed majestically" beside the steamer, "harmoniz[ing] well with the grand magnificence of the shore."[23] As the steamer approached Cooks Landing in Ticonderoga, the captain sounded a bugle. Upon landing, the passengers rushed to the "stage wagon" for the journey to the steamboat dock on Lake Champlain, making stops along the way for travelers to view the lower falls on the La Chute River and the ruins of Fort Ticonderoga.[24]

Although the steamers *William Caldwell* and *John Jay* had navigated Lake George for a total of 16 years without a state charter, a reincarnated Lake George Steam Boat Company was chartered in 1854 by the state legislature. In 1853 the steamer *John Jay* with all her equipment was purchased from Harris for $18,000 by the new company.[25] The *John Jay* was described at the time as "a fine, staunch vessel" under the command of Hosea B. Farr, operating with "a due regard to speed and to the higher importance, confident safety to the traveller."[26]

The *John Jay* continued her successful but uneventful career until July 29, 1856, when the one and only fatal steamboat accident of the Lake George Steam Boat Company occurred, destroying the boat and taking six lives. The steamer had departed from Ticonderoga under Captain James Gale at six o'clock in the evening, a later departure than usual. According to the boat's pilot, Elias S. Harris, brother of the builder of the *John Jay*, the boat began "taking fire when passing Friends Point."[27] The steamer, with 80 passengers aboard, was then about five miles south of her Ticonderoga dock. According to Harris, a gale wind from a severe thunderstorm had stopped the draft in the smokestack, causing high pressure to "burst open both doors of the furnace," spewing red-hot embers into a pile of nearby wood.[28] A newspaper account written a few days after the accident, however, suggested that the fire had been caused by burning "pitch-pine wood, which choked up the smoke-pipe, so as to drive the fire and smoke into the fireroom."[29] Pitch pine, although somewhat dangerous, was often used to coax extra speed from a steamer. The burning vessel continued past Waltonian Island as the crew attempted to land the boat on the Hague shore.

The hero of the disaster, at least by his account, was Pilot Elias Harris. Although blinded by the smoke and steam from the erupting boilers and the burning vessel, Harris felt his way to the stern where he attempted to jury-rig the tiller bar, the ropes connecting the steering wheel to the rudder having been burned away. Harris, guessing at his course, somehow managed to steer the blazing vessel to shore just to the south of Temple Knoll Island. The *Glens Falls Republican* on August 5, 1856, reported: "After striking the rocks she shot out into the Lake some thirty or forty rods. At this point the passengers became alarmed, and as the flames raged with fury, driving them from place to place, they jumped overboard and many saved themselves by clinging to chairs, trunks, life-preservers, tables, etc., that had been thrown overboard."[30] Pilot Harris later maintained that "jumping over the rail forward of the moving wheels was the cause of the most of the drownings," since the turning paddle wheels created a current which pulled the victims into deeper water.[31] Five of the bodies were recovered immediately after the wreck; but despite a company reward of $100 and a search for the body, no trace of a Connecticut woman was ever found.

There were many heroic acts during the catastrophe. William George, a carpenter on the steamer, saved a "young lady" who had pleaded with him to save her life: "She threw both arms around his neck and as the boat struck, he jumped to the shore with the lady upon his back."[32] When George later discovered Captain Gale struggling in the lake, he scrambled into the water, despite an injury, and dragged him ashore by his hair. William Brunet, who worked at Garfield's Hotel (across from the present-day Hague Town Beach), assisted many women to shore after the crash and also recovered three bodies.

Richard Shear, known as "Old Dick" or the "rattlesnake man," was aboard the *John Jay* with his box of rattlesnakes, which he displayed to tourists for a fee. In the confusion of the disaster, the box of rattlesnakes was thrown overboard. A little girl, the daughter of a Ticonderoga resident, was placed on the box and safely drifted to the shore, despite the elevated heads of the rattlers, which had poked themselves through the broken top of the box to silently witness the calamity.[33]

Not all the witnesses to the disaster, however, were as altruistic as the heroes who saved the passengers. "A young man living there threw off his outer clothing, saved six persons from the burning vessel, and while he was doing it some public spirited person stole his watch"[34] A *New York Herald* reporter noted that the "land sharks" or "vultures" on the night of the disaster "had a great pile of shawls, bunnets, bags, parasols, hats, canes, & c., which they were pulling over."[35]

The cause of the accident was never conclusively determined. Whether the engine was over stoked with pine pitch to make up for the late departure that evening is unknown. The rock that the *John Jay* hit that night has since been known as Calamity Rock.

Twelve days after the tragedy in Hague, the directors of the steamboat company, meeting at the Fort William Henry Hotel, decided to build a new steamboat at a cost limited to $20,000. The engine, boilers, and machinery were to be salvaged from the wreckage of the *John Jay*. The keel of the new steamer was laid on November 7, 1856, on the west shore of Lake George at Caldwell. Thomas Collyer, who had earlier built the steamers *Francis Saltus* and *America* on Lake Champlain, was in charge of building the new 260-ton craft at Lake George. The 140-foot steamer with a beam of 22-24 feet was finished in a record six months at a cost of approximately $26,000. The *Minne-Ha-Ha*, meaning "Laughing Water" in Henry Wadsworth Longfellow's poem "Hiawatha," was launched on May 12, 1857, "ami[d] the plaudits of the multitude [estimated at 1,500] who assembled to witness the spectacle."[36] The 400-passenger *Minne-Ha-Ha* had a single smokestack and two decks with the forward top deck open. She burned six cords of wood on each round trip. The steamer was a financial success, but the disruption of the Civil War, which drastically reduced the tourist trade, cut revenues in half for the *Minne-Ha-Ha*. After the Civil War the steamer's business recovered and notable passengers such as Major General George B. McClellan, former commander in chief of the Union Army, traveled on the vessel, as did 12-year-old Theodore Roosevelt.

By the late 1860s, expanding railroad lines and business consolidations, which had affected many sectors of the American economy, impacted Lake George. As early as 1866, the Champlain Transportation Company, under the presidency of Colonel LeGrand Cannon, had purchased enough stock in the Lake George Steam Boat Company to replace the officers, including the president. The new president, Colonel LeGrand Cannon himself, following an amendment to the charter of the Lake George Steam Boat Company, completed a full takeover of the company by the CTC in 1868. The Champlain Transportation Company was itself the target of a friendly takeover in 1868 by the Rensselaer and Saratoga Railroad, whose president, George H. Cramer, was Cannon's brother-in-law. With the expiration of the Lake George Steam Boat Company's charter in 1869, steamboats on Lake George operated under the name of the Champlain Transportation Company. On May 1, 1871, the Delaware and Hudson Canal Company (Colonel Cannon was also a member of the board of directors) leased in perpetuity all of the assets of the Rensselaer and Saratoga, including the two steamboat lines. The coordination of the Delaware and Hudson's train schedules with the lake steamer runs was soon accomplished, which allowed continuous service between New York City and Montreal. Four years later, the Delaware and Hudson constructed a railroad line from the Baldwin Landing on northern Lake George to the Montcalm Landing at Ticonderoga on Lake Champlain. By 1882 the Delaware and Hudson had also connected its rail lines from Glens Falls to Caldwell.

With the infusion of new capital into the Lake George operation, Colonel Cannon and the board of the Champlain Transportation Company authorized funds to build a second steamer at Lake George. Elijah Root, the chief engineer of the CTC, was directed to supervise construction of the vessel. In the late spring of 1869, the firm of Neafie and

Above: The *Minnie-Ha-Ha* after renovation as a hotel/dining facility at Black Mountain Point. Photo by Seneca Ray Stoddard. (New York State Museum)

Top left: The 140-foot *Minne-Ha-Ha* at her Caldwell dock, the *Ganouskie* in the background. (Special Collections, Bailey/Howe Memorial Library, UVM)

Top right: The *Minne-Ha-Ha* as a hotel at Black Mountain Point. Photo by Seneca Ray Stoddard (New York State Museum)

Below: The *Minne-Ha-Ha* falling in ruin at Black Mountain Point during the 1890s. (Aaron Feigen Collection, courtesy of Betty Ahearn Buckell)

Levy of Philadelphia completed the 64-foot *Ganouskie*, an Indian name for present-day Northwest Bay. The propeller-driven vessel had one main deck with only a pilot house and a larger observation cabin in the aft section of the upper deck. The dependable little steamer was converted from a wood-burner to coal in 1877. The *Ganouskie*'s first captain, Arnold Hulett, had the habit of exaggerating his maritime experiences and knowledge of Lake George to curious passengers. "There is not a single rock or reef in the waters of Lake George that I don't know," Hulett once boasted, only to have the steamer scrape over a rocky reef, to which he nimbly observed, "There's one of them now."[37]

Left: The *Ganouskie* at Huletts Landing. (Lake George Historical Association)
Right: An early photograph of the 64-foot *Ganouskie* without her canopy roof.
(Special Collections, Bailey/Howe Memorial Library, UVM)
Below: The 195-foot *Horicon*, 1877-1911. (Lake George Historical Association)

In 1872 the board of directors of the Champlain Transportation Company decided to resurrect the steamboat company on Lake George as a separate corporation. The Champlain Transportation Company had always endeavored to monopolize the steamboat trade on Lake Champlain. With the expiration of the old Lake George Steam Boat Company's charter, the CTC may have sought a new charter for Lake George from New York State to forestall any potential competitors who might solicit a charter in the future. In 1872 the New York legislature approved a charter of the Lake George Steamboat Company until 1887. The new president, Colonel LeGrand B. Cannon, was president of the last Lake George company and the president of the CTC at the time. The charter of the Lake George Steamboat Company was renewed in 1887, 1902, and 1916. The 1916 recharter was extended to 2417!

Following a "request" from the CTC, the Lake George Steamboat Company built the largest steamboat on the lake to date at Cooks Landing, Ticonderoga, during 1876-1877. The 643-ton, 195-foot *Horicon*, a name from James Fenimore Cooper's *Last of the Mohicans*, could achieve 14 miles per hour with her 270-horsepower steam engine. The engine and boiler for the new steamer were salvaged from the steamer *Champlain*, wrecked north of Westport on Lake Champlain in 1875. The 1,000-passenger *Horicon*, the first large steamer built under the Champlain Transportation Company umbrella, was elegantly furnished throughout with a main saloon on the promenade deck, 108 feet in length and 27 feet wide, finished in butternut and black walnut. Built at a cost of $64,000, the *Horicon* required "80 [rail] carloads of timber, machinery, iron, dressed lumber and joiner work."[38] According to Charles Possons' 1888 travel guide, the vessel also had three staterooms and an unheard of crew at the time of "three officers and twenty-four men."[39]

By the 1880s tourism at Lake George had changed with the addition of more hotels and boarding houses along the lake and in the picturesque Narrows. An enlarged Fort William Henry Hotel, the Kattskill House, Marion House, Algonquin, Sagamore, Kenesaw House, Pearl Point House, Hundred Island House, Hulett House, Phoenix House, Trout House, Island Harbor House, Rogers Rock Hotel and more than a dozen other hotels were part of the landscape as the flood of tourists reached Lake George via expanding rail connections.

With the operation of the *Horicon*, the Lake George Steamboat Company sold the old *Minne-Ha-Ha* to Cyrus Butler, owner of both the Horicon Iron Company in Ticonderoga and a small hotel at Black Mountain Point in the Narrows. In 1877 Butler towed the engineless vessel to the small bay at Black Mountain adjacent to his hotel, the Horicon Pavilion. Butler had earlier attempted to construct a canal between Red Rock Bay and Paradise Bay with the intention of mooring the *Minne-Ha-Ha* as a hotel on the latter bay, but the project was abandoned as too costly. At Black Mountain Point the vessel was converted into a 25-room hotel and dining facility. Following a fire on April 21, 1889, which destroyed the Horicon Pavilion, the old *Minne-Ha-Ha* was abandoned in the bay. In July 1893 a local newspaper reported that "storms and ice are fast causing the craft to fall into ruin, and it will not be very many years before the boat totally disappears."[40] To clear the channel and avoid accidents by curious visitors, the upper portion of the old steamer was dismantled and the hull later dynamited.

As a period of prosperity unfolded for the steamboat line on Lake George during the 1880s, the company decided to build a larger steamboat to replace the *Ganouskie*. The financing of the new vessel was facilitated by the separation of the Lake George profits from the Champlain Transportation Company's income. The 172-foot *Ticonderoga*, the first passenger vessel to bear the famous name, was the last of the firm's large steamboats built completely of wood. Constructed by the company's carpenters at Cooks Landing, the last of the classic nineteenth-century designs exhibited hog-frames, masts, swinging oil lamps, and hand steering gear. The vessel was completed in 1884 at a cost of $76,707.31.[41] The *Ticonderoga* was the last of the Lake George Steamboat Company's vessels launched at Cooks Landing. Today, one can still observe the remains of the old wooden ways (launching structure) in the shallow water on the western shore.

Overleaf:
Top: The 172-foot *Ticonderoga*. The steamboat was lengthened by 15 feet in 1896.
Photo by Seneca Ray Stoddard. (New York State Museum)
Middle: Ticonderoga burning at Hawkeye Point, August 29, 1901.
(Lake George Historical Association)
Bottom: "Steamboat Graveyard." Detroit Photographic Co. (Library of Congress)

The two steamers, *Horicon* and *Ticonderoga*, operated during the heyday of nine-teenth-century tourism. The company's 1885 slogan, "The Most Delightful One Day Excursion on the American Continent," was echoed by many of the travelers of the day, including General William T. Sherman of Civil War fame.[42] By the 1880s, travel/history guides by B. F. DeCosta, Charles Possons, T. E. Roessle, Seneca Ray Stoddard, the R. S. Styles' Printing House, and others spread Lake George's reputation for beauty and historical lore. As the demand for day excursions increased, the steamboat line began picnic lunch stops on the grounds of various hotels along the lake. In 1888, after complaints of litter at the hotels, the Lake George Steamboat Company purchased Fourteen Mile Island at the entrance to the Narrows for its excursion stopovers. The acquisition included the 48-room Kenesaw House (formerly called the Fourteen Mile Island House), which was leased to a concessionaire. A shooting gallery and other attractions were built on the island, but the public eventually wearied of the same stop. The hotel closed in 1896 and the company sold the island in 1905.

The pending introduction of the *Ticonderoga* resulted in the retirement of the *Ganouskie* to Cooks Landing at the end of the 1883 season. Although the idea of transferring the vessel to Lake Champlain as a tug was considered, the *Ganouskie* was sold in 1885 to G. W. Howard, who towed the vessel to a mooring at Big Burnt Island in the Narrows. Prior to her sale, the engine and boiler had been removed from the vessel and sent to the Champlain Transportation Company's shipyard at Shelburne Harbor.[43] The *Ganouskie* remained at Big Burnt Island for several years as a floating saloon. The business failed, however, after the novelty of the floating bar, which displayed a large glass box of rattlesnakes, wore off. The hull was towed to the old *Meteor* dock in Ticonderoga Creek, where it rotted away after the superstructure was dismantled and taken to Whitehall.[44]

The original configuration of the first *Mohican*
(1894), Paradise Bay. (New York State Museum)

In February 1895 the Lake George Steamboat Company purchased the 93-foot, propeller-driven steamer *Mohican* from Captain Everett Harrison of Glens Falls for $13,000. Harrison had built the *Mohican* to replace his 90-foot steamer *Island Queen*, which had been destroyed by fire. The *Island Queen*, known as the *L.G.A.* (Lake George Assembly) during her first year of operation in 1890, was a 250-passenger propeller steamer "double-decked from stem to stern."[45] The *Island Queen* made two regular round-trips each day from Caldwell to Paradise Bay during the regular tourist season. The vessel burned early on the morning of November 12, 1892, while tied up at Cedar Landing on Kattskill Bay.[46]

The *Mohican*, built for H. G. Burleigh and Everett Harrison in 1893-1894, was designed as an excursion boat by Henry T. Marvin of Brooklyn, New York. The *Mohican*'s 350-horsepower engine was built in Glens Falls, while the sturdy oak vessel itself was finished in Caldwell by shipbuilder Hiram Hyde.[47] The *Mohican* operated for only one year before her sale to the Lake George Steamboat Company. Although just prior to the purchase, the Lake George Steamboat Company considered building a smaller steamer that could navigate Paradise Bay with excursion parties, these plans were reportedly dropped as too expensive. The company's decision to buy the *Mohican*, however, may well have been made to eliminate potential competition, a policy that had been used effectively throughout the nineteenth century by the Champlain Transportation Company. After remodeling to accommodate more passengers, the *Mohican* began local passenger service in the summer of 1895, making 32 stops on the lake during her daily runs.

Top left: The *Meteor* at Black Mountain Point. (Lake George Historical Association) *Bottom left:* The 80-foot steam launch *Ellide.* (Bolton Historical Society) *Right:* The 61-foot steamer *Lillie M. Price* at the Lake House dock. (Lake George Historical Association)

By the end of the nineteenth century, smaller steamers accounted for a notable amount of traffic on Lake George. In her last year of operation in 1888, the 61-foot steamer *Lillie M. Price* offered two excursions daily from her dock at Caldwell to the Narrows, "making a complete tour of the famous Hundred Islands, and into Paradise Bay, touching at all hotels on the way, and affording an enchanting trip."[48] Other small nineteenth-century commercial steamers included the *Hiawatha, River Queen, Julia, E. D. Lewis, Meteor, Owl, Mamie, Locust, H. Colvin,* and *Mary Anderson*. Private steam yachts, charter steam launches, and naptha yachts also became familiar sights on the lake by the turn of the century.* The yachts became the main attraction at annual regattas, the first of which

---

* Partial lists of steam yachts published in the *Lake George Mirror* (1882–1899): *Latona, Nonowantuck, Minnette, Caprice, Danellia, Paragon, Cosey, Waterbelle, Eva B, Orient, Fanita, Crickett, Cyric, Pocahontas, Geneva, Wanda, Vagabond, Theta, Pampero, Pastime, Helen, Isolde, Gladys, Katrina, Nahma, Mirror, Marie Louise, Helen R, Camper, Ruth, Vanadis, Crusader, Majorie, Middy,* and *Echo*; charter steam yachts: *Marion, Rover, Comus, Mamie, Olive, Kismet, Camera, Saranac,* and *Neptune*; the *Oneita, Marie Louise,* and *Saunterer* were listed as naptha yachts. The Hague-built, Sexton boats, not listed above, included the *Cecilia, Ella, Gypsy, Locust, Mohawk, Passaic,* and *Uncas.*[49]

was held in Hague in 1888. One of the most unusual excursion boats of the period was the 80-foot *Ellide*, originally built as a private steam yacht for E. Burgess Warren of Green Island. The 800-horsepower, mahogany steamer cut through the water at more than 40 miles per hour, breaking the world record for a steam launch. In later years, the *Ellide*, under Captain W. W. Burton, made three excursion trips daily with more than 30 possible stops per trip for a one dollar ticket. As late as the 1920s, the "speed yacht" *Ellide* was listed in the *Lake George Mirror* under steamboat service available to the public for short trips.[50] The *Ellide* was eventually stored in a boathouse at Green Island, and was broken up years later.

One of the smaller steamers was involved in an accident that claimed the greatest loss of life on Lake George during the steamboat era. On the night of August 3, 1893, the one-year-old steamer *Rachel* sank near the shore in the Narrows. Twenty-seven passengers, bound for a dance at the Hundred Island House on the eastern shore of the Narrows, departed at 8:45 P.M. from the Kenesaw House aboard the 55-foot steamer. Claude Granger, a two-season employee of the hotel on Fourteen Mile Island, was in temporary command of the vessel because the regular pilot had fallen ill. In the darkness, the vessel crashed into the submerged remains of an old pier south of the Hundred Island House. Granger blew the *Rachel*'s whistle as a distress call until the vessel sank. Tourists and employees rushed from the Hundred Island House to the lakeside with lanterns. Although the rescuers quickly launched rowboats, seven women and a mother and son lost their lives. Some of the victims had been trapped under the shade deck as the vessel sank "on her side with her port bow stove in and seven feet of water above her smoke stack."[51] In the aftermath, the newspapers called for legislation to require an examination and licensing of pilots and engineers on Lake George. The *Rachel*, which had been valued at $4,000, was raised four days later with the use of two scows.[52]

Eight years after the *Rachel* disaster, the steamer *Ticonderoga* was totally destroyed by fire at the northern end of the lake. Following a moonlight excursion to Fourteen Mile Island on the evening of August 28, 1901, the *Ticonderoga* departed from her Baldwin dock without passengers at 7:20 the next morning for another trip to the southern end of the lake. Just before she reached her first stop at the Rogers Rock landing, a fire, apparently smouldering all night under the boiler-room floor, "burst from the engine room. Hurriedly, the crew manned the pumps and worked bravely to save the steamer. But instantly and almost mysteriously the entire steamer was enveloped in flames."[53] The elegant wooden steamer, remodeled and lengthened by 15 feet in 1896, was steered by Captain Frank G. White into the Rogers Rock dock. The crew frantically tied the *Ticonderoga* to the dock and cut holes through the deck in two or three places in order to pour buckets of water on the flames. The blaze, however, soon set fire to the dock and burned the ropes away. Captain White and his crew escaped, and two women employed in the kitchen in the aft section narrowly eluded disaster when they were saved by one of the crew in a small boat at the stern of the burning vessel. Engulfed in flames, the unmanned steamer drifted northward to Hawkeye Point, where it ran aground on the reef and burned completely to the waterline within two hours as horrified onlookers from the shore and steamer *Horicon* watched helplessly. The unsightly wreckage of the *Ticonderoga*, potentially discouraging to steamboat passengers, was subsequently removed from the lake.[54] On October 24, 1901, the *Ticonderoga Sentinel* reported that "the wreck of the steamer *Ticonderoga* has been sold to the Green Mountain Junk Company in Burlington, that firm being the highest bidder."[55] A week later the newspaper noted that "a force of men are at work blasting the wreck of the burned *Ticonderoga*."[56]

Following the calamity of the *Ticonderoga*, the Lake George Steamboat Company made immediate arrangements to build the first modern steel-hulled sidewheeler on the

lake. The keel of the steamer *Sagamore*, a name again drawn from Cooper's *Last of the Mohicans*, was laid at Pine Point in Caldwell on March 3, 1902. Launched on April 23, after having been built in record time, the 203-foot *Sagamore* had "the same dimensions, model, machinery, and general arrangement as the steamer *Chateaugay*," built by the Champlain Transportation Company in 1888.[57] The elegant 1,500-passenger boat had a dining hall on the main deck, a hurricane deck for sightseeing, lavish furnishings in the cherry-trimmed interior, electric lights, a barbershop, and a powerful searchlight for night trips. The silver and china were stamped with the *Sagamore* monogram, the interior halls completed with hazel wood and mirrors, the ceilings decorated in gold leaf on white, and an upper-hall floor covered by a lavish red carpet with green plush rosewood chairs. Within a few weeks of operation, the *Sagamore* exhibited a top-heavy condition because of the extra headroom provided between decks. In September 1902 the vessel was withdrawn from service, cut in half amidship, and lengthened 20 feet to increase stability.

The *Sagamore* re-entered passenger service in 1903 with a length of 223 feet and a 1,125-ton displacement. The work on the *Sagamore* was completed on a parcel of land purchased in 1885 on the Baldwin shoreline (Heart Bay today). Previously, steamers had been built and repaired at the rented Cooks Landing facility. The set of ways used on the *Sagamore*'s repair, still solid after nearly a century underwater, can be observed in the waters off the Baldwin shore. Another set of ways, built in 1910 and enlarged in 1927 with a marine railway, lies east of the original ways on Heart Bay.

Because of a host of design and mechanical problems, the company decided to replace the 13-year-old *Mohican* with a new steel-hulled vessel. The building of the hull and engines of the new *Mohican* was contracted to the W. and A. Fletcher Company of New Jersey. The hull, subcontracted to the T. S. Marvel Shipbuilding Company, was built in sections

Above: The *Mohican II* and *Mountaineer II* at the Lake George docks. (Special Collections, Bailey/Howe Memorial Library, UVM) *Facing page:, top:* The *Sagamore* under construction at Pine Point, 1902. (Lake George Historical Association) *Middle:* The *Sagamore* at the Baldwin shipyard. (Lake George Historical Association) *Bottom:* The 1,500-passenger *Sagamore*. (Postcard, author's collection)

at Newburgh, New York, and shipped to the Baldwin yard for re-assembly in 1907. Completed the following year, the 115-foot *Mohican II* utilized two 275-horsepower steam engines with twin-screw propellers. The new vessel, similar in design and appearance to the original *Mohican*, made her "official trial trip" on May 6, 1908, running from the Baldwin shipyard to the Caldwell dock in two hours and 17 minutes.[58] The first *Mohican* was brought to the Baldwin shipyard, where the vessel was dismantled and cut up. The *Mohican II*, although rebuilt several times, survives today as the oldest vessel in service at Lake George. During the early decades of operation, the *Mohican II* handled full-lake trips in the slack season while supplementing the larger steamers during the summer. In addition, the *Mohican II* offered regular Paradise Bay excursions.

An examination of the aging *Horicon* in the fall of 1908 revealed the need for expensive repairs on the hull and machinery. During the following year, the steamboat company made plans for its replacement with the largest and most powerful steamboat ever completed at Lake George. The W. and A. Fletcher Company again received the contract and once more engaged the T. S. Marvel Shipbuilding Company to build the hull. The hull, built in Newburgh, was re-assembled at Baldwin for a December 1, 1910, launching.[59] The 230-1/2-foot *Horicon II*, built at a cost of $202,000, began service in late July 1911 (commissioned on August 20) by taking the *Sagamore*'s route; the latter steamer assumed the schedule of the original *Horicon*. The huge *Horicon II* had three levels: the main, saloon, and hurricane decks, which originally were designed to accommodate 1,500–1,700 passengers. The vessel's accommodations included finely-upholstered furniture, a 100-seat dining room, eight observation and overnight staterooms, and a closed sewage system with pump-out facilities at the Lake George dock. The luxurious interior was finished in natural wood with butternut and cherry trim. The 1,280-horsepower engines propelled the *Horicon II*'s 22-1/2-foot paddle wheels at a speed of 21 miles per hour, one mile per hour faster than the *Sagamore*. The handsome new steamer was an immediate financial success, carrying a large share of the 120,000 passengers who traveled on the company's three steamboats in 1911.

Just before the time of the launch of the new *Horicon II*, the Lake George Steamboat Company began operation of its first regularly-scheduled gasoline yachts. The company leased the 45-foot, 25-passenger *Mercury* in 1909 to service the southern end of the lake. In June 1910 the company purchased the 54-foot *Pampero* for $1,200 from Harrison B. Moore, a former commodore of the New York Yacht Club and summer resident of northern Lake George. The *Pampero*, built in 1876 and exhibited at the Philadelphia Centennial in that same year, was a finely-finished steam yacht of teak and mahogany with stamped sheet metal frames (ribs). The long narrow vessel with a 36-foot canopy top was brought to Lake George in 1877. When the Lake George Steamboat Company acquired the vessel, the steam engine had already been replaced with a gasoline model. The boat was to be used to pick up passengers at small private docks which were either too small or too shallow to handle the larger steamboats. The 20-passenger *Pampero* made four round trips daily in the southern basin, with occasional charters in the evening after her scheduled seven o'clock cruise.[60]

Facing page, top: Hull of *Horicon II* under construction at the Baldwin shipyard, 1910. (Lake George Historical Association) *Middle:* Construction of the superstructure on the *Horicon II* at Baldwin, 1911. The bow of the *Mohican II* is in the foreground and the stern of the first *Horicon* in the background. (Special Collections, Bailey/Howe Memorial Library, UVM) *Bottom:* The 230-1/2 -foot *Horicon II*, the largest steamboat ever built at Lake George. (Special Collections, Bailey/Howe Memorial Library, UVM)

The Lake George Steamboat Company began operation of the 54-foot gasoline yacht *Pampero* in 1910. (Special Collections, Bailey/Howe Memorial Library, UVM)

The *Pampero*, abandoned on the shore of Lambshanty Bay. Photo by the author.

Following two profitable seasons for the *Pampero*, the Lake George Steamboat Company decided to build a larger gasoline yacht for local service on the lake. The 70-foot *Mountaineer II*, named for the second steamboat on Lake George, was completed by yacht builder Alexander McDonald in June 1912 at Mariners' Harbor, Staten Island, New York. The 75-passenger *Mountaineer II*, equipped with a 125-horsepower gasoline engine, began service in July.[61] The vessel's hull was constructed of white ash, the deck was yellow pine, and the enclosed cabin, framed in mahogany with large glass windows, extended for 54 feet on the deck. The *Mountaineer II* made four scheduled trips daily, one hour after the departures of the *Pampero*. After two years of operation, it became clear that passengers preferred the comfort of the larger *Mountaineer II* to that of the *Pampero*. Consequently, the *Pampero* was retired at the end of the 1913 season and sold to James McCabe of Ticonderoga in 1916. A large, deteriorated vessel presently on the wooded shore of Lambshanty Bay on the east side of the lake has been identified as the old *Pampero*.[62] In the twilight of her career, the *Pampero* hauled logs and loggers to a sawmill located on the shore of the bay. Except for 1919, the *Mountaineer II* remained in commission through 1921. By the 1920s the *Mountaineer*'s six cylinder engine, no longer an efficient powerplant, consumed large quantities of gasoline and was incapable of moving the vessel at the higher speeds of more modern boats. In 1927 the *Mountaineer II* was sold for $500 and converted into a cruiser/houseboat.

The *Mountaineer II* was not the only yacht offering tour boat rides during the World War I era and the 1920s.* On June 27, 1915, the 75-foot steamer *Scioto*, which had been

---

* During the first decades of the twentieth century, a number of other vessels were also available for commercial passenger service, some of which had been private yachts: *Antlers, Bertha, Blue Bird, Cadet, Cecilia, Clio, Echo, Elizabeth, Ella, Fanita, Getaway, Gypsy, Heron, Iroquois, Katrina, Locust, Marion, Naomi,* and *Shirley*.[63]

Left: The 75-foot *Scioto* at a regatta in Hague. The *Sayonara* is in background. (Collection of Jim Shaughnessy) *Right:* Wreckage of tour boat *Scioto* sunk near the southwest corner of Canoe Island. Photo by the author.

on the lake since the turn of the century, began regular service under owner Captain Frank Hamilton's "Kattskill Bay Line" on the southern section of the lake.[64] The 50-passenger *Scioto* had a small enclosed cabin just aft of the mid-section with a canopied roof over much of the remaining length of the vessel. During the 1920s, Hamilton made summer and early fall trips to Paradise Bay with the *Scioto*, in addition to regular summer evening cruises by searchlight (after 1924). Paul Goodness acquired the vessel from Hamilton and continued the Paradise Bay cruises during the 1930s. Although one published report stated that "the *Scioto* became unseaworthy and was deliberately sunk by its owners in the narrows," other veterans of lake history have identified the wreck on the southwest side of Canoe Island as the *Scioto*.[65] The wreck at Canoe Island has been observed by local residents at least since the early 1940s. After the *Scioto*, Paul Goodness purchased the *Mountaineer II*, rebuilt its superstructure in 1938, and operated the vessel briefly as the tour boat *Scioto II*. After having a few more owners, the *Mountaineer II* ended her career abandoned on the rocks at the southern end of Warner Bay on the east side of the lake. Later the vessel was broken up.

By the 1920s Lake George was undergoing yet another transformation caused by changes in transportation and the economy. The availability of the automobile to the general population opened the beauty of Lake George to thousands of short-term visitors. Old hotels and boarding houses were soon facing competition from cabins catering to the motoring public. In place of wealthy families spending leisurely summers at the lake, tourists with only a week's vacation came to dominate the economy of the villages along the lake. Millionaires Row, a 10-mile stretch from Lake George Village to Bolton Landing consisting of the palatial estates of prosperous financiers, publishers, statesmen, etc., was eventually supplanted by cabins and motels.

While the changes brought more intensive utilization of the land, the islands and the shoreline in the Narrows have largely returned to a natural state. During the nineteenth century, New York State had leased or sold islands for private summer cottages, some for as low as ten dollars. The Narrows also encompassed five large summer hotels serviced by the steamboats. Portions of the mountainous shores were often denuded by the lumber industry earlier in the ninteenth century. By the 1880s the new forest commission (Department of Environmental Conservation today) took a more preservationist attitude toward state land at Lake George. Legislation and the "forever wild" constitutional amendment further solidified the movement toward conservation. Hotels and lumbering activity disappeared from the middle of the lake, and after the turn of the century the state began taking back the islands, requiring removal of private bungalows. The state continued to acquire land during the twentieth century, including the 1941 purchase of much of the huge estate at Shelving Rock of George O. Knapp, co-founder of the Union Carbide Corporation.

The *Sagamore* half-submerged after colliding with Anthony's Nose on July 1, 1927.
(Special Collections, Bailey/Howe Memorial Library, UVM)

The steamboat business continued with routine service until 1927 when a dramatic accident nearly resulted in tragedy. The *Sagamore* had departed from Ticonderoga in dense fog about seven o'clock on the morning of July 1, 1927. After successfully negotiating the first landing at Rogers Rock, the first pilot was forced to navigate by compass while the second pilot counted the paddle wheel revolutions to measure distance. "With a blanket of fog so dense that the captain and pilot were unable to see the main deck from the pilot's house," the *Sagamore*, while turning for the Glenburnie Landing, crashed head-on into the vertical rock ledges of Anthony's Nose shortly before nine o'clock.[66] The screeching of the steel hull against the immovable stone promontory echoed across the lake. The stricken vessel was backed away from the mountain by Captain John L. Washburn as the frantic crew pressed mattresses into the openings of the crumpled hull plates. The *Sagamore* steamed a half mile to the Glenburnie dock where the passengers and mail were safely unloaded. The vessel then settled in 18 feet of water north of the dock. Three weeks later, the *Sagamore* was raised and towed to the Baldwin shipyard for extensive repairs. To haul the *Sagamore* out of the water, a marine railroad was constructed at the site of the ways that had been built in 1910 for the *Horicon II*. Before the use of the 540-foot marine railway, steamers had to be laboriously hauled out of the water by teams of horses. After repairs, the *Sagamore* returned to service during the first week of May 1928. The marine railway, built during the summer and fall of 1927, is still in operation at this writing.

The late 1920s and 1930s ushered in significant changes for steamboat activity on Lake George. While the automobile had been present for quite some time, it was not until the early 1930s that paved roads connected the entire western side of the lake from Lake George Village to Ticonderoga. By 1932, following the completion in 1925 of a paved road from Hague to Ticonderoga, the state completed a paved roadway over the sharp prominence of Tongue Mountain between Bolton and Hague.[67] Competition from private automobiles, combined with the significant drop in traffic as a result of the Great

Depression, caused the Delaware and Hudson to suffer a $200,000 deficit in its steamboat business on Lake George and Lake Champlain. The Lake George steamers carried only 50,000 passengers in 1932 compared to 110,000 in 1923.[68] At the beginning of 1933, the board of directors of the Delaware and Hudson decided to discontinue steamer service on Lake George.

After considerable dialogue with area residents and the Delaware and Hudson, Frederick W. Kavanaugh, a former state senator, established the Lake George Transportation Corporation, which subsequently leased the three steamers and marine facilities from the D and H.[69] The new company immediately invested $25,000 in the transformation of the *Horicon II* into a showboat, complete with dining accommodations, three cocktail lounges, and a grand ballroom on the second deck. Beginning on July 1, 1933, the 1,000-passenger steamer, under the command of Captain Alanson A. Fisher and Pilot Martin Fisher and a staff of 60, began moonlight cruises with big-name bands every evening during the summer. The *Mohican II* continued to run daily round-trips over the length of the lake from the Baldwin Landing while the *Sagamore* completed similar trips from Lake George Village. In 1934 the *Horicon II* was leased to the Lake George Show-Boat, Inc., operated by Frederick Kavanaugh and Hoyt Austin, while the *Mohican II* was leased to George H. Stafford, a former captain of the *Mohican II* and an employee of the steamboat company for more than two decades.[70]

During the following summer of 1935, the *Mohican II* continued passenger service under a lease arrangement with George Stafford, and in late July, Hoyt Austin began the operation of the leased *Horicon II* Show-Boat.[71] Both leasees continued their enterprises during the summer of 1936.[72] Meanwhile, the idled *Sagamore*'s wooden superstructure began to deteriorate at the Baldwin dock. Beginning on November 1, 1935, the once-proud sidewheeler was slowly dismantled for scrap.[73] In order to provide employment for loyal company workers, the CTC handled the salvage work on the *Sagamore*, rather than selling the vessel outright to scrap dealers. On September 3, 1936, Daniel A. Loomis, the CTC general manager, wrote that "the boat is pretty well stripped," but the sale of equipment, furnishings, and scrap, and the final cutting of the hull into sections required another two years.[74]

The Champlain Transportation Company, a subsidiary of the Delaware and Hudson Railroad, was sold on April 1, 1937 (see chapter 11), but the Lake George Steamboat Company remained under the D & H for two more years. Captain George Stafford leased both the *Mohican II* and the *Horicon II* Show-Boat for the summer of 1937, but revenue from the latter vessel, which supported a staff of 60, fell short of expectations for the season and Stafford leased only the *Mohican II* in 1938.[75] The new president of the D & H, Joseph N. Nuelle, decided to dispose of the Lake George Steamboat Company as soon as "a reasonable offer" was received.[76] On July 1, 1939, George H. Stafford purchased the Lake George Steamboat Company, whose principal assets in 1939 included the steamers *Horicon II* and *Mohican II* as well as the Caldwell dock, the Baldwin shipyard, numerous buildings, and eight acres at Baldwin, including 1,800 feet of lakeshore property.[77]

The *Horicon II*, built at a cost of $202,000 in 1911 and renovated in 1933 for $25,000, was sold to a scrap dealer in the fall of 1939 for $5,000. To expedite the scrapping process, the wooden superstructure of the *Horicon II* was burned. The last sidewheeler was gone forever from Lake George. During World War II, the reliable *Mohican II* maintained her daily round-trips over the length of the lake. At the same time, Stafford dispensed with much of the Baldwin property, selling shorefront lots for as little as $150 and new dishes from the steamers for ten cents each. The remaining assets were sold in November 1945 to Wilbur E. Dow, Jr., an admiralty lawyer with years of maritime experience. The new Lake George Steamboat Company, under the energetic leadership of Dow, was revived

 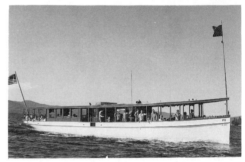

Above: The tour boat *Roamer* at Paradise Bay. (Postcard, author's collection) *Top:* The 80-foot tour boat *Ranger*. Photo by Richard Dean. *Middle:* The 81-foot tour boat *Sayonara* with a raised pilot house during the ownership period of Lake George Marine Industries, Inc. (ca. 1960s) and in the early 1970s. Photos by Richard Dean.

as a major tourist attraction at the southern end of the lake. The first changes occurred after the end of the 1946 season when the *Mohican*'s Fletcher steam engines were replaced with four diesels and the wooden superstructure on the vessel was remodeled along more modern lines.[78]

From the 1930s through the 1950s, the Lake George Steamboat Company was not the only tour boat business on the lake. Not only did the yacht *Scioto* operate during the early 1930s, but large sightseeing speedboats, including the *Empress* and *Sea Sled*, became popular with tourists. During this time, the 45-foot tour boat *Forward*, owned by Alden Shaw and Leonard Irish, sank off Diamond Island. Originally built in 1906 for William Bixby, the vessel had a long, open cockpit with twin 30-horsepower gasoline engines and propellers. While on a fishing outing near Diamond Island, the boat reportedly caught fire and sank. Rediscovered by divers decades later, the *Forward* is partially intact today with no evidence of fire damage. On May 25, 1938, Alden Shaw and Walter Harris, son of Captain Elias S. Harris, made the maiden voyage in their new 48-foot tour boat *Roamer*. The *Roamer*, built by John E. Lindsey and his son at a cost of $10,000 at Alexandria Bay on the St. Lawrence River, had arrived via truck in late November 1937. The 60-passenger vessel, which began Paradise Bay tours in June 1938, had a long cabin, providing passenger seating for most of the boat's length.[79]

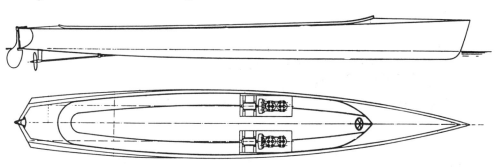

Blueprint drawing of the 45-foot launch *Forward*.
(Courtesy of Ted Caldwell and W. K. Bixby Family)

By 1940 Paul Goodness had acquired the 81-foot yacht *Sayonara* from George O. Knapp. The vessel had once served as the private steam yacht for Knapp's palatial estate at Shelving Rock. After his 65-foot steam yacht *Vanadis* burned at her dock in the fall of 1909, Knapp commissioned the building of the *Sayonara* during the following year. The long, narrow vessel had an elongated glass enclosed cabin of East India mahogany with handcrafted panels and cabinets that extended for much of her length. After a brief stint as a tour boat under Paul Goodness, the *Sayonara* was purchased during the 1940s by Alden Shaw and Harmel Burton. The handsome tour boat plied the lake for a few years beginning in 1946, before being placed in temporary storage in her old boathouse at Shelving Rock. During the 1940s, the firm of Alden Shaw and Doug and Harmel Burton, operating as the Lake George Marine Industries, Inc., also owned a fleet of 10 large sightseeing runabouts known as the "Miss Lake George Speed Boats."

In 1946 the Lake George Marine Industries, Inc., purchased an 80-foot PT boat built during World War II for the navy by the Elco Boat Company of Bayonne, New Jersey. On May 31, 1947, the 40-ton *Ranger*, converted to a tour boat and named for the rangers of French and Indian War fame, was launched at Lake George Village. The sleek *Ranger* had an enclosed 40-foot cabin built of African mahogany with a permanent canopy that extended 20 feet from the rear of the cabin to the stern of the boat. The 150-passenger

Ranger cruised at 20 knots with three 225-horsepower General Motors diesel engines driving three propellers. The vessel made two trips daily; one involved a complete cruise of the length of Lake George.[80] By the mid-1950s, the *Ranger* was retired, taken out of the lake and cut up due to deterioration of the plywood hull. By June 1756, the yacht *Sayonara* had returned to service after hull repairs and the installation of twin Chrysler marine engines. Lake George Marine Industries under Alden Shaw continued to run the *Roamer* cruise boat during the entire period.

As the popularity of Lake George increased as a vacation destination during the post-war era, the Lake George Steamboat Company decided to add another large vessel to its operation. In late 1949, following the rejection of expensive bids on a brand new vessel, Wilbur Dow, Jr., purchased the 168-foot Landing Craft 1085 from the McAllister Lighterage Company for $11,000. Built by the DeFoe Shipbuilding Company of Michigan in 1944, the vessel had served in the Pacific during World War II. Decommissioned in August 1947, the 1085 served as the mother ship for a mothball fleet on the east coast. The vessel reached Lake Champlain via the Champlain Canal, whereupon the hull was cut into four sections and carried by truck to Lake George in early 1950. After being reassembled and fitted with a new superstructure, decking, and interior, the 360-ton, 900-horsepower vessel began her career on Lake George as the cruise boat *Ticonderoga II*.[81] The vessel was further modified during the 1950s with the addition of a large dining room and an expanded cocktail lounge. The *Ticonderoga II* renewed the steamboat company's round-trip service over the entire length of the lake. At the time of the introduction of the *Ticonderoga II*, the *Mohican II* was assigned to trips departing from the Baldwin dock. In 1961 the *Mohican II* returned to the Lake George Village dock as the demand for shorter sightseeing cruises increased on the southern part of the lake. During the fall of 1966 and the following spring, the *Mohican II* underwent extensive remodeling, in which the entire wooden superstructure and decking were replaced with steel. Although the rebuilt *Mohican II* exhibits larger glass windows and painted steel, the vessel has a more classic shape with a tall smokestack and a more prominent pilot house reminiscent of the original *Mohican* configuration (1894, 1908).

Following World War II, the estates located between Lake George Village and Bolton Landing were largely subdivided into cabins and motels to accommodate the burgeoning tourist trade. The completion of the Adirondack Northway (Interstate 87) during the late 1960s made Lake George more accessible than ever by automobile. The Northway accelerated the movement to more motel rooms and encouraged the development of second homes along the lake. The increase in the number of tourists led the Lake George Steamboat Company to add a third vessel to its fleet in order to provide vacationers with one-hour lake excursions. Concluding that the new vessel should be an attraction in itself, Wilbur Dow, Jr., decided on a steam-powered vessel. Since the contemplated vessel would have a length of only 100 feet, a Mississippi sternwheel riverboat was built rather than a sidewheeler, which might have appeared stubby. The hull, built at the company's drydock in Baldwin, was launched in little more than two months in late 1968. Completed at Lake George Village in the spring of 1969, the 103-foot *Minne-Ha-Ha II*, named for the nineteenth-century steamer, utilized a 200-horsepower steam engine with 12-foot paddle

Facing page, top: The 168-foot *Ticonderoga II* at the Lake George Steamboat Company's dock in Lake George Village. Photo by the author.
Middle: Dismantling of the *Ticonderoga II* at Baldwin during the fall of 1993. Photo by the author.
Bottom: The 137-foot *Minnie-Ha-Ha II* following a 1998/1999 renovation, which lengthened the steamboat by 34 feet. Photo by Richard Dean.

wheels. The engine room was enclosed in glass to allow passengers to observe the marvels of the steam engine and the bell signals between the engineer and pilot. On August 1, 1969, the *Minne-Ha-Ha II* began her daily schedule of six hourly trips. At seven miles per hour, however, steamboat never traveled out of view of the steel pier on her hourly cruises. The boat, nevertheless, was a captivating sight on the lake with her chugging steam engine and calliope reverberating along the shoreline. In the fall of 1998 the *Minne-Ha-Ha II* was lengthened by 34 feet at the company's Baldwin shipyard and a 180-horsepower diesel engine was installed in the steamboat, providing a second means of propulsion. The twin-decorative smokestacks were replaced with a single operational one. Modifications to the superstructure were completed at the company's steel pier at Lake George Village in time for the 137-foot, 500-passenger vessel to begin the 1999 season.

Alden Shaw's tour boat operation, Lake George Marine Industries, was also an active business at Lake George during the 1960s. In the fall of 1965 Shaw purchased the 65-foot *Patricia*, then in operation near the Straits of Mackinac in Michigan. The one-year-old steel vessel, originally built in Erie, Pennsylvania, was powered by twin 671 Detroit diesels. The *Patricia* operated from 1966 to 1970, after which the business was sold to Peter and Donald Smith. The Smiths continued with the tour boats *Roamer*, *Sayonara*, and *Patricia* at a dock on Beach Road in Lake George Village. The Lake George Steamboat Company, also located on Beach Road, began litigation which would remove the competing boats owned by the Smith Brothers from their dockage on the road. Based on the contention that a local government did not have the right to lease public land to private enterprise, the Lake George Steamboat Company eventually won the case after a series of court appeals against the Smiths. The Smiths subsequently moved the three tour boats to a dock on the western shoreline. Because of the less-visible location, the profits from the *Roamer*, *Sayonara*, and *Patricia* dropped precipitously. In 1973 Alden Shaw, who held the note on the three boats, foreclosed on the Smiths. The Lake George Steamboat Company subsequently purchased all three vessels during the late summer of 1973, thereby eliminating any potential competition.

After operating briefly and unprofitably for the Lake George Steamboat Company from Bolton Landing, the *Roamer* was sold in 1981 and continued her long career on Skaneateles Lake, New York, as the tour boat *Barbara S. Wiles*. The *Patricia*, renamed the *Sunshine City*, was sold by the steamboat company to a sightseeing firm in Tampa, Florida, during the fall of 1973.[82] The *Sayonara*, however, was not as lucky. The vessel was placed in her boathouse at Shelving Rock where she sat largely untouched for more than ten years. The vessel was later sold by the steamboat company to George Owen Knapp II and Sarah Knapp Sprole for $1. After an unsuccessful attempt to sell the vessel, a New Hampshire salvager removed much of the mahogany superstructure and plans were made to burn the rest of the vessel. After learning of the planned burning of the *Sayonara*, I initiated the "Save the *Sayonara* Committee." After a year-long effort to save the vessel by proposing the creation of an underwater historic preserve adjacent to state forest lands in the upper Narrows of Lake George, the committee's application was rejected by the state. A state fire permit was granted and on May 7, 1988, the *Sayonara*, along with her boathouse at Shelving Rock, was burned.

The removal from Lake George of the *Roamer*, *Sayonara*, and *Patricia* did not end the competition in sightseeing rides on the lake. By the summer of 1977, James Quirk, operator of the U-Drive Boat Rentals at Lake George, had brought three 40-foot fiberglass cruise boats to Lake George from the Thames River in Connecticut. The 58-passenger boats, built in 1974 by Anchorage, Inc., of Warren, Rhode Island, were propelled by 150-horsepower diesels. The Lake George Boat Tours, located adjacent to Beach Road on the western shore, began a schedule of lake tours every half-hour during the summer of

Above: The 85-foot *Horicon*, built by the Scarano Boat Building Company for Shoreline Cruises, began operating on Lake George in 1988. Photo by the author.

Right: The 72-foot *Morgan* passing through the west channel of the Dollar Islands. Photo by the author.

1977. The three canopied boats, the *Ethan Allen*, *Algonquin*, and *De Champlain*, continue to offer one-hour cruises on the half-hour in season. Renamed Shoreline Cruises, the company purchased the double-deck, 65-foot *Defiance* in 1983 at New London, Connecticut. The *Defiance* is virtually identical to the old *Patricia*, having been constructed by the same shipyard (Nolan Brothers). The 600-horsepower steel *Defiance*, remodeled in 1996, continues to offer narrated one-hour trips and sunset cruises at the time of this writing. In 1987 Shoreline Cruises contracted with the Scarano Boat Building Company of Albany to build an 85-foot tour boat. The *Horicon*, the third tour boat with the same name on the lake, is a triple-deck boat made entirely of mahogany, teak, and yellow pine. The boat has an appearance somewhat similar to the original *Mohican* of the Lake George Steamboat Company. Powered by two 250-horsepower diesel engines, the 300-passenger *Horicon* began operating in 1988 and today offers Paradise Bay tours, lunch and dinner cruises, and late evening entertainment trips .

Another addition to the fleet of tour boats on the lake was built in late 1986 for the owners of the restored Sagamore Hotel on Green Island in Bolton Landing. The 72-foot *Morgan*, built by Bill Morgan of Silver Bay, utilized a wood frame encased in fiberglass. Morgan, the owner of the Hacker Boat Company of Hague, fabricated the entire vessel with local craftsmen at the Sagamore Hotel site. Today, the 80-ton tour boat, powered by a 250-horsepower diesel engine, offers sightseeing and dinner cruises with seating for 130 hotel guests and area visitors.

During the years of expansion by its new rivals, the Lake George Steamboat Company was not idle. In the early 1970s Wilbur Dow, Jr., and his son William Dow inaugurated the New Orleans Steamboat Company as a subsidiary of the Lake George company with

The 190-foot *Lac du Saint Sacrement* completed at Lake George in 1989.
Photo by Richard Dean.

the eventual acquisition of five vessels. A significant step was taken by the company in
August 1979 when the keel was laid for the largest tour boat on the lake since the departure
of the *Horicon II* in 1939. The 190-foot *Lac du Saint Sacrement*, a name that Father Isaac
Jogues had given to the lake in 1646, was designed as a three-quarter scale replica of the
classic Hudson River Day Line steamer *Peter Stuyvesant*. The *Saint* required ten years to
complete, over eight years being spent at the company's drydock in Baldwin. For much
of the 1980s, curious onlookers flocked to the Baldwin shore to observe the mammoth
hull under construction. The lengthy building process resulted from the decision to rely
on the company's Lake George profits each year to fund the purchase of parts and supplies.
The total cost approximated $4.25 million dollars for the vessel. Nearly all the work was
accomplished by skilled local workers, most of whom spent the whole decade on the boat
as their sole occupation.

Finished in June 1989, the 190-foot by 40-foot wide *Lac du Saint Sacrement*, with her four decks, dwarfs her sister ships at the steel pier at Lake George Village. Powered by two 625-horsepower Caterpiller diesel engines with twin 66-inch propellers, the 500-ton vessel cruises at 14 miles per hour, leaving only a minimal wake. The vessel carries an extensive array of electronic gear and radar in the wheel house and has electric-hydraulic steering, bridge wings, a 200-horsepower bow thruster for docking maneuvers, and four lifeboats. Amenities such as the mirrored ceiling over the dance floor and a grand double staircase with brass railings are reminiscent of the heyday of luxurious steamers such as the *Horicon II*. The *Saint* assumed the *Ticonderoga II*'s cruises. The *Ticonderoga II*, retired in 1989, remained at the company's steel pier until October 13, 1993, when the old veteran made her final voyage to the Baldwin shipyard, where the vessel was dismantled for scrap.

At the turn of the twenty-first century, one wonders if Lake George will survive the intensity of use that had increased significantly over the last two decades? At the time of this writing, the controversy over the spreading milfoil beds and the deterioration of water clarity in the southern basin of the lake had led to widespread discussion of environmental issues. As a young boy from Connecticut in 1952, I was amazed by the clarity of Lake George. I could actually see my feet on the bottom of the lake at the "Million Dollar Beach"! The beauty of Lake George and the transparency of its water were often noted by eighteenth-century soldiers, who had trudged to its shores during the French and Indian War. While it may be normal for some deterioration of water quality to occur over centuries, it is unnatural for the waters of a spring-fed lake to degenerate visibly during only one lifetime. The Task Force for the Future of the Lake George Park aptly recognized the risk that Lake George was in danger of being "loved to death."[83] The outlook for the lake, however, is not entirely gloomy. Significant strides have been made in recent years in protecting Lake George, including support provided to organizations for lake preservation activities by the Lake George Fund, lake-saving projects funded by the Lake George Association, submerged cultural resource management by Bateaux Below, Inc., recreational and environmental management by the Lake George Park Commission and the Department of Environmental Conservation, lake quality monitoring by the Darrin Fresh Water Institute, and the protection of over 4,000 acres and 26,550 feet of Lake George shoreline by the Lake George Land Conservancy. The survival of the lake in the end will not only depend upon basin-wide planning but upon individual observance of environmentally-safe practices, including the maintenance of septic systems, avoidance of lawn fertilizers, use of sealed boat toilets, etc.

In less than two centuries, Lake George and Lake Champlain have gone from a totally primitive state to the hustle and bustle of the twentieth century with its concomitant problems. The native Americans who once inhabited the two lakes had minimal impact on the environment, but they were quickly dislodged during the ensuing military rivalries. As "highways of empire," the two lakes witnessed the English and French and later the Americans and British vie for control of their strategic waters. Where men once anxiously awaited the onslaught of enemy soldiers in laboriously-constructed forts, summer visitors today calmly examine the relics that once determined the very beginning of a nation. Where the thunder of cannons from war fleets once shattered the silence of the wilderness, modern sailboats leisurely glide over tranquil waters. Below the serene surface, however, lie fragments of history in quiet solitude as reminders of the turbulent days of long ago. Likewise, the schooners, steamers, and canal boats that rest on the bottom of the lakes are mute testimony to the once-thriving commercial era. As the sun slowly sinks to the edge of the rugged mountains on the western shores of each lake, glimmering sparkles dance across their surfaces, belying the once tempestuous past of each lake.

Archaeological Discoveries

Although the shipwrecks of the steamboats *James Caldwell* and *William Caldwell*, once lying in shallow water at the southern end of the lake, were the first steamboat wrecks to draw the attention of tourists, the wreckage of the steamer *John Jay* has sustained the interest of the public for nearly a century and a half. In 1856 the *John Jay* burned and sank with the loss of six lives at Hague. The steam engine, boilers, and other equipment were removed from the wreck and installed in the steamboat *Minnie-Ha-Ha*, but the frames of the *John Jay* remained relatively intact where the vessel sank, south of Temple Knoll (Cooks Islands) in the shallow water off the Hague shore, adjacent to Calamity Rock. The memory of the incident was further sustained by the sale of postcards showing the rock. At the turn of the twentieth century, W. S. Howard, writing for the *Rudder*, "anchored [one] night on the south side of Calamity Rock. . .the moon was so bright and the water so clear that we could plainly see the outline of the old steamboat hull down in the water, which was wrecked there some forty-three years ago."[84] Today, the broken wreckage of the steamer is still visible from the surface. She lies south of Buoy B5 in the shallow water directly in front of a private residence. Its length of approximately 122 feet (maximum width of 17 feet) is still present on the lake bottom. The stern section of the *John Jay* is intact at a 10-foot depth with its white paint yet visible if you brush away the light silt with your hand. Frames (ribs), the keelson, keel, a section of the apron and inner stempost, and other scattered wreckage lie in the shallow water adjacent to Calamity Rock. Charred parts of the steamboat can be found 60 feet down an underwater bank near the site of the wreckage. Because the site lies close to the shore near private homes and the Lake George Park Commission regulations prohibit anchoring within 200 feet of a private shoreline, the wreck site is not easily accessible to the public.

Left: Stern section of steamer *John Jay* sunk in Hague, N.Y., 1856.
Right: Wreckage of the *Minnie-Ha-Ha* at Black Mountain Point. Photos by the author.

The wreckage of the next large steamboat on the lake, the *Minnie-Ha-Ha*, also lies in shallow water today. After being sold by the steamboat company in 1877, the *Minnie-Ha-Ha* was moored in a cove on the north side of Black Mountain Point and used as a hotel and dining hall for a dozen years. The vessel was later abandoned, ravaged by ice and storms, and finally dismantled, and its hull dynamited. The main wreckage of the

Minnie-Ha-Ha lies across the bay, oriented in an east-west direction in approximately ten feet of water, north of the public docks. The huge beams, keelson, frames, and boards are cleary visible from the surface.

Very little evidence of the steamboat *Ticonderoga*, which burned and sank in 1901 on the west shore at Hawkeye Point, exists because most of the wreckage was removed immediately from the lake (see main text). For years souvenir hunters picked over the scant remains of the wreckage. However, one large piece of the vessel, the nine-by-six-foot rudder, lay undisturbed in eight to ten feet of water near the reef until 1948 when two young summer residents, George Chapman Singer and Douglass S. Bruce, raised the 1,600-pound relic. The following year the rudder was varnished for use as a table inside the new clubhouse of the Northern Lake George Yacht Club, but unfortunately, it was placed outside as a picnic table and totally disintegrated over the years.[85] Today, only china fragments, spikes, boards, and a few large beams lie scattered at 5- to 30-foot depths on both sides of the reef at Hawkeye Point.

Stern of the launch *Forward*. Photo by the author.

The remains of many smaller steam- and gasoline-powered vessels have been found in Lake George. The 1906 launch *Forward*, one of the earliest gasoline-powered vessels on the lake, sank during the late 1930s east of Diamond Island. Through the efforts of Bateaux Below, Inc., a non-profit archaeological group certified by the Education Department of the state of New York, the 45-foot wreck, lying in 35-45 feet of water, was designated a Submerged Heritage Preserve by the state in 1993. The preserve was subsequently expanded into an "Underwater Classroom," with signs describing the vegetation and geology of the lake bottom for divers, as well as a monitoring station for zebra mussels.[86] Underwater preserves have been created across the country in an effort to protect underwater cultural resources. In 1988 Congress passed the Abandoned Shipwreck Act, whose purpose is "to promote cooperative efforts...to locate and protect abandoned historic shipwrecks on, in or under state submerged lands."[87] With encouragement from this legislation and Vermont's example, Bateaux Below and the state of New York began planning for likely preserve sites in state waters. The Lake George Park Commission and the Department of Environmental Conservation, supported by several other state agencies, began an approval process in 1991 for the lake's first underwater preserve.

In 1997 Bateaux Below discovered the 48-foot steamboat *Cadet* in the waters of Bolton Landing during a side-scan sonar survey conducted by Vincent J. Capone of Marine Search & Survey, Inc. The *Cadet* was originally built in 1893 as the 40-foot launch *Olive* and equipped with a triple-expansion steam engine. In 1894 the *Olive*'s first owner, N. E. Porter, sold the steam launch to Raphael Potter, who operated the vessel as an excursion boat. John Boulton Simpson, president of the Sagamore Hotel group, purchased the *Olive* in 1898 and "rebuilt and lengthened" the steamer during the following winter, renaming the vessel the *Cadet*.[88] Captain Fred R. Smith acquired the steam launch a short time later and by 1901 he had rebuilt the boat, and operated it as a charter vessel.[89] Oral history suggests that the *Cadet* may have been scuttled around 1910. In 1999 Bateaux Below, Inc., sponsored a full archaeological study of the vessel under the direction of Dr. D. K. Abbass, director of the Rhode Island Marine Archaeology Project, and Joseph W. Zarzynski, executive director of Bateaux Below and site manager for the project. Although the machinery on the vessel had been removed prior to her scuttling, the archaeological team concluded that the *Cadet* "exhibits great structural integrity with many intact construction details."[90] An inventory of artifacts at the wreck site included an incomplete steam funnel, metal rudder, four-bladed propeller, firebrick, and various ornamental features. Even the exterior paint scheme was discernible.[91]

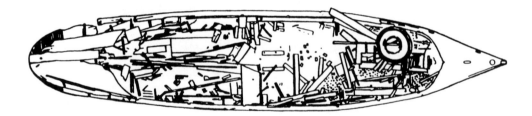

Remains of launch *Cadet*. Preliminary drawing by Robert Benway
and Joseph W. Zarzynski. (Bateaux Below, Inc.)

Bateaux Below's efforts to document underwater cultural resources in Lake George, with the use of side-scan sonar and diver verification, have resulted in a clearer understanding of the types of vessels that once plied the lake. The remains of numerous small craft have been located and studied during the last decade, including steam launches, early gasoline-powered boats, guideboats, and even the 1960 submarine *Baby Whale*. One of the most unusual submerged cultural resources surveyed by the organization involved a study of the Delaware & Hudson Company's marine railroad, located at the southern end of the lake. The railway was constructed in 1910 to launch and retrieve private launches/yachts, using railroad boxcars and flatcars as platforms. Although the D & H removed hundreds of feet of track in 1950, the archaeological team discovered 122-1/2 feet of intact track and another 80-foot section of bedding timbers submerged at depths of five to 15 feet.[92]

A multi-year survey of shipwrecks located at the northern outlet of Lake George (Ticonderoga) was conducted under project director Scott Padeni with the assistance of members of Bateaux Below, Inc., the New York State Archaeological Association, and support from the Lake Champlain Maritime Museum. Padeni documented the remains of a colonial-era shipwreck, seven nineteenth-century barges, a 25-foot nineteenth-century sailboat, a 44-foot propeller-driven steamboat, and three smaller steamboat wrecks.[93]

Underwater cultural resources need to be treated as unique historic objects that deserve a comprehensive management plan and public support for their protection. Many of these wooden vessels have outlived any comparable land-based cultural resources. For example, no original wooden fort from the eighteenth century has survived intact—yet both the 1758 radeau *Land Tortoise* and the 1776 gunboat *Spitfire* are completely intact. The discovery of these vessels and others has provided the public with a new understanding of America's maritime heritage. Before the radeau *Land Tortoise* and the sailing canal boat *General Butler* were found, no one actually understood the nature of these vessels. Technology has created the opportunity to discover vessels centuries old, but society must devise policies and methods to ensure the protection of these finite resources.

Engine in a turn-of-the-century launch in the town of Putnam
(probably a Sexton-built boat from Hague). Photo by the author.

Steam Ferry.

24th April, 1830.

THE STEAM-BOAT

GEN. GREENE,

CAPTAIN DAN LYON,

WILL run until further notice in the following order, viz:

𝕷𝖊𝖆𝖛𝖊 𝕭𝖚𝖗𝖑𝖎𝖓𝖌𝖙𝖔𝖓 at half past 8 o'clock in the morning, Sundays excepted, touching at Port Kent, and arrive at Plattsburgh at 12 o'clock.

𝕷𝖊𝖆𝖛𝖊 𝕻𝖑𝖆𝖙𝖙𝖘𝖇𝖚𝖗𝖌𝖍 at 2 o'clock P. M., and PORT KENT at 4 o'clock, and arrive at Burlington at half past 5 the same evening.

The following are the established rates of Ferriage
TO AND FROM PORT KENT.

Every four wheel pleasure Carriage on springs, drawn by two Horses, including driver,	$2 00
Every two wheel pleasure Carriage on springs, drawn by one Horse, including driver,	1 50
Every Wagon or Sleigh drawn by two Horses, including driver,	1 50
Every Wagon, Cart or Sleigh drawn by one Horse, including driver,	1 25
Every Cart drawn by two Oxen, including driver	1 50
Every additional person, Horse or Ox,	50
Every foot passenger, (children under 12 years of age, half price,)	50
Cattle in droves, each	25
Sheep and Hogs in droves, each	6
Parties of pleasure going and returning the same day, not less than 12 persons, each	25

A reasonable sum will be added to the above prices to and from Plattsburgh.

The above rates will be charged, until the first day of November, after which time the company reserve to themselves the right of charging those rates of ferriage which are established and allowed by law.

Broadside (poster) of the Champlain Ferry Company 1830.
(Special Collections, Bailey/Howe Memorial Library, UVM)

Notes

Abbreviations

AAS	American Antiquarian Society, Worcester, Massachusetts
A5	Peter Force, ed., *American Archives, Fifth Series*, 3 vols. (Washington, D.C.: M. St. Clair Clarke and Peter Force, 1848-53)
AB	Abercromby Papers, Huntington Library, San Marino, California
BFTM	*The Bulletin of the Fort Ticonderoga Museum*
Coll. Conn. HS	*Collections of the Connecticut Historical Society*
Coll. NYHS	*Collections of the New-York Historical Society*
CSL	Connecticut State Library, Archives Division, Hartford, Connecticut
CTC	Champlain Transportation Company Papers, Special Collections, Bailey/Howe Library, University of Vermont, Burlington, Vermont
EIHC	*The Essex Institute Historical Collections*
GFR	*Glens Falls Republican*
LCMM	Lake Champlain Maritime Museum, Basin Harbor, Vermont
LGM	*Lake George Mirror*
LO	Loudoun Papers, Huntington Library, San Marino, California
MAH	*The Magazine of American History*
MASS HS	Massachusetts Historical Society, Boston
NAC	National Archives of Canada, Ottawa
NDAR	William Bell Clark and William James Morgan, eds., *Naval Documents of the American Revolution*, 9 vols. (Washington, D.C.: Naval History Division, Department of the Navy, 1964-86)
NEHGR	*New-England Historical and Genealogical Register*
NRCNA	Naval Records Collection, National Archives, Washington, D.C.
NYSL	New York State Library, Albany, New York
NYCD	E. B. O'Callaghan, ed., *Documents Relative to the Colonial History of the State of New York*, 10 vols. (Albany: Weed, Parsons and Company, 1853-58)
NYD	E. B. O'Callaghan, ed., *The Documentary History of the State of New York*, 4 vols. (Albany: Weed, Parsons & Co.: Charles Van Benthuysen, Public Printer, 1849-51)
PRO	Public Record Office, London
	CO Colonial Office Papers
	WO War Office Papers

Introduction

1. Una Pope-Hennessy, ed., *The Aristocratic Journey* (New York: G. P. Putnam's Sons, 1931), 59; S. H. Hammond and L. W. Mansfield, *Country Margins and Rambles of a Journalist* (New York: J. C. Derby, 1855), 288.

1. Years of Conflict

1. Louis Antoine de Bougainville, *Adventure in the Wilderness: The American Journals of Louis Antoine de Bougainville 1756-1760*, trans. and ed. Edward P. Hamilton (Norman, OK: University of Oklahoma Press, 1964), 246.

2. Ibid.

3. For information on the archaeological sites of the native population at Lake Champlain see William A. Haviland and Marjory W. Power, *The Original Vermonters* (Hanover, N.H.: University Press of New England, 1981), 31, 38, 54, 59, 95, 105, 148-55, 199, and John C. Huden, comp., *Archaeology in Vermont* (Rutland, VT.: Charles E. Tuttle Company, Inc., 1970), 3-6, 73-74, 100.

4. Floyd G. Lounsbury, *Iroquois Place-Names in the Champlain Valley* (Albany: The University of the State of New York, 1965), 23-66; Floyd G. Lounsbury, "Iroquois Place - Names in the Champlain Valley" in *Neighbors and Intruders: An Ethnohistorical Exploration of the Indians of Hudson's River*, ed. by Laurence M. Hauptman and Jack Campisi (Ottawa: National Museums of Canada, 1978), 105-49; PRO, CO 5/46, UP microfilm reel 1, frame 638.

5. H. P. Biggar, ed., *The Works of Samuel De Champlain* (Toronto: The Champlain Society, 1925), Volume 2, 1608-1613, 91-92.

6. Majorie L. Porter, "The Champlain Monster," *Vermont Life*, Summer 1970, 47; For an excellent overview of the history of Champ sightings see Joseph W. Zarzynski, *Champ--Beyond the Legend* (Wilton, N.Y.: M-Z Information, 1988).

7. Biggar, 93.

8. Ibid., 96.

9. John Wagner, "Au Plaisir," *Adirondack Life*, January/February 1988, 55.

10. Biggar, 99.

11. Ibid., 101.

12. Guy Omeron Coolidge, *The French Occupation of the Champlain Valley from 1609 to 1759* (1938; reprint ed., Harrison, N.Y.: Harbor Hill Books, 1979), 17.

13. Reuben Gold Thwaites, ed., *Travels and Explorations of the Society of Jesus Missionaries in New France* (Cleveland: The Burrows Brothers Company, 1898), Volume 29, 49.

14. *NYD*, 1: 69.

15. *NYD*, 1: 70; Coolidge, 36.

16. *NYCD*, 9: 423.

17. Coolidge, 59.

18. *NYCD*, 4: 193.

19. Ibid., 196.

20. Ibid.

21. *NYD*, 2: 287, for John Schuyler's entire diary see 285-88.

22. For some details of the Phips' expedition, see *NYCD*, 9: 455-58. See also Chaplain John Wise's diary of the Phips' expedition in Samuel A. Green, ed., *Two Narratives of the Expedition Against Quebec, A. D. 1690* (Cambridge, MA: John Wilson and Son, 1902), 3-29; R. James Ringer, "Phips's Fleet," *National Geographic*, August 2000, 72-80.

23. Coolidge, 76.

24. For more on the military career of Francis Nicholson see Stephens Saunders Webb, "The Strange Career of Francis Nicholson," *The William and Mary Quarterly* 23 (October 1966): 515-48.

25. *NYCD*, 9: 843.

26. For a diary of the Nicholson expedition see Rev. Thomas Buckingham, "A Diary of the Land Expedition Against Crown Point in the Year 1711," in *Roll and Journal of Connecticut Service in Queen Anne's War* (Hartford, CT.: Acorn Club, 1916), 28-45.

27. Peter S. Palmer, *History of Lake Champlain*, 4th ed. (1886; reprint ed., Harrison, N.Y.: Harbor Hill Books, 1983), 56; See also "Rock Inscription at the Ruins of Old Fort St. Frederick at Crown Point," *Proceedings of the New York State Historical Association* 10 (1911): 107-13.

28. Coolidge, 97-98.

29. Ibid., 116-17.

30. Ibid., 122-23.

31. John C. Huden, "The Admiral of Lake Champlain," *Vermont History* 30 (January 1962): 67.

32. James Sullivan, ed., *The Papers of Sir William Johnson* (Albany: The University of the State of New York, 1922), Volume 2, 75.

33. Edward P. Hamilton, *The French and Indian Wars* (Garden City, N.Y.: Doubleday & Company, Inc., 1962), 123.

34. Coolidge, 147.

35. Adolph B. Benson, ed., *Peter Kalm's Travels in North America* (New York: Dover Publications, Inc., 1937), 391; Phineas Stevens also wrote a detailed description of Fort St. Frédéric in 1749. Phineas Stevens, "Journal of Capt. Phineas Stevens to and from Canada 1749," *Collections of the New-Hampshire Historical Society* 5(1837): 204; See also Chaplain John Norton's 1746 description in Arthur Latham Perry, *Origins of Williamstown*, 3rd ed. (Williamstown, MA.: A.L. Perry, 1900), 169-70.

36. Coolidge, 150; "Rock Inscription," 112; *NYCD*, 6: 582; Stoddert (Stoddard) was killed at the Battle of Lake George in 1755. *NYCD*, 6: 1005; Sullivan, 9: 238; For additional information on Stoddard, see *NYCD*, 10: 211-16.

2. Battle of Lake George

1. "Journal of the Proceedings of the Congress Held at Albany, in 1754," *Collections of the Massachusetts Historical Society* 5 (3rd Series) (1836): 6-7.

2. *NYD*, 2: 648-53.

3. Fred Anderson, *A People's Army ----Massachusetts Soldiers and Society in the Seven Years' War* (New York: W. W. Norton & Company, 1985), 8.

4. Palmer, 56; *NYD*, 2: 65.

5. John W. Krueger, *A Most Memorable Day: The Battle of Lake George, September 8, 1755* (Saranac Lake, N.Y.: North Country Community College Press, 1980), 8; Anderson, 10; The "Beating Orders" issued for recruitment specified men between 18 and 35, "free from all bodily ails and of perfect limbs," and "no Roman Catholic, nor any that are under five feet four inches high without their shoes." Arthur J.C. Sowdon, "Commemoration of the Battle of Lake George, September 8, 1903," *The Society of Colonial Wars of the Commonwealth of Massachusetts* (1906): 153-54.

6. Seth Pomeroy, *The Journals and Papers of Seth Pomeroy*, ed. by Louis Effingham De Forest (New York: Society of Colonial Wars in the State of New York, 1926), 105.

7. Sullivan, 1: 883; Captain Richard Godfrey from Taunton, Massachusetts, described a "fort house" on August 13 "one hundred foot one way, 18 foot the other and near half an acre picketed in, and another guard house 30 foot one way, 14 ye other." Richard Godfrey, "A Journal of the March of Captain Richard Godfrey's Company, 1755, in *History of Taunton, Mass.*, by Samuel H. Emery (Syracuse, N.Y.: D. Mason, 1893), 421-22; See also Pomeroy, 107-8.

8. Sullivan, 2:66; For references to the name Fort Lyman see Daniel Emerson, "A Journal of My Procedure with the Army to Crown Point--Begun July Ye 8, 1755," in *Ipswich Emersons*, by Benjamin Kendall Emerson (Boston: Press of David Clapp & Son, 1900), 90; Thomas Williams, "Correspondence of Doctor Thomas Williams of Deerfield, Mass., A Surgeon in the Army," *The Historical Magazine* 7(April 1870): 212; Sullivan, 2:63; *NYD*, 4:168-69.

9. Christopher Champline, 14 August 1755, unpublished letter (M-202B), Thompson-Pell Research Center, Fort Ticonderoga Museum.

10. James Gilbert, "A Journal Kept by James Gilbert," *Magazine of New England History* 3(1893): 191.

11. Delphina L. H. Clark, *Phineas Lyman----Connecticut's General* (Springfield, MA.: Connecticut Valley Historical Museum, 1964), 16.

12. Sullivan, 1: 783.

13. Ibid., 1: 861.

14. *NYD*, 1: 69.

15. John Gardner, "Famous Boat Type in Transitional Stage, " *National Fisherman*, May 1967, 28-A; See also David J. Christofferson, *Batteau, Battoe: A Pictorial Collection* (St. Paul: Fox in Circle Productions, 1986), Volume1, 1-12.

16. Gilbert, 193; See also Pomeroy, 111; *NYCD, 6: 998-99.*

17. James Hill, "The Diary of a Private on the First Expedition to Crown Point," ed. by Edna V. Moffett, *The New England Quarterly* 5 (1932): 608; See also John Burk, "John Burk's Diary," in *History of the Town of Bernardston*, by Lucy Cutler Kellogg (Greenfield, MA.: Press of E. A. Hall & Co., 1902), 45; Gilbert, 194.

18. Sullivan, 2: 10; There were continuing problems with the wagoners. Rev. Samuel Chandler noted on November 23, 1755, that "some of the waggoners who were hired to carry down the sick have turned them out in the woods & left them some of whom died." Samuel Chandler, "Extracts from the Diary of Rev. Samuel Chandler," *NEHGR* 17 (October 1863): 352.

19. Gilbert, 193.

20. Sullivan, 2: 10.

21. Ibid., 13.

22. Ibid., 19; Governor Vaudreuil, however, estimated the total force at 3,573. *NYCD*, 10: 319; See also PRO, CO 5/46, University Publications of America microfilm reel 1, frame 236.

23. Roger R. P. Dechame, "Why Carillon?" *BFTM* 13(Fall 1980): 432-46.

24. PRO, CO 5/46, UP microfilm reel 1, frame 638; See also Lawrence M. Hauptman and Jack Campisi, eds., *Neighbors and Intruders* (Ottawa: National Museums of Canada, 1978), 128-32.

25. *NYCD*, 10: 319, 335.

26. *NYCD*, 10: 344.

27. Ibid., 335. The figures vary on the Dieskau Expedition, see Sullivan, 2: 26-27, 58, 72.

28. *NYCD*, 6: 1004.

29. Gilbert, 194; Daniel Claus, *Daniel Claus' Narrative of His Relations with Sir William Johnson and Experiences in the Lake George Fight* (New York: Society of Colonial Wars in the State of New York, 1904), 12; *NYCD*, 6: 1005.

30. *NYD*, 2: 691.

31. *NYCD*, 10: 342; Claus, 13; See also *The London Magazine* (October 1759): 534.

32. Johnson reported that a wagoner "heard a gun fire, and a man call upon heaven for mercy, which he judged to be Adams." *NYD*, 2: 691; See also Claus, 12; *NYCD*, 10: 367.

33. Krueger, *Most Memorable Day*, 13, 15.

34. Gilbert, 195; Sullivan, 2: 691.

35. *NYCD*, 10: 342; Sullivan, 2: 72-73; Krueger, *Most Memorable Day*, 28, 30; William A. Pew, *Colonel Ephraim Williams: An Appreciation* (Williamstown, MA.: Williams College, 1919), 22; There are a variety of stories regarding the origin of the first shot, see Wyllis E. Wright, *Colonel Ephraim Williams: A Documentary Life* (Pittsfield, MA.: Berkshire County Historical Society, 1970), 136.

36. *NYCD,* 10: 318.

37. Claus, 14; Decades later John Norton repeated the Mohawk oral history of the incident: "Stand aside,-- for our Father only makes War against the English, and does not desire to hurt any of his Children,-- the Native Tribes." Carl F. Klinck and James J. Talman, eds., *The Journal of Major John Norton 1816* (Toronto: The Champlain Society, 1970), 266.

38. Ibid.

39. Ibid.

40. Daniel Claus noted that "the Breastwork w[hi]ch consisted of some Trees cut down in a hurry at the front of the Camp in some places not above a foot & half high & which waggons were the principal Shelter." Claus, 15. A French report mentioned that "the intrenchment consisted of bateaux turned upside down and of wagons." *NYCD,* 10: 367.

41. Charles Henry Lincoln, ed., *Correspondence of William Shirley* (New York: The Macmillan Company, 1912), Volume 2, 255; See also Gilbert, 195.

42. M. Pouchot, *Memoir Upon the Late War in North America Between the French and English,* 1755-60, trans. and ed. Franklin B. Hough (Roxbury, MA.: W. Elliot Woodward, 1866), 47; Pierre Pouchot, *Memoir Upon the Late War in North America Between the French and English,* trans. Michael Cardy and ed. Brian Leigh Dunnigan (Youngstown, N.Y.: Old Fort Niagara Association, Inc., 1994), 88.

43. D. Clark, *Phineas Lyman,* 19.

44. There is some dispute as to the time when Johnson retired, see Milton W. Hamilton, *Sir William Johnson,* (Port Washington, N.Y.: Kennikat Press, 1976), 165, 173-74, 357; Krueger, *Most Memorable Day,* 37; C. Lincoln, *William Shirley,* 2: 260.

45. *NYCD,* 6: 1005.

46. Emerson, 91.

47. Williams, 211-12.

48. D. Clark, *Phineas Lyman,* 19; Hill, 609; M. W. Hamilton, *Sir William Johnson,* 164; Some of the booty was brought into the Lake George camp by troops from Fort Lyman, see Godfrey, 423; See also *The London Magazine* (October 1759): 533.

49. *NYCD,* 10: 343; See also Claus, 15-16; Lawrence Henry Gipson, *The Great War for the Empire: The Years of Defeat, 1754-1757* (New York: Alfred A. Knopf, 1946), 6: 173.

50. *NYCD,* 10: 343.

51. In his journal on September 9, 1758, James Henderson noted an ambush of an English party between Lake George and the Halfway Brook post: "It was near the Bloody Pond." James Henderson, "James Henderson's Journal," in *The First Century of the Colonial Wars in the Commonwealth of Massachusetts* (Boston: Society of Colonial Wars, Mass., 1944), 200; An American officer marching along the road to Lake George in 1776, noted that "many Hundred were killed and thrown into a pond [in 1755] which gave it the name Bloody pond, many Bones are now to be seen in the Pond and about

it." *From Cambridge to Champlain* (Middleboro, MA.: Lawrence B. Romaine, 1957), 28.

52. Ibid.

53. Sullivan, 2: 45.

54. Ibid., 184.

55. C. Lincoln, *William Shirley,* 2: 257-58.

56. Wright, 148; *NYCD,* 10: 354; See also Allan W. Eckert, *Wilderness Empire* (Boston: Little, Brown and Company, 1969), 345; Sullivan, 9: 234-38.

57. Claus, 17; See also Thomas, 213; Armand Francis Lucier, ed., *French and Indian War Notices Abstracted from Colonial Newspapers 1754-1755* (Bowie, MD.: Heritage Books, Inc., 1999), Volume 1, 302.

58. Pomeroy, 115.

59. C. H. Lincoln, *William Shirley,* 2: 258.

60. Sullivan, 2: 196, 199.

61. Pomeroy, 116.

62. Sullivan, 2: 49.

63. Ibid., 214.

64. *NYCD,* 10: 325.

65. E. P. Hamilton, *French and Indian Wars,* 213; See also Bougainville, 51.

66. Sullivan, 2: 9; This letter was written after King Hendrick's speech on September 4 in which the Mohawk sachem related Shirley's negative comments about Johnson. *NYCD,* 6: 998-99.

67. C. H. Lincoln, *William Shirley,* 2: 270.

68. Sullivan, 2: 40.

69. Ibid., 53, 150.

70. C. H. Lincoln, *William Shirley,* 2: 282.

71. Sullivan, 2: 193.

72. Ibid., 166, 169; See also M. W. Hamilton, *Sir William Johnson,* 174.

73. J. Hill, "Diary," 608; Burk, 45; Gilbert, 194.

74. Sullivan, 2: 152, see also 63, 117, 135, 138.

75. Sullivan, 1: 863, 875.

76. Sullivan, 2: 160.

77. Scott Padeni, "Skirmish at The Isle of Mutton," *The Lake George Nautical Newsletter* 3 (1994): 1, 8.

78. Sullivan, 2: 305.

79. Ibid., 319.

80. Nathaniel Dwight, "The Journal of Capt. Nathaniel Dwight of Belchertown, Mass., During the Crown Point Expedition, 1755," *The New York Geneological and Biographical Record* 33 (April 1902): 65-66.

81. Sullivan, 2: 279.

82. Lyman's role in the engagement had immediately raised a storm of controversy after the publication of his letter in newspapers, which gave much of the credit for the 1755 victory to the Connecticut troops. See Milton W. Hamilton, "Battle Report: General William Johnson's Letter to the Governors, Lake George, September 9-10, 1755," *Proceed-*

ings of the American Antiquarian Society 74 (Part 1, 1964): 28-29.

83. *The London Magazine* (October 1759): 535.

3. Defeat at Fort William Henry

1. Anderson, 170; See also Gipson, 6:207.

2. Anderson, 174.

3. Ibid., 185.

4. PRO, CO 5/47, UP microfilm reel 2, frame 23; See also Stanley M. Gifford, *Fort William Henry: A History* (Lake George, N.Y.: Fort William Henry Museum, 1955), 32; Early in September 1756 Major General Winslow accompanied troops on a "Tour round the Lake" aboard "One Sloop with two Six pounders One Seven Inch Mort[a]r and Eight Swivels fifty men, One Sloop four Swivels forty men, One Ditto two Swivels and thirty men." LO 1710. On October 16, 1756, Dr. Cutter noted that "the Fleet consists of 1 sloop about 40 tons, 2 smaller about 20 tons each, another sloop on ye Ways ready to Launch of ye Bigness of former." Ammi Ruhamah Cutter, "Dr. A. R. Cutter's Journal of his Military Experience, 1756-1758," in *A History of the Cutter Family of New England*, by William Richard Cutter (Boston: David Clapp & Son, 1871), 66; See also William Hervey, *Journals of Hon. William Hervey* (Bury St. Edmund's: Paul & Mathew, Butter Market, 1906), 38.

5. *Boston Gazette and Country Journal*, 13 September 1756; Nathan L. Swayze, *Engraved Powder Horns* (Yazoo City, MS.: Gun Hill Pub. Co., 1978), 219; One of the vessels on the lake in 1756 was a sailing barge, see Jeduthan Baldwin, "Journal Kept by Capt. Jeduthan Baldwin While on the Expedition Against Crown Point, 1755-56," *Journal of the Military Service Institute* 39 (July-August 1906): 129.

6. LO 1776; See also Bougainville, 33.

7. Rogers, 28-29, 36; LO 1776; See also LO 1219.

8. Luther Roby, *Reminiscences of the French War; Rogers' Expeditions and Maj. Gen. John Stark* (Concord, N.H.: Luther Roby, 1831), 22-23.

9. Bougainville, 46; Roby, 31.

10. For Rogers' original report on the battle see LO 2704.

11. PRO, CO 5/48, UP microfilm reel 2, frame 374.

12. Ibid., frame 373.

13. Bougainville, 96.

14. Roby, 43.

15. PRO, CO 5/48, UP microfilm reel 2, frame 350; a subsequent letter noted the time as one o'clock. Ibid., frame 357.

16. PRO, CO 5/48, UP microfilm reel 2, frame 359, see also frames 346-49, 352-53; See also Thomas Mante, *The History of the Late War in North----America* (1772; reprint ed., New York: Research Reprints Inc., n.d.), 84.

17. Bougainville, 97; See also PRO, CO 5/48, UP microfilm reel 2, frame 361.

18. Bougainville, 97; See also *NYCD*,10: 545.

19. PRO, CO 5/48, UP microfilm reel 2, frame 362; Stanley McCrory Pargellis, *Lord Loudoun in North America* (Hamden, CT.: Archon Books, 1968), 235.

20. PRO, CO 5/48, UP microfilm reel 2, frame 546.

21. Bougainville, 119.

22. *The London Magazine* (September 1757): p.n.a.; See also *NYCD*, 10: 599.

23. Bougainville, 132; Reuben Gold Thwaites, ed., *Travels and Explorations of the Jesuit Missionaries in New France* (Cleveland: The Burrows Brothers Company, 1900), Volume 70, 105.

24. Bougainville, 138.

25. Ibid., 140; See also *NYCD*, 10:591, 594, 647; Arthur G. Doughty, ed., *Report of the Public Archives for the Year 1929* (Ottawa: F.A. Acland, 1930), 98.

26. *NYCD*, 10: 647; James Montresor, "Journals of Col. James Montresor," *Coll. NYHS* 14 (1881): 22.

27. *NYCD*, 10: 599; See also Mante, 85.

28. Bougainville, 142; *NYCD*, 10: 647.

29. Bougainville, 143.

30. Thwaites, 125.

31. Ibid., 155.

32. Bougainville, 144.

33. PRO, CO 5/48, UP microfilm reel 2, frame 545.

34. Ibid

35. *NYCD*, 10: 734; See also Seth Tinkham, "Diary of Seth Tinkham," in *History of Plymouth County, Massachusetts*, comp. by D. Hamilton Hurd (Philadelphia: J.W. Lewis & Co., 1884), 996; Thwaites, 139-41.

36. *NYCD*, 10: 606-7; Bougainville's figures in his journal (152, 153) differ slightly from his official report; See also D. Peter MacLeod, *The Canadian Iroquois and the Seven Years' War* (Toronto: Dundurn Press, 1996), 100, 212 (note 18).

37. Bougainville, 146.

38. Ibid., 147.

39. Ibid., 156; One of the British officers "who Saw the Platforms for Cannon which the Enemy brought upon the boats...speaks of them as a good invention." LO 4385; See also PRO, CO 5/48, UP microfilm reel 2, frame 541.

40. Pouchot (Hough), 86; Bougainville, 158; James Furnis, "An Eyewitness Account by James Furnis of the Surrender of Fort William Henry, August 1757," ed. by William S. Ewing, *New York History* 42 (July 1961): 311; PRO, CO 5/48, UP microfilm reel 2, frame 556; Mante, 90; *NYCD*, 10: 611.

41. Joseph Frye, "A Journal of the Attack of Fort William Henry," Parkman Papers 42: 140-41, MASS HS; See also James L. Kochan, ed., "Joseph Frye's Journal and Map of the Siege of Fort William Henry, 1757," *BFTM* 15 (1993): 348; Mante, 91.

42. PRO, CO 5/48, UP microfilm reel 2, frame 557.

43. PRO, CO 5/47, UP microfilm reel 2, frame 22; Anderson, 95.

44. PRO, CO 5/48, UP microfilm reel 2, frame 552.

45. Furnis, 311; LO 4479; Father Roubaud described the entrenched camp as "a fortified rock faced with palisades secured by heaps of stones." Thwaites, 155.

46. Francis Parkman, *France and England in North America* (Boston: Little, Brown, and Company, 1885), 496; See also LO 4479.

47. PRO, CO 5/48, UP microfilm reel 2, frame 557.

48. George Bartman, "The Siege of Fort William Henry, Letters of George Bartman," *Huntington Library Quarterly* 12 (August 1949): 419.

49. PRO, CO 5/48, UP microfilm reel 2, frame 558.

50. Frye, 143; See also Bartman, 420-21; Mante, 92; Bougainville, 163.

51. "A Journal Kept During the Siege of Fort William Henry, August, 1757," *Proceedings of the American Philosophical Society* 37 (1898): 147.

52. Bougainville, 166-67.

53. "Journal During the Siege," 148.

54. LO 5309; According to Lieutenant Colonel Monro, the garrison in the fort during the siege consisted of 100 regulars, 300 provincials, two officers of the 35th Regiment, one officer of the Royal American Regiment, and 30 sailors. LO 4479.

55. Twenty-two-year-old Seth Metcalf at Fort Edward wrote that the cannon firings began in the morning in "a most terrible manner and So continued all Day by Spel[l]s." Seth Metcalf, *Diary and Journal of Seth Metcalf* (Boston: The Historical Records Survey, 1939), 9.

56. PRO, CO 5/48, UP microfilm reel 2, frame 554-55; See also Francis Parkman, *Montcalm and Wolfe* (1884; reprint ed., New York: Atheneum, 1984), 291-92.

57. Sullivan, 2: 730; See also Samuel Angell, "Camp Fort Edward, 14th August 1757," *Historical Magazine* 8 (November 1870): 259.

58. Bartman, 422-23.

59. D. Clark, *Phineas Lyman*, 34-35; See also M.A. Stickney, "Massacre at Fort William Henry, 1757," *EIHC* 3 (1861): 81.

60. Frye, 146; Kochan, 352; "Journal During the Siege," 149; See also Lawrence Henry Gipson, *The Great War for the Empire: The Victorious Years, 1758-1760* (New York: Alfred A. Knopf, 1949), 7: 83.

61. Pouchot (Hough), 88; Mante, 93-94; *NYCD*, 10: 618.

62. Bougainville, 170; The chiefs acquiesced to the terms of the surrender, rather than agreed. See MacLeod, 106; See also Ian K. Steele, *Betrayals: Fort William Henry and the "Massacre"* (New York: Oxford University Press, 1990), 111.

63. Thwaites, 179; See also LO 4660; *The London Chronicle*, 11-13 October 1757.

64. Doughty, 96; Frye, 151; Kochan, 355; See also *NYCD*, 10: 633.

65. Frye, 151; Kochan, 356; Furnis, 313.

66. Frye, 151; Kochan, 356.

67. *The Universal Magazine* (October 1757): 183.

68. "Affidavit of Miles Whitworth," in Parkman, *Montcalm and Wolfe*, 560.

69. Furnis, 313.

70. *NYCD*, 10: 633.

71. Frye, 152; Kochan, 356; See also Thwaites, 179; Metcalf, 10; Furnis, 313.

72. Frye, 152; Kochan, 356; See also Furnis, 313; Angell, 259; *The London Magazine* (October 1757): 494.

73. Jonathan Carver, *Travels Through the Interior Parts of North America in the Years 1766, 1767, and 1768* (1778; reprint ed., Minneapolis: Ross and Haines, Inc., 1956), 319; See also *NYCD*, 10: 633; Frye, 152; Kochan, 356.

74. "The Colden Papers–1755-1760," *Coll. NYHS* 5 (1921): 168; Carver, 316.

75. "Journal During the Siege," 10; Russell P. Bellico, *Chronicles of Lake George: Journeys in War and Peace* (Fleischmanns, N.Y.: Purple Mountain Press, 1995), 74.

76. PRO, CO 5/48, UP microfilm reel 2, frame 566.

77. Angell, 259.

78. Metcalf, 10; See also Thwaites, 181, 187, 189; Jabez Fitch, Jr., *The Diary of Jabez Fitch, Jr., in the French and Indian War 1757* (Fort Edward: Earl and Jean Stott, 1986), 19.

79. *The London Chronicle*, 11-13 October 1757; *The London Magazine* (October 1757): 494-95; The same story was published earlier in colonial newspapers. Armand Francis Lucier, *French and Indian War Notices Abstracted from Colonial Newspapers*, Volume 2: 1756-1757 (Bowie, MD.: Heritage Books, 1999), 295; Colonial Joseph Frye noted "women and children, some of which later they killed and Scalp't in the road." Frye, 152; Kochan, 356.

80. Frye, 152; Kochan, 356-57; Carver, 318.

81. Parkman, *France and England*, 510.

82. *NYCD*, 10: 616, 619, 633.

83. Scott A. Padeni, "The Role of Blacks in New York's Northern Campaigns of the Seven Years' War," *BFTM* 16 (1999): 153-69; Steele, 140.

84. *NYCD*, 10: 633; Bougainville, 174; See also Luke Gridley, *Luke Gridley's Diary of 1757* (Hartford, CT.: Acorn Club, 1906), 49.

85. The numbers are low considering the number of troops that had been at Fort William Henry. According to Bougainville's journal, there were 2,339 men at the fort and camp when the garrison finally surrendered. The troops included 713 regulars from the 50th and 60th Regiments, 798 from the Massachusetts militia, 302 from New Jersey, 231 from New Hampshire, 57 from New York, 113 from two independent militia companies, 30 from the Royal Artillery and 95 rangers. Bougainville, 176.

86. Steele, 135, 139; see also 133-34.

87. Bougainville, 177-78; See also *NYCD*, 10: 625, 629.

88. Montresor, 37; See also *NYCD*, 10: 605.

89. Furnis, 314; See also PRO, CO 5/48, UP microfilm reel 2, frame 546-47.

90. Bougainville, 177.

91. *Boston Evening Post*, 12 September 1757.

92. LO 4407; LO 5314; See also Scott A. Padeni, *Final Report of the Literature Review and Shipwreck Inventory of Lake George's Northern End* (Ballston Spa, N.Y.: Scott A. Padeni, 1999), 20-23.

93. Lemuel Wood, "Diaries Kept by Lemuel Wood, of Boxford," *Essex Institute Historical Collections* 20 (1883): 156; PRO 283/1, WO 30/50, fol. 58.

94. David R. Starbuck, *The Great Warpath: British Military Sites from Albany to Crown Point* (Hanover, N.H.: University Press of New England, 1999), 83-110.

4. Abercromby Expedition

1. "Petition of James Scott," September 1, 1766, "Petition of Hugh Jackson," September 22, 1766, "Petition of William Friend," September 16, 1766, *New York Colonial Manuscripts, Indorsed Land Papers*, Volume 21, 134, 152, 149 (a) (b), NYSL; During the American Revolution, the cliff was also known as Rogers Rock. Horatio Rogers, ed., *Hadden's Journal and Orderly Books: A Journal Kept in Canada and Upon Burgoyne's Campaign in 1776 and 1777* (1884; reprint ed., Boston: Gregg Press, 1972), 104; Jeduthan Baldwin, *The Revolutionary Journal of Col. Jeduthan Baldwin 1775-1778*, ed. Thomas Williams Baldwin (Bangor, M.E.: DeBurians, 1906), 100.

2. William Parkman, "Journal of William Parkman," *Proceedings of the Massachusetts Historical Society* 7 (1879-80): 243; One report, however, stated that Abercromby was "in perfect health" on the day of the army's departure for Ticonderoga. AB 431.

3. E. C. Dawes, ed., *Journal of Gen. Rufus Putnam 1757-1760* (Albany: Joel Munsell's Sons, 1886), 66.

4. *The Scots Magazine* (September 1758): 442; [Ann Grant], *Memories of an American Lady* (1808; reprint ed., New York: Research Reprints, Inc., 1970), Volume 2, 67-68.

5. PRO, CO 5/50, UP microfilm reel 3, frame 4.

6. Captain John Knox, *An Historical Journal of the Campaigns in North America*, Volume 1, (1769; edited by Arthur G. Doughty, 1914-1916; reprint ed., Freeport, N.Y.: Books for Libraries Press, 1970), 181.

7. AB 397; AB 436; LO 5772; PRO CO 5/50, UP microfilm reel 2, frame 981; For an analysis of the immense logistical problems encountered in raising and equipping the army during 1758, see M. John Cardwell, "The British Expedition Against Fort Ticonderoga in 1758," (M.A. thesis, The University of New Brunswick, 1990), 20-32, 143; M. John

Cardwell, "Mismanagement: The 1758 British Expedition Against Carillon," *BFTM* 15 (1992): 246-66.

8. Anderson, 76; Amos Richardson, "Amos Richardson's Journal, 1758," *BFTM* 12 (September 1968): 274.

9. Anderson, 40-41; Harold E. Selesky, *War and Society in Colonial Connecticut* (New Haven: Yale University Press, 1990), 156-61, 176-77.

10. *Boston Gazette and Country Journal*, 20 November 1758; AB 436; PRO, CO 5/50, UP microfilm reel 2, frame 981.

11. William Sweat, "Captain William Sweat's Personal Diary of the Expedition Against Ticonderoga," *EIHC* 93 (1957): 42; Garrett Albertson, "A Short Account of the Life and Travels of Garrett Albertson, Sr.," *BFTM* 4 (July 1936): 44; Abel Spicer, "Diary of Abel Spicer from June 5th Until September 29th, 1758," in *History of the Descendants of Peter Spicer*, comp. by Susan Spicer Meech and Susan Billings Meech (Boston: F. H. Gilson, 1911), 394; Bellico, *Chronicles of Lake George*, 100.

12. Dr. James Searing, "The Battle of Ticonderoga, 1758," *Proceedings of the New York Historical Society* 5 (1847): 113; Peter Pond, an 18-year-old provincial from Connecticut, later noted that the fleet also included "Gondoloes, Rogalleys & Gunboats." Peter Pond, "Experiences in Early Wars in America," *The Journal of American History* 1 (1907): 91; Colonel Melancthon Taylor Woolsey, aboard the fleet, only mentions the "900 bateaux, 135 whale-boats, artillery on flat-boats." Melancthon Taylor Woolsey, *Letters of Melancthon Taylor Woolsey* (Champlain, N.Y.: Moorsfield Press, 1927), 12; *The New-York Mercury* noted "two floating castles with two Pieces of Cannon mounted on each, of four Pounders." *New-York Mercury*, 24 July 1758.

13. LO 5505.

14. F. Parkman, *Montcalm and Wolfe*, 357; Gipson, 7: 218.

15. AB 407; See also PRO 291/2, WO 34/76, fol. 148; Nathan Whiting, *Orderly Book of Colonel Nathan Whiting: Second Connecticut Regiment at Lake George 1758* (Hartford: Connecticut State Library, 1940), 34.

16. Roby, 69; Samuel Fisher, "Diary of Operations Around Lake George 1758," MS, Library of Congress.

17. J. Knox, *An Historical Journal*, 1: 190; See also AB 431.

18. *NYCD*, 10: 722, 738, 742; See also Pouchot (Hough), 111-12; Pouchot (Card and Dunnigan), 140; "Detailed Statement of Operations at Ticonderoga, 1758," *Pennsylvania Archives*, ed. by Samuel Hazard (Philadelphia: Joseph Severns & Co., 1853), Volume 3, 472.

19. Charles Lee, "Narrative--Enclosed in Letter of September 16th 1758," *Collections of the New-York Historical Society* (1871): 9 (See Lee's original letter in the Fort Ticonderoga Thompson-Pell Research Center); See also PRO, CO 5/50, UP microfilm reel 2, frame 982; AB 445; Searing, 114; Spicer, 394.

20. *NYCD*, 10: 747.

21. Robert Rogers, *Journals of Major Robert Rogers* (1765; reprint ed., Ann Arbor, MI.: University Microfilms, Inc., 1966), 113-14; See also Nicholas Westbrook, comp. and ed., " 'Like roaring lions breaking from their chains': The Highland Regiment at Ticonderoga," *BFTM* 16 (1998): 38.

22. David Perry, "Recollections of an Old Soldier," *BFTM* 14 (Summer 1981): 5; Dr. Caleb Rea noted that the "Battle lasted but 6 or 8 minutes...as many Thousand Guns fired, which made a most terrible ro[a]ring in the woods." Caleb Rea, "The Journal of Dr. Caleb Rea, Written During the Expedition Against Ticonderoga in 1758," *EIHC* 18 (1881): 103.

23. Joshua Loring, Chatham Papers, PRO 30/8/96, fol. 97.

24. Ibid.; Lee, 10; See also Albertson, 45.

25. Joseph Nichols, "Joseph Nichols Military Journal 1758-59," Henry E. Huntington Library, HM 89, 20.

26. AB 436.

27. Richardson, 275.

28. Samuel Thompson, *Diary of Lieut. Samuel Thompson*, ed. by William R. Cutter (Boston: Press of David Clapp & Son, 1896), 9.

29. S. H. P. Pell, *Fort Ticonderoga, A Short History* (Ticonderoga, N.Y.: Fort Ticonderoga Museum, 1978), 29.

30. R. Rogers, *Journals*, 114; See also PRO 272, WO 34/30, fol. 22.

31. *NYCD*, 10: 726.

32. Winslow C. Watson, *The Military and Civil History of the County of Essex, New York* (Albany: J. Munsell, 1869), 89; *NYCD*, 10: 739; Abercromby also mentioned "a vast number of Pointed Stakes Drove into the Ground" on the road to the French breastwork. AB 445.

33. Westbrook, 27; Loring, fol. 98; See also Searing, 116; Spicer, 395; Pond, 92; Woolsey, 14; AB 437; PRO 272, WO 34/30, fol. 23; *The Scots Magazine* (August 1758): 437.

34. Alexander Colden, "Eye-Witnesses' Accounts of the British Repulse at Ticonderoga," *The Canadian Historical Review* 2 (December 1921): 362; See also Rea, 105; Westbrook, 57; *The Scots Magazine* (December 1758): Appendix, 698-99.

35. A. G. Bradley, *The Fight with France for North America* (New York: E. P. Dutton and Company, 1900), 246; Lee, 12; See also E. P. Hamilton, *French and Indian Wars*, 220-21; *NYCD*, 10: 727; Westbrook, 80.

36. Westbrook, 56; Searing, 115; R. Rogers, *Journals*, 114; Loring, fol. 98; Hervey, 50; AB 445; AB 436; *NYCD*, 10:726; Joseph Smith, "Journal of Joseph Smith, of Groton," *Connecticut Society of Colonial Wars Proceedings* 1 (1896): 306.

37. Hervey, 50; Westbrook, 56; Alexander Colden, a veteran of the campaign, mentioned that Colonel John Bradstreet "with an engineer was sent to reconnoitre the French Lines." Colden, 361.

38. Loring, fol. 98; Hervey, 50; See also *The Scots Magazine* (December 1758): Appendix, 698.

39. Caleb Stark, *Memoir and Official Correspondence of Gen. John Stark, With Notices of Several Other Officers of the Revolution* (1860; reprint ed., Gregg Press, 1972), 26.

40. Westbrook, 53; *The Scots Magazine* (December 1758): Appendix, 698.

41. AB 445.

42. Seth Tinkham, "The Diary of Seth Tinkham," in *History of Plymouth County, Massachusetts*, by D. Hamilton Hurd (Philadelphia: J. W. Lewis. & Co., 1884), 996.

43. W. Parkman, "Journal," 244; See also David Waterbury, "Personal Roster and Diary of Captain David Waterbury in the Lake George Campaign," typed transcript, 8-9, Fort Ticonderoga Thompson-Pell Research Center.

44. Spicer, 395; Bellico, *Chronicles of Lake George*, 101; Benjamin Jewett similarly observed that the regulars were "cut down amazin." Benjamin Jewett, "The Diary of Benjamin Jewett--1758," *National Magazine* 17 (1892-93): 63; One British officer remarked that the French were able "to mow us down like a field of corn." *The Scots Magazine* (December 1758): Appendix, 699.

45. Perry, 6; See also Archelaus Fuller, "Journal of Col. Archelaus of Middleton, Mass.," in the Expedition Against Ticonderoga in 1758," *EIHC* 46 (1910): 214.

46. Westbrook, 69, 65-67; "Plan du Fort de Carillon" shows Abercromby's position. Cartographic and Architectural Division, National Archives of Canada (c13277); See also Pond, 92; One of the first books to detail the history of the Seven Years' War in America, *The History of the Late War in North America*, was written by Thomas Mante in 1772. Mante suggested that Abercromby "remained during the greatest part of the attack, at the Saw-mills." Mante, 151. Subsequent historians followed this account until fresh documents were released by the Fort Ticonderoga Museum two and a quarter centuries later (see Westbrook above). There is no definitive evidence available at this time to indicate a family relationship between Major General James Abercromby and Captain James Abercrombie, although Robert Rogers mentioned in his journal that "Captain Abercrombie, Aid[e]-de-Camp and nephew of General Abercrombie." R. Rogers, *Journals*, 37.

47. Westbrook, 41.

48. Lemuel Lyon, "Military Journal for 1758," in *The Military Journals of Two Private Soldiers, 1758-1775*, by Abraham Tomlinson (1854; reprint ed., New York: Books for Libraries Press, 1970), 22; See also W. Parkman, "Journal," 244. Henry Champion, "The Journal of Colonel Henry Champion," in *Champion Genealogy*, by Francis Bacon Trowbridge (New Haven, CT.: F. B. Trowbridge, 1891), 419; See original "Accounts & Journals of Captain Henry Champion of Colchester, Campaign of 1758," CSL.

49. Spicer, 407.

50. Benjamin Glasier, "French and Indian War Diary of Benjamin Glasier of Ipswich, 1758-1760," *EIHC* 86 (1950): 76; Dawes, 69; See also *NYCD*, 10: 735.

51. Searing, 116.

52. Spicer, 407, 394.

53. Westbrook, 85; Captain Alexander Monypenny's 1758 map shows a "Battery of Cannon proposed to Flank the entrenchment on Rattlesnake Hill." Westbrook, insert, 54-55.

54. J. Knox, *An Historical Journal*, 1: 192.

55. Colden, 362.

56. Spicer, 395; Parkman, *Montcalm and Wolfe*, 366.

57. Pouchot (Hough), 118-19; Pouchot (Cardy and Dunnigan), 148; See also Spicer, 395. As a result of the flag deception, Joseph Nichols suggested that the French soldiers were able to fire "upon our men & Cut them Down Like Grass." Nichols, HM 89, 22.

58. Eleanor S. Murray, "Manuscripts As Resources," *Vermont Quarterly* 20 (April 1952): 92.

59. *NYCD*, 10: 740.

60. Bradley, 254-56; E. P. Hamilton, *French and Indian Wars*, 225; Ralph Nading Hill, *Lake Champlain: Key to Liberty* (Montpelier, VT.: Vermont Life Magazine, 1976), 61-63; F. Parkman, *France and England*, 433-36; F. Parkman, *Montcalm and Wolfe*, 561-63; Wallace E. Lamb, *Lake George: Facts and Anecdotes* (Glens Falls, N.Y.: Glens Falls Post Co., 1938), 133-35; Carroll V. Lonergan, *Ticonderoga: Historic Portage* (Ticonderoga, N.Y.: Fort Mount Hope Society Press, 1959), 47-53; Frederick B. Richards, *The Black Watch* (Ticonderoga, N.Y.: Fort Ticonderoga Museum, 1926), 34-60.

61. Bougainville, 233.

62. Gertrude Selwyn Kimball, ed., *Correspondence of William Pitt* (New York: The Macmillan Company, 1906), Volume 1, 300; *NYCD*, 10: 727; See also PRO 272, WO 34/30, fol. 23; AB 445; AB 436.

63. Pond, 92.

64. Loring, fol. 99; See also Lee, 13.

65. Loring, fol. 99; Rea, 106; Spicer, 407; Hervey, 50; Dawes, 71; Searing, 117; Barrows, 97; Glasier, 77; Westbrook, 43-44; Obadiah Harris, "Journal of Obadiah Harris 1758," HM 591, 10-11, Huntington Library.

66. Perry, 6-7; Abner Barrows had the same observation as Perry. "I fear a great many Wounded men fell Into the hands of our Enemy & the Slain all Lay on the spot." Abner Barrows, "Diary of Abner Barrows," in *History of the Town of Middleboro*, by Thomas Weston (New York: Houghton Mifflin, 1906), 97; Garrett Albertson wrote that the French "were out plundering our dead and wounded with candles and lanterns." Albertson, 47.

67. Fuller, 214.

68. Dawes, 71-72.

69. Spicer, 407; See also Pond, 91; Putnam, 71.

70. Nichols, HM 89, 24.

71. Lyon, 23; See also Joseph Smith, "Journal of Joseph Smith, of Groton," *Connecticut Society of Colonial Wars Proceedings* 1 (1896): 307.

72. W. Parkman, "Journal," 244; See also Hervey, 50; Lee, 14; Because some of the men had departed during the night, the remaining bateaux were overloaded on the morning of the 9th with "30 men into Each Battoe." Fisher, MS, Library of Congress.

73. John Cleaveland, "The Journal of the Rev. John Cleaveland," *EIHC* 12 (July 1874): 185-86.

74. Cleaveland, *EIHC* 13 (1877): 63.

75. AB 436; See also PRO 272, WO 34/30, fol. 23; AB 425; AB 445; Kimball, 300.

76. *NYCD*, 10: 744; Bougainville, 236.

77. Perry, 7; See also Barrows, 97; Fuller, 214.

78. George Francis Dow, *History of Topsfield, Massachusetts* (Topsfield: The Topsfield Historical Society, 1940), 161-62.

79. Bougainville, 249.

80. Pouchot (Hough), 121; Pouchot (Cardy and Dunnigan), 150; *NYCD*, 10: 725.

81. Bougainville, 235; *NYCD*, 10: 725, 733, 746, 753, 848; See also François de Lévis, *Journal Des Champagnes Du Chevalier De Lévis En Canada De 1756 à 1760* (Montreal: C.O. Beauchemin & Fils, 1889), 139.

82. Westbrook, 74-75; For additional discussion of Abercromby's strategy see Tim J. Todish, "The 1758 Attack on Fort Ticonderoga," *Muzzleloader*, January/February 2000, 47- 48.

83. Allan Rogers, *Empire and Liberty* (Berkeley, CA.: University of California Press, 1974), 72.

84. Westbrook, 76; See also Brian Connell, *The Savage Years* (New York: Harper & Brothers Publishers, 1959), 159; Lawrence Henry Gipson, *The Great War for the Empire: The Victorious Years, 1758-1760* (New York: Alfred A. Knopf, 1949), Volume 7, 232.

85. Gipson, 7: 232; D. Clark, *Phineas Lyman*, 41; Another veteran of the assault, Alexander Colden, suggested that the provincial troops "upon the whole...behaved extremely well." Colden, 363.

86. D. Clark, *Phineas Lyman*, 41.

87. Cleaveland, *EIHC* 12 (1874): 185.

88. Dawes, 72; See also Lee, 13.

89. Joseph Holt, "Journals of Joseph Holt, of Wilton, N.H.," *NEHGR* 10 (January 1856): 308; See also Thomas Alexander, "Ens. Alexander's Diary," in *History of Northfield, Massachusetts*, by J. H. Temple and George Sheldon (Albany: Joel Munsell, 1875), 304; Samuel Abbott Green, *Papers Relating to Captain Thomas Lawrence's Company* (Cambridge, MA.: John Wilson and Son, 1890), 7; Asa Foster, "Diary of Capt. Asa Foster of Andover, Mass.," *NEHGR* 54 (January 1900): 185; John Cleaveland, "The Journal of Rev. John Cleaveland Kept While Chaplain in the French and Indian War," *BFTM* 10 (1959): 201-2; Lyon, 25; Rea, 112; J. Smith, 307;

Spicer, 397; Bougainville, 245; PRO, CO 5/50, UP microfilm reel 3, frame 30.

90. *NYCD*, 10:750, 818; Bougainville, 253; R. Rogers, *Journals*, 117; Leonard Spaulding, "French and Indian War Record," in *The Vermont Historical Gazetteer*, Volume 5, ed. by Abby Maria Hemenway (Brandon, VT.: Carrie E. H. Page, 1891), 28; John Noyes, "Journal of John Noyes of Newbury in the Expedition Against Ticonderoga, 1758," *EIHC* 45 (1909): 74; Alexander, 304; Cleaveland, *BFTM* 10 (1959): 205; Foster, 185; A. Fuller, 216; Holt, 308; Lyon, 26; Rea, 117; Spicer, 398; AB 495; Abercromby later maintained that the Indians who attacked the convoy "had got themselves so intoxicated" on the liquor aboard the wagons that "it wou'd have been a very easy matter to have cut them all to Pieces...but Col. Hart whose Party consisted of 300 [provincials], refusing to come up, the Enemy got off unhurt." PRO, CO 5/50, UP microfilm reel 3, frame 33.

91. For more details on the ordeal of Putnam, see F. Parkman, *Montcalm and Wolfe*, 377-78; See also Mante, 159; Pouchot (Hough), 123; Pouchot (Cardy and Dunnigan), 152-53; R. Rogers, *Journals*, 117-19.

92. R. Rogers, *Journals*, 119; Bougainville, 261; AB 522; Alexander, 304; Rea, 180; Spaulding, 29; Spicer, 401; In a letter to William Pitt, describing Rogers' encounter with Marin's force, Abercromby praised the ranger leader: "I must not omit, doing Rogers the Justice to say, that he merits much to be commended, he having, by Report of a very good officer in the Light Infantry, who was on this Party, acted the whole Time with great Calmness and Officer like." PRO, CO 5/50, UP microfilm reel 3, frame 40.

93. Samuel Cobb, "The Journal of Captain Samuel Cobb," *BFTM* 14 (Summer 1981): 20; Cobb's journal was first published in 1871 with a notation that the author was unknown, "Journal of a Provincial Officer, in the Campaign, in Northern New York, in 1758," *The Historical Magazine* 10 (July 1871): 113-22.

94. Henry Champion, "The Journal of Colonel Henry Champion," in *Champion Genealogy*, by Francis Bacon Trowbridge (New Haven, CT.: F. B. Trowbridge, 1891), 420; See original "Accounts & Journal of Captain Henry Champion of Colchester, Campaign of 1758," CSL; Thomas Alexander recorded that he participated in the construction of "a breastwork at the south-east end of the Lake." Alexander, 304.

95. Rea, 107, 102, 111, 113; See also Foster, 185; Holt, 307; A. Fuller "*EIHC*," 215-16; Glasier, 75, 77; Spicer, 403; Westbrook, 31; Fisher, MS, Library of Congress.

96. AB 397.

97. Spicer, 398.

98. Lois M. Feister, "Archaeological Testing at Fort Gage, a Provincial Redoubt of 1758 at Lake George, New York," *The Bulletin and Journal of Archaeology of New York State* 90 (Spring 1985): 40-59;

Starbuck, *The Great Warpath* 114-18; Scott A. Padeni, "A Review of Potential Sites for the Archaeological Study of Military Life at Lake George's Southern End during the French and Indian War and American Revolution," MS, Empire State College, 1994; Bellico, *Chronicles of Lake George*, 59, 185, 379.

99. Abercromby to Pitt, 19 August 1758, MASS HS, Parkman Papers 42: 253; PRO, CO 5/50, UP microfilm reel 3, frame 28.

100. *Boston Gazette and Country Journal*, 28 August 1758; Loring, fol. 100; PRO, CO 5/50, UP microfilm reel 3, frame 28; Spicer, 402; Major General Phineas Lyman suggested that the *Halifax* "mounts Sixteen carriage guns" and another participant in the campaign noted "sixteen a board the sloop" were fired on August 28 during the celebration of the news of the capture of Louisbourg. D. Clark, 42; "Anonymous Journal," *BFTM* 12 (September 1968): 294; See also Rea, 190; Shubael Griswold, "Journal During Service in French and Indian Wars," CSL; *New-York Mercury*, 11 September 1758.

101. Bougainville, 279; *NYCD*, 10: 853.

102. Cobb, 24; See also Glasier, 81; Rea, 184, 186; Nichols, 74.

103. Rea, 191; See also D. Clark, *Phineas Lyman*, 42.

104. John Cleaveland, "Journal of Rev. John Cleaveland Kept While Chaplain in the French and Indian War 1758-1759," *BFTM* 10 (no. 3, 1959): 277; Harrison Bird, *Navies in the Mountains* (New York: Oxford University Press, 1962), 232.

105. PRO 281/2, WO 34/46B, fol. 1.

106. Cleaveland, *BFTM*, 229; *Boston Gazette and Country Journal*, 8 October 1759; See also Samuel Niles, "A Summary Historical Narrative of the Wars in New-England with the French and Indians, in Several Parts of the Country [1760]," *Collections of the Massachusetts Historical Society* 6 (3rd Series) (1837): 524.

107. Champion, 431.

108. Rea, 199.

109. Christopher Comstock, "Diary of Christopher Comstock 1758-59," Connecticut Historical Society.

110. Sweat, 54; On October 18, Dr. Rea recorded that "Two of the Row Gally missing, I suppose sunk," Rea, 203; Abel Spicer noted on October 3 that "one of the row gallies out of the lake loaded on a pair of wheels," Spicer, 405.

111. Cobb, 30; In September Abel Spicer had mentioned the planned construction of a vessel "50 foot long and 20 foot wide," Spicer, 404.

112. Cobb, 30.

113. Ibid.

114. Noyes, 76; Rea, 203; Nichols, 86; Cleaveland, *BFTM*, 229; Holt, 310.

115. Champion, 433.

116. Noyes, 76; Thompson, 18; Spaulding, 30.

117. AB 802. Loring was probably including the 30-foot radeau in the count of the three row galleys. Other whaleboats were "hid in the woods in Order that they may be at Hand for any scouting." PRO, CO 5/50, UP microfilm reel 3, frame 115; See also Spicer, 406.

118. Thompson, 19; See also Rea, 203; Noyes, 76; AB 802.

119. Bougainville, 292.

120. Ibid.

121. AB 450.

122. Ian McCulloch, trans. and ed., " 'Believe Us, Sir, This Will Impress Few People!' Spin-Doctoring--18th Century Style," *BFTM* 16 (1998): 105, see also 92-107; See also Stanley Pargellis, ed., *Military Affairs on North America 1748-1765* (New Haven: Archon Books, 1969), 425-27.

123. PRO, CO 5/50, UP microfilm reel 3, frames 129, 270.

124. PRO 272, WO 34/30, fol. 36.

125. S. R. Stoddard, *Lake George: (Illustrated) A Book of To-Day* (Glens Falls, N.Y.: S. R. Stoddard, 1887), 56; See also Henry Marvin, *A Complete History of Lake George* (New York: Sibells & Maigne Printers, 1853), 48-49; B. F. DeCosta, *Lake George: Its Scenes and Characteristics* (New York: Anson D. F. Randolph & Co., 1869), 63.

126. Ogden J. Ross, *The Steamboats of Lake George 1817 to 1932* (Albany: Press of the Delaware and Hudson Railroad, 1932), 33; Captain E. S. Harris, *Lake George: All About It* (Glens Falls, N.Y.: Glens Falls Republican, 1903), 27.

127. *LGM*, 11 July 1903.

128. Charles H. Possons, *Possons' Guide to Lake George, Lake Champlain and Adirondacks* (Glens Falls, N.Y.: Chas. H. Possons, Publisher, 1888), 77-78.

129. *LGM*, 5 August 1960; *The Times-Union*, 31 July 1960; *The Saratogian*, 30 September 1960.

130. *LGM*, 10 June 1893; See also *LGM*, 10 September 1898.

131. *LGM*, 12 August 1960.

132. PRO 160/1, WO 34/57, fol. 21.

133. John Gardner, "Bateau 'Reconstructed' from Remains, Drawing," *National Fisherman*, August 1967, 8-A; See also George F. Bass, ed., *Ships and Shipwrecks of the Americas* (New York: Thames and Hudson, 1988), 133, 136-37.

134. *New York Times*, 27 June 1965.

135. *The Lake George Nautical Newsletter*, Volume 4, 1995, 1, 8.

136. *Post-Star*, 3 August 1995; *Times Union*, 7 August 1995; *The Chronicle*, 17 August 1995.

137. The 1990 team included Joseph W. Zarzynski, Russell P. Bellico, Robert R. Benway, Vincent J. Capone, James T. Crandall, John P. Farrell, and David Van Aken.

138. Three of the gunport lids from the *Land Tortoise* were raised by Bateaux Below and preserved at the archaeological lab of East Carolina University. The lids are presently held by the New York State Museum. For a discussion of the possible type of armament planned for the radeau *Land Tortoise* see Gary Paine, "Ord's Arks: Angles, Artillery, and Ambush on Lakes George and Champlain," *The American Neptune* 58 (Spring 1998): 105-21.

139. PRO 291, WO 34/75-76, fol. 251; PRO 285/1, WO 34/64, fol. 208.

140. Sweat, 54.

141. Joseph W. Zarzynski et al., "'Ring-Around-A-Radeau,' or, Fencing in a 1758 Shipwreck for Public Access and Preservation," *Underwater Archaeology* (1996): 35-40.

142. Scott A. Padeni, *Final Report of the Literature Review and Shipwreck Inventory of Lake George's Northern End* (Ballston Spa, N.Y.: Scott A. Padeni, 1999), 18.

143. Arthur B. Cohn, et. al., *Lake Champlain Cultural Resources Survey--Volume 2: 1997 Results; Volume 3: 1998 Results* (Vergennes, VT.: Lake Champlain Maritime Museum, 2000), 174-82.

5. Amherst Sweeps the Lakes

1. Bougainville, 246.

2. PRO, CO 5/55, UP microfilm reel 4, frame 419.

3. Henry True, *Journal and Letters of Rev. Henry True* (Marion, OH.: Star Press, 1900), 18; William Henshaw, "William Henshaw's Journal," *Proceedings of the Worcester Society of Antiquity* 25 (1909): 56; See also Samuel Warner, "Extracts from Samuel Warner's Journal," in *An Historical Address ---- Town of Wilbraham*, by Rufus P. Stebbins (Boston: George C. Rand & Avery, 1864), 210; PRO 293/2, 34/80, fol. 114.

4. Francis Grant, "Journal from New York to Canada, 1767," *Proceedings of the New York State Historical Association* 30 (1932): 321; See also Lord Adam Gordon's 1765 description of "a Small Stockade Fort, tumbling down" and "a little above this (and now Called Fort George) we have a Complet[e] Bastion built of Stone, the Casemates of Wood. It mounts ten Guns." Newton D. Mereness, *Travels in the American Colonies* (1916; reprint ed., New York: Antiquarian Press, LTD., 1961), 445.

5. J. Clarence Webster, ed., *The Journal of Jeffery Amherst* (Toronto: The Ryerson Press, 1931), 128.

6. Ibid., 131; Salah Barnard, "Journal of Major Salah Barnard," MS, Fort Ticonderoga Thompson-Pell Research Center.

7. Lemuel Wood, "Diaries Kept by Lemuel Wood, of Boxford," *EIHC* 19 (1882): 143; See also Bellico, *Chronicles of Lake George*, 132; This is probably the same vessel that Captain Philip Skene, who would play a significant role in the settlement of Lake Champlain, discovered in the lake: "We have weighed a large boat that was sunk at the close of the campaign in forty fathom water." (The depth

was actually 40 feet.), J. Knox, *An Historical Journal*, 1: 492.

8. Gary Zaboly, "A Royal Artillery Officer with Amherst: The Journal of Captain-Lieutenant Henry Skinner, 1 May--28 July 1759," *BFTM* 15 (1993): 379; For the original account see Henry Skinner, "Proceedings of the Army Under the Command of General Amherst, for the Year 1759," *The Universal Magazine* (December 1759): 285.

9. *Boston Gazette and Country Journal*, 8 October 1759; Other witnesses mention smaller cannons on the row galleys in addition to the one 18-pounder. See Samuel Merriman, "Journal of Samuel Merriman," in *A History of Deerfield*, by George Sheldon (1895-96; reprint ed., Somersworth, N.H.: New Hampshire Publishing Company, 1972), 666.

10. Zaboly, "Skinner," 374, 378-79, (see diary entries for July 7, 14, 16); L. Wood, "Diaries," 19: 149; See also Knox, 1: 485.

11. PRO, CO 5/56, UP microfilm reel 4, frames 501-2; John Clarence Webster, ed., *Journal of William Amherst in America* (London: Butler & Tannes, Ltd., 1927), 42-43; Barnard, p.n.a.; *Boston Gazette and Country Journal*, 8 October 1759; Warner, 210; J. Knox, *An Historical Journal*, 1; 490-91; Constantine Hardy, "Extracts from the Journal of Constantine Hardy," *New-England Historical and Genealogical Register* 60 (1906): 237; Jonathan Knap, "Journal of Jonathan Knap of Killington, Connecticut," CSL.

12. Zaboly, "Skinner," 372.

13. J. C. Webster, *Journal of Jeffery Amherst*, 141.

14. *BFTM* 6 (January 1942): 84.

15. Zaboly, "Skinner," 381; One Massachusetts provincial, referring to the *Invincible*, recorded that "They call it an Ark of Redoubt." James Henderson, "James Henderson's Journal," in *The First Century of the Colonial Wars in the Commonwealth of Massachusetts* (Boston: Society of Colonial Wars, Mass., 1944), 204.

16. PRO, CO 5/56, UP microfilm reel 4, frame 502; See also PRO, CO 5/56, fol. 89.

17. Zaboly, "Skinner," 381.

18. Barnard, p.n.a.; Montresor, 83; See also "Diary of a Soldier at Crown Point, etc., 1759," French and Indian War Collections Octavo 2, AAS; Montresor, 83; John Woods, "John Woods His Book," French and Indian War Collections, Octavo, 1, AAS; PRO 285/1, WO 34/64, fol. 175; PRO 283, WO 34/50, fol. 6.

19. J. C. Webster, *Journal of Jeffery Amherst*, 138; Zaboly, "Skinner," 378.

20. PRO 285/1, WO 34/64, fol. 182; PRO, CO 5/54, UP microfilm reel 3, frame 861.

21. Mante, 210; See also the following sources for details on the sailing order of the fleet: J. Knox, *An Historical Journal*, 1: 501-2; Commissary Wilson, *Commissary Wilson's Orderly Book,1759*, (Albany: J. Munsell, 1857), 88; John Hawks, *Orderly Book and Journal of Major John Hawks 1759-1760* (n.a., N.Y.: Society of Colonial Wars, 1911), 42; J.C.

22. Merriman, 664; Wood, 19: 145; See also Barnard, p.n.a.; True, 10; Hardy, 237; Dawes, 88; Bellico, *Chronicles of Lake George*, 125, 134.

23. *NYCD*, 10: 1055; J. Knox, *An Historical Journal*, 1: 503.

24. S. H. P. Pell, *Fort Ticonderoga*, 49; Colonel Nathan Whiting of Connecticut wrote that "the General appears to me to be cool & very clever & every thing Looks with a favorable aspect." Lemuel Aiken Welles, ed., "Letters of Col. Nathan Whiting Written from Camp during the French and Indian War," *Papers of the New Haven Colony Historical Society* 6(1900): 142.

25. "Lieutenant Brehm's Report," *BFTM* 11(December 1962): 38-42.

26. J. C. Webster, *Journal of Jeffery Amherst*, 144; See also L. Wood, "Diaries," 19: 148.

27. Robert Webster, "Robert Webster's Journal," *BFTM* 2 (July 1931): 133; See also L. Wood, "Diaries," 19: 148.

28. Lemuel Wood noted that Townshend "was Cut of[f] in two Parts with a Can[n]on Ball as he was Riding at ye generals Side near ye Trenches." L. Wood, "Diaries," 19: 148.

29. Ibid., 149.

30. J. C. Webster, *Journal of William Amherst*, 50; Mante, 213.

31. J. C. Webster, *Journal of William Amherst*, 49; See also Henderson, 205; R. Rogers, *Journals*, 141.

32. J. C. Webster, *Journal of Jeffery Amherst*, 147; PRO, CO 5/56, UP microfilm reel 4, frame 516.

33. L. Wood, "Diaries," 20: 156; See also PRO 293/3, WO 34/81, fol.37.

34. Zaboly, "Skinner," 383; See also PRO 283/1, WO 30/50, fol. 58.

35. S. H. P. Pell, *Fort Ticonderoga*, 51.

36. L. Wood, "Diaries," 19: 185-86; For Amherst's description and assessment of the condition of the fort see *The London Magazine* (September 1759): 499; *The Universal Magazine* (September 1759): 147.

37. J. C. Webster, *Journal of Jeffery Amherst*, 146; See also PRO, CO 5/56, UP microfilm reel 4, frame 496.

38. J. C. Webster, *Journal of Jeffery Amherst*, 148, see also 157; *The Scots Magazine* (August 1759): 439; *The London Magazine* (December 1759): 661.

39. Huden, "The Admiral of Lake Champlain," 66.

40. As early as May, Amherst had informed Loring that he needed "Two Briggs. . .and. . . two Snows, capable of Mounting Eighteen Six Pounders" for Lake Champlain. PRO 285/1, WO 34/64, fol. 198, see also fol. 196.

41. L. Wood, "Diaries," 19: 149.

42. S. H. P. Pell, *Fort Ticonderoga*, 51.

43. J. C. Webster, *Journal of Jeffery Amherst*, 151; See also *The Universal Magazine* (September 1759): 147.

44. Henderson, 206.

45. Welles, 143.

46. F. Parkman, *Montcalm and Wolfe*, 445.

47. J. C. Webster, *Journal of Jeffery Amherst*, 163; See also Barnard, p.n.a.; *New York-Mercury*, 24 September 1759.

48. Haldimand Papers, "Misc. Papers Relating to the Provincial Navy 1775-1780," NAC, Microfilm H-1649, Volume 1, B144, fol. 99; "Endorsed List of the Vessels...1762," PRO, CO 5/62, UP microfilm reel 7, frame 446.

49. PRO 285/1, 34/64, fol. 212.

50. J. C. Webster, *Journal of Jeffery Amherst*, 174; For information on the building materials and problems involved in the construction of the radeau *Ligonier* see PRO 285/1, WO 34/64, fols. 152, 155, 207-8, 212; See also *Boston Gazette and Country Journal*, 8 October 1759; Early in November the radeau *Ligonier* transported cargo between Ticonderoga and Crown Point, taking "1600 barrels of provisions and went back again." John Hurlbut, "The Journal of a Colonial Soldier," *The Magazine of American History* 39 (1893): 395.

51. PRO 285/1, WO 34/64, fol. 157; See also D. Clark, *Phineas Lyman*, 47; See also PRO 285/1, WO 34/64, fols. 164-65, 215, 218.

52. PRO 278/2, WO 34/42, fol. 229; See also Haldimand Papers, "Misc. Papers Relating to the Provincial Navy 1775-1780," NAC Microfilm H-1649, Volume 1, B144, fol. 99; *The London Magazine* (December 1759): 662; PRO, CO 5/62, UP microfilm reel 7, frame 446.

53. *The London Magazine* (December 1759): 662.

54. PRO 285/1, WO 34/64, fol. 212.

55. *NYCD*, 10: 1055.

56. Thomas M. Charland, "The Lake Champlain Army and the Fall of Montreal," *Vermont History* 28 (October 1960): 294.

57. PRO 285/1, WO 34/64, fol. 225.

58. Merriman, 666; A newspaper account noted "5 Row Gallies, which mount 18 Pounders, each of them one; the Gun is placed fore and aft, and fires out at the Head, they row with 14 Oars on each side, carry 30 Men each." *Boston Gazette and Country Journal*, 8 October 1759; See also J. C. Webster, *Journal of Jeffery Amherst*, 179; Wilson, 184; PRO 293/3, WO 34/81, fol. 66.

59. Burt Garfield Loescher, *Genesis: Rogers Rangers, The First Green Berets* (San Mateo, CA.: B. G. Loescher, 1969), Volume 2, 65; See also L. Wood, "Diaries," 20: 290, 296.

60. PRO 272/1, WO 34/30, fol. 87.

61. Ibid., fols. 87-88; *The London Magazine* (December 1759): 662.

62. J. C. Webster, *Journal of Jeffery Amherst*, 180.

63. Wilson, 185; *The London Magazine* (December 1759): 662.

64. *NYCD*, 10: 1056.

65. *The London Magazine* (December 1759): 662.

66. PRO 272/1, WO 34/30, fol. 88; To retrieve the cannons, the French set a pattern of anchors and cables which could be snagged later with a drag line. George F. Bass, ed., *A History of Seafaring* (New York: Walker Publishing Co., Inc., 1972), 288-89.

67. J. C. Webster, *Journal of Jeffery Amherst*, 185; PRO 272/1, WO 34/30, fol. 86; Comstock, p.n.a.

68. PRO 278/2, WO 34/42, fol. 26.

69. PRO 285/1, WO 34/64, fol. 232.

70. PRO, CO 5/57, UP microfilm reel 4, frames 901-8.

71. Ebenezer Dibble, "Diary of Ebenezer Dibble," *Society of Colonial Wars in the State of Connecticut Proceedings* 1 (1903): 318.

72. PRO 283/1, WO 34/50, fol. 5.

73. Ibid., fol. 8; For information on the debate on winter protection for the vessels see fols. 5, 160, and PRO 285/1, WO 34/64, fol. 229.

74. PRO, CO 5/58, UP microfilm reel 5, frame 660.

75. Ibid., frame 662.

76. P. M. Woodwell, ed., *Diary of Thomas Moody* (South Berwick, ME.: The Chronicle Print Shop, 1976), 18.

77. Samuel MacClintock, *Rev. Samuel MacClintock's Journal 1760* (Crown Point, N.Y.: Crown Point Road Association, Inc., 1972), 11; For a report of the on-going construction at Fort Ticonderoga in 1760, which included barracks, a hospital, a sewage system that emptied into the lake, redoubts, and the covered way, see PRO 283/1, WO 34/50, fol. 23.

78. Woodwell, 24; David Holden, "Journal of Sergeant David Holden," *Proceeding of the Massachusetts Historical Society* 4 (2nd Series) (1887-1889): 396; See also Samuel A. Green, ed., *Three Military Diaries* (Cambridge, MA.: John Wilson & Son, 1901), 59; MacClintock, 14; *New-York Mercury*, 25 August 1760; PRO 285/1, WO 34/65, fol. 137; PRO 284/2, WO 34/52, fol. 23; PRO 284/1, WO 34/51, fols. 67, 54.

79. John Bradbury, "Diary of Old John Bradbury," in *Bradbury Memorial*, comp. by William Berry Lapham (Portland, ME.: Brown Thurston & Company, 1890), 275.

80. MacClintock, 13; R. Rogers, *Journals*, 189-90; Woodwell, 25; Jacob Bayley, "Capt. Jacob Bayley's Journal," in *History of Newbury, Vermont*, by Frederic P. Wells (St. Johnsbury, VT.: The Caledonian Company, 1902), 379.

81. Woodwell, 25.

82. Holden, 397; See also True, 29; L. Wood, "Diaries," 20: 291; Bradbury, 276; MacClintock, 14; Woodwell, 26; Bayley, 379; John Frost, Jr., "Expedition Against Canada," *Old Eliot* 8(1908): 114; Samuel Jenks, "Samuel Jenks, his Journal of the Campaign in 1760," *Proceedings of the Massachusetts Historical Society* 5 (2nd Series) (1889-90): 368; *New-York Mercury*, 1 September 1760.

83. Bradbury, 279.

84. *NYCD*, 10: 1103; See also PRO, CO 5/50, UP microfilm reel 3, frame 42; *New-York Mercury*, 25 August 1760; PRO 284/1, WO 34/51, fols. 24-25, 57-58.

85. Woodwell, 30; R. Rogers, *Journals*, 191; Bradbury, 279; *NYCD*, 10: 1104.

86. Holden, 398; The captured vessels were listed differently in other journals, see L. Wood, "Diaries," 20: 293; MacClintock, 16; True, 30; Frost, 115; Samuel Jenks, "Samuel Jenks, his Journal of the Campaign in 1760," *Proceedings of the Massachusetts Historical Society* 5 (2nd Series) (1889-90): 371, see also 374; Woodwell, 30; *New-York Mercury*, 8 September 1760.

87. Haldimand Papers, fol. 99; "Endorsed List...1762," frame 446.

88. Woodwell, 31; See also Holden, 399; Frost, 115; MacClintock, 17.

89. J.Knox, *An Historical Journal*, 2: 418.

90. Bougainville, 326.

91. Welles, 147.

92. PRO 278/2, WO 34/42, fol. 280; See also PRO 284/2, WO 34/52, fols. 90, 93.

93. J.C. Webster, *Journal of Jeffery Amherst*, 262.

94. Woodwell, 39.

95. PRO 278/2, WO 34/42, fol. 283; PRO 285/1, WO 34/65, fol. 40, 162; PRO 284/1, WO 34/51, fols. 101-2; PRO 283/1, WO 34/50, fol. 140.

96. PRO 283/1, WO 34/50, fols. 54, 209; See also PRO 283/1, WO 34/50, fols. 50, 61, 62, 114, 157, 216; PRO 284/1, WO 24/51, fols. 129, 131, 135; PRO 287/1, WO 34/68, fol. 141.

97. PRO 283/1, WO 34/50, fol. 217.

98. PRO 284/1, WO 34/51, fol. 209; PRO 283/1, WO 34/50, fol. 83; See also PRO 283/1, WO 34/50, fol. 86; PRO 284/2, 34/52, fol. 240.

99. PRO 283/1, WO 34/50, fol. 83.

100. PRO 284/2, WO 34/52, fol. 205; PRO 284/1, WO 34/51, fol. 218; The radeau *Ligonier*, called the "Great Radeau," was also used to carry provisions on Lake Champlain. PRO 284/1, WO 34/51, fols. 157, 218.

101. PRO 287/2, WO 34/69, fols. 36, 38; True, 22.

102. F. Grant, "Journal," 319; For Lord Adam Gordon's description of Crown Point in 1765, see Mereness, 443-44; See also Bellico, *Chronicles of Lake Champlain*, 171-72.

103. Ammi R. Robbins, "Journal of the Rev. Ammi R. Robbins," in *History of Norfolk*, comp. by Theron Wilmot Crissey (Everett, MA.: Massachusetts Publishing Company, 1900), 101.

104. F. Grant, "Journal," 320; See also "List of the Vessels on the Different Lakes; with their present State...Novʳ· 1762." PRO 285/2, WO 34/65, fol. 109.

105. Haldimand Papers, fol. 99.

106. PRO 285/2, WO 34/54, fol. 60.

107. Amherst Family Papers, U1350 014, fol. 139, Centre for Kentish Studies, Kent, Great Britain; Haldimand Papers, fol. 99.

108. PRO 283/1, WO 34/50, fol. 59, see also fol. 214.

109. Ibid, fol.65; See also PRO 284/1, WO 34/51, fol. 178.

110. PRO 284/1, WO 34/51, fol. 27; PRO 159/1, WO 34/54, fol. 183, see also fol. 213; PRO 283/1, WO 34/50, fol. 65, see also fols. 14, 179; James Walker, "Capt. James Walker's Journal," in *History of Bedford New Hampshire* (Concord, N.H.: Town of Bedford, 1903), 477; Two scows, which had been raised by Amherst's troops in 1759 (originally captured and sunk by Montcalm's men in 1757), were present at Fort George in 1760. PRO 159/1, WO 34/54, fol. 212; See also note 33 above.

111. William Gilliland, Willisborough Town-Book Commencing the 8th Day of June 1765, MS, Plattsburgh Public Library, New York, 2.

112. *Plattsburgh Evening News*, 18 December 1908; *Ticonderoga Sentinel*, 4 March 1909; *Ticonderoga Sentinel*, 1 April 1909; See also *LGM*, 1 July 1922.

113. "Arnold's Ships," *BFTM* 9 (Winter 1954): 227; See also "The Revenge," *BFTM* 1 (July 1928): 6-11; *Ticonderoga Sentinel*, 1 April 1909.

114. Peter Barranco, April 15, 1970, personal communication; *Times-Union* (Albany), 16 September 1954; *Ticonderoga Sentinel*, 16 September 1954.

115. Edwin Rich, "Arnold's Fleet 1771-1790," (unpublished paper, 1964), 64.

116. *BFTM* 14 (Fall 1985): 335-440; Bass, *Ships and Shipwrecks*, 142-47.

117. Peter Barranco, March 25, 2000, personal communication; contemporary photographs and postcards.

118. Arthur Cohn and Kevin Crisman, *Report of the Phase 1 In-Water Archaeological Survey in the Waters Surrounding Crown Point State Historic Site* (Basin Harbor, VT.: Lake Champlain Maritime Museum, 1990), 49. For information on the land-based archaeology of the Crown Point State Historic Site see Charles L. Fisher, "The Archaeology of Provincial Officers' Huts at Crown Point State Historic Site," *Northeast Historical Archaeology* 24 (1995): 65-85; Lois M. Feister, *Archaeological Excavations at the Crown Point Soldiers' Barracks, 1976 and 1977* (Waterford, N.Y.: Bureau of Historic Sites, New York Office of Parks, Recreation and Historic Preservation, 1998), 1-205.

119. J. Knox, *An Historical Journal*, 3: 74.

120. James T. Hays, David E. Mize, and Richard W. Ward, "Guns Under Lake Champlain," *York State Tradition*, Winter 1969, 10.

121. *Plattsburgh Press Republican*, 18 August 1987.

122 *Plattsburgh Press Republican*, 14 April 1987.

123. André Lépine, "An 18th Century Wreck in the Richelieu River, Quebec, Canada," *The International Journal of Nautical Archaeology and Underwater Exploration* 8.4 (1979): 340-46; André Lépine, "A Wreck Believed to Be a French 'Bateau' Sunk During Action in 1760 off Isle-aux-noix in the

Richelieu River, Quebec, Canada," *The International Journal of Nautical Archaeology and Underwater Exploration* 10.1 (1981): 41-50.

6. From Champlain to Canada

1. [E.B.O'Callaghan], comp., *Calendar of N.Y. Colonial Manuscripts: Indorsed Land Papers 1643-1863* (1864; reprint ed., Harrison, N. Y.: Harbor Hill Books, 1987), 339, 354, 356, 358-59; Doris Begor Morton, *Philip Skene of Skenesborough* (Granville, N.Y.: The Grastorf Press, 1959), 24-25; *History of Washington County, New York* (1878; reprint., Interlaken, N.Y.: Heart of the Lakes Publishing, 1991), 34.

2. Bellico, *Chronicles of Lake Champlain*, 171-85.

3. [E.B. O'Callaghan], *Indorsed Land Papers*, 474; [Peter S. Palmer], *Historical Sketch of Plattsburgh, New York* (Plattsburgh, N.Y.: Plattsburgh *Republican*, 1893), 3; Allan S. Everest, *Briefly Told, Plattsburgh, New York, 1784-1984* (Plattsburgh, N.Y.: Clinton County Historical Association, 1984), 1; Marjorie Lansing Porter, *Old Plattsburgh* (Plattsburgh, N.Y.: Clinton Press, Inc., 1944), 3; Adolphus Benzel, "Adolphus Benzel's 1772 Notes on Lake Champlain," *BFTM* 12 (December 1969): 362.

4. *NDAR*, 1: 162; See also James Jeffry, "Journal Kept in Quebec in 1775 by James Jeffry," *EIHC* 50 (April 1914): 105; *AA* 4, 2: 243-44.

5. *NDAR*, 1: 267; See also Thomas Jones, *History of New York* (New York: The New-York Historical Society, 1879), Volume 1, 546-47; *AA* 4, 2: 750-51; "Who Took Ticonderoga," *BFTM* 4 (January 1937): 57-58.

6. Ethan Allen, "Ethan Allen to Philip Skene," *BFTM* 6 (January 1943): 165-66.

7. *NDAR*, 1: 316; See also "Papers Relating to the Expedition to Ticonderoga," *Collections of the Connecticut Historical Society* 1 (1860): 171-72.

8. *NDAR*, 1:314, see also 312-13, 751-52; See also Ephaphras Bull, "Journal of Ephaphras Bull," *BFTM* 8 (July 1948): 40; For more details see Bellico, *Chronicles of Lake Champlain*, 189-203.

9. Royal R. Hinman, comp., *A Historical Collection of the Part Sustained by Connecticut* (Hartford: E. Gleanson, 1842), 29; See also "Papers Relating," 175.

10. Four years later, Ethan Allen wrote that he had demanded the surrender of the fort "In the name of the great Jehovah, and the Continental Congress." Ethan Allen, *A Narrative of Colonel Ethan Allen's Captivity Containing His Voyages & Travels* (1779; reprint ed., Rutland, VT.: Vermont Statehood Bicentennial Commission, 1988), 8. Years later, another eyewitness to the event suggested that Allen's real words were, "Come out of here, you d----d old rat." William Cleaves Todd, "Lord Timothy Dexter," *The Historical and Genealogical Register* 40 (October 1886): 380; See also James Austin Holden, ed., "What Ethan Allen Really Said at Ticon-

deroga," *Proceedings of the New York State Historical Association* 9 (1910):355.

11. Aaron Barlow, "The March to Montreal and Quebec, 1775," ed. by Charles Burr Todd, *American Historical Register* 2 (1895): 644.

12. PRO, CO 5/91, UP microfilm reel 1, frames 306-7, 311, 314, 324, 355, 378, 505.

13. Bull, 41; In his petition to the Provincial Congress of New York, the fort's nominal commander, Captain John Nordberg, mentioned that "Mr. Romans came & took possession of Fort George, Mr. Romans behaved very genteel and civil to me." B.F. DeCosta, *Notes on the History of Fort George* (New York: J. Sabin & Sons, 1871), 11-12; See also Nordberg to Provincial Congress in New York, December 1775, *Proceedings of the New York State Historical Association* 9 (1910): 387-88.

14. *NDAR*, 1: 313.

15. "Benedict Arnold's Regimental Memorandum Book," *BFTM* 14 (Winter 1982): 71.

16. Ibid., 364-67; See also "Journal Kept by Eleazer Oswald on Lake Champlain," *BFTM* 13 (1977): 341.

17. Haldimand Papers, "Misc. Papers Relating to the Provincial Navy, 1775-1780," NAC, Microfilm H-1649, Volume 1, B144, fol. 99; *NDAR* 1: 319; See also Oscar E. Bredenberg, "The American Champlain Fleet, 1775-77," *BFTM* 12 (September 1964): 249-51.

18. *NDAR*, 1: 539.

19. Ibid., 366, 358.

20. "Arnold's Regimental Memorandum Book," 77.

21. *NDAR*, 1: 808.

22. Ibid., 763.

23. Don R. Gerlach, *Proud Patriot----Philip Schuyler and the War of Independence, 1775-1783* (Syracuse, N.Y.: Syracuse University Press, 1987), 10, 21.

24. *NDAR*, 1: 1217; On September 6, 1775, Rudolphus Ritzema recorded in his journal that each gondola had only one cannon. Rudolphus Ritzema, "Journal of Col. Rudolphus Ritzema," *MAH* 1 (1877): 99.

25. Benjamin Trumbull, "A Concise Journal or Minutes of the Principal Movements Towards St. John's," *Coll. Conn. HS* 7 (1899): 146; Bredenberg, "Champlain Fleet," 257; Oscar R. Bredenberg, "The Royal Savage," *BFTM* 12 (September 1966): 138.

26. John Joseph Henry, *Account of Arnold's Campaign Against Quebec* (1877; reprint ed., New York: The New York Times & Arno Press, 1968), 94; Henry also noted that Montgomery "was well limbed, tall and handsome, though his face was much pockmarked." Ibid; Captain John Topham described Montgomery as "a genteel polite man, tall and slender...bald on the top of his head. Resolute mild and of a fine temper & an excellent gen[1]." John Topham, "The Journal of Captain John Topham, 1775-6," *The Magazine of History* 50 (1916): 115.

27. *NDAR*, 1: 1044, 1043, 1055, 1215.

28. B. Trumbull, "Concise Journal," 141; "The Montgomery Expedition, 1775," *BFTM* 1 (January 1927): 12, 141; See also Ritzema, 99.

29. B. Trumbull, "Concise Journal," 143.

30. *NDAR*, 2: 150-51.

31. Ethan Allen, *A Narrative of Colonel Ethan Allen's Captivity* (1930; reprint ed., Rutland, VT.: Vermont Heritage Press, 1988), 19-20; See also George F. G. Stanley, *Canada Invaded* (Toronto: A. M. Hakkert Ltd., 1973), 44-48.

32. Ibid., 21-22; Urieh Cross, one of the three Americans who managed to escape, later wrote that "the last I saw of Allen he was surrounded, had hold with both hands [of] the muzzle of a gun swinging it round and round." Urieh Cross, "Narrative of Urieh Cross in the Revolutionary War," *Vermont Quarterly* 15 (July 1947): 182.

33. R. N. Hill, *Lake Champlain*, 88.

34. "Papers Relating to the Surrender of Fort St. Johns and Fort Chambly," in *Report of the Work of the Public Archives for the Years 1914 and 1915*, ed. by Arthur G. Doughty (Ottawa: Public Archives of Canada, 1916), 20.

35. Henry Livingston, "Journal of Major Henry Livingston, 1775," ed. by Gaillard Hunt, *The Pennsylvania Magazine of History and Biography* 12 (1898): 18; John André, however, mentioned only "a 24 lb^{er}" aboard the row galley. "Papers Relating to the Surrender," 21.

36. B. Trumbull, "Concise Journal," 146; See also a rendition of the *Enterprise* and *Liberty* carved on a powder horn in 1775 shown in Swayze, 141, 212.

37. Livingston, 17.

38. Ritzema, 101; See also Judah Frisbie, "Journal as a Soldier in the Revolution," in *History of the Town of Wolcott*, by Rev. Samuel Orcutt (Waterbury, CT.: Press of the American Printing Company, 1874), 308-9.

39. "Papers Relating to the Surrender." 23.

40. *NDAR*, 2: 891.

41. See B. Trumbull, "Concise Journal," 171; Stanley, 59-60; See also John Fassett, "Diary of Lieutenant John Fassett," in *The Follett-Dewey, Fassett-Safford Ancestry*, by Harry Parker Ward (Columbus, Ohio: Champlin Printing, 1896), 225-28.

42. B. Trumball, "Concise Journal," 155, 160.

43. B. Trumbull, "Concise Journal," 156.

44. *NDAR*, 2: 1390.

45. Bredenberg, "The Royal Savage," 134, 137, 138-39. See also Livingston, 17-18. Livingston's journal indicated that the vessel had been brought to Ticonderoga. Livingston, 32.

46. *NDAR*, 2: 431.

47. Henry Dearborn, *Revolutionary War Journals of Henry Dearborn, 1775-1783*, ed. by Lloyd A. Brown and Howard H. Peckham (1939; reprint ed., New York: Da Capo Press, 1971), 50; See also Henry, 59-60.

48. Topham, 105; See also Dearborn, 53.

49. "A Journal of a March from Cambridge, on an Expedition against Quebec in Colonel Benedict Arnold's Detachment, Sept. 13, 1775," *Proceedings of the Massachusetts Historical Society* 2 (2nd Series) (1885-1886): 270; See also "Expedition Against Quebec," *NEHGR* 6 (January 1852): 131; For a discussion of the author of this journal see Justin H. Smith, *Arnold's March from Cambridge to Quebec* (1903; reprint ed., Bowie, MD.: Heritage Books, Inc., 1998), 44-55.

50. Edwards Park, "Could Canada Have Ever Been Our Fourteenth Colony," *Smithsonian*, December 1987, 46; Jeremiah Greenman, *Diary of a Common Soldier in the American Revolution, 1775-1783*, ed. by Robert C. Bray & Paul E. Bushnell (DeKalb, Ill.: Northern Illinois University Press, 1978), 18; Henry, 71-72.

51 Doyen Salsig, ed., *Parole: Quebec; Countersign: Ticonderoga----Second New Jersey Regimental Orderly Book, 1776* (Cranbury, N.J.: Associated University Presses, Inc., 1980), 26.

52. B. Trumbull, "Concise Journal," 162.

53. "The Montgomery Expedition, 1775," *BFTM* 1 (July 1928): 33; See also B. Trumbull, "Concise Journal," 167; Alan S. Everest, ed., *The Journal of Charles Carroll of Carrollton* (Fort Ticonderoga, N.Y.: The Champlain–Upper Hudson Bicentennial Committee, 1976), 52.

54. *NDAR*, 2: 1056; The two gondolas *Hancock* and *Schuyler* were also referred to as "row gallies." Barlow, 645.

55. Charles Bracelen Flood, *Rise, and Fight Again* (New York: Dodd, Mead & Co., 1976), 51

56. Dearborn, 60; Greenman, 22; Henry, 94.

57. Henry Knox, "Knox's Diary During His Ticonderoga Expedition," *NEHGR* 30 (1876): 323; See also Wm. L. Bowne, *Y^e Cohorn Caravan, The Knox Expedition in the Winter of 1775-76* (Schuylerville, N.Y.: NaPaul Publishers, Inc., 1975), 21.

58. *NDAR*, 2: 1390.

59. H. Knox, "Diary," 323.

60. *NDAR*, 3: 251; See also Willard M. Wallace, *Traitorous Hero* (1954; reprint ed., Freeport, N.Y.: Books for Libraries Press, 1970), 81-82; James Kirby Martin, *Benedict Arnold: Revolutionary Hero* (New York: New York University Press, 1997), 158-59, 164-65.

61. Dearborn, 65; Greenman, 23, (Jeremiah Greenman recorded the date as December 23); See also Topham, 118.

62. Greenman, 23; Henry, 107; "Expedition against Quebec," 132; Others suggested that the operation began at four o'clock in the morning. Dearborn, 66; *NDAR*, 2: 1399; Charles Porterfield, "Memorable Attack on Quebec, December 21, 1775," *MAH* 21 (April 1889): 319.

63. "Journal of the Most Remarkable Occurrences in Quebec, 1775-1776," *Coll. NYHS* 13 (1880): 187-88.

64. Ritzema, 105.

65. *NDAR*, 3: 315; See also Henry, 108; and "Journal in Quebec," *Coll. NYHS* 13 (1880): 188.

66. Simeon Thayer, "Account of the Assault" in *The Journal of James Melvin----Private Soldier in Arnold's Expedition Against Quebec in the Year 1775*, ed. by Andrew A. Melvin (Portland, ME.: The Wardwell Press, 1902), 61; Porterfield, 319.

67. Dearborn, 68.

68. "Journal of Remarkable Occurrences," 190.

69. Dearborn, 68-69.

70. Thayer, 61; See also Henry, 114-15.

71. Thayer, 62; Captain Henry Dearborn characterized his confinement on January 1 with similar language: "I began this year in very disagreeable Circumstances." Dearborn, 77; Captain John Topham referred to his first night in captivity as "a sorrowful night." Topham, 124.

72. Henry, 135.

73. Ibid., 132.

74. *NDAR*, 3: 1072.

75. Everest, *Journal of Carroll*, 30-31; See also Bellico, *Chronicles of Lake George*, 156-73.

76. Everest, *Journal of Carroll*, 32.

77. Ibid., 34.

78. "John Trumbull at Ticonderoga from His Autobiography," *BFTM* 3 (January 1933): 5.

79. Everest, *Journal of Carroll*, 37-38; Lieutenant Colonel Rudolphus Ritzema referred to the *Revenge* as one of "two Schooners" at the time of the surrender of Fort St. Jean. Ritzema, 103.

80. Boylan, 67.

81. "Journal of a March...against Quebec," 273; Lewis Beebe, "Journal of a Physician on the Expedition Against Canada, 1776," *The Pennsylvania Magazine of History and Biography* 59 (October 1935): 327; See also *NDAR*, 5: 22; Charles Henry Jones, *History of the Campaign for the Conquest of Canada in 1776* (1882; reprint ed., New York: Research Reprints, Inc., 1970), 44.

82. Elizabeth Cometti, ed., *The American Journals of Lt. John Enys* (Syracuse, N.Y.: The Syracuse University Press, 1976), 12; "Journal of Remarkable Occurrences," 235; See also Topham, 126-27.

83. *NDAR*, 4: 1456; George M. Wrong, *Canada and the American Revolution* (New York: The Macmillan Company, 1935), 313.

84. Beebe, 328.

85. Salsig, 113.

86. *NDAR*, 5: 390.

87. Vose, 257-58; One American participant, however, suggested that the incursion into the swamp occurred only after the battle had started, when the Americans were "exposed to a very galling fire from all the vessels, seventeen in number." John Almon, ed., *The Remembrancer; Or Impartial Repository of Public Events* (London: J. Almon, 1776), Part 2, 304; See also Joshua Pell, Jr., "Diary of Joshua Pell, Junior," *MAH* 2 (1878): 43; R. Lamb,

Journal of Occurrences During the Late American War (Dublin: Wilkinson & Courtney, 1809), 107-8.

88. Cometti, 14.

89. *NDAR*, 5: 444.

90. Beebe, 331, 342.

91. Ibid., 336; *NDAR*, 5: 614, 694; See also Elisha Porter, "The Diary of Mr. Elisha Porter of Hadley," *MAH* 29 (1893): 197.

92. Cometti, 16.

93. Beebe, 336; See also William Chamberlin, "Letter of General William Chamberlin," *Proceedings of the Massachusetts Historical Society* 10 (2nd Series) (1896): 498.

94. R. Lamb, *Journal*, 109; Almon, 305.

7. Battle of Valcour Island

1. *NDAR*, 5: 701, see also 873.

2. Ibid., 731.

3. Ibid., 710.

4. *NDAR*, 6: 3; See also *NDAR*, 5: 309-10, 498, 988, 1088-89, 1113.

5. Henry Steele Commager and Richard B. Morris, ed., *The Spirit of 'Seventy-Six* (Indianapolis, IN.: The Bobbs-Merrill Company, Inc., 1949), Volume 1, 221; "Colonel John Trumbull to His Father, Governor Jonathan Trumbull of Connecticut," *BFTM* 6 (July 1942): 144.

6. Salsig, 163.

7. Ibid., 165; See also Gerlach, *Proud Patriot*, 168-69.

8. *AA5*, 1: 376; Others, however, claim that the gondolas did correspond to the "Delaware mould," *AA5*, 1: 682.

9. Jeduthan Baldwin, *The Revolutionary Journal of Col. Jeduthan Baldwin 1775-1778*, ed. by Thomas Williams Baldwin (Bangor, ME.: De Burians, 1906), 59, 61, 70, 78, 85; Ebenezer Elmer, "Journal of Lieutenant Ebenezer Elmer," *Proceedings of the New Jersey Historical Society* 3 (1848-1849): 44; Donald H. Wickman, "Built with Spirit, Deserted in Darkness: The American Occupation of Mount Independence 1776-1777," (master's thesis, University of Vermont, 1993), 12-13, 15, 17-19, 26-27, 34.

10. *AA* 5, 1: 630; Baldwin, 63; The news of the Declaration of Independence was celebrated earlier at Crown Point as Colonel Elisha Hadley noted on July 16: "This morning we rec'd the agreeable news of Independence being declared by the Congress. About noon 2 or 3 kettles of Brandy Grog evidenced our joy at the news which we expressed in proper toasts." Porter, 201.

11. *AA* 5, 1: 649.

12. Ibid., 582.

13. Ibid., 649, see also 51, 340, 512; Christopher Ward, *The War of the Revolution* (New York, The Macmillan Company, 1952), Volume 1, 388; Supervision of the construction of the vessels at Skenesborough was accomplished through a mixture of officers dur-

ing the spring and summer of 1776. Initially, Assistant Deputy Quartermaster General Harmanus Schuyler (no relation to Philip Schuyler) began the gondola construction; later Colonel Cornelius Wynkoop, commander of a New York infantry regiment, helped oversee a good deal of the ship-building and work at the sawmills. After arriving on July 14, Brigadier General David Waterbury from Connecticut, who had served during the 1775 St. Jean campaign, was sent by Gates to Skenesborough to command the militia arriving there and eventually participated in the supervision of naval construction.

14. *NDAR*, 5: 1282.

15. *AA* 5, 1: 1273.

16. Ibid.,1268; See also Allan S. Everest, *Moses Hazen and the Canadian Refugees in the American Revolution* (Syracuse, N.Y.: Syracuse University Press, 1976), 44-45; *AA5*, 1: 1273-75.

17. Bayze Wells, "Journal of Bayze Wells," *Coll. Conn. HS 7* (1899): 268.

18. *NDAR*, 6: 215.

19. Ibid., 1073.

20. Many accounts of the fleet suggest that the *Revenge* was built at Ticonderoga. Ward, 387; Frederic F. Van De Water, *Lake Champlain and Lake George* (Indianapolis, IN.: The Bobbs-Merrill Company, 1946), 191; "A List of Ships in the American and British Fleets in the Battle of Valcour Island," *BFTM* 1 (July 1928): 13.

21. *AA5*, 1: 1268.

22. *NDAR*, 5: 1168.

23. The dimensions of the British vessels may be found in the Haldimand Papers, "Misc. Papers Relating to the Provincial Navy, 1775-1780," NAC, Microfilm H-1649, Volume 1, B144, fols. 15, 142, and Microfilm C-3242, Volume 722A, fol. 20.

24. *NDAR*, 1: 1271; *NDAR*, 6: 1341; Howard I. Chapelle, *The History of the American Sailing Navy* (New York: Bonanza Books, 1949), 103.

25. "A Journal of Carleton's and Burgoyne's Campaigns," Part 1, *BFTM* 11 (December 1964): 256; See also William L. Stone, trans. and ed., *Letters of Brunswick and Hessian Officers During the American Revolution* (Albany, N.Y.: Joel Munsell's Sons, Publishers, 1891), 51.

26. PRO, CO 5/125, fol. 365.

27. Helga Doblin, trans. and Mary C. Lynn, ed., *An Eyewitness Account of the American Revolution and New England Life: The Journal of J. F. Wasmus, German Company Surgeon, 1776-1783* (Westport, CT.: Greenwood Press, 1990), 30; Eleanor M. Murray, "The Burgoyne Campaign," *BFTM* 8 (January 1948): 6; See also *AA* 5, 2: 1179; *NDAR*, 6: 1344; R. Lamb, *Journal*, 110.

28. *AA5*, 1: 826.

29. Ibid., 1267; See also Wells, 271.

30. *NDAR*, 6: 734; See also Wells, 275.

31. *NDAR*, 735.

32. *AA5*, 2: 113.

33. Ibid., 440; See also Rufus Wheeler, "Journal of Lieut. Rufus Wheeler of Rowley," *EIHC* 68 (October 1932): 373; Doblin and Lynn, *Journal of J. F. Wasmus*, 30.

34. *AA5*, 2: 591.

35. Ibid., 440.

36. *NDAR*, 6: 1237.

37. Ibid., 1117.

38. *AA5*, 2: 421.

39. *NDAR*, 6: 857-58; A letter to Benedict Arnold dated September 23, 1776, from Lieutenant Colonel Thomas Hartley seems to imply that the British had a radeau: "The Grand Diable (which I understand is the largest vessel of the Enemy)." The letter was among Arnold's papers taken by the British before the *Royal Savage* was destroyed. "Documents sur la Révolution Américaine," *La Revue De L'Université Laval, Québec* 2 (June 1948): 928.

40. *NDAR*, 6: 1081-82; *AA5*, 2: 566; Intelligence reports include *AA5,2*: 421, 481-82, 835, 982; General James Wilkinson, *Memoirs of My Own Times* (1816; reprint ed., New York: AMS Press Inc., 1973), 87.

41. *AA5*, 2: 933.

42. Ibid., 834.

43. Horatio Rogers, ed., *Hadden's Journal and Orderly Books: A Journal Kept in Canada and Upon Burgoyne's Campaign in 1776 and 1777, by Lieut. James M. Hadden, Roy. Art.* (1884; reprint ed., Boston: Gregg Press, 1972), 17.

44. John Schank, John Starke, and Edward Longcroft, "An Open Letter to Captain Pringle," *BFTM* 1 (July 1928): 18; J. Robert Maguire, "Dr. Robert Knox's Account of The Battle of Valcour, October 11-13, 1776," *Vermont History* 46 (Summer 1978): 148.

45. William L. Stone, trans., *Memoirs, Letters, and Journals of Major General Riedesel* (1868; reprint ed., New York: The New York Times & Arno Press, 1969), Volume 1, 70; *NDAR*, 6: 1277, 858; Wells, 283. Arnold reported two British gondolas carrying three cannons each, Lieutenant Wells aboard the *Providence* reported observing two British sloops in addition to the four larger ships at Valcour, and Sergeant Eli Stiles, reconnoitering St. Jean in September, also noticed two gondolas.

46. Maguire, 148.

47. *AA5*, 2: 1224.

48. Arnold saw 28 gondolas—*NDAR*, 6: 1277; Pascal De Angelis observed 30 sail in the whole fleet—Charles M. Snyder, "With Benedict Arnold at Valcour Island: The Diary of Pascal De Angelis," *Vermont History* 42 (summer 1974): 198; Twenty-eight gunboats and 4 armed longboats were on a September 1776 British list—*NDAR*, 6: 883-84; Captain Georg Pausch mentioned 27 armed bateaux (gunboats)—William L. Stone, ed., *Journal of Captain Pausch* (Albany, N.Y.: Joel Munsell's Sons, 1886), 82; An anonymous British journal listed 29 gunboats—"A Journal of Carleton's and Bur-

goyne's Campaigns," 256; Lieutenant James Hadden listed 22 gunboats—H. Rogers, *Hadden's Journal*, 16; both Sergeant R. Lamb and Ensign John Enys noted 20 gunboats—R. Lamb, *Journal*, 110, and Cometti, 18; Captain Charles Douglas reported 20 gunboats and 4 armed longboats—*NDAR*, 6: 1344.

49. Synder, 198; E. Vale Smith, *History of Newburyport* (Newburyport, MA.: pub.n.a., 1854), 357.

50. *NDAR*, 7: 123; Charles Terrot, "Naval Action on Lake Champlain, 1776" *American Neptune* 8: 3 (1948): 256; See also Charles Terrot to John Frott, 17 October 1776, Fort Ticonderoga Thompson-Pell Research Center. This correspondence is believed to be the basis for William Faden's famous map of the battle. Faden's original map engraving entitled "The Attack and Defeat of the American Fleet under Benedict Arnold, by the King's Fleet Commanded by Captn. Thos. Pringle, upon Lake Champlain. The 11th of October 1776" is in the collection of the Fort Ticonderoga Museum.

51. H. Rogers, *Hadden's Journal*, 23; See also PRO, CO 5/125, fol. 365.

52. W. Stone, *Journal of Pausch*, 83-84.

53. Arnold recorded that two British gondolas sank and one blew up—*NDAR*, 6: 1277; William Briggs, a seaman on the *Washington*, said that two English gunboats sank—*AA5*, 2: 1028; Joshua Pell, Jr., an officer with the British army on Lake Champlain but not at Valcour, noted 2 British gunboats sank—Joshua Pell, Jr., "Diary of Joshua Pell, Junior," *MAH* 2 (1878): 46; General Burgoyne, General Carleton, Lieutenant Digby, Lieutenant Hadden and Dr. Knox mentioned that only one gunboat sank—*Plattsburgh Republican*, 25 December 1897 (Burgoyne, Canadian Archives); *NDAR*, 6: 1272-74 (Carleton); James Phinney Baxter, ed., *The British Invasion from the North, The Campaigns of Generals Carleton and Burgoyne from Canada, 1776-1777, With the Journal of Lieut. William Digby* (Albany, N.Y.: Joel Munsell's Sons, 1887), 159; H. Rogers, *Hadden's Journal*, 23; Maguire, 148 (Knox).

54. Pascal Charles Joseph De Angelis, "The Lake Champlain Fight," diary 1776, Marshall Family Papers, MS 9, Penfield Library, State University of New York at Oswego. A shortened version of the De Angelis diary published in 1974 (note 48) omitted about half of his October 11 entry.

55. Donald Wickman, ed., "A Most Unsettled Time on Lake Champlain: The October 1776 Journal of Jahiel Steward," *Vermont History* 64 (Spring 1996): 92.

56. Edward Osler, *The Life of Admiral Viscount Exmouth* (London: Smith Elder & Co., 1835), 12-13; See also Philip Stephens, "A British View on the Battle of Valcour," (letter, Canadian Archives) *North Country Notes*, April 1963, 3; Wells, 284.

57. Schank, Starke, and Longcroft, 18.

58. W. Stone, *Journal of Pausch*, 83.

59. Schank, Starke, and Longcroft, 18.

60. De Angelis, Marshall Family Papers.

61. *NDAR*, 6: 1235.

62. De Angelis, Marshall Family Papers.

63. Ibid.

64. Wickman, "Journal of Jahiel Stewart," 92.

65. Benedict Arnold's papers from the *Royal Savage* are now held by Laval University in Quebec. The papers include letters from other officers which date from September 21, 1775, and end on October 5, 1776. Although some of the letters have been published in Peter Force's *American Archives* (Fifth Series, Volume 2) and William James Morgan's *Naval Documents of the American Revolution* (Volume 6), others apparently have not been published in the United States. In addition to the military correspondence, some letters, written by his sister Hannah Arnold, deal with news about his young sons. "Documents, sur la Révolution Américaine," *La Revue De L'Université Laval*, Québec 2 (December 1947): 344-49; 2 (March 1948): 642-48; 2 (April 1948): 742-48; 2 (May 1948): 838-46; 2 (June 1948): 926-34.

66. W. C. Watson, "Arnold's Retreat After the Battle of Valcour," *MAH* 6 (June 1881): 414-17; Palmer, 111; Gardner W. Allen, *A Naval History of the American Revolution* (New York: Russell & Russell, Inc., 1913), 173; Most British officers believed that the Americans passed through their lines--see Cometti, 20; H. Rogers, *Hadden's Journal*, 24; Schank, Starke, and Longcroft, 19; "Carleton's Prize," Melvin Barnes, *Reprint of a Short Biography of Colonel Ebenezer Allen* et al. (Plattsburgh, N.Y.: J. W. Tuttle Book and Job Printer, 1852), 26-27.

67. De Angelis, Marshall Family Papers; *AA5*, 2: 1224; See also *History of Oneida County, New York* (Philadelphia: Everts & Fariss, 1878), 569.

68. *AA5*, 2: 1069.

69. Schank, Starke, and Longcroft, 19.

70. W. Stone, *Memoirs of Riedesel*, 1: 71.

71. *NDAR*, 6: 1274.

72. Cometti, 20; Hadden's journal also states that the Americans were "scarcely out of sight" the next morning. H. Rogers, *Hadden's Journal*, 26.

73. *AA5*, 2: 1079; De Angelis, Marshall Family Papers; Snyder, 198.

74. *NDAR*, 6: 1245; *AA5*, 2: 1179; "Journal of Carleton's and Burgoyne's Campaigns," 257; Baxter, 162; Haldimand Papers, NAC, Microfilm C-3242, Volume 722A, fol. 21.

75. Cometti, 20, 22.

76. Edward Wigglesworth, "Colonel Wigglesworth's Diary Containing His Account of the Naval Battles on Lake Champlain, Oct. 11 and 13, 1776," in Stan. V. Henkels, Jr., *Autographs: Letters--Documents--Manuscripts Catalogue No. 1464* (Philadelphia: Stan. V. Henkels, Jr., 1932), 52; "A Return of the fleet belonging to the United States of America on Lake Champlain...October 22, 1776," MS, Lake Champlain Maritime Museum; Art Cohn and Peter Barranco, "Determining the Identity of the Re-

cently Discovered Gunboat," Lake Champlain Maritime Museum, 1999, 15.

78. *AA5*, 2: 1079.

79. Ibid., 1224; *NDAR*, 7: 1295.

80. Wigglesworth, 52.

81. De Angelis, Marshall Family Papers; Snyder, 198.

82. *AA5*, 2: 1079; Bayze Wells recorded that he was "against the mouth of Gillilands Creek [Boquet River]." Wells, 284; Bellico, *Chronicles of Lake Champlain*, 231; For the departure time of the British fleet see H. Rogers, *Hadden's Journal*, 28; Enys noted that the fleet left early on October 13, Cometti, 20; See also Maquire, 148.

83. *AA5*, 2: 1069; R. Lamb, *Journal*, 110.

84. Wickman, "Journal of Jahiel Stewart," 94.

85. *NDAR*, 6: 1258; "Return of the fleet," MS, Lake Champlain Maritime Museum. See also Cometti, 22; W. Stone, *Memoirs of Riedesel*, 1:73; Wilkinson, 91.

86. *AA5*, 2: 1079.

87. Ibid., 1224.

88. Wigglesworth, 52; See also E. Smith, *History of Newburyport*, 358.

89. *History of Oneida County*, 569.

90. Wilkinson, 91; Morris F. Glenn, *The Story of Three Towns* (Ann Arbor, Mich.: Braun-Brumfield, 1977), 102-3.

91. *AA5*, 2: 1069; Maguire, 148; Wigglesworth, 52; E. Smith, *History of Newburyport*, 358; De Angelis, Marshall Family Papers; Snyder, 199; Wickman, "Journal of Jahiel Stewart," 94.

92. Persifer Frazer, "Letters from Ticonderoga, 1776," *BFTM* 10 (January 1962): 453; Sewall also "Heard a cannonading down the lake in the morning." Henry Sewall, "The Diary of Henry Sewall," *Historical Magazine* 10 (August 1871): 132; Ingalls recorded firing "till 2 or 3 o'clock," Phineas Ingalls."Revolutionary War Journal, Kept By Phineas Ingalls of Andover, Mass.," *EIHC* 53 (1917): 90; Dr. Beebe noted "incessant fire from daybreak, till afternoon." Beebe, 354; At 11:30 A.M., Colonel Thomas Hartley at Crown Point stated that the enemy "have been firing, for two hours past, a few heavy guns." Thomas Hartley, "Hartley, Thomas—to General Gates," *BFTM* 4 (July 1938): 46; Jonathan Burton remarked that "in the morning we hear[d] a very heavy firing Down the Lake." Jonathan Burton, *Diary and Orderly Book of Sergeant Jonathan Burton*, ed. by Isaac W. Hammond (Concord., N. H.: Republican Press Association, 1885), 34; Reverend Ammi Robbins' prayer service was compromised because "the attention of the people [was] taken up by a smart cannonading from the fleets which began in the morning." Robbins, 119.

93. *NDAR*, 7: 1295; Snyder, 199; See also Stephens, 3.

94. Wigglesworth, 52; E. Smith, *History of Newburyport*, 358-59.

95. *AA5*, 2: 1080.

96. Wilkinson, 91; See also Charles R. Smith, *Marines in the Revolution: A History of the Continental Marines in the American Revolution 1775-1783* (Washington, D.C.: History and Museums Division, Headquarters, U.S. Marine Corps, 1975), 32; Surgeon Julius Friedrich Wasmus, who accompanied the German troops, wrote "that [Arnold] did not abandon his ship any sooner than when she was everywhere ablaze. Thus, he wished to prevent any of the English coming aboard and lowering the American flag, that remained hoisted until the ship was consumed by the flames." Doblin and Lynn, *Journal of J. F. Wasmus*, 33.

97. Maguire, 148.

98. W. Stone, *Memoirs of Riedesel*, 80.

99. Max Von Eelking, *The German Allied Troops in the North American War of Independence 1776-1783*, trans. J. G. Rosengarten (Albany: Joel Munsell's Sons, Publishers, 1893), 96.

100. Art Cohn, "An Incident Not Known to History: Squire Ferris and Benedict Arnold at Ferris Bay, October 13, 1776," *Vermont History* 55 (Spring 1987): 108-10; P. C. Tucker, Esq., *General Arnold and the Congress Galley* (Vergennes, VT.: booklet originally written, 1861), 3.

101. Samuel Swift, *History of the Town of Middlebury* (Middlebury, VT.: A. H. Copeland, 1859), 89; See also Rowland E. Robinson, *Vermont, A Study of Independence* (Boston: Houghton Mifflin Company, 1892), 136.

102. Wells, 284-85.

103. *AA5*, 2: 1080.

104. Jeduthan Baldwin, *The Revolutionary Journal of Col. Jeduthan Baldwin 1775-1778*, ed. Thomas Williams Baldwin (Bangor, ME.: De Burians, 1906), 80; Chaplain Enos Hitchcock chronicled that "firing continued to about 2 °Clock. a number of boats with Inhabitants came up about four ye hospital Sloop [Enterprise] & Schooner [Revenge] came up with ye wounded about Sunset, ye Trumb[u]l[l], Co^l· Wigglesworth & ye Gund[o]la [New York] & ye Schooner Liberty." Enos Hitchcock, "Diary of Enos Hitchcock," MS, Rhode Island Historical Society, Providence, Rhode Island.

105. Hartley, 46; *AA5*, 2: 1028.

106. Schank, Starke, and Longcroft, 19.

107. Doblin and Lynn, *Journal of J. F. Wasmus*, 33.

108. Baxter, 160-61.

109. *NDAR*, 6: 1274.

110. John Trumbull, *Autobiography, Reminiscences and Letters of John Trumbull from 1756 To 1841* (New Haven, CT.: B. L. Hamlen, 1841), 35-36.

111. Baldwin, *Revolutionary Journal*, 81.

112. *AA5*, 2: 1040-41; *NDAR*, 6: 1257-58; Carleton may also have been influenced by Ensign Thomas McCoy, an American captive in Canada, who suggested on September 25, "that there were 20,000 men at Crown Point and Ticonderoga well supplied with cannon, provisions & c." Baxter, 147.

113. *AA5*, 2: 1041; Cometti, 20, 22; Haldimand Papers, NAC, Microfilm C-3242, Volume 722A, fol. 21; See also Thomas H. Canfield, "Discovery, Navigation, and Navigators of Lake Champlain," in Abby Maria Hemenway, ed., *The Vermont Historical Gazetteer* (Burlington, VT.: A. M. Hemenway, 1867), Volume 1, 665.

114. *AA5*, 2: 1080; Captain Ichabod Norton, serving with the Americans at Ticonderoga, recorded in his orderly book that Gates "returns his h[e]arty thanks to General Arnold, officers, se[a]m[e]n and marines of the fleet for the Galant Defence they made against the Super[i]ority of the Enemy. More such Brave behavour Will Establish the fame of the American arms Throughout the Globe." Ichabod Norton, *Orderly Book of Capt. Ichabod Norton of Col. Mott's Regiment of Connecticut Troops Destined for the Northern Campaign in 1776* (Fort Edward, N.Y.: Press of Keating & Barnard, 1898), 13.

115. Elmer, 44; See also Donald Wickman, ed., "The Diary of Timothy Tuttle," *New Jersey History* 113 (Fall/Winter 1995): 72-75.

116. *AA5*, 2: 1186.

117. Beebe, 355.

118. Baldwin, *Revolutionary Journal*, 82.

119. Baxter, 147.

120. *NDAR*, 6: 1336.

121. Helga Doblin, trans. and Mary C. Lynn, ed., *The Specht Journal: A Military Journal of the Burgoyne Campaign* (Westport, CT.: Greenwood Press, 1995), 33; Doblin and Lynn, *Journal of J. F. Wasmus*, 34; Major General Riedesel suggested that orders for winter quarters were received on October 18. W. Stone, *Memoirs of Riedesel*, 75.

122. Frazer, "Letters from Ticonderoga, 1776," 455.

123. Ibid.; See also Persifer Frazer, "An Account of a Skirmish on or Near Lake Champlain," 28 Oct. 1776, NYSL, #14007: 5; Wells, 286; Baldwin, *Revolutionary Journal*, 84; Sewall, 133; AA5, 2: 1314-15; Wheeler, 376; Nathaniel Dodge, "A Letter and Diary of 1776," *Vermont Quarterly* 21 (1953): 35; Micah Hildreth, "Micah Hildreth of Dracutt His Book," in *History of Dracut*, by Silas R. Coburn (Lowell, MA.: Press of the Courier-Citizen Co., 1922), 150; Simon Mudge, "A Journal of the March to Continental Army," in *Memorials: Mudge*, by Alfred Mudge (Boston: Alfred Mudge & Son, 1868), 205; Ingalls, 91; Burton, 35; Norton, 48.

124. J. Trumbull, *Autobiography*, 36.

125. Baxter, 176.

126. Anthony Wayne, *Orderly Book of the Northern Army at Ticonderoga and Mount Independence, from October 17th, 1776, to January 8th, 1777* (Albany, N.Y.: J. Munsell, 1859), 134. The *New York* gondola was also mentioned on 110; See also Elmer, 53; A return of vessels dated October 22, 1776, referred to the gondola *New York* as the *Success*. "Return of the fleet," MS, Lake Champlain Maritime Museum.

127. Doblin and Lynn, *Journal of J. F. Wasmus*, 32.

128. *AA5*, 2: 1192.

129. Ibid., 1143.

130. *NDAR*, 7: 29.

131. Paul David Nelson, "Guy Carleton versus Benedict Arnold: The Campaign of 1776 in Canada and on Lake Champlain," *New York History* 57 (July 1976): 361.

132. W. Stone, *Memoirs of Riedesel*, 83.

133. A. T. Mahan, *War of American Independence* (Boston: Little, Brown, and Co., 1913), 25.

8. Invasion of the Lakes

1. *NDAR*, 7: 621; See also *AA5*, 3: 1592.

2. Ibid., 784.

3. *NDAR*, 8: 528.

4. *BFTM* 5 (January 1939): 37.

5. *NDAR*, 7: 1190.

6. Arthur Cohn, *The Great Bridge "From Ticonderoga to Independent Point"* (Lake Champlain Basin Program, 1995), Report 4C, 20-21; Kevin Crisman, *The 1992 Mount Independence Phase One Underwater Archaeological Survey* (Lake Champlain Basin Program, 1995), Report 4B, 48-49.

7. James Thacher, M.D., *Military Journal of the American Revolution* (Hartford, CT.: Hurlbut, Williams & Company, 1862), 80; Thacher may have taken the measurements from Burgoyne's work published in 1780. John Burgoyne, *A State of the Expedition from Canada* (1780; reprint ed., New York: The New York Times & Arno Press, 1969), Appendix VII, xxx.

8. *NDAR*, 8: 187-88; See also *NDAR*, 7: 1255-56, 627.

9. Gerlach, *Proud Patriot*, 222.

10. Burgoyne, 12, 16.

11. Doblin and Lynn, *Journal of J. F. Wasmus*, 51; Johann Friedrich Specht also mentioned that the "radeau [was] enlarged." Helga Doblin, trans. and Mary C. Lynn, ed., *The Specht Journal: a Military Journal of the Burgoyne Campaign* (Westport, CT.: Greenwood Press, 1995), 40; Charlotte S. J. Epping, trans., *Journal of Du Roi the Elder* (Philadelphia: University of Pennsylvania, 1911), 87.

12. Sources for the vessels include: Haldimand Papers, "Misc. Papers Relating to the Provincial Navy, 1775-1780," NAC, Microfilm H-1649, Volume 1, B144, fols. 15, 142, and Microfilm C-3242, Volume 722A, fols. 20-25, 30-31; *NDAR*, 7: 830-31; *NDAR*, 8: 986; *NDAR*, 9: 331-33; Rich, 42-43; H. Rogers, *Hadden's Journal*, 53; Joshua Pell, Jr., an officer with the British expedition, also noted a seven-gun vessel called the *Land Crab*, carrying 30 men. Pell, however, may have called the flat-bottomed gondola *Loyal Convert* the *Land Crab* since he omitted the former vessel from his list; J. Pell, *Diary*, 107.

13. Thomas Anburey, *Travels Through the Interior Parts of America* (Boston: Houghton Mifflin Company, 1923), Volume 1, 181-82; Julius Friedrich

Wasmus remarked that "the beauty of this sight is beyond description." Doblin and Lynn, *Journal of J. F. Wasmus*, 53.

14. Burgoyne, Appendix VI, xxii-xxiv; See also Anbury, 283, 286-87.

15. W. Stone, *Memoirs of Riedesel*, 1: 108-9.

16. "The Trial of Major General Schuyler, October 1778," *Coll. NYHS* 12 (1879): 14.

17. "The Trial of Major General St. Clair, August 1778,"*Coll. NYHS* 13(1880): 24-25, see also 74-75.

18. Baldwin, *Revolutionary Journal*, 100; See also Wickman, "Built with Spirit," 86-87; Dennis E. Howe, *This Ragged, Starved, Lousy, Pocky Army* (Concord, N. H.: The Printed Word, 1996), 20-21; David R. Starbuck, "Military Hospitals on the Frontier of Colonial America," *Expedition* 39 (No. 1, 1997): 35-38.

19. Doblin and Lynn, *Journal of J. F. Wasmus*, 59; Anburey, 187; See also Doblin and Lynn, *Specht Journal*, 53; Epping, 97.

20. Simon Fraser, "Gen. Fraser's Account of Burgoyne's Campaign on Lake Champlain and the Battle of Hubbardton," *Proceedings of the Vermont Historical Society* (October 18 and November 2, 1898): 140-41 (See also Simon Fraser, "Inquisition of a Spy," 18 June 1777, Fort Ticonderoga Thompson-Pell Research Center and *BFTM* 10 (1959): 240-45.

21. Baldwin, *Revolutionary Journal*, 95-96; Wickman, "Built with Spirit," 72-73; See also Bellico, *Chronicles of Lake George*, 176-77.

22. "The Trial of St. Clair," 116.

23. "Trial of Schuyler," 158.

24. Ibid., 13.

25. "Trial of St. Clair," 69; See also Baldwin, *Revolutionary Journal*, 108; Enos Stone, "Capt. Enos Stone's Journal," *NEHGR* 15 (January 1861): 300; Thomas Blake, "Lieutenant Thomas Blake's Journal," in *History of the First New Hampshire Regiment*, by Frederic Kidder (Albany: Joel Munsell, 1868), 26.

26. Fraser, "Gen. Fraser's Account," 143.

27. Burgoyne, Appendix VI, xxix; See also Fraser, "Gen. Fraser's Account," 144; Anburey, 190.

28. Lieutenants James Hadden, August Wilhelm Du Roi, and William Digby and Colonel Christian Prätorius recorded that the road to the summit of Mount Defiance was under construction on July 4. H. Rogers, *Hadden's Journal*, 84; Epping, 93; Baxter, 204-5; Helga Doblin, tran. and ed., "Journal of Lt. Colonel Christian Julius Prätorius 2 June 1777-17 July 1777," *BFTM* 15 (Winter 1991): 64. Prätorius also suggested that some of the cannons brought to the summit were taken from the radeau *Thunderer*. Ibid.

29. Thacher, 82.

30. Wilkinson, 184; Other American participants observed British troops on Mount Defiance on July 5, 1777. Baldwin, *Revolutionary Journal*, 109; Blake, 27-28; Donald H. Wickman, " 'Breakfast on Choco-

late': The Diary of Moses Greenleaf, 1777," *BFTM* 15 (1997): 497; John Calfe, "Capt. John Calfe's Book," in *A Memorial of the Town of Hampstead, New Hampshire*, comp. by Harriette Eliza Noyes (Boston: George B. Reed, 1899), 290; William B. Weeden, ed., "Diary of Enos Hitchcock, D. D., A Chaplain in the Revolutionary Army with a Memoir," *Publications of the Rhode Island Historical Society* 7 (1899): 117; See also Bellico, *Chronicles of Lake Champlain*, 265.

31. Wilkinson, 185.

32. "Trial of St. Clair," 93, 88; See also Blake, 28; Wickman, "Moses Greenleaf," 497; E. Stone, "Capt. Enos Stone's Journal," 301; Calfe, 290.

33. "Trial of St. Clair," 55.

34. Ibid., 111.

35. Wickman, "Moses Greenleaf," 497; Doblin and Lynn, *Specht Journal*, 52; Doblin, *Journal of Prätorius*, 64; Helga Doblin, trans. and Mary C. Lynn, ed., *The American Revolution, Garrison Life in French Canada and New York: Journal of an Officer in the Prinz Friedrich Regiment, 1776-1883* (Westport, CT.: Greenwood Press, 1993), 74.

36. Thacher, 83; See also Weeden, 117-18.

37. Ibid.

38. Anburey, 192-93.

39. W. Stone, *Memoirs of Riedesel*, 1:113; H. Rogers, *Hadden's Journal*, 85; Blake, 29; Doblin and Lynn, *Specht Journal*, 53.

40. Burgoyne, Appendix VII, xxx; Doblin and Lynn, *Journal of J. F. Wasmus*, 59.

41. Calfe, 290; See also Thacher, 83-84; Weeden, 118.

42. Burgoyne, Appendix VII, xxx.

43. "A Journal of Carleton's and Burgoyne's Campaigns," Part 2, *BFTM* 11 (September 1965): 312; See also James Minor Lincoln, *The Papers of Captain Rufus Lincoln of Wareham, Mass.* (1904; reprint ed., Arno Press, Inc., 1971), 14; Pell, "Diary," 108; H. Rogers, *Hadden's Journal*, 91; Philip Skene Petition, NYSL, #7308.

44. "A Journal of Carleton's and Burgoyne's Campaigns," Part 2: 321; This list is virtually identical to one published in the *Connecticut Gazette* on December 5, 1777. *NDAR*, 9: 225.

45. H. Rogers, *Hadden's Journal*, 89.

46. Doblin and Lynn, *Journal of J. F. Wasmus*, 60.

47. Thacher, 84; See also J. Lincoln, *Rufus Lincoln*, 14.

48. Anburey, 194; See also Charles I. Bushnell, ed., *The Narrative of Ebenezer Fletcher* (1827; reprint ed., Freeport N. Y.: Books for Libraries Press, 1970), 12.

49. E. Stone, "Capt. Enos Stone's Journal," 301.

50. Wickman, "Moses Greenleaf," 497.

51. Anburey, 199; See also J. Lincoln, *Rufus Lincoln*, 14; J. Pell, "Diary," 107-8; Boatner, 526-28; William L. Stone, *The Campaign of Lieut. Gen. John Burgoyne* (Albany: Joel Munsell, 1877), 22.

52. Fraser, "Gen. Fraser's Account," 146; Burgoyne, Appendix VII, xxxiii; J. Pell, "Diary," 108; H. Rogers, *Hadden's Journal*, 86; Baxter, 210.

53. Weeden, 119; Brigadier General Johann Specht suggested that Fort Anne was "nothing but a square of palisades in which embrasures [openings for cannons] have been fitted. Before leaving, the enemy has set fire to it whereby a wooden barrack and a similar magazine, which had stood in this square, had been reduced to ashes. Actually no more than half of the palisades had burned; for a sudden, heavy rain must have extinguished the flames." Doblin and Lynn, *Specht Journal*, 59.

54. J. Lincoln, *Rufus Lincoln*, 15; See also Thacher, 85.

55. Epping, 114; See also F. J. Hudleston, *Gentleman Johnny Burgoyne* (Garden City, N.Y.: Garden City Publishing Co., 1927), 162; Doris Begor Morton, *Philip Skene of Skenesborough* (Granville, N.Y.: The Grastorf Press, 1959), 54; R. N. Hill, *Lake Champlain*, 116; Van De Water, 213.

56. Burgoyne, 17; See also B. F. DeCosta, *Notes on the History of Fort George During the Colonial and Revolutionary Periods* (New York: J. Sabin & Sons, 1871), 45; See also a summary of debate on the issue in H. N. Muller and David A. Donath," 'The Road Not Taken': A Reassessment of Burgoyne's Campaign," *BFTM* 13 (1973): 272-85.

57. Burgoyne, 17-18.

58. Burgoyne, Appendix XII, lxxxv; See also DeCosta, *Fort George*, 38; *NDAR*, 8: 1000.

59. *NDAR*, 9: 331-32; See also Anburey, 213; William Gordon, *The History of the Rise, Progress, and Establishment of the Independence of the United States of America* (New York: Samuel Campbell, 1794), Volume 2, 210.

60. H. Rogers, *Hadden's Journal*, 103.

61. Ibid., 107.

62. DeCosta, *Fort George*, 36-37; Riedesel, however, described the fort as having 12 cannons, barracks for 1,000 men east of the fort, and to the west of the magazine"where Fort William Henry formerly stood, is the large hospital, a building of great dimensions...surrounded by palisades, and to have a small redoubt on the hill south of it." W. Stone, *Memoirs of Riedesel*, 1:296.

63. Palmer, 129.

64. Gerlach, *Proud Patriot*, 283-84; Muller and Donath, 276; Lawrence Cortesi, "The Tragic Romance of Jane McCrea," *American History Illustrated*, April 1985, 10-15.

65. Bruce MacGregor, "A Failure to Communicate," *American History Illustrated*, October 1985, 19.

66. Doblin and Lynn, *Specht Journal*, 62-63.

67. Wilkinson, 198; See also Thacher, 86.

68. "Trial of St. Clair," 67-68, 76, 83, 108, 111, 120, 171; "Trial of Schuyler," 6-182.

69. W. Stone, *Memoirs of Riedesel*, 1:130.

70. Roby, 250.

71. Ibid., 192; Chaplain Enos Hitchcock noted 664 men captured (more than half German soldiers) and 280 killed or wounded. Weeden, 128; Burgoyne later blamed Major General Riedesel for the idea of the ill-fated expedition: "It was at this time Major-general Riedesel conceived the purpose of mounting his regiment of drago[o]ns." Burgoyne, 18; Although Riedesel had suggested a raid for horses earlier, he later maintained that Bennington was a dangerous undertaking "being at too great a distance," but Burgoyne "was not a man to be dissuaded." W. Stone, *Memoirs of Riedesel*, 1:127.

72. Burgoyne, Appendix XIII, lxxxi.

73. Robert T. Pell, "John Brown and the Dash for Ticonderoga," *BFTM* 2 (January 1930): 32; Peter Nelson, "The Battle of Diamond Island," *Quarterly Journal of the New York State Historical Association*, (January 1922): 43.

74. "Brown's Attack of September 1777," *BFTM* 11 (July 1964): 212; See also Scott Padeni, "John Brown's Attack on Diamond Island, Lake George," *The Lake George Nautical Newsletter* 3 (No. 2, 1994): 5.

75. R. T. Pell, "John Brown," 31.

76. Ibid., 36.

77. "General Powell to Sir Guy Carleton, 19 September 1777," *BFTM* 7 (July 1945): 30.

78. *NDAR*, 9: 939; See also B. F. DeCosta, "The Fight at Diamond Island," *NEHGR* 26 (January 1872): 150.

79. Jn. Starke, "Remarks on Affairs at the Portage Between Ticonderoga and Lake George, and the Mount Independence, in Sept. 1777," *BFTM* 11 (July 1964): 207-8; See also MS (M-2126) in the Fort Ticonderoga Thompson-Pell Research Center.

80. Burgoyne, Appendix XIV, xciv.

81. Starke, "Remarks on Affairs," 209.

82. "Powell to Carleton," 32.

83. Burgoyne, Appendix XIV, xcv.

84. *NDAR*, 9: 968; William L. Stone, *The Campaign of Lieut. Gen. John Burgoyne and the Expedition of Lieut. Col. Barry St. Leger* (Albany: Joel Munsell, 1877), 351; The additional cannons aboard the sloop had been captured from the British near Fort Ticonderoga and Mount Defiance. John C. Dann, *The Revolution Remembered: Eyewitness Accounts of the War for Independence* (Chicago: The University of Chicago Press, 1980), 95.

85. P. Nelson, "Diamond Island," 48; Captain Lemuel Roberts, *Memoirs of Captain Lemuel Roberts* (1809; reprint ed., New York: The New York Times & Arno Press, 1969), 62; *NDAR*, 9: 968.

86. Roberts, 62.

87. R. T. Pell, "John Brown," 39.

88. "General Powell to Sir Guy Carleton, 27 September 1777," *BFTM* 7 (July 1945): 34.

89. *NDAR*, 9: 968.

90. Ibid., 969.

91. Dann, 95.

92. Burgoyne, Appendix XIV, xcv.

93. DeCosta, "Diamond Island," 151.

94. Thomas Reeves Lord, *Stories of Lake George, Fact and Fancy* (Pemberton, N.J.: Pinelands Press, 1987), 36; Rod Canham, "New York's Lake George, Queen of American Lakes," *Skin Diver Magazine*, October 1983, 43.

95. W. Stone, *Memoirs of Riedesel*, 1:134, 274, 276; *NDAR*, 9: 969; DeCosta, "Diamond Island," 151.

96. Richardson, 284; See also Benson Lossing, ed., *The Military Journals of Two Private Soldiers 1758-1775* (Poughkeepsie, N.Y.: Abraham Tomlinson, 1855), 24.

97. Alexander Monypenny, "Monypenny Orderly Book," *BFTM* 7 (October 1970): 444; See also Champion, 421, 426, 433, which mention the "first Island" in the lake as "Diamond Island."

98. Benjamin Silliman, *Remarks Made on a Short Tour Between Hartford and Quebec in the Autumn of 1819*, 2nd ed. (New Haven, CT.: S. Converse, 1824), 153.

99. Elizabeth Eggleston Seelye, *Lake George in History*, 2nd ed. (Lake George, N.Y.: Elwyn Seelye, 1896), 107; W. Lamb, *Lake George*, 42; See also Henry Marvin, *A Complete History of Lake George* (New York: Sibells & Maigne, Printers, 1853), 54-56; W. Max Reid, *Lake George and Lake Champlain* (New York: G. P. Putnam's Sons, 1910), 331.

100. "Powell to Carleton, 27 September 1777," 34; "A Journal of Carleton's and Burgoyne's Campaigns," Part 3, *BFTM* 7 (March 1966): 32. This journal reported that the "principal vessel, and gun boats were retaken."; See also Walter B. Sturtevant, "John Brown's Raid--September, 1777," *Infantry Journal* 36 (May 1930): 484.

101. Burgoyne, Appendix XIV, lxxxix.

102. Ibid., 26.

103. Ibid; Appendix XV, cii; Simon Alexander, a Massachusetts militiaman, years later recounted that the day before the "cessation of arms" the Americans fired a cannonball which struck "a small red house"; the day after the end of the hostilities "some of the British soldiers came over into our camp, and one of them told me that Burgoyne and his officers were holding a council of war in that house at the time the ball passed through it." Dann, 110.

104. Gerlach, *Proud Patriot*, 319.

105. W. Stone, *Letters*, 128.

106. Ibid., 129.

107. Epping, 110; Doblin and Lynn, *American Revolution, Garrison Life*, 86.

108. Doblin and Lynn, *American Revolution, Garrison Life*, 86; See also Epping, 110.

109. Epping, 110.

110. Haldimand Papers, NAC, Microfilm C-3242, Volume 722A, fols. 30-31, Microfilm H-1649, Volume 1, B144, fol. 142.

111. Ibid.

112. Ida H.Washington and Paul A.Washington, *Carleton's Raid* (Canaan, N.H.: Phoenix Publishing, 1977), vii.

113. For the Ferris story see Samuel Swift, *History of the Town of Middlebury* (Middlebury, VT.: A. H. Copeland, 1859), 89-93; See also Washington and Washington, 56, 65, 67, 69.

114. Gavin K. Watt, *The Burning of the Valleys: Daring Raids from Canada Against the New York Frontier in the Fall of 1780* (Toronto: Dundurn Press, 1997), 137-49.

115. Ibid., 103.

116. Cometti, 46-47; Brian Burns, "Carleton in the Valley or the Year of the Burning," *BFTM* 13 (Fall 1980): 404.

117. Cometti, 46.

118. Ibid., 48.

119. Winston Adler, ed., *Their Own Voices: Oral Accounts of Early Settlers in Washington County, New York* (Interlaken, N. Y.: Heart of the Lakes Publishing, 1983), 101.

120. Ibid., 120.

121. Oscar E. Bredenberg, *Military Activities in the Champlain Valley after 1777* (Champlain, N.Y.: Moorsfield Press, 1962), 30.

122. Ibid., 30-31; See also Don R. Gerlach, "The British Invasion of 1780 and 'A Character. . .Debased Beyond Description,' " *BFTM* 14 (Summer 1984): 316.

123. Philip Schuyler to George Washington, 2 November 1781, MS (1999.1134), Fort Ticonderoga Thompson-Pell Research Center.

124. Charles A. Jellison, *Ethan Allen, Frontier Rebel* (Syracuse, N.Y.: Syracuse University Press, 1969), 283-84; See also Van De Water, 236; Schuyler to Washington, MS.

125. Jellison, 285.

126. Morris F. Glenn, "New York's Chain of 'Ghost' Blockhouses on Lake Champlain," (unpublished paper, 1999).

127. Bredenberg, "The Royal Savage," 149.

128. Palmer, 109.

129. *Plattsburgh Republican*, 21 March 1868; See also *Plattsburgh Republican*, 31 July 1880.

130. *LGM*, 6 July 1901. The article suggested that two of the gun carriages would be sent to the Smithsonian Institution and "the other has been given to the city of Burlington."

131. *Glens Falls Daily Times*, 23 October 1908; *Plattsburg Evening News*, 16 October 1908; *Ticonderoga Sentinel*, 22 October 1908.

132. John B. Ferguson, "Whatever Happened to the Royal Savage," *Yankee*, November 1975, 269; See also John Williams, "I Saw the Savage," *Champlain Maritime Society Soundings*, Fall/Winter 1985, 4-5, 9.

133. Sterling Martin, "Memoir of a Summer 'Dig,' " *BFTM* 15 (1992): 320.

134. Lorenzo F. Hagglund to Charles C. Adams, 29 October 1930, New York State Museum.

135. Hagglund to Adams, 9 September 1929, New York State Museum; Adams replied that by law any relics discovered belonged to the state museum and pledged cooperation since the museum was about to make "important additions" to its collections. Adams to Hagglund, 18 September 1929, New York State Museum.

136. Hagglund to Adams, 29 October 1930, New York State Museum.

137. Hagglund to Adams, 1 September 1932, New York State Museum.

138. Hagglund to Adams, 3 May 1934, New York State Museum.

139. Horace Sawyer Mazet, "Lake Champlain Yields Historic Relics," *Motor Boating,* February 1935, 294.

140. Hagglund to Adams, 18 September 1934, New York State Museum.

141. Robert G. Skerrett, "Wreck of the Royal Savage Recovered," *U.S. Naval Institute Proceedings,* (November 1935): 1652.

142. Hagglund to Adams, 2 April 1935; Adams to Hagglund, 5 April 1935, New York State Museum.

143. Sidney Ernest Hammersley, *The Lake Champlain Naval Battles of 1776-1814* (Waterford, N.Y.: Col. Sidney E. Hammersley, 1959), 21.

144. "The Continental Gondola 'Philadelphia' Raised from the Depths after 158 years," *Burlington Daily News,* Special Historical Tabloid, August-September 1935, 2.

145. Hagglund to Adams, 22 July 1935, New York State Museum.

146. Lorenzo Frederick Hagglund, *A Page from the Past:The Story of the Continental Gondola "Philadelphia"* (Whitehall, N. Y.: The Whitehall Times, 1936), 19; See also L. F. Hagglund, *A Page from the Past: The Story of the Continental Gundelo PHILADELPHIA on Lake Champlain--1776-1949,* 2nd ed. (Lake George, N.Y.: Adirondack Resorts Press, 1949), 20.

147. *Burlington Daily News,* Special Historical Tabloid, 8.

148. Ibid.

149. Adams to George P. Burns, 9 March 1936, New York State Museum.

150. Curtis B. Norris, "The Gundalow of Valcour Bay," *Yankee,* September 1966, 164; Hagglund, *A Page from the Past,* 2nd ed., 29.

151. Charles Adams, Alexander Flick, and Dorothy Smith, *Report of Committee--Concerning the "Philadelphia,"* December 11, 1936, New York State Museum. The report mentioned that the Fort Ticonderoga Association offered $5,000 for the *Philadelphia,* the New York Historical Society $10,000, and that the City of Philadelphia and the University of Vermont also wished to acquire the vessel.

152. Ibid.; William Leland Thompson to Owen D. Young, April 24, 1937; See also William Leland Thompson to William J. Wallin, April 22, 1937, New York State Museum.

153. Philip K. Lundeberg, *The Gunboat Philadelphia and the Defense of the Lake Champlain in 1776* (Basin Harbor, VT.: Lake Champlain Maritime Museum, 1995), 42-43.

154. *NDAR,* 6: 1276, 1389.

155. *AA5,* 2: 1179.

156. John R. Spears, *The History of Our Navy* (New York: Charles Scribner's Sons, 1897), Volume 1, 109.

157. *AA5,* 2: 1143.

158. *NDAR,* 6: 1245; Baxter, 162; "A Journal of Carleton's and Burgoyne's Campaigns," Part 1, *BFTM* 11 (December 1964): 257 (original in West Point Library); "An Account of the Expedition of the British Fleet on Lake Champlain under the command of Captain Thomas Pringle & the Defeat of the Rebel Fleet commanded by Benedict Arnold on the 11 & 13 of October 1776," NYSL, #1008.

159. Cometti, 20, 22.

160. As early as the 1930s, Hagglund suggested raising one or two more historic vessels. Lloyd L. Cheney to Frank P. Graves, 17 May 1937; Hagglund to Adams, 19 November 1940, New York State Museum.

161. Philip K. Lundeberg, *Search for Continental Gunboats at Schuyler Island, Lake Champlain, New York* (Washington, D.C.: National Geographic Society Research Reports, 1968 Projects, 1976), 223.

162. *Valley News,* 2 March 1988.

163. *The New York Times,* 24 September 1989; *Burlington Free Press,* 22 September 1989.

164. *LCMM News,* Fall/Winter 1997, 3; Barranco, *Naval Inventory,* 54; *The New York Times,* 1 July 1997; *Vermont Times,* 30 July 1997; Lois Fecteau, "Benedict Arnold's Long-Lost Gunboat," *Soundings,* January 1998, A32.

165. "A Revolutionary Discovery in Lake Champlain," *Sea History,* Autumn 1997, 36.

166. Cohn and Barranco, "Determining the Identity," 18; *The Post-Star,* 9 May 1999.

167. "Return of the fleet," MS, Lake Champlain Maritime Museum.

168. W. Stone, *Memoirs of Riedesel,* 1: 80.

169. Cometti, 176.

170. Mazet, 100.

171. *Schenectady Daily Gazette,* 17 March 2000; *LCMM News,* Spring/Summer 2000.

172. Zadock Thompson, *History of Vermont* (Burlington, VT.: Chauncey Goodrich, 1842), Part 3, 135.

173. Hemenway, 1: 80; See also H. P. Smith, ed., *History of Addison County* (Syracuse: D. Mason & Co. Pub., 1886), 581.

174. Philip C. Tucker, *General Arnold and the Congress Galley* (Vergennes, VT.: pub., n.a., 1861), 6.

175. Mazet, 101.

176. *Vergennes Vermonter*, 30 October 1891.

177. Russell L. Kent, the great, great, great, grandson of Peter Ferris, wrote to me that "a cane from the 'Congress' lays before me now...I sent Gen. Eisenhower a brace from the 'Congress' and I have his letter of thanks and I learn it is in Abilene with my name on it." Russell L. Kent, 26 March 1985, personal communication.

178. Reid, 357.

179. *New York Times*, 23 November 1952.

180. *Lake Placid News*, 28 May 1954; The ambitious plans included a "main exhibition hall 156 feet wide in the front, sloping to 252 feet in the rear and 112 feet in length...another exhibition hall 252 feet wide by 124 feet deep. The ceiling of the main section and rear section will be about 40 feet above the floor to allow for the masts and spars of the vessels." Offering Circular, 100,000 Shares of Common Stock, Lake Champlain Associates, Inc., May 18, 1954, 3-9.

181. *Whitehall Times*, 11 September 1958.

182. Lundeberg, *Search for Continental Gunboats*, 215.

183. Arthur B. Cohn, afterward to *The Gunboat Philadelphia and the Defense of Lake Champlain in 1776* by Philip K. Lundeberg (Basin Harbor, VT.: Lake Champlain Maritime Museum, 1995), 61-84.

184. Cohn and Barranco, "Determining the Identity," 22; See also *LGM*, 2 September 1910.

185. *Ticonderoga Sentinel*, 16 November 1911.

186. "A Journal of Carleton's and Burgoyne's Campaigns," Part 2: 321; J. Lincoln, *Rufus Lincoln*, 14.

187. Cohn and Barranco, "Determining the Identity," 6, 22.

188. Haldimand Papers, "Misc. Papers Relating to the Provincial Navy, 1775-1780," NAC, Microfilm H-1649, Volume 2, B145, fol. 55.

189. Ibid., 120; See also John W. Krueger, ed., "Simon Metcalfe's 'Little Book,' " *BFTM* 15 (Winter 1988): 30, 32.

190. Haldimand Papers, UP microfilm reel 71, fol. 116; The *Liberty* was reported to be "old but repairable" as late as 1790. Bredenberg, "The American Champlain Fleet," 263.

191. Allan S. Everest, *Point au Fer on Lake Champlain* (Plattsburgh, N. Y.: Clinton County Historical Association, 1992), 38; See also H. N. Muller III, *The Commercial History of the Lake Champlain-Richelieu River, 1760-1815* (Ph.D. diss., University of Rochester, N.Y., 1968), 101.

192. André Lepiné, *La Richelieu Archeologique* (Montreal: La Societé du Musée Militaire et Maritime, 1983), 29-30.

193. Peter Barranco, April 15, 1970, personal communication; *Times Union* (Albany), 16 September 1954; *Ticonderoga Sentinel*, 16 September 1954.

194. Edward P. Hamilton, "An Historic Mortar," *BFTM* 10 (February 1960): 299-303; See also Baldwin, *Revolutionary Journal*, 63-64.

195. Starbuck, *The Great Warpath*, 133, 136-57; Howe, 15-58.

196. Arthur Cohn, *The 1992 Fort Ticonderoga-Mount Independence Submerged Cultural Resource Survey* (Lake Champlain Basin Program, 1995), Report 4A; Kevin Crisman, *The 1992 Mount Independence Phase One Underwater Archaeological Survey* (Lake Champlain Basin Program, 1995), Report 4B; Arthur Cohn, *The Great Bridge "From Ticonderoga to Independant Point"* (Lake Champlain Basin Program, 1995), Report 4C.

197. *LGM*, 21 July 2000; *Post-Star*, 27 July 2000; See also Russell Bellico, "The Need for a Fort George Visitor Center," *Proceedings: First Annual Conference of Heritage Tourism in the Adirondack Region*, (Glens Falls: Adirondack Regional Chambers of Commerce, 1997), 61-64.

9. War Of 1812: Plattsburgh Bay

1. Hugh Ll. Keenleyside, *Canada and the United States* (Port Washington, N.Y.: Kennikat Press, 1971), 79.

2. Allan S. Everest, *The War of 1812 in the Champlain Valley* (Syracuse, N.Y.: Syracuse University Press, 1981), 45; H. N. Muller III, *Commercial History*, 210; Doris B. Morton, *Whitehall in the War of 1812* (Whitehall, N.Y.: Washington County Historical Society, 1964, Mimeographed), 2; Walter Hill Crockett, *Vermont: The Green Mountain State* (New York: The Century History Co., 1921), 43.

3. Rodney Macdonough, *Life of Commodore Thomas Macdonough* (Boston: The Fort Hill Press, 1909), 108; William S. Dudley, *The Naval War of 1812: A Documentary History* (Washington, D.C.: Department of the Navy, 1985), Volume 1, 319.

4. Everest, *War of 1812*, 64; Dudley, 1: 325; *The Battle of Plattsburgh: What Historians Say About It* (1914; New York State Commission Plattsburgh Centenary; reprint ed., Elizabethtown, N.Y.: Crown Point Press, Inc., 1968), 60; Dennis M. Lewis, *British Naval Activity on Lake Champlain during the War of 1812* (Plattsburgh: Clinton Historical Association, 1994), 2, 46; H. N. Muller III, "Commercial History," 159, 264.

5. Walter Hill Crockett, *A History of Lake Champlain 1609-1909* (Burlington, VT.: Hobart J. Shanley & Co., 1909), 293; H. N. Muller III, *Commercial History*, 159, 264; A. Peter Barranco, Jr., et. al., *Lake Champlain, Lake George, and the Upper Richelieu River Naval and Military Vessel Inventory 1742-1836* (Basin Harbor, VT.: Lake Champlain Maritime Museum, 1999), 187.

6. Dudley, 1: 371.

7. Everest, *War of 1812*, 92; See also Wallace E. Lamb, *The Lake Champlain and Lake George Valleys* (New York: The American Historical Company, Inc., 1940), Volume 1, 312-13 .

8. Dennis M. Lewis, "An Expedition Upon Lake Champlain: Murray's Raid, 1813," *Proceedings of the Champlain Valley Symposium*, ed. by Bruce P.

Stark (Plattsburgh, N.Y.: Clinton County Historical Association, 1982), 31; Macdonough, 116.

9. Macdonough, 116.

10. Charles G. Muller, *The Proudest Day* (New York:
The John Day Company, 1960), 343; For the Brit-
ish version see NAC, Record Group 8, Microfilm
C-3502, Volume 1170, fol. 226.

11. Macdonough, 120.

12. Glenn, *Story of Three Towns*, 340; Everest, *War of
1812*, 120; Crockett, *Lake Champlain*, 293.

13. Van De Water, 251; Bird, 268, 276.

14. NAC, Record Group 8, Microfilm C-3173, Volume 679, fol. 291.

15. Everest, *War of 1812*, 116.

16. Macdonough, 123; For information on
Burlington's role during the war see Karen Stites
Campbell, "Propaganda, Pestilence, and Prosperity:
Burlington's Camptown Days During the War of
1812," *Vermont History* 64 (Summer 1996); Cannonballs found at Battery Park in Burlington were
reportedly the "remnants" of the battle on August
2, 1813. *Burlington Free Press*, 350th Lake Champlain Festival Edition, 3 July 1959.

17. NAC, Record Group 8, Microfilm C-3173, Volume 679, fol. 341.

18. Macdonough, 126; Chapelle, *American Sailing
Navy*, 275-76; NRCNA, Record Group 45, Microcopy 147, Roll 5, Part 2, fol. 144b.

19. K. Jack Bauer, *The New American State Papers: Na-
val Affairs* (Wilmington, DE.: Scholarly Resources,
Inc., 1981), Volume 4, 385; Byron N. Clark, *A List
of Pensioners of the War of 1812* (Burlington, VT.:
Research Publication Company, 1904), 60;
Chapelle, *American Sailing Navy*, 298, 532-33, 545;
Theodore Roosevelt, *The Naval War of 1812* (New
York: G. P. Putnam's Sons, 1882), 377.

20. Everest, *War of 1812*, 135.

21. NRCNA, Record Group 45, Microcopy 149, Roll
11, fol.163; See also Chapelle, *American Sailing
Navy*, 274-76.

22. NRCNA, Record Group 45, Microcopy 149, Roll
11, fol. 223; See also Noah Brown, "The Remarkable Statement of Noah Brown," *The Journal of
American History* 8 (1914): 107. Brown's recollection of the size and armament of the vessels was erroneous, however.

23. Ibid.

24. A. Bowen, *The Naval Monument* (Boston: George
Clark, 1830), 152; *Niles' Weekly Register*, 1 October
1814; Clark, *Pensioners*, 60; Chapelle, *American Sailing Navy*, 298, 532-34, 541, 556; See also Norman
Ansley, *Vergennes, Vermont and the War of 1812*
(Severna Park, MD.: Brooke Keefer Ltd. Editions,
1999), 3, 42.

25. Kevin J. Crisman, *The Eagle* (Shelburne, VT.: The
New England Press, 1987), 19.

26. Kevin James Crisman, *The History and Construction of the United States Schooner Ticonderoga* (Alex-

andria, VA.: Eyrie Publications, 1983), 4; Macdonough, 144.

27. Crisman, *Ticonderoga*, 13.

28. NRCNA, Record Group 45, Microcopy 147, Roll
5, Part 2, fol. 115.

29. NAC, Record Group 8, Microfilm C-3174, Volume 683, fol. 160, Microfilm C-3526, Volume 1219,
fol. 89; See also Joyce Gold, *The Naval Chronicle*
(London: Joyce Gold, 1814), Volume 32, 157; Lewis, *British Naval Activity*, 46-47.

30. NRCNA, Record Group 45, Microcopy 147, Roll
5, Part 2, fol. 128a, 128b; Macdonough, 142.

31. Glenn, *Story of Three Towns*, 245; See also Palmer,
183.

32. Macdonough, 147; On August 14, Joseph Heatly
Dulles, a 19-year-old graduate of Yale College, described the *Saratoga* as "very low [in the water] for
her size and her appearance is deceptive; she is
much broader than she appears [36-foot beam], having fine quarters." Dulles also mentioned the six galleys and four gunboats of the American fleet: "the
large gallies have a long 24 pounder in the head and
a car[r]onade in the stern, has 60 men on board, is
sharp each end; the small ones have about 40 men
and one gun. They have a large 4 sided sail which is
placed in the middle of the boat." Joseph Heatly
Dulles, "Extracts from the Diary of Joseph Heatly
Dulles," *The Pennsylvania Magazine of History and
Biography* 35 (1911): 280.

33. Glenn, *Story of Three Towns*, 215; "Essex: An Architectural Guide," Essex Community Heritage Organization, pamphlet, 1986, 1; Alfred H. Trost and
Robert C. DeLong, eds., *A History Celebrating the
150th Anniversary of the Town of Essex, N.Y. 1805-
1955* (Malone, N.Y.: The Industrial Press, 1955),
p.n.a.

34. NRCNA, Record Group 45, Microcopy 147, Roll
5, Part 2, fol. 145a.

35. H. N. Muller III, "A 'Traitorous and Diabolical
Traffic': The Commerce of the Champlain–
Richelieu Corridor During the War of 1812," *Ver-
mont History* 44 (Spring 1976): 83.

36. Everest, *War of 1812*, 139, 151-52.

37. J. F. C. Fuller, *Decisive Battles of the U.S.A.* (New
York: Harper & Brothers Publishers, 1942), 117;
A. T. Mahan, *Sea Power in Its Relations to the War
of 1812* (Boston: Little, Brown, and Company,
1905), Volume 2, 364.

38. H. N. Muller III, *Commerical History*, 311.

39. Mahan, *Sea Power*, 363; See also Waldo H. Heinrichs, Jr., "The Battle of Plattsburgh, 1814–The Losers," *American Neptune* 21 (January 1961): 50.

40. Macdonough, 150; H. N. Muller III, "Diabolical
Traffic," 90; C. G. Muller, *Proudest Day*, 254-55; Everest, *War of 1812*, 152; Joel Abbot Papers, Microfilm, No. 25, fol. 173, Special Collections, Nimitz
Library, U.S. Naval Academy, Annapolis, MD.;
NRCNA, Record Group 45, Microcopy 147, Roll
5, Part 2, fol. 153.

41. B. Clark, *Pensioners*, 61; Bowen, 153; William James, *Naval Occurrences* (London: T. Egerton, 1817), 409; William Wood, *Select British Documents of the Canadian War of 1812* (Toronto: The Champlain Society, 1926), Volume 3, Part 1, 402, 406, 429-30, 433, 450, 459, 476; The *Tecumseh* was listed by Macdonough as a British galley that had participated in the battle; the number of gunboats was listed as 12 in NAC, Record Group 8, Microfilm C-3840, Volume 1709, fol. 116, Microfilm C-3526, Volume 1219, fol. 279; *The Weekly Messenger* (Boston), 7 October 1814; *Charleston Courier*, 4 October 1814; Lewis, *British Naval Activity*, 46-47.

42. *Niles' Weekly Register*, 1 October 1814; James, 420; Bauer, 385; Crisman, *Eagle*, 216; Lewis, *British Naval Activity*, 47.

43. J. Mackay Hitsman, *The Incredible War of 1812* (Toronto: University of Toronto Press, 1965), 217; William Wood, *Select British Documents of the Canadian War of 1812* (Toronto: The Champlain Society, 1920), Volume 1, 121.

44. Crisman, *Eagle*, 48.

45. NRCNA, Record Group 45, Microcopy 147, Roll 5, Part 3, fol. 12.

46. James MacGregor Burns, *The Vineyard of Liberty* (New York: Alfred A. Knopf, Inc., 1981), 213; Frank B. Latham, *Jacob Brown and the War of 1812* (New York: Cowles Book Company, Inc., 1971), 99.

47. Macdonough, 158.

48. Everest, *War of 1812*, 166.

49. Hitsman, 215.

50. NAC, Record Group 8, Microfilm C-3527, Volume 1222, fols. 194-95.

51. Leonard F. Guttridge and Jay D. Smith, *The Commodores* (New York: Harper & Row, Publishers, 1969), 257; J. F. C. Fuller, *Decisive Battles*, 117.

52. Everest, *War of 1812*, 158; Hitsman, 219.

53. Everest, *War of 1812*, 164.

54. B. Clark, *Pensioners*, 49, 53; Everest, *War of 1812*, 167; W. Wood, *Select British Documents*, 1: 117; Byron N. Clark, "Accounts of the Battle of Plattsburgh, 11 September, 1814," *The Vermont Antiquarian* 1 (March 1903): 79.

55. Everest, *War of 1812*, 178; C. G. Muller, *Proudest Day*, 347.

56. Macdonough, 162; Everest, *War of 1812*, 166.

57. Crisman, *Eagle*, 61.

58. W. Wood, *Select British Documents*, 3: 378, 461-62, 469; For information on the controversy regarding the change of command see Robert Malcomson, *Lords of the Lake: The Naval War on Lake Ontario 1812-1814* (Annapolis: Naval Institute Press, 1998), 303.

59. W. Wood, *Select British Document*, 3: 368.

60. Ibid., 380.

61. Ibid., 470.

62. Nell Jane Barnett Sullivan and David Kendall Martin, *A History of the Town of Chazy* (Burlington, VT.: George Little Press, Inc., 1970), 102.

63. W. Wood, *Select British Documents*, 1: 125, see also 3: 414, 441-42, 459, 463, 470.

64. Ibid., 3: 47; See also NAC, Record Group 8, Microfilm C-3526, Volume 1219, fol. 280.

65. B. Clark, *Pensioners*, 57; W. Wood, *Select British Documents*, 3: 369, 482, 495; NRCNA, Record Group 45, Microcopy 125, Roll 39, fol. 51; See also Joyce Gold, *The Naval Chronicle* (London: Joyce Gold, 1815), Volume 33, 255; Crisman, *Eagle*, 226.

66. W. Wood, *Select British Documents*, 3: 381, see also 396; Macdonough, 171.

67. John M. Stahl, *The Battle of Plattsburg; A Study in and of the War of 1812* (Illinois: The Van Trump Company, 1918), 117-18; Everest, *War of 1812*, 181.

68. Joseph Allen, *Battles of the British Navy; From A.D. 1000 to 1840* (London: A. H. Baily & Co., 1842), Volume 2, 481; Everest, *War of 1812*, 185.

69. *What Historians Say*, 38; Roosevelt, 390; Macdonough, 178; *Niles' Weekly Register*, 1 October 1814; "Biographical Sketch of Captain Thomas Macdonough," *Analectic Magazine and Naval Chronicle* 7 (March 1816): 224; Benson J. Lossing, *Pictorial Field-Book of the War of 1812* (New York: Harper & Brothers, Publishers, 1869), 867; Bowen, 159.

70. James, 410; C. G. Muller, *Proudest Day*, 349; W. Wood, *Select British Documents*, 3: 374.

71. W. Wood, *Select British Documents*, 3: 369, 407, 422-23, 426, 497.

72. Everest, *War of 1812*, 185.

73. C. H. J. Snider, *In the Wake of the Eighteen-Twelvers* (1913; reprint ed., London: Cornmarket Press Limited, 1969), 218-19; James Russell Soley, *The Boys of 1812* (Boston: Estes and Lauriat, 1887), 288; B. Clark, *Pensioners*, 48; Macdonough, 182.

74. J. Fenimore Cooper, *The History of the Navy of the United States of America* (Philadelphia: Lea & Blanchard, 1839), Volume 2, 444-45; Lossing, *War of 1812*, 872.

75. W. Wood, *Select British Documents*, 3: 402, 406, 429, 433.

76. Ibid., 406, 429-33, 462, 490-91; James, 409.

77. W. Wood, *Select British Documents*, 3: 483.

78. NRCNA, Record Group 45, Old Subject File NI, Report of Thomas Macdonough, May 6, 1815, fol. 3.

79. Ibid., 473.

80. Ibid., 483, see also 496.

81. NRCNA, Record Group 45, Microcopy 125, Roll 39, fol. 55; W. Wood, *Select British Documents*, 3: 384.

82. Crisman, *Eagle*, 74.

83. Nathaniel Coburn, "An Accurate & brief account of the War of 1812 with an account of Corp[l.] Nath[l.] Coburn, 2nd Regiment, U.S. Infantry, Feb-

ruary 1, 1816," MS, Rensselaer County Historical Society, Troy, N.Y.

84. Bowen, 157-58.

85. NRCNA, Record Group 45, Microcopy 125, Roll 39, fol. 51; Bowen, 148. Captain Daniel Pring's report noted that the movement of the *Eagle* "enabled us to direct our fire against the division of the enemy's gunboats and ship [*Saratoga*]." *Naval Chronicle*, 33:255.

86. NRCNA, Record Group 45, Old Subject File NI, Report of Thomas Macdonough, May 6, 1815, fol. 1.

87. W. Wood, *Select British Documents*, 3: 384, 422.

88. Ibid., 374.

89. Ibid., 375.

90. Ibid., 375, 474.

91. NRCNA, Record Group 45, Microcopy 125, Roll 39, fol. 51; Bowen, 148; James, 412.

92. W. Wood, *Select British Documents*, 3: 351; See note 41, the galley *Tecumseh* appears in American records; NAC, Record Group 8, Microfilm C-3840, Volume 1709, fol. 116, Microfilm C-3526, Volume 1219, fol. 279.

93. Bess H. Langworthy, *History of Cumberland Head* (Plattsburgh, N.Y.: pub., n.a., 1961), 23; Allan S. Everest, *Recollections of Clinton County and the Battle of Plattsburgh 1800-1840* (Plattsburgh, N.Y.: Clinton Historical Association, 1964), 26, 49.

94. *What Historians Say*, 39-40.

95. Crisman, *Eagle*, 79-80; Bowen, 149, 154; NRCNA, Record Group 45, Microcopy 125, Roll 39, fol. 51; After the battle, Benajah Phelps of South Hero Island remarked that the sides of the *Confiance* were "stuck solid full of [cannon]balls that looked just like some of the new fashioned houses, plastered on the outside." James A. Holden, ed., *The Centenary of the Battle of Plattsburgh* (Albany: The University of the State of New York, 1914), 30.

96. NRCNA, Record Group 45, Microcopy 125, Roll 39, fol. 51; Bowen, 149; W. Wood, *Select British Documents*, 3: 408, 413; See also James, 415; Macdonough, 168; Roosevelt, 379; James Fenimore Cooper (*History of the Navy of the United States*) maintained that "the Americans found a furnace on board the Confiance, with eight or ten heated shot in it." Cooper, 441.

97. Bowen, 152; Everest, *War of 1812*, 185; James, cixii; W. Wood, *Select British Documents*, 3: 479; Oscar Bredenberg, *The Battle of Plattsburgh Bay* (Plattsburgh, N.Y.: Clinton County Historical Association, 1978), 21.

98. *Plattsburgh Press Republican*, 11 September 1987 (diary extracts of William Miller).

99. NAC, Record Group 8, Microfilm C-3526, Volume 1219, fol. 280; Prevost's letter of September 16, 1814, reasoned that "the impracticability of carrying on any operations without a sufficient Naval cooperation has caused me to turn the whole of my attention to upper Canada." Microfilm C-3527, Volume 1222, fol. 195; See also W. Wood, *Select British*

Documents, 3: 352, 359; Fuller, 122; Everest, *War of 1812*, 186; B. Clark, *Pensioners*, 54-55.

100. W. Wood, *Select British Documents*, 3: 360.

101. Ibid., 400.

102. NRCNA, Record Group 45, Microcopy 125, Roll 40, fol. 105; See also *Plattsburgh Republican*, 3 December 1814.

103. Macdonough, 185; NRCNA, Record Group 45, Microcopy 125, Roll 39, fol. 38.

104. Macdonough, 185.

105. Ibid., 190; See also *Naval Chronicle*, 33:257.

106. W. Wood, *Select British Documents*, 3: 402, 458, see also 385-86, 440, 447, 486; *Naval Chronicle*, 33:254.

107. W. Wood, *Select British Documents*, 402, 459, see also 440, 491.

108. Mahan, 381; Winston S. Churchill also suggested that the Battle of Plattsburgh was "the most decisive engagement of the war." Winston S. Churchill, *Churchill's History of the English-Speaking Peoples*, ed. by Henry Steele Commager (New York: Dodd, Mead & Company, 1965), 319.

109. Roosevelt, 398-99.

110. NRCNA, Record Group 45, Microcopy 149, Roll 11, fol. 492.

111. Crisman, *Eagle*, 98-101.

112. John M. Duncan, *Travels Through Part of the United States and Canada in 1818 and 1819* (Glasgow: Hurst, Robinson, & Company, 1823), Volume 2, 233.

113. Silliman (2nd ed.), 192-93.

114. Crisman, *Eagle*, 106-7.

115. Silliman (2nd ed.), 192.

116. Crisman, *Eagle*, 107-10; The notice of the sale of the Lake Champlain squadron in 1825 apparently had wide distribution. See *The National Gazette and Literary Register* (Philadelphia), 11 June 1825.

117. *LCMM News*, Fall/Winter 1999-2000, 7; Morton, *Whitehall*, 8. The latter source suggested that a portion of the hull of the *Confiance* had swung out from the Poultney River during the high waters of 1869; Benson J. Lossing mentioned that he "saw the remains of this vessel [*Saratoga*] and the *Confiance* there [Whitehall] as late as 1850." Lossing, *War of 1812*, 873.

118. Silliman (2nd ed.), 208; See also Duncan, 2: 229; Theodore Dwight, Jr., *The Northern Traveller and Northern Tour with Routes to Springs, Niagara & Quebec*, 4th ed. (New York: J. & J. Harper, 1831), 192.

119. Hammersley, 24.

120. *The Whitehall Times*, 20 October 1949; Erika L. Washburn, "The Story of HMS *Linnet*, a Brig from the War of 1812," *Underwater Archaeology* (1996): 118. The principals involved in raising the vessels included Steve and Tony Galick and Fred Stevens. Sidney Hammersley later made some measurements and suggested that the combined

wreckage "was about 100 feet long." Hammersley, 24.

121. *The Whitehall Times*, 20 October 1949; *Ticonderoga Sentinel*, 13 October 1949. The second cannon was raised by Noah Raymond and his son, Frank Bessette, and Albert Yell.

122. *The Whitehall Times*, 20 October 1949.

123. Hamilton, "An Historic Mortar," 299-303.

124. Washburn, 119-20.

125. Steve and John Galick directed the salvage operation; Fred Stevens and Dar Lamphere worked on the recovery; and Frank Martucci of the Bicentennial Committee had overall charge of the project. *The Whitehall Times*, 12 March 1959.

126. Crisman, *Ticonderoga*, 36-38.

127. Ibid., 39-58.

128.. Morton, *Whitehall*, 9; Crisman, *Eagle*, 128; interviews with local residents.

129. *Ticonderoga Sentinel*, 3 October 1957; "3 Colonial Ships Found in Lake Champlain," newspaper, p.n.a.

130. Craig Lonergan, interview by author, 30 August 2000.

131. Russ Bellico, "The Battle of Plattsburgh," *Adirondack Life*, September/October 1977, 48.

132. Crisman, *Eagle*, 118, 151, 235-43; Bass, *Ships and Shipwrecks*, 185-86; Arthur B. Cohn, ed., *A Report on the Nautical Archeology of Lake Champlain: Results of the 1982 Field Season of the Champlain Maritime Society* (Burlington, VT.: The Champlain Maritime Society, 1984), 47-71; R. Montgomery Fischer, ed., *A Report of the Nautical Archeology of Lake Champlain: Results of the 1983 Field Season of the Champlain Maritime Society* (Burlington, VT.: The Champlain Maritime Society, 1985), 13-19.

133. Eric B. Emery, " 'Gallies are Unquestionably the Best Description of Vessels for the Northern Parts of this Lake': The Excavation and Study of the U.S.N. Row Galley *Allen* on Lake Champlain," *Underwater Archaeology* (1996): 134-39.

134. *Press-Republican*, 31 August 1996; *Burlington Free Press*, 23 September 1998; *LCMM News*, Spring/Summer 1997, 5; *LCMM News*, Fall/Winter 1998, 5; For the methods used to conserve the anchor see *LCMM News*, Spring/Summer 2000, 4.

135. *Press-Republican*, 18 August 1981.

136. *The Saratogian*, 22 August 1999; *LCMM News*, Spring/Summer 2000, 5.

10. Champlain Canal Boats

1. Fred Copeland, "Champlain Canal Days," *The Vermonter*, August 1941, 157.

2. Everest, *Journal of Carroll*, 24.

3. See Ronald E. Shaw, *Erie Water West* (Lexington, KY.: University of Kentucky Press, 1966), 12-16; Alvin F. Harlow, *Old Towpaths* (New York: D. Appleton and Company, 1926), 29-32; *A Canalboat*

Primer on the Canals of New York State (Syracuse, N.Y.: The Canal Museum, 1981), 5; Henry Wayland Hill, *An Historical Review of Waterways and Canal Construction in New York State* (Buffalo: Buffalo Historical Society, 1908), 58-64.

4. Jonathan Hughes, *American Economic History* (Glenview, IL.: Scott, Foresman and Company, 1983), 175.

5. Gertrude E. Cone, "Studies in the Development of Transportation in the Champlain Valley to 1876," (M.A. thesis, The University of Vermont, 1945), 74.

6. G. W., "A Sketch of the Great Northern or Champlain Canal," 1823, Special Collections, NYSL, 7.

7. Noble E. Whitford, *History of the Canal System of the State of New York* (Albany, Brandow Printing Company, 1906), Volume 1, 412, 414-15. The bottom width, however, may have been 26 feet rather than 28. Whitford, 2: 1031, 1466.

8. *Albany Argus*, 30 November 1819.

9. Ibid.

10. Horatio Gates Spafford, *A Gazetteer of the State of New York* (Albany: B.D. Packard and Horatio Gates Spafford, 1824), 97.

11. Arthur Cohn and Marshall True, "The Wreck of the *General Butler* and the Mystery of Lake Champlain's Sailing Canal Boats," *Vermont History* 60 (Winter 1992): 35; See also W. S. Rann, *History of Chittenden Country* (Syracuse: D. Mason & Co., Pub., 1886), 312.

12. Theodore Dwight, Jr., *The Northern Traveller and Northern Tour with Routes to Springs, Niagara & Quebec*, 4th ed. (New York: J. & J. Harper, 1831), 185.

13. Cohn and True, 37.

14. John L. Sullivan, *Commentary on the New System of Naval Architecture of William Annesley* (Troy, N. Y.: William S. Parker, 1823), Appendix, 1; Cohn and True, 37.

15. Sullivan, Appendix, 1.

16. Cohn and True, 33.

17. Champlain Transportation Company Papers, A Collection, "Lake Champlain--Sloop List 1822-1890," carton 10, folder 9, Special Collections, Bailey-Howe Library, University of Vermont, Burlington, VT.; Rann, 314.

18. CTC Papers, "Sloop List."

19. Ulysses Prentiss Hendrick, *A History of Agriculture in the State of New York* (Albany: New York State Agricultural Society, 1933), 246; See also F. Daniel Larkin, *New York Canals: A Short History* (Fleischmanns, N. Y.: Purple Mountain Press, 1998), 48.

20. Harlow, 146.

21. Howard S. Russell, *A Long, Deep Furrow: Three Centuries of Farming in New England* (Hanover, N. H.: University Press of New England, 1976), 327.

22. John E. O'Hara, "Erie's Junior Partner," (Ph.D. diss. Columbia University, 1951), 131-32.

23. P. André Sévigny, *Trade and Navigation on the Chambly Canal: A Historical Review* (Ottawa: National Historic Parks and Sites Branch, Parks Canada, 1983), 40, 66.

24. Arthur B. Cohn, et al., *The Archaeological Reconstruction of the Lake Champlain Canal Schooner General Butler* (Ferrisburg, VT.: Lake Champlain Maritime Museum, 1996), 26; CTC Papers, "Sloop List."

25. CTC Papers, "Sloop List."

26. Cohn and True, 39.

27. CTC Papers, "Sloop List."; Glenn, *Story of Three Towns*, 342-43; Morris F. Glenn, *Lake Champlain Album* (Alexandria, VA.: Morris F. Glenn, 1979), Volume 2, 29.

28. CTC Papers, "Sloop List."; Rann, 314.

29. Harlow, 352.

30. Ibid.; See also Lamb, *Lake Champlain and Lake George*, 2: 578.

31. O'Hara, 186.

32. Ibid., 175; H. Hill, *Waterways and Canal Construction*, 145.

33. O'Hara, 175.

34. Ibid., 176.

35. Whitford, 1: 427; See also Thomas X. Grasso, *Champlain Canal* (Syracuse, N.Y.: The Canal Society of New York State, 1985), 4. The first enlargement of locks on the Champlain Canal was not completely finished until 1858; by then the second enlargement of locks had begun.

36. Whitford, 1: 428, 982.

37. Ibid., 430; H. Hill, *Waterways and Canal Construction*, 156.

38. Whitford, 2: 959, 964, 432.

39. Andrew G. Meiklejohn, "The Champlain Canal—Remarks of Hon. Andrew G. Meiklejohn," 5 April 1864, Special Collections, NYSL, 2-3; See also Grasso, 4.

40. H. Hill, *Waterways and Canal Construction*, 157; Whitford, 1: 432-33.

41. Whitford, 1: 983; In 1870 the New York legislature authorized a further enlargement of the Champlain Canal prism to 58' x 44' x 7', but the work was never completed. Whitford, 2: 1056, 1031.

42. Ibid., 984; Grasso, 4.

43. CTC Papers, "Sloop List." The 86-foot canal schooner *Itasca* was built at Essex, New York, in 1861.

44. Ibid.; Rann, 314; Glenn, *The Story of Three Towns*, 342-343. Some additional Essex-built vessels, completed between 1861 and 1870, may also have been sailing canal boats: *G.W. Palmer, J.G. Randall,* and *John Hoskins.* The 93-foot *Dreadnought,* built at Ticonderoga in 1877, was listed as a schooner-rigged canal boat. CTC Papers, "Sloop List." The 91-foot canal schooner *Gleaner* was built in 1883 at Champlain, N.Y., as was the 88-foot canal sloop *H. H. Adams* two years later. Certificate of Enrollment, No. 4, 1897 and No. 1, 1898, Bureau of Marine Inspection and Navigation, Record Group 41, National Archives, Washington, D.C.

45. R. S. Styles, *A Descriptive and Historical Guide to the Valley of Lake Champlain and the Adirondacks* (Burlington, VT.: R. S. Styles' Steam Printing House, 1871), 29.

46. See Richard Garrity, *Canal Boatman* (Syracuse, N.Y.: Syracuse University Press, 1977), 50; and Capt. Frank H. Godfrey, *The Godfrey Letters,* (Syracuse, N.Y.: The Canal Society of New York State, 1973), 29-30, for details on canal boat operations.

47. *Canal Regulations, Rates of Tolls, and Distances on the New-York State Canals* (Albany: E. Croswell, Printer to the State, 1830), 9; Capt. Frank H. Godfrey, *The Godfrey Letters,* 19.

48. Ethel M. Springer and Thomas F. Hahn, *Canal Boat Children* (Shepherdstown, W. VA.: The American Canal & Transportation Center, 1981), 34; See also Fred G. Godfrey, *The Champlain Canal: Mules to Tugboats* (Monroe, N.Y.: LRA, Inc., 1994), 84, 87.

49. Martha Robbins Juckett, *My Canaling Days,* ed. by Dorothy M. Parker (reprint, Whitehall, N.Y.: Historical Society of Whitehall, 1972), 10.

50. Juckett, 8.

51. *LCMM News,* Spring/Summer 2000, 7.

52. Ibid.

53. For stories of children who fell from canal boats see Howard Pyle, "Through Inland Waters," *Harpers New Monthly Magazine,* May 1896, 837; Bellico, *Chronicles of Lake Champlain,* 394.

54. Springer and Hahn, 8; See also James Lee, ed., *Tales the Boatmen Told* (Exton, PA.: Canal Press Incorporated, 1977), 101.

55. Springer and Hahn, 9.

56. O'Hara, 142; Cone, 82-84.

57. O'Hara, 144-49.

58. Ibid., 219.

59. Flavius J. Cook, *Home Sketches of Essex County: Ticonderoga* (Keeseville, N.Y.: W. Lansing & Son, 1858), 71.

60. Glenn, *The Story of Three Towns,* 342-43; Gertrude E. Cone, "Early Sailing Craft on Lake Champlain," *North Country Life,* Winter 1950, 42.

61. Glenn, *The Story of Three Towns,* 348-49.

62. Meiklejohn, 4.

63. Godfrey, *Godfrey Letters,* 27.

64. Ibid., 28.

65. H. Hill, *Waterways and Canal Construction,* 178; Harlow, 156. The Hoskins and Ross shipyard at Essex completed its last sailing canal boat in 1878. Cohn, *The Archaeological Reconstruction General Butler,* 27. Perhaps one of the last canal schooners to sail Lake Champlain was observed by eight-year-old John Williams in 1916 from the Plattsburgh Dock and Coal Company wharf. *LCMM News,* Fall/Winter 1993-1994, 4.

66. Michele A. McFee, *A Long Haul: The Story of the New York State Barge Canal* (Fleischmanns, N.Y.: Purple Mountain Press, 1998), 40-41.

67. Francis P. Kimball, *New York--The Canal State* (Albany: The Argus Press, 1937), 36-37; See also Charles T. O'Malley, *Low Bridges and High Water on the New York State Barge Canal* (Utica, N.Y.: North Country Books, 1991), 12-13; McFee, 42.

68. McFee, 45-51; See also O'Malley, 14-15.

69. Frank M. Williams, *The Story of the New York State Canals* (Albany: J. B. Lyon Company, Printers, 1916), 7.

70. Patrick F. Farrell, *Through the Light Hole: A Saga of Adirondack Mines and Men* (Utica, N.Y.: North Country Books, 1996), 97-98; Godfrey, *Godfrey Letters*, 27.

71. McFee, 181-82; See also *The Erie Canalway: A Special Resource Study of the New York State Canal System* (Boston: National Park Service, 1998), 76.

72. *Post-Star*, 8 August 2000; See also *Post-Star*, 16 August 1997.

73. *Boston Globe*, 17 November 1978; *New York Times*, 19 November 1978; *Burlington Free Press* 20 November 1978.

74. See Cohn, *1982 Field Season*, 31-39; and Fischer, 27-35, for more details.

75. Early documents listed the *General Butler* as 86 feet long. CTC Papers, "Sloop List."; Certificate of Enrollment, No. 7, 1862, Bureau of Marine Inspection and Navigation, Record Group 41, National Archives.

76. Fischer, 21-24; Russell Bellico, "The General Butler," *Skin Diver*, September 1985, 100, 104-8.

77. Cohn, *Archaeological Reconstruction General Butler*, 97.

78. Ibid., 139-245; Cohn and True, 29-31.

79. Arthur B. Cohn et al., *Underwater Preserve Feasibility Study of the Lake Champlain Canal Schooner O. J. Walker* (Ferrisburg, VT.: Lake Champlain Maritime Museum, 1996), 31-32; CTC Papers, "Sloop List."; Certificate of Enrollment, No. 5, 1862, Bureau of Marine Inspection and Navigation, Record Group 41, National Archives. The certificates 74(1881), 30(1883), 4(1892), and 7(1893) listed the *O. J. Walker's* length as 85 1/2 feet.

80. Cohn, *Underwater Preserve O. J. Walker*, 44.

81. *Burlington Free Press and Times*, 13 May 1895.

82. Cohn, *Underwater Preserve O. J. Walker*, 44.

83. Ibid., 43.

84. Ibid., 49-50, 121-36.

85. J. Cozzi, "The Lake Champlain Sailing Canal Boat," *Underwater Archaeology* (1996): 130.

86. *Burlington Free Press and Times*, 18 November 1897; Certificate of Enrollment, No. 26, 1894, Bureau of Marine Inspection and Navigation, Record Group 41, National Archives; See also Morris F. Glenn, *Glenn's History of Lake Champlain: Occasional Lists of Shipping on Lake Champlain* (Alexandria, VA.: Morris F. Glenn, 1980), Volume 2, 18;

Cohn, *Archaeological Reconstruction General Butler*, 40.

87. The annual side-scan sonar surveys included project director Arthur B. Cohn with historian and navigator A. Peter Barranco, Jr., boat captain and engineer Fred Fayette, and sonar operators/geologists Patricia and Thomas Manley.

88. Arthur B. Cohn, et al., *Lake Champlain Underwater Cultural Resources Survey--Volume 3: 1998 Results* (Vergennes, VT.: Lake Champlain Maritime Museum, 2000), 85-89.

89. Caroline Halstead Royce, *Bessboro: A History of Westport, Essex Co., N.Y.* (Elizabethtown, N.Y.: C. H. Royce, 1904), 344; "The Schooner *Troy* Discovered: A Tragic Lake Mystery Solved!" Lake Champlain Maritime Museum Press Release, 7 August 2000.

90. Royce, 344.

91. "The Schooner *Troy* Discovered."

92. Ibid.

93. Cohn, *Cultural Resources Survey*, 20-24, 67-69, 70-75, 80-85, 112, 127, 129-30; *LCMM News*, Fall/Winter 1997-1998, 5; *LCMM News*, Fall/Winter 1998-1999, 6, 7; *LCMM News*, Fall/Winter 1999-2000,1; *LCMM News*, Spring/Summer 2000, 3.

94. Cohn, *Cultural Resources Survey*, 24-25.

95. Ibid., 136; See also *LCMM News*, Fall/Winter 1998, 6, 7.

96. "Lake Champlain Maritime Museum and Lake Champlain Transportation Company Announce a New Project: To Build a Full-Size Replica of a 19th Century Sailing Canal Schooner on the Burlington Waterfront," Lake Champlain Maritime Museum Press Release, 20 September 2000.

11. Steamboats of Lake Champlain

1. Thomas H. Canfield, "Discovery, Navigation, and Navigators of Lake Champlain," in Abby Maria Hemenway, ed., *The Vermont Historical Gazetteer* (Burlington, VT.: A. M. Hemenway, 1867), Volume 1, 688; Glenn, *Occasional Lists*, 2: 8; Rann, 39.

2. For details on early steamboat history see James Thomas Flexner, *Steamboats Come True* (New York: The Viking Press, 1944), 16, 68-69; Thompson Westcott, *Life of John Fitch* (Philadephia: J. B. Lippincott & Co., 1857), 177-78, 180, 184-85, 198; Ralph Nading Hill, *Sidewheeler Saga* (New York: Rinehart & Company, Inc., 1953), 3-45; Arthur G. Adams, *The Hudson Through the Years* (New York: Fordham University Press, 1996), 41-48.

3. Canfield, 670; Palmer, 164; Rann, 311; Crockett, *Lake Champlain*, 291, 293; H. N. Muller III, *Commercial History*, 159; Glenn, *Story of Three Towns*, 340; Morris F. Glenn, *The Capture and Burning of the Sloop Essex* (Alexandria, VA.: Morris F. Glenn, 1981), 1. The original table has been adjusted to reflect additional information. Some of the vessels listed on the table apparently had new owners

(Guy and Moses Catlin, Deering Speers, Ephraim Lake etc.) in subsequent years, according to customs records. Frederick M. Hocker, "The Development of the Sailing Carrying Trade on Lake Champlain 1742-1823" (master's thesis, Middlebury College, 1984), 47-51.

4. David J. Blow, "*Vermont I*: Lake Champlain's First Steamboat," *Vermont History* 34 (April 1966), 117-18. Joseph Lough, along with John and James Winans, organized the company that financed the *Vermont*. Blow, 117; See also Crockett, *Lake Champlain*, 294; Ogden J. Ross, *The Steamboats of Lake Champlain 1809 to 1930* (Albany: Press of the Delaware and Hudson Railroad, 1930), 24.

5. Hill, *Sidewheeler Saga*, 47.

6. "Grant from Robert R. Livingston and Robert Fulton, September 15, 1812, of exclusive right of Navigation of Lake Champlain," Champlain Transportation Company Papers, A Collection, carton 1, folder 1, Special Collections, Bailey-Howe Library, University of Vermont, Burlington, VT.

7. Rebecca Davison, ed., *Phoenix Project* (Burlington, VT.: Champlain Maritime Society, 1981), 7.

8. Canfield, 690.

9. "Burning of the Steamboat *Phoenix*," CTC Papers, B Collection, carton 3, folder 65.

10. Fred Erving Dayton, *Steamboat Days* (New York: Frederick A. Stokes Company, 1925), 91, 93. Richard W. Sherman was the grandfather of James S. Sherman, who served as vice-president of the United States from 1909-1912.

11. "Burning of the Steamboat *Phoenix*," CTC Papers.

12. Ronald A. Anderson, *Government and Business*, 4th ed. (Cincinnati: South-Western Publishing Co., 1981), 124.

13. Silliman (2nd ed.), 191.

14. Bellico, *Chronicles of Lake Champlain*, 329-47.

15. Dayton, 92; Ross, *Steamboats of Lake Champlain*, 35.

16. Basil Hall, *Travels in North America* (1829; reprint ed., Akademische Druck, 1964), Volume 2, 5; See also Allen Penfield Beach, *Lake Champlain As Centuries Pass* (1959; reprint ed., Basin Harbor: Basin Harbor Club and the Lake Champlain Maritime Museum, 1994), 85.

17. Una Pope-Hennessy, ed., *The Aristocratic Journey* (New York: G. P. Putnam's Sons, 1931), 59.

18. Kevin J. Crisman and Arthur B. Cohn, *When Horses Walked on Water: Horse-Powered Ferries in Nineteenth-Century America* (Washington, D. C.: Smithsonian Institution Press, 1998), 70-73.

19. Silliman (2nd ed.), 68; See also Bellico, *Chronicles of Lake George*, 231; Crisman and Cohn, *Horse-Powered Ferries*, 73-74.

20. Crisman and Cohn, *Horse-Powered Ferries*, 115-126; See also Z. Thompson, *Guide to Lake George, Lake Champlain, Montreal and Quebec* (Burlington: Chauncey Goodrich, 1845), 22.

21. Ross, *Steamboats of Lake Champlain*, 50.

22. On November 22, 1831, the CTC signed a contract for $4,250 with Jahaziel Sherman to haul out the steamer *Franklin* "to put on a false bow to be twenty five feet in length," adding decking and finishing the interior of the bow with "plain berths." "Agreement between the Champ. Transp. Co. & J. Sherman for new Bow to Steam Boat Franklin," 22 November 1831, CTC Papers, A Collection, carton 1, folder 162.

23. Ell B. Rockwell, "Various Recollections," Captain E. Rockwell Papers, Special Collections, Bailey-Howe Library, University of Vermont, Burlington, VT.

24. Crisman and Cohn, *Horse-Powered Ferries*, 122; Canfield, 707.

25. Royce, 417.

26. "Articles of Agreement between the Champ. Transp. Co. [and] Van Ness & Follett," 30 March 1829, CTC Papers, A Collection, carton 1, folder 92; Newspaper article, CTC Papers, A Collection, carton 8, folder 24.

27. "Articles of Agreement," 30 March 1829.

28. "Minutes of Directors' Meetings," (extract) 9 March 1829, CTC Papers, B Collection, carton 3, folder 60.

29. "Articles of Agreement Between Ch. Transp. Company & Isaiah Townsend," 29 January 1831, CTC Papers, A Collection, carton 1, folder 157, see also folder 159; See also Gideon Lathrop, "The Diary of Gideon Lathrop," 25, Special Collections, Bailey-Howe Library, University of Vermont.

30. "Isaiah Townsend to The Ch. Tr. Company - - Conveyance of Boats & c." 22 February 1833, CTC Papers, A Collection, carton 1, folder 178, see also folder 179.

31. Although early sources listed the *Water Witch* with a length of 90 feet, the vessel today measures 83 feet "from the stern rabbet to the after edge of the taffrail [and] 80 ft. on the deck." Elizabeth Robinson Baldwin, "The Steamboat Wrecks of Lake Champlain," *Underwater Archaeology* (1996): 123.

32. "Agreement between Jah. Sherman & Ch. Transp. Co., 21 Nov. 1833," CTC Papers, A Collection, carton 1, folder 188.

33. "Report of Committee," 27 January 1835, CTC Papers, A Collection, carton 1, folder 242; "Mem. of the new organization of the consolidation stock of the Champ. Transp. Co.," CTC Papers, A Collection, carton 1, folder 241.

34. Rockwell Papers, "Various Recollections."

35. *The Daily Free Press*, 27 April 1866. The *Trader* was listed as an 86-foot canal schooner. CTC Papers, "Sloop List."

36. *Burlington Free Press*, 4 June 1906.

37. Charles Dickens, *American Notes* (1892; reprint ed., New York: St. Martin's Press, 1985), 194.

38. Ross, *Steamboats of Lake Champlain*, 61; See also Canfield, 696.

39. Ross, *Steamboats of Lake Champlain*, 63.

40. State of New-York. No. 64. In Assembly, 22 January 1841, 1, author collection.

41. *Plattsburgh Republican*, 6 August 1841; See also *A Century of Progress: History of the Delaware and Hudson Company 1823-1923* (Albany, N.Y.: J. B. Lyon Company, 1925), 710.

42. See the *Plattsburgh Republican*, 5 September 1846, for the Champlain Transportation Company's explanation of the unsuccessful agreement.

43. Crisman and Cohn, *Horse-Powered Ferries*, 120; Rann, 324; Ell B. Rockwell suggested that the vessel was originally designed as a horse boat powered by six horses, with three "on a side," and converted into a steamboat. Rockwell Papers, "Various Recollections."

44. For a list of steamers which includes dimensions and final dispositions see Canfield, 707; Rockwell Papers, "Various Recollections"; F. H. Wilkins, "Lake Champlain Steamers," *The Vermonter* 21 (January 1916): 14-15.

45. Cone, "Studies," 60.

46. Touring Lake Champlain, S. H. Hammond described the steamboat *America* as "a staunch and beautiful boat...furnished with great elegance and care" and questioned why travelers had neglected to praise Lake Champlain, which "is one of the most beautiful sheets of water in the world." S. H. Hammond and L. W. Mansfield, *Country Margins and Rambles of a Journalist* (New York: J. C. Derby, 1855), 287-88.

47. "Minutes of Directors' Meetings," (extract) 1856, CTC Papers, B Collection, carton 3, folder 60.

48. Ibid., 1868.

49. The length of the *Oakes Ames* has been listed as 258 feet. Wilkins, 14; D. A. Loomis, CTC Papers, B Collection, carton 3, folder 60; Rann, 324. However, the registration papers for Burlington indicate that the *Oakes Ames* had a length of 244 feet. Elizabeth R. Baldwin, et al., *Underwater Historic Preserve Feasibility Study of the Lake Champlain Steamboat Champlain II Westport, Essex County, New York* (Ferrisburg, VT: Lake Champlain Maritime Museum, 1996), 58; Another source suggested that the *Champlain II* was 250 feet in length. D. A. Loomis, "Steamers Which Have Been Engaged in Regular Traffic on Lake Champlain During 124 Years," *The Vermonter*, February 1933, 32.

50. Ross, *Steamboats of Lake Champlain*, 125.

51. Rockwell Papers, "The Story of the Wreck," 2; *Plattsburgh Sentinel*, 23 July 1875; Royce, 576.

52. Rockwell Papers, "The Story of the Wreck," 2; R. N. Hill, *Sidewheeler Saga*, 266; Lynn H. Bottum, "*Oakes Ames/Champlain*: The Biography of a Lake Champlain Steamboat," *Vermont History* 51 (Summer 1983): 133.

53. John Eldredge, "Statement of John Eldredge, Pilot--Testimony concerning wreck of steamer *Champlain* July 1875," CTC Papers, A Collection, carton 8, folder 21; Eldredge suggested that he was alone in the pilot house. Apparently, wheelman Edwin Rockwell should have been present since regu-

lations required two employees in the pilot house while underway.

54. George Rushlow, "Statement of George Rushlow, Captain--Testimony concerning wreck of steamer *Champlain* July 1875," CTC Papers, A Collection, carton 8, folder 21, 1-4.

55. Ell B. Rockwell, "Statement of E. B. Rockwell, Pilot--Testimony concerning wreck of steamer Champlain 1875," CTC Papers, A Collection, carton 8, folder 21, 4.

56. Abijah North, "Statement of Abijah North, Clerk--Testimony concerning wreck of steamer *Champlain* 1875," CTC Papers, A Collection, carton 8, folder 21, 7.

57. *Plattsburgh Sentinel*, 23 July 1875; See also "Statement of E. B. Rockwell," 2.

58. *Plattsburgh Sentinel*, 23 July 1875.

59. There was also a tug *J. G. Witherbee* in use during the late nineteenth century. Morris F. Glenn, *Glenn's History of Lake Champlain: Steam Navigation* (Alexandria, Va.: Morris F. Glenn, 1980), Volume 3, Section K, F-1.

60. Alex Markee, "Statement of Alex Markee, Pilot--Testimony concerning wreck of steamer *Champlain* July 1875," CTC Papers, A Collection, carton 8, folder 21, 1.

61. *Plattsburgh Sentinel*, 23 July 1875; Eldredge later suggested that he "was so much overcome by the accident that I rendered no assistance after the occurrence--but went ashore." "Statement of John Eldredge," 2. It would take Eldredge nearly three days after the crash of the *Champlain II* to reach his home at Colchester, Vermont.

62. "Statement of Abijah North," 14-16; Bottum, 154.

63. Rockwell Papers, "The Wreck of the 'Champlain' in 1875," 4.

64. Rockwell Papers, "The Story of the Wreck," 4.

65. Rockwell Papers, "The Wreck of the 'Champlain' in 1875," 3.

66. E. Baldwin, *Preserve Feasibility Champlain II*, 43.

67. *Plattsburgh Sentinel*, 23 July 1875.

68. The steamer *A. Williams* was "hauled out and lengthened about 12 feet" in 1878. "Minutes of Directors' Meetings," (extract) 1878, CTC Papers, B Collection, carton 3, folder 60. The length of the *A. Williams* has been listed as 132 feet. Wilkins, 15; Ross, *Steamboats of Lake Champlain*, 135; D. A. Loomis, "Steamers" (*Vermonter*), 32. However, several sources have different lengths for the steamer, ranging from 125 feet to 130 feet. Crockett, *Lake Champlain*, 310; CTC Papers, "Sloop List"; Rann, 324.

69. Ell B. Rockwell noted that the *Maquam* "operated to and including 1905. Hull cut up at Shelburne Harbor during the summer of 1906." Rockwell Papers, "Various Recollections." The *Maquam* and *Vermont II* were hauled out "and cut...into firewood because there wasn't room enough without obstructing the channel to put on the bottom another wreck [at Shelburne Harbor]." CTC Papers,

B Collection, carton 8, folder 31; See also *Ticon-deroga Sentinel*, 6 September 1906.

70. CTC Papers, "Sloop List"; Wilkins, 14. Other source suggest that the *Reindeer* had a length of 180 feet or 181 feet. Rann, 324; Crockett, *Lake Champlain*, 312.

71. R. N. Hill, *Sidewheeler Saga*, 268.

72. Ibid.

73. "Record of Steamer Service from 1809 to 1929," CTC Papers, B Collection, carton 3, folder 60; D. A. Loomis, 30 January 1933, CTC Papers, B Collection, carton 3, folder 60; CTC Papers, Daniel A. Loomis Diary, July 10-12, 1925.

74. Richard M. Strum, *Ticonderoga: Lake Champlain Steamboat* (Shelburne, VT.: Shelburne Museum, 1998), 65, 97.

75. CTC Papers, B Collection, carton 8, folder 73.

76. Ralph Nading Hill, "Two Centuries of Ferry Boating on Lake Champlain," in *Lake Champlain Ferryboats*, ed. by Jerry P. Williams (Burlington: Lake Champlain Transportation Company, 1990), 19-20; Arthur B. Cohn, afterward to *The Steamboats of Lake Champlain 1809 to 1930*, by Ogden Ross (1930; reprint ed., Quechee, VT.: Vermont Heritage Press, 1997), 186-87; Glenn, *Steam Navigation*, section G.

77. Strum, 66-67; CTC Papers, B Collection, carton 6, folder 164; carton 7, folder 35, 115; For information regarding the CTC operation during the late 1930s see Cohn, afterward to *Steamboats of Lake Champlain*, 188-90; R. Hill, "Ferry Boating," 23; "Champlain Transportation Co., Including All Three Steamers, Is Sold to Horace W. Corbin," newspaper clipping 1937, CTC Papers.

78. Jerry Aske, Jr., and Gardiner Lake, *History of the Shelburne Shipyard and Its Shipbuilding Activities During World War II and the Korean Conflict* (Essex Junction, VT.: Chittenden County Regional Planning Commission, 1992), 17, 21, 23-24. Three of the sub-chasers sank during a typhoon enroute to the U.S.S.R. under a lend-lease program.

79. Ibid., 24-25, 31-32; See also Ralph N. Hill, "Shelburne Shipyard," *Vermont Life*, Autumn 1953, 8-13, 60.

80. Cohn, afterward to *Steamboats of Lake Champlain*, 194-201; R. Hill, "Ferry Boating," 24-32, 35.

81. R. Hill, "Ferry Boating," 18-35; Gordon C. and Elsie L. Sherman, *An Illuminating History of the Champlain Valley and Adirondack Mountains, 1814-1929* (Elizabethtown, N. Y.: Denton Publications, Inc., 1977), Volume 2, 42-45, 64-80.

82. For more information on the *Juniper* see Russ Bellico, "The Cruise of the *Juniper*," *Adirondack Life*, May/June 1978, 38-40.

83. Lynn Watt, "Is Champlain Doomed?" *Vermont Life*, Spring 1969, 46-50; See also Lori Fisher, "The Battle of Burlington: Sewage Hits the Beaches," *Lake Champlain Committee Newsletter*, Summer/Fall 1987, 2.

84. Lake Placid News, 28 May 1954; Barney Fowler, *Adirondack Album* (Schenectady, N. Y.: Outdoor Associates, 1974),Volume 1, 31; In June 1937 Daniel A. Loomis, former general manager of the Champlain Transportation Company (After April 1, 1937, he managed the Delaware and Hudson Company's Lake George Steamboat Company.), began making a series of inquiries to Canadian authorities regarding the location of the wreck of the *Vermont* in the Richelieu River. CTC Papers, B Collection, carton 7, folders 20, 22.

85. Davison, 15; Jack Chase, "Phoenix--Silent Mistress of Lake Champlain," *Adirondac*, July 1982, 6; Other divers also explored the *Phoenix* during this time period. *Champlain Maritime Society Soundings*, Spring/Summer 1985, 6; Derek R. Grout, "The *Phoenix* Lives!," *Skin Diver*, August 1981, 70, 84-85, 92-93.

86. Fischer, 47-53; *Champlain Maritime Society Soundings*, Fall/Winter 1984, 3, 10. A 12-foot anchor raised four decades ago at Colchester Reef and displayed at the Shelburne Museum was "believed to be from the...*Phoenix*." Hanson Carroll, "Skin Diving," *Vermont Life*, Summer 1960, 44.

87. Kevin Crisman, *Of Sailing Ships and Sidewheelers* (Montpelier: Division of Historic Preservation, 1986), 30.

88. *Burlington Free Press*, 2 August 1984.

89. Donald G. Shomette, "Heyday of the Horse Ferry," *National Geographic*, October 1989, 548-56. The National Geographic Society donated $5,000 to the VDHP to help protect the wreck of the Burlington Bay horse ferry.

90. Crisman and Cohn, *Horse-Powered Ferries*, 173, 160-75; See also Kevin J. Crisman and Arthur B. Cohn, *The Burlington Bay Horse Ferry Wreck and the Era of Horse-powered Watercraft* (Basin Harbor, VT.: Lake Champlain Maritime Museum, 1993), 69-70, 101-2. A limited number of artifacts were recovered from the vessel, including broken horseshoes, fragments of horse collars, harness fragments, buckles, gears, caulking irons, spikes, and ring bolts. Crisman and Cohn, *Horse-Powered Ferries*, 167, 170, 173-74; Crisman and Cohn, *Burlington Bay Horse Ferry Wreck*, 83, 91-93, 150-219.

91. Crisman and Cohn, *Burlington Bay Horse Ferry Wreck*, 134. The dimensions of the Burlington Bay horse boat are similar to those reported in letters by the Langdons, which are held in the New York State Archives (Isaiah Townsend Papers). Kevin Crisman, letter to author, 22 August 2000.

92. *LCMM News*, Spring/Summer 1994, 7; Elizabeth Robinson Baldwin, "The Steamboat Wrecks of Lake Champlain," *Underwater Archaeology* (1996): 123.

93. Fischer, 56-61, for measurements of the sunken steamers; Jack S. Chase, "The Steamboat Graveyard--A Preliminary Report," *Champlain Maritime Society Soundings*, Fall/Winter 1984, 4.

94. Fischer, 55-61; Merritt Carpenter, "The Wrecks of Shelburne Harbor," *Champlain Maritime Society Soundings*, August 1981, 2; See also *Burlington Free*

Press, 4 June 1906; *Burlington Free Press*, 350th Lake Champlain Festival Edition, 3 July 1959.

95. Russ Bellico, "Historic Preservation: The Wreck of the *Champlain*," *Adirondack Life*, July/August 1989, 26-28.

96. Ross, *Steamboats of Lake Champlain*, 128.

97. E. Baldwin, *Preserve Feasibility Champlain II*, 91.

98. Ibid., 58; *LCMM News*, Fall/Winter 1998-1999, 8.

99. Peter Barranco, Jr., *Ticonderoga's Floating Drawbridge; 1871-1920* (Lake Champlain Basin Program, 1995), Report 4E, 10-16, 18-40, 48-55.

100. *LCMM News*, Spring/Summer 2000, 3. The Lake Champlain Maritime Museum has also discovered other relics from the railroad era, including two flatbed railroad cars that rolled off the deck of the sloop *General Scott* in 1849 near Schuyler Island. The railcars were found during a 1989 side-scan survey and relocated during another survey in 1998. Cohn, *Cultural Resources Survey*, 125.

12. Steamboats of Lake George

1. Sarah N. Randolph, *The Domestic Life of Thomas Jefferson* (New York: Harper & Brothers Publishers, 1871), 201; See also J. Robert Maguire, ed., *The Tour to the Northern Lakes of James Madison & Thomas Jefferson May-June 1791* (Ticonderoga, N.Y.: Fort Ticonderoga, 1995), 28-29.

2. Codman Hislop, *Albany: Dutch, English, and American* (Albany: The Argus Press, 1936), 210; Alexander C. Flick, ed., *History of the State of New York* (New York: Columbia University Press, 1933), Volume 4, 333-34. James Caldwell was also a director of Albany's first bank. Hislop, 217.

3. Alfred F. Young, *The Democratic Republicans of New York: The Origins 1763-1797* (Chapel Hill: The University of North Carolina Press, 1967), 538-39; Hislop, 210-11.

4. David E. Mix, *Catalogue Maps and Surveys, in the Office of the Secretary of State, State Engineer and Surveyor* (Albany: Charles Van Benthuysen, 1859), 166; H. P. Smith, *History of Warren County* (Syracuse, N.Y.: D. Mason & Co., Publishers, 1885), 565. In 1785 James Caldwell had petitioned for a lease of the "Fort George landing" and was also involved in land patents in other areas of the lake, as well as Lake Champlain. [E. B. O'Callaghan], comp., *Calendar of N.Y. Colonial Manuscripts: Indorsed Land Papers 1643-1863* (1864; reprint ed., Harrison, N.Y.: Harbor Hill Books, 1987), 656, 767, 981; Mix, 221, 236-37, 240.

5. F. Grant, "Journal," 320; Betty Ahearn Buckell, *Old Lake George Hotels* (Lake George, N.Y.: Buckle Press, 1986), 66.

6. Cometti, 47; Silliman (1st ed.), 149; Buckell, *Hotels*, 30.

7. Silliman (1st ed.), 149; See also Bellico, *Chronicles of Lake George*, 236.

8. Marvin, 32.

9. *GFR*, 19 May 1857.

10. Silliman (1st ed.), 153; The tavern mentioned in Silliman's book was probably the Lake House, first built in 1800 on the present site of Shepard Park in Lake George Village. See Buckell, *Hotels*, 25.

11. *GFR*, 19 May 1857.

12. Ibid.

13. E. S. Harris, *Lake George*, 26; See also Ross, *Steamboats of Lake George*, 53; Canfield, 693; S. R. Stoddard, *Lake George: A Book of To-day* (Albany: Van Benthuysen & Sons, Printers, 1880), 59.

14. Sullivan, Appendix, 1. Other sources suggest that the *Mountaineer* was 102 feet in length. *GFR*, 19 May 1857.

15. *GFR*, 19 May 1857; E. S. Harris, *Lake George*, 26.

16. Betty Ahearn Buckell, *Lake George Boats* (Lake George, N.Y.: Buckle Press, 1990), 7; Miscellaneous Records, Book 1, 388, Warren County Clerk, Municipal Center, Queensbury, N.Y.

17. Data on the dimensions of the steamer *William Caldwell* vary considerably, see *GFR*, 19 May 1857; Ross, *Steamboats of Lake George*, 57; Canfield, 693.

18. Marvin, 49-50. The steamer *William Caldwell*'s "saloon deck was towed to Bolton and hauled out on the Mohican House lawn." *LGM*, 22 August 1892.

19. John Jay Harris Collection, M95.08, Box 3, Ticonderoga Historical Society, Ticonderoga, N.Y.

20. Ibid.

21. Ibid.

22. Ross, *Steamboats of Lake George*, 63.

23. Mrs. John J. Van Winkle, "Mrs. John J. Van Winkle Travel Journal," MS, Fort Ticonderoga Thompson-Pell Research Center, Ticonderoga, N.Y.

24. Ibid.

25. *GFR*, 19 May 1857.

26. Marvin, 53.

27. E. S. Harris, *Lake George*, 10.

28. *LGM*, 26 August 1893.

29. *GFR*, 5 August 1856.

30. Ibid.

31. *LGM*, 26 August 1893.

32. *GFR*, 5 August 1856.

33. Ibid.

34. Stoddard, 60.

35. *GFR*, 5 August 1856.

36. *GFR*, 19 May 1857.

37. Ross, *Steamboats of Lake George*, 81.

38. "Minutes of Directors' Meetings," (extract) 1876 and 1877, CTC Papers, B Collection, carton 3, folder 60.

39. Charles H. Possons, *Possons' Guide to Lake George, Lake Champlain and Adirondacks* (Glens Falls, N.Y.: Chas. H. Possons, Publisher, 1888), 46.

40. *LGM*, 8 July 1893.

41. "Minutes of Directors' Meetings," (extract) 1884, CTC Papers, B Collection, carton 3, folder 60.

42. Ross, *Steamboats of Lake George*, 101.

43. "Minutes of Directors' Meetings," (extract) 1884 and 1885, CTC Papers, B Collection, carton 3, folder 60.

44. Buckell, *Lake George Boats*, 23-24; telephone interview with Betty Buckell, 8 April 1990.

45. *LGM*, 6 July 1892; For more information on the *Island Queen* see *Glens Falls Daily Times*, 14 November 1892, see also 29 August 1901; *LGM*, 18 July 1891, 6 June 1891, 1 August 1891, 16 July 1892; Fred T. Stiles, "Tales of Lake George," *York State Tradition*, Summer 1963, 50; Buckell, *Lake George Boats*, 64; For additional details on Everett Harrison's operation see *LGM*, 18 July 1891, 2 September 1893, 1 June 1895.

46. *Glens Falls Daily Times*, 14 November 1892.

47. *LGM*, 3 June 1893, 2 September 1893.

48. Possons, 47; See also T. E. Roessle, *Lake George: A Descriptive and Historical Sketch* (Lake George, N. Y.: T. E. Roessle, 1887), 16.

49. *LGM*, 13 August 1892, 5 September 1896, 12 June 1897, 3 June 1899; Dorothy Backus Offensend, *The Sexton Boatbuilders of Hague* (Pawlet, VT.: D. B. Offensend, 1982), 56, 64, 65, 71, 90, 94, 98; See also Buckell, *Lake George Boats*, 67-78.

50. *LGM*, 7 July 1923.

51. Ibid., 12 August 1893; See also *Glens Falls Daily Times*, 4 August 1893.

52. Buckell, *Lake George Boats*, 70-71.

53. *Glens Falls Daily Times*, 29 August 1901; See also *LGM*, 31 August 1901.

54. Lape, 208; Telephone interview with Dr. George Peter Cook of Ticonderoga whose father helped remove the wreckage.

55. *Ticonderoga Sentinel*, 24 October 1901.

56. Ibid., 31 October 1901.

57. CTC Papers, B Collection, carton 8, folder 47, see also folder 65. The new steamer *Sagamore* carried an anchor that had been used on both the *John Jay* and *Minnie-Ha-Ha*. *Ticonderoga Sentinel*, 24 April 1902.

58. CTC Papers, B Collection, carton 8, folder 69.

59. Ibid., carton 3, folder 65; See also *LGM*, 17 June 1911; William Preston Gates, *Turn-of-the-Century Scrapbook of Jonathan Streeter Gates* (Glens Falls: Gates Publishing Company, 1999), 75.

60. *LGM*, 2 September 1911, 28 June 1913.

61. Ibid., 22 June 1912, see also 18 July 1914, 29 July 1916, 9 September 1916. In 1917 the *Mountaineer II* offered service as far north as French Point in the Narrows, where General Electric had established a camp for young female employees. CTC Papers, B Collection, carton 7, folder 65.

62. Buckell, Bernard. Interview by Russell Bellico, 28 August 1988.

63. CTC Papers, B Collection, "Steam Yachts of Lake George," carton 8, folder 70.

64. *LGM*, 17 July 1915; E. S. Harris, *Lake George*, 15; For other details about the *Scioto*'s subsequent career see *LGM*, 15 July 1922, 4 September 1926, 2 July 1927, 30 June 1934, 16 July 1937; Glens Falls newspapers also carried stories about the *Scioto II* in June 1938 and June 1939.

65. Frederick C. Thorne, *Pilot Knob Story: An Historical Report of Its Life and Times* (Pilot Knob, N. Y.: F. C. Thorne, 1977), 38; Burleigh, Captain Gordon. Interview by Russell Bellico, 25 July 1990.

66. *LGM*, 2 July 1927.

67. *LGM*, 5 July 1925; Thomas Reeves Lord, *Still More Stories of Lake George Fact and Fancy* (Pemberton, N.J.: Pinelands Press, 1999), 125.

68. *Mountain Steamboats*, 15.

69. CTC Papers, B Collection, carton 7, folder 101.

70. Ibid., carton 3, folder 90; carton 8, folder 10; CTC Papers, Daniel A. Loomis Diary, May 15, 1934; *LGM*, 30 June 1934, 14 July 1934. By early July 1934 George Stafford, operator of the *Mohican II*, complained to the CTC general manager of the "cut-throat game" being played by the management of the *Horicon II*, who offered discount fares to entice passengers who might otherwise travel on the *Mohican II*. CTC Papers, B Collection, carton 8, folder 67; See also *LGM*, 8 August 1934.

71. CTC Papers, B Collection, carton 7, folders 67, 41, 119.

72. Ibid., carton 8, folder 67; carton 7, folders 108, 93, 89, 104. Although round-trip tickets were priced as low as one dollar, Hoyt Austin's 1936 *Horicon II* operation appeared to be profitable with $22,663.93 in gross revenue and only a $2,008.89 lease payment to the CTC. Ibid., carton 7, folder 89; See also *LGM*, 17 July 1936.

73. CTC Papers, B Collection, carton 8, folder 48.

74. Ibid., carton 7, folders 49, 40, 48. In December 1935 the CTC offered to sell the *Sagamore* without her steam engine for $4,000 to the Indian Kettles Club in Hague for use as a night club, but the latter firm was interested in purchasing the *Horicon II* Show-Boat at the time. Ibid., carton 8, folder 48. A considerable amount of equipment from the *Sagamore* was sold to the Mariners Museum in Newport News, Virginia. Ibid., carton 7, folder 2; carton 8, folder 5.

75. Ibid., carton 7, folder 58; see also carton 6, folder 164; *LGM*, 3 July 1937, 16 July 1937; CTC Papers, B Collection, carton 7, folders 14, 35; carton 8, folder 5.

76. CTC Papers, B Collection, carton 8, folder 67.

77. Ibid., carton 7, folder 49; *LGM*, 28 July 1939. The *LGM* article revealed that the purchase of the Lake George Steamboat Company was in the name of Concetta Stafford, wife of Captain George Stafford. At the time of the sale of the steamboat company, the president of the Sagamore Hotel made an inquiry regarding the purchase of the *Horicon II* with-

out her engine, but nothing further transpired. CTC Papers, B Collection, carton 8, folder 67.

78. *LGM*, 30 August 1946, 27 June 1947, 4 July 1947.

79. *Glens Falls Times*, 26 May 1938; Tom Hirchburg, "Remembering the *Roamer*," Special Supplement, *LGM* Summer 2000. The *Roamer* also operated during World War II. *LGM*, 18 August 1944, 6 July 1945.

80. Some details on the *Ranger* may be found in the *LGM*, 28 June 1946, 5 July 1946, 27 June 1947, 4 July 1947, 11 July 1947; "PT Boat Converted to Pleasure Craft," *Motorship Magazine*, August 1947, 42-43.

81. *LGM*, 7 July 1950, 6 July 1951.

82. *Post-Star*, 8 November 1973.

83. *The Plan for the Future of the Lake George Park* (Lake George, N. Y.: The Task Force for the Future of the Lake George Park, 1985), 5.

84. W. S. Howard, "A Rough House Cruise to Lake George," in *On River and Canal to Lake Champlain* (New York: The Rudder Publishing Company, 1907), 54. (reprinted from *The Rudder*).

85. *LGM*, 30 July 1999; George Chapman Singer, "The Burning of the Steamer *Ticonderoga* 29 August 1901," MS, 17 July 1975.

86. Joseph W. Zarzynski, ed., *Lake George's Forward: Historic Vessel, Shipwreck Preserve, and "Underwater Classroom"* (Wilton, N.Y.: Bateaux Below, Inc., 1998); See also *The Lake George Nautical Newsletter*, June 1992, 3.

87. *Abandoned Historic Shipwreck Protection Act*, H. R. 2071, lines 17-22.

88. Joseph W. Zarzynski and D. K. Abbass, *The Lake George, New York Steam Launch Cadet Shipwreck Study--1998 Report* (Wilton, N.Y.: Bateaux Below, Inc., 1999), 16; Buckell, *Lake George Boats*, 84.

89. Zarzynski and Abbass, *Cadet Shipwreck Study*, 16-17; See also *LGM*, 22 August 1896, 12 June 1897; Buckell, *Lake George Boats*, 78.

90. Joseph W. Zarzynski, "The 1999 *Cadet* ex *Olive* Shipwreck Project at Lake George" (paper presented at the annual meeting of the New York State Archaeological Association, Lake George, New York, May 6, 2000), 8.

91. Ibid., 7.

92. Joseph W. Zarzynski and Bob Benway, *Lake George, New York's D & H "Submarine Railway": A Report on Its History and Bateaux Below, Inc.'s Archaeological Survey* (Wilton, N.Y.: Bateaux Below, Inc., 2000), 34.

93. Padeni, *Final Report*, 20-31; Cohn, *Cultural Resources Survey*, 174-82; "Remains of Colonial Shipwreck Studied in Lake George," Scott A. Padeni Press Release, 24 September 2000.

Ruins of Fort George in 1920. (New York State Museum)

Select Bibliography

Journals and Primary Sources

Abbot, Joel. Papers. Microfilm 25. Special Collections, Nimitz Library, U.S. Naval Academy, Annapolis, MD.

Abercromby, James. Papers. Huntington Library, San Marino, California.

Adler, Winston, ed. *Their Own Voices: Oral Accounts of Early Settlers in Washington County, New York*. Interlaken, N.Y.: Heart of the Lakes Publishing, 1983.

Albertson, Garrett. "A Short Account of the Life and Travels of Garrett Albertson, Sr." *BFTM* 4 (July 1936): 43-47.

Alexander, Thomas. "Ens. Alexander's Diary." In *History of Northfield, Massachusetts*, by J. H. Temple and George Sheldon. 303-5. Albany: Joel Munsell, 1875.

Allen, Ethan. "Ethan Allen to Philip Skene." *BFTM* 6 (January 1943): 164-66.

_____. *A Narrative of Colonel Ethan Allen's Captivity*. 1930; Reprint. Rutland, VT.: Vermont Heritage Press, 1988.

Almon, John, ed. *The Remembrancer; Or Impartial Repository of Public Events*. Part 2. London: J. Almon, 1776.

Amherst, Jeffery. Amherst Family Papers. Centre for Kentish Studies, Kent, Great Britain.

Amherst, Jeffery. Amherst Papers, 22 vols. Public Record Office, London.

Anburey, Thomas. *Travels Through the Interior Parts of America*. Vol. 1. Boston: Houghton Mifflin Company, 1923.

[André, John.] "Papers Relating to the Surrender of Fort St. Johns and Fort Chambly." In *Report of the Work of the Public Archives for the Years 1914 and 1915*, Edited by Arthur G. Doughty. 3-25. Ottawa: Public Archives of Canada, 1916.

Angell, Samuel. "Camp Fort Edward, 14th August 1757." *Historical Magazine* 8 (November 1870): 257-59.

"The Anonymous Journal of the French and Indian War." *BFTM* 12 (September 1968): 291-97.

Arnold, Benedict. "Benedict Arnold's Regimental Memorandum Book." *BFTM* 14 (Winter 1982): 71-80.

Baldwin, Jeduthan. "Journal Kept by Capt. Jeduthan Baldwin While on the Expedition Against Crown Point, 1755-56." *Journal of the Military Service Institute* 39 (July-August 1906): 123-30.

Baldwin, Thomas Williams, ed. *The Revolutionary Journal of Col. Jeduthan Baldwin 1775-1778*. Bangor, ME.: DeBurians, 1906.

Bangs, Nathaniel. *Orderly Book Kept by Nathaniel Bangs at Fort Edward, 1758*. MASS HS.

Barlow, Aaron. "The March to Montreal and Quebec." *The American Historical Register* 2 (September 1894–February 1895): 641-49.

Barnard, Salah. "Journal of Major Salah Barnard." MS. Fort Ticonderoga Thompson-Pell Research Center.

Barrows, Abner. "Diary of Abner Barrows." In *History of the Town of Middleboro*, Edited by Thomas Weston. 95-98. New York: Houghton Mifflin, 1906.

Bartman, George. "The Siege of Fort William Henry, Letters of George Bartman." *Huntington Library Quarterly* 12 (August 1949): 415-24.

Bauer, K. Jack, ed. *The New American State Papers: Naval Affairs*. Vol. 4. Wilmington, DE.: Scholarly Resources, Inc., 1981.

Baxter, James Phinney, ed. *The British Invasion from the North, The Campaigns of Generals Carleton and Burgoyne from Canada, 1776-1777, With the Journal of Lieut. William Digby*. Albany: Joel Munsell's Sons, 1887.

Bayley, Jacob. "Part of the Journal of Capt. Jacob Bayley, in the Old French War." In *History of Newbury, Vermont*, by Frederic P. Wells. 376-80. St. Johnsbury, VT.: The Caledonian Company, 1902.

Beebe, Lewis. "Journal of a Physician on the Expedition Against Canada, 1776." *The Pennsylvania Magazine of History and Biography* 59 (October 1935): 321-61.

Benson, Adolph B., ed. *Peter Kalm's Travels in North America*. New York: Dover Publications, Inc., 1937.

Benzel, Adolphus. "Remarks on Lake Champlain, 1772." *BFTM* 12 (December 1969): 358-64.

Biggar, H. P., ed. *The Works of Samuel De Champlain*. Vol. 2, 1608-1613. Toronto: The Champlain Society, 1925.

Blake, Thomas. "Lieutenant Thomas Blake's Journal." In *History of the First New Hampshire Regiment in the War of the Revolution*, by Frederic Kidder. 25-56. Albany: Joel Munsell, 1868.

Bougainville, Louis Antoine de. *Adventure in the Wilderness. The American Journals of Louis Antoine de Bougainville 1756-1760*. Translated and Edited by Edward P. Hamilton. Norman, OK: University of Oklahoma Press, 1964.

Bowen, A. *The Naval Monument*. Boston: George Clark, 1830.

Bradbury, John. "Diary of Dea. John Bradbury." In *Bradbury Memorial*, Compiled by William Berry Lapham. 261-95. Portland, ME: Brown Thurston & Company, 1890.

Brehm, Diedrick. "Brehm's Report." *BFTM* 11 (December 1962): 37-42.

Brown, Noah. "The Remarkable Statement of Noah Brown." *The Journal of American History* 8 (1914): 103-8.

Buckingham, Thomas. "A Diary of the Land Expedition Against Crown Point in the Year 1711." In *Roll and Journal of Connecticut Service in Queen Anne's War*, 28-45. Hartford, CT.: Acorn Club, 1916.

Bull, Ephraphas. "Journal of Ephaphras Bull." *BFTM* 8 (July 1948): 38-46.

Burgoyne, John. *A State of the Expedition from Canada*. 1780; Reprint. New York: The New York Times & Arno Press, 1969.

Burk, John. "John Burk's Diary." In *History of the Town of Bernardston*, by Lucy Cutler Kellogg. 40-47. Greenfield, MA.: Press of E. A. Hall & Co., 1902.

Burr, Asa. "Diary of Asa Burr, 1758." Octavo Volume 1, AAS.

Burton, Jonathan. *Diary and Orderly Book of Sergeant Jonathan Burton.* Edited by Isaac W. Hammond. Concord., N. H.: Republican Press Association, 1855.

Bushnell, Charles I., ed. *The Narrative of Ebenezer Fletcher, A Soldier of the Revolution.* 1866. Reprint. Freeport, N.Y.: Books for Libraries Press, 1970.

Calfe, John. "Capt. John Calfe's Journal, 1777." In *A Memorial of the Town of Hampstead, New Hampshire,* by Harriette Eliza Noyes. 288-95. Boston: George B. Reed, 1899.

"Campaign in Canada & c Under G. Carleton." *BFTM* 11 (December 1964): 235-69; 11 (September 1965): 307-35; 12 (March 1966): 5-37.

Campbell, John. Loudoun Papers. Huntington Library, San Marino, California.

Carleton, Major. "Articles of Capitulation. . .at Fort George." *BFTM* 7 (July 1946): 25.

Carver, Jonathan. *Travels Through the Interior Parts of North America in the Years 1766, 1767, and 1768.* 1778. Reprint. Minneapolis: Ross & Haines, Inc., 1956.

Certificates of Enrollment. Bureau of Marine Inspection and Navigation, Record Group 41, National Archives, Washington, D.C.

Chamberlin, William. "Letter of General William Chamberlin." *Proceedings of the Massachusetts Historical Society* 10, Second Series (1895, 1896): 490-504.

Champion, Henry. "Accounts & Journals of Captain Henry Champion of Colchester, Campaign of 1758." CSL.

_____. "The Journal of Colonel Henry Champion." In *Champion Genealogy,* by Francis Bacon Trowbridge. 417-38. New Haven: F. B. Trowbridge, 1891.

Champlain Transportation Company Papers. Special Collections, Bailey-Howe Library, University of Vermont, Burlington, Vermont.

Chandler, Samuel. "Extracts from the Diary of Rev. Samuel Chandler." *NEHGR* 17 (October 1863): 346-54.

Clark, Byron N. "Accounts of the Battle of Plattsburgh, 11 September, 1814." *Vermont Antiquarian* 1 (March 1903): 75-93.

_____. ed. *A List of Pensioners of the War of 1812.* Burlington, VT.: Research Publication Company, 1904.

Clark, William Bell and William James Morgan, eds. *Naval Documents of the American Revolution.* 9 vols. Washington, D.C.: Naval History Division, Department of the Navy, 1964-86.

Claus, Daniel. *Daniel Claus' Narrative of His Relations with Sir William Johnson and Experiences in the Lake George Fight.* New York: Society of Colonial Wars in the State of New York, 1904.

Cleaveland, John. "The Journal of the Rev. John Cleaveland." *EIHC* 12 (April 1874): 85-103; (July 1874): 179-96; 13 (1877): 53-63.

_____. "Journal of Rev. John Cleaveland Kept While Chaplain in the French and Indian War, 1758-1759." *BFTM* 10 (No. 3, 1959). 192-234.

Cobb, Samuel. "The Journal of Captain Samuel Cobb." *BFTM* 14 (Summer 1981): 12-31.

Coburn, Nathaniel. "An Accurate & brief account of the War of 1812 with an account of Corp.l Nath.l Coburn, 2nd Regiment, U. S. Infantry, February 1, 1816." MS. Rensselaer County Historical Society, Troy, N.Y.

Colden, Alexander. "Eye-Witnesses' Accounts of the British Repulse at Ticonderoga." *The Canadian Historical Review* 2 (December 1921): 360-63.

Cometti, Elizabeth, ed. *The American Journals of Lt. John Enys.* Syracuse, N.Y.: Syracuse University Press, 1976.

Comstock, Christopher. "Diary of Christopher Comstock 1758-59." Connecticut Historical Society.

Cross, Urieh. "Narrative of Urieh Cross in the Revolutionary War." *Vermont Quarterly* 15 (July 1947): 177-87.

Cutter, Ruhamah Ammi. "Dr. A. R. Cutter's Journal of his Military Experience 1756-1758." In *A History of the Cutter Family of New England,* by Richard Cutter. 60-72. Boston: David Clapp & Son, 1871.

Cutter, William R., ed. *Diary of Lieut. Samuel Thompson.* Boston: Press of David Clapp & Son, 1896.

Dawes, E. C., ed. *Journal of Gen. Rufus Putnam 1757-1760.* Albany: Joel Munsell's Sons, 1886.

De Angelis, Pascal Charles Joseph. "The Lake Champlain Fight." Marshall Family Papers. MS 9. Penfield Library, State University of New York at Oswego.

Dearborn, Henry. *Revolutionary War Journals of Henry Dearborn, 1775-1783.* Edited by Lloyd A. Brown and Howard H. Peckham. 1939. Reprint. New York: Da Capo Press, 1971.

"Detailed Statement of Operations at Ticonderoga, 1758." *Pennsylvania Archives.* Volume 3, 472-73. Edited by Samuel Hazard. Philadelphia: Joseph Severns & Co., 1853.

"Diary of a Soldier at Crown Point 1759." French and Indian War Collection. AAS.

Dibble, Ebenezer. "Diary of Ebenezer Dibble." *Proceedings of the Society of Colonial Wars in the State of Connecticut* 1 (1903): 313-29.

Doblin, Helga, trans. and ed. "Journal of Lt. Colonel Christian Julius Prätorius 2 June 1777-17 July 1777." *BFTM* 15 (Winter 1991): 56-68.

Doblin, Helga, tran. and Mary C. Lynn, ed. *An Eyewitness Account of the American Revolution and New England Life: The Journal of J. F. Wasmus, German Company Surgeon, 1776-1783.* Westport, CT.: Greenwood Press, 1990.

_____. *The American Revolution, Garrison Life in French Canada and New York: Journal of an Officer in the Prinz Friedrich Regiment, 1776-1883.* Westport, CT.: Greenwood Press, 1993.

_____. *The Specht Journal: A Military Journal of the Burgoyne Campaign.* Westport, CT.: Greenwood Press, 1995.

"Documents, sur la Révolution Américaine." *La Revue De L'Université Laval, Québec* 2 (December 1947): 344-49; 2 (March 1948): 642-48; 2 (April 1948): 742-48; 2 (May 1948): 838-46; 2 (June 1948): 926-34.

Dodge, Nathaniel Brown. "A Letter and Diary of 1776." *Vermont Quarterly* 21 (1953): 29-35.

Doughty, Arthur G., ed. *Report of the Public Archives for the Year 1929.* Ottawa: F. A. Acland, 1930.

Douglas, Charles. "A British View on the Battle of Valcour." *North Country Notes,* April 1963, 2-3.

Dudley, William S. *The Naval War of 1812: A Documentary History*. Vol. 1. Washington, D.C.: Department of the Navy, 1985.

Dulles, Joseph Heatly. "Extracts from the Diary of Joseph Heatly Dulles." *The Pennsylvania Magazine of History and Biography* 35 (1911): 276-89.

Dwight, Nathaniel. "The Journal of Capt. Nathaniel Dwight of Belchertown, Mass., During the Crown Point Expedition, 1755." *The New York Genealogical and Biographical Record* 33 (1902): 3-10, 65-70.

Elmer, Ebenezer. "Journal of Lieutenant Ebenezer Elmer." *Proceedings of the New Jersey Historical Society* 3 (1848-1849): 21-102.

Emerson, Daniel. "A Journal of My Procedure with the Army to Crown Point--Begun July Ye 8, 1755." In *Ipswich Emersons*, by Benjamin Kendall Emerson. 86-91. Boston: Press of David Clapp & Son, 1900.

Epping, Charlotte S. J., trans. *Journal of Du Roi the Elder*. Philadelphia: University of Pennsylvania, 1911.

Everest, Allan S., ed. *The Journal of Charles Carroll of Carrollton*. Fort Ticonderoga, N.Y.: The Champlain-Upper Hudson Bicentennial Committee, 1976.

"Expedition Against Quebec." *NEHGR* 6 (January 1852): 129-41.

Fassett, John. "Diary of Lieutenant John Fassett." In *The Follett-Dewey, Fassett-Safford Ancestry*, by Harry Parker Ward. 225-28. Columbus, OH.: Champlin Printing, 1896.

Fisher, Samuel. "Diary of Operations Around Lake George 1758." MS. Library of Congress.

Fitch, Jabez, Jr. *The Diary of Jabez Fitch, Jr. in the French and Indian War 1757*. 3rd ed. Fort Edward, N.Y.: Rogers Island Historical Association, 1986.

Forbush, Eli. "Camp at Ticonderoga or Fort Carillon, Aug. 4, 1759." In *Fort Ticonderoga, A Short History*, by S. H. P. Pell. Ticonderoga: N.Y.: Fort Ticonderoga Museum, 1978.

Force, Peter, ed. *American Archives*. Fourth Series, Vol. 3-4. Washington, D.C.: M. St. Clair Clarke and Peter Force, 1840, 1846; Fifth Series, Vol. 1-3. Washington, D.C.: M. St. Clair Clarke and Peter Force, 1848-53.

Foster Asa. "Diary of Capt. Asa Foster of Andover, Mass." *NEHGR* 213 (1900): 183-88.

Fraser, Simon. "Gen. Fraser's Account of Burgoyne's Campaign on Lake Champlain and the Battle of Hubbardton." *Proceedings of the Vermont Historical Society* (October 18 and November 2, 1898): 139-47.

Fraser, Simon. "Inquisition of a Spy." *BFTM* 10 (1959): 240-45.

Frazer, Persifer. "Letters from Ticonderoga, 1776." *BFTM* 10 (January 1962): 450-59.

Freiberg, Malcolm. "The Reverend William Gordon's Autumn 1776 Tour of the Northeast." *The New England Quarterly* 65 (September 1992): 469-80.

French and Indian War Collection 1754-1774, "A Soldier at Fort William Henry, 1756." Octavo Volume 2, AAS.

Frisbie, Judah. "Journal as a Soldier in the Revolution." In *History of the Town of Wolcott*, by Rev. Samuel Orcutt. 306-11. Waterbury, CT.: Press of the American Printing Company, 1874.

From Cambridge to Champlain. Middleboro, MA.: Lawrence B. Romaine, 1957.

Frost, John Jr. "Diary of Lieut. John Frost, Jr., 1760." *Old Eliot* 8 (1908): 109-17.

Frye, Joseph. "A Journal of the Attack of Fort William Henry." *Parkman Papers* 42: 137-62. MASS HS.

Fuller, Archelaus. "Journal of Col. Archelaus Fuller of Middleton, Mass." *EIHC* 46 (1910): 209-20.

_____. "The Journal of Archelaus Fuller May--Nov. 1758." *BFTM* 13 (December 1970): 5-17.

Furnis, James. "An Eyewitness Account by James Furnis of the Surrender of Fort William Henry, August 1757." Edited by William S. Ewing. *New York History* 42 (July 1961): 307-16.

Gage, Thomas. *The Correspondence of General Thomas Gage with the Secretaries of State, and with the War Office and Treasury 1763-1775*. Compiled and Edited by Clarence Edwin Carter. Vol. 1-2. Archon Books, 1969.

Gates, Horatio. Horatio Gates Papers 1726-1828. (microfilm, State University of New York at Albany).

Gilbert, James. "Journal Kept by James Gilbert." *Magazine of New England History* 3 (1893): 188-95.

Gilliland, William. Willisborough Town-Book Commencing the 8th Day of June 1765. MS. Plattsburgh Public Library, Plattsburgh, New York.

Glasier, Benjamin. "French and Indian War Diary of Benjamin Glasier of Ipswich, 1758-1760." *EIHC* 86 (1950): 65-92.

Godfrey, Richard. "A Journal of the March of Captain Richard Godfrey's Company, 1755." In *History of Taunton, Mass.*, by Samuel H. Emery. 419-24. Syracuse, N.Y.: D. Mason, 1893.

Gold, Joyce. *The Naval Chronicle*. Vol. 32, 33. London: Joyce Gold, 1814 & 1815.

Goodrich, Josiah. "The Josiah Goodrich Orderbook." *BFTM* 13 (Fall 1980): 410-31.

Graham, John. "The Journal of the Rev. John Graham." *MAH*, Part 1 (1882): 206-12.

[Grant, Ann]. *Memories of an American Lady*. 1808. Reprint. Vol. 2. New York: Research Reprints, Inc., 1970.

Grant, Francis. "Journal from New York to Canada, 1767." *Proceedings of the New York State Historical Association* 13 (1932): 181-322.

Grant, W. L., ed. *Voyages of Samuel De Champlain 1604-1618*. New York: Charles Scribner and Sons, 1907.

Green, Samuel Abbott. *Papers Relating to Captain Thomas Lawrence's Company*. Cambridge, MA.: John Wilson and Son, 1890.

Green, Samuel A., ed. *Three Military Diaries*. Cambridge, MA.: John Wilson & Son, 1901.

_____. *Two Narratives of the Expedition Against Quebec, A. D. 1690*. Cambridge, MA: John Wilson and Son, 1902.

Greenleaf, Samuel. *Account Book and Journal*, 1756. MASS HS.

Greenman, Jeremiah. *Diary of a Common Soldier in the American Revolution, 1775-1783*. Edited by Robert C. Bray and Paul E. Bushnell. DeKalb, IL.: Northern Illinois University Press, 1978.

Gridley, Luke. *Luke Gridley's Diary of 1757*. Hartford, CT.: The Acorn Club, 1906.

Griswold, Shubael. "Journal During Service in French and Indian Wars." CSL.

Guild, Joseph. "Journal of Captain Joseph Guild." *The Dedham Historical Register* 7 (1896): 43-47.

Haldimand Papers. National Archives of Canada, Ottawa. "Misc. Papers Relating to the Provincial

Navy, 1775-1780." Microfilm H-1649, Vol. 1, B144, Vol 2, B145; Microfilm C-3242, Vol. 722A.

Hardy, Constantine. "Extracts from the Journal of Constantine Hardy." *NEHGR* 60 (1906): 236-39.

Harris, John Jay. John Jay Harris Collection, Ticonderoga Historical Society, Ticonderoga, N.Y.

Harris, Obadiah. "Journal of Obadiah Harris 1758." HM 591. Huntington Library.

Hawks, John. *Orderly Book and Journal of Major John Hawks 1759-1760.* New York: Society of Colonial Wars, 1911.

Hawley, Elisha. "Capt. Hawley's Journal." In *History of Northampton, Massachusetts.* Vol. 2. by James R. Trumbull. 254-59. Northampton, MA.: Press of Gazette Printing Co., 1902.

Haynes, Thomas. "Memorandum of Colonial French War A.D. 1758-." *BFTM* 12 (October 1967): 193-203.

Henderson, James. "James Henderson's Journal." In *The First Century of the Colonial Wars in the Commonwealth of Massachusetts*, 195-209. Boston: Society of Colonial Wars, Mass., 1944.

Henry, John Joseph. *Account of Arnold's Campaign Against Quebec.* 1877. Reprint. New York: The New York Times & Arno Press, 1968.

Henshaw, William. "William Henshaw's Journal." *Proceedings of the Worcester Society of Antiquity* 25 (1912): 43-64.

Hervey, William. *Journals of the Hon. William Hervey.* Bury St. Edmund's: Paul & Mathew, Butter Market, 1906.

Hildreth, Micah. "Micah Hildreth of Dracutt His Book." In *History of Dracut, Massachusetts*, by Silas R. Coburn. 147-52. Lowell, MA.: Press of the Courier-Citizen Co., 1922.

Hill, James. "The Diary of a Private on the First Expedition to Crown Point." Edited by Edna V. Moffett. *New England Quarterly* 5 (1932): 602-18.

Hitchcock, Enos. "Diary of Enos Hitchcock [1776]." MS. Rhode Island Historical Society, Providence, R.I.

Holden, David. "Journal of Sergeant Holden." *Proceedings of the Massachusetts Historical Society* 4, Second Series (1887-1889): 384-409.

Hollister, Josiah. *The Journal of Josiah Hollister.* Illinois: Romanzo Norton Bunn, d.n.a.

Holt, Joseph. "Journals of Joseph Holt, of Wilton, N.H." *NEHGR* (1856): 307-11.

Hurlbut, John, Jr. "The Journal of a Colonial Soldier." *MAH* 39 (1893): 395-96.

Ingalls, Phineas. "Revolutionary War Journal, Kept by Phineas Ingalls of Andover, Mass, April 19, 1775 - December 8, 1776." *EIHC* 53 (1917): 81-91.

Jeffry, James. "Journal Kept in Quebec in 1775 by James Jeffry." *EIHC* 50 (April 1914): 97-150.

Jenks, Samuel. "Samuel Jenks, his Journal of the Campaign in 1760." *Proceedings of the Massachusetts Historical Society* 5, Second Series (1889-1890): 353-91.

Jewett, Benjamin. "The Diary of Benjamin Jewett--1758." *National Magazine* 17 (1892-93): 60-64.

"A Journal Kept During the Siege of Fort William Henry, August, 1757." *Proceedings of the American Philosophical Society* 37 (1898): 143-50.

"A Journal of a March from Cambridge on an Expedition against Quebec in Colonel Benedict Arnold's Detachment, Sept. 13, 1775." *Proceedings of the Massachusetts Historical Society* 2 (2nd Series) (1885-1886): 267-75.

"Journal of the Most Remarkable Occurrences in Quebec, 1775-1776." *Coll. NYHS* 13 (1880): 177-236.

"Journal of the Proceedings of the Congress Held at Albany, in 1754." *Collections of the Massachusetts Historical Society* 5 (3rd Series) (1836): 5-74.

"Journal of a Provincial Officer in the Campaign in Northern New York in 1758." *The Historical Magazine* 10 (July 1871): 118-22.

"Journal in Quebec." *Coll. NYHS* 13 (1880): 173-236.

Kimball, Gertrude Selwyn, ed. *Correspondence of William Pitt.* Vol. 1. New York: The Macmillan Company, 1906.

Klinck, Carl F., and James J. Talman, eds. *The Journal of Major John Norton 1816.* Toronto: The Champlain Society, 1970.

Knap, Jonathan. "Journal of Jonathan Knap of Killington, Connecticut." CSL.

Knox, Captain John. *An Historical Journal of the Campaigns in North America.* 3 vols. 1769. by Arthur G. Doughty 1914-1916. Reprint. Freeport, N.Y.: Books for Libraries Press, 1970.

Knox, Henry. "Knox's Diary During His Ticonderoga Expedition." *NEHGR* 119 (July 1876): 321-27.

_____. "Diary of Henry Knox." In *Ye Cohorn Caravan*, by Wm. L. Bowne. Schuylerville, N.Y.: NaPaul Publishers, Inc., 1975.

Kochan, James L., ed. "Joseph Frye's Journal and Map of the Siege of Fort William Henry, 1757." *BFTM* 15 (1993): 339-61.

Kruger, John W., ed. "Simon Metcalfe's 'Little Book.'" *BFTM* 15 (Winter 1988): 28-36.

Lamb, R. *Journal of Occurrences During the Late American War.* Dubin: Wilkinson & Courtney, 1809.

Lathrop, Gideon. "The Diary of Gideon Lathrop." Special Collections, Bailey-Howe Library, University of Vermont, Burlington, VT.

Lee, Charles. "Narrative--Enclosed in Letter of September 16th 1758." *Collections of the New-York Historical Society* (1871): 9-15.

"Letters of Benedict Arnold, Guy Carleton, Horatio Gates, Thomas Hartley et al." *BFTM* 4 (July 1938): 20-56.

"Letters of General Gates, 1776." *BFTM* 5 (January 1939): 9-34.

"Letters of General Powell, 1777." *BFTM* 7 (July 1945): 29-35.

Lévis, François de. *Journal Des Champagnes Du Chevalier De Lévis En Canada De 1756 à 1760.* Montreal: C. O. Beauchemin & Fils, 1889.

Lincoln, Charles Henry, ed. *Correspondence of William Shirley.* Vol. 2. New York: The Macmillan Company, 1912.

Lincoln, James Minor. comp. *The Papers of Captain Rufus Lincoln of Wareham, Mass.* 1904. Reprint. New York: Arno Press Inc., 1971.

Livingston, Henry. "Journal of Major Henry Livingston 1775." Edited by Gaillard Hunt. *The Pennsylvania Magazine of History and Biography* 22 (1898): 9-33.

Lyon, Lemuel. "Military Journal for 1758." In *The Military Journals of Two Private Soldiers 1758-1775*, by Abraham Tomlinson. 11-45. 1854. Reprint. Freeport, N.Y.: Books for Libraries Press, 1970.

MacClintock, Samuel. *Rev. Samuel MacClintock's Journal.* 1760. Crown Point, N.Y.: Crown Point Road Association, Inc., 1972.

Maguire, Robert J. "Dr. Robert Knox's Account of the Battle of Valcour, October 11-13." *Vermont History* 46 (Summer 1978): 141-50.

Melvin, James. *The Journal of James Melvin----Private Soldier in Arnold's Expedition Against Quebec in the Year 1775.* Edited by Andrew A. Melvin. Portland, ME.: The Wardwell Press, 1902.

Merriman, Samuel. "Journal of Samuel Merriman." In *A History of Deerfield,* by George Sheldon. 661-68. 1895. Reprint. Somersworth, N.H.: New Hampshire Publishing Company, 1972.

Metcalf, Seth. *Diary and Journal of Seth Metcalf.* Boston: The Historical Records Survey, 1939.

Montresor, James. "Journals of Col. James Montresor." *Coll. NYHS* 14 (1881): 17-111.

Monypenny, Alexander. "Monypenny Orderly Book." *BFTM* 12 (October 1970): 434-61.

Mudge, Simon. "Journal of the March to Continental Army." In *Memorials: Mudge,* by Alfred Mudge. 204-5. Boston: Alfred Mudge and Son, 1868.

National Archives of Canada, Ottawa. Record Group 8. British Military and Naval Records. Microfilm C-3173, Vol. 679; Microfilm C-3174, Vol. 683; Microfilm C-3233, Vol. 690; Microfilm C-3243, Vol. 730; Microfilm C-3502, Vol. C.1170; Microfilm C-3526, Vol. 1219; Microfilm C-3527, Vols. 1222 and 1225; Microfilm C-3840, Vol. 1709.

Naval Records Collection of the Office of Naval Records and Library. Washington, D.C.: National Archives. Record Group 45, Microcopies 125, 147, 149.

Nichols, Joseph. "Joseph Nichols Military Journal 1758-59." HM 89. Huntington Library, San Marino, California.

Norton, Ichabod. *Orderly Book of Capt. Ichabod Norton of Col. Mott's Regiment of Connecticut Troops Destined for the Northern Campaign in 1776.* Fort Edward, N.Y.: Press of Keating & Barnard, 1898.

Nourse, Henry S. *The Military Annals of Lancaster, Massachusetts 1740-1865.* Lancaster, MA.: Henry S. Nourse, 1889.

Noyes, John. "Journal of John Noyes of Newbury in the Expedition Against Ticonderoga, 1758." *EIHC* 45 (1909): 73-77.

O'Callaghan, Edmund B. ed. *The Documentary History of the State of New York.* 4 vol. Albany: Weed, Parsons & Co.; Charles Van Benthuysen, Public Printer, 184 -51.

_____. *Documents Relative to the Colonial History of the State of New York.* 10 vol. Albany: Weed, Parsons and Company, 1853-1858.

Oswald, Eleazer. "Journal Kept by Eleazer Oswald on Lake Champlain." *BFTM* 13 (1977): 341.

"Papers Relating to the Expedition to Ticonderoga." *Collections of the Connecticut Historical Society* 1 (1860): 171-72.

Parkman, Francis. Parkman Papers. Vol. 42. MASS HS.

Parkman, William. "Journal of William Parkman." *Proceedings of the Massachusetts Historical Society* 17 (1879-80): 243-45.

Pell, Joshua, Jr. "Diary of Joshua Pell, Junior." *MAH* 2 (1878): 43-47, 107-11.

Perry, David. "Recollections of an Old Soldier." *BFTM* 14 (Summer 1981): 4-11.

Pomeroy, Seth. *The Journals and Papers of Seth Pomeroy.* Edited by Louis Effingham De Forest. New York:

Society of Colonial Wars in the State of New York, 1926.

Pond, Peter. "Experience in Early Wars in America." *The Journal of American History* 1 (1907): 89-93.

Porter, Elisha. "Diary of Mr. Elisha Porter of Hadley." *MAH* 29 (1893): 185-206.

Porterfield, Charles. "Memorable Attack on Quebec, December 21, 1775." *MAH* 21 (1889): 318-19.

Pouchot, M. *Memoir Upon the Late War in North America Between the French and English* 1755-60. Translated and Edited by Franklin B. Hough. Roxbury, MA.: W. Elliot Woodward, 1866.

Pouchot, Pierre. *Memoir Upon the Late War in North America Between the French and English.* Translated by Michael Cardy and Edited by Brian Leigh Dunnigan. Youngstown, N.Y.: Old Fort Niagara Association, Inc., 1994.

Rea, Caleb. "The Journal of Dr. Caleb Rea, Written During the Expedition Against Ticonderoga in 1758." *EIHC* 18 (1881): 81-120, 177-205.

"A Return of the fleet belonging to the United States of America on Lake Champlain...Octob^{er} 22, 1776." MS. Lake Champlain Maritime Museum, Basin Harbor, VT.

Revolutionary War Manuscripts. Albany: New York State Library and Archives. Documents #224, 671, 1008, 1382, 1477, 1484, 1570, 1572, 1633, 7308, 7312, 11107, 14007.

Richardson, Amos. "Amos Richardson's Journal, 1758." *BFTM* 12 (September 1968): 267-91.

Ritzema, Rudolphus. "Journal of Col. Rudolphus Ritzema." *MAH* 1 (1877): 98-105.

Robbins, Ammi R. "Journal of Rev. Ammi R. Robbins, A Chaplain in the American Army." In *History of Norfolk,* by Theron Wilmot Crissey. 97-121. Everett, MA.: Massachusetts Publishing Company, 1900.

Roberts, Lemuel. *Memoirs of Captain Lemuel Roberts.* 1809. Reprint. New York: The New York Times & Arno Press, 1969.

Roby, Luther. *Reminiscences of the French War; Roger's Expeditions and Maj. Gen. John Stark.* Concord, N.H.: Luther Roby, 1831.

Rockwell, Ell B. Papers. Special Collections, Bailey-Howe Library, University of Vermont, Burlington, VT.

Rogers, Horatio, ed. *Hadden's Journal and Orderly Books: A Journal Kept in Canada and Upon Burgoyne's Campaign in 1776 and 1777.* 1884. Reprint. Boston: Gregg Press, 1972.

Rogers, Robert. *Journals of Major Robert Rogers.* 1765. Reprint. Ann Arbor, Mich.: University Microfilms, Inc. 1966.

Schank, John, John Starke, and Edward Longcroft. "An Open Letter to Captain Pringle." *BFTM* 1 (July 1928): 14-20.

Searing, James. "The Battle of Ticonderoga, 1758." *Proceedings of the New-York Historical Society* 5 (1847): 112-17.

Sewall, Henry. "Diary of Captain Henry Sewall of the Army of the Revolution, 1776-1783." *The Historical Magazine* 10 (July 1871): 128-35.

_____. "The Diary of Henry Sewall." *BFTM* 11 (September 1963): 75-92.

Smith, E. Vale. "Diary of Colonel Edward Wigglesworth." In *History of Newburyport*, 357-59. Newburyport, MA.: pub.n.a., 1854.

Smith, Joseph. "Journal of Joseph Smith, of Groton." *Proceedings of the Society of Colonial Wars in the State of Connecticut* 1 (1903): 305-10.

Snyder, Charles M. "With Benedict Arnold at Valcour Island: The Diary of Pascal De Angelis." *Vermont History* 42 (summer 1974):195-200.

Spaulding, Leonard. "French and Indian War Record." In *The Vermont Historical Gazetteer*. Vol. 5. Edited by Abby Maria Hemenway. 28-33. Brandon, VT.: Carrie E. H. Page, 1891.

Spicer, Abel. "Diary of Abel Spicer from June 5th Until September 29th, 1758." In *History of the Descendants of Peter Spicer*, by Susan Spicer Meech and Susan Billings Meech. 388-409. Boston: F. H. Gilson, 1911.

Stark, Caleb. *Memoir and Official Correspondence of Gen. John Stark, With Notices of Several Other Offices of the Revolution.* 1860. Reprint. Gregg Press, 1972.

Starke, Jn. "Remarks on Affairs at the Portage Between Ticonderoga and Lake George, and the Mount Independence, in Sept. 1777." *BFTM* 11 (July 1964): 207-10.

Stevens, Phineas. "Journal of Capt. Phineas Stevens to and from Canada 1749." *Collections of the New-Hampshire Historical Society* 5 (1837): 199-205.

Stickney, M.A. "Massacre at Fort William Henry, 1757." *EIHC* 3 (1861): 79-84.

Stone, Enos. "Capt. Enos Stone's Journal." *NEHGR* 15 (January 1861): 299-303.

Stone, William L., ed. *Journal of Captain Pausch*. Albany: Joel Munsell's Sons, 1886.

———. trans. and ed. *Letters of Brunswick and Hessian Officers During the American Revolution*. Albany: Joel Munsell's Sons, Publishers, 1891.

———. trans. *Memoirs, Letters, and Journals of Major General Riedesel*. 2 vols. 1868. Reprint. New York: The New York Times & Arno Press, 1969.

Sullivan, James, ed. *The Papers of Sir William Johnson*. 2 vol. Albany: The University of the State of New York, 1921-1922.

Sweat, William. "Captain William Sweat's Personal Diary of the Expedition Against Ticonderoga, May 2–November 7, 1758." *EIHC* 93 (1957): 36-57.

Terrot, Charles. "Naval Action on Lake Champlain, 1776." *American Neptune* 8 (1948): 255-56.

Thacher, James. *Military Journal of the American Revolution*. Hartford, CT.: Hurlbut, Williams & Company, 1862.

Thompson, Samuel. "Diary of Lieut. Samuel Thompson of Woburn." In *The History of Woburn*, by Samuel Sewall. 547-59. Boston: Wiggin and Lunt Publishers, 1868.

Thwaites, Reuben Gold, ed. *Travels and Explorations of the Jesuit Missionaries in New France*. Vol. 70. Cleveland: The Burrows Brothers Company, 1900.

Tinkham, Seth. "The Diary of Seth Tinkham." In *History of Plymouth County, Massachusetts*, by D. Hamilton Hurd. 944-98. Philadelphia: J. W. Lewis & Co., 1884.

Topham, John. "The Journal of Captain John Topham,1775-6." *The Magazine of History* 50 (1916): 97-127.

"The Trial of Major General St. Clair, August 1778." *Coll. NYHS* 13 (1880): 1-171.

"The Trial of Major General Schuyler, October 1778." *Coll. NYHS* 12 (1879): 1-181.

True, Henry. *Journal and Letters of Rev. Henry True*. Marion, OH.: Star Press, 1900.

Trumbull, Benjamin. "A Concise Journal or Minutes of the Principal Movements Towards St. John's." *Coll. Conn. HS* 7 (1899): 137-73.

———. "The Montgomery Expedition, 1775." *BFTM* 1 (January 1927, July 1927, July 1928): 11-18; 26-33; 21-35.

Trumbull, John. *Autobiography, Reminiscences and Letters of John Trumbull from 1756 to 1841*. New Haven, CT.: B. L. Hamlen,1841.

———. "John Trumbull at Ticonderoga from His Autobiography." *BFTM* 3 (January 1933): 3-12.

Van Winkle, Mrs. John J. "Mrs. John J. Van Winkle Travel Journal." MS. Fort Ticonderoga Thompson-Pell Research Center, Ticonderoga, N.Y.

Vose, Joseph. "Journal of Lieutenant-Colonel Joseph Vose." *Publications of the Colonial Society of Massachusetts: Transactions* 7 (1900-1902): 248-262.

Walker, James. "Capt. James Walker's Journal." In *History of Bedford New Hampshire*. 474-49. Concord, N.H.: The Town of Bedford, 1903.

Ware, Joseph. "Expedition Against Quebec." *NEHGR* 6 (April 1852): 129-45.

Warner, Samuel. "Extracts from Samuel Warner's Journal Kept on the Expedition to Crown Point, 1759." In *An Historical Address Delivered at the Centennial Celebration of the Incorporation of the Town of Wilbraham*, by Rufus P. Stebbins. 208-13. Boston: George C. Rand & Avery, Printers, 1864.

Warren, Benjamin. "Diary of Capt. Benjamin Warren on Battlefield of Saratoga." *The Journal of American History* 3 (1909): 201-16.

Waterbury, David. "Personal Roster and Diary of Captain David Waterbury in the Lake George Campaign." typed transcript. Fort Ticonderoga Thompson-Pell Research Center.

Wayne, Anthony. *Orderly Book of the Northern Army at Ticonderoga and Mount Independence, from October 17th 1776, to January 8th, 1777*. Albany: J. Munsell, 1859.

Webster, Clarence J., ed. *The Journal of Jeffery Amherst*. Toronto: The Ryerson Press, 1931.

Webster, John Clarence, ed. *Journal of William Amherst in America*. London: Butler & Tannes, Ltd., 1927.

Webster, Robert. "Robert Webster's Journal." *BFTM* 2 (July 1931): 120-59.

Weeden, William B., ed. "Diary of Enos Hitchcock, D. D., A Chaplain in the Revolutionary Army with a Memoir." *Publications of the Rhode Island Historical Society* 7 (1899): 87-134, 147-63.

Welles, Lemuel Aiken, ed. "Letters of Col. Nathan Whiting Written from Camp during the French and Indian War." *Papers of the New Haven Colony Historical Society* 6 (1900): 133-50.

Wells, Bayze. "Journal of Bayze Wells." *Coll. Conn. HS* 7 (1899): 239-96.

Wheeler, Rufus. "Journal of Lieut. Rufus Wheeler of Rowley." *EIHC* 68 (1932): 371-77.

Whiting, Nathan. *Orderly Book of Colonel Nathan Whiting: Second Connecticut Regiment at Lake George 1758.* Hartford: Connecticut State Library, 1940.

Wickman, Donald, ed. "The Diary of Timothy Tuttle." *New Jersey History* 113 (Fall/Winter 1995): 61-80.

_____. "A Most Unsettled Time on Lake Champlain: The October 1776 Journal of Jahiel Steward." *Vermont History* 64 (Spring 1996): 89-98.

_____. "Breakfast on Chocolate: The Diary of Moses Greenleaf, 1777." *BFTM* 15 (1997): 482-506.

Wigglesworth, Edward. "Colonel Wigglesworth's Diary Containing His Account of the Naval Battles on Lake Champlain, Oct. 11 and 13, 1776." In *Autographs: Letters--Documents--Manuscripts Catalogue No. 1464*, by Stan. V. Henkels, Jr., 51-52. Philadelphia: Stan V. Henkels, Jr., 1932.

Wild, Ebenezer. "A Journal of a March from Cambridge, on an Expedition against Quebec in Colonel Benedict Arnold's Detachment, Sept. 13, 1775." *Proceedings of the Massachusetts Historical Society* 2, Second Series (1885-1886): 267-85.

Wilkinson, James. *Memoirs of My Own Times.* 1816. Reprint. New York: AMS Press Inc., 1973.

Williams, Thomas. "Correspondence of Doctor Thomas Williams, of Deerfield, Mass., A Surgeon in the Army." *The Historical Magazine* 7 (April 1870): 109-216.

Wilson, Commissary. *Commissary Wilson's Orderly Book, 1759.* Albany: J. Munsell, 1857.

Wood, Lemuel. "Diaries Kept by Lemuel Wood, of Boxford." *EIHC* 19 (1882): 61-80, 143-92; 20 (1883): 156-60, 198-208, 289-96; 21 (1884): 63-68.

_____. "Extract from the Diary of Lemuel Wood in Colonel Willard's Regiment of Massachusetts Militia." *BFTM* 2 (July 1932): 252-53.

Wood, William. *Select British Documents of the Canadian War of 1812.* Vol. 1, 3. Toronto: The Champlain Society, 1920-1926.

Woods, John. "Diary of John Woods June 10, 1759--November 4, 1759." Octavo Vol. 1, AAS.

Woodwell, P. M., ed. *Diary of Thomas Moody.* South Berwick, ME.: The Chronicle Print Shop, 1976.

Woolsey, Melancthon Taylor. *The Letters of Melancthon Taylor Woolsey.* Champlain, N.Y.: Moorsfield Press, 1927.

Zaboly, Gary. "A Royal Artillery Officer With Amherst: The Journal of Captain-Lieutenant Henry Skinner, May 1 - July 28, 1759." *BFTM* 15 (1993): 362-87.

Books and Monographs

Adams, Arthur G. *The Hudson Through the Years.* New York: Fordham University Press, 1996.

Allen, Joseph. *Battles of the British Navy; From A.D. 1000 to 1840.* Vol. 2. London: A. H. Baily & Co., 1842.

Anderson, Fred. *A People's Army--Massachusetts Soldiers and Society in the Seven Years' War.* New York: W. W. Norton & Company, 1985.

Ansley, Norman. *Vergennes, Vermont and the War of 1812.* Severna Park, MD.: Brooke Keefer Ltd. Editions, 1999.

Aske, Jerry, Jr., and Gardiner Lake. *History of the Shelburne Shipyard and Its Shipbuilding Activities During World War II and the Korean Conflict.* Essex Junction,

VT.: Chittenden County Regional Planning Commission, 1992.

Baldwin, Elizabeth R., et al. *Underwater Historic Preserve Feasibility Study of the Lake Champlain Steamboat Champlain II Westport, Essex County, New York.* Ferrisburg, VT: Lake Champlain Maritime Museum, 1996.

Barkley, Alexander. *Rival Routes from the West.* Albany: Report of Canal Commissioner, 1875.

Barnes, James. *Naval Actions of the War of 1812.* New York: Harper & Brothers Publishers, 1896.

[Barnes, Melvin]. *Reprint of a Short Biography of Colonel Ebenezer Allen . . .Lieutenant Samuel Allen.* Plattsburgh, N.Y.: J. W. Tuttle, Book and Job Printer, 1852.

Barranco, Peter, Jr. *Ticonderoga's Floating Drawbridge; 1871-1920.* Lake Champlain Basin Program, 1995.

Barranco, A. Peter, Jr., et. al. *Lake Champlain, Lake George, and the Upper Richelieu River Naval and Military Vessel Inventory 1742-1836.* Basin Harbor, VT.: Lake Champlain Maritime Museum, 1999.

George F. Bass, ed. *A History of Seafaring.* New York: Walker Publishing Co., Inc., 1972.

_____. *Ships and Shipwrecks of the Americas.* New York: Thames and Hudson, 1988.

The Battle of Plattsburgh---- What Historians Say About It. Albany: J. B. Lyon Company, Printers, 1914.

Beach, Allen Penfield. *Lake Champlain As Centuries Pass.* 1959. Reprint. Basin Harbor: Basin Harbor Club and the Lake Champlain Maritime Museum, 1994.

Bellesiles, Michael A. *Revolutionary Outlaws: Ethan Allen and his Struggle for Independence on the Early American Frontier.* Charlottesville, Va.: University Press of Virginia, 1993.

Bellico, Russell P. *Chronicles of Lake George: Journeys in War and Peace.* Fleischmanns, N.Y.: Purple Mountain Press, 1995.

_____. *Chronicles of Lake Champlain: Journeys in War and Peace.* Fleischmanns, N.Y.: Purple Mountain Press, 1999.

Bielinski, Stefan, ed. *A Guide to the Revolutionary War Manuscripts in the New York State Library.* Albany: New York State American Revolution Bicentennial Commission, 1976.

Bird, Harrison. *Navies in the Mountains.* New York: Oxford University Press, 1962.

Boatner, Mark Mayo, III. *Encyclopedia of the American Revolution.* New York: David McKay Company, Inc., 1966.

Bradley, A. G. *The Fight with France for North America.* New York: E. P. Dutton and Company, 1900.

Bredenberg, Oscar E. *Military Activities in the Champlain Valley after 1777.* Champlain, N.Y.: Moorsfield Press, 1962.

_____. *The Battle of Plattsburgh Bay.* Plattsburgh, N.Y.: Clinton County Historical Association, 1978.

Brown, William H., ed. *History of Warren County New York.* Glens Falls, N.Y.: Board of Supervisors of Warren County, 1963.

Buckell, Betty Ahern, ed. *No Dull Days at Huletts.* Glens Falls, N.Y.: Guy Printing Co., Inc., 1984.

_____. *Old Lake George Hotels.* Lake George, N.Y.: Buckle Press, 1986.

_____. *Lake George Boats.* Lake George, N.Y.: Buckle Press, 1990.

Burns, James MacGregor. *The Vineyard of Liberty*. New York: Alfred A. Knopf, Inc., 1981.

Butler, B. C. *Lake George and Lake Champlain*. Albany: Weed, Parsons and Co., 1868.

Callahan, Edward W., ed. *List of Officers of the Navy of the United States and of the Marine Corps from 1775 to 1900*. 1901. Reprint. New York: Haskell House Publishers, LTD., 1969.

A Canalboat Primer on the Canals of New York State. Syracuse, N.Y.: The Canal Museum, 1981.

Canal Regulations, Rates of Tolls, and Distances on the New-York State Canal. Albany: E. Croswell, Printer to the State, 1830.

Canfield, Thomas H. *Discovery: Navigation and Navigators of Lake Champlain*. 1859. Reprint. Burlington, VT.: Burlington Savings Bank, 1959.

Cardwell, M. John. "The British Expedition Against Fort Ticonderoga in 1758." Master's thesis, The University of New Brunswick, 1990.

Carpenter, Warwick Stevens. *The Summer Paradise in History*. Albany: The Delaware and Hudson Company, 1914.

A Century of Progress: History of the Delaware and Hudson Company 1823-1923. Albany, J. B. Lyon Company, 1925.

Chapelle, Howard I. *The History of American Sailing Ships*. New York: W. W. Norton & Company, Inc., 1935.

_____. *The History of the American Sailing Navy*. New York: W. W. Norton & Company, Inc., 1949.

Churchill, Winston S. *Churchill's History of the English-Speaking Peoples*. Edited by Henry Steele Commager. New York: Dodd, Mead & Company, 1965.

Clark, Delphina L. H. *Phineas Lyman----Connecticut's General*. Springfield, MA.: Connecticut Valley Historical Museum, 1964.

Clark, Raymond C. *A View of Westport, N.Y. on Lake Champlain*. Elizabethtown, N.Y.: Denton Publications, Inc., 1972.

Cohn, Arthur. *The Great Bridge "From Ticonderoga to Independent Point."* Lake Champlain Basin Program, 1995. Report 4C.

_____. Afterward to *The Steamboats of Lake Champlain 1809 to 1930.* by Ogden Ross. 1930. Reprint. Quechee, VT.: Vermont Heritage Press, 1997.

Cohn, Arthur B., ed. *A Report on the Nautical Archeology of Lake Champlain: Results of the 1982 Field Season of the Champlain Maritime Society*. Burlington, VT.: The Champlain Maritime Society, 1984.

_____. *The 1992 Fort Ticonderoga-Mount Independence Submerged Cultural Resource Survey*. Lake Champlain Basin Program, 1995, Report 4A.

Cohn, Arthur, and Kevin Crisman. *Report of the Phase 1 In-Water Archaeological Survey in the Waters Surrounding Crown Point State Historic Site*. Basin Harbor, VT.: Lake Champlain Maritime Museum, 1990.

Cohn, Arthur B., et al. *The Archaeological Reconstruction of the Lake Champlain Canal Schooner General Butler*. Ferrisburg, VT.: Lake Champlain Maritime Museum, 1996.

_____. *Underwater Preserve Feasibility Study of the Lake Champlain Canal Schooner O. J. Walker*. Ferrisburg, VT.: Lake Champlain Maritime Museum, 1996.

_____. *Lake Champlain Cultural Resources Survey--Volume 2: 1997 Results; Volume 3: 1998 Results*. Vergennes, VT.: Lake Champlain Maritime Museum, 2000.

Commager, Henry Steele, and Richard B. Morris, ed. *The Spirit of 'Seventy-Six*. Indianapolis, IN.: The Bobbs - Merrill Company, 1949.

Cone, Gertrude E. "Studies in the Development of Transportation in the Champlain Valley to 1876." Master's thesis, The University of Vermont, 1945.

Connell, Brian. *The Savage Years*. New York: Harper & Brothers Publishers, 1959.

Cook, Flavius J. *Home Sketches of Essex County: Ticonderoga*. Keeseville, N.Y.: W. Lansing & Son, 1858.

Cook, Joseph, and Edward J. Owen. *Extracts from Sketches of Ticonderoga; Burial of Lord Howe*. Ticonderoga, N.Y.: n. d.

Coolidge, Guy Omeron. *The French Occupation of the Champlain Valley from 1609 to 1759*. 1938. Reprint. Harrison, N.Y.: Harbor Hill Books, 1979.

Cooper, J. Fenimore. *The History of the Navy of the United States of America*. Vol. 1-2. Philadelphia: Lea & Blanchard, 1839.

Copeland, Fred. *Lake Champlain*. Rutland, VT.: Charles E. Tuttle Co., 1950.

Crisman, Kevin J. *The History and Construction of the United States Schooner Ticonderoga*. Alexandria, VA.: Eyrie Publications, 1983.

_____. *Of Sailing Ships and Sidewheelers*. Montpelier, VT.: Division of Historic Preservation, 1986.

_____. *The Eagle*. Shelburne, VT.: The New England Press, 1987.

_____. *The 1992 Mount Independence Phase One Underwater Archaeological Survey*. Lake Champlain Basin Program, 1995, Report 4B.

Crisman, Kevin J., and Arthur B. Cohn. *The Burlington Bay Horse Ferry Wreck and the Era of Horse-powered Watercraft*. Basin Harbor, VT.: Lake Champlain Maritime Museum, 1993.

_____. *When Horses Walked on Water: Horse-Powered Ferries in Nineteenth-Century America*. Washington, D. C.: Smithsonian Institution Press, 1998.

Crockett, Walter Hill. *A History of Lake Champlain 1609-1909*. Burlington, VT.: Hobart J. Shanley & Co., 1909.

_____. *Vermont: The Green Mountain State*. New York: The Century History Co., 1921.

Currier, John J. *History of Newburyport, Mass. 1764-1905*. Newburyport, MA.: John J. Currier, 1906.

Dann, John C. *The Revolution Remembered: Eyewitness Accounts of the War for Independence*. Chicago: The University of Chicago Press, 1980.

Davison, Rebecca, ed. *Phoenix Project*. Burlington, VT.: Champlain Maritime Society, 1981.

Dayton, Fred Erving. *Steamboat Days*. New York: Frederick A. Stokes Company, 1925.

DeCosta, B. F. *A Narrative of Events at Lake George*. New York: B. F. DeCosta, 1868.

_____. *Lake George; Its Scenes and Characteristics*. New York: Anson D. F. Randolph & Co., 1869.

_____. *Notes on the History of Fort George During the Colonial and Revolutionary Periods*. New York: J. Sabin & Sons, 1871.

_____. *The Fight at Diamond Island, Lake George*. New York: J. Sabin & Sons, 1872.

Diamant, Lincoln. *Bernard Romans*. Harrison, N.Y.: Harbor Hill Books, 1985.

Dickens, Charles. *American Notes*. 1892. Reprint. New York: St. Martin's Press, 1985.

Dow, George Francis. *History of Topsfield, Massachusetts*. Topsfield, MA.: The Topsfield Historical Society, 1940.

Duncan, John M. *Travels Through Part of the United States and Canada in 1818 and 1819*. Glasgow: Hurst, Robinson, & Company, 1823.

Dwight, Theodore, Jr. *The Northern Traveller and Northern Tour with Routes to Springs, Niagara & Quebec*. 4th ed. New York: J. & J. Harper, 1831.

Eckert, Allan W. *Wilderness Empire*. Boston: Little, Brown and Company, 1969.

Eller, E. M. *Riverine Warfare: The U.S. Navy's Operations on Inland Waters*. Washington, D.C.: Naval History Division, Department of the Navy, 1969.

Everest, Allan S. *Recollections of Clinton County and the Battle of Plattsburgh 1800-1840*. Plattsburgh, N.Y.: Clinton Historical Association, 1964.

_____. *Moses Hazen and the Canadian Refugees in the American Revolution*. Syracuse, N.Y.: Syracuse University Press, 1976.

_____. *The War of 1812 in the Champlain Valley*. Syracuse, N.Y.: Syracuse University Press, 1981.

_____. *Briefly Told, Plattsburgh, New York, 1784-1984*. Plattsburgh, N.Y.: Clinton County Historical Association, 1984.

_____. *Point au Fer on Lake Champlain*. Plattsburgh, N.Y.: Clinton County Historical Association, 1992.

Farrell, Patrick F. *Through the Light Hole: A Saga of Adirondack Mines and Men*. Utica, N.Y.: North Country Books, 1996.

Favreau, J. Arthur. *La Grande Semaine*. Worcester, MA.: Société Historique Franco-Américaine, 1909.

Feister, Lois M. *Archaeological Excavations at the Crown Point Soldiers' Barracks, 1976 and 1977*. Waterford, N.Y.: Bureau of Historic Sites, New York Office of Parks, Recreation and Historic Preservation, 1998.

Fischer, Montgomery, ed. *A Report of the Nautical Archeology of Lake Champlain: Results of the 1983 Field Season of the Champlain Maritime Society*. Burlington, VT.: The Champlain Maritime Society, 1985.

Flexner, James Thomas. *Steamboats Come True*. New York: The Viking Press, 1944.

_____. *Mohawk Baronet*. 1950. Reprint. Syracuse, N.Y.: Syracuse University Press, 1989.

Flick, Alexander C., ed. *History of the State of New York*. Vol. 4. New York: Columbia University Press, 1933.

Flood, Charles Bracelen. *Rise, And Fight Again*. New York: Dodd, Mead & Co., 1976.

Folsom, William R. *Vermonters in Battle and Other Papers*. Burlington, VT.: Lane Press, 1953.

Fowler, Barney. *Adirondack Album*. Schenectady, N.Y.: Outdoor Associates, 1974.

_____. *Adirondack Album*. Vol. 3. Schenectady, N.Y.: Outdoor Associates, 1982.

Fowler, William M., Jr. *Rebels Under Sail*. New York: Charles Scribner's Sons, 1976.

Gardner, John. *The Dory Book*. Mystic, CT.: Mystic Seaport Museum, Inc., 1987.

Garrity, Richard. *Canal Boatman*. Syracuse, N.Y.: Syracuse University Press, 1977.

Gates, William Preston. *Turn-of-the-Century Scrapbook of Jonathan Streeter Gates*. Glens Falls: Gates Publishing Company, 1999.

Gerlach, Don R. *Proud Patriot----Philip Schuyler and the War of Independence, 1775--1783*. Syracuse, N.Y.: Syracuse University Press, 1987.

Gifford, Stanley M. *Fort William Henry: A History*. Lake George, N.Y.: Fort William Henry Museum, 1955.

Gipson, Lawrence Henry. *The Great War for the Empire: The Years of Defeat, 1754-1757*. Vol. 6. New York: Alfred A. Knopf, 1946.

_____. *The Great War for the Empire: The Victorious Years, 1758-1760*. Vol. 7. New York: Alfred A. Knopf, 1949.

_____. *The Great War for the Empire: The Culmination, 1760-1763*. Vol. 8. New York: Alfred A. Knopf, 1954.

Glenn, Morris F. *The Story of Three Towns*. Ann Arbor, MI.: Braun-Brumfield, 1977.

_____. *Lake Champlain Album*. Vol. 2. Alexandria, VA.: Morris F. Glenn, 1979.

_____. *Glenn's History of Lake Champlain: Occasional Lists of Shipping on Lake Champlain*. Vol. 2. Alexandria, VA.: Morris F. Glenn, 1980.

_____. *Glenn's History of Lake Champlain: Steam Navigation*. Vol. 3. Alexandria, Va.: Morris F. Glenn, 1980.

_____. *The Capture and Burning of the Sloop Essex*. Alexandria, VA.: Morris F. Glenn, 1981.

_____. *Glenn's History of Lake Champlain: Canal Boats*. Vol. 4. Alexandria, VA.: Morris F. Glenn, n.d.

Godfrey, Frank H. *The Godfrey Letters*. Syracuse, N.Y.: The Canal Society of New York, 1973.

Godfrey, Fred G. *The Champlain Canal: Mules to Tugboats*. Monroe, N.Y.: LRA, Inc., 1994.

Gordon, William. *The History of the Rise, Progress, and Establishment of the Independence of the United States of America*. Vol. 2. New York: Samuel Campbell, 1794.

Grasso, Thomas X. *Champlain Canal*. Syracuse, N.Y.: The Canal Society of New York State, 1985.

Guttridge, Leonard F. and Jay D. Smith. *The Commodores*. New York: Harper & Row, Publishers, 1969.

Hall, Basil. *Travels in North America*. Vol. 2. 1829. Reprint. Akademische Druck, 1964.

Hamilton, Edward P. *Lake Champlain and the Upper Hudson Valley*. Ticonderoga, N.Y.: Fort Ticonderoga Association, 1959.

_____. *The French and Indian Wars*. Garden City, N.Y.: Doubleday & Company, Inc., 1962.

_____. *Fort Ticonderoga----Key to a Continent*. Boston: Little, Brown and Company, 1964.

Hamilton, Milton W. *Sir William Johnson*. Port Washington, N.Y.: Kennikat Press, 1976.

Hammersley, Sidney Ernest. *The Lake Champlain Naval Battles of 1776-1814*. Waterford, N.Y.: Col. Sidney E. Hammersley, 1959.

Hammond, S. H., and L. W. Mansfield. *Country Margins and Rambles of a Journalist*. New York: J. C. Derby, 1855.

Harlow, Alvin F. *Old Towpaths*. New York: D. Appleton and Company, 1926.

Harris, Captain E. S. *Lake George: All About It*. Glens Falls, N.Y.: Glens Falls Republican, 1903.

Hauptman, Lawrence M., and Jack Campisi, ed. *Neighbors and Intruders: An Ethnohistorical Exploration of* the Indians of Hudson's River. Ottawa: National Museums of Canada, 1978.

Haviland, William A. and Marjory W. Power. *The Original Vermonters.* Hanover, N.H.: University Press of New England, 1981.

Heitman, Francis B. *Historical Register of Officers of the Continental Army during the War of the Revolution.* Washington, D.C.: The Rare Book Shop Publishing Company, Inc., 1914.

Hemenway, Abby Maria, ed. *The Vermont Historical Gazetteer.* Vol. 1. Burlington, VT. A. M. Hemenway, 1867.

Hendrick, Ulysses Prentiss. *A History of Agriculture in the State of New York.* Albany: New York State Agricultural Society, 1933.

Hill, Henry Wayland. *Waterways and Canal Construction in New York State.* Buffalo, N.Y.: Buffalo Historical Society, 1908.

_____. *The Champlain Tercentenary 1909.* 2 vols. Albany: J. B. Lyon Company, State Printers, 1913.

Hill, Ralph Nading. *Sidewheeler Saga.* New York: Rinehart & Company, Inc., 1953.

_____. *Two Centuries of Ferry Boating.* Burlington, VT.: Lake Champlain Transportation Co., Inc., 1972.

_____. *Lake Champlain: Key to Liberty.* Montpelier, VT.: Vermont Life Magazine, 1976.

_____. "Two Centuries of Ferry Boating on Lake Champlain." In *Lake Champlain Ferryboats.* Edited by Jerry P. Williams. 7-32. Burlington: Lake Champlain Transportation Company, 1990.

Hinman, Royal R. comp. *A Historical Collection of the Part Sustained by Connecticut.* Hartford: E. Gleason, 1842.

Hislop, Codman. *Albany: Dutch, English, and American.* Albany: The Argus Press, 1936.

History of Oneida County, New York. Philadelphia: Everts & Fariss, 1878.

History of Washington County, New York. 1878: Reprint. Interlaken, N.Y.: Heart of the Lakes Publishing, 1991.

Hitsman, J. MacKay. *The Incredible War of 1812.* Toronto: University of Toronto Press, 1965.

Hocker, Frederick M. "The Development of the Sailing Carrying Trade on Lake Champlain 1742-1823." Master's thesis, Middlebury College, 1984.

Holden, James A., ed. *The Centenary of the Battle of Plattsburgh.* Albany: The University of the State of New York, 1914.

Howe, Dennis E. *This Ragged, Starved, Lousy, Pocky Army.* Concord, N.H.: The Printed Word, 1996.

Huden, John C., comp. *Archaeology in Vermont.* Rutland, VT.: Charles E. Tuttle Company, 1971.

Hudleston, F. J. *Gentleman Johnny Burgoyne.* Garden City, N.Y.: Garden City Publishing Co., 1927.

James, William. *A Full and Correct Account of the Chief Naval Occurrences of the Late War Between Great Britain and the United States of America.* London: T. Egerton, 1817.

Jellison, Charles A. *Ethan Allen, Frontier Rebel.* Syracuse, N.Y.: Syracuse University Press, 1969.

Jones, Charles Henry. *History of the Campaign for the Conquest of Canada in 1776.* 1882. Reprint. New York: Research Reprints, Inc., 1970.

Jones, Thomas. *History of New York.* Vol. 1. New York: The New-York Historical Society, 1879.

Keenleyside, Hugh Ll. *Canada and the United States.* Port Washington, N.Y.: Kennikat Press, 1971.

Kellogg, Lewis. *A Sketch of the History of Whitehall.* Whitehall, N.Y.: S. B. Fairman, Printer, 1847.

Ketchum, Richard M. *Saratoga: Turning Point of America's Revolutionary War.* New York: Henry Holt and Company, Inc., 1997.

Kimball, Francis P. *New York----The Canal State.* Albany: The Argus Press, 1937.

Knight, Arthur S., ed. *The Adirondack Guide ---- Vacationland: In Picture, Story and History.* Lake George, N.Y.: Press of Lake George Printing Co., 1929.

_____. *Vacationland: In Picture, Story and History.* Lake George, N.Y.: Adirondack Resorts Press, Inc., 1946-1960.

Krueger, John W. *A Most Memorable Day: The Battle of Lake George, September 8, 1775.* Saranac Lake, N.Y.: North Country Community College Press, 1980.

Lake Champlain Tercentenary. Albany, N.Y.: New York State Education Department, 1909.

Lamb Wallace E. *Lake George: Facts and Anecdotes.* Glens Falls, N.Y.: Glens Falls Post Co., 1938.

_____. *The Lake Champlain and Lake George Valleys.* Vol. 1 and 2. New York: The American Historical Company, Inc., 1940.

Langworthy, Bess H. *History of Cumberland Head.* Plattsburgh, N.Y.: pub.n.a., 1961.

Lape, Jane M., ed. *Ticonderoga----Patches and Patterns from Its Past.* Ticonderoga, N.Y.: The Ticonderoga Historical Society, 1969.

Larkin, F. Daniel. *New York Canals: A Short History.* Fleischmanns, N.Y.: Purple Mountain Press, 1998.

Latham, Frank B. *Jacob Brown and the War of 1812.* New York: Cowles Book Company, Inc., 1971.

Leach, Douglas Edward. *Roots of Conflict: British Armed Forces and the Colonial Americans, 1667-1763.* Chapel Hill, N.C.: The University of North Carolina Press, 1986.

Lee, James, ed. *Tales the Boatmen Told.* Exton, Pa: Canal Press Incorporated, 1977.

Lépine, André. *La Richelieu Archeologique.* Montreal: La Societé du Musée Militaire et Maritime, 1983.

Lewis, Dennis M. *British Naval Activity on Lake Champlain during the War of 1812.* Plattsburgh: Clinton Historical Association, 1994.

Loescher, Burt G. *The History of Rogers Rangers.* Vol. 1. San Francisco: Burt G. Loescher, 1946.

_____. *The History of Rogers Rangers: Officers and Noncommissioned Officers.* Vol. 3. Burlingame, CA.: Burt Garfield Loescher, 1957.

_____. *Geneis: Rogers Rangers the First Green Berets.* Vol. 2. San Mateo, CA.: B. G. Loescher, 1969.

Lonergan, Carroll Vincent. *Ticonderoga: Historic Portage.* Ticonderoga, N.Y.: Fort Mount Hope Society Press, 1959.

Lord, Thomas Reeves. *Stories of Lake George, Fact and Fancy.* Pemberton, N.J.: Pinelands Press, 1987.

_____. *Still More Stories of Lake George Fact and Fancy.* Pemberton, N.J.: Pinelands Press, 1999.

Lossing, Benson J. *The Pictorial Field-Book of the Revolution.* Vol. 1. 1851. Reprint. Freeport, N.Y.: Books for Libraries Press, 1969.

_____. *Pictorial Field-Book of the War of 1812.* New York: Harper & Brothers, Publishers, 1869.

_____. *The Life and Times of Philip Schuyler*. Vol. 2. New York: Sheldon & Company, 1873.

Lundeberg, Philip K. *The Continental Gunboat Philadelphia and the Northern Campaign of 1776*. Washington, D.C.: Smithsonian Institution, 1966.

_____. *The Gunboat Philadelphia and the Defense of the Lake Champlain in 1776*. Basin Harbor, VT.: Lake Champlain Maritime Museum, 1995.

MacDonald, James N., ed. *Historical Sketches of the Town of Plattsburgh*. Elizabethtown, N.Y.: Denton Publications, 1975.

Macdonough, Rodney. *Life of Commodore Thomas Macdonough*. Boston: The Fort Hill Press, 1909.

MacLeod, D. Peter. *The Canadian Iroquois and the Seven Years' War*. Toronto: Dundurn Press, 1996.

Maguire, Robert, ed. *The Tour to the Northern Lakes of James Madison & Thomas Jefferson May-June 1791*. Ticonderoga, N.Y.: Fort Ticonderoga, 1995.

Mahan, A. T. *Sea Power in Its Relations to the War of 1812*. Vol. 2. Boston: Little, Brown, and Company, 1905.

_____. *War of American Independence*. Boston: Little, Brown, and Co., 1913.

Mante, Thomas. *The History of the Late War in North-America*. 1772. Reprint. New York: Research Reprints, Inc., n.d.

Martin, James Kirby. *Benedict Arnold: Revolutionary Hero*. New York: New York University Press, 1997.

Marvin, Henry. *A Complete History of Lake George*. New York: Sibells & Maigne, Printers, 1853.

Mason, Richard A., ed. *Exploring Rogers Island*. Fort Edward, N.Y.: The Rogers Island Historical Association, 1969.

McFee, Michelle A. *A Long Haul: The Story of the New York State Barge Canal*. Fleischmanns, N.Y.: Purple Mountain Press, 1998.

McKelvey, William J., Jr. *Champlain to Chesapeake*. Exton, PA.: Canal Press Inc., 1978.

Mereness, Newton D. *Travels in the American Colonies*. 1916. Reprint. New York: Antiquarian Press, LTD., 1961.

Mix, David E. *Catalogue Maps and Surveys, in the Office of the Secretary of State, State Engineer and Surveyor*. Albany: Charles Van Benthuysen, 1859.

Morton, Doris Begor. *Philip Skene of Skenesborough*. Granville, N.Y.: The Grastorf Press, 1959.

_____. comp. *Day Before Yesterday*. Whitehall: Town Board of Whitehall, 1977.

Mountain Steamboats. Lake George, N.Y.: The Lake George Steamboat Company, 1981.

Muller, Charles G. *The Proudest Day*. New York: The John Day Company, 1960.

Muller, H. N. III. *The Commerical History of the Lake Champlain-Richelieu River Route 1760-1815*. Ann Arbor, MI.: University Microfilms, 1969.

Murray, W. H. H. *Lake Champlain and Its Shores*. Boston: DeWolfe, Fiske & Co., 1890.

Nelson, Paul David. *General Horatio Gates*. Baton Rouge, LA.: Louisiana State University Press, 1976.

O'Brien, Kathryn E. *The Great and the Gracious on Millionaires' Row*. Sylvan Beach, N.Y.: North Country Books, 1978.

[O'Callaghan, E. B.], comp. *Calendar of N.Y. Colonial Manuscripts: Indorsed Land Papers 1643-1803*. 1864. Reprint. Harrison, N.Y.: Harbor Hill Books, 1987.

Offensend, Dorothy Backus. *The Sexton Boatbuilders of Hague*. Pawlet, VT.: D. B. Offensend, 1982.

O'Hara, John E. "Erie's Junior Partner." Ph.D. diss., Columbia University, 1951.

O'Malley, Charles T. *Low Bridges and High Water on the New York State Barge Canal*. Utica, N.Y.: North Country Books, 1991.

Osler, Edward, Esq. *The Life of Admiral Viscount Exmouth*. London: Smith Elder & Co., 1835.

Padeni, Scott A. *Final Report of the Literature Review and Shipwreck Inventory of Lake George's Northern End*. Ballston Spa, N.Y.: Scott A. Padeni, 1999.

[Palmer, Peter S.]. *Historical Sketch of Plattsburgh, New York*. Plattsburgh Republican, 1893.

Palmer, Peter S. *History of Lake Champlain*. 1886. Reprint. Harrison, N.Y.: Harbor Hill Books, 1983.

Pargellis, Stanley McCrory. *Lord Loudoun in North America*. Hampden, CT.: Archon Books, 1968.

_____. ed. *Military Affairs in North America 1748-1765*. New Haven: Archon Books, 1969.

Parkman, Francis, *Montcalm and Wolfe*. 1884. Reprint. New York: Atheneum, 1984.

_____. *France and England in North America*. Boston: Little, Brown, and Company, 1885.

Paullin, Charles Oscar. *The Navy of the American Revolution*. 1906. Reprint. New York: Haskell House Publishers Ltd., 1971.

Pell, S. H. P. *Fort Ticonderoga, A Short History*. Ticonderoga, N.Y.: Fort Ticonderoga Museum, 1978.

Perry, Arthur Latham. *Origins of Williamstown*. 3rd ed. Williamstown, MA.: A. L. Perry, 1900.

Pew, William A. *Colonel Ephraim Williams: An Appreciation*. Williamstown, MA.: Williams College, 1919.

Pope-Hennessy, Una, ed. *The Aristocratic Journey*. New York: G.P. Putnam's Sons, 1931.

Porter, Marjorie Lansing. *Old Plattsburgh*. Plattsburgh, N.Y.: Clinton Press, Inc., 1944.

Possons, Charles H. *Possons's Guide to Lake George, Lake Champlain and Adirondacks*. Glens Falls, N.Y.: Chas. H. Possons, Publisher, 1888.

Powers, M. J. *A Summer Paradise*. Albany: The Delaware and Hudson Railroad, 1932.

Randall, Willard Sterne. *Benedict Arnold: Patriot and Traitor*. New York: William Morrow and Company, Inc., 1990.

Randolph, Sarah N. *The Domestic Life of Thomas Jefferson*. New York: Harper & Brothers Publishers, 1871.

Rann, W. S., ed. *History of Chittenden County Vermont*. Syracuse, N.Y.: D. Mason & Co., 1886.

Reid, Max W. *Lake George and Lake Champlain*. New York: G. P. Putnam's Sons, 1910.

Richards, Frederick B. *The Black Watch*. Ticonderoga, N.Y.: Fort Ticonderoga Museum, 1926.

Robinson, Rowland E. *Vermont, A Study of Independence*. Boston: Houghton Mifflin Company, 1892.

Roessele, T. E. *Lake George: A Descriptive and Historical Sketch*. Lake George, N.Y.: T. E. Roessele, 1887.

Rogers, Allan. *Empire and Liberty*. Berkeley, CA.: University of California Press, 1974.

Roosevelt, Theodore. *The Naval War of 1812*. New York: G. P. Putnam's Sons, 1882.

Ross, Ogden, J. *The Steamboats of Lake Champlain 1809 to 1930*. Albany: Press of the Delaware and Hudson Railroad, 1930.

_____. *The Steamboats of Lake George 1817 to 1932*. Albany: Press of the Delaware and Hudson Railroad, 1932.

Royce, Caroline Halstead. *Bessboro: A History of Westport, Essex Co., N.Y.* Elizabethtown, N.Y.: C. H. Royce, 1904.

Russell, Howard S. *A Long, Deep Furrow: Three Centuries of Farming in New England*. Hanover, N.H.: University Press of New England, 1976.

Salsig, Doyen, ed. *Parole: Quebec: Countersign: Ticonderoga----Second New Jersey Regimental Orderly Book, 1776*. Cranbury, N.J.: Associated Presses, Inc., 1980.

Seelye, Elizabeth Eggleston. *Lake George in History*. 2nd ed. Lake George, N.Y.: Elwyn Seelye, 1896.

_____. *Saratoga and Lake Champlain in History*. Lake George, N.Y.: Elwyn Seelye, 1898.

Selesky, Harold E. *War and Society in Colonial Connecticut*. New Haven: Yale University Press, 1990.

Sévigny, P. André. *Trade and Navigation on the Chambly Canal: A Historical Review*. Ottawa: National Historic Parks and Sites Branch, Parks Canada, 1983.

Shaughnessy, Jim. *Delaware & Hudson*. Berkeley, CA.: Howell - North Books, 1967.

_____. *The Rutland Road*. 2nd ed. Syracuse: Syracuse University Press, 1997.

Shaw, Ronald E. *Erie Water West*. Lexington, KY.: University of Kentucky Press, 1966.

Shelton, Hal T. *General Richard Montgomery and the American Revolution*. New York: New York University Press, 1994.

Sherman, Gordon C., and Elsie L. Sherman. *An Illuminating History of the Champlain Valley and the Adirondack Mountains, 1814-1929*. Vol. 2. Elizabethtown, N.Y.: Denton Publications, Inc., 1977.

Silliman, Benjamin. *Remarks Made on a Short Tour Between Hartford and Quebec in the Autumn of 1819*. 2nd ed. New Haven, CT.: S. Converse, 1824.

Smith, Charles R. *Marines in the Revolution: A History of the Continental Marines in the American Revolution 1775-1783*. Washington, D.C.: History and Museums Division, Headquarters, U.S. Marine Corps, 1975.

Smith, Edgar Newbold. *American Naval Broadsides: A Collection of Early Naval Prints (1745-1815)*. New York: Philadelphia Maritime Museum and Clarkson N. Potter, Inc. Publisher, 1974.

Smith, H. P., ed. *History of Warren County*. Syracuse, N.Y.: D. Mason & Co. Pub., 1885.

_____. *History of Addison County*. Syracuse, N.Y.: D. Mason & Co. Pub., 1886.

Smith, Justin H. *Arnold's March from Cambridge to Quebec*. 1903. Reprint. Bowie, MD.: Heritage Books, Inc., 1998.

Smith, R. P. *Historical and Statistical Gazetteer of New York State*. Syracuse, N.Y.: R. P. Smith, 1860.

Smith, William Henry. *The Life and Public Services of Arthur St. Clair*. Cincinnati, OH.: Robert Clarke & Co., 1882.

Snider, C. H. J. *In the Wake of the Eighteen-Twelvers*. 1913. Reprint. London: Cornmarket Press Limited, 1969.

Soley, James Russell. *The Boys of 1812*. Boston: Estes and Lauriat, 1887.

Spafford, Horatio Gates. *A Gazetteer of the State of New York*. Albany: B.D. Packard and Horatio Gates Spafford, 1824.

Spears, John R. *The History of Our Navy*. New York: Charles Scribner's Sons, 1897.

Springer, Ethel M. and Thomas F. Hahn, *Canal Boat Children*. Shepherdstown, W. VA.: The American Canal & Transportation Center, 1981.

Stahl, John M. *The Battle of Plattsburgh; A Study in and of the War of 1812*. Illinois: The Van Trump Company, 1918.

Stanley, George F. G. *Canada Invaded*. Toronto: A. M. Hakkert Ltd., 1973.

Starbuck, David R. *The Great Warpath: British Military Sites from Albany to Crown Point*. Hanover, N.H.: University Press of New England, 1999.

Steele, Ian K. *Betrayals: Fort William Henry and the "Massacre"*. New York: Oxford University Press, 1990.

Steinback, Elsa Kny. *Sweet Peas and a White Bridge: On Lake George When Steam Was King*. Burlington, VT.: The George Little Press, 1974.

Stevenson, Robert Louis. *Ticonderoga: A Legend of the West Highlands*. 1887. Reprint. New York: The Fort Ticonderoga Museum, 1947.

Stoddard, S. R. *Ticonderoga: Past and Present*. Albany: Weed, Parsons and Company, Printers, 1873.

_____. *Lake George: A Book of To-day*. Albany, N.Y.: Van Benthuysen & Sons, Printers, 1880.

_____. *Lake George and Lake Champlain a Book of To-day*. Glens Falls, N.Y.: S. R. Stoddard, 1900, 1901, 1906.

Stone, R. G. *An Account of the Anniversary of the Battle of Plattsburgh*. Plattsburgh, N.Y.: Plattsburgh Republican, 1843.

Stone, William L. *The Campaign of Lieut. Gen. John Burgoyne*. Albany: Joel Munsell, 1877.

_____. *The Campaign of Lieut. Gen. John Burgoyne and the Expedition of Lieut. Col. Barry St. Leger*. Albany: Joel Munsell, 1877.

Stott, Earl E. *Exploring Rogers Island*. Fort Edwards, N.Y.: The Rogers Island Historical Association, 1969.

Strum, Richard M. *Ticonderoga: Lake Champlain Steamboat*. Shelburne, VT.: Shelburne Museum, 1998.

Styles, R. S. *A Descriptive and Historical Guide to the Valley of Lake Champlain and the Adirondacks*. Burlington, VT.: R. S. Styles' Steam Printing House, 1871.

Sullivan, John L. *Commentary on the New System of Naval Architecture of William Annesley*. Troy, N.Y.: William S. Parker, 1823.

Sullivan, Nell Jane Barnett, and David Kendall Martin. *A History of the Town of Chazy*. Burlington, VT.: George Little Press, Inc., 1970.

Swayze, Nathan L. *Engraved Powder Horns*. Yazoo City, MS.: Gun Hill Pub. Co., 1978.

Swift, Samuel. *History of the Town of Middlebury*. Middlebury, VT.: A. H. Copeland, 1859.

Taylor, Daniel T. *The Shores of Champlain*. Champlain, N.Y.: Moorsfield Press, 1979.

Thompson, Zadock. *History of Vermont*. Part 3. Burlington, VT.: Chauncey Goodrich, 1842.

_____. *Guide to Lake George, Lake Champlain, Montreal and Quebec*. Burlington: Chauncey Goodrich, 1845.

_____. *History of the State of Vermont*. Burlington, VT.: Smith & Co., 1858.

Thorne, Frederick C. *Pilot Knob Story: An Historical Report of Its Life and Times*. Pilot Knob, N.Y.: F. C. Thorne, 1977.

Todish, Timothy J. *America's First World War.* Grand Rapids, Mich.: Suagothel Productions Ltd., 1982.

Trost, Alfred H., and Robert C. DeLond, eds. *A History Celebrating the 150th Anniversary of the Town of Essex, N.Y. 1805-1955.* Malone, N.Y.: The Industrial Press, 1955.

Tucker, Spencer C. *The Jeffersonian Gunboat Navy.* Columbia, S.C.: University of South Carolina Press, 1993.

Tyrell, William G. *Champlain and the French in New York.* Albany: The University of the State of New York, the State Education Department, 1959.

Van De Water, Frederic F. *Lake Champlain and Lake George.* Indianapolis: The Bobbs-Merrill Company, 1946.

Von Eelking, Max. *The German Allied Troops in the North American War of Independence 1776-1783.* Translated by J. G. Rosengarten. Albany: Joel Munsell's Sons, Publishers, 1893.

Ward, Christopher. *The War of the Revolution.* New York: The Macmillan Company, 1952.

Warner, C. B., and C. Eleanor Hall. *History of Port Henry.* Rutland, VT.: The Tuttle Co., 1931.

Washington, Ida H., and Paul A. Washington. *Carleton's Raid.* Canaan, N.H.: Phoenix Publishing, 1977.

Watson, Winslow C. *The Military and Civil History of the County of Essex, N.Y.* Albany: J. Munsell, 1869.

Watt, Gavin K. *The Burning of the Valleys: Daring Raids from Canada Against the New York Frontier in the Fall of 1780.* Toronto: Dundurn Press, 1997.

Westcott, Thompson. *Life of John Fitch.* Philadelphia: J. B. Lippincott & Co., 1857.

Whitehall Bicentennial. Whitehall, N.Y.: Whitehall Bicentennial Association, 1959.

Whitford, Noble E. *History of the Canal System of the State of New York.* Vol. 1-2: Albany: Brandow Printing Company, 1906.

Whittemore, Charles P. *A General of the Revolution, John Sullivan of New Hampshire.* New York: Columbia University Press, 1961.

Whittier, Bob. *Paddle Wheel Steamers and Their Giant Engines.* Duxbury, Ma.: Seamaster Boats, Inc., 1983.

Wickman, Donald H. "Built with Spirit, Deserted in Darkness: The American Occupation of Mount Independence 1776-1777." Master's thesis, University of Vermont, 1993.

Williams, Frank M. *The Story of the New York State Canals.* Albany: J.B. Lyon Company, Printers, 1916.

Wright, Wyllis E. *Colonel Ephraim Williams: A Documentary Life.* Pittsfield, MA.: Berkshire County Historical Society, 1970.

Wrong, George M. *The Conquest of New France.* New Haven, CT.: Yale University Press, 1921.

_____. *Canada and the American Revolution.* New York: The Macmillan Company, 1935.

Wyld, Lionel D. *40'x 28'x 4': The Erie Canal----150 Years.* Rome, N.Y.: Oneida County Erie Canal Commemoration Commission, 1967.

Wynkoop, William. "The Wynkoop Family." In *A Collection of Papers Read Before the Bucks County Historical Society,* Edited by Harman Yerkes et al. Riegelsville, PA.: B. F. Fackenthal, Jr. 1909.

Young, Alfred F. *The Democratic Republicans of New York: The Origins 1763-1797.* Chapel Hill: The University of North Carolina Press, 1967.

Zarzynski, Joseph W. *Monster Wrecks of Lock Ness and Lake Champlain.* Wilton, N.Y.: M-Z Information, 1986.

_____. *Champ----Beyond the Legend.* Wilton, N.Y.: M-Z Information, 1988.

_____. *Lake George's Forward: Historic Vessel, Shipwreck Preserve, and "Underwater Classroom".* Wilton, N.Y.: Bateaux Below, Inc., 1998.

Zarzynski, Joseph W., and D. K. Abbass. *The Lake George, New York Steam Launch Cadet Shipwreck Study--1998 Report.* Wilton, N.Y.: Bateaux Below, Inc., 1999.

Zarzynski, Joseph W., and Bob Benway. *Lake George, New York's D & H "Submarine Railway": A Report on Its History and Bateaux Below, Inc.'s Archaeological Survey.* Wilton, N.Y.: Bateaux Below, Inc., 2000.

Magazines, Pamphlets, Periodicals, and Unpublished Papers

Abass, D. K., Robert Cembrola, and Joseph W. Zarzynski. "The Lake George Radeau: An Intact Vessel of 1758." *Underwater Archaeology* (1992): 142-47.

Baldwin, Elizabeth Robinson. "The Steamboat Wrecks of Lake Champlain." *Underwater Archaeology* (1996):. 122-27.

Barker, Elmer Eugene. *The Story of Crown Point Iron.* Ironville, N.Y.: The Penfield Foundation, 1969.

Bellico, Russell. "Gateway in the North: Lake Champlain." *Skin Diver,* March 1973.

_____. "Sails and Steamers in the Mountains." *Aquarius,* Fall 1974.

_____. "Diving into History." *Adirondack Life,* Fall 1976.

_____. "The Battle of Plattsburgh." *Adirondack Life,* September/October 1977.

_____. "The Cruise of the Juniper." *Adirondack Life,* May/June 1978.

_____. "The Search for Arnold's Navy." *Adirondack Life,* September/October 1980.

_____. "Beneath Lake George: Underwater Paradise." *Lake Champlain Waterways,* June 1982.

_____. "The Abercromby Expedition." *Adirondack Life,* July/August 1983.

_____. "Battle on Lake Champlain." *American History Illustrated,* March 1985.

_____. "The Search for Benedict Arnold's Navy." *American History Illustrated,* March 1985.

_____. "The *General Butler.*" *Skin Diver,* September 1985.

_____. "Littered With History." *Scubapro Diving,* Summer 1986.

_____. "Lake Champlain, A Storehouse of Marine History." *Scubapro Diving,* Fall 1987.

_____. "Historic Preservation: The Wreck of the *Champlain.*" *Adirondack Life,* July/August 1989.

_____. "Ghost from the Depths." *American History Illustrated,* March/April 1992.

_____. "Radeau Below: On the Floor of Lake George Since 1758--North America's Oldest Intact Warship." *Sea History,* Autumn 1992, 18-19.

_____. "The Need for a Fort George Visitor Center." *Proceedings: First Annual Conference of Heritage Tour-*

ism in the Adirondack Region. Glens Falls: Adirondack Regional Chambers of Commerce, 1997, 61-64.

_____. *The Lake George Nautical Newsletter*. 6 vols. 15 articles. (1992-1997).

_____. with Joseph W. Zarzynski and D. K. Abbass. "Strange Bedfellows: Research and Politics of the *Land Tortoise*, Lake George's 1758 Radeau Shipwreck." *Underwater Archaeology* (1994): 74-79.

"Biographical Sketch of Captain Thomas Macdonough." *Analectic Magazine and Naval Chronicle* 7 (March 1816): 201-24.

Blow, David J. "*Vermont I*: Lake Champlain's First Steamboat." *Vermont History* 34 (April 1966): 115-22.

Bottum, Lynn H. "*Oakes Ames/Champlain*----The Biography of a Lake Champlain Steamboat." *Vermont History* 51 (Summer 1983): 133-57.

Bredenberg, Oscar E. "The American Champlain Fleet, 1775-77." *BFTM* 12 (September 1964): 249-63.

_____. "The Royal Savage," *BFTM* 12 (September 1966): 128-49.

Burns, Brian. "Carleton in the Valley or the Year of the Burning." *BFTM* 13 (Fall 1980): 398-411.

Campbell, Karen Stites. "Propaganda, Pestilence, and Prosperity: Burlington's Camptown Days During the War of 1812." *Vermont History* 64 (Summer 1996): p.n.a.

Cardwell, M. John. "Mismanagement: The 1758 British Expedition Against Carillon." *BFTM* 15 (1992): 236-91.

Carroll, Hanson. "Skin Diving." *Vermont Life*, Summer 1960.

Charland, Thomas M. "The Lake Champlain Army and the Fall of Montreal." *Vermont History* 28 (October 1960): 293-301.

Chase, Jack. "Phoenix--Silent Mistress of Lake Champlain." *Adirondac*, July 1982, 4-7.

_____. "The Steamboat Graveyard--A Preliminary Report." *Champlain Maritime Society Soundings*, Fall/Winter 1984, 4.

Cohn, Arthur B. "The Fort Ticonderoga King's Shipyard Excavation: 1984 Field---Season Report." *BFTM* 14 (Fall 1985): 337-55.

_____. "An Incident Not Known to History: Squire Ferris and Benedict Arnold at Ferris Bay, October 13, 1776." *Vermont History* 55 (Spring 1987): 108-10.

Cohn, Arthur, and Marshall True. "The Wreck of the *General Butler* and the Mystery of Lake Champlain's Sailing Canal Boats." *Vermont History* 60 (Winter 1992): 29-45.

Cone, Gertrude E. "Early Sailing Craft on Lake Champlain." *North Country Life*, Winter 1950.

Cook, Joseph. *An Historical Address*. Ticonderoga, N.Y.: Ticonderoga Historical Society, 1864.

Copeland, Fred. "Champlain Canal Days." *The Vermonter*, August 1941.

Cortesi, Lawrence. "The Tragic Romance of Jane McCrea." *American History Illustrated*, April 1985.

Cozzi, J. "The Lake Champlain Sailing Canal Boat." *Underwater Archaeology* (1996): 128-33.

Crisman, Kevin J. "The Construction of the Boscawen." *BFTM* 14 (Fall 1985): 357-70.

_____. "The Fort Ticonderoga King's Shipyard Excavation: The Artifacts." *BFTM* 14 (Fall 1985): 375-436.

Dawson, Henry B. "The Battle of Bennington." *The Historical Magazine* 7 (May 1870): 289-305.

Dechame, Roger R. P. "The First Fort at Fort Ticonderoga." *BFTM* 15 (Winter 1988): 8-14.

_____. "Why Carillon?" *BFTM* 13 (Fall 1980): 432-46.

DeCosta, B. F. "The Fight at Diamond Island." *NEHGR* 26 (April 1872): 147-52.

Dufour, Madeleine M. "Samuel De Champlain and the Discovery of the Lake." *BFTM* 14 (Summer 1984): 271-76.

Emery, Eric B. " 'Gallies are Unquestionably the Best Description of Vessels for the Northern Parts of this Lake': The Excavation and Study of the U.S.N. Row Galley *Allen* on Lake Champlain." *Underwater Archaeology* (1996): 134-39.

Fecteau, Lois. "Benedict Arnold's Long-Lost Gunboat." *Soundings*, January 1998, A32.

Feister, Lois M. "Archaeological Testing at Fort Gage, a Provincial Redoubt of 1758 at Lake George, New York." *The Bulletin and Journal of Archaeology of New York State* 90 (Spring 1985): 40-59.

Fisher, Charles L. "The Archaeology of Provincial Officers' Huts at Crown Point State Historic Site." *Northeast Historical Archaeology* 24 (1995): 65-85.

Frise, Joseph R. "A Trumbull Map of Fort Ticonderoga." *BFTM* 13 (June 1971): 129-36.

Gardner, John. "Famous Boat Type in Transitional Stage." *National Fisherman*, May, August 1967.

Gerlach, Don R. "The Fall of Ticonderoga in 1777: Who Was Responsible." *BFTM* 14 (Summer 1982): 131-57.

_____. "The British Invasion of 1780 and 'A Character. . . Debased Beyond Description.' " *BFTM* 14 (Summer 1984): 311-21.

Grout, Derek R. "The *Phoenix* Lives!." *Skin Diver*, August 1981, 70, 84-85, 92-93.

Hagglund, L. F. *A Page from the Past*, 2nd ed. Lake George, N.Y.: Adirondack Resorts Press, 1949.

Hamilton, Edward P. "An Historic Mortar." *BFTM* 10 (February 1960): 299-303.

Hamilton, Milton W. "Battle Report: General William Johnson's Letter to the Governors, Lake George, September 9-10, 1755." *Proceedings of the American Antiquarian Society* 74 (Part 1, 1964): 19-36.

Hays, James T., David E. Mize, and Richard W. Ward. "Guns Under Lake Champlain." *York State Tradition*, Winter 1963.

Heinrichs, Jr., Waldo H. "The Battle of Plattsburgh, 1814-The Losers." *American Neptune*. 21 (January 1961): 42-56.

Hill, Ralph N., Jr. "Shelburne Shipyard." *Vermont Life*, Autumn 1953.

_____. "Sidewheeler for Shelburne." *American Heritage*, April 1955.

_____. "The One. . .The Only Ti." *Vermont Life*, Summer 1961.

_____. "A New Era for Lady Ti." *Yankee*, November 1983.

Holden, James Austin. "What Ethan Allen Really Said at Ticonderoga." *Proceedings of the New York State Historical Association* 9 (1910): 351-56.

Huden, John C. "The Admiral of Lake Champlain." *Vermont History* 30 (January 1962): 66-69.

Hunt, Livingston. "A Forgotten Commodore--Thomas Macdonough." *United States Naval Institute* (November 1931): 1485-87.

Juckett, Martha Robbins. *My Canaling Days.* Edited by Dorothy M. Parker. Reprint. Whitehall: N.Y.: Historical Society of Whitehall, 1972.

Kane, Roberta. "The Fort That Almost Lived Twice." *Adirondack Bits 'n Pieces,* Winter 1983-84.

Kellogg, Lewis. *A Sketch of the History of Whitehall.* Whitehall, N.Y.: S. B. Fairman, Printer, 1847.

Krueger, John W. "Troop Life at the Champlain Valley Forts During the American Revolution." *BFTM* 14 (Summer 1982): 158-64; (Fall 1983): 220-49; (Summer 1984): 277-310.

Lépine, André. "An 18th Century Wreck in the Richelieu River, Quebec, Canada." *The International Journal of Nautical Archaeology and Underwater Exploration* 8.4 (1979): 340-46.

_____. "A Wreck Believed to Be a French 'Bateau' Sunk During Action in 1760 off Isle-aux-noix in the Richelieu River, Quebec, Canada." *The International Journal of Nautical Archaeology and Underwater Exploration* 10.1 (1981):41-50.

Lewis, Dennis M. "An Expedition Upon Lake Champlain: Murray's Raid, 1813." *Proceedings of the Champlain Valley Symposium,* Edited by Bruce P. Stark. Plattsburgh, N.Y.: Clinton County Historical Association, 1982.

_____. "The Naval Campaign of 1759 on Lake Champlain." *BFTM* 14 (Fall 1983): 203-16.

Loomis, D. A. "Steamers Which Have Been Engaged in Regular Traffic on Lake Champlain During 124 Years." *The Vermonter,* February 1933, 32.

Lundeberg, Philip K. *Search for Continental Gunboats at Schuyler Island, Lake Champlain, New York.* Washington, D.C.: National Geographic Society Research Reports, 1976.

MacGregor, Bruce. "A Failure to Communicate." *American History Illustrated,* October 1985.

Martin, Sterling. "Memoir of a Summer 'Dig.' " *BFTM* 15 (1992): 316-22.

Mazet, Horace Sawyer. "Lake Champlain Yields Historic Relics." *Motor Boating,* February 1935.

McCulloch, Ian, trans. and ed. " 'Believe Us, Sir, This Will Impress Few People!' Spin-Doctoring--18th Century Style." *BFTM* 16 (1998): 92-107.

Meiklejohn, Andrew G. "The Champlain Canal---Remarks of Hon. Andrew G. Meiklejohn." 5 April 1964, NYSL.

Miksch, Heidi. "The Fort Ticonderoga King's Shipyard Excavation: The Conservation Program." *BFTM* 14 (Fall 1985): 371-74.

Mize, David E. *Scuba Explorers Research.* Plattsburgh, N.Y.: Clinton County Historical Association, 1967.

Morton, Doris Begor. *Whitehall in the War of 1812.* Whitehall, N.Y.: Washington County Historical Society, 1964.

_____. *Birth of the United States Navy.* Whitehall, N.Y.: Whitehall Times, 1982.

_____. "Birth of a Navy." *Adirondack Bits 'n Pieces,* Winter 1983-84.

Muller, H. N., III. "A 'Traitorous and Diabolical Traffic': The Commerce of the Champlain---Richelieu Corridor During the War of 1812." *Vermont History* 44 (Spring 1976):78-96.

Muller, H. N. and David A. Donath. " 'The Road Not Taken': A Reassessment of Burgoyne's Campaign." *BFTM* 13 (1973):272-85.

Muller, H. Nicholas, III, and Marshall M. True. "All Unquiet on the Waterfront." *Vermont Life,* Summer 1985.

Muratori, Marisa. "The Lac du Saint Sacrement." *Adirondack Life,* September/October 1989.

Murray, Eleanor S. "The Invasion of Northern New York." *BFTM* 7 (July 1946):3-21.

_____. "Resume of the Court Martial of General St. Clair Resulting from the Evacuation of Fort Ticonderoga and Mount Independence July 6, 1777." *BFTM* 7 (July 1947):3-19.

_____. "The Burgoyne Campaign." *BFTM* 8 (January 1948):4-16.

_____. "Manuscripts as Resources." *Vermont Quarterly* 20 (April 1952): 89-104.

Nelson, Paul David. "Guy Carleton versus Benedict Arnold: The Campaign of 1776 in Canada and on Lake Champlain." *New York History* 57 (July 1976): 339-66.

Nelson, Peter. "The Battle of Diamond Island." *Quarterly Journal of the New York State History Association* (January 1922): 36-53.

_____. "John Brown and the Dash for Ticonderoga." *BFTM* 2 (January 1930): 23-40.

Niles, Samuel. "A Summary Historical Narrative of the Wars in New-England with the French and Indians, in Several Parts of the Country [1760]." *Collections of the Massachusetts Historical Society* 6, Third Series (1837): 154-279; 5, Fourth Series (1861): 309-589.

Noble, Henry Harmon. *A Sketch of the History of the Town of Essex, New York.* Champlain, N.Y.: Moorsfield Press, 1940.

Norris, Curtis B. "The Gundalow of Valcour Bay." *Yankee,* September 1966.

Olsen, Godfrey, J. "Archaeology of Ticonderoga." *Proceedings of the New York State Historical Association* 32 (1934): 407-11.

Osler, Edward. "The Battle of Valcour Island." *BFTM* 2 (January 1932):163-68.

Padeni, Scott. "John Brown's Attack on Diamond Island, Lake George." *The Lake George Nautical Newsletter* 3 (No. 2, 1994): 1, 5, 8.

_____. "A Review of Potential Sites for the Archaeological Study of Military Life at Lake George's Southern End during the French and Indian War and American Revolution." MS. Empire State College, 1994.

_____. "Skirmish at The Isle of Mutton," *The Lake George Nautical Newsletter* 3 (No. 3, 1994): 1, 8.

_____. "The Role of Blacks in New York's Northern Campaigns of the Seven Years' War." *BFTM* 16 (1999): 153-69.

Paine, Gary. "Ord's Arks: Angles, Artillery, and Ambush on Lake George and Champlain." *The American Neptune* 58 (Spring 1998): 105-21.

Paltsits, Victor H. and W. Max Reid. "Rock Inscription at the Ruins of Old Fort St. Frederick at Crown Point." *Proceedings of the New York State Historical Association* 10 (1911):107-13.

Park, Edwards. "Could Canada Have Ever Been Our Fourteenth Colony." *Smithsonian,* December 1987.

Peebles, Giovanna N., and David C. Skinas. "Vermont's Underwater Historic Preserves: Challenges, Benefits, Problems, and Process." *Underwater Archaeology Proceedings* (1989):49-53.

Pell, John H. G. "General George Washington's Visit to Fort Ticonderoga in July 1783." *BFTM* 14 (Fall 1983): 260-62.

Pell, Robert T. "John Brown and the Dash for Ticonderoga." *BFTM* 2 (January 1930): 23-40.

Pines, Paul. "Lake George: Milfoil, Moratoriums and Controversy." *Adirondack Life*, July/August 1987.

Pollard, Louise. "The Champlain Transportation Company." *The Vermonter*, February 1933.

Porter, Majorie L. "The Champlain Monster." *Vermont Life*, Summer 1970.

Pyle, Howard. "Through Inland Waters." *Harper's New Monthly Magazine*, May 1896, 828-39; June 1896, 63-75.

"The Revenge." *BFTM* 1 (July 1929):6-11.

Rich, Edwin. "Arnold's Fleet 1771-1790." unpublished paper, 1964.

Shomette, Donald G. "Heyday of the Horse Ferry." *National Geographic,* October 1989.

Singer, George Chapman. "The Burning of the Steamer *Ticonderoga* 29 August 1901." MS. 17 July 1975.

Skerrett, Robert G. "Wreck of the Royal Savage Recovered." *U.S. Naval Institute Proceedings* (November 1935): 1646-52.

Smith, Dorothy U. "Historic War Vessels in Lake Champlain and Lake George." *New York State Museum Bulletin* 313 (October 1937): 123-36.

Sowdon, Arthur J. C. "Commemoration of the Battle of Lake George, September 8, 1903." *The Society of Colonial Wars of the Commonwealth of Massachusetts* (1906): 139-208.

Starbuck, David R. "Military Hospitals on the Frontier of Colonial America." *Expedition* 39 (No. 1, 1997): 35-38.

Stephens, Philip. "A British View of the Battle of Valcour." *North Country Notes*, April 1963.

Stiles, Fred T. "Tales of Old Canal Days." *North Country Life*, Winter 1959.

Sturtevant, Walter B. "John Brown's Raid--September, 1777." *Infantry Journal* 36 (May 1930): 475-85.

Todish, Tim J. "The 1758 Attack on Fort Ticonderoga." *Muzzleloader*, January/February 2000.

Trumbull, J. H. *The Origin of the Expedition Against Ticonderoga in 1775.* Hartford, CT.: J. H.Trumbull, 1869.

Tucker, Philip C. *General Arnold and the Congress Galley.* Vergennes, VT.: pub., n.a., 1861.

Wagner, John. "Au Plaisir." *Adirondack Life*, January/February 1988.

"Was Washington to Blame for the Loss of Ticonderoga in 1777?" *BFTM* 11 (September 1963): 65-74.

Watson, W.C. "Arnold's Retreat After the Battle of Valcour." *MAH* 6 (June 1881):414-17.

Watt, Lynn. "Is Champlain Doomed?" *Vermont Life*, Spring 1969.

Webb, Stephen Saunders. "The Strange Career of Francis Nicholson." *The William and Mary Quarterly* 23 (October 1966): 513-48.

Westbrook, Nicholas, comp. and ed. " 'Like roaring lions breaking from their chains': The Highland Regiment at Ticonderoga." *BFTM* 16 (1998): 16-91.

W. G. "A Sketch of the Great Northern or Champlain Canal." Albany: New York State Library, 1823.

Wilkins, F. H. "Lake Champlain Steamers." *The Vermonter*, January 1916.

Williams, John. "I Saw the Savage." *Champlain Maritime Society Soundings*, Fall/Winter 1985, 4-5, 9.

Zaboly, Gary. "The Battle on Snowshoes." *American History Illustrated*, December 1979.

Zarzynski, Joseph W., et al. *The Atlantic Alliance for Maritime Heritage Conservation 1987 Lake George, New York Underwater Archaeology Workshop and Field Report.* AALGBRT, 1987.

_____. "The 1758 *Land Tortoise* Radeau Shipwreck--Creating a Seamless Photomosaic Using Off-the-Shelf Technology." *Underwater Archaeology* (1995): 181-85.

_____. " 'Ring-Around-A-Radeau,' or, Fencing in a 1758 Shipwreck for Public Access and Preservation." *Underwater Archaeology* (1996): 35-40.

Zarzynski, Joseph W., D. K. Abbass, and Russell P. Bellico. "Strange Bedfellows: Research and Politics of the *Land Tortoise,* Lake George's 1758 Radeau Shipwreck." *Underwater Archaeology* (1994): 74-79.

Newspapers, Newsletters, and Early Magazines

Albany Argus
Boston Evening Post
Boston Gazette and Country Journal
Burlington Free Press
Champlain Journal
Champlain Maritime Society Soundings
Daily Free Press (Burlington)
Glens Falls Daily Times
Glens Falls Republican
Lake Champlain Committee Newsletter
Lake Champlain Maritime Museum News
Lake George Mirror
Lake George Nautical Newsletter
London Chronicle
London Magazine
Newspapers, Newsletters, and Early Magazines
New-York Mercury
New York Times
Niles Weekly Register
Plattsburgh Daily Press
Plattsburgh Evening News
Plattsburgh Press Republican
Plattsburgh Sentinel
Post-Star (Glens Falls)
The Saratogian
Scots Magazine
Ticonderoga Sentinel
Times-Union (Albany)
Universal Magazine
Valley News (Elizabethtown)
Vergennes Enterprise
Vergennes Vermonter
Warrensburg News
Whitehall Times

Index

Other important books by Russell Bellico available from Purple Mountain Press:

Chronicles of Lake George: Journeys in War and Peace

"The central role of Lake George in both military and social history emerges in the words of eyewitnesses, and Bellico's extended introductions to each chronicle provide the best compact history of the lake to date." —Robert Foulke, Professor Emeritus at Skidmore College and Patricia Foulke, authors of *Colonial America*

Chronicles of Lake Champlain: Journeys in War and Peace

"This imaginatively-crafted work combines superbly detailed, researched narrative with gripping passages sagely drawn from contemporary accounts." —Philip K. Lundeberg, Curator Emeritus, Armed Forces Collection, Smithsonian Institution

For information or a free catalog, write Purple Mountain Press, Ltd., P.O. Box 309, Fleischmanns, NY 12430-0379 or call 845-254-4062 or fax 845-254-4476 or email purple@catskill.net

http://www.catskill.net/purple